YEARBOOK OF AMERICAN & CANADIAN CHU
1993

Sixty-first issue

Annual

YEARBOOK OF AMERICAN & CANADIAN CHURCHES 1993

Edited by Kenneth Bedell

Prepared and edited for the Education, Communication and Discipleship Unit of the National Council of Churches of Christ in the U.S.A. 475 Riverside Drive, New York, NY 10115-0050

Published and Distributed by Abingdon Press Nashville

Yearbook of American
and Canadian Churches
1993

Joan Brown Campbell
Publisher

J. Martin Bailey
Editorial Director

Printed in the United States of America
ISBN 0687-46648-2
ISSN 0195-9034
Library of Congress catalog card number:
16-5726

Kenneth Bedell
Editor

Alice M. Jones
Editorial Associate

Larry Ramey
Assistant Editor

Freda Brown
Production Assistant

Preparation of this Year-
book is an annual project of
the National Council of
Churches of Christ in the
United States of America.

This is the sixty-first edition of a yearbook that was
first published in 1916. Previous editions have been enti-
tled, Federal Council
Yearbook (1916-1917),
Yearbook of the Churches
(1918-1925), The Handbook
of the Churches (1927), The
New Handbook of the
Churches (1928), Yearbook
of American Churches (1933-
1972) and Yearbook of
American and Canadian
Churches (1973-present).

Introduction

The *Yearbook* tells the story of religious life in the United States and Canada. It is only a snap shot of religious activity. Just days before the book goes to the printer letters arrive telling about a church leader who has retired, died or simply been replaced. All the organizations described in this volume are in constant flux.

While it is impossible to determine a trend by looking at the change that happens in one year, it is important to closely examine the pulse of religious activity periodically. Like a doctor checking a patient's blood pressure, one measurement is not sufficient to make a complete diagnosis, but each test contributes to the development of our understanding of the role religion plays in our society.

The temptation is to look for quick confirmation of long held beliefs about the church. But reality is always much more complex. In collecting information for the *Yearbook* I made several observations that challenged my own previously held beliefs about religion in our society.

Individuals are not constrained to one denomination

George Gallup argues in an article published in this *Yearbook* that the forces shaping the churches are no longer "top down," but are changing to "bottom up." It appears that the "bottom" people are not constrained to expressing religion through a single denomination. This is particularly true in African-American denominations, but there is evidence in many other places as well.

For this edition we attempted to obtain more complete data on denominations that have largely African-American membership. In the process we developed a list a African-American denominations and their membership. To this we added estimates of the African-American participation in denominations with majority white membership. We estimated that there are at least one million African-American Moslems. When these numbers were all added together they came up to almost 100 percent of the total African-American population in the United States.

Wardell Payne, the editor of the *Directory of African American Religious Bodies* was very helpful at this point. He explained that people often participate in several different organizations and are, therefore, counted more than once. The same may be true for a whole congregation that participates in several denominational associations so it is counted more than once. We cannot add the numbers of adherents and subtract that number from the total population to calculate the number of people who are non-participants in religious organizations. So increasing numbers of total participants in denominations is partly an indication of participation of individuals across denominational lines.

Religion in the U.S. is becoming less white

Ask anyone "What was the fastest growing religious denomination in the United States during the 1980s that has a membership of over one million?" If they guess the Assemblies of God, they are naming the highly visible, largely white denomination that grew about one third as fast during the 1980s and has less than half as many members as the Church of God in Christ denomination. Both denominations share a pentecostal tradition. Sherry DuPree and Herbert Dupree write in this volume what may be an introduction for some to this denomination that is currently the fifth largest denomination in the United States.

It is often noted that a large number of denominations have small membership of less than 10,000 and that the majority of church participation can be accounted for by the membership of a few very large denominations. But, denominations that are very visible in the public media like the Presbyterian Church (U.S.A.), the Episcopal Church and the United Church of Christ are not even in the top seven largest denominations. There are, however, two African-American denominations in the top seven: The National Baptist Convention (U.S.A.) and the Church of God in Christ. They are joined by the Roman Catholic Church, the Southern Baptist Convention, the United Methodist

Church, the Evangelical Lutheran Church in America, and the Church of Jesus Christ of Latter-day Saints. Another evidence that African-American denominations do not receive the attention that they deserve is the fact that of the 14 largest denominations, six have largely African-American membership.

As Eric Lincoln and Lawrence Mamiya point out in an article in this volume, "The seven major black denominations have not suffered the kind of severe decline in membership experienced by some mainstream white denominations."

Regional ecumenical activity increasingly volunteer

The *Yearbook* collects information to update listings by mailing requests to every organization listed. We have the lowest percent of response from the regional ecumenical agencies. This year all the agencies that did not respond were telephoned to obtain updated information. We discovered that the person answering the telephone is often a committed volunteer. Usually these people had never heard of the *Yearbook*, but they were eager to be as helpful as possible with a project that sounded like it helped people work together.

This is another example of the "bottom up" activity that George Gallup discusses. Individuals are participating in organizations that take them beyond a particular denomination.

Another example of this shift can be seen in the expanded listing of "Cooperative Organizations" found in this directory. We contacted the religious service organizations listed in previous editions and asked them if they wanted to be listed as "Cooperative Organizations." The response was overwhelming. This year we list 69 U.S. and 32 Canadian organizations. This is an increase from 44 U.S. and 13 Canadian listings last year.

Discovering meaning for the word *Ecumenical*

This *Yearbook* will be used for many purposes. It is an imperfect description of religious life in the United States and Canada. Yet, its imperfections are partly the result of the rich diversity and complexity of religion in North America. That story is partly told in the annual changes in membership and financial giving. The story is partly told in the descriptions of organizations and denominations. It is partly told in the trend articles.

I believe that the most important thing we can learn from the pages of this *Yearbook* is that people are discovering how to work together. As Joan Brown Campbell pointed out in an article in the 1992 edition of the *Yearbook*, "The typical church member lives ecumenically." Sometimes the evidence is subtle. For example, the Association of Theological Schools added seven United States and two Canadian schools last year. This demonstrates that schools of theology are interested in cooperative efforts. Other evidence is much more direct, such as the vitality of cooperative organizations. These changes give meaning to the word "Ecumenical."

As the editor of this *Yearbook* it is my dream that the contents will not simple describe this discovery of religious cooperation. I hope that the directories and other information will help people and organizations learn about each other so that they can identify each other and discover how to be ecumenical.

Ken Bedell
Editor

CONTENTS

I. The Church in the '90s:
Trends and Developments

II. Directories

III. Statistical Section

IV. A Calendar for Church Use

Indexes

Challenges to the Black Church

The Black Church and the Twenty-First Century

Eric Lincoln
Duke University
and
Lawrence Mamiya
Vassar College

At the beginning of the last decade of the twentieth century the black churches are, on the whole, still healthy and vibrant institutions. While there has been some chipping away at the edges, particularly among unchurched underclass black youth and some college educated, middle-class young adults, black churches still remain the central institutional sector in most black communities.

Based on the indices of church membership, church attendance, and charitable giving in 1987, different studies have pointed out the following: about 78 percent of the black population claimed church membership and attended once in the last six months; blacks (44 percent) tend to have slightly higher rates of weekly church attendance than white Protestants (40 percent); and they have the highest rates of being superchurched (attending church more than on Sundays) among all Americans (37 versus 31 percent). Furthermore, if time and money are an indication of loyalty, black churches received a far higher percentage of the charitable dollar and more volunteer time than that given to any other organization by black people.[1] The seven major black denominations have not suffered the kind of severe decline in membership experienced by some mainstream white denominations like the Disciples of Christ (40 percent), the United Presbyterian Church (33 percent) or the Episcopal Church (33 percent).[2]

The Challenge of Two Black Americas and Two Black Churches?

The process of secularization in black communities has always meant a diminishing of the influence of religion and an erosion in the central importance of black churches. Secularization is accompanied by the twin processes of increasing differentiation and increasing pluralism that tend to diminish the cultural unity provided by the black sacred cosmos.[3] There is some evidence that the present and past central importance of the Black Church may be threatened by the virtual explosion of opportunities which are now be-

Excerpted from Chapter 13, "The Black Church and the Twenty-First Century: Challenges to the Black Church" in *The Black Church in the African American Experience*, C. Eric Lincoln and Lawrence H. Mamiya, Durham: Duke University Press, 1990. Reprinted with permission of the publisher.

coming available to recent black college graduates. An officially segregated society contributed to the dominant role black churches were able to maintain as one of the few cohesive black institutions to emerge from slavery. Talented black men and women developed their leadership skills in black churches and used them as launching pads for professional careers in the church or elsewhere in black society like education, music, and entertainment. With the breakdown of official law, medicine, politics, and business have opened up as never before. Also, many white colleges, universities, and graduate schools have been seeking black students to bolster their black enrollment. As Freeman has pointed out in his study of black elites, recent black college graduates have been able to achieve income parity with their white counterparts for the first time in history, an occurrence beyond the reach of the vast majority of black workers.[4] Even with some decline in black college enrollment during the Reagan years, the total numbers of black college graduates since the 1960s will still represent an unprecedented phenomenon in black history. How black churches and their leadership grapple with this challenge will determine whether they will be faced with the same problems of attrition and decline now affecting several white mainstream denominations. Whether black churches will have the clergy with educational training equal to that of their lay members is also in question. At one time black clergy were among the most highly educated members of the community, and a number of black colleges and universities were founded for the training of the clergy. However, that is no longer the case. With the proliferation in available professions for young people, the question of whether the ministry of the Black Church will continue to attract the best and the brightest is still unresolved.

Some studies have pointed out the increasing bifurcation of the black community into two main class divisions: a coping sector of middle-income working class and middle-class black communities, and a crisis sector of poor black communities, involving the working poor and the dependent poor.[5] The demographic movement of middle-income blacks out of inner city areas and into residential parts of the cities, older suburbs, or into newly created black suburbs, has meant a growing physical and social isolation of the black poor. For example, since the 1960s, 48 percent of the black population of Atlanta has moved out of the central city into surrounding counties.[6] The gradual emergence of two fairly distinct black Americas along class lines - of two nations within a nation - has raised a serious challenge to the Black Church. The membership of the seven historic black denominations is composed largely of middle-income working-class and middle-class members, with a scattering of support from poorer members, especially those in southern rural areas who tend to be among the most loyal members.[7] But black pastors and churches have had a difficult time in attempting to reach the hard-core urban poor, the black underclass, which is continuing to grow.[8] In past generations some of the large urban black churches were one of the few institutions that could reach beyond class boundaries and provide a semblance of unity in black communities.[9] The challenge for the future is whether black clergy and their churches will attempt to transcend class boundaries and reach out to the poor, as these class lines continue to solidify with demographic changes in black communities. If the traditional Black Church fails in its attempt to include the urban poor, the possibility of a Black Church of the poor may emerge, consisting largely of independent, fundamentalist, and Pentecostal storefront churches. There also may emerge cults and sectarian forms of new religious movements among the black poor, similar to those exotic groups that emerged in the 1930s like those of Father Divine, Daddy Grace, Mother Horne, Elder Solomon Lightfoot Michaux, Rabbi Cherry, and Elijah Muhammad.[10] One of the few hopeful signs that the historic black churches will be able to provide a measure of unity beyond class boundaries involves the rise of a neo-Pentecostal movement in some black denominations.

The Islamic Challenge to the Black Church

The resurgence of Islamic fundamentalism has been a worldwide phenomenon in recent years and it has implications for the general religious situation in the

United States and for black Christian churches. Black communities have been particularly vulnerable to the Islamic challenge since the largest indigenous sector of Americans who have become Muslims are from the black population. The influence of varieties of Islam among blacks in the United States has had a long history, stemming from the African Muslims who were brought to North America as slaves and who constituted as much as 20 percent of the slave population on some large southern plantations.[11] However, much of the African Islamic influence did not survive the period of slavery, and the main bearers of that tradition, came through the writings of intellectuals like Edward Wilmot Blyden, a late-nineteenth-century advocate of African Islam.[12] But it was the leaders of "proto-Islamic" movements during the black urban migrations of the twentieth century who prepared the way for a much wider acceptance of Islam. Muslim advocates such as Noble Drew Ali of the Moorish Science Temple in 1913 and Master Wali Fard and the Honorable Elijah Muhammad of the Nation of Islam during the years of the Great Depression opened the door of Islam to black America with a dramatic appeal to heritage and history.[13] The nation of Islam survived to become the nucleus of a rapidly proliferating Islamic growth in America transcending racial and ethnic boundaries.

The Nation of Islam, which was founded by Master Farad Muhammad in 1930 and led by Elijah Muhammad from 1934 until 1975, has a challenging and controversial history.[14] Under the influence of Minister Malcolm X, Elijah's national representative, the Nation made its greatest impact on the black community and American society during the 1960s and early 1970s when America was searching for change but adamantly resisting changing. Malcolm X and the Nation are credited with the primary ideological foundations that led to the development of the concepts of "black power," "black pride," and "black consciousness" which stirred black youth and reverberated all through the civil rights movement of the period. Malcolm X was more deeply aware than many less controversial leaders that the struggle for civil rights and integration were meaningless if the integrity and independence of black

selfhood were drowned in a sea of whiteness. Malcolm's biting critique of the "so-called Negro" and his emphasis upon the recovery of an independent black selfhood helped to change the language and vocabulary of an entire society from "Negro" to "black."[15]

Under Wali Fard and Elijah Muhammad the Nation of Islam was essentially a proto-Islamic religious black nationalism that was often at odds with the traditional doctrines of orthodox Islam.

Since the death of Elijah Muhammad in 1975, many members of the Nation of Islam, or the Black Muslims, have followed their new leader Imam Warith Deen Muhammad in making the transition to orthodox Sunni Islam. Warith began dismantling the exclusive black "nation" by accepting whites into the movement and then proceeded to gradually discard all the precepts and practices taught by Elijah, which he considered to be in violation of the spirit and the letter of orthodox Islam. "There is no black Muslim or white Muslim," he declared, "all are Muslims, all children of God."[16] Under Warith Muhammad the movement changed its name, first to the World Community of Islam in the West, then to the American Muslim Mission, finally finding its long-sought "true" identity in the world brotherhood of traditional Islam. Imam Warith Muhammad was recognized and accepted by world Muslim leaders, who honored him with the office of certification for Muslims from the United States who go on the annual pilgrimage, or Hajj, to Mecca. Muslim imams or leaders of the "Jummah," or Friday prayer services, are now commonly accepted as members of black ministerial alliances across the country.

An estimated 100,000 former members of Elijah Muhammad's old Nation of Islam followed Warith Deen Muhammad into Islamic orthodoxy as Sunni Muslims. Imam Muhammad's newspaper, *The Muslim Journal,* has also been one of the pioneers in using the term African American in reference to black Americans. Perhaps another 20,000 or so are led by Minister Louis Farrakhan, who continues the provincial black nationalist teachings of Master Fard and Elijah Muhammad. Farrakhan's followers retained the original designation of the Nation of Islam along with its ideology. While there have

3

been smaller splinter groups led by rival leaders, the fluidity of membership in these groups has made it very difficult to obtain an accurate assessment of membership figures. However, over the fifty-eight-year history of the Nation and its evolution to orthodox Islam, it is estimated that several million black people, mostly black men, have passed through these various Islamic and proto-Islamic movements.[17] In 1989 the *New York Times* estimated that about 1 million of the 6 million Muslims in the United States are African Americans, and close to 90 percent of the new converts are black.[18]

Islam has proven itself to be a viable religious alternative to black Christian churches, especially for black males, who have experienced difficulty with normative social and economic adjustments. In fact, the membership of Islamic masjids or mosques has always tended to be heavily made up of black men, a segment of the black population which black churches have had great difficulty in recruiting. The attraction of Islamic movements to black males may be due to several reasons, among them the legacy of the militant and radical black nationalist Malcolm X has been a profound influence on these young men. As a culture hero, Malcolm X was seen as the uncompromising critic of American society. Another reason is that the Muslims project a more macho image among black men. The Qur'an advocates self-defense while the Christian Bible counsels turning the other cheek. The *lex talionis,* "an eye for an eye, a life for a life," has a persuasive appeal to the oppressed whose cheeks are weary of inordinate abuse. Black sports heroes such as Muhammad Ali and Kareem Abdul-Jabbar have further legitimated the Islamic option by converting to Islam and taking on Muslim names. Black parents who are not Muslims frequently give their children Muslim names as a statement of solidarity with some features of Islam and as a way of announcing their independence from Western social conventions, or as a means of identifying with an African cultural heritage. Finally, many black men have been attracted to Islamic alternatives because the Muslims have been very active in working in prisons and on the streets where they are, a ministry which is not pronounced in most black Christian churches.

A full decade after the turn of the twenty-first century, if the estimate of 6 million Muslims in the United States is reasonably accurate, Islam has become the second-largest religion in America, after Protestant and Catholic Christianity. American Judaism with a steadily declining membership, is now third. While much of this Islamic growth is independent of the black community, the possibility of a serious impact on the Black Church cannot be peremptorily dismissed. The phenomenon of more black males preferring Islam while more black females adhere to traditional black Christianity is not as bizarre as it sounds. It is already clear that in Islam the historic black church denominations will be faced with a far more serious and more powerful competitor for the souls of black folk than the white churches ever were. When is the question, not whether.

"E Pluribus Unum," Out of Many, One?: The Challenge of Black Ecumenism

The potential power of the Black Church as a social institution has never been fully realized and it probably never will be so long as sectarianism is the norm. However, there have been men and women throughout the black history who have dared to dream that out of the denominational pluralism that has characterized the situation of black churches, there might one day arise a unity, and perhaps an organic union and merger, so that the several black churches could speak with one effective voice and move with one unified spirit and singleness of purpose. They have dreamed that these churches could pool their financial, material, and human resources to better serve their people, eliminating the duplication and replication of services such as multimillion-dollar publishing houses for each denomination. From the very beginnings of the historic black denominations there were serious discussions between black Methodist leaders of Philadelphia-Baltimore and New York City about merging into one denomination. In fact, the New York leaders of the A.M.E. Zion Church did adopt as their official name "the African Methodist Episcopal Church in America" before relationships between the communions degenerated and the word "Zion" was added to differentiate themselves from the Philadelphia-Baltimore Methodist movement that became known as the A.M.E. Church.[19] Throughout the nineteenth and twentieth centuries there have been sporadic efforts at ecumenical merger between various members of the historic black denominations. For example, the National Baptist Convention, U.S.A., Inc., was formed in 1895 through the merger of three Baptist groups, but two schisms in 1915 and in 1961 also produced two new and independent denominations, the National Baptist Convention of America, and the Progressive National Baptist Convention. Another cooperative attempt, the Fraternal Council of Churches which was founded in 1934 by A.M.E. Bishop Reverdy C. Ransom, was active in the 1940s and 1950s.[20] The period of civil rights ferment and black consciousness has also spawned a wide variety of black ecumenical movements such as the Southern Christian Leadership Conference, the National Black Evangelical Association, and the National Conference of Black Churchmen.[21] One of the more successful ventures in black ecumenism was the Interdenominational Theological Center, founded in 1957. ITC represents the cooperative efforts of six denominational bodies, including black Episcopalians and black United Methodists, to provide a common center for theological training by pooling their separate resources and services.

During the decade of the 1980s several other major efforts in black ecumenism have emerged: Partners in Ecumenism (PIE); and the Congress of National Black Churches (CNBC). A merger of three black denominations is planned, consisting of the African Methodist Episcopal Zion Church, the Christian Methodist Episcopal Church and the Union American Methodist Episcopal Church. Both PIE and CNBC were established as ecumenical groups in 1978, although with different purposes and constituencies. Founded under the auspices of the National Council of Churches to promote social change programs through the common efforts of black and white churches, Partners in Ecumenism challenged the NCC and white denominations to be more responsive to black concerns, and provided a platform for progressive black and white clergy. In contrast, the Congress of National Black Churches, which began with a membership restricted to black denominations with a national constituency, is concerned with social and economic programs that promote institution building in black communities through such programs as collective purchasing, banking, insurance, and communications.[22] Plans call for a cooperative publishing house adequate to meet the printing and publishing needs of member denominations and secular black writers. The congress also sponsors a large-scale social program called Project Spirit which attempts to relate black churches, families, and children in after-school programs focused on developing self-esteem among the children in an enriched cultural ethos in Atlanta, Indianapolis, and Oakland.

The planned merger of the C.M.E. Church, the A.M.E. Zion Church, and the U.A.M.E. Church may be completed in the 1990s, thereby strengthening historic black Methodistism at a time when membership in some of the churches involved is beginning to decline. Merger may help to resolve some problems common to black churches such as an aging clergy, dwindling financial resources, inefficient use of duplicated church properties and personnel. However church mergers are among the most complicated of human endeavors, and the restructuring of ecclesiastical entities seem to founder more often than they succeed. Human interests vested in positions of power and leadership must be resolved once the doctrinal and ritual preferences have been resolved. Traditions are not readily relinquished, even in the face of the obvious, and emotions sometimes speak with more authority than either reason or practicality.[23] Nevertheless, the planned merger of these three black Methodist denominations has heightened speculations about the possibility of their merger with the A.M.E. Church at some time in the future, and of the possibility that the black Baptist denominations may also consider reunion with each other. The split between the National Baptist Convention, U.S.A., Inc., and the Progressive National Baptist Convention is fairly recent and probably not irreparable, though the divisions of separation between the two older Baptist conventions have had more time to harden. But the hopes among some black and white Christians that the black Church will eventually merge into mainline white Christianity seem increasingly unrealistic as these racial communions seem more and more resigned to the realities of religious separation in a society where secular separation remains the ideological norm.

As the United States moves into the technological space age of the twenty-first century, the collective efforts of black ecumenical groups will become increasingly important both to preserve their religious and cultural integrity and to oppose the subtle manipulations of an information society.

End Notes

1. For data on church membership and rates of being unchurched, see Princeton Religion Research Center *Emerging Trends*, vol. 9, no. 5 (May 1987): 5

2. Research group on Congregational Studies, sponsored by the Lilly Endowment. Also see Roof and McKinney, *American Mainline Religion*, New Brunswick, N.J.: Rutgers University Press, 1987.

3. For general theoretical descriptions of the effects of the process of secularization on religion, see Peter Berger, *The Sacred Canopy*, Garden City, N.Y.: Doubleday, 1967, chapters 2, 3

4. Freeman, Richard B., *Black Elite: The New Market for Highly Educated Black Americans*, pp. 27-40

5. For example, see William Julius Wilson, *The Truly Disadvantaged: The Inner City, the Underclass, and Public Policy*, Chicago: University of Chicago Press, 1980. Also see the socioeconomic data of the National Urban League in the annual publication, *The State of Black America*, 1986, 1987, 1988. The terms "coping" and "crisis" sectors of the black community are derived from Professor Martin Kilson in a presentation on Afro-American Religion and Politics, at the W.E.B. Du Bois Institute, Harvard University, Oct. 29, 1988.

6. Smothers, Ronald, "Atlanta Still on a Roll, but New Doubts Arise," *New York Times*, June 29, 1988, A-14

7. Nelsen, Hart M., "Unchurched Black Americans: Patterns of Religiosity and Affiliation," *Review of Religious Research 29*, June 1998, no. 4:398-412

8. Stepp, Laura Sessions, "Black Church Losing Historic Role: Drug Use, Teen Pregnancies Seen as Consequences," *Washington Post*, Aug. 20, 1988, p. A-6

9. Drake, St. Clair, and Cayton, Horace, *Black Metropolis: A Study of Negro Life in the North*, vol. 2, New York: Harper and Row, 1962

10. Washington, Joseph, *Black Sects and Cults*, Garden City, N.Y.: Anchor/Doubleday, 1973. For an overview of five major groups, see Mamiya, Lawrence H. and Lincoln, C. Eric, "Black Militant and Separatist Movements," *Encyclopedia of the American Religious Experience*, Charles Lippy and Peter W. Williams, editors. New York: Charles Scribner's Sons, 1988, 2:755-71

11. Austin, Allan D., *African Muslims in Antebellum America: A Sourcebook*, New York: Garland, 1984

12. Blyden, Edward W., *Islam and the Negro Race*, London: Edinburgh University, 1967 reprint. Also see Hollis Lynch, *Edward Wilmot Blyden: Pan Negro Patriot*, New York: Oxford University Press, 1970

13. For overviews of the Moorish Science Temple and the Nation of Islam, see Mamiya and Lincoln, "Black Militant and Separatist Movements." The term "proto-Islam" was coined by C. Eric Lincoln, "The American Muslim Mission in the Context of American Social History," in *The Muslim Community in North America*, edited by Earle H. Wauh, Baha Au-Laban, and Regula B. Qureshi.

14. For overview of the origins of the movement, see Lincoln, C. Eric, *The Black Muslims in America*, Boston: Beacon, 1961

15. Mamiya and Lincoln, "Black Militant and Separatist Movement," p. 767

16. "Rule Switch Allows Whites as Muslims," *Nashville Tennessean*, June 19, 1975

17. Gans, Bruce M. and Lowe, Walter L., "The Islam Connection," *Playboy*, May 1980

18. Goldman, Ari L., "Mainstream Islam Rapidly Embraced by Black Americans," *New York Times*, Feb. 21, 1989, pp. I, B-4

19. Walls, William J., *The African Methodist Episcopal Zion Church: Reality of the Black Church*, Charlotte, N.C.: A.M.E. Zion Publishing House, 1974

20. Sawyer, Mary, "Black Ecumenical Movements: Proponents of Social Change," *Review of Religious Research 30* (December 1988), no. 2:152-53

21. Ibid, see figure I

22. Sawyer, "Black Ecumenical Movements," pp. 154-55

23. Mamiya and Lincoln, "Policy and Planning Implications of the Christian Methodist Episcopal Church Survey"

The Explosive Growth of the African American Pentecostal Church

Sherry Sherrod DuPree
University of Florida, Institute of Black Culture,
Research Librarian, Santa Fe Community College
and
Herbert C. DuPree
Administrator in the Marion County Schools

From Azusa Street, Los Angeles, to northern cities, African American pentecostals have built the fastest-growing church in the United States. They have formed denominations totalling more than 6.3 million members, including the Church of God in Christ (COGIC), the fastest-growing major denomination in the United States and the nation's fifth-largest denomination overall. With a combination of dynamic worship (Andrae Crouch and the Winans gospel music singers came from COGIC congregations) and social outreach, African American pentecostal churches have surged in the past decade.

Figure 1: Spatial Distribution of Selected Migration Routes of African Americans: 1914 to 1960

Major African American Migration Routes
Atlanta
Regional Routes

SOURCE: Blacks in the U.S.: A Geographic Perspective
by Davis and Donaldson
Black Metropolis by Drake and Clayton

Figure 2: Spatial Diffusion of the Church of God in Christ Churches 1901 to 1920

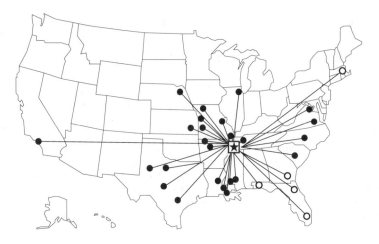

● 1 Church
☐ 4 Churches
★ Original Church Location
○ 1 Church...Approximate Location

SOURCE: Sherry S. DuPree Collection

For example:

* World Changers Ministries, an independent charismatic church in the Atlanta suburb of College Park, Ga., gained 3,250 members in 1990.

* West Angeles Church of God in Christ gained more than 2,000 members in 1990, and now has more than 8,000 members.

* Imani Temple, which started with 500 members in 1989 at Howard University in Washington, D.C., reported having more than 5,000 members in 1991. Congregations spread to Norfolk and Richmond, Va., Philadelphia, and Houston.

* Full Gospel Church of the Lord's Mission, International, Inc., started with 750 members in Silver Springs, Md., in 1989. It had 5,000 members by 1991, with congregations in the District of Columbia, Virginia, Tennessee, Florida, and Haiti.

* Deliverance Evangelistic Church, founded in 1960 in a Philadelphia house, now has 83,000 members in 32 congrega-

tions, mostly in major cities along the East Coast.

* The Church of God in Christ has averaged gaining nearly 200,000 members and 600 congregations per year since 1982.

The roots of American Pentecostalism can be traced to the 19th Century Methodist Holiness groups, emphasizing justification, sanctification, and baptism in the Holy Spirit as evidenced by speaking in tongues.[1] Speaking in tongues was practiced, but it was not viewed as a distinguishing doctrinal difference.[2]

Data on the African American pentecostals has been sketchy at best, where a rich oral tradition has not lent itself to accurate record-keeping. But the development of the African American pentecostal church can be seen in the explosive growth of the Church of God in Christ. It is:

* With 5.5 million members, more than twice the size of the Assemblies of God, which grew from a black-white split in

COGIC in 1914 to become the largest predominantly white pentecostal denomination;

* The second-largest African American denomination, behind the 8-million member National Baptist Convention, U.S.A.;

* The fifth-largest U.S. denomination, behind the Roman Catholic Church, the Southern Baptist Convention, the United Methodist Church, and the National Baptist Convention, U.S.A.; and

* The fastest-growing major U.S. denomination in the 1980s. It grew by 48.3 percent between 1982 and 1991, compared to 22.3 percent for the Church of Jesus Christ of Latter-day Saints, 22 percent for the Assemblies of God, 14.4 percent for the Roman Catholic Church, and 9.1 percent for the Southern Baptist Convention.[3]

The Azusa Street Revival, which gave birth to most of the pentecostal denominations, was started in 1906 by a black Holiness minister named William Joseph Seymour, during a visit to Los Angeles.[5] The euphoria of the racial harmony of the revival was short-lived, as white dissatisfaction with the prominent roles which blacks played in the revival led to open criticism of how it was being conducted.[5] Schisms soon developed along racial lines with the conclusion of the revival in 1909. Nevertheless, during this brief period of interracial harmony among pentecostalists, the Church of God in Christ, as the sole incorporated pentecostal body between 1907 and 1914, ordained hundreds of white ministers from independent congregations, who did not have a recognized ecclesiastical body to ordain them.[6]

The Rev. Charles Harrison Mason, who along with fellow Baptist the Rev. Charles Price Jones had established a Holiness Church in 1895 in Lexington, Miss.,[7] attended the Azusa Street Revival in 1907.[8] Under Mason's leadership, the Church of

Figure 3: Spatial Diffusion of the Church of God in Christ Churches: 1921 to 1945

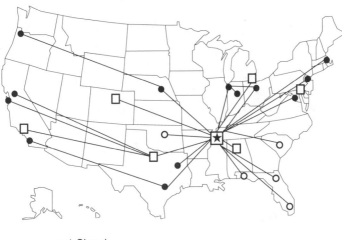

● 1 Church
☐ 4 Churches
★ Original Church Location
○ 1 Church...Approximate Location

SOURCE: Sherry S. DuPree Collection

God in Christ was formed. For the next 54 years, he led the spread of COGIC throughout the United States.

The greatest growth came in the years following World War I and II, when blacks migrated en masse to the industrial cities of the North and West, to escape the agrarian poverty that blighted much of the South. The spatial spread reached its greatest extent by 1945, with 750 churches, including practically every state, branching out from its Memphis headquarters to New York, Philadelphia, Boston, Chicago, Omaha, Los Angeles, and Jacksonville, Fla.[9]

The spread of the African American pentecostal church can be seen by comparing the migration of African Americans (Fig. 1) to the diffusion of the Church of God in Christ (Fig. 2-3).

Maps furnish a unique opportunity to view African American Pentecostal denominations geographically, which heretofore had been listed sporadically and often inaccurately. This method of analysis illustrated certain spatial patterns, however, one should remember that sites were frequently determined by a leader's personal network. An eastern orientation of denominations probably meant that acquaintances lived in that direction. Chronicles were replete with requests to the "original" churches to send "saints" to evangelize an area and eventually establish churches.

End Notes

1. *Standard Manual and Constitution and By-Laws of the United Holy Church of America, Inc.*, 1980. Durham, N.C.: Service Printing Co. p. 4

2. Melton, J. Gordon, 1987, *The Encyclopedia of American Religions*, 2nd Edition, Gale Pulishing Co., p. 41

3. Calculations were made using data published in the *Yearbook of American and Canadian Churches* 1983 and 1992 editions.

4. Tinney, James S., Fall, 1976, "William J. Seymour: Father of Modern-Day Pentecostalism," *Journal of Interdenominational Theological Center*, Vol. 4, p. 24-44

5. Patterson, J.O.; Ross, German; and Atkins-Mason, Julia; 1959. *History of Formative Years of the Church of God in Christ.* Memphis, Tenn.: Church of God in Christ Publishing House. p. 17-20

6. Synan, Vinson, 1971. *The Holiness Pentecostal Movement in the United States*, Grand Rapids, Mich.: W. Eerdman's Publishing Co. p. 169

7. DuPree, Sherry Sherrod, 1989. *Biographical Dictionary of African-American, Holiness-Pentecostals: 1880-1990*, Washington, D.C., Middle Atlantic Regional Press, page 177

8. *Official Manual with the Doctrine and Discipline of the Church of God in Christ 1973.* Memphis: Church of God in Christ Publishing House, p. XXVI

9. Synan, *The Holiness-Pentecostal Movement*, p. 176

A COUNTY BY COUNTY VIEW OF RELIGION IN THE U.S.

Richard Houseal and Dale E. Jones
Church Growth Research Center
Church of the Nazarene

Church affiliation and membership rates vary greatly throughout the United States. Statistics published in Churches and Church Membership in the United States, 1990[1] provide county level data from which these variations can be studied. Sponsored by the Association of Statisticians of American Religious Bodies, it represents the most complete church affiliation data available for the United States.

The study asked each denomination to list their number of churches, members, and total adherents for each county in the United States. In many cases, denominations provided yearbooks or other printouts so that the study's researchers could determine county locations. Since there is no common way of defining membership, each denomination used their own membership definition in determining their membership figures. The adherent figure was defined as all members, their children, and the number of other regular participants who are not considered members. If a group was unable to provide an adherent figure a formula was used to estimate the figure.[2] The adherent figure therefore provides comparable data between groups. In all cases, a printout was sent to the denominational contact person for checking and approval.

Two factors make Churches and Church Membership unique. First, it provides a listing for 133 denominational groupings for every county in the United States. This is important since the Census Bureau stopped asking questions related to religion in 1936. While many phone surveys have provided information on religious affiliation at the national level, they cannot provide data at the state or county level. Having county level data also means that it can be compared to any other data aggregated by county (e.g., census data). Second, Churches and Church Membership receives its data directly from denominational headquarters or yearbooks.[3] This method counts fewer people with a church affiliation than other surveys which ask individuals to self-identify their religion; however, this may be more accurate in describing church affiliation since the denomination has been notified of one's claimed preference.

When the data is looked at nationally, religious patterns begin to emerge. Map 1 shows the predominant family group[4] by counties of the United States. For this map, predominance is based on the percentage of church adherents—not the entire population. Immediately one sees that the South is basically Baptist; the Northeast, West, and areas that are ports of entry into the United States are considerably Catholic; Utah and some surrounding areas are mostly Mormon; the mid-North is largely Lutheran; and there is a path of Methodism from Delaware to Nebraska. Table 1 shows the number of counties in which a particular family group was predominant.

Another way to view the data is in comparison to the entire population. Map 2 shows the percentage of the population not claimed by any of the 133 groups reporting. Here it becomes obvious that people living in the western half of the United States are less likely to have a church affiliation. In fact, with the exception of areas predominately Mormon, less than half of the western population is claimed by a church or synagogue. Florida, parts of the Northeast, Michigan, Indiana, and Ohio are also highly un-claimed. The Bible-belt is visible, stretch-ing across the South from North Carolina through Texas; however, there is also a vertical band (a North-South Bible-belt?) of highly claimed counties from North Dakota through Texas.

Churches and Church Membership also shows a continuing loss in adherents for most mainline denominations: Episcopal Church, Evangelical Lutheran Church in America, Presbyterian Church (USA), United Church of Christ, and the United Methodist Church. Groups such as the Catholic Church, Southern Baptist Con-vention, Latter-day Saints and the Assem-blies of God show considerable increases. Table 2 compares 1980[5] and 1990 adher-ent figures.

Denominational planners, local churches, demographers, sociologists, or anyone else interested in understanding religious affiliation in the United States will find this data invaluable. Do you know the religious make-up for the county in which you live?

Table 1: Number of Counties with a Predominant group

Family Group	No. of Counties Where Predominant
Baptist	1,322
Catholic	959
Lutheran	266
Methodist	249
Latter-day Saints	83
Christian	54
Reformed	8
Mennonite	7
United Church of Christ	6
Pentecostal	5
Presbyterian	5
Brethren	2
Jewish	2
Moravian	2
Adventist	1
Episcopal	1
Friends	1

MAJOR DENOMINATIONAL FAMILIES

BY COUNTIES OF THE UNITED STATES: 1990

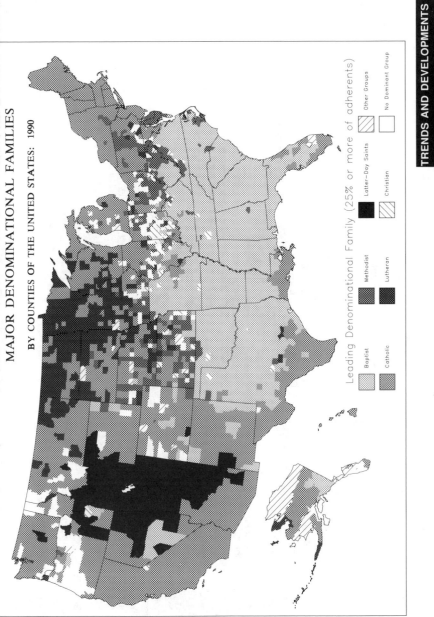

Leading Denominational Family (25% or more of adherents)

Baptist   Methodist   Latter-Day Saints   Other Groups

Catholic   Lutheran   Christian   No Dominant Group

13

Table 2: 1980-1990 Comparison of U.S. Denominations

Denomination	1980-1990 % Change in Adherents	Denomination	1980-1990 % Change in Adherents
Advent Christian Church	-32.9%	Church of the Brethren	-10.3%
African Methodist Episcopal Zion	4.5%	Church of the Lutheran Brethren of Amer.	62.7%
American Baptist Churches USA	-2.5%	Church of the Lutheran Confession	-6.4%
Apostolic Christian Church (Nazarene)	20.6%	Church of the Nazarene	.3%
Apostolic Lutheran Church of America	.1%	Churches of Christ	5.1%
Armenian Apostolic Ch. Amer., E.Prelacy	619.1%	Congr. Christian Churches, Nat'l Assoc. of	-17.3%
Assemblies of God	34.0%	Conservative Congregation Christian Conf.	28.0%
Assoc. Reformed Presbyterian Church	18.8%	Cumberland Presbyterian Church	.4%
Baptist General Conference	11.0%	Episcopal Church	-13.4%
Baptist Missionary Association of Amer.	5.6%	Estonian Evangelical Lutheran Church	-43.1%
Beachy Amish Mennonite Churches	39.6%	Evangelical Bible Churches, Fellowship of	-24.0%
Berean Fundamental Church	46.6%	Evangelical Congregational Church	-2.7%
Bible Church of Christ, Inc.	119.6%	Evangelical Free Church of America	155.4%
Brethren Church (Ashland, Ohio)	-11.1%	Evangelical Lutheran Church in America*	-2.8%
Brethren in Christ Church	7.2%	Evangelical Lutheran Synod	7.4%
Catholic Church	12.4%	Evangelical Mennonite Church, Inc.	11.5%
Christ Catholic Church	-40.2%	Evangelical Methodist Church	-5.8%
Christian & Missionary Alliance	59.3%	Fire Baptized Holiness Church (Wesleyan)	-2.0%
Christian Brethren	29.1%	Free Lutheran Congregations, The Assoc. of	88.9%
Christian Church (Disciples of Christ)	-14.4%	Free Methodist Church of North America**	-59.5%
Christian Churches & Churches of Christ	7.6%	Friends-USA	-5.0%
Christian Reformed Church	6.7%	General Conf. of Mennonite Brethren Chs.	14.7%
Church of God (Anderson, Indiana)**	-56.5%	Internat'l Church of the Foursquare Gospel	59.4%
Church of God (Cleveland, Tennessee)	46.5%	Jewish (estimate)**	645.3%
Church of God (Seventh Day), Denver, Colo.	89.8%	Latvian Evang. Lutheran church in Amer.	5.0%
Church of God Gen. Conf. (Abrahamic Faith)	-14.1%	Lutheran Church—Missouri Synod	-.7%
Church of God in Christ (Mennonite)	68.2%	Mennonite Church	30.4%
Church of Jesus Christ of Latter-day Saints	31.9%		

Table 2: 1980-1990 Comparison of U.S. Denominations—Continued

Denomination	1980-1990 % Change in Adherents
Mennonite Church, The General Conference	-12.7%
Missionary Church	26.8%
Moravian Church in America, Alaska Prov.	22.1%
Moravian Church in America, Northern Prov.	-4.1%
Moravian Church in America, Southern Prov.	1.0%
North American Baptist Conference	4.4%
Old Order Amish Church	42.1%
Pentecostal Holiness Church, Inc.	29.2%
Presbyterian Church (USA)*	-11.5%
Presbyterian Church in America*	95.7%
Primitive Advent Christian Church	-21.2%
Primitive Methodist Church, U.S.A.	-34.7%
Protestant Conference (Lutheran), The	-21.8%
Reformed Church in America	-2.2%
Reformed Episcopal Church	-10.9%
Salvation Army, The**	-64.7%
Seventh Day Baptist General Conference	4.8%

Denomination	1980-1990 % Change in Adherents
Seventh-day Adventists	35.1%
Southern Baptist Convention	16.3%
Syrian Orthodox Church of Antioch	25.1%
Unitarian Universalist Association**	21.7%
United Christian Church	-2.3%
United Church of Christ	-4.9%
United Methodist Church, The	-4.0%
Wisconsin Evangelical Lutheran Synod	3.8%
Total	12.4%

The national population changed 9.8%. The unclaimed population is 44.9% of the country.

* 1980 figures include denominations that merged during the decade.
** Methodology for reporting adherents differed in 1980 and 1990.
See *Churches and Church Membership in the United States, 1990* for methodology.

Notes:
1. Martin Bradley et al., Churches and Church Membership in the United States, 1990 (Atlanta: Glenmary Research Center, 1992). This publication lists statistics for Judaeo-Christian groups; however, there are a number of groups that are unable or unwilling to participate. This study is also related to three previous studies which collected data in 1952, 1971, and 1980. Publications are available through the Glenmary Research Center, 750 Piedmont Avenue NE, Atlanta, GA 30308. Datatapes are available through the Roper Center at the University of Connecticut in Storrs.
2. Many protestant denominations do not include children in membership, and a number of groups could not provide adherent data; therefore, an estimating formula was used to include children. The inclusion of children and other non-members is why this study's adherent figures are higher than the Yearbook's membership figures.
3. There are four exceptions to this in the 1990 study. Survey data was used to count Independent, Charismatic and Independent, non-Charismatic churches and adherents, Jewish synagogues and adherents, and Black Baptist adherents.
4. A listing of the family groupings can be found in the *Churches and Church Membership in the United States, 1990* publication on page xvi.
5. Bernard Quinn et al., *Churches and Church Membership in the United States, 1980* (Atlanta: Glenmary Research Center, 1982).

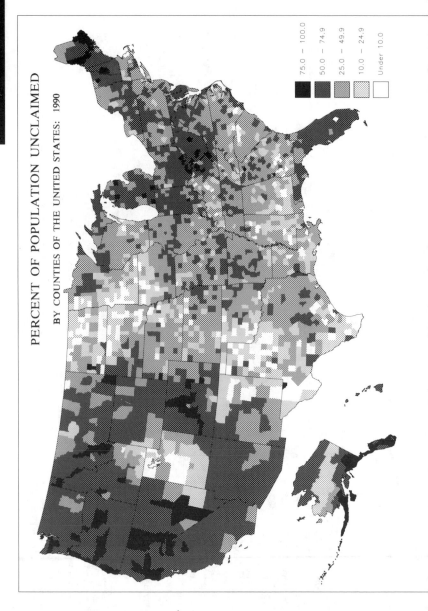

PERCENT OF POPULATION UNCLAIMED

BY COUNTIES OF THE UNITED STATES: 1990

75.0 — 100.0

50.0 — 74.9

25.0 — 49.9

10.0 — 24.9

Under 10.0

Empowering the Laity

George H. Gallup Jr.
Chairman, The George H. Gallup International Institute

To a growing extent, survey evidence indicates, the church of the future will be shaped from the "bottom up" rather than the "top down." And so it becomes increasingly important to give the laity a voice in the leadership of churches. In one survey we discovered that Americans by a 6 to 1 ratio said the laity (the people who attend religious services) should have greater influence in their churches. The ratio is yet higher among young upscale groups, who will provide a large share of the leadership of churches in the future.

One would have to conclude that if church leaders are not sensitive to the growing demands of the laity to have a role in leadership, organized religion could show further signs of slippage in the years ahead. This does not mean, of course, that the laity should take over the leadership of a given church — the clergy in charge are the authorities in spiritual matters — but the laity can do much to relieve the burden of the clergy.

Surveys can help open up the communications process in a church. The key role of a leader of a church, many would maintain, is to lead parishioners to ever deeper levels of faith. To do this, surveys can be very helpful in shedding light on levels of religious belief, practice and knowledge, as well as spiritual problems and needs — and to measure the degree of progress or lack of progress.

Let's take a moment to examine the role of religion in the United States in the broad sense. What is often missing from the media coverage of religion is the people in the pews, the people whose lives are influenced by the actions of church leaders and who, literally, make up the church's body. The "top down" approach characterizes much of organized religious life. When it comes to religion, Americans do not see their role, as it once was, to "pay, pray, and obey." They see their role as taking part fully in church life; the church, they believe, serves them, not the other way around.

Certainly, every good pastor, just like any other leader in society, has a sense of the nature and needs of this people. But social science surveys — public opinion polls — can provide unique and vital information about people. It's common in religious circles to talk dismissively about not wanting to "govern by the polls." Of course, religious leaders should no more govern by polls than should any other leader — if so doing means changing core beliefs to suit every change in fashion. But no one can truly lead without knowing what the people think and believe, and polls can provide that vital information.

Polls are in many ways a populist device: They empower the people themselves by letting them know what their neighbors, what all other Americans believe. And above all, they give the people a voice in leadership — whether of churches or of the nation.

Surveys enhance the listening process in churches. In his book, *Between Two Worlds,* the English author and evangelist John Stott offers this advice about listening:

"The best preachers know the people and understand the human scene in all its pain and pleasure, glory and tragedy. And the quickest way to gain such an understanding is to shut our mouths and open our eyes and ears. We need to ask people questions and get them talking. Clergy should encourage people to talk about and tell about their home and family life, their job, their expertise, and their spare time interests. We need to penetrate beyond their doing into the thinking."

One way of listening is to conduct a survey in a congregation or community to find out what people are thinking, what they know, what they believe, and what they see as needs for their church. This knowledge will improve the quality of congregational planning. But it will also improve the quality of communication within the church, improving listening skills, and helping people to talk more openly with one another.

Survey findings can replace hunches,

guesswork, and wishful thinking with objective information. Using a church survey can be a constructive and creative experience that can inform and build up the community and generate participation at every level.

In one sense, a survey can serve effectively as a tool of evangelism, as well as a measurement of faith. It can pose questions which challenge the reader to make choices than can relate to the basic tenets of faith. Responding honestly to such questions has the potential to change a person, or to start him on the road to change. For many, acknowledging unbelief is the first step toward belief.

Finally, a word about the follow-up to a survey. A survey is not worth undertaking unless it leads to specific action steps. What are the strengths upon which a church should build? What are the major challenges? What specific steps can be undertaken to deepen the faith of the parishioners? What can be done to maintain a productive balance between inner renewal and social renewal?

Many churches have excellent clergy that serve them well. But without the active support of the laity, they can do only so much. It's up to you!

II
DIRECTORIES

1. UNITED STATES COOPERATIVE ORGANIZATIONS, NATIONAL

The organizations listed in this section are cooperative religious organizations that are national in scope. All organizations are listed alphabetically including the National Council of the Churches of Christ in the USA.

American Bible Society

In 1816, pastors and laymen representing a variety of Christian denominations gathered in New York City to establish a truly interconfessional effort "to disseminate the Gospel of Christ throughout the habitable world." Since that time the American Bible Society (ABS) has continued to provide God's Word, without doctrinal note or comment, wherever it is needed and in the language and format the reader can most easily use and understand. The ABS is the servant of the denominations and local churches. It provides Scriptures at exceptionally low costs in various attractive formats for their use in outreach ministries here in the United States and all across the world.

Today the ABS has the endorsement of more than 100 denominations and agencies, and its board of managers is composed of distinguished clergy and laity drawn from these Christian groups.

Forty-six years ago the American Bible Society played a leading role in the founding of the United Bible Societies, that is involved in Scripture translation, publication, and distribution in more than 200 countries and territories around the world. The ABS contributes 40.3 percent of the support provided by the UBS to those national Bible Societies financially unable to meet the total Scripture needs of people in their own countries.

The work of the ABS is supported through gifts from individuals, local churches, denominations and cooperating agencies. Their generosity made possible the distribution of 259,930,278 copies of the Scriptures during 1990, out of a total of 639,249,849 copies of the Scriptures distributed by all member societies of the UBS.

HEADQUARTERS

1865 Broadway, New York, NY 10023 Tel. (212)408-1200

Media Contact, Dir., Pub. Rel., William P. Cedfeldt, Tel. (212)408-1419 Fax (212)408-1456

OFFICERS

Chpsn., James Wood
Vice-Chpsn., Mrs. Norman Vincent Peale
2nd Vice-Chpsn., Mrs. Sally Shoemaker Robinson
Pres. & CEO, Dr. Eugene B. Habecker
Vice-Pres. for Natl. Programs, Maria I. Martinez
Vice-Pres. for Dev., Arthur Caccese
Vice-Pres. of Fin. & Treas., Daniel K. Scarberry
Departmental Heads: Dir., Natl. Program Dev., Rev. Fred A. Allen; Dir., Translation & Scripture Res. Dev., Rev. David G. Burke; Dir., Public Relations, William P. Cedfeldt; Dir., Human Resources, Robert P. Fichtel; Dir., Production & Supply, Gary R. Ruth; Dir., Systems, George Balinski; Dir. Library & Archival Services, Dr. Peter Wosh

American Council of Christian Churches

Founded in 1941, The American Council of Christian Churches (ACCC) is comprised of major denominations—Bible Presbyterian Church, Evangelical Methodist Church, Fellowship of Fundamental Bible Churches (formerly Bible Protestant), Fellowship of Independent Methodists, Free Presbyterian Church of North America, Fundamental Methodist Church, General Association of Regular Baptist Churches, Independent Baptist Fellowship and Independent Churches Affiliated, along with hundreds of independent churches. The total membership nears 2 million. Each denomination retains its identity and full autonomy, but cannot be associated with the World Council of Churches, National Council of Churches, or National Association of Evangelicals.

The ACCC stands as an agency for fellowship and cooperation on the part of Bible-believing churches, for the maintenance of a pure testimony to the great fundamental truths of the Word of God: the inspiration and inerrancy of Scripture; the triune God—Father, Son, and Holy Spirit; the virgin birth; substitutionary death and resurrection of Christ, and His second coming; total depravity of man; salvation by grace through faith; and the necessity of maintaining the purity of the church in doctrine and life.

HEADQUARTERS

P.O. Box 816, Valley Forge, PA 19482 Tel. (215)566-8154

OFFICERS

Pres., Dr. E. Allen Griffith
Vice-Pres., Rev. Mark Franklin
Exec. Sec., Dr. Ralph Colas
Sec., Rev. David Natale
Treas., Mr. William H. Worrilow, Jr.
Commissions: Chaplaincy; Education; Laymen; Literature; Missions; Radio & Audio Visual; Relief; Youth

American Friends Service Committee

The American Friends Service Committee began 75 years ago as a World War I Quaker effort to provide humanitarian assistance to civilians whose lives were devastated by violence. Since then, AFSC has evolved into a complex organization addressing an array of the most pressing issues before the human family.

AFSC's recent programs illustrate common themes that have emerged over nearly eight decades of multi-faceted Quaker witness to the dignity of all people. During the Gulf War, AFSC's role again expressed Friends' opposition to all war and support for those whose convictions lead them to reject participation in killing. AFSC's assistance to Iraqis who suffered the violence of war represents continuing Quaker service to war victims regardless of nationality and politics. Development and training programs in Cambodia reflect AFSC's commitment to move from emergency assistance to programs that aid in the rebuilding of people's lives.

These and other programs illustrate the work for justice, peace and development which is based in timeless religious faith and the commitment of our predecessors in Quaker Service.

HEADQUARTERS

1501 Cherry St., Philadelphia, PA 19102 Tel. (215)241-7000 Fax (215)864-0104
Media Contact, Lady Borton

OFFICERS

Chpsn., Dulaney O. Bennett
Treas., Lois Forrest
Exec. Sec., Kara Newell

The American Theological Library Association, Inc.

The American Theological Library Association, Inc. (ATLA) is a special library association that works to improve theological and religious libraries and librarianship by providing continuing education, developing standards, promoting research and experimental projects, encouraging cooperative programs and publishing and disseminating research tools and aids. Founded in 1947, ATLA currently has a membership of over 180 institutions and 500 individuals.

HEADQUARTERS

820 Church St., Ste. 300, Evanston, IL 60201 Tel. (708)869-7788
Media Contact, Exec. Sec., Joanne Juhnke

OFFICERS

Pres., Mary Bischoff, Jesuit/Krauss/McCormick Library, 1100 E. 55th St., Chicago, IL 60615
Vice-Pres., Linda Corman, Trinity College Library, 6 Hoskin Ave., Toronto, ON M5S 1H8
Sec., David J. Wartluft, Krauth Memorial Library, 7301 Germantown Ave., Philadelphia, PA 19119-1794
Exec. Dir./CEO, Albert E. Hurd

American Tract Society

The American Tract Society is a nonprofit, nonsectarian, interdenominational organization, instituted in 1825 through the merger of most of the then-existing tract societies. As one of the earliest religious publishing bodies in the United States, ATS has pioneered in the publishing of Christian books, booklets, and leaflets. The volume of distribution has risen to more than 25 million pieces of literature annually.

HEADQUARTERS

P.O. Box 462008, Garland, TX 75046 Tel. (214)276-9408 Fax (214)272-9642
Media Contact, Dir. of Marketing, Perry Brown

OFFICERS

Chpsn., Stephen E. Slocum, Jr.
Vice-Chpsns., Arthur J. Widman, Philip E. Worth
Sec., Edgar L. Bensen
Treas., Raymond P. Negris

The American Waldensian Society

The American Waldensian Society (AWS) promotes ministry linkages, broadly ecumenical, between U.S. churches and Waldensian-Methodist (Reformed) constituencies in Italy and Waldensian constituencies in Argentina-Uruguay. Founded in 1906, AWS aims to enlarge mission discovery and partnership among overseas Waldensian-Methodist forces and denominational forces in the U.S.

AWS is governed by a national ecumenical board, although it consults and collaborates closely with the three overseas Waldensian-Methodist boards. The Waldensian experience is the earliest continuing Protestant experience.

HEADQUARTERS

475 Riverside Dr., Rm. 1850, New York, NY 10115 Tel. (212)870-2671 Fax (212)870-2499
Media Contact, Exec. Dir., Rev. Frank G. Gibson, Jr.

OFFICERS

Pres., Rev. Laura R. Jervis
Vice-Pres., Rev. Gilbert W. Bowen, D.Min.
Sec., Rev. Ralph E. Ahlberg
Treas., Lon Haines
Exec. Dir., Rev. Frank G. Gibson, Jr.

The Associated Church Press

The Associated Church Press was organized in 1916. Its member publications include major Protestant, Anglican, and Orthodox groups in the U.S. and Canada. Some Roman Catholic publications and major ecumenical journals are also members. It is a professional religious journalistic association seeking to promote better understanding among editors, raise standards, and represent the interests of the religious press. It sponsors seminars, conventions, awards programs, and workshops for editors, staff people, and business managers.

HEADQUARTERS

502 Edgeworthe S.E., Grand Rapids, MI 49546
Media Contact, Exec. Dir., Rev. John Stapert, P.O. Box 162, Ada, MI 49301 Tel. (616)676-1017

OFFICERS

Pres., Tom McGrath, 205 W. Monroe, Chicago, IL 60606
Exec. Dir., Rev. John Stapert, P.O. Box 162, Ada, MI 49301 Tel. (616)676-1190
Treas., Chris Woehr, P.O. Box 28001, Santa Ana, CA 92799

The Associated Gospel Churches

Organized in 1939, The Associated Gospel Churches (AGC) endorses chaplains primarily for Fundamental Independent Baptist Churches to the U.S. Armed Forces. The AGC has been recognized by the U.S. Department of Defense for more than

50 years as an Endorsing Agency, and it supports a strong national defense. The AGC also endorses VA chaplains, police and prison chaplains.

The AGC provides fellowship and missionary support for Fundamental Independent Churches and represents their seminaries, colleges, and Bible Institutes.

The AGC believes in the sovereignty of the local church; the historic doctrines of the Christian faith and the infallibility of the Bible; and practices separation from apostasy.

HEADQUARTERS

114 West Hackney Road, Greer, SC 29650 Tel. (803)292-8610

OFFICERS

Pres. & Chpsn., Comm. on Chaplains, Dr. Everette J. Thomas, USA (Ret.)
Vice-Pres. & Vice-Chpsn., Comm. on Chaplains, George W. Baugham, D.D., AGC Admn. Ofc., P.O. Box 10777, Killeen, TX 76547 Tel. (817)539-4666 Fax (817)539-4242
Sec.-Treas., Mrs. Eva Baugham
Natl. Field Rep., Rev. Charles Flesher

Association for the Development of Religious Information Systems

The Association for the Development of Religious Information Systems (or Services) was established in 1971 to facilitate coordination and cooperation among information services that pertain to religion. Its goal is a worldwide network that is interdisciplinary, inter-faith and interdenominational to serve both administrative and research applications.

HEADQUARTERS

2619 E. Newberry Blvd., Milwaukee, WI 53211 Tel. (414)964-3465
Media Contact, Coord., David O. Moberg

Association of Catholic Diocesan Archivists

The Association of Catholic Diocesan Archivists, which began in 1979, has been committed to the active promotion of professionalism in the management of diocesan archives. The Association meets annually: in the even years it has its own summer conference, in the odd years it meets in conjunction with the Society of American Archivists. Publications include Standards for *Diocesan Archives* and an *Access Policy for Diocesan Archives.*

HEADQUARTERS

Archives & Records Center, 5150 Northwest Hwy., Chicago, IL 60630 Tel. (312)736-5150 Fax (312)736-0488
Media Contact, Ms. Nancy Sandleback

OFFICERS

Episcopal Moderator, Archbishop of Chicago, Joseph Cardinal Bernardin
Pres., Rev. George C. Michalek, 300 W. Ottawa St., Lansing, MI 48933 Tel. (517)342-2455
Vice-Pres., Mr. John J. Treanor
Sec.-Treas., Sr. Catherine Louise LaCoste, C.S.J., P.O. Box 85728, San Diego, CA 92186-5728 Tel. (619)574-6309
Bd. Members: Msgr. Francis J. Weber, 15151 San Fernando Mission Blvd., Mission Hills, CA 91345 Tel. (818)365-1501; Ronald D. Patkus, 2121 Commonwealth Ave., Brighton, MA 03235 Tel. (617)254-0100; Johanna Mims, P.O. Box 36776, Charlotte, NC 28236 Tel. (704)377-6871; Rev. Dale McFarlane, P.O. Box 1399, Great Falls, MT 59403 Tel. (406)727-6683
Newsletter Editor, Nancy Sandleback

Association of Regional Religious Communicators (ARRC)

ARRC is a professional association of regional, ecumenical and interfaith communicators who work with local, state and regional religious agencies to fulfill their needs by providing occasional syndicated television and radio programs to members. ARRC also publishes the quarterly *ARRC Newsletter*. ARRC provides local representation on the Communication Commission of the National Council of Churches, before the Federal Communications Commission, and with the denominations. ARRC offers fellowship by participation at the annual convention of the North American Broadcast Section of the World Association for Christian Communication, by updating names and addresses of national and local communicators.

OFFICERS

Pres., Margaret Hoepfl, Ecumenical Communications of NW Ohio, 1102 Sandusky, Ste. M, Perrysburg, OH 43552 Tel. (409)874-3932

Association of Statisticians of American Religious Bodies

This Association was organized in 1934 and grew out of personal consultations held by representatives from *The Yearbook of American Churches*, *The National* (now *Official*) *Catholic Directory*, the Jewish Statistical Bureau, The Methodist (now The United Methodist), the Lutheran, and the Presbyterian churches.

ASARB has a variety of purposes: to bring together those officially and professionally responsible for gathering, compiling, and publishing denominational statistics; to provide a forum for the exchange of ideas and sharing of problems in statistical methods and procedure; and to seek such standardization as may be possible in religious statistical data.

HEADQUARTERS

c/o American Baptist Churches,USA, P.O. Box 851, Valley Forge, PA 19082-0851 Tel. (215)768-2480 Fax (215)768-2470
Media Contact, Sec.-Treas., Dr. Norman M. Green, Jr., c/o American Baptist Churches

OFFICERS

Pres., Dale E. Jones, Church of the Nazarene, 6401 The Paseo, Kansas City, MO 64131 Tel. (816)333-7000 Fax (816)333-1683
1st Vice-Pres., Lou McNeil, Glenmary Research Center, 750 Piedmont Ave. N.E., Atlanta, GA 30308 Tel. (404)876-6518 Fax (404)876-0604
2nd Vice-Pres., Ms. Greta Lauria, Presbyterian Church (USA), 100 Witherspoon St. #4420, Louisville, KY 40202-1396 Tel. (502)569-5360 Fax (502)569-8005
Sec.-Treas., Dr. Norman M. Green, Jr., American Baptist Churches, U.S.A., P.O. Box 851, Valley Forge, PA 19082-0851 Tel. (215)768-2480 Fax (215)768-2470

Campus Crusade for Christ International

Campus Crusade for Christ International is an interdenominational, evangelistic and discipleship ministry dedicate to helping fulfill the Great Commission through the multiplication strategy of win-build-send. Formed in 1951 on the campus of UCLA, the organization now includes 40 separate ministries reaching out to almost every segment of society. There are more than 40,000 full-time, trained associate and volunteer staff in 152 countries, with the numbers expanding almost daily. The NewLife 2000 (Reg) strategy to give every person on earth an opportunity to say "yes" to Jesus Christ by the year 2000 includes thousands of churches of all denominations and 350 mission groups.

HEADQUARTERS
100 Sunport La., Orlando, FL 32809 Tel. (407)826-2000 Fax (407)826-2120
Media Contact, Sid Wright

OFFICERS
Pres., William R. Bright
Exec. Vice-Pres., Stephen B. Douglass
Vice-Pres. of Admn. & Chief Financial Officer, Kenneth P. Heckmann
Vice-Pres. of Intl. Ministries, Bailey E. Marks

CARA—Center for Applied Research in the Apostolate

CARA—the Center for Applied Research in the Apostolate is a not-for-profit research organization, founded by a group of Roman Catholic laity, bishops, clergy and religious (men and women) on the premise that not only theological principles but also the findings of secular sciences, especially sociology and psychology, must be the basis for pastoral care.

CARA performs a wide range of studies and services including church management, religious life research and planning, church personnel, education, health care ministry, parish development. Since its roots are Roman Catholic, many of its studies are done for dioceses, religious orders, educational institutions, hospitals and social service agencies. Interdenominational studies are also performed.

HEADQUARTERS
Georgetown University, P.O. Box 1601, Washington, DC 20057 Tel. (202)687-8080 Fax (202)687-8083
Media Contact, Msgr. Edward C. Foster

OFFICERS
Exec. Dir., Msgr. Edward C. Foster
Senior Research Assoc., Sr. Eleace King, Ed.D.
Research Assoc., Dr. Joseph O'Hara, Ph.D.

Center for Parish Development

The Center for Parish Development is an ecumenical, non-profit research and development agency whose mission is to facilitate major and profound change in church organizations in today's post-Christendom era. Founded in 1968, the Center's goals are to develop an *ecclesial* paradigm (to challenge the current *privacy* and *societal* paradigms), to develop and test transformation theory and practice in church systems, to apply systems theory to the work of church transformation, and to contribute to the practical theology conversation.

The Center staff provides research, consulting, and training resources for church organizations engaging in major change. The Center is governed by a 12-member Board of Directors.

HEADQUARTERS
5407 S. University Ave., Chicago, IL 60615 Tel. (312)752-1596
Media Contact, Exec. Dir., Paul M. Dietterich

OFFICERS
Chairperson, Eugene L. Delves, 9142 S. Winchester Ave., Chicago, IL 60620
Vice-Chair, Pastor Gordon Nusz, United Methodist Church, 2458 W. State Rd., West Branch, MI 48661
Sec., Raymond L. Alley, 5916 Cresthaven Ln, #527B, Toledo, OH 43614
Treas., Robert J. Schreiter, C.P.P.S., Catholic Theological Union, 5401 S. Cornell Ave., Chicago, IL 60615
Past Chair, Anthony Shipley, The United Methodist Church, 475 Riverside Dr., Ste. 300, New York, NY 10115
Exec. Dir., Paul M. Dietterich

Christian Endeavor International

Christian Endeavor is a Christ-centered, youth-oriented ministry which assists the local church in reaching young people with the gospel of Jesus Christ, discipling them in the Christian faith and equipping them for Christian ministry and service in their local church, community, and world. It reaches across denominational, cultural, racial, and geographical boundaries.

Christian Endeavor Internation produces materials for program enrichment, provides seminars for equipping youth leaders for effective ministry, and holds conferences and conventions for Christian inspiration, spiritual growth, and fellowship.

Organized in Portland, Maine, in February 18881, there now are active Christian Endeavor groups in approximately 78 nations and island groups, totaling over 2 million members.

HEADQUARTERS
1221 E. Broad St., P.O. Box 1110, Columbus, OH 43216-1110 Tel. (614)258-9545 Fax (614)2522-2311

OFFICERS
Pres., Rev. Richard Cattermole
Exec. Dir., Rev. David G. Jackson

Christian Holiness Association

The Association is a coordinating agency of those religious bodies that hold the Wesleyan-Arminian theological view. It was organized in 1867.

HEADQUARTERS
CHA Center, S. Walnut St., P.O. Box 100, Wilmore, KY 40390 Tel. (606)858-4091

OFFICERS
Pres., Dr. Thomas Hermiz, World Gospel Mission, Box WGM, Marion, IN 46952
Exec. Dir., Burnis H. Bushong, World Gospel Mission, Box WGM, Marion, IN 46952

AFFILIATED ORGANIZATIONS
Bible Holiness Movement
Brethren in Christ Church
Churches of Christ in Christian Union
Evangelical Christian Church
Evangelical Church of North America

Evangelical Friends Alliance
Evangelical Methodist Church
Free Methodist Church in North America
The Church of the Nazarene
The Salvation Army
The Salvantion Army in Canada
United Brethren in Christ Church (Sandusky Conference)
The Wesleyan Church
Japan Immanuel Church

Christian Management Association

Christian Management Association is a member-based association devoted to educating, equipping, and encouraging its members to improve their management skills. More than 3,200 members nationwide, both individually and organizationally, we have 60 local chapters participating in strengthening, encouraging, and challenging one another to perform the Lord's work with excellence and integrity.

As a nonprofit organization, CMA understands the complex and demanding needs of churches, parachurch organizations and other Christian ministries. Whether your area of responsibility is in church management, planning, leading, fund raising, administration, data processing, finance, accounting, law or a related field, CMA has the resources and services to help you do a better job.

Through seminars, books, tapes, newsletters, bi-monthly chapter meetins, and much more, CMA strives in every way to live out its credo "Members Serving Members".

HEADQUARTERS
22632 Golden Springs, Ste. 390, Diamond Bar, CA 91765 Tel. (909)861-8861 Fax (909)860-8247
Media Contact, Dir., Sylvia Nash

OFFICERS
Chairman of the Board, Commissioner James Osborne, The Salvation Army, 615 Slaters Lane, Alexandria, VA 22313
Vice-Chairman, Patrick Clements, Church Extension Plan, P.O. Box 12629, Salem, OR 97309
Treas., C. E. Crouse, Jr., Capin, Crouse & Company, 720 Executive Park Drive, Greenwood, IN 46143
Sec., Frederick Rudy, Good News Publishers, 1300 Crescent St., Wheaton, IL 60187
Dir., Silvia Nash

A Christian Ministry in the National Parks

The Ministry is an independent ecumenical movement providing interdenominational religious services in 65 National Parks, Monuments, and Recreation Areas. For 20 years it was administered in the National Council of Churches. On Jan. 1, 1972, it became an independent movement representing more than 40 denominations, 60 local park committees, more than 300 theological seminaries, and 16 separate religious organizations. The program recruits and staffs 300 positions, winter and summer, in 65 areas.

HEADQUARTERS
222 1/2 E. 49th St., New York, NY 10017 Tel. (212) 758-3450

Religious News Service photo

Starving in Somalia
Churches rushed to aid starving Somalians in the civil war-torn African country. In December, President George Bush sent U.S. troops to open up food supply routes cut off by rival clans. This starving, elderly woman fled with hundreds of thousands of Somalians to a squalid camp in neighboring Ethiopia.

OFFICER
Dir., Dr. Warren W. Ost

Church Growth Center

The Church Growth Center is an interfaith, nonprofit, professional organization of men and women who have the responsibility for promoting, planning, and/or managing meetings, workshops, conferences, and consultation services for churches, assemblies and other religious organizations.

Founded in 1978, the Church Growth Center ministry always strives toward bringing about the transformational change of the Christian Church toward the effective implementation of the Lord's Great Commission to make disciples of all peoples.

With focus on the Great Commission, today the Church Growth Center provides resources in the form of books, workshop materials, and services, which has not only been used nationally but internationally.

The Church Growth Center has conducted annual conferences and meetings that have gone to Africa, Cambodia, Japan, Korea, and many other places.

HEADQUARTERS
1230 U. S. Highway Six, P.O. Box 145, Corunna, IN 46730 Tel. (219)281-2452 Fax (219)281-2167
Media Contact, Operations Mgr., Franklin L. Grepke

OFFICERS

Pres., Dr. Kent R. Hunter, D. Min.
Vice-Pres., Walter J. Kuleck, Ph.D., Cognitive Processes Inc., 3631 Fairmount Blvd., Cleveland, OH 44118
Sec.-Treas., Paul Griebel, M.Div., St. John Lutheran Church, 312 S. Oak Street, Kendallville, IN 46755

Church Women United in the U.S.A.

Church Women United in the U.S.A. is an ecumenical lay movement providing Protestant, Orthodox, and Roman Catholic and other Christian women with programs and channels of involvement in church, civic, and national affairs. CWU has some 1,750 units formally organized in communities in all 50 states, greater Washington, D.C., and Puerto Rico.

HEADQUARTERS

475 Riverside Dr., Rm. 812, New York, NY 10115 Tel. (212)870-2347 Fax (212)870-2338
Other Offices: 777 United Nations Plz., New York, NY 10017 Tel. (212)661-3856; CWU Washington Ofc., 110 Maryland Ave. NE, Rm. 108, Washington, DC 20002 Tel. (202)544-8747

OFFICERS

Pres., Ann B. Garvin, New York, N.Y.
1st Vice-Pres., Van Lynch, Indianapolis, Ind.
2nd Vice-Pres., Jo Walton, Tuskegee, Ala.
Sec./Treas., Helen Quirino, Portland, Ore.
Regional Coordinators: Central, Miriam Cline, Urbandale, Iowa; East Central, Helen Hokenson, Huntington Woods, Mich.; Mid-Atlantic, Hatti Hamilton, Philadelphia, Pa.; Northeast, Carolyn Hill, Moorestown, N.J.; Northwest, Nadine Riley, Portland, Ore.; South Central, Marjorie Troeh, Independence, Mo.; Southeast, Catharine Vick, Durham, N.C.; Southwest, Beverley Wolfard, Phoenix, Ariz.

STAFF

Gen. Dir., Patricia J. Rumer, Tel. (212)870-2343
Comptroller, Anne Martin, Tel. (212)870-2345
Dir. of Admn. Services, Beverly Oates, Tel. (212)870-3035
Ecumenical Action Office, ——, Tel. (212)870-3054
Dir. of Ecumenical Celebrations, Mary Cline Detrick, (212)870-2348-New York, (703)432-5568-Virginia
Dir. of Fin. Dev./Comp. Services, Marcia Parker, Tel. (212)870-3047
Communications Office, ——, (212)870-2364
Dir. of Ecumenical Development, Robina Winbush, Tel. (212)870-3046
Prog. Coord. (United Nations Ofc.), Winnie Arceo, Tel. (212)661-3856
Dir., Washington, D.C. Ofc., Nancy Chupp, 110 Maryland Ave. N.E., Rm. 108, Washington, DC 20002 Tel. (202)544-8747

CODEL—Coordination in Development

CODEL is a membership association of Orthodox, Protestant and Roman Catholic mission-sending agencies, communions and Christian organizations working together in international development. Founded in 1969, CODEL is committed to an ecumenical approach in the development process. The 40 U.S.-based member organizations combine expertise, funds, planning, project implementation and evaluation in a spirit of Christian unity working toward self-sufficiency of the poorest peoples and communities of the world.

There are more than 80 projects in 30 countries in health, agriculture, community development, and informal education. Other CODEL programs include current issues, development education activities, environment and development projects and workshops.

CODEL's budget for 1991/92 was $1,968,000.

HEADQUARTERS

475 Riverside Dr., Rm. 1842, New York, NY 10115 Tel. (212)870-3000 Fax (212)870-3545
Media Contact, Exec. Dir., Boyd Lowry

OFFICERS

Pres., The Very Rev. John Lynch
1st Vice-Pres., Sr. Margaret Rogers
Sec., Mr. Kelly Miller
Treas., Rev. Theo Feldbrugge

STAFF

Exec. Dir., Rev. Boyd Lowry
Coord. for Africa, Dr. Caroline W. Njuki
Coord. for Asia & the Pacific, Dr. A. C. Bartholomew
Coord. for Latin America & Caribbean, ——
Environment & Development, Sr. Mary Ann Smith
Ecumenical Relations/Development Educ., Rev. Nathan VanderWerf
Accountant, Florence Tees

Consultation on Church Union

Officially constituted in 1962, the Consultation on Church Union is a venture in reconciliation of nine American communions. It has been authorized to explore the formation of a united church, truly catholic, truly evangelical, and truly reformed. In 1992 the participating churches are African Methodist Episcopal Church, African Methodist Episcopal Zion Church, Christian Church (Disciples of Christ), Christian Methodist Episcopal Church, The Episcopal Church, International Council of Community Churches, Presbyterian Church (U.S.A.), United Church of Christ, and The United Methodist Church.

The Plenary Assembly, which normally meets every four or five years, is composed of 10 delegates and 10 associate delegates from each of the participating churches. Included also are observer-consultants from more than 20 other churches, other union negotiations, and conciliar bodies. The most recent Plenaries have been held in 1984 (Baltimore) and 1988 (New Orleans.)

The Executive Committee is composed of the president, two representatives from each of the participating churches, and the secretariat. The Secretariat consists of the full-time executive staff of the Consultation, all of whom are based at the national office in Princeton, N.J. Various task groups are convened to fulfill certain assignments. In 1990 there were four task groups: Communications, Unity & Justice, Theology, and Special Gifts. In addition there was an Editorial Board for the annual Lenten Booklet of devotional meditations.

HEADQUARTERS

151 Wall St., Princeton, NJ 08540 Tel. (609)921-7866 Fax (609)921-0471

OFFICERS

Gen. Sec., Dr. David W. A. Taylor

Treas./Bus. Mgr., Christine V. Bilarczyk
Conf. Proj. Mgr., Dr. Robert L. Polk

OFFICERS
Pres., Dr. Vivian U. Robinson, 125 Hernlen St., Augusta, GA 30901
Vice-Pres.: Bishop Vinton R. Anderson, P.O. Box 6416, St. Louis, MO 63107; Rev. Alice C. Cowan, Trinity Episcopal Church, Oxford, OH 456566
Sec., Rev. Clyde H. Miller, Jr., 7000 Broadway, A.B.S. Bldg., Denver, CO 80221

REP. FROM PARTICIPATING CHURCHES
African Methodist Episcopal Church: Bishop Vinton R. Anderson, 4144 Lindell Blvd., Ste. 222, St. Louis, MO 63108; Bishop Frederick C. James, 3700 Forest Drive, #5022, Columbia, SC 29204
African Methodist Episcopal Zion Church: Bishop J. Clinton Hoggard, 1511 K. St. N.W., Ste. 1100, Washington, DC 20005; Bishop Cecil Bishop, 5401 Broadwater St., Temple Hill, MD 20748
Christian Church (Disciples of Christ): Rev. Dr. Paul A. Crow, Jr., P.O. Box 1986, Indianapolis, IN 46206; Rev. Dr. Albert M. Pennybacker, 120 E. Main St., Apt. 2101, Lexington, KY 40507
Christian Methodist Episcopal Church: Bishop Marshall Gilmore, 109 Holcomb Dr., Shreveport, LA 71103; Dr. Vivian U. Robinson, 1256 Hernlen St., Augusta, GA 30901
The Episcopal Church: Rt. Rev. William G. Burrill, 935 East Ave., Rochester, NY 14607; Rev. Alice C. Cowan, Holy Trinity Episcopal Church, Oxford, OH 45656
Intl. Council of Community Churches: Rev. Dr. Jeffrey R. Newhall, 7808 College Dr., Ste. 2-SE, Palos Hts., IL 60463; Mr. Abraham Wright, 1909 East-West Hwy., Silver Springs, MD 20910
Presbyterian Church (U.S.A.): Rev. Michael E. Livingston, CN-821, Princeton, NJ 08542; Rev. Lewis H. Lancaster, Jr., 100 Witherspoon St., Rm. 3418, Louisville, KY 40202
United Church of Christ: Rev. Clyde H. Miller, Jr., 7000 Broadway, A.B.S. Bldg., Ste. 420, Denver, CO 80221; Rev. Dr. Thomas E. Dipko, 4041 N. High St., Ste. 301, Columbus, OH 43214
The United Methodist Church: Bishop William B. Grove, 234 Lark Street, Albany, NY 12210; Rev. Dr. Larry D. Pickens, 5600 S. Indiana Ave., Chicago, IL 60649

The Evangelical Church Alliance

The Evangelical Church Alliance was incorporated in 1928 in Missouri as The World's Faith Missionary Association and was later known as The Fundamental Ministerial Association. The title Evangelical Church Alliance was adopted in 1958.

ECA (1) licenses and ordains ministers who are qualified and provides them with credentials from a recognized ecclesiastical body; (2) provides through the Bible Extension Institute courses of study to those who have not had seminary or Bible school training; (3) provides an organization for autonomous churches so they may have communion and association with one another; (4) provides an organization where members can find companionship through correspondence, Regional Conventions, and General Conventions; (5) cooperates with churches in finding new pastors when vacancies occur in their pulpits.

ECA is an interdenominational, nonsectarian, Evangelical organization. Total ordained and licensed clergy members—1,802.

HEADQUARTERS
205 W. Broadway St., P.O. Box 9, Bradley, IL 60915 Tel. (815)937-0720

OFFICERS
Exec. Dir., Rev. George L. Miller
Pres., Dr. Charles Wesley Ewing, 321 W. Harrison St., Royal Oak, MI 48067
1st Vice-Pres., Dr. Sterling L. Cauble, Sunman Bible Church, P.O. Box 216, Sunman, IN 47041
2nd Vice-Pres., Rev. Richard J. Sydnes, P.O. Box 355, Des Moines, IA 50302

Evangelical Council for Financial Accountability

Founded in 1979, the Evangelical Council for Financial Accountability has the purpose of helping Christ-centered, evangelical, nonprofit organizations earn the public's trust through their ethical practices and financial accountability. ECFA assists its over 700 member organizations in making appropriate public disclosure of their financial practices and accomplishments, thus materially enhancing their credibility and support potential among present and prospective donors.

HEADQUARTERS
2411 Dulles Corner Park, Ste. 140, Herndon, VA 22071-3430 Tel. (703)713-1414 Fax (703)713-1133
P.O. Box 17456, Washington, DC 20041-0456
Media Contact, Pres., Clarence Reimer

OFFICERS
Pres., Clarence Reimer
Deputy Exec. Officer, Martha James
Dir. of Member Services, Lucinda McCord

Evangelical Press Association

The Evangelical Press Association is an organization of editors and publishers of Christian periodicals which seeks to promote the cause of Evangelical Christianity and enhance the influence of Christian journalism.

OFFICERS
Pres., Robert Ingram, Tabletalk Magazine, P.O. Box 7500, Orlando, FL 32854
Sec., Jonathan Singer, The Christian Jew Foundation, Box 470654, Charlotte, NC 28247-0654
Treas., W. Terry Whalin, Decision Magazine, 1300 Harmon Pl., Minneapolis, MN 55403
Exec. Dir., Ronald Wilson, 485 Panorama Rd., Earlysville, VA 22936 Tel. (804)973-5941 Fax (804)973-2710

Fellowship of Reconcilliation

The Fellowship of Reconciliation is an interfaith pacifist organization that has been working for peace and justice since 1915. The FOR has programs in the areas of international peace, social justice, and nonviolence education in an effort to respond creatively and compassionately to issues of violence and injustice.

HEADQUARTERS
Box 271, Nyack, NY 10960 Tel. (914)358-4601 Fax (914)358-4924
Media Contact, Ed. and Communications Dir., Robin Washington

OFFICERS

Chair, Natl. Council, Karim Alkadhi, 1556 Castle Ct., Houston, TX 77006-5706
Vice-Chair, Natl. Council, Paula Green, 49 Richardson Rd., Leverett, MA 01054
Exec. Sec., C. Douglas Hostetter

RELIGIOUS PEACE FELLOWSHIPS

Presbyterian Peace Fellowship
Jewish Peace Fellowship
Baptist Peace Fellowship of N. America
Buddhist Peace Fellowship
Sojourners Peace Ministry
NISBCO
Pax Christi USA
World Peacemakers
Church of God Peace Fellowship
Episcopal Peace Fellowship
Disciples Peace Fellowship
Methodist Peace Fellowship
Catholic Peace Fellowship
Lutheran Peace Fellowship
Unitarian Universalist Peace Fellowship
New Call to Peacemaking
Orthodox Peace Fellowship
United Church of Christ FOR
Brethren Peace Fellowship
Disciples Peace Fellowship
Hutterian Fellowship

Glenmary Research Center

The Research Center is a department of the Glenmary Home Missioners, a Catholic society of priests and brothers. The Center was established in 1966 to serve the rural research needs of the Catholic Church in the United States. Its research has led it to serve ecumenically a wide variety of church bodies. Local case studies as well as quantitative research is done to understand better the diversity of contexts in the rural sections of the country. The Center's statistical profiles of the nation's counties cover both urban and rural counties.

HEADQUARTERS

750 Piedmont Ave., NE, Atlanta, GA 30308 Tel. (404)876-6518
Media Contact, Dr. Clifford Granmich

OFFICERS

Pres., Rev. Robert A. Dalton, P.O. Box 465618, Cincinnati, OH 45246-5618
1st Vice-Pres., Rev. Gerald Dorn, P.O. Box 465618, Cincinnati, OH 45246-5618
2nd Vice-Pres., Bro. Terrence O'Rourke, P.O. Box 465618, Cincinnati, OH 45246-5618
Treas., Mr. Robert Knueven, P.O. Box 465618, Cincinnati, OH 45246-5618
Dir., Rev. Lou McNeil

Higher Education Ministries Team

The Higher Education Ministries Team has emerged out of United Ministries in Education. It embodies the covenant-based ministry coalition created more than thirty years ago and carries forward the work of United Campus Christian Fellowship, United Ministries in Education and Ministries in Public Education (K-12). HEMT works with churches and educational institutions as they seek to express their concern about the ways in which educating forces affect quality of life. HEMT focuses on the goal to design, manage, facilitate, nurture, and participate in partnerships with regional and denominational organizations in support of ministry in higher education. Current programs include mission and resource partnerships, campus ministry training for fundraising, AIDS prevention education, strategic conversations for developing models and planning strategies at the state and regional levels, training for new campus ministers and chaplains, personnel services, support and network for Christian student organizations including the World Student Christian Federation and the Council for Ecumenical Student Christian Ministry and promoting the informal networking of people, resources and experiences of people in the field.

OFFICERS

Admn. Coord., Clyde O. Robinson, Jr., 7407 Steele Creek Rd., Charlotte, NC 28217 Tel. (704)588-2182 Fax (704)588-3652
Treas., Gary Harke, P. O. Box 386, Sun Prairie, WI 53590 Tel. (608)837-0537 Fax (608)825-6610
Personnel Service, Lawrence S. Steinmetz, 11780 Borman Dr., Ste. 100, St.Louis, MO 63146 Tel. (314)991-3000 Fax (314)993-9018
Resource Center, Linda Freeman, 7407 Steele Creek Rd., Charlotte, NC 28217 Tel. (704)588-2182 Fax (704)588-3652

PARTICIPATING DENOMINATIONS

Christian Church (Disciples of Christ)
Church of the Brethren
Moravian Church (Northern Province)
Presbyterian Church (U.S.A.)
United Church of Christ

Institutes of Religion and Health

The Institutes of Religion and Health is dedicated to helping people overcome emotional obstacles by joining mental health expertise with religious faith and values. Its Blanton-Peale Graduate Institute provides advanced training in marriage and family therapy, psychotherapy and pastoral care for ministers, rabbis, sisters, priests and other counselors. Its Blanton-Peale Counselor Centers provide counseling for individuals, couples, families and groups. IRH also offers a nationwide telephone support service for clergy and social service agencies and promotes interdisciplinary communication among theology, medicine and the behavioral sciences. IRH was founded in 1937 by Dr. Norman Vincent Peale and psychiatrist Smiley Blanton, M.D.

HEADQUARTERS

3 W. 29th St., New York, NY 10001 Tel. (212)725-7850 Fax (212)689-3212
Media Contact, Anne E. Impellizzeri

OFFICERS

Chmn., Neal Gilliatt
Vice-Chmn., Arthur Caliandro
Sec., E. Virgil Conway
Treas., Bruce Gregory
Pres. & CEO, Anne E. Impellizzeri

Interchurch Communications

Interchurch Communications is made up of the communication units of the Anglican Church of Canada, the Evangelical Lutheran Church in Canada, the Presbyterian Church in Canada, the Canadian Conference of Catholic Bishops (English Sector), and the United Church of Canada. ICC members collaborate on occasional video or print coproductions and on addressing public policy issues affecting religious communications.

Chairperson, Douglas Tindal, Anglican Church of Canada, 600 Jarvis St., Toronto, ON M4Y 2J6 Tel. (416)924-9192 Fax (416)968-7983

Vice-Chair, Rev. Randy Naylor, United Church of Canada, 85 St. Clair Ave. E., Toronto, ON M4T 1M8 Tel. (416)925-5931 Fax (416)925-9692

Sec., Mr. Dennis Gruending, Canadian Conference of Catholic Bishops, 90 Parent Ave., Ottawa, ON K1N 7B1 Tel. (613)136-9461 Fax (613)236-8117

MEMBERS

Mr. Merv Compone, Evangelical Lutheran Church in Canada, 21415-76th Ave., R.R. #1, Langley, BC V3A 6Y3 Tel. (604)888-4562 Fax (604)888-3162

Rev. Glenn Cooper, Presbyterian Church in Canada, Box 1840, Pictou, NS B0K 1H0 Tel. (902)485-1561 Fax (902)485-1562

Rev. Rod Booth, United Church of Canada, 315 Queen St. E., Toronto, ON M5A 1S7 Tel. (416)366-9221 Fax (416)368-9774

Mr. Jim Hodgson, Canadian Council of Churches, 40 St. Clair Ave. E., Toronto, ON M5A 1M9 Tel. (416)921-4152 Fax (416)921-7478

Interfaith Impact for Justice and Peace

Interfaith Impact for Justice and Peace is the religious community's united voice in Washington. It helps Protestant, Jewish, Muslim and Catholic national organizations have clout on Capitol Hill and brings grassroots groups and individual and congregational members to Washington and shows them how to turn their values into votes for justice and peace. Interfaith Impact for Justice and Peace is the recently merged organization of Interfaith Action for Economic Justice and National Impact.

Interfaith Impact for Justice and Peace has established the following Issue Networks to advance the cause of justice and peace: domestic poverty and human needs; international peace; civil, human and voting rights; economic policy and sustainable development; energy, environment and agriculture; health care; and justice for women and families. The Interfaith Impact Foundation provides an annual Legislative Briefing for their members.

Members receive the quarterly magazine, periodic Action alerts on initiatives, voting records, etc., and a free subscription to the Issue Network of their choice.

HEADQUARTERS

110 Maryland Ave. N.E., Ste. 509, Washington, DC 20002 Tel. (202)543-2800 Fax (202)547-8107

OFFICERS

Exec. Dir., Rev. James M. Bell

Chair of Bd., Kay Dowhower, Evangelical Lutheran Church in America, Office for Governmental Affairs

Communications Director, Robert Greenwood, 110 Maryland Ave. NE, Washington, DC 20002 Tel. (202)543-2800 Fax (202)547-8107

MEMBERS

American Baptist Churches, USA
American Ethical Union
American Muslim Council
Center of Concern
Christian Methodist Episcopal (EME) Church
Christian Church (Disciples of Christ)
Church of the Brethren
Church Women United
Columban Fathers
Commission on Religion in Appalachia
Episcopal Church
Episcopal Urban Caucus
Evangelical Lutheran Church in America
Federation of Southern Cooperatives/LAF
Friends Committee on National Legislation
Federator for Rural Empowerment
Jesuit Social Ministries
Maryknoll Fathers and Brothers
Moravian Church in America
National Council of Churches of Christ: Church World Service; Washington Office
National Council of Jewish Women
NETWORK
Peoria Citizens Committee
Presbyterian Church (USA)
Progressive National Baptist Convention
Presbyterian Hunger Fund
Reformed Church in America
Rural Advancement Fund
Society of African Missions
Southwest Organizing Project
Southwest Voter Registration/Education Project
Toledo Metropolitan Ministries
Union of American Hebrew Congregations
Unitarian Universalist Association
Unitarian Universalist Service Committee
United Church of Christ: Bd. for Homeland Ministries; Bd. for World Ministries; Hunger Action Ofc.; Ofc. of Church in Society
United Methodist Church: Gen. Bd. of Church & Society; Gen. Bd. of Global Ministries Natl. Div.; Gen. Bd. of Global Ministries Women's Div.; Gen. Bd. of Global Ministries World Div.
Virginia Council of Churches
Western Organization of Resource Councils

International Christian Youth Exchange (ICYE)

ICYE sponsors the exchange of young people between nations as a means of international and ecumenical education in order to further commitment to and responsibility for reconciliation, justice, and peace. Exchangees 16-30 years of age spend one year in another country and participate in family, school, church, voluntary service projects and community life. Short-term, ecumenical, international work camp experiences are also available for those 18-35 years of age.

The U.S. Committee works in cooperation with national committees in 28 other countries and the Federation of National Committees for ICYE, which has headquarters in Berlin, Germany. ICYE is one of the only two U.S. youth exchange programs operating in Africa.

Exchanges for American youth going abroad and for overseas youth coming to the United States are frequently sponsored by local churches and/or community groups. Participation is open to all regardless of religious affiliation. Denominational agencies are sponsors of ICYE, including: American Baptist Churches in the U.S.A.; Christian Church (Disciples of Christ); Church of the Brethren; Episcopal Church; Evangelical Lutheran Church in America; Presbyterian Church (U.S.A.); Reformed Church in America; United Church of Christ; and The United Methodist Church. Collaborating organizations include the National Federation of Catholic Youth Ministry and the National Catholic Education Association. Scholarships covering part of the cost are provided by most sponsoring denominations.

HEADQUARTERS

134 W. 26th St., New York, NY 10001 Tel. (212)206-7307 Fax (212)633-9085

OFFICERS

Exec. Dir., Ms. Frances C. Waldron

Interreligious Foundation for Community Organization (IFCO)

IFCO is a national ecumenical agency created in 1966 by several Protestant, Roman Catholic, and Jewish organizations, to be an interreligious, interracial agency for support of community organization and education in pursuit of social justice. Through IFCO, national and regional religious bodies collaborate in development of social justice strategies and provide financial support and technical assistance to local, national, and international social-justice projects.

IFCO serves as a bridge between the churches and communities, and acts as a resource for ministers and congregations wishing to better understand and do more to advance the struggles of the poor and oppressed. IFCO conducts training workshops for community organizers and uses its vast national and international network of organizers, clergy, and other professionals to crystallize, publicize, and act in the interest of justice.

HEADQUARTERS

402 W. 145th St., New York, NY 10031 Tel. (212)926-5757 Fax (212)926-5842
Media Contact, Dir. of Communications, Gail Walker

OFFICERS

Pres., Dr. Ernest Newborn, Christian Church (Disciples of Christ), Dir, Reconciliation Committee
Vice-Pres., Dr. Benjamin Greene, Jr., American Baptist Churches in the U.S.A., Dir., Comm. Dev., Natl. Ministries

Inter-Varsity Christian Fellowship of the U.S.A. (IFCO)

Inter-Varsity Christian Fellowship is a nonprofit, interdenominational student movement that ministers to college and university students in the United States. Inter-Varsity began in the United States when students at the University of Michigan invited C. Stacey Woods, then General Secretary of the Canadian movement, to help establish an Inter-Varsity chapter on their campus. Inter-Varsity Christian Fellowship-USA was incorporated two years later, in 1941. Inter-Varsity's uniqueness as a campus ministry lies in the fact that it is student-initiated and student-led. Inter-Varsity strives to build collegiate fellowships that engage their campus with the gospel of Jesus Christ and develop disciples who live out biblical values. Inter-Varsity students are encouraged in evangelism, spiritual discipleship, serving the church, human relationships, righteousness, vocational stewardship and world evangelization. A triennial missions conference held in Urbana, Ill., jointly sponsored with Inter-Varsity-Canada, has long been a launching point for missionary service.

HEADQUARTERS

6400 Schroeder Road, P.O. Box 7895, Madison, WI 53707 Tel. (608)274-9001 Fax (608)274-7882

Media Contact, Dir. of Development Services, Carole Sharkey, P.O. Box 7895, Madison, WI 53707 Tel. (608)274-9001 Fax (608)274-7882

OFFICERS

Pres. & CEO, Stephen A. Hayner
Vice-Pres.: C. Barney Ford; Robert A. Fryling; Robert Peitscher; Samuel Barkat; Dan Harrison
Sec., H. Yvonne Vinkemulder
Treas., Thomas H. Witte
Bd. Chpsn., Karen Mains
Bd. Vice-Chpsn., Thomas Boyle

Laymen's National Bible Association, Inc.

The Laymen's National Bible Association, Inc. (LNBA) is an autonomous, interfaith organization of lay people who advocate regular Bible reading. LNBA sponsors National Bible Week (Thanksgiving week) each November. Program activities include public service advertising, distribution of nonsectarian literature and thousands of local Bible Week observances by secular and religious organizations. LNBA also urges constitutionally acceptable use of the Bible in public school classrooms. All support comes from individuals, corporations and foundations.

LNBA was founded in 1940 by a group of business and professional people. It publishes a quarterly newsletter and has the IRS nonprofit status of a 501(c)(3) educational association.

HEADQUARTERS

1865 Broadway, 12th floor, New York, NY 10023 Tel. (212)408-1390 Fax (212)408-1448
Media Contact, John Winslow, Tel. (212)408-1439

OFFICERS

Pres., Dr. Victor W. Eimicke
Chrm., Kenneth S. Giniger
Vice-Pres., Max Chopnick, Esq. George Q. Nichols, Dr. Martin S. Quigley
Treas., Henry W. Wyman
Sec., Stewart S. Furlong
Exec. Dir., Thomas R. May

The Liturgical Conference

Founded in 1940 by a group of Benedictines, the Liturgical Conference is an independent, ecumenical, international association of persons concerned about liturgical renewal and meaningful worship. The Liturgical Conference is known chiefly for its periodicals, books, materials, and sponsorship of regional and local workshops on worship-related concerns in cooperation with various church groups.

HEADQUARTERS

1017 12th St., NW, Washington, DC 20005 Tel. (202)898-0885
8750 George Ave., Ste. 123, Silver Spring, MD 20910-3621 Tel. (301)495-0885
Media Contact, Exec. Dir., Ralph R. Van Loon

OFFICERS

Pres., Shawn Madigan, CSJ
Vice-Pres., John B. Foley, SJ
Sec., Eleanor Bernstein, CSJ
Treas., Frank Senn
Exec. Dir., Ralph R. Van Loon

The Lord's Day Alliance of the United States

The Lord's Day Alliance of the United States, founded in 1888 in Washington, D.C., is the only national organization whose sole purpose is the preservation and cultivation of Sunday, the Lord's Day, as a day of rest and worship. The Alliance also seeks to safeguard a Day of Common Rest for all people regardless of their faith. Its Board of Managers is composed of representatives from 25 denominations.

It serves as an information bureau, publishes a magazine *Sunday*, furnishes speakers and a variety of materials such as pamphlets, a book, *The Lord's Day*, videos, posters, radio spot announcements, decals, cassettes, news releases, articles for magazines and television programs, and a new 15-minute motion picture.

HEADQUARTERS

2930 Flowers Road South, Ste. 16, Atlanta, GA 30341 Tel. (404)936-5376 Fax (404)454-6081

OFFICERS

Exec. Dir. & Ed., Dr. Jack P. Lowndes
Pres., Dr. Paul Craven, Jr.
Vice-Pres.: Donald R. Pepper; Roger A. Kvam; Timothy E. Bird; John H. Schaal
Vice-Pres: Faith Willard
Vice-Pres.: W. David Sapp
Sec., Rev. Ernest A. Bergeson
Treas., Mr. E. Larry Eidson

Lutheran World Relief

Lutheran World Relief (LWR) is an overseas development and relief agency based in New York City which responds quickly to natural and man-made disasters and supports more than 160 long-range development projects in countries throughout Africa, Asia, the Middle East and Latin America.

Founded in 1945 to act in behalf of Lutherans in the United States, LWR has as its mission "to support the poor and oppressed of less-developed countries in their efforts to meet basic human needs and to participate with dignity and equity in the life of their communities; and to alleviate human suffering resulting from natural disaster, war, social conflict or poverty."

HEADQUARTERS

390 Park Avenue South, New York, NY 10016 Tel. (212)532-6350 Fax (212)213-6081
Exec. Dir., Norman E. Barth
Media Contact, William B. Dingler

The Mennonite Central Committee

The Mennonite Central Committee is the relief and service agency of North American Mennonite and Brethren in Christ Churches. Representatives from Mennonite and Brethren in Christ groups make up the MCC, which meets annually in February to review its program and to approve policies and budget. Founded in 1920, MCC administers and participates in programs of agricultural and economic development, education, health, self-help, relief, peace, and disaster service. MCC has about 950 workers serving in 50 countries in Africa, Asia, Europe, Middle East, and South, Central, and North America.

MCC has service programs in North America that focus both on urban and rural poverty areas.

Additionally there are North American programs focusing on such diverse matters as handicap concerns, community conciliation, employment creation and criminal justice issues. These programs are administered by two national bodies—MCC U.S. and MCC Canada.

Contributions from North American Mennonite and Brethren in Christ churches provide the largest part of MCC's support. Other sources of financial support include the contributed earnings of volunteers, grants from private and government agencies, and contributions from Mennonite churches abroad. The total income in 1991, including material aid contributions, amounted to $33,431,578.

MCC tries to strengthen local communities by working in cooperation with local churches or other community groups. Many personnel are placed with other agencies, including missions. Programs are planned with sensitivity to locally felt needs.

HEADQUARTERS

Box 500, 21 S. 12th St., Akron, PA 17501 Tel. (717)859-1151 Fax (717)859-2171
Canadian Office, 134 Plaza Dr., Winnipeg, MB R3T 5K9 Tel. (204)261-6381 Fax (204)269-9875
Media Contact, Exec. Sec., John A. Lapp, P.O. Box 500, Akron, PA 17501 Tel. (717)859-1151 Fax (717)859-2171

OFFICERS

Exec. Secs.: International, John A. Lapp; Canada, Daniel Zehr; U.S.A., Lynette Meck

National Association of Ecumenical Staff

This is the successor organization to the Association of Council Secretaries which was founded in 1940. The name change was made in 1971.

NAES is an association of professional staff in ecumenical and interreligious services. It was established to provide creative relationships among them and to encourage mutual support and personal and professional growth. This is accomplished through training programs, through exchange and discussion of common concerns at conferences, and through the publication of the *Corletter*.

HEADQUARTERS

475 Riverside Dr., Rm. 868, New York, NY 10115 Tel. (212)870-2156 Fax (212)870-2158
Media Contact, Dr. Kathleen S. Hurty

OFFICERS

Pres., Rev. Dr. Mel Luetchens, NCC/CWSW P.O. Box 968, Elkhart, IN 46515
Vice-Pres., Dorthy Rose, Interreligious Council of New York, 910 Madison St., Syracuse, NY 13210
1993 Program Chair, Rev. Stan Bratton, Buffalo Area Council of Churches, 1272 Delaware Avenue, Buffalo, NY 14209. Tel. (716)882-4793
Sec., Ms. Janet Leng, Associated Min. of Tacoma/Pierce Co., 1224 South I St., Tacoma, WA 98405 Tel. (206)383-3056

The National Association of Evangelicals

The National Association of Evangelicals is a voluntary fellowship of evangelical denominations, churches, schools, organizations and individuals. Its purpose is not to eliminate denominations, but to protect them; not to force individual churches into a mold of liberal or radical sameness, but to provide a means of cooperation in evangelical witness; not to do the work of the churches, but to stand for the right of churches to do their work as they feel called by God.

Based upon the affirmation of a common faith resting squarely in God's Word, the Bible, NAE provides evangelical identification for 50,000 churches from more than 77 denominations; with a service constituency of more than 15 million through its commissions, affiliates, and subsidiary.

HEADQUARTERS
450 Gundersen Dr., Carol Stream, IL 60188 Tel. (708)665-0500 Fax (708)665-8575
Office of Public Affairs, 1023 15th St. N.W., Ste. 500, Washington, DC 20005 Tel. (202)789-1011 Fax (202)842-0392

OFFICERS
Pres., Dr. Don Argue, 910 Elliott Ave. S., Minneapolis, MN 55404
1st Vice-Pres., Dr. David Rambo, P.O. Box 35000, Colorado Springs, CO 80935
2nd Vice-Pres., Rev. Leonard J. Hofman, 2850 Kalamazoo Ave. SE, Grand Rapids, MI 49560
Sec., Dr. Jack Estep, P. O. Box 828, Wheaton, IL 60189
Treas., Mr. Paul Steiner, 1825 Florida Dr., Ft. Wayne, IN 46805

STAFF
Exec. Dir., Dr. Billy A. Melvin
Dir. of Field Services, Rev. Darrel L. Anderson
Dir. of Information, Rev. Donald R. Brown
Dir. of Business Admn., Darrell L. Fulton
Natl. Field Rep., Rev. David L. Melvin
Dir. of Public Affairs, Dr. Robert P. Dugan, Jr.
Public Policy Analyst, Rev. Richard Cizik
Counsel, Forest Montgomery, 1023 15th St., NW, Ste. 500, Washington, DC 20005 Tel. (202)789-1011

COMMISSIONS, AFFILIATES, SERVICE AGENCIES
Commissions: Chaplains; Christian Higher Educ.; Churchmen; Evangelism & Home Mission; Hispanic; Natl. Christian Educ.; Social Action; Women's
Affiliates: Christian Stewardship Assoc.; Evangelical Child & Family; Evangelical Fellowship of Mission Agencies; National Religious Broadcasters
Subsidiary: World Relief Corp.
Service Agency: New Hope Family Services

MEMBER DENOMINATIONS
Advent Christian General Conference
Assemblies of God
Baptist General Conference
Brethren Church (Ashland, OH)
Brethren in Christ Church
Christian Catholic Church (Evang. Prot.)
Christian Church of North America
Christian and Missionary Alliance
Christian Reformed Church in N.A.
Christian Union
Church of God (Cleveland, TN)
Church of God of the Mountain Assembly
Church of the Nazarene
Church of the United Brethren in Christ
Churches of Christ in Christian Union
Congregational Holiness Church
Conservative Baptist Assoc. of America
Conservative Congregational Christian Conf.
Conservative Lutheran Association
Elim Fellowship
Evangelical Church of North America
Evangelical Christian Church
Evangelical Congregational Church
Evangelical Free Church of America
Evangelical Friends Intl./North America
Evangelical Mennonite Church
Evangelical Methodist Church
Evangelical Presbyterian Church
Evangelistic Missionary Fellowship
Fellowship of Evangelical Bible Churches
Fire-Baptized Holiness Church of God of the Americas
Free Methodist Church of North America
General Association of General Baptists
Intl. Church of the Foursquare Gospel
Intl. Pentecostal Church of Christ
Intl. Pentecostal Holiness Church
Mennonite Brethren Churches, USA
Midwest Congregational Christian Fellowship
Missionary Church
Open Bible Standard Churches
Pentecostal Church of God
Pentecostal Free Will Baptist Church
Presbyterian Church in America
Primitive Methodist Church, USA
Reformed Church in America, Synods of Far West and Mid-America
Reformed Episcopal Church
Reformed Presbyterian Church of N.A.
Salvation Army
Wesleyan Church

National Conference of Christians and Jews
The National Conference of Christians and Jews (NCCJ) is a non-profit human relations organization engaged in a nationwide program of intergroup education so that people of different religious, racial, and ethnic backgrounds learn to live together without bigotry and discrimination and without compromising distinctive faiths or identities. Founded in 1928, the NCCJ promotes education for citizenship in a pluralistic democracy and attempts to help diverse groups discover their mutual self-interest. Primary program areas include interfaith and interracial dialogue, youth intercultural communications, training for the administration of justice, and the building of community coalitions. The NCCJ has 65 offices nationally, staffed by approximately 240 people. Nearly 200 members comprise the National Board of Trustees and members from that group form the 22-member Executive Board. Each regional office has its own local board of trustees with a total of about 2,800. The National Board of Trustees meets once annually; the Executive Board at least three times annually.

HEADQUARTERS
71 Fifth Ave., New York, NY 10003 Tel. (212)206-0006
Media Contact, Communications Officer, Christopher Bugbee, Fax (212)255-6177

OFFICER
Pres., Gillian Martin Sorensen

National Conference on Ministry to the Armed Forces
The Conference is an incorporated civilian agency. Representation in the Conference with all

privileges of the same is open to all endorsing or certifying agencies or groups authorized to provide chaplains for any branch of the Armed Forces.

The purpose of this organization is to provide a means of dialogue to discuss concerns and objectives and, when agreed upon, to take action with the appropriate authority to support the spiritual ministry to and the moral welfare of Armed Forces personnel.

HEADQUARTERS
4141 N. Henderson Rd., Ste. 13, Arlington, VA 22203 Tel. (703)276-7905 Fax (703)276-7906

STAFF
Coord., Clifford T. Weathers
Admn. Asst., Maureen Francis

OFFICERS
Chpsn., Lloyd Lyngdal
Chair-elect, Lewis Burnett
Sec., Curt Bowers
Treas., Robert Crick
Committee Members: Catholic Rep., Msgr. John Glynn; Protestant Rep., Rev. Vincent McMenamy; Jewish Rep., Rabbi David Lapp; Orthodox Rep., Gregory Havrilak; Member-at-Large, Rev. Dr. James E. Townsend

National Council of Churches of Christ in the U.S.A.
The National Council of the Churches of Christ in the U.S.A. is the preeminent expression in the United States of the movement toward Christian unity. The NCC's 32 member communions, including Protestant, Orthodox and Anglican church bodies, work together on a wide range of activities that further Christian unity, that witness to the faith and that serve people throughout the world. More than 45 million U.S. Christians belong to churches that hold Council membership. The Council was formed in 1950 in Cleveland, Ohio, by the action of representatives of the member churches, and by the merger of 12 previously existing ecumenical agencies, each of which had a different program focus. The roots of some of these agencies go back to the 19th century.

HEADQUARTERS
475 Riverside Dr., New York, NY 10115. Tel.(212)870-2511

GENERAL OFFICERS
Pres., Rev. Dr. Syngman Rhee
Gen. Sec., Rev. Joan B.Campbell
Pres.-Elect, Rev. Dr. Gordon L.Sommers
Immediate Past Pres., V. Rev. Leonid Kishkovsky
Sec., Mary A. Love
Treas., Dr. Shirley M. Jones
Vice-Pres./Unit Chpsns.: Dr. William Watley (Unity & Relationships); Dr. Mary D. Matz (Educ., Communication & Discipleship); Rev. Benjamin F. Chavis, Jr. (Prophetic Justice);Dr. Belle Miller McMaster (ChurchWorld Service & Witness)

ELECTED STAFF
OFFICE OF THE GENERAL SECRETARY
Tel. (212)870-2138 Fax (212)870-2817
Gen. Sec., Rev. Dr. Joan B. Campbell
Deputy Gen. Sec., James A. Hamilton
Assoc. for Ecumenical Relations, Rev. Eileen W.Lindner
Assoc. for Inclusiveness & Justice, Lois M.Dauway

Assoc. for Public Witness, James A.Hamilton
Coord. for Governance Services, MelRose B.Corley
Washington, D.C.: Mailing Address, NCC, Ste. 108, 110 Maryland Ave., NE, Washington, DC 20002. Tel. (202)544-2350; Fax(202)543-1297.
Dir. of the Washington Ofc., James A.Hamilton
Assoc. Dir., Mary Anderson Cooper
Dir. of the CWS/LWR Ofc. on Development Policy, Carol Capps

EDUCATION, COMMUNICATION AND DISCIPLESHIP
Tel. (212)870-2049 Fax (212)870-2030
Unit Dir./Assoc. Gen. Sec., Rev. J. Martin Bailey
Dir., Finance, ———-
Communication, Department of
Dir., Rev. J. Martin Bailey
Dir., News Services, Carol Fouke
Dir., Electronic Media, Rev. David W.Pomeroy
Dir., Interpretation Resources, Sarah Vilankulu
Assoc. Dir., Electronic Media, Rev. Roy T.Lloyd
Ministries in Christian Education
Dir., Dorothy Savage
Education for Mission
Dir., Educ. for Mission/Friendship Press, Dr. Audrey A. Miller
Editor, Friendship Press, Margaret S. Larom
Audio-Visual Coord., Rev. David W.Pomeroy
Professional Church Leadership
Staff Assoc., Peggy L. Shriver
Women in Ministry, Elizabeth Verdesi
Bible Translation and Utilization
Dir., Rev. Arthur O. Van Eck
Evangelization
Staff Assoc., Patricia Brown
Worship
Staff Assoc., Herman E. Luben

CHURCH WORLD SERVICE AND WITNESS
Tel. (212)870-2257 Fax (212)870-2055
Unit Dir./Assoc. Gen. Sec., Lani J.Havens
Dir., Financial Management, Howard Jost
Dir., Constituency Information & Development, Melvin Lehman
Global Ecumenical Mission
Interim Dir., Global Ecumenical Mission, Dr. Yen-with K. Whitney
Dir., Agricultural Missions, Sinforonso Atienza
Dir., Human Rights, Frederick Bronkema
Dir., World Community, David W. Briddell
Dir., Global Educ., Loretta Whalen, 2115 N. CharlesSt., Baltimore, MD 21218. Tel. (301)727-6106
Dir., CWS/LWR Ofc. on Development Policy, CarolCapps, 110 Maryland Ave., NE, Ste. 108, Washington, DC 20002. Tel.(202)543-6336
Dir., Resource Sharing, Lowell Brown
Dir., Disaster Response, Kenlynn Schroeder
Acting Dir., Immigration & Refugee Program, Ronald E. Stenning
Dir., Material Resources, Soon-Young Hahn
Dir., Leadership Development, John W. Backer
Dir., Overseas Personnel, Paul W. Yount, Jr.
Dir., Intl. Congregations & Lay Ministry, Arthur O. Bauer
Dir., Africa, Willis H. Logan
Dir., Caribbean & Latin America, Oscar Bolioli, Fax (212)870-3220
Dir., East Asia & the Pacific, Victor W. C. Hsu
Assoc. Dir./Dir. China Program, Franklin J.Woo
Dir., Japan North America Commission (JNAC), Patricia Patterson
Acting Dir., Europe/USSR, L. NewtonThorber
Dir., Middle East, Dale Bishop

Dir., Southern Asia, R. Lawrence Turnipseed
Community Education and Fund Raising
Tel. (219)264-3102 Fax (219)262-0966
Dir., Community Educ. & Fund Raising Subunit,
The Rev. Melvin H. Luetchens, P.O. Box 968,
Elkhart, IN 46515
Dir. of Community Outreach, Douglas R.Beane

PROPHETIC JUSTICE

Tel (212)870-2491
Dir. Finance, Mr. Robert Temmler
Unit Dir./Assoc. Gen. Sec., Dr. Kenyon C.Burke
Program Dir., Racial Justice/Ecumenical Minority
Bail Bond Fund, Rev. Joseph E. Agne
Program Dir., Justice for Women, Ms. Karen Hessel
Program Dir., Health Justice, ——-
Program Dir., Economic & Environmental Justice/Hunger Concerns, Dr. N. Jean Sindab
Child & Family Justice, Ms. Margery Freeman
Religious & Civil Liberty, Rev. Dean M. Kelley
Related Movements of Prophetic Justice
Tel. (212)870-2293 Fax (212)870-2023
Council on Native American Ministries, Rev.
Lawrence Hart, RR#4, Box 230, Clinton, OK
73601. Tel. (405)323-624
Hispanic American Ministries Taskforce, German
Acevedo-Delgado, P.O. Box 708, Perth Amboy,
NJ 08862. Tel.(908)324-7969
Interfaith Center for Corporate Responsibility, Mr.
Timothy Smith
Natl. Farm Worker Ministry, Sr. Patricia Drydyk,
O.S.F., 1337 W. Ohio, Chicago, IL 60622. Tel.
(312)829-6436 or Dr. Jon A. Lacey, P.O. Box
4897, East Lansing, MI 48826. Tel.(517)351-
4780

UNITY AND RELATIONSHIPS

Tel. (212)870-2157 Fax (212)870-2158
Unit Dir./Assoc. Gen. Sec., Dr. Constance Tarasar.
Tel. (212)870-2923
Ecumenical Networks
Dir., Dr. Kathleen S. Hurty. Tel. (212)870-2155
Inter-Faith Relations
Christian-Jewish Concerns: Dir., Dr. Jay T. Rock.
Tel. (212)870-2560
Christian-Muslim Concerns: Dir., ——-, 77 Sherman St., Hartford, CT 06105. Tel. (203)232-
4451
Faith and Order
Interim Dir., Rev. Norman A. Hjelm. Tel.
(212)870-2569

FINANCE AND ADMINISTRATION

Tel. (212)870-2094 Fax (212)870-3112
Dir., Robert K. Soong
Financial Management
Controller, Leo Lamb
Deputy Controller, Marian Perdiz
Asst. Controller, William B. Price
Business Services
Dir., Phyllis Sharpe
Publication Services
Dir. ——-
Management Information Systems
Dir., Rev. Nelson Murphy
Office of Personnel
Dir., Emilio F. Carrillo, Jr.
Dir. of Compensation & Benefits, Michael W.Mazoki

CONSTITUENT BODIES OF THE NATIONAL
COUNCIL (with membership dates)

African Methodist Episcopal Church (1950)
African Methodist Episcopal Zion Church (1950)
American Baptist Churches in the U.S.A. (1950)
The Antiochian Orthodox Christian Archdiocese
of North America (1966)
Armenian Church of America, Diocese of the
(1957)
Christian Church (Disciples of Christ) (1950)
Christian Methodist Episcopal Church (1950)
Church of the Brethren (1950)
The Coptic Orthodox Church (1978)
The Episcopal Church (1950)
Evangelical Lutheran Church in America (1950)
Friends United Meeting (1950)
Greek Orthodox Archdiocese of North & South
America(1952)
Hungarian Reformed Church in America (1957)
Intl. Council of Community Churches (1977)
Korean Presbyterian Church in America, Gen.Assembly of the (1986)
Moravian Church in America (1950)
Natl. Baptist Convention of America (1950)
Natl. Baptist Convention, U.S.A., Inc. (1950)
Orthodox Church in America (1950)
Philadelphia Yearly Meeting of the Religious Society of Friends (1950)
Polish Natl. Catholic Church of America (1957)
Presbyterian Church (U.S.A.) (1950)
Progressive Natl. Baptist Convention, Inc. (1966)
Reformed Church in America (1950)
Russian Orthodox Church in the U.S.A., Patriarchal Parishes of the (1966)
Serbian Orthodox Church in the U.S.A. & Canada
(1957)
Swedenborgian Church (1966)
Syrian Orthodox Church of Antioch (1960)
Ukrainian Orthodox Church in America (1950)
United Church of Christ (1950)
The United Methodist Church (1950)

National Interfaith Coalition on Aging

The National Interfaith Coalition on Aging (NICA), an affiliate of the National Council on Aging, is composed of Protestant, Roman Catholic, Jewish, and Orthodox organizations and individuals concerned about the needs of older people and the religious community's response to problems facing the aging population in the United States.

Primary objectives of NICA are: to enable religious organizations to serve older adults; to encourage religious communities to promote ministry by and with older adults; to support religious workers in aging in their many roles; to be a forum for religious dialogue about aging; and to be an advocate for older adults' concerns.

NICA supports development of programs and services for older people by religious organizations, agencies, judicatories and congregations; develops and distributes resources that help churches and synagogues develop ministries that respond to the needs and improve the quality of life of older people; convenes national and regional conferences for those who work with older adults; sponsors training and continuing education programs concerned with quality of life and religious programming for older people.

HEADQUARTERS

c/o NCOA, 409 Third St., SW (2nd Fl.), Washington, DC 20024 Tel. (202)479-6689 Fax
(202)479-0735
Chair, Communications Committee, Dr. Lynn
Huber, 1609 Harmony Way, Bowling Green, KY
42103 Tel. (902)843-6162 Fax (615)242-5197

Chair, Dr. Carol S. Pierskalla
Chair-Elect, Elaine Tiller
Past Chair, Rev. Harry J. Ekstam
Sec., Mrs. Maj. Carolyn Peacock
Prog. Mgr., Rev. John F. Evans

National Interfaith Hospitality Networks

The National Interfaith Hospitality Network is a non-profit organization which works with interdenominational congregations to form Networks which provide shelter, meals, and assistance to homeless families. The program mobilizes exising community resources: churches and synagogues for overnight lodging, congregations for volunteers, social service agencies for screening and referrals and existing facilities for day programs. The Network also employs a director who provides assistance and advocacy to Network families as they seek housing and jobs.

NIHN offers speakers, videotapes, guides, and manuals for successful programs.

HEADQUARTERS
120 Morris Ave., Summit, NJ 07901 Tel. (908)273-1100
Media Contact, Ofc. Mgr., Nancy Kadri

National Interreligious Service Board for Conscientious Objectors

NISBCO, formed in 1940, is a nonprofit service organization sponsored by a broad coalition of national religious bodies. NISBCO responds to the needs of conscientious objectors by: providing information on how to register and document one's convictions as a conscientious objector; providing professional counseling for those who are working through convictions of conscientious objection and training religious conscientious objector counselors; alerting citizens to the latest developments in the drive to bring back the draft and the efforts to institute compulsory national service; aiding conscientious objectors in the armed forces who seek noncombatant transfer or discharge; maintaining an extensive referral service to local counseling agencies in all areas of the country and to attorneys who can aid those in need of legal counsel; acting as a national resource center for those interested in conscientious objector/peace witness of all religious bodies in the United States: encouraging citizens through articles, speaking engagements, and NISBCO publications to decide for themselves what they believe about participation in war based upon the dictates of their own consciences.

HEADQUARTERS
Ste. 750, 1601 Connecticut Ave., NW,, Washington, DC 20009 Tel. (202)483-4510 Fax (202)265-8022

OFFICERS
Exec. Dir., L. William Yolton

National Religious Broadcasters

National Religious Broadcasters is an association of more than 800 organizations which produce religious programs for radio and television or operate stations carrying predominately religious programs. NRB member organizations are responsible for more than 75 percent of all religious radio and television in the United States, reaching an average weekly audience of millions by radio and television.

Dedicated to the communication of the Gospel, NRB was founded in 1944 to safeguard free and complete access to the broadcast media. By encouraging the development of Christian programs and stations, NRB helps make it possible for millions to hear the good news of Jesus Christ through the electronic media.

HEADQUARTERS
7839 Ashton Ave., Manassas, VA 22110 Tel. (703)330-7000 Fax (703)330-7100

OFFICERS
Exec. Dir., E. Brandt Gustavson
Pres., David Clark, KMC Media, Dallas, TX
1st Vice-Pres., Robert Straton, Walter Bennett Communications, Ft. Washington, PA
2nd Vice-Pres., Richard Mason, Radio Bible Class, Grand Rapids, MI
Sec., Sue Bahner, WWWG Radio, Rochester, NY
Treas., Brian Erickson, Back to the Bible, Lincoln, NE
Dir. of PR, Ron Kopczick, NRB, 7839 Ashton Ave., Manassas, VA 22110 Tel. (703)330-7000 Fax (703)330-7100

National Woman's Christian Temperance Union

The National WCTU is a not-for-profit, non-partisan, inter-denominational organization, dedicated to the education of our nation's citizens, especially children and teens, on the harmful effects of alcoholic beverages, other drugs, and tobacco on the human body and the society in which we live. We believe in a strong family unit and, through legislation, education and prayer, fight for everything that will protect the home and family.

WCTU, which began in 1874 with the motto, "For God and Home and Every Land," is organized in 72 countries.

HEADQUARTERS
1730 Chicago Ave., Evanston, IL 60201 Tel. (708)864-1396
Media Contact, Michael C. Vitucci, Tel. (813)394-1343

OFFICERS
Pres., Rachel Kelly
Vice-Pres., Merry Lee Christy, Rt. 1, Box 26, Rivesville, WV 26588
Promotion Dir., Nancy Zabel
Treas., Marilyn Staples
Recording Sec., Mildred Roland, 3802 Rolling Hill Ave. NW, Roanoke, VA 24017

MEMBER ORGANIZATIONS
Loyal Temperance Legion (LTL), for boys and girls ages 6-12
Youth Temperance Council (YTC), for teens through college age

North American Academy of Ecumenists

Organized in 1967, the stated purpose of the NAAE is "to inform, relate, and encourage men and women professionally engaged in the study, teaching, and other practice of ecumenism."

33

Mailing Address, c/o Eugene Zoeller, 2001 New-burg Rd., Louisville, KY 40205

OFFICERS

Pres., Rev. Ernest R. Falardeau, S.S.S., Natl. Assoc. of Diocesan Ecum. Officers, Albuquerque, NM

Vice-Pres & Pres.-Elect, Dr. George Vandervelde, Institute for Christian Studies, Toronto, ON

Rec. Sec., Dr. Thomas Prinz, 1300 Collingwood Dr., Alexandria, VA 22308

Membership Sec. & Treas., Eugene Zoeller, 2001 Newburg Rd., Louisville, KY 40205

North American Baptist Fellowship

Organized in 1964, the North American Baptist Fellowship is a voluntary organization of Baptist Conventions in Canada and the United States, functioning as a regional body within the Baptist World Alliance. Its objectives are: (a) to promote fellowship and cooperation among Baptists in North America, and (b) to further the aims and objectives of the Baptist World Alliance so far as these affect the life of the Baptist churches in North America. Its membership, however, is not identical with the North American membership of the Baptist World Alliance.

Church membership of the Fellowship bodies is more than 28 million.

The NABF assembles representatives of the member bodies once a year to exchange information and views in such fields as evangelism and education, missions, stewardship promotion, laymen's activities, and theological education. It conducts consultations for denominational leaders on as church extension. It encourages cooperation at the city and county level where churches of more than one member group are located.

HEADQUARTERS

Baptist World Alliance Bldg., 6733 Curran St., McLean, VA 22101

OFFICERS

Pres., Dr. Richard Coffin, Canadian Baptist Federation, 7185 Millcreek Drive, Mississauga, ON L5N 5R4

Vice-Pres., Dr. Arthur Walker, 901 N. Commerce St., Ste. 600, Nashville, TN 37203

MEMBER BODIES

American Baptist Churches in the USA
Canadian Baptist Federation
General Association of General Baptists
National Baptist Convention of America
National Baptist Convention, USA, Inc.
Progressive National Baptist Convention, Inc.
Seventh Day Baptist General Conference
North American Baptist Conference
Southern Baptist Convention

North American Broadcast Section, World Association for Christian Communicators

This group was created in 1970 to bring together those persons in Canada and the United States who have an interest in broadcasting from a Christian perspective.

An annual conference is held during the week after Thanksgiving in the United States that draws more than 200 persons from at least 25 communions.

HEADQUARTERS

1300 Mutual Building, Detroit, MI 48226 Tel. (313)962-0340

OFFICERS

Bus. Mgr., Rev. Edward Willingham

Parish Resource Center, Inc.

Parish Resource Center, Inc. promotes, establishes, nurtures and accredits local Affiliate Parish Resource Centers. Affiliate Centers educate, equip and strengthen subscribing congregations of all faiths by providing professional consultants, resource materials and workshops. The Parish Resource Center was founded in 1976. In 1992, there are six free-standing Affiliates located in Lancaster, Pa.; Long Island, N.Y.; South Bend, Ind.; Denver, Colo.; Dayton, Ohio; and New York City. These Centers serve congregations from 32 faith traditions.

HEADQUARTERS

633 Community Way, Lancaster, PA 17603 Tel. (717)299-2223 Fax (717)299-7229
Media Contact, Exec. Dir., Dr. D. Douglas Whiting

OFFICERS

Pres., Richard G. Greiner, Esq.
Vice-Pres., Dr. James D. Glasse
Sec., Dr. Robert Webber
Treas., R. Leslie Ellis

Pentecostal Fellowship of North America

The fellowship was organized at Des Moines, Iowa, in October 1948 shortly after the first World Conference of Pentecostal Believers was held in Zurich, Switzerland, in May, 1947. The PFNA has the following objectives: 1) to provide a vehicle of expression and coordination of efforts in matters common to all member bodies including missionary and evangelistic effort; 2) to demonstrate to the world the essential unity of Spirit-baptized believers; 3) to provide services to its constituents to facilitate world evangelism; 4) to encourage the principles of community for the nurture of the body of Christ, endeavoring to keep the unity of the Spirit until we all come to the unity of the faith.

The PFNA has local chapters in communities where churches of the member groups are located, and fellowship rallies are held. On the national level, representatives of the member bodies are assembled for studies and exchange of views in the fields of home missions, foreign missions, and youth.

HEADQUARTERS

Media Contact, Chairman, Rev. B. E. Underwood, P.O. Box 12609, Oklahoma City, OK 73157 Tel. (405)787-7110 Fax (405)789-3957

OFFICERS

Chpsn., Bishop B. E. Underwood
1st Vice-Chpsn., Ray E. Smith, 2020 Bell Ave., Des Moines, IA 50315
2nd Vice-Chpsn., Dr. John Holland, 1910 Sunset Blvd., Los Angeles, CA 90026
Sec., Rev. Joe Edmonson, 13334 E. 14th, Tulsa, OK 64802
Treas., Dr. James D. Gee, P.O. Box 850, Joplin, MO 64802
Custodial Sec., Wayne E. Warner, 1445 Boonville Ave., Springfield, MO 65802

Anchor Bay Evangelistic Association
Apostolic Church of Canada
Assemblies of God
Christian Church of North America
Church of God
Church of God of Apostolic Faith
Church of God, Mountain Assembly
Congregational Holiness Church
Elim Fellowship
Free Gospel Church, Inc.
Karl Coke Evangelistic Assn.
International Church of the Foursquare Gospel
International Pentecostal Church of Christ
International Pentecostal Holiness Church
Italian Pentecostal Church of Canada
Open Bible Standard Churches, Inc.
Pentecostal Assemblies of Canada
Pentecostal Assemblies of Newfoundland
Pentecostal Church of God
Pentecostal Free-Will Baptist Church
Pentecostal Holiness Church of Canada

Project Equality, Inc.

Project Equality is a non-profit national interfaith program for affirmative action and equal employment opportunity.

Project Equality serves as a central agency to receive and validate the equal employment commitment of suppliers of goods and services to sponsoring organizations and participating institutions, congregations, and individuals. Employers filing an accepted Annual Participation Report are included in the Project Equality "Buyer's Guide."

Workshops, training events, and consultant services in affirmative action and equal employment practices in recruitment, selection, placement, transfer, promotion, discipline, and discharge are also available to sponsors and participants.

HEADQUARTERS
Pres., 1020 E. 63rd St., Ste. 102, Kansas City, MO 64110 Tel. (816)361-9222 Fax (816)361-8997
Media Contact, Pres., Rev. Maurice E. Culver, 1020 E. 63rd St., Ste. 102, Kansas City, MO 64110 Tel. (816)361-9222 Fax (816)361-8997

OFFICERS
Chpsn., Emilio Carrillo, Dir. of Human Resources, Natl. Council of Churches
Vice-Chpsn., Dr. Lillian Anthony, Assoc. for Equal Employment Opportunity, Presbyterian Church (USA)
Sec., John Colon, Dir. of Human Resources, The Episcopal Church
Treas., Dr. Ernest J. Newborn, Admn. Dir., Reconciliation, Christian Church (Disciples of Christ)
Pres., Rev. Maurice E. Culver

SPONSORS/ENDORSING ORGANIZATIONS
American Baptist Churches in the U.S.A.
American Friends Service Committee
American Jewish Committee
Central Conference of American Rabbis
Christian Church (Disciples of Christ)
Church of the Brethren
Church Women United
Consultation on Church Union
The Episcopal Church
Evangelical Lutheran Church in America
Intl. Council of Community Churches
National Association of Ecumenical Staff
National Association of Church Personnel Administration
National Catholic Conf. for Interracial Justice

National Council of Churches of Christ in the U.S.A.
National Education Association
Presbyterian Church (USA)
Progressive National Baptist Church
Reformed Church in America
Roman Catholic Dioceses & Religious Orders
Unitarian Universalist Association
Union of American Hebrew Congregations
United Church of Christ
United Methodist Assoc. of Health & Welfare Ministries
United Methodist Church
YWCA of the USA

Protestant Radio and Television Center, Inc.

The Protestant Radio and Television Center, Inc. (PRTVC) is an interdenominational organization dedicated to the purpose of creating, producing, marketing and distributing audio-visual products for the non-profit sector. Its primary constituency is religious, educational, and service-oriented groups.

Chartered in 1949, PRTVC provides a state-of-the-art studio facility, professional staff and a talent pool for radio, TV, cassettes and other forms of media production.

Affiliate members include the Episcopal Church, Evangelical Lutheran Church in America, Presbyterian Church (U.S.A.), Agnes Scott College, Candler School of Theology, Emory University, and Columbia Theological Seminary.

HEADQUARTERS
1727 Clifton Rd., NE, Atlanta, GA 30329 Tel. (404)634-3324 Fax (404)634-3326
Media Contact, William W. Horlock

OFFICERS
Bd. Chair, Don Heald
Vice-Chair, Dr. Gerald Troutman
Sec.-Treas., William W. Horlock
Pres., William W. Horlock

Religion In American Life, Inc.

Religion In American Life (RIAL) is a unique cooperative program of some 50 major national religious groups (Catholic, Eastern Orthodox, Jewish, Protestant, Muslim, etc.). It provides services for denominationally-supported, congregation-based outreach and growth projects such as the current Invite a Friend program. These projects are promoted through national advertising campaigns reaching the American public by the use of all media. The ad campaigns are produced by a volunteer agency with production/distribution and administration costs funded by denominations and business groups, as well as by individuals. Since 1949, RIAL ad campaign projects have been among the much coveted major campaigns of The Advertising Council. This results in as much as $20 million worth of time and space in a single year, contributed by media as a public service. Through RIAL, religious groups demonstrate respect for other traditions and the value of religious freedom. The RIAL program also includes seminars and symposia, research, leadership awards programs, and Worship Directories in hotels, motels, and public places throughout the nation.

HEADQUARTERS
2 Queenston Pl., Rm. 200, Princeton, NJ 08540 Tel. (609)921-3639 Fax (609)921-0551

EXECUTIVE COMMITTEE

Natl. Chpsn., O. Milton Gossett, (SSAW)

Chpsn. of Bd., Rabbi Joseph B. Glasser, (CCAR)

Vice-Chpsns.: Bishop Khajag Barsamian, Primate (Amen. Ch. of Am.); Rev. Bryant Kirkland, (Presbyterian Church, USA); John Cardinal O'Connor, (Archbishop of New York); Rabbi Ronald B. Sobel, (Cong. Emmanu-El of the City of N.Y.)

Sec., Beverly Campbell, (Church of Jesus Christ of LDS)

Treas., Francis J. Palamara, (ARA Service)

STAFF

Pres., Dr. Nicholas B. van Dvck

Exec. Asst., Sharon E. Lloyd

Worship Directory Mgr., Ms. Jane Kelly

Religion Newswriters Association

Founded in 1949, the RNA is a professional association of religion news editors and reporters on secular daily and weekly newspapers, news services, and news magazines. It sponsors four annual contests for excellence in religion news coverage in the secular press. Annual meetings during a major religious convocation.

OFFICERS

Pres., Jim Jones, Ft. Worth Star-Telegram, 400 W. 7th Street, Ft. Worth, TX 76102 Tel. (817)390-7707 Fax (817)390-7789

1st Vice-Pres., Richard Dujardin, Providence Journal-Bulletin, Providence, RI 02902

2nd Vice-Pres., Cecile Holmes White, Houston Chronicle, Houston, TX 77210

Sec., Joan Connell, Newhouse News Service, 2000 Pennsylvania Ave. NW, Washington, DC

Treas., Judith Weidman, Religious News Service, New York, NY 10101

Religious Conference Management Association, Inc.

The Religious Conference Management Association, Inc. (RCMA) is an interfaith, nonprofit, professional organization of men and women who have responsibility for planning and/or managing meetings, seminars, conferences, conventions, assemblies, or other gatherings for religious organizations.

Founded in 1972, RCMA is dedicated to promoting the highest professional performance by its members and associate members through the mutual exchange of ideas, techniques, and methods.

Today RCMA has more than 1,600 members and associate members.

The association conducts an annual conference and exposition which provide a forum for its membership to gain increased knowledge in the arts and sciences of religious meeting planning and management.

HEADQUARTERS

One Hoosier Dome, Ste. 120, Indianapolis, IN 46225 Tel. (317)632-1888

Media Contact, Exec. Dir., DeWayne S. Woodring, Tel. (3317)632-1888

OFFICERS

Pres., Melvin L. Worthington, Natl. Assoc. of Free Will Baptists, P.O. Box 5002, Antioch, TN 37011-5002

Vice-Pres., Rainer B. Wilson, Sr., Church of Christ, Holiness, U.S.A., 819 Hampton Ave., Newport News, VA 23607

Sec.-Treas., Rudy Becton, United Pentecostal Church Intl., 8855 Dunn Rd., Hazelwood, MO 63042

Exec. Dir., DeWayne S. Woodring, Religious Conf. Mgt. Assoc., One Hoosier Dome, Ste. 120, Indianapolis, IN 46225

Religious News Service

Religious News Service is an interfaith news service marketed to daily newspapers and religious publications and agencies across the country.

Founded in 1933, RNS also sponsors research, fellowship, and intern programs in support of religious journalism. Since 1991 RNS has been syndicated by the New York Times.

The service was founded and sponsored for 50 years by the National Conference of Christians and Jews. In 1983 it was taken over by the United Methodist Reporter, the flagship publication of an ecumenical publishing company in Dallas. RNS is editorially independent.

HEADQUARTERS

P.O. Box 1015, Radio City Station, New York, NY 10101 Tel. (212)315-0870 Fax (212)315-5850

Media Contact, Exec. Ed., Judith Weidman, 301 W. 53 St., Ste. 6C, New York, NY 10019

OFFICERS

Publisher, Ronald Patterson, P.O. Box 660275, Dallas, TX 75226 Tel. (214)630-6495 Fax (214)630-0079

The Religious Public Relations Council, Inc.

RPRC is an international, interfaith, interdisciplinary association of professional communicators who work for religious groups and causes. It was founded in 1929 and is the oldest non-profit professional public relations organization in the world. RPRC's 600 members include those who work in communications and related fields for church-related institutions, denominational agencies, non- and interdenominational organizations, and communications firms who primarily serve religious organizations.

Members represent a wide range of faiths, including Presbyterian, Baptist, Methodist, Lutheran, Episcopalian, Mennonite, Roman Catholic, Seventh-Day Adventist, Jewish, Salvation Army, Brethren, Bahá'í, Disciples, Latter-Day Saints, and others.

On the national level, RPRC sponsors an annual three-day convention, and has published four editions of a *Religious Public Relations Handbook* for churches and church organizations, and a videostrip, *The Church at Jackrabbit Junction*. Members receive a quarterly newsletter (*Counselor*), and a quarterly digest of professional articles (*MediaKit*). From time to time, RPRC sponsors national teleconferences and a summer institute in religious communications. There are 13 regional chapters.

RPRC administers the annual Wilbur Awards competition to recognize high quality coverage of religious values and issues in the public media. Wilbur winners include producers, reporters, editors and broadcasters nationwide. To recognize communications excellence within church communities, RPRC also sponsors the annual DeRose-Hinkhouse Awards for its own members.

In 1970, 1980 and 1990, RPRC initiated a global Religious Communications Congress bringing together thousands of persons from western, eastern and third-world nations who are involved in communicating religious faith. Another Congress is planned for 2000.

HEADQUARTERS

357 Righters Mill Rd., P.O. Box 315, Gladwyne, PA 19035 Tel. (215)642-8895

OFFICERS

Pres., David B. Smith, Dir. Dev. & Public Relations, AMC, 1100 Rancho Conejo Blvd., Box O, Thousand Oaks, CA 91360 Tel. (805)373-7733 Fax (805)3733-7702
Vice-Pres., Rev. Daniel R. Gangler, Dir. of Communications, 2641 North 49th St., P.O. Box 4553, Lincoln, NE 68504 Tel. (402)464-5994 Fax j(402)466-7931
Exec. Dir., J. Ron Byler, RPRC, P.O. Box 315, Gladwyne, PA 19035

Standing Conference of Canonical Orthodox Bishops in the Americas

This body was established in 1960 to achieve cooperation among the various Eastern Orthodox Churches in the United States. The Conference is "a voluntary association of the Bishops in the Americas established to serve as an agency to centralize and coordinate the mission of the Church. It acts as a clearing house to focus the efforts of the Church on common concerns and to avoid duplication and overlapping of services and agencies. Special departments are devoted to campus work, Christian education, military and other chaplaincies, regional clergy fellowships, and ecumenical relations."

HEADQUARTERS

8-10 East 79th St., New York, NY 10021 Tel. (212)570-3500 Fax (212)861-2163
Media Contact, Ecumenical Officer, Rev. Dr. Milton B. Efthimiou, 10 E. 79th St., New York, NY 10021 Fax (212)861-2163

OFFICERS

Chpsn., Most Rev. Archbishop Iakovos
Vice Chpsn., Most Rev. Metropolitan Philip
Treas., Bishop Nicholas of Amissos
Sec., Most Rev. Metropolitan Joseph
Rec. Sec., V. Rev. Paul Schneirla

MEMBER CHURCHES

Albanian Orthodox Diocese of America
American Carpatho-Russian Orthodox Greek Catholic Ch.
Antiochian Orthodox Christian Archdiocese of All N.A.
Bulgarian Eastern Orthodox Church
Greek Orthodox Archdiocese of North & South America
Orthodox Church in America
Romanian Orthodox Church in America
Serbian Orthodox Church for the U.S.A. & Canada
Ukrainian Orthodox Church of America
Ukrainian Orthodox Church of Canada

T.H.E.O.S.

T.H.E.O.S. is a nonprofit, nondenominational self-help support network of men and women who provide emotional assistance to the widowed. Established in 1960, T.H.E.O.S. holds monthly group meetings so that bereaved people can help themselves and others through the process of grieving. The organization also publishes a magazine called *Survivor's Outreach*, the brochure "What Do You Say to a Widowed Person?" and a grief bibliography. In addition, T.H.E.O.S. hosts an international annual conference.

T.H.E.O.S. is comprised of more than 500 volunteers throughout the United States and Canada.

HEADQUARTERS

1301 Clark Building, 717 Liberty Ave., Pittsburgh, PA 15222 Tel. (412)471-7779
Media Contact, Cathy Smith

OFFICERS

Pres., Barbara Moore
Sec., Janet Nataro
Treas., Carol Lampe
Public Educ. & Information Committee, Mimi Wilson

Vellore Christian Medical College Board (USA), Inc.

The Vellore Christian Medical College Board has been linked since 1900 to the vision of the young American medical doctor, Ida S. Scudder. Dr. Ida's dream initially was to ensure quality health care for women and children in India.

American women and men representing several church denominations wanted to be a part of Dr. Ida's dream and in 1916 recommended Vellore as the site for the proposed Missionary Medical College for Women. Since 1947 the Christian Medical College has admitted women and men. The hospital has a commitment to serve all regardless of ability to pay. The partnership between Vellore India and Vellore USA has continued uninterrupted to the present time.

HEADQUARTERS

475 Riverside Dr., Rm. 243, New York, NY 10115 Tel. (212)870-2640 Fax (212)870-2173
Media Contact, Exec. Dir., Linda L. Pierce

OFFICERS

Pres., Jane Cummings, 675 Upton Rd., NW, Atlanta, GA 30318
Vice-Pres., Alfred E. Berthold, 2452 Club Rd., Columbus, OH 43221
Sec., Betty J. Letzig, 475 Riverside Dr., Rm. 300, New York, NY 10115
Treas., Peter Fetterolf, 6 Beardsley La., Huntington, NY 11743

World Conference on Religion and Peace, The

The World Conference on Religion and Peace in the United States (WCRP/USA) provides a forum for the nation's religious bodies based upon respect for religious differences and the recognition that in today's world cooperation among religions offers an important opportunity to mobilize and coordinate the great capacities for constructive action inherent in religious communities.

WCRP/USA provides American religious bodies with opportunities for the following: to clarify their respective orientation to both national and international social concerns; to coordinate their efforts with other religious groups on behalf of widely-shared concerns; to design, undertake, and evaluate joint action projects; and to communicate and collaborate with similar national religious forums organizaed by WCRP around the world.

HEADQUARTERS

WCRP/USA OFFICE, 777 United Nations Plaza, New York, NY 10017 Tel. (212)687-2163 Fax (212)861-2757

Media Contact, Sec. Gen., Dr. William F. Vendley

OFFICERS

Pres., Ms. Mary Jane Patterson
Sec. Gen., Dr. William M. Vendley
Vice-Pres., Dr. Viqar A. Hamdani, Ms. Judith M. Hertz, Rev. Malcolm R. Sutherland, Rev. Robert Smylie
Sec., Ms. Edna McCallion
Treas., Rev. Robert McClean
Officer Ex Officio:, Mrs. Norma U. Levitt, International President
Officer Ex Officio:, The Rt. Rev. Sir Paul Reeves, International President
Exec. Committee Officers: Dr. John Borelli, Edward Doty, Dr. Jane Evans, Mrs. Betty Golumb, Dr. Anand Mohan, Sr. Mary Beth Reissen, Rev. Katsuji Suzuki

YMCA of the USA

The YMCA is one of the largest private voluntary organizations in the world, serving about 30 million people in more than 100 countries. In the Untied States, about 2,000 local branches, units, camps, and centers annually serve almost 13 million people of all ages, races, and abilities. About half of those served are female. No one is turned away because of an inability to pay.

The YMCA is best known for health and fitness. The Y teaches kids to swim, organizes youth basketball games, and offers adult aerobics. But the Y represents more than fitness—it works to strengthen families and help people develop values and behavior that are consistent with Christian principles.

The Y offers hundreds of programs, including day camp for kids, child care, exercise for people with disabilities, teen clubs, environmental programs, substance abuse prevention, family nights, job training, and many more programs from infant mortality prevention to overnight camping for seniors.

The kind of programs offered at a YMCA will vary; each is controlled by volunteer board members who make their own program, policy, and financial decisions based on the special needs of their community. In its own way, every Y promotes good health, strong families, confident kids, solid communities, and a better world.

The YMCA was founded in London, England, in 1844 by George Williams and friends who lived and worked together as clerks. Their goal was to save other live-in clerks from the wicked life of the London streets. The first members were evangelical Protestants who prayed and studied the Bible as an alternative to vice. The Y has always been nonsectarian and today accepts those of all faiths at all levels of the organization.

HEADQUARTERS

101 N. Wacker Dr., Chicago, IL 60649 Tel. (312)977-0031 Fax (312)977-9063

OFFICERS

Board Chpsn., Barbara Roper
Exec. Dir., David R. Mercer
Public Relations Assoc., Leslie Cohn

Young Women's Christian Association of the United States

The YWCA of the U.S.A. is comprised of some 425 affiliates in communities and on college campuses across the United States and serving some 2 million members and program participants. It seeks to empower women and girls and to enable them, coming together across lines of age, race, religious belief, economic and occupational status to make a significant contribution to the elimination of racism and the achievement of peace, justice, freedom and dignity for all people. Its leadership is vested in a National Board, whose functions are to unite into an effective continuing organization the autonomous member Associations for furthering the purposes of the National Association and to participate in the work of the World YWCA.

HEADQUARTERS

726 Broadway, New York, NY 10003 Tel. (212)614-2700 Fax (212)677-9716

OFFICERS

Pres., Ann Stallard
Sec., Anne H. Perkins
Exec. Dir., Gwendolyn Calvert Baker

Youth for Christ/USA

Founded in 1945, the mission of YFC is to communicate the life-changing message of Jesus Christ to every young person.

Locally controlled YFC programs serve in 220 cities and metropolitan areas of the United States.

YFC's Campus Life Club program involves teens who attend approximately 1,365 high schools in the United States. YFC's staff now numbers approximately 1,000. In addition, nearly 10,000 part-time and volunteer staff supplement the full-time staff. Youth Guidance, a ministry for nonschool-oriented youth includes group homes, court referrals, institutional services, and neighborhood ministries. The year-round conference and camping program involves approximately 35,000 young people each year. A family-oriented ministry designed to enrich individuals and church family education programs is carried on through Family Forum, a daily five-minute radio program on more than 300 stations. Independent, indigenous YFC organizations also work in 65 countries overseas.

HEADQUARTERS

U.S. Headquarters, P.O. Box 228822, Denver, CO 80222 Tel. (303)843-9000 Fax (303)843-9002
Canadian Organization, 220 Attwell Dr., Unit #1, Rexdale, ON M9W 5B2
Media Contact, Sr. Vice-Pres. - Admin. (COO), James Neal, Box 228822, Denver, CO 80222 Tel. (303)843-9000 Fax (303)843-9002

OFFICERS

United States, CEO, Roger Cross
Canada, Pres., ———
Intl. Organization: Singapore, Pres., Gerry Gallimore

2. CANADIAN COOPERATIVE ORGANIZATIONS, NATIONAL

The list of Canadian Cooperative Organizations has been expanded for this edition. Many of the organizations previously listed in the Canadian Service Agencies section are now listed here. In most cases the organizations listed here work on a national level and cooperate across denominational lines.

Aboriginal Rights Coalition (Project North)

ARC is a coalition for education and action on issues of Aboriginal justice in Canada. It works in partnership with Native organizations and local network groups. The major focus is on the just settlement of Aboriginal land rights, impacts of major resource development, self-determination, and related military and environmental concerns.

HEADQUARTERS

151 Laurier E., Ottawa, ON K1N 6N8 Tel. (613)235-9956
Media Contact, Exec. Dir., Lorna Schwartzentruber

OFFICERS

Co-chairs, Lorraine Land, John Siebert
Exec. Dir., Lorna Schwartzentruber

MEMBER ORGANIZATIONS

Anglican Church of Canada
Council of Christian Reformed Churches in Canada
Evangelical Lutheran Church in Canada
Mennonite Central Committee
Oblate Conference of Canada
Presbyterian Church of Canada
Religious Society of Friends (Quakers)
Society of Jesus (Jesuits)
United Church of Canada.

Alliance For Life — Alliance Pour La Vie

Alliance For Life was incorporated in 1972 to promote the right to life from conception to natural death. A registered charity for the purpose of education, Alliance conducts research on all life issues: abortion, infanticide, euthanasia and more. Alliance publishes materials to disseminate the information gained through that research. Alliance has prepared a one-hour documentary on untimely pregnancy and maintains a toll free line to counsel women with inconveniently timed pregnancies and to help others suffering from post-abortion syndrome.

Alliance is the umbrella organization for 245 pro-life organizations in Canada. Governed by a Board of Directors, composed of representatives from all provinces, it holds annual conferences in alternating provinces. Conferences are open to the public.

In 1992, Alliance For Life was split to permit the establishment of Alliance Action, Inc., a non-profit, non-charitable entity which is mandated to do advocacy work which Alliance For Life cannot do as a charity. It is located at the same address and publishes *Pro Life News*, a monthly newsmagazine.

HEADQUARTERS

B1-90 Garry St., Winnipeg, MB R3C 4H1 Tel. (204)942-4772

ALLIANCE FOR LIFE OFFICERS

Pres., Bernadette Mysko
1st Vice-Pres., Regina Weidinger
2nd Vice-Pres., Wayne MacMillan
Treas., Denise Boutilier
Sec., Levina Luymes

ALLIANCE ACTION OFFICERS

Pres., Regina Weidinger
1st Vice-Pres., Denise Boutilier
Treas., Wayne MacMillan
Sec., Nancy Jahn

Association of Canadian Bible Colleges

The Association brings into cooperative association Bible colleges in Canada that are evangelical in doctrine and whose objectives are similar. Services are provided to improve the quality of Bible college education in Canada and to further the interests of the Association by means of conferences, seminars, cooperative undertakings, information services, research, publications and other projects.

HEADQUARTERS

Box 173, Three Hills, AB T0M 2A0 Tel. (403)443-5511
Media Contact, Pres., Dr. Paul Magnus

OFFICERS

Pres., Dr. Paul Magnus, Briercrest Bible College, 510 College Dr., Caronport, SK S0H 0S0 Tel. (306)756-3200 Fax (306)756-3366
Vice-Pres., Dr. James Richards, Western Pentecostal Bible College, Box 1700, Abbotsford, BC V2S 7E7 Tel. (604)853-7491 Fax (604)853-8951
Sec./Treas., Dr. Charlotte Kinvig Bates, Prairie Bible College, Box 173, Three Hills, AB T0M 2A0 Tel. (403)443-5511
Members-at-Large: Rev. James Cianca, London Baptist Bible College, 30 Grand Ave., London, ON N6C 1K8 Tel. (519)434-6801; Dr. Arnold Friesen, Providence College, General Delivery, Otterburne, MB R0A 1G0 Tel. (204)433-7488 Fax (204)433-7158; Dr. Walter Unger, Columbia Bible College, 2940 Clearbrook Rd., Clearbrook, BC V2T 2Z8 Tel. (604)853-3358 Fax (604)853-3063

Canadian Association Pastoral Education/Association Canadienne Pour l'Éducation Pastorale

Canadian Association for Pastoral Education/Association Canadienne Pour l'Éducation Pastorale is an association committed to the professional education, certification and support of those endorsed by their faith communities in ministries of pastoral care, counselling and education.

HEADQUARTERS

Business Mgr., Verda Rochon

Canadian Bible Society

As early as 1805, the British and Foreign Bible Society was at work in Canada. The Bible Society branch at Truro, Nova Scotia, has been functioning continually since 1810. In 1904, the various auxiliaries of the British and Foreign Bible Society joined to form the Canadian Bible Society.

The Canadian Bible Society has 17 district offices across Canada, each managed by a District Secretary. The Society holds annual meetings consisting of one representative of each district, plus members appointed by the General Board of the CBS. Each year contributions, bequests, and annuity income of nearly $10 million come from Canadian supporters. Through the Canadian Bible Society's membership in the United Bible Societies' fellowship, more than 83 million Bibles, Testaments and portions, in more than 900 languages, were distributed globally in 1990.

The Canadian Bible Society is nondenominational. Its mandate is to translate, publish, and distribute the Scriptures, without note or comment, in languages that can be easily read and understood.

HEADQUARTERS

10 Carnforth Road, Toronto, ON M4A 2S4 Tel. (416)757-4171

Media Contact, Dir., Ministry Funding, Barbara Walkden, 10 Carnforth Rd., Toronto, ON M4A 2S4 Tel. (416)757-4171

OFFICER

Gen. Sec., Dr. Floyd C. Babcock

Canadian Centre for Ecumenism

The Centre was founded in 1963 for the promotion of interdenominational dialogue in Montréal. It grew by stages to become a national, bilingual, ecumenical resource centre. The centre established an interchurch board of directors in 1976 and obtained a federal charter. Collaborating with the Canadian Council of Churches in work for Christian Unity, the Centre is an office related to the Canadian bishops and offers its services to other churches as well as other religions.

The Centre has three major areas of activity: education, dialogue, and prayer/sharing of spiritual riches. Its quarterly magazine Ecumenism/Oecuménism is published in English and French and goes out to 44 countries. A specialized library is open to the public M-F, 9-5.

HEADQUARTERS

2065, Sherbrooke St. West, Montréal, QC H3H 1G6 Tel. (514)937-9176

Media Contact, Bernice Baranowski

OFFICERS

Pres., Fr. Irénée Beaubien, S.J., 25 Jarry Street West, Montréal, QC H2P 1S6 Tel. (514)597-1468

Vice-Pres., Pamela McBeth, 170 Beacons Hill, Beaconsfield, QC H9W 1T6 Tel. (514)695-5492

Treas., George Cervinka, 3676 St. Hubert, Montréal, QC H2L 4A2 Tel. (514)877-3378 Fax (514)934-1200

Exec. Dir., Fr. Thomas Ryan, C.S.P.

Canadian Council of Christians and Jews

The Canadian Council of Christians and Jews builds bridges of understanding between Canadians. Its techniques of effecting social change are dialogue and education. The CCCJ believes that there exist in any community in Canada the reservoirs of good will, the mediating skills, and the enlightened self-interest which make accommodation to change and the creation of social justice possible.

The CCCJ was established in Toronto in 1947 by a group of business, civic and religious leaders.

Its mandate is: "to promote justice, friendship, cooperation and understanding among people differing in race, religion, or nationality."

HEADQUARTERS

49 Front St., E., Toronto, ON M5E 1B3 Tel. (416)364-3101.

STAFF

Natl. Exec. Dir., Ms. Elyse Graff

The Canadian Council of Churches

The Canadian Council of Churches was organized in 1944. Its basic purpose is to provide the churches with an agency for conference and consultation and for such common planning and common action as they desire to undertake. It encourages ecumenical understanding and action throughout Canada through local councils of churches. It also relates to the World Council of Churches and other agencies serving the worldwide ecumenical movement.

The Council has a Triennial Assembly, a Governing Board which meets semiannually, and an Executive Committee. Program is administered through three commissions—Faith and Witness, Justice and Peace, and Ecumenical Education and Communication.

HEADQUARTERS

40 St. Clair Ave. E, Ste. 201, Toronto, ON M4T 1M9 Tel. (416)921-4152

Media Contact, Education/Communication

OFFICERS AND STAFF

Pres., The Very Rev. Bruce McLeod

Vice-Pres.: Anne Thomas; Rev. Joe Williams; Rev. Dr. Ronald Watts

Treas., Mr. John Hart

Gen. Sec., Dr. Stuart E. Brown

Assoc. Sec.: Rev. Douglas duCharme; Mr. James Hodgson

AFFILIATED INSTITUTION

The Canadian Churches' Forum for Global Ministries, Co-Dirs: Ms. Patricia Talbot, Rev. Tim Ryan, 11 Madison Ave., Toronto, ON M5R 2S2 Tel. (416)924-9351

MEMBERS

The Anglican Church of Canada
The Armenian Church of America—Diocese of Canada
Baptist Convention of Ontario and Québec
British Methodist Episcopal Church*
Canadian Conference of Catholic Bishops*
Christian Church (Disciples of Christ)
Coptic Orthodox Church of Canada
Ethiopian Orthodox Church in Canada
Evangelical Lutheran Church in Canada
Greek Orthodox Diocese of Toronto (Canada)
Orthodox Church in America, Diocese of Canada
Polish National Catholic Church
Presbyterian Church in Canada
Ethiopian Orthodox Church in Canada
Reformed Church in Ameraica—Classis of Ontario
Religious Society of Friends—Canada Yearly Meeting
Salvation Army—Canada and Bermuda
The Ukrainian Orthodox Church
The United Church of Canada
*Associate Member

Canadian Evangelical Theological Association

In May 1990, about sixty scholars, pastors, and other interested persons met together in Toronto to form a new theological society. Arising out of the Canadian chapter of the Evangelical Theological Society, the association established itself as a distinctly Canadian group with a new name. It sponsored its first conference as CETA in Kingston, Ontario, in May 1991.

CETA provides a forum for scholarly contributions to the renewal of theology and church in Canada. CETA seeks to promote theological work which is loyal to Christ and his Gospel, faithful to the primacy and authority of Scripture, and responsive to the guiding force of the historic creeds and Protestant confessions of the Christian Church. In its newsletters and conferences, CETA seeks presentations that will speak to a general theologically-educated audience, rather than to specialists.

CETA has special interest in evangelical points of view upon and contributions to the wider conversations regarding religious studies and church life. Members therefore include pastors, students, and other interested persons as well as professional academicians. The last category includes professors at public universities, Christian liberal arts universities, seminaries, Bible schools, and other institutions. CETA currently includes nearly 100 members, many of whom attend its annual conference in the early summer.

HEADQUARTERS

c/o John G. Stackhouse, Dept. of Religion, University of Manitoba, Winnipeg, MB R3T 2N2 Tel. (204)474-6277
Media Contact, John G. Stackhouse

OFFICERS

Pres. and Western representative, John G. Stackhouse, Jr., The University of Manitoba
Sec./Treas., Dr. Douglas Harink
Publications Coord., Dr. Mark Parent, The King's College, Edmonton
Eastern representative, Dr. Barry Smith, Atlantic Baptist College, Moncton
Central representative, Dr. Kevin Quast, Ontario Theological Seminary

Canadian Society of Biblical Studies/Société des Études Bibliques

The society was founded in 1933 to stimulate the critical investigation of classical biblical literature and related areas of research by exchange of scholarly research in published form and in public forum.

The CSBS/SCEB has 283 members and meets annually in conjunction with the Learned Societies of Canada. Every year the Society publishes a Bulletin and is a member of the Canadian Corporation for the Study of Religion/Corporation Canadienne des Sciences Religieuses, which publishes Studies in Religion/Sciences religieuses quarterly.

HEADQUARTERS

Dept. of Religious Studies, Memorial University of Newfoundland, St. John's, NF A1C 5S7 Tel. (709)737-8166
Media Contact, Exec. Sec., Dr. David J. Hawkin

OFFICERS

Pres., David Jobling, St. Andrew's College, 1121 College Dr., Saskatoon, SK S7N 0W3 Tel. (306)966-8978
Vice-Pres., Harold Remus, Dept. of Religion and Culture, Wilfrid Laurier University, Waterloo, ON N2L 3C5 Tel. (519)884-1970 Fax Tel Ext.2051
Sec., Dr. David J. Hawkin, Dept. of Religious Studies, Memorial University of Newfoundland, St. John's, NF A1C 5S7 Tel. (709)737-8173
Treas., Terry Donaldson, College of Emmanuel & St. Chad, 1337 College Dr., Saskatoon, SK S7N 0W6 Tel. (306)975-1050
Publications Coord., Lyle Eslinger, Dept. of Religious Studies, Univ. of Calgary, 2500 University Dr. NW, Calgary, AB T2N 1N4 Tel. (403)220-5886
Programme Coord., Susan Slater-Kuzak, Atlantic School of Theloty, 640 Francklyn St., Halifax, NS B3H 3B5 Tel. (902)425-7051
Member-at-Large, Margaret MacDonald, Dept. of Religious Studies, Univ. of Ottawa, 177 Waller, Ottawa, ON K1N 6N5 Tel. (613)564-3308

Canadian Tract Society

The Canadian Tract Society was organized in 1970 as an independent distributor of Gospel leaflets to provide Canadian churches and individual Christians with quality materials proclaiming the Gospel through the printed page. It is affiliated with the American Tract Society, which encouraged its formation and assisted in its founding, and for whom it serves as an exclusive Canadian distributor. The CTS is a nonprofit international service ministry.

HEADQUARTERS

Box 2156, Bramalea, ON L6T 3S4

OFFICERS

Pres., Stanley D. Mackey
Sec., Robert J. Burns

The Church Army in Canada

The Church Army in Canada has been involved in evangelism and Christian social service since 1929.

HEADQUARTERS

397 Brunswick Ave., Toronto, ON M5R 2Z2 Tel. (416)924-9279

Dir., Capt. Walter W. Marshall
Asst. Dir., Capt. R. Bruce Smith
Dir. of Training, Capt. Roy E. Dickson
Field Sec., Capt. Reed S. Fleming
Bd. Chmn., Ivor S. Joshua, C.A.

Churches' Council on Theological Education in Canada: An Ecumenical Foundation, The

The Churches' Council (CCTE: EF) maintains an overview of theological education in Canada on behalf of its constituent churches and functions as a bridge between the schools of theology and the churches which they serve.

Founded in 1970, and with a national and ecumenical mandate, the CCTE: EF provides resources for research into matters pertaining to theological education, opportunities for consultation and cooperation, and a limited amount of funding in the form of grants for the furtherance of ecumenical theological education.

HEADQUARTERS

60 St. Clair Avenue E, Ste. 302, Toronto, ON M4T 1N5 Tel. (416)928-3223
Media Contact, Exec. Dir., Dr. Thomas Harding

OFFICERS

Board of Directors, Chair, Dr. H. M. Mills, The United Church of Canada, 85 St. Clair Avenue East, Toronto, ON M4T 1M8
Board of Directors, Vice Chair, The Rev. Jean Armstrong, The Presbyterian Church in Canada, 50 Wynford Dr., Don Mills, ON M3C 1J7
Treas., Donald Hall, 80 Strathallan Blvd., Toronto, ON M5N 1S7
Exec. Dir., Dr. Thomas Harding

MEMBER ORGANIZATIONS

The General Synod of the Anglican Church of Canada
The Canadian Baptist Federation
The Evangelical Lutheran Church in Canada
The Presbyterian Church in Canada
The Canadian Conference of Catholic Bishops
The United Church of Canada

Concerns, Canada: a corporate division of Alcohol & Drug Concerns, Inc.

Concerns, Canada is a registered, non-profit, charitable organization that has been closely associated with the Christian Church throughout its long history. The organization's mandate is "to promote and encourage a positive lifestyle free from dependence upon alcohol, tobacco and other drugs."

The organization was granted a national charter in 1987, moving from an Ontario charter dating back to 1934. Among its services are: Toc Alpha (its youth wing for 14-to-24 year olds; PLUS (Positive Life-Using Skills), a teacher curriculum for grades 4 to 8; two Institutes on Addiction Studies; courses for clients of the Ontario Ministry of Corrections; and educational materials for target groups.

HEADQUARTERS

11 Progress Ave., Ste. 200, Scarborough, ON M1P 4S7 Tel. (416)293-3400
Media Contact, Exec. Dir., Rev. Karl N. Burden

Pres., Linda Mills, 31 Sunnydene Cres., Toronto, ON M4N 3J5
Vice-Pres.: Keith Farraway, Douglas Dr., R.R. #2, Bracebridge, ON P1L 1W9; Mary Fleming, 177 Parkston Cr., Richmond Hill, ON L4C 4S2; Larry Gillians, P.O. Box 226, Newburgh, ON K0K 2S0
Treas., Jean Desgagne, Price Waterhouse, 1 First Canadian Pl., Ste. 3300, Toronto, ON M5X 1H7
Exec. Dir., Rev. Karl N. Burden

Ecumenical Coalition for Economic Justice (ECEJ)

Ecumenical Coalition for Economic Justice (ECEJ) is a national project of five Canadian churches (Anglican, Roman Catholic, Lutheran, Presbyterian, and United) mandated to assist popular groups and progressive church organizations struggling for economic justice in Canada and the Third World. ECEJ pursues these objectives through research, popular education, and political action. ECEJ is guided by an Administrative Committee composed of representatives from each of the sponsoring churches.

Research priorities for the next two years include international trade and trading agreements, women and economic justice, coalition building, and social policy.

HEADQUARTERS

11 Madison Ave., Toronto, ON M5R 2S2 Tel. (416)921-4615

OFFICERS

Chairperson, David Pollock, Anglican Church of Canada

STAFF

Researcher, Joan Dillon
Programme Coord., Women & Economic Justice, Lorraine Michael
Education Programme Coord., Dennis Howlett
Admin. Coord., Diana Gibbs

Evangelical Fellowship of Canada

The Fellowship was formed in 1964. There are 100 denominations, 100 organizations, and 800 local churches, and thousands of individual members.

Its purposes are: "Fellowship in the gospel" (Phil. 1: 5), "the defence and confirmation of the gospel" (Phil. 1: 7), and "the furtherance of the gospel" (Phil. 1: 12). The Fellowship believes the Holy Scriptures, as originally given, are infallible and that salvation through the Lord Jesus Christ is by faith apart from works.

In national and regional conventions the Fellowship urges Christians to live exemplary lives and to openly challenge the evils and injustices of society. It encourages cooperation with various agencies in Canada and overseas that are sensitive to social and spiritual needs.

HEADQUARTERS

Office: 175 Riviera Dr., Markham, ON L3R 5J6 Tel. (416)479-5885
Mailing Address: PO Box 8800, Stn. B, Willowdale, ON M2K 2R6
Media Contact, Exec. Dir., Dr. Brian C. Stiller, 175 Riviera Dr., Markham, ON L3R 5J6 Tel. (416)479-5885

Exec. Dir., Dr. Brian C. Stiller
Pres., Dr. John Redekop
Vice-Pres., Dr. Donald Jost
Treas., Rev. Grover Crosby
Sec., Major John Wilder
Past Pres., Bishop Donald Bastian
Committee Members-at-Large: Mrs. Moira Hunt; Rev. David Collins; Dr. W. Harold Fuller; Mr. Donald Simmonds; Rev. Ron Swanson; Mrs. Linda Tripp; Dr. John Vissers; Rev. Andrew Wong
Co-Chpsn., Social Action Commission: Dr. Paul Marshall; Mrs. Aileen VanGinkel
Chpsn., Task Force on Evangelism: Dr. William McRae
Chpsn., Task Force on the Family: Dr. Mavis Olesen
Chpsn., Task Force on Canada's Future: Dr. Paul Marshall
Chpsn., Religious Liberties Commission, Dr. Peter Marshall

Inter-Varsity Christian Fellowship of Canada

Inter-Varsity Christian Fellowship is a non-profit, interdenominational Canadian student movement centering on the witness to Jesus Christ in campus communities: universities, colleges, high schools, and through a Canada-wide Pioneer Camping program. It also ministers to professionals and teachers through Nurses and Teachers' Christian Fellowship. IVCF was officially formed in 1928-29 through the late Dr. Howard Guinness, whose arrival from Britain challenged students to follow the example of the Inter-Varsity Fellowship from which he came, in organizing themselves in prayer and Bible Study fellowship groups. Inter-Varsity has always been a student-initiated movement, emphasizing and developing leadership on the campus to call Christians to outreach, challenging other students to a personal faith in Jesus Christ, and study of the Bible as God's revealed truth within a fellowship of believers. A strong stress has been placed on missionary activity, and the triennial conference held at Urbana, Ill. (jointly sponsored by U.S. and Canadian IVCF) has been a means of challenging many young people to service in Christian vocation. Inter-Varsity works closely with, and is a strong believer in, the work of local and national churches.

HEADQUARTERS
Unit 17, 40 Vogell Rd., Richmond Hill, ON L4B 3N6 Tel. (416)884-6880
Media Contact, Gen. Dir., James E. Berney, Unit 17, 40 Vogell Rd., Richmond Hill, ON L4B 3N6 Tel. (416)884-6880

OFFICERS
Gen. Dir., James E. Berney

John Howard Society of Ontario

The John Howard Society of Ontario, Inc., is a registered non-profit charitable organization providing services to individuals, families, and groups at all stages in the youth and criminal justice system, community education on critical issues in the justice system, and advocacy for reform of the justice system. The mandate of the Society is the prevention of crime through service, community education, advocacy, and reform.

Founded in 1929, the Society has grown from a one-office service in Toronto to 17 local branches providing direct services in the major cities of Ontario and a provincial office providing justice policy analysis, advocacy for reform, and support to branches.

HEADQUARTERS
6 Jackson Place, Toronto, ON M6P 1T6 Tel. (416)604-8412
Media Contact, Exec. Dir., Graham Stewart

OFFICERS
Pres., Angela Hildyard, Ofc. of Field Service & Research, 252 Bloor St. W, 12th Fl., Rm. 130, Toronto, ON M5S 1V6
Vice-Pres., Gerry Treble, 595 Trafalgar St., London, ON N5Z 1E6
Treas., Hugh Peacock, Ontario Labour Relations Board, 400 University Ave., 4th Fl., Toronto, ON M7A 1V4
Sec., Susan Reid-MacNevin, Dept. of Sociology, University of Guelph, Guelph, ON N1G 2W1
Exec. Dir., Graham Stewart

LOCAL SOCIETIES
Oshawa, Hamilton, Kingston, London, Toronto, Collins Bay, St. Catherines, Ottawa, Brampton, Peterborough, Sarnia, Sault Ste. Marie, Sudbury Thunder Bay, Lindsay, Waterloo, Joyceville and Millhaven

John Milton Society for the Blind in Canada

The John Milton Society for the Blind in Canada is an interdenominational Christian charity whose mandate is producing Christian publications for Canadian adults or young people who are visually impaired or blind. As such, we produce *Insight*, a large-print magazine, *Insound*, a cassette magazine, and *In Touch*, a braille magazine. We also feature an audio cassette library called our *Library In Sound*, which contains Christian music, sermons, seasonal materials, workshops, etc.

Founded in 1970, the Society is committed to seeing that accessible Christian materials find their way by mail to people who can no longer manage small print.

HEADQUARTERS
40 St. Clair Avenue East, Ste. 202, Toronto, ON M4T 1M9 Tel. (416)960-3953
Media Contact, Debbie Wraith

OFFICERS
Pres., Kenneth Holmes, 90 Albertus Ave., Toronto, ON M4T 1J7
Vice-Pres., William Lawson, 65 Wynford Hghts. Cres., Apt. 1808, Don Mills, ON M3C 1L7
Vice-Pres., Miss Ruth Cowan, 267 Lawrence Ave. East, Toronto, ON M4N 1T6
Exec. Dir., M. Gisela Côté, 4 Mossbrook Crescent, Scarborough, ON M1W 2W9

Lutheran Council in Canada

The Lutheran Council in Canada was organized in 1967 and is a cooperative agency of the Evangelical Lutheran Church in Canada and the Lutheran Church-Canada.

The Council's activities include communications, coordinative service, and national liaison in social ministry, chaplaincy, and scout activity.

HEADQUARTERS
1512 S. James St., Winnipeg, MB R3H 0L2 Tel. (204)786-6707

Media Contact, Pres., Bishop D. W. Sjoberg, 1512 St. James St., Winnipeg, MB R3H 0L2 Tel. (204)786-6707

OFFICERS

Pres., Rev. Edwin Lehman

Mennonite Central Committee Canada (MCCC)

Mennonite Central Committee Canada was organized in 1964 to continue the work which several regional Canadian inter-Mennonite agencies had been doing in relief, service, immigration, and peace. All but a few of the smaller Mennonite groups in Canada belong to MCC Canada.

MCCC is part of the binational Mennonite Central Committee (MCC) which has its headquarters in Akron, Pa., from where the overseas development and relief projects are administered. In 1991 MCCC's budget was $19,790,000, about 40 percent of the total MCC budget. There were 429 Canadians of a total of 953 MCC workers serving one to three year terms in North America and abroad during the same time period.

The MCC office in Winnipeg administers projects located in Canada. Domestic programs of Voluntary Service, Native Concerns, Peace and Social Concerns, Food Program, Employment Concerns, Ottawa Office, Victim/Offender Ministries, Mental Health and immigration are all part of MCC's Canadian ministry. Whenever it undertakes a project, MCCC attempts to relate to the church or churches in the area.

HEADQUARTERS

134 Plaza Dr., Winnipeg, MB R3T 5K9 Tel. (204)261-6381

OFFICER

Exec. Dir., Daniel Zehr

Religious Television Associates

Religious Television Associates was formed in the early 1960s for the production units of the Anglican, Baptist, Presbyterian, Roman Catholic Churches, and the United Church of Canada. In the intervening years, the Baptists have withdrawn and the Lutherans have come in. RTA provides an ecumenical umbrella for joint productions in broadcasting and development education. The Directors are the heads of the Communications Departments participating in Interchurch Communications.

HEADQUARTERS

315 Queen St. East, Toronto, ON M5A 1S7 Tel. (416)366-9221
Media Contact, Exec. Dir., Rod Booth

OFFICERS

Chair, Douglas Tindal, 600 Jarvis St., Toronto, ON M4Y 2J6
Sec., Dennis Gruending, 90 Parent Ave., Ottawa, ON K1N 7B1
Treas., Carolyn Pringle, 85 St. Clair Ave. E, Toronto, ON M4T 1M8

MEMBER ORGANIZATIONS

The Anglican Church of Canada
Canadian Conference of Catholic Bishops
The Canadian Council of Churches
The Evangelical Lutheran Church in Canada
The Presbyterian Church in Canada
The United Church of Canada

Scripture Union

Scripture Union is an international interdenominational missionary movement working in over 100 countries.

Scripture Union aims to work with the churches to make God's Good News known to children, young people, and families and to encourage people of all ages to meet God daily through the Bible and prayer.

In Canada, a range of daily devotional booklets are offered on a no-charge basis to individuals from ages four years old through adults.

A program of youth evangelism, including beach missions and community-based evangelistic holiday clubs, is also undertaken.

DIRECTORS

Dr. Emily Berkman, 217 Melrose Ave., Ottawa, ON K1Y 1V3
Alan Cairnie, R.R. #6, Renfrew, ON K7V 3Z9
Duane Morrison, 17765 Merryhill Crt., Monument, CO 80132 Tel. USA
Dr. Paul Pill, 5 Bendale Blvd., Scarborough, ON M1J 2B1
Ross Reid, 8 Fabray Ct., Agincourt, ON M1W 3W5
Ruth Russell, 14 Caronridge Cres., Agincourt, ON M1W 1L2
L. Claude Simmonds, Windfield Terr. E, Ste. 301, 1200 Don Mills Rd., Don Mills, ON M3B 3N8
Michael White, 251 Jefferson Sideroad, R.R. #1, Richmond Hill, ON L4C 4X7
Dr. Ruth Whitehead, 3002 Southmore Dr. E, Ottawa, ON K1V 6Z4

Student Christian Movement of Canada

The Student Christian Movement of Canada was formed in 1921 from the student arm of the YMCA. It has its roots in the Social Gospel movements of the late 19th and early 20th centuries. Throughout its intellectual history, the SCM in Canada has sought to relate the Christian faith to the living realities of the social and political context of each student generation.

The present priorities are built around the need to form more and stronger critical Christian communities on Canadian campuses within which individuals may develop their social and political analyses, experience spiritual growth and fellowship, and bring Christian ecumenical witness to the university.

The Student Christian Movement of Canada is affiliated with the World Student Christian Federation.

HEADQUARTERS

310 Danforth Ave., Ste. C3, Toronto, ON M4K 1N6 Tel. (416)463-4312
Media Contact, Gen. Sec., Bruce Gilbert, 310 Danforth Ave., Ste. C3, Toronto, ON M4K 1N6 Tel. (416)463-4312

OFFICER

Gen. Sec., Bruce Gilbert

Taskforce on the Churches and Corporate Responsibility

The Taskforce on the Churches and Corporate Responsibility is a national ecumenical coalition of the major Christian churches in Canada founded in 1975 to assist its members in implementing policies adopted by them in the area of corporate social responsibility. Areas of special concern include human rights and aboriginal rights, environment, military exports, and corporate governance. The Taskforce facilitates communication on these and other issues between church shareholders and other shareholders and corporate managers.

HEADQUARTERS
129 St. Clair Ave., W., Toronto, ON M4V 1N5 Tel. (416)923-1758
Media Contact, Coord., Bill Davis, Tel. (416)923-1758

OFFICERS
Coord., Bill Davis
Bd. Chpsn., Rev. Dr. Ray Hodgson
Treas., Mike Kelly
Chair, Corp. Governance Committee, Ann Stafford

MEMBERS
Anglican Church of Canada
Canadian Conference of Catholic Bishops
Catholic Church Extension Society of Canada
Congregation of Notre Dame
Evangelical Lutheran Church in Canada
Grey Sisters of the Immaculate Conception
Jesuit Fathers of Upper Canada
Oblates of Mary Immaculate—Grandin Province
Oblates of Mary Immaculate—St. Paul's Province
Presbyterian Church in Canada
Redemptorist Fathers
Religious Hospitallers of St. Joseph
Scarboro Foreign Mission Society
Sisterhood of St. John the Divine
Sisters of Charity—Mount St. Vincent
Sisters of Charity of the Immaculate Conception
Sisters of the Holy Names of Jesus & Mary
Sisters of Mercy Generalate
Sisters of St. Joseph—Diocese of London
Sisters of St. Joseph—Toronto
Les Soeurs de Sainte-Anne
United Church of Canada
Ursulines of Chatham Union
Canadian University Service Overseas
Young Women's Christian Association

Ten Days for World Development
Supported by five of Canada's major Christian denominations and by the Canadian International Development Agency (CIDA), Ten Days is dedicated to helping people discover, examine and reflect on the ways global and domestic structures and policies promote and perpetuate poverty and injustice for the majority of the world's people. The program collaborates in defining goals and human values which insist that social structures respond justly to the needs of the poor and vulnerable. As it engages in action, it attempts to influence the policies and practice of Canadian churches, government, business, labour, education and the media.

HEADQUARTERS
85, St. Clair Ave. E., Toronto, ON M4T 1M8 Tel. (416)922-0591
Media Contact, Natl. Coordinator, Dennis Howlett

STAFF
Natl. Coordinator, Dennis Howlett
Coord. for Leadership Dev. & Regional Communication, David Reid
Resource Coord., Debbie Culbertson

Admn. Asst., Ramya Hemachandra

MEMBER ORGANIZATIONS
Anglican Church of Canada
Canadian Cath. Orgn. for Dev. & Peace
Evangelical Lutheran Church in Canada
Presbyterian Church in Canada
United Church of Canada

Women's Interchurch Council of Canada
The council is an ecumenical movement through which Christians may express their unity by prayer, fellowship, study, action. The purpose is to enable Christian women across Canada to live in love and fellowship so that all people may find fullness of life in Christ. WICC sponsors the World Day of Prayer and the Fellowship of the Least Coin in Canada. Human rights projects are supported and ecumenical study kits produced. A newsletter is issued four times a year.

The council is affiliated with Ecumenical Decade for Churches in Solidarity with Women.

HEADQUARTERS
815 Danforth Ave., Ste 402, Toronto, ON M4J 1L2 Tel. (416)462-2528
Media Contact, Exec. Dir., Vivian Harrower, 815 Danforth Ave., Ste 402, Toronto, ON M4J 1L2 Tel. (416)462-3915

OFFICERS
Pres., Diane Steffer
Exec. Dir., Vivian Harrower

World Vision Canada
World Vision Canada is a Christian humanitarian relief and development organization. Although its main international commitment is to translate child sponsorship into holistic, sustainable community development, World Vision also allocates resources to help Canada's poor and complement the mission of the church.

World Vision's Reception Centre assists government-sponsored refugees entering Canada. The NeighbourLink program mobilizes church volunteers to respond locally to people's needs. A quarterly publication, *Context*, provides data on the Canadian family to help churches effectively reach their communities. The development education program provides resources on development issues. During the annual 30-Hour Famine, people fast for 30 hours while discussing poverty and raising funds to support aid programs.

HEADQUARTERS
6630 Turner Valley Rd., Mississauga, ON L5N 2S4 Tel. (416)821-3030
Media Contact, Senior Information Officer, Mr. Philip Maher, Tel. (416)567-2726

OFFICERS
Pres., J. Don Scott
Vice-Pres.: Internation & Gov't Relations, Linda Tripp; Natl. Programs, Don Posterski; Donor Development, Dave Toycen; Fin. and Admin., Don Epp

Young Men's Christian Association in Canada
The YMCA began as a Christian association to help young men find healthy recreation and meditation, as well as opportunities for education, in the industrial slums of 19th century England. It came

Religious News Service Photo

We are the earth

The Dalai Lama, Tibet's spiritual leader, joins Amazon Indians during the Earth Summit in Rio de Janeiro, Brazil. Religious leaders from around the world came to Brazil to hold meetings on the future of the planet, during the Earth Summit.

to Canada in 1851 with the same mission in mind for young men working in camps and on the railways.

Today, the YMCA maintains its original mission — helping individuals to grow and develop in spirit, mind, and body — but attends to those needs for men and women of all ages and religious beliefs. The YMCA registers almost 2 million participants and 250,000 annual members, in 69 autonomous Associations representative of their communities.

The program of each Association differs, according to the needs of the community, but most offer one or more programs in each of the following categories: community support, housing and shelters, guidance and counselling, camping and outdoor education, leadership development, refugee and immigrant services, international development, and education.

The YMCA encourages people of all ages, races, abilities, income, and beliefs to mix in an environment which promotes balance in life, breaking down barriers, and helping to create healthier communities.

HEADQUARTERS

2160 Yonge St., Toronto, ON M4S 2A9 Tel. (416)485-9447

Media Contact, Dir., Communications, Donald S. McCraig, 2160 Yonge St., Toronto, ON M4S 2A9 Tel. (416)485-9447

OFFICERS

Chpsn., Betty Black
CEO, Sol Kasimer
Dir., Intl. Programs, Alan Hatton

Young Women's Christian Association of/du Canada

The YWCA of/du Canada is a national voluntary organization serving 45 YWCAs and YM-YWCAs across Canada. Dedicated to the development and improved status of women and their families, the YWCA is committed to service delivery, to being a source of public education on women's issues, and an advocate of social change. Services provided by YWCAs and YM-YWCAs include adult education programs, residences and shelters, child care, fitness activities, wellness programs and international development education. As a member of the World YWCA, the YWCA of/du Canada is part of the largest women's organization in the world.

HEADQUARTERS

80 Gerrard St.E., Toronto, ON M5B 1G6 Tel. (416)593-9886

Media Contact, Dir., Communications, Alissa Lee, 80 Gerrard St., E., Toronto, ON M5B 1G6 Tel. (416)593-9886

OFFICERS

CEO, Judith Wiley
Pres., Sally Ballingall

Youth for Christ/Canada

Youth For Christ is an interdenominational organization founded in 1944 by Torrey Johnson. Under the leadership of YFC's 34 national board of directors, Youth For Christ/Canada cooperates with churches and serves as a mission agency reaching out to young people and their families through a variety of ministries.

YFC seeks to have maximum influence in a world of youth through high-interest activities and personal involvement. Individual attention is given to each teenager through small group involvement and counselling. These activities and relationships become vehicles for communicating the message of the Gospel.

HEADQUARTERS

220 Attwell Dr., #1, Rexdale, ON M9W 5B2 Tel. (416)674-0466

OFFICERS

Vice-Pres., Ron Adams, 7115 Codlin Ave., Misissauga, ON L4T 2M3 Tel. (416)674-0466

TYFC Exec. Dir., Paul Robertson, 58 Bridekirk Pl., Brampton, ON L6Y 2V8 Tel. (416)674-0466

Natl. Min. Coord., John Wilkinson, 26 Lanewood Cres., Agincourt, ON M1W 1X1 Tel. (416)674-0466

3. RELIGIOUS BODIES IN THE UNITED STATES

The following lists were supplied by the denominations. They are printed in alphabetical order by the official name of the organization. A list of religious bodies by family group is found at the end of this section.

Information found in other places in this yearbook is not repeated. The denominational listing points you to additional information. Specifically, addresses and editors' names for periodicals are found in the listing of United States Periodicals. Also, statistical information is found in the statistical section.

When an organization supplied a headquarters address it is listed immediately following the description of the organization. This address, telephone number, and fax number is not reprinted for entries that have exactly the same address and numbers. An address or telephone number is only printed when it is known to be different from the headquarters'. Individuals listed without an address can be contacted through the headquarters.

Denominations were asked to provide the name of a media contact. Many responded with a specific person that newspaper or other reporters can contact for official information. These people are listed with the headquarters address.

The organizations listed here represent the denominations to which the vast majority of church members in the United States belong. It does not include all religious bodies functioning in the United States. *The Encyclopedia of American Religions* (Gale Research Inc., P.O. Box 33477, Detroit MI 48232-5477) contains names and addresses of additional religious bodies.

Advent Christian Church

The Advent Christian Church is a conservative, evangelical denomination, which grew out of the Millerite movement of the 1830s and 1840s. The members stress the authority of Scripture, justification by faith in Jesus Christ alone, the importance of evangelism and world missions, and the soon visible return of Jesus Christ.

Organized in 1860, the Advent Christian Church maintains headquarters in Charlotte, N.C., with regional offices in Rochester, N.H.; Augusta, Ga.; Fort Worth, Texas; Lewiston, Idaho; and Lenoir, N.C. Missions are maintained in India, Nigeria, Japan, Malaysia, the Philippines, Mexico and Memphis, Tenn.

The Advent Christian Church maintains doctrinal distinctives in three areas: conditional immortality, the sleep of the dead until the return of Christ, and belief that the kingdom of God will be established on earth made new by Jesus Christ.

HEADQUARTERS

P.O. Box 23152, Charlotte, NC 28212 Tel. (704)545-6161 Fax (704)545-2558
Media Contact, Exec. Vice-Pres., David E. Ross, Fax (704)573-0712

OFFICERS

Pres., Rev. Glennon Balser, 6315 Studley Rd., Mechanicsville, VA 23111
Exec. Vice-Pres., David E. Ross
Sec., Rev. John Gallagher, P.O. Box 551, Presque Isle, ME 04769
Appalachian Vice-Pres., Rev. Marshall Tidwell, 1002 Grove Ave., SW, Lenoir, NC 28645
Central Vice-Pres., Rev. Clarence DuBois, 1401 Illinois Ave., Mendota, IL 61342
Eastern Vice-Pres., Rev. Irvin Verrill, 20 Highland Cliff Rd., Windham, ME 04062
Southern Vice-Pres., Rev. Larry Withrow, 318 Crescent Dr., Clayton, NC 27520
Western Vice-Pres., Mr. Larry McIntyre, 1629 Jamie Cr., West Linn, OR 97068
The Woman's Home & Foreign Mission Soc., Pres., Mrs. Bea Moore, Rt. 8, Box 274, Loudon, NH 03301

PERIODICALS

Advent Christian Witness, The; Advent Christian News; Maranatha; Insight

African Methodist Episcopal Church

This church began in 1787 in Philadelphia when persons in St. George's Methodist Episcopal Church withdrew as a protest against color segregation. In 1816 the denomination was started, led by Rev. Richard Allen, who had been ordained deacon by Bishop Francis Asbury, and who was ordained elder and elected and consecrated bishop.

OFFICERS

Senior Bishop, Bishop Vernon Byrd Tel. (615)242-6814
Gen. Sec., Dr. Cecil Howard Tel. (314)534-5118
Council of Bishops: Pres., Bishop Harold B. Senatle, 18 Cor. Phillips & Anderson St., P.O. Box 261306 Excom. 2023, Johannesburg, Rep. of South Africa; Sec., Bishop Henry A. Belin, Jr., 604 Locust St., N. Little Rock, AR 42114
Genl. Bd.: Pres., Bishop Frederick C. James, Landmark East, 3700 Forest Dr., Ste. 402, Columbia, SC 29204
Treas., Dr. Joseph C. McKinney, 2311 M St., N.W., Washington, DC 20037 Tel. (202)337-3930
Historiographer, Dr. Dennis Dickerson, P.O. Box 301, Williamstown, MA 02167
Judical Council, Pres., Atty. P. A. Townsend, 1010 Macvicar St., Topeka, KS 66604

DEPARTMENTS

Missions, Dr. Frederick C. Harrison, 475 Riverside Dr., Rm. 1926, New York, NY 10115 Tel. (212)870-2258
Church Extension, Sec.-Treas., Dr. Hercules Miles, 3526 Dodier, St. Louis, MO 63107 Tel. (314)534-4272
Christian Education, Sec., Dr. Edgar Mack, 500 8th Ave., S., Nashville, TN 37203 Tel. (615)242-1420

Sunday School Union, Sec-Treas., Dr. A. Lee Henderson, 500 Eighth Ave., S., Nashville, TN 37203 Tel. (615)256-5882

Evangelism, Dir., Yale B. Bruce, 5728 Major Blvd., Orlando, FL 82819 Tel. (305)352-6515

Publications, Sec.-Treas., Dr. A. Lee Henderson, 500 8th Ave., S., Nashville, TN 37203 Tel. (615)256-5882

Pension, Sec.-Treas., Dr. J. Anderson Todd, 500 8th Ave., S., Nashville, TN 37203 Tel. (615)256-7725

Fin. Dept., Dr. Joseph C. McKinney, 2311 M St., N.W., Washington, DC 20037 Tel. (202)337-3930

Statistical Dept., ———-

Minimum Salary, Dr. Alonzo W. Holman, 280 Hernando St., Memphis, TN 38126 Tel. (901)526-4281

Religious Lit. Dept., Ed.-in-Chief, Dr. Cyrus S. Keller, Sr., P.O. Box 5327, St. Louis, MO 63115 Tel. (314)535-8822

Women's Missionary Soc., Pres., Mrs. Delores L. K. Williams, 2311 M St., N.W., Washington, DC 20037 Tel. (212)337-1335

Lay Organization, Connectional Pres., Dr. Kathryn M. Brown, 171 Ashby St., Atlanta, GA 30314

BISHOPS IN THE U.S.A.

First District, Frank C. Cummings, 5070 Parkside, Ste. 1410, Philadelphia, PA 19131 Tel. (215)877-3771

Second District, H. Hartford Brookins, 6209 Stoneham Ln., McLean, VA Tel. (703)442-0261

Third District, Richard Allen Hildebrand, 700 Bryden Rd., Ste. 135, Columbus, OH 43215 Tel. (614)461-6496

Fourth District, J. Haskell Mayo, Jr., P.O. Box 53539, 400 E. 41st St., Ste. 114, Chicago, IL 60653 Tel. (312)373-6587

Fifth District, Vinton R. Anderson, P.O. Box 6416, St. Louis, MO 63107 Tel. (314)534-4274

Sixth District, John H. Adams, 208 Auburn Ave. N.E., Atlanta, GA 30303 Tel. (404)524-8279

Seventh District, Frederick C. James, 370 Forest Dr., Ste. 402, Columbia, SC 29204

Eighth District, Donald G. Ming, 2138 St. Bernard Ave., New Orleans, LA 70119 Tel. (504)948-4251

Ninth District, Cornelius E. Thomas, 2101 Magnolia, Birmingham, AL 35205 Tel. (205)252-2612

10th District, J. Robert L. Pruitt, Republic Bank Tower, Oak Cliff, Ste. 813, Dallas, TX 75208 Tel. (214)941-9323

11th District, Philip R. Cousin, P.O. Box 2970, Jacksonville, FL 32203 Tel. (904)355-8262

12th District, Henry A. Belin, Jr., 604 Locust St., North, Little Rock, AR 72114 Tel. (501)375-4310

13th District, Vernon R. Byrd, 500 8th Ave., S., Nashville, TN 37203 Tel. (615)242-6814

14th District, John R. Bryant, P.O. Box 4191, Monrovia, Liberia, W. Africa

15th District, Robert Thomas, Jr., 28 Walmer Rd., Woodstock 7925, Capetown, Rep. of S. Africa

16th District, Henry A. Belin, Jr., 131 Ashford Rd., Cherry Hill, NJ 08003 Tel. (609)751-7288

17th District, Richard A. Chapelle, P.O. Box 183, St. Louis, MO 63166 Tel. (314)355-7371

18th District, Richard A. Chappelle, P.O. Box MS 223, Maseru, 100, Lesotho

19th District, Harold Ben Senatle, P.O. Box 12, Residensia 1980, Rep. of S. Africa

Ecumenical Ofc., Frederick H. Talbot, P.O. Box 684, Frederiksted, St. Croix, U. S. Virgin Islands, 00840 Tel. (809)772-0723

Located, Rembert E. Stokes, 783 Hidden Circle, Dayton, OH 45459 Tel. (513)436-7347

RETIRED BISHOPS

Henry W. Murph, 5940 Holt Ave., Los Angeles, CA 90056 Tel. (213)410-0266

D. Ward Nichols, 2295 Seventh Ave., New York, NY 10030 Tel. (516)427-0225

Ernest L. Hickman, 1320 Oakcrest Dr., S.W., Atlanta, GA 30311 Tel. (404)349-1336

Harrison J. Bryant, 4000 Bedford Rd., Baltimore, MD 21207 Tel. (301)484-7508

H. Thomas Primm, 2820 Monaco Parkway, Denver, CO 80207 Tel. (303)335-9545

Hubert N. Robinson, 357 Arden Park, Detroit, MI 48202 Tel. (313)875-4967

PERIODICALS

Christian Recorder, The; A.M.E. Review; Journal of Christian Education; Secret Chamber; Women's Missionary Magazine; Voice of Missions

African Methodist Episcopal Zion Church

The A.M.E. Zion Church is an independent body, having withdrawn from the John Street Methodist Church of New York City in 1796. The first bishop was James Varick.

HEADQUARTERS

Dept. of Records & Research, P.O. Box 32843, Charlotte, NC 28232 Tel. (704)332-3851 Fax (704)333-1769

Media Contact, Gen. Sec.-Aud., Dr. W. Robert Johnson, III

OFFICERS

Senior Bishop, Bishop Ruben L. Speaks, 1238 Maxwell St., P.O. Box 986, Salisgury, NC 28144

Bd. of Bishops, Sec., Bishop John Henry Miller, Sr., 8605 Caswell Ct., Raleigh, NC 27612

Bd. of Bishops, Asst. Sec., Bishop Marshall H. Strickland, 2000 Cedar Circle Dr., Baltimore, MD 21228

Bd. of Bishops, Treas., George W. Walker, Sr., 3654 Poplar Rd., Flossmoor, IL 60422

GENERAL OFFICERS AND DEPARTMENTS

Gen. Sec., Rev. W. Robert Johnson, III

Fin. Sec., Miss Madie L. Simpson, P.O. Box 31005, Charlotte, NC 28230 Tel. (704)333-4847 Fax (704)333-6517

A.M.E. Zion Publishing House: Gen. Mgr., Dr. Lem Long, Jr., P.O. Box 30714, Charlotte, NC 28230 Tel. (704)334-9596

The Star of Zion: Editor, Dr. Morgan W. Tann, P.O. Box 31005, Charlotte, NC 28231 Tel. (704)377-4329 Fax (704)333-1769

A.M.E. Zion Quarterly Review: Ed., Rev. James D. Armstrong, P.O. Box 31005, Charlotte, NC 28231 Tel. (704)392-9540 Fax (704)333-1769

Dept. of Overseas Missions: Sec.-Ed., Rev. Dr. Kermit J. DeGraffenreidt, 475 Riverside Dr., Rm. 1935, New York, NY 10115 Tel. (212)870-2952 Fax (212)870-2055

Dept. Brotherhood Pensions & Minst. Relief: Sec.-Treas., Rev. David Miller, P.O. Box 34454, Charlotte, NC 28234-4454 Tel. (704)333-3779 Fax (704)333-3867

Christian Education Department: Sec., Rev. Raymon Hunt, P.O. Box 32305, Charlotte, NC 28231 Tel. (704)332-9323 Fax (704)332-9332

Dept. of Church School Literature: Ed., Ms. Mary A. Love, P.O. Box 31005, Charlotte, NC 28231 Tel. (704)332-1034 Fax (704)333-1769

Dept.of Church Extension & Home Missions: Sec.-Treas., Dr. Lem Long, Jr., P.O. Box 31005, Charlotte, NC 28231 Tel. (704)334-2519

Dept. of Evangelism: Dir., Dr. Norman H. Hicklin, P.O. Box 561071, Charlotte, NC 28256 Tel. (704)537-9247

Dir. of Public Affairs: Dr. Thaddeus Garrett, Jr., 1730 M St., NW, Ste. 808, Washington, DC 20036 Tel. (202)332-0200 Fax (202)872-0444

Dept. of Health & Social Concerns: Dir., Dr. James E. Milton, 910 Church St., Tuskegee, AL 36083 Tel. (205)727-4601

Judicial Council: Pres., Judge Adele M. Riley, 625 Ellsworth Dr., Dayton, OH 45426

BISHOPS

Piedmont: Bishop Ruben L. Speaks, 1238 Maxwell St., P.O. Box 986, Salisbury, NC 28144 Tel. (704)637-1471; Office, 217 W. Salisbury, Salisbury, NC 28144 Tel. (704)637-6018

Mid-Atlantic I: Bishop Cecil Bishop, 5401 Broadwater St., Temple Hills, MD 20748 Tel. (301)894-2165; Bishop Cecil Bishop, 5401 Broadwater St., Temple Hills, MD 20748 Tel. (301)894-2165

North Eastern Region: Bishop George W. Walker, Sr., 3654 Poplar Road, Flossmoor, IL 60422 Tel. (708)799-5599

Mid-Atlantic II: Bishop Milton A. Williams, 1015 Pineburr Rd., Jamestown, MC 27282 Tel. (919)454-4875; Office, P.O. Box 7441, Greensboro, NC 27417

Eastern West Africa: Bishop S. Chuka Ekemam, Sr., 98 Okigwe Rd., P.O. Box 1149, Owerri, W. Africa, Tel. (083)232-271; Office, Tel. 083-232-271 Fax 234-83-232-271

South Atlantic: Bishop George E. Battle, Jr., 8233 Charles Crawford Lane, Charlotte, NC 28213 Tel. (704)547-7405; Office, P.O. Box 26396, Charlotte, NC 28221-6396 Tel. (704)332-7600 Fax (704)343-3743

Southwestern Delta: Bishop Joseph Johnson, 4 Russwood Cove, Little Rock, AK 72211; Mailing, P.O. Box 56058, Little Rock, AR 72215 Tel. (501)228-9711

Cahaba: Bishop Richard K. Thompson, 1420 Missouri Ave. NW, P.O. Box 55458, Washington, DC 20040 Tel. (202)723-8993

Mid-West: Bishop Enoch B. Rochester, 32 Trebling, Willingboro, NJ 08046 Tel. (609)871-2759 Fax (800)243-LOVE

Western West Africa: Bishop Marshall H. Strickland, 2000 Cedar Circle Dr., Baltimore, MD 21228 Tel. (410)744-7330; Office, Tel. (410)764-0876

Western: Bishop Clarence Carr, 2600 Normandy Dr., Greendale, MO 63121 Tel. (314)727-2931; Office, Tel. (314)727-2940

PERIODICALS

Star of Zion; Quarterly Review; Missionary Seer; Church School Herald

Albanian Orthodox Archdiocese in America

The Albanian Orthodox Church in America traces its origins to the groups of Albanian immigrants which first arrived in the United States in 1886, seeking religious, cultural, and economic freedoms denied them in the homeland.

In 1908 in Boston, the Rev. Fan Stylian Noli (later Archbishop) served the first liturgy in the Albanian language in 500 years, to which Orthodox Albanians rallied, forming their own diocese in 1919. Parishes began to spring up through New England and the Mid-Atlantic and Great Lakes states. In 1922, clergy from the United States traveled to Albania to proclaim the self-governance of the Orthodox Church in the homeland at the Congress of Berat.

In 1971 the Albanian Archdiocese sought and gained union with the Orthodox Church in America, expressing the desire to expand the Orthodox witness to America at large, giving it an indigenous character. The Albanian Archdiocese remains vigilant for its brothers and sisters in the homeland and serves as an important resource for human rights issues and Albanian affairs, in addition to its programs for youth, theological education, vocational interest programs, and retreats for young adults and women.

HEADQUARTERS

523 E. Broadway, S. Boston, MA 02127
Media Contact, Sec., Ms. Dorothy Adams, Tel. (617)268-1275 Fax (617)268-3184

OFFICERS

Metropolitan Theodosius, 529 E. Broadway, Boston, MA 02127 Tel. (617)268-1275

Chancellor, V. Rev. Arthur E. Liolin, 60 Antwerp St., East Milton, MA 02186 Tel. (617)698-3366

Lay Chpsn., Thomas Sotir, 145 Highland St., Newton, MA 02102 Tel. (617)244-5670

Treas., Ronald Nasson, 26 Enfield St., Jamaica Plains, MA 02130 Tel. (617)522-7715

Albanian Orthodox Diocese of America

This Diocese was organized in 1950 as a canonical body administering to the Albanian faithful. It is under the ecclesiastical jurisdiction of the Ecumenical Patriarchate of Constantinople (Istanbul).

HEADQUARTERS

6455 Silver Dawn Ln., Las Vegas, NV 89118-1186 Tel. (702)221-8245

OFFICER

Vicar General, The Rev. Ik. Ilia Katre

Allegheny Wesleyan Methodist Connection (Original Allegheny Conference)

This body was formed in 1968 by members of the Allegheny Conference (located in eastern Ohio and western Pennsylvania) of the Wesleyan Methodist Church, which merged in 1966 with the Pilgrim Holiness Church to form The Wesleyan Church.

The Allegheny Wesleyan Methodist Connection is composed of persons "having the form and seeking the power of godliness, united in order to pray together, to receive the word of exhortation, and to watch over one another in love, that they may help each other to work out their salvation." There is a strong commitment to congregational government and to holiness of heart and life. There is a strong thrust in church extension within the United States and in missions worldwide.

1827 Allen Dr., Salem, OH 44460 Tel. (216)337-9376

Media Contact, Pres., Rev. John B. Durfee

Pres., Rev. John B. Durfee

Vice-Pres., Rev. William Cope, 1231 Conser Dr., Salem, OH 44460

Sec., Rev. W. H. Cornell, Box 266, Sagamore, PA 16250

Treas., Mr. Clair Taylor, 858 E. Philadelphia Ave., Youngstown, OH 44502

Allegheny Wesleyan Methodist, The

Amana Church Society

The Amana Church Society was founded by a God-fearing, God-loving, and pioneering group not associated with any other church or organization. It had its beginning as the Community of True Inspiration in 1714 in the province of Hesse, Germany. The members were much persecuted in Germany because of their belief in the "power of divine inspiration," because they would not send their children to the 10 established schools, and because they were pacifistic.

The Community of True Inspiration had its humble beginning under the inspired leadership of Eberhard Ludwig Gruber and Johann Friedrich Rock. Beginning in 1842, Christian Metz, while divinely inspired, led the community to the West and the New World, where they established the Ebenezer Community near Buffalo, N.Y. Because of deterring and worldly influences, the Ebenezer lands were abandoned in 1854. The Amana Colonies were founded in Iowa in 1855.

The Amana Church Society does no proselyting or missionary work. It believes in a peaceful, quiet, "brotherly" way of life. Although many of the stricter church rules have been relaxed over the years, the Amana Church Society maintains its simple, unostentatious churches and rituals. There have been no divinely inspired leaders since the demise of Barbara Landman in 1883, but the faith is still paramount in divine revelation of the Word of God through God's chosen representatives, and the testimonies of the aforementioned religious leaders are read in all the regular services. This small group over the years attests to a faith in God that makes the term *Amana* meaningful—"as a rock" or "to remain faithful."

OFFICERS

Pres., Kirk Setzer, Amana, IA 52203 Tel. (319)622-3799

Vice-Pres., Steward Geiger, Cedar Rapids, IA 52203

Sec., Martin Roemig, Amana, IA 52203 Tel. (319)622-3262

Treas., Henry Schiff, Amana, IA 52203

The American Baptist Association

The American Baptist Association (ABA) is an international fellowship of independent Baptist churches voluntarily cooperating in missionary, evangelistic, benevolent, and Christian education activities throughout the world. Its beginnings can be traced to the landmark movement of the 1850s. Led by James R. Graves and J. M. Pendleton, a significant number of Baptist churches in the South, claiming a New Testament heritage, re-jected as extrascriptural the policies of the newly formed Southern Baptist Convention (SBC). Because they strongly advocated church equality, many of these churches continued doing mission and benevolent work apart from the SBC, electing to work through local associations. Meeting in Texarkana, Texas, in 1924, messengers from the various churches effectively merged two of these major associations—the Baptist Missionary Association of Texas and the General Association—forming the American Baptist Association.

Since 1924, mission efforts have been supported in Canada, Mexico, Central and South America, Australia, Africa, Europe, Asia, India, New Zealand, Korea, and Japan. An even more successful domestic mission effort has changed the ABA from a predominantly rural southern organization to one with churches in 45 states.

Through its publishing arm in Texarkana, the ABA publishes literature and books numbering into the thousands. Major seminaries include the Missionary Baptist Seminary, founded by Dr. Ben M. Bogard in Little Rock, Ark.; Texas Baptist Seminary, Henderson, Tex.; Oklahoma Missionary Baptist College in Marlow, Okla.; and Florida Baptist Schools in Lakeland, Fla.

While no person may speak for the churches of the ABA, all accept the Bible as the inerrant Word of God. They believe Christ was the virgin-born Son of God, that God is a triune God, that the only church is the local congregation of scripturally baptized believers, and that the work of the church is to spread the gospel.

HEADQUARTERS

4605 N. State Line Ave., Texarkana, TX 75503 Tel. (903)792-2783

Media Contact, P.R. Dir., Wayne Sewell, P.O. Box 1828, Texarkana, AR 75504-1828 Tel. (903)792-2783

OFFICERS

Pres., J. O. Phillips, P.O. Box 561, Mauldin, SC 29662

Vice-Pres.: James F. Homes, 109 Tanglewood Dr., North Little Rock, AR 72118; Art Richardson, 457 Mark Ave., Shafter, CA 93263; Marlin Gipson, 1526 N. Mulberry Ave., Panama City, FL 32405

Rec. Clks.: Larry Clements, P.O. Box 234, Monticello, AR 71655; Gene Smith, 1208 W. 35th St., Pine Bluff, AR 71601

Publications: Ed.-in-Chief, Dr. Bill Johnson, P.O. Box 502, Texarkana, AR 75504; Bus. Mgr., Tom Sannes, Box 1828, Texarkana, AR 75501

Meeting Arrangements, Dir., Edgar N. Sutton, P.O. Box 240, Alexandria, AR 72002

Sec.-Treas., D. S. Madden, P.O. Box 1050, Texarkana, TX 75504

American Baptist Churches in the U.S.A.

Originally known as the Northern Baptist Convention, this body of Baptist churches changed the name to American Baptist Convention in 1950 with a commitment to "hold the name in trust for all Christians of like faith and mind who desire to bear witness to the historical Baptist convictions in a framework of cooperative Protestantism."

In 1972 American Baptist Churches in the U.S.A. was adopted as the new name. Although national missionary organizational developments began in 1814 with the establishment of the American Baptist Foreign Mission Society and continued with the organization of the American Baptist Publication Society in 1824 and the American Baptist Home Mission Society in 1832, the general denominational body was not formed until 1907. American Baptist work at the local level dates back to the organization by Roger Williams of the First Baptist Church in Providence, R. I. in 1638.

HEADQUARTERS

P.O. Box 851, Valley Forge, PA 19482 Tel. (215)768-2000 Fax (215)768-2320

Media Contact, Dir., ABC News Service, Richard W. Schramm, Tel. (215)768-2077 Fax (215)768-2320

OFFICERS

Pres., James A. Scott
Vice-Pres., Hector M. Gonzales
Budget Review Officer, Dorothy J. Herrin
Gen. Sec., Daniel E. Weiss
Assoc. Gen. Sec.-Treas., Cheryl H. Wade

REGIONAL ORGANIZATIONS

Central Region, Fred W. Thompson, Box 4105, Topeka, KS 66614-4105

Metro Chicago, Duane J. Gibson, 28 E. Jackson Blvd., Ste. 210, Chicago, IL 60604-2207

Cleveland, Dennis E. Norris, 1737 Euclid Ave., Ste. 603, Cleveland, OH 44115-2141

Connecticut, Lowell H. Fewster, 100 Bloomfield Ave., Hartford, CT 06105-1097

Dakotas, Ronald E. Cowles, 1524 S. Summit Ave., Sioux Falls, SD 57105-1697

District of Columbia, Bapt. Conv., W. Jere Allen, 1628 16th St., NW, Washington, DC 20009-3099

Great Rivers Region, Malcolm G. Shotwell, P.O. Box 3786, Springfield, IL 62708-3786

Indiana, L. Eugene Ton, 1650 N. Delaware St., Indianapolis, IN 46202-2493

Greater Indianapolis, Larry D. Sayre, 1350 N. Delaware St., Indianapolis, IN 46202-2493

Los Angeles Bapt. City Mission Soc., Emory C. Campbell, 1212 Wilshire Blvd., Ste. 201, Los Angeles, CA 90017-1902

Maine, Gary G. Johnson, P.O. Box 667, Augusta, ME 04332-0667

Massachusetts, Linda C. Spoolstra, 20 Milton St., Dedham, MA 02026-2967

Metropolitan New York, James D. Stallings, 475 Riverside Dr., Rm. 432, New York, NY 10115-0001

Michigan, Robert E. Shaw, 4578 S. Hagadorn Rd., East Lansing, MI 48823-5335

Mid-America, Telfer L. Epp, Ste. 15, 2400 86th St., Des Moines, IA 50322-4380

Nebraska, Dennis D. Hatfield, 6404 Maple St., Omaha, NE 68104-4079

New Jersey, A. Roy Medley, 161 Freeway Dr. E., East Orange, NJ 07018-4099

New York State, Harrison E. Willims, Int., 3049 E. Genesee St., Syracuse, NY 13224-1699

Northwest, Gaylord L. Hasselblad, 321 First Ave. W., Seattle, WA 98119-4103

Ohio, Robert A. Fisher, P.O. Box 376, Granville, OH 43023-0376

Oregon, James T. Ledbetter, 0245 SW Bancroft St., Ste. G, Portland, OR 97201-4270

Pacific Southwest, John J. Jackson, 970 Village Oaks Dr., Covina, CA 91724-3679

Pennsylvania & Delaware, Richard E. Rusbuldt, P.O. Box 851, Valley Forge, PA 19482-0851

Philadelphia, Larry K. Waltz, 100 N. 17th St., Philadelphia, PA 19103-2736

Pittsburgh, Clayton R. Woodbury, 1620 Allegheny Bldg., 429 Forbes Ave., Pittsburgh, PA 15219-1604

Puerto Rico, E. Yamina Apolinaris, Mayaguez #21, Hato Rey, PR 00917

Rhode Island, Donald H. Crosby, 734 Hope St., Providence, RI 02906-3535

Rochester/Genessee Region, Carrol A. Turner, 151 Brooks Ave., Rochester, NY 14619

Rocky Mountains, ———, 1344 Pennsylvania St., Denver, CO 80203-2499

South, Walter L. Parrish, II, 525 Main St., Ste. 105, Laurel, MD 20707-4995

Vermont/New Hampshire, Robert W. Williams, P.O. Box 796, Concord, NH 03302-0796

West, Robert D. Rasmussen, P.O. Box 23204, Oakland, CA 94623-0204

West Virginia, Lloyd D. Hamblin, Jr., P.O. Box 1019, Parkersburg, WV 26101-1019

Wisconsin, George E. Daniels, 15330 W. Watertown Plank Rd., Elm Grove, WI 53122-2391

BOARDS

Board of Educational Ministries: Exec. Dir., Jean B. Kim; Pres., ———

American Baptist Assembly: Green Lake, WI 54941; Pres., Paul W. LaDue; Chpsn., J. Ralph Beaty

American Baptist Historical Society: 1106 S. Goodman St., Rochester, NY 14620; or P.O. Box 851, Valley Forge, PA 19482-0851; Archivist, Beverly C. Carlson; Pres., John F. Mandt

American Baptist Men: Exec. Dir., Richard S. McPhee; Pres., Richard A. Renquest

American Baptist Women's Ministries: Exec. Dir., Donna M. Anderson; Pres., Ruth Housam

Commission on the Ministry: Exec. Dir., Craig A. Collemer

Board of International Ministries: Exec. Dir., John A. Sundquist; Pres., Michael A. Buckles

Board of National Ministries: Exec. Dir., Aidsand F. Wright-Riggins; Pres., G. Elaine Smith

Ministers & Missionary Benefit Board: Exec. Dir., Gordon E. Smith

Ministers & Missionaries Benefit Board: Pres., John W. Reed, 475 Riverside Dr., New York, NY 10115

Minister Council: Dir., Harley D. Hunt; Pres., Wendell A. Johnson

PERIODICALS

Baptist Leader; Secret Place, The; American Baptist Quarterly; American Baptists in Mission

The American Carpatho-Russian Orthodox Greek Catholic Church

The American Carpatho-Russian Orthodox Greek Catholic Church is a self-governing diocese that is in communion with the Ecumenical Patriarchate of Constantinople. The late Patriarch Benjamin I, in an official Patriarchal Document dated Sept. 19, 1938, canonized the Diocese in the name of the Orthodox Church of Christ.

HEADQUARTERS

Johnstown, PA 15906 Tel. (814)536-4207

Media Contact, Chancellor, V. Rev. Msgr. Frank Miloro, 312 Garfield St., Johnstown, PA 15906 Tel. (814)539-8086 Fax (814)536-4699

OFFICERS

Bishop, Rt. Bishop Nicholas (Smisko), 312 Garfield St., Johnstown, PA 15906

Vicar General, V. Rev. Msgr. John Yurcisin, 249 Butler Ave., Johnstown, PA 15906

Chancellor, V. Rev. Msgr. Frank P. Miloro, 312 Garfield St., Johnstown, PA 15906

Treas., V. Rev. Msgr. Ronald A. Hazuda, 115 East Ave., Erie, PA 16503

PERIODICAL

Cerkovnyj Vistnik—Church Messenger

American Evangelical Christian Churches

Founded in 1944, the AECC is composed of individual ministers and churches who are united in accepting "Seven Articles of Faith." These seven articles are: the Bible as the written word of God; the Virgin birth; the deity of Jesus Christ; Salvation through the atonement; guidance of our life through prayer; the return of the Saviour; and the establishment of the Millenial Kingdom.

The organization offers credentials (licenses and ordinations) to those who accept the Seven Articles and who put unity in Christ above indidvual interpretations and are approved by A.E.C.C.

A.E.C.C. seeks to promote the gospel through its ministers, churches and missionary activities.

Churches operate independently with all decisions concerning local government left to the individual churches.

The organization also has ministers in Canada.

HEADQUARTERS

64 South Street, Indianapolis, IN 46227

Media Contact, Natl. Mod., Dr. Ben Morgan, Indianapolis, IN 46227 Tel. (317)784-9726

OFFICERS

Mod., Dr. Ben Morgan

Sec., Dr. Charles Wasielewski, 64 South St., Southport, IN 46227 Tel. (317)784-9726

American Rescue Workers

Founded in 1884 as a national religious and charitable movement which operates on a quasimilitary basis. Membership includes officers (clergy); soldiers/adherents (laity); members of various activity groups; and volunteers who serve as advisors, associates, and committed participants in ARW service functions.

The American Rescue Workers, founded in 1884, is an evangelical part of the Universal Christian Church.

The motivation of the organization is the love of God. Its message is based on the Bible. This is expressed by its spiritual Ministry, the purposes of which are to preach the gospel of Jesus Christ and to meet human needs in his name without discrimination.

HEADQUARTERS

2827 Frankford Ave., P.O. Box 4766, Philadelphia, PA 19134 Tel. (215)739-6524

Washington DC Capital Area Office, 716 Ritchie Rd., Capitol Heights, MD 20743 Tel. (301)336-6200

Field Office, 1209 Hamilton Blvd., Hagerstown, MD 21742 Tel. (301)797-0061

Media Contact, Natl. Communication Sec., Col. Robert N. Coles, Natl. Field Ofc., Fax (301)797-1480

OFFICERS

Commander-In-Chief & Pres. of Corp., General Paul E. Martin

Chief of Staff, Col. Claude S. Astin, Jr.

Natl. Bd. Pres., Col. George B Gossett

Special Services/Aide-de-Camp, Col. Robert N. Coles, Natl. Field Ofc.

Natl. Chief Sec., Col. Joyce Gossett

PERIODICAL

Rescue Herald, The

The Anglican Orthodox Church

This body was founded on Nov. 16, 1963, in Statesville, N.C., by the Most Rev. James P. Dees. The church holds to the Thirty-Nine Articles of Religion, the 1928 Book of Common Prayer, the King James Version of the Bible, and basic Anglican traditions and church government. It upholds biblical morality and emphasizes the fundamental doctrines of the virgin birth, the incarnation, the atoning sacrifice of the cross, the Trinity, the resurrection, the second coming, salvation by faith alone, and the divinity of Christ.

Branches of the worldwide Orthodox Anglican Communion are located in South India, Madagascar, Pakistan, Liberia, Nigeria, the Philippines, the Fiji Islands, South Africa, Kenya, and Colombia.

The entire membership totals over 300,000.

An active program of Christian education is promoted both in the United States and on a worldwide basis. This includes but is not limited to weekly Sunday School Bible study classes and weekday youth clubs.

The Anglican Orthodox Church operates Cranmer Seminary in Statesville, N. C., to train men for holy orders.

HEADQUARTERS

P.O. Box 128, Statesville, NC 28677 Tel. (704)873-8365

Media Contact, Admn. Asst., Mrs. Betty Hoffman

OFFICER

Presiding Bishop, The Most Rev. George C. Schneller, 323 Walnut St., P.O. Box 128, Statesville, NC 28677 Tel. (704)873-8365

PERIODICAL

News, The

The Antiochian Orthodox Christian Archdiocese of North America

The spiritual needs of Antiochian faithful in North America were first served through the Syro-Arabian Mission of the Russian Orthodox Church in 1892. In 1895, the Syrian Orthodox Benevolent Society was organized by Antiochian immigrants in New York City. Raphael Hawaweeny, a young Damascene clergyman serving as professor of Arabic language at the Orthodox theological academy in Kazan, Russia, came to New York to organize the first Arabic-language parish in North America in 1896, after being canonically received under the omophorion of the head of the Russian Church in North America. Saint Nicholas Cathedral, now located at 355 State St. in Brooklyn, is considered the "mother parish" of the Archdiocese.

On March 12, 1904, Hawaweeny became the first Orthodox bishop to be consecrated in North America. He traveled throughout the continent and established new parishes. The unity of Orthodoxy in the New World, including the Syrian Greek Orthodox community, was ruptured after the death of Bishop Raphael in 1915 and by the Bolshevik revolution in Russia and the First World War. Unity returned in 1975 when Metropolitan Philip

Saliba, of the Antiochian Archdiocese of New York, and Metropolitan Michael Shaheen of the Antiochian archdiocese of Toledo, Ohio, signed the Articles of Reunification, ratified by the Holy Synod of the Patriarchate. Saliba was recognized as the Metropolitan Primate and Shaheen as Auxiliary Archbishop. A second auxiliary to the Metropolitan, Bishop Antoun Khouri, was consecrated at Brooklyn's Saint Nicholas Cathedral, in 1983. A third auxiliary, Bishop Basil Essey, was consecrated at Wichita's St. George Cathedral, in 1992.

The Archdiocesan Board of Trustees (consisting of 50 elected and appointed clergy and lay members) and the Metropolitan's Advisory Council (consisting of clergy and lay representatives from each parish and mission) meet regularly to assist the Primate in the administration of the Archdiocese.

HEADQUARTERS

358 Mountain Rd., Englewood, NJ 07631 Tel. (201)871-1355 Fax (201)871-7954
Media Contact, Vicar, The V. Rev. George S. Corey, 52 78th St., Brooklyn, NY 11209 Tel. (718)748-7940 Fax (718)855-3608

OFFICERS

Primate, Metropolitan Philip Saliba
Auxiliary, Archbishop Michael Shaheen
Auxiliary, Bishop Antoun Khouri
Auxiliary, Bishop Basil Essey

PERIODICAL

Word, The

Apostolic Catholic Assyrian Church of the East, North American Dioceses

The Holy Apostolic Catholic Assyrian Church of the East is the Ancient Christian Church that developed within the Persian Empire from the day of Pentecost. The Apostolic traditions testify that the Church of the East was established by Sts. Peter, Thomas, Thaddaeus and Bartholomew from among the Twelve and by the labors of Mar Mari and Aggai of the Seventy. The Church grew and developed carrying the Christian Gospel into the whole of Asia and Islands of the Pacific. Prior to the Great Persecution at the hands of Tamer'leng the Mongol, it is said to have been the largest Christian church in the world.

The doctrinal identity of the church is that of the Apostles. The church stresses two natures and two Qnume in the One Person, Perfect God-Perfect man. The church gives witness to the original Nicene Creed, the Ecumenical Councils of Nicea and Constantinople, and the church fathers of that era. Since God is revealed as Trinity, the appellation "Mother of God" is rejected for the Ever Virgin Blessed Mary Mother of Christ, we declare that she is Mother of Emmanuel, God with us!

The church has maintained a line of Catholicos Patriarchs from the time of the Holy Apostles until this present time. Today the present occupant of the Apostolic Throne is His Holiness Mar Dinkha IV, 120th successor to the See of Selucia Ctestiphon.

PATRIARCHAL OFFICES

Catholicos Patriarch, His Holiness Mar Dinkha, IV, Metropolitanate Residence, The Assyrian Church of the East, Baghdad, Iraq

Media Contact, Chancellor to the Bishop, The Rev. Chancellor C. H. Klutz, 7201 N. Ashland, Chicago, IL 60626 Tel. (312)465-4777 Fax (312)465-0776

BISHOPS

Diocese Eastern USA: His Grace Bishop Mar Aprim Khamis, 8908 Birch Ave., Morton Grove, IL 60053 Tel. (312)465-4777 Fax (708)966-0012
Diocese Western USA: His Grace Bishop Mar Bawai Soro, St. Joseph Cathedral, 680 Minnesota Ave., San Jose, CA 95125 Tel. (408)286-7377 Fax (408)286-1236
Diocese of Canada: His Grace Bishop Mar Emmanuel Joseph, St. Mary Cathedral, 57 Apted Ave., Weston, ON M9L 2P2 Tel. (416)744-9311

PERIODICAL

Qala min M'Dinkha (Voice from the East)

Apostolic Christian Church (Nazarene)

This body was formed in America by an immigration from various European nations, from a movement begun by Rev. S. H. Froehlich, a Swiss pastor, whose followers are still found in Switzerland and Central Europe.

HEADQUARTERS

Apostolic Christian Church Foundation, 1135 Sholey Rd., Richmond, VA 23231 Tel. (804)222-1943
Media Contact, Sec.-Treas., Eugene R. Galat, Tel. (309)925-5162 Fax (309)925-5162

OFFICERS

Exec. Dir., James Hodges

Apostolic Christian Churches of America

The Apostolic Christian Church of America was founded in the early 1830s in Switzerland by Samuel Froehlich, a young divinity student who had experienced a religious conversion based on the pattern found in the New Testament. The church, known then as Evangelical Baptist, spread to surrounding countries. A Froehlich associate, Elder Benedict Weyeneth, established the church's first American congregation in 1847, in upstate New York. In America, where the highest concentration today is in the Midwest farm belt, the church became known as Apostolic Christian.

Church doctrine is based on a literal interpretation of the Bible, the infallible Word of God. The church believes that a true faith in Christ's redemptive work at Calvary is manifested by a sincere repentance and conversion. Members strive for sanctification and separation from worldliness, as a consequence of salvation, not a means to obtain it. Security in Christ is believed to be conditional based on faithfulness. Uniform observance of scriptural standards of holiness are stressed. Holy Communion is confined to members of the church. Male members are willing to serve in the military, but do not bear arms. The holy kiss is practiced and women wear head coverings during prayer and worship.

Doctrinal authority rests with a council of elders, each of whom serves as a local elder (bishop). Both elders and ministers are chosen from local congregations, do not attend seminary, and serve without compensation. Sermons are delivered extemporaneously as led by the Holy Spirit, using the Bible.

3420 N. Sheridan Rd., Peoria, IL 61604
Media Contact, Sec., Dale R. Eisenmann, 6913
Wilmette, Darien, IL 60561 Tel. (708)969-7021

SECRETARY

Elder (Bishop) Dale R. Eisenmann, 6913 Wilmette, Darien, IL 60561 Tel. (708)969-7021

PERIODICAL

The Silver Lining

Apostolic Faith Mission Church of God

The Apostolic Faith Mission Church of God was
founded and organized July 10, 1906, by Bishop F.
W. Williams in Mobile, Ala.

Bishop Williams was saved and filled with the
Holy Ghost at a revival in Los Angeles under Elder
W. J. Seymour of The Divine Apostolic Faith
Movement. After being called into the ministry,
Bishop Williams went out to preach the gospel in
Mississippi, then moved on to Mobile.

On Oct. 9, 1915, the Apostolic Faith Mission
Church of God was incorporated in Mobile under
Bishop Williams, who was also the general over-
seer of this church.

HEADQUARTERS

Ward's Temple, 806 Muscogee Rd., Cantonment,
FL 32533
Media Contact, Natl. Sunday School Supt., Elder
Thomas Brooks, 3298 Toney Dr., Decatur, GA
30032 Tel. (404)284-7596

OFFICERS

Board of Bishops: Presiding Bishop, T. C. Tolbert,
226 Elston Ave., Anniston, AL 36201 Tel.
(205)237-5502; Billy Carter; J. L. Smiley; T. L.
Frye; D. Brown; T. C. Tolbert

NATIONAL DEPARTMENTS

Missionary Dept., Pres., Sr. Sarah Ward, Cantonment, Fla.
Youth Dept., Pres., W. J. Wills, Lincoln, Ala.
Sunday School Dept., Supt., Thomas Brooks, Decatur, Ga.
Mother Dept., Pres., Mother Juanita Phillips, Birmingham, Ala.

Apostolic Faith Mission of Portland, Oregon

The Apostolic Faith Mission of Portland, Oregon, was founded in 1907. It had its beginning in
the Latter Rain outpouring on Azusa Street in Los
Angeles in 1906.

Some of the main doctrines are justification by
faith; spiritual new birth, as Jesus told Nicodemus
and as Martin Luther proclaimed in the Great
Reformation; sanctification, a second definite
work of grace, the Wesleyan teaching of holiness,
the baptism of the Holy Ghost as experienced on
the Day of Pentecost, and again poured out at the
beginning of the Latter Rain revival in Los Angeles.

Florence L. Crawford, who had received the
baptism of the Holy Ghost in Los Angeles, brought
this Latter Rain message to Portland on Christmas
Day 1906. It has spread to the world by means of
literature which is still published and mailed eve-
rywhere without a subscription price. Collections
are never taken in the meetings and the public is not
asked for money.

Camp meetings have been held annually in Port-

land, Ore., since 1907, with delegations coming
from around the world.

Missionaries from the Portland headquarters
have established churches in Korea, Japan, the
Philippines and many countries in Africa.

HEADQUARTERS

6615 SE 52nd Ave., Portland, OR 97206 Tel.
(503)777-1741 Fax (503)777-1743
Media Contact, Gen. Overseer, Loyce C. Carver

OFFICER

Gen. Overseer, Rev. Loyce C. Carver

PERIODICAL

Light of Hope, The

Apostolic Lutheran Church of America

Organized in 1872 as the Solomon Korteniemi
Lutheran Society, this Finnish body was incorporated in 1929 as the Finnish Apostolic Lutheran
Church in America and changed its name to Apostolic Lutheran Church of America in 1962.

This body stresses preaching the Word of God
and there is an absence of liturgy and formalism in
worship. A seminary education is not required of
pastors. Being called by God to preach the Word is
the chief requirement for clergy and laity. The
church stresses personal absolution and forgive-
ness of sins, as practiced by Martin Luther, and the
importance of bringing converts into God's kingdom.

HEADQUARTERS

Rt 1 Box 462, Houghton, MI 49931 Tel. (906)482-
8269
Media Contact, Sec., James Johnson

OFFICERS

Pres., Rev. Ralph Davidson, Rt. 1, 66 Keinanen
Rd., Moose Lake, MN 03452
Sec., James Johnson, Rt. 1, Box 462, Houghton, MI
49931
Treas., Richard Sakrisson, 7606 NE Vancouver
Mall Dr., #14, Vancouver, WA 98662

PERIODICAL

Christian Monthly

Apostolic Overcoming Holy Church of God, Inc.

The Rt. Rev. William Thomas Phillips (1893-
1973) was thoroughly convinced in 1912 that
Holiness was a system through which God wanted
him to serve. In 1916 he was led to Mobile, Ala.,
where he organized the Ethiopian Overcoming
Holy Church of God. In 1941 the church was
incorporated in Ala. under its present title.

Each congregation manages its own affairs,
united under districts governed by overseers and
diocesan bishops, and assisted by an executive
board comprised of bishops, ministers, laymen,
and the National Secretary. The General Assembly
convenes annually (June 1-10).

The church's chief objective is to enlighten
people of God's holy Word and to be a blessing to
every nation. The main purpose of this church is to
ordain elders, appoint pastors, and send out divinely called missionaries and teachers. This
church enforces all ordinances enacted by Jesus
Christ. The church believes in water baptism (Acts
2: 38, 8: 12, and 10: 47); administers the Lord's
Supper; observes the washing of feet (John 13:
4-7); believes that Jesus Christ shed his blood to

sanctify the people and cleanse them from all sin; and believes in the resurrection of the dead and the second coming of Christ.

HEADQUARTERS

1120 N. 24th St., Birmingham, AL 35234
Media Contact, Natl. Exec. Sec., Juanita R. Arrington, Tel. (205)324-2202

OFFICERS

Senior Bishop & Exec. Head, Rt. Rev. Jasper Roby
Associate Bishops: G. W. Ayers, 2257 St. Stephens Rd., Mobile, AL 36617; L. M. Bell, 2000 Pio Nono Ave., Macon, GA 31206; Gabriel Crutcher, 526 E. Bethune St., Detroit, MI 48202; John Mathews, 12 College St., Dayton, OH 45407; Bishop Joe Bennett, 15718 Drexel Ave., Dalton, IL 60419
Exec. Sec., Mrs. Juanita R. Arrington

Armenian Apostolic Church of America

Widespread movement of the Armenian people over the centuries caused the development of two seats of religious jurisdiction of the Armenian Apostolic Church in the World: the See of Etchmiadzin, in Armenia, and the See of Cilicia, in Lebanon.

In America, the Armenian Church functioned under the jurisdiction of the Etchmiadzin See from 1887 to 1933, when a division occurred within the American diocese over the condition of the church in Soviet Armenia. One group chose to remain independent until 1957, when the Holy See of Cilicia agreed to accept them under its jurisdiction.

Despite the existence of two dioceses in North America, the Armenian Church has always functioned as one church in dogma and liturgy.

HEADQUARTERS

138 E. 39th St., New York, NY 10016 Tel. (212)689-7810 Fax (212)689-7168
Media Contact, Exec. Dir., Vasken Ghougassian

OFFICERS

Eastern Prelacy, Prelate, Archbishop Mesrob Ashjian
Eastern Prelacy, Chpsn., Nerses Chitjian
Western Prelacy, Prelate, Archbishop Datev Sarkissian, 4401 Russell Ave., Los Angeles, CA 90026 Fax (213)663-0438
Western Prelacy, Chpsn., Khajug Dikidjian
Exec. Dir., Vasken Ghougassian

DEPARTMENTS

AREC, Armenian Religious Educ. Council, Exec. Coord., Deacon Shant Kazanjian
ANEC, Armenian National Educ. Council, Exec. Coord., Hourig Sahagian-Papazian

PERIODICAL

Outreach

Armenian Church of America, Diocese of the

The Armenian Apostolic Church was founded at the foot of the biblical mountain of Ararat in the ancient land of Armenia, where Saints Thaddeus and Bartholomew preached Christianity. In A.D. 301 the historic Mother Church of Etchmiadzin was built by Saint Gregory the Illuminator, the first Catholicos of All Armenians. This cathedral still stands and serves as the center of the Armenian Church. A branch of this Church was established in North America in 1889 and the first Armenian

Diocese was set up in 1898 by the then-Catholicos of All Armenians, Khrimian Hairig. Armenian immigrants built the first Armenian church in the new world in Worcester, Mass., under the jurisdiction of Holy Etchmiadzin.

In 1927, the churches and the parishes in California were formed into a Western Diocese and the parishes in Canada formed their own diocese in 1984. The Armenian Apostolic Church also includes the Catholicate of Cilicia, now located in Lebanon, the Armenian Patriarchate of Jerusalem and the Armenian Patriarchate of Constantinople.

HEADQUARTERS

Eastern Diocese: 630 Second Ave., New York, NY 10016-4885 Tel. (212)686-0710 Fax (212)779-3558
Western Diocese: 1201 N. Vine St., Hollywood, CA 90038 Tel. (213)466-5265
Canadian Diocese: 615 Stuart Ave., Outremont, QC H2V 3H2 Tel. (514)276-9479 Fax (514)276-9960
Media Contact, Dir., Zohiab Information Ctr., V. Rev. Fr. Krikor Maksoudian, Eastern Diocese

OFFICERS

Eastern Diocese
Primate, His Eminence Archbishop Khajag Barsamian
Vicar Gen., V. Rev. Fr. Haigazoun Najarian
Diocesan Council, Chpsn., Vincent Gurahian, Macauley Rd., RFD 2, Katonah, NY 10536
Diocesan Council, Sec., Edward Onanian, 13010 Hathaway Dr., Wheaton, MD 20906
Western Diocese
Primate, His Em. Archbishop Vatche Hovsepian, Western Diocese Ofc.
Diocesan Council, Chpsn., The Rev. Fr. Vartan Kasparian, St. Mary Armenian Church, P.O. Box 367, Yettem, CA 93670
Diocesan Council, Sec., Armen Hampar, 6134 Pat Ave., Woodland Hills, CA 91367
Canadian Diocese
Primate, His Eminence Bishop Hovnan Derderian,

PERIODICAL

Mother Church, The

Assemblies of God

From a few hundred delegates at its founding convention in 1914 at Hot Springs, Ark., the Assemblies of God has become the largest church group in the modern Pentecostal movement worldwide. Throughout its existence it has emphasized the power of the Holy Spirit to change lives and the participation of all members in the work of the church.

The revival that led to the formation of the Assemblies of God and numerous other church groups early in the 20th century began during times of intense prayer and Bible study. Believers in the United States and around the world received spiritual experiences like those described in the Book of Acts. Accompanied by baptism in the Holy Spirit and its initial physical evidence of "speaking in tongues," or a language unknown to the person, their experiences were associated with the coming of the Holy Spirit at Pentecost (Acts 2), so participants were called Pentecostals.

The church also believes that the Bible is God's infallible Word to man, that salvation is available only through Jesus Christ, that divine healing is made possible through Christ's suffering, and that Christ will return again for those who love him. In recent years, this Pentecostal revival has spilled over into almost every denomination in a new wave of revival sometimes called the charismatic renewal.

Assemblies of God leaders credit their church's rapid and continuing growth to its acceptance of the New Testament as a model for the present-day church. Aggressive evangelism and missionary zeal at home and abroad characterize the denomination.

Assemblies of God believers observe two ordinances—water baptism by immersion and the Lord's Supper, or Holy Communion. The church is trinitarian, holding that God exists in three persons, Father, Son, and Holy Spirit.

HEADQUARTERS

1445 Boonville Ave., Springfield, MO 65802 Tel. (417)862-2781 Fax (417)862-8558

Media Contact, Sec. of Information, Juleen Turnage

EXECUTIVE PRESBYTERY

Gen. Supt., G. Raymond Carlson
Asst. Supt., Everett R. Stenhouse
Gen. Sec., Joseph R. Flower
Gen. Treas., Thomas E. Trask
Foreign Missions, Exec. Dir., Loren O. Triplett
Great Lakes, Robert K. Schmidgall, P.O. Box 296-1155, Aurora Ave., Naperville, IL 60540
Gulf, Phillip Wannenmacher, 1301 N. Boonville, Springfield, MO 65802
North Central, Herman H. Rohde, 1351 Portland Ave. S, Minneapolis, MN 55404
Northeast, Almon Bartholomew, P.O. Box 39, Liverpool, NY 13088
Northwest, R. L. Brandt, 1702 Colton Blvd., Billings, MT 59102
South Central, Paul Lowenberg, 6015 E. Ninth St., Wichita, KS 67208
Southeast, J. Foy Johnson, P.O. Box 24687, Lakeland, FL 33801
Southwest, Glen D. Cole, 9470 Micron Rd., Sacramento, CA 95827

INTERNATIONAL HEADQUARTERS

General Supt.'s Office Administration, Gen. Supt., G. Raymond Carlson
Gen. Secretary's Office Administration, Gen. Sec., Joseph R. Flower
Division of the Treasury, Gen. Treas., Thomas E. Trask
Division of Christian Education, Natl. Dir., David Torgerson
Division of Christian Higher Education, Natl. Dir., David Bundrick
Division of Church Ministries, Natl. Dir., Terry Raburn
Division of Communications, Natl. Dir., ——-
Division of Foreign Missions, Exec. Dir., Loren O. Triplett
Division of Home Missions, Natl. Dir., Charles Hackett
Div. of Publication, Gospel Publishing House, Natl. Dir., Joseph Kilpatrick

PERIODICALS

Advance; At Ease; Caring; Sunday School Curriculum & Literature; High Adventure; Memos: A Magazine for Missionettes Leaders; Mountain Movers; Paraclete; Pentecostal Evangel; Sunday School Counselor; Woman's Touch

Assemblies of God International Fellowship (Independent/Not affiliated)

April 9, 1906 is the date commonly accepted by Pentecostals as the 20th-century outpouring of God's spirit in America, which began in a humble gospel mission at 312 Azusa Street in Los Angeles.

This spirit movement spread across the United States and gave birth to the Independent Assemblies of God (Scandinavian). Early pioneers instrumental in guiding and shaping the fellowship of ministers and churches into a nucleus of independent churches included Pastor B. M. Johnson, founder of Lakeview Gospel Church in 1911; Rev. A. A. Holmgren, a Baptist minister who received his baptism of the Holy Spirit in the early Chicago outpourings and was publisher of Sanningens Vittne, a voice of the Scandinavian Independent Assemblies of God, and also served as secretary of the fellowship for many years; Gunnar Wingren, missionary pioneer in Brazil; and Arthur F. Johnson, who served for many years as chairman of the Scandinavian Assemblies.

In 1935, the Scandinavian group dissolved its incorporation and united with the Independent Assemblies of God of the U.S. and Canada which by majority vote of members formed a new corporation in 1986, Assemblies of God International Fellowship (Independent/Not Affiliated).

HEADQUARTERS

8504 Commerce Ave., San Diego, CA 92121 Tel. (619)530-1727 Fax (619)530-1543

Media Contact, Exec. Dir. & Ed., Rev. T. A. Lanes

OFFICERS

Exec. Dir., Rev. T. A. Lanes
Vice-Pres., Rev. Winston Mattsson-Boze
Sec., Rev. Clair Hutchins
Treas., Dr. Joseph Bohac
Canada, Sec., Harry Nunn, Sr., 15 White Crest Ct., St. Catherines, ON 62N 6Y1

PERIODICAL

Fellowship Magazine, The

Associate Reformed Presbyterian Church (General Synod)

The Associate Reformed Presbyterian Church (General Synod) stems from the 1782 merger of Associate Presbyterians and Reformed Presbyterians. In 1822, the Synod of the Carolinas broke with the Associate Reformed Church (which eventually became part of the United Presbyterian Church of North America).

The story of the Synod of the Carolinas began with the Seceder Church, formed in Scotland in 1733 and representing a break from the established Church of Scotland. Seceders, in America called Associate Presbyterians, settled in South Carolina following the Revolutionary War. They were joined by a few Covenanter congregations, which, along with the Seceders, had protested Scotland's established church. The Covenanters took their name from the Solemn League and Covenant of 1643, the guiding document of Scotch Presbyterians. In 1790, some Seceders and Covenanters formed the Presbytery of the Carolinas and Georgia at Long Cane, S.C. Thomas Clark and John Boyse led in the formation of this presbytery, a unit within the Associate Reformed Presbyterian Church. The presbytery represented the southern segment of that church.

In 1822 the southern church became independent of the northern Associate Reformed Presbyterian Church and formed the Associate Reformed Presbyterian Church of the South. "Of the South" was dropped in 1858 when the northern group joined the United Presbyterian Church and "General Synod" was added in 1935. The General Synod is the denomination's highest court; it is composed of all the teaching elders and at least one ruling elder from each congregation.

Doctrinally, the church holds to the Westminster Confession of Faith. Liturgically, the synod has been distinguished by its exclusive use of psalmody; in 1946 this practice became optional.

HEADQUARTERS

Associate Reformed Presbyterian Center, One Cleveland St., Greenville, SC 29601 Tel. (803)232-8297

Media Contact, Prin. Clk., Rev. C. Ronald Beard, D.D., 3132 Grace Hill Rd., Columbia, SC 29204 Tel. (803)787-6370

OFFICERS

Mod., Mr. Harold N. Morris, P.O. Box 1709, Lake Placid, FL 33852

Principal Clk., Rev. C. Ronald Beard, D.D., 3132 Grace Hill Rd., Columbia, SC 29204

AGENCIES AND INSTITUTIONS

Ofc. of Admn. Services, Dir., Mr. Ed Hogan

Assoc. Reformed Presb. Foundation, Inc.

Assoc. Reformed Presb. Retirement Plan

Ofc. Of Christian Education, Dir., Rev. J. B. Hendrick, D. Min.

Ofc. of Church Extension, Dir., Rev. James T. Corbitt

Ofc. of Synod's Treasurer, Mr. Guy H. Smith, III

Ofc. of Secretary of World Witness, Exec. Sec., John E. Mariner, Tel. (803)233-5226

Bonclarken Assembly, Dir., Mr. James T. Brice, 500 Pine St., Flat Rock, NC 28731 Tel. (704)692-2223

Erskine College, Pres., James W. Strobel, Ph.D., Due West, SC 29639 Tel. (803)379-8759

Erskine Theological Seminary, Dean, Rev. Randall R. Ruble, Ph.D., Due West, SC 26939 Tel. (803)379-8885

PERIODICALS

Associate Reformed Presbyterian, The; Adult Quarterly, The

Bahá'í Faith

The Bahá'í Faith is an independent world religion with adherents in virtually every country. Bahá'ís are followers of Bahá'u'lláh (1817-1892). The religion upholds the basic principles of the oneness of God, the oneness of religion, and the oneness of humankind. The central aim of the Bahá'í Faith is the unification of mankind.

The Bahá'í administrative order consists of elected local Spiritual Assemblies, National Spiritual Assemblies and the Universal House of Justice. The Local and National Spiritual Assemblies are elected annually. The Universal House of Justice is elected every five years. There are 165 National Assemblies and approximately 20,000 local Spiritual Assemblies worldwide. Literature of the Bahá'í Faith has been published in 802 languages.

The period from April 21, 1992 to April 20, 1993 was designated a Holy Year by the Bahá'í Faith. The Holy Year commemorates the centenary of the passing of Bahá'u'lláh, the Prophet-Founder of the religion.

HEADQUARTERS

National Spiritual Assembly, 536 Sheridan Rd., Wilmette, IL 60091 Tel. (708)869-9039 Fax (708)869-0247

Media Contact, Dir., Ofc. of Information, Ronald B. Precht

OFFICERS

Chpsn., Judge James Nelson

Sec. Gen., Robert Henderson

Sec. for External Affairs, Firuz Kazemzadeh

Baptist Bible Fellowship International

Organized on May 24, 1950 in Fort Worth, Tex., the Baptist Bible Fellowship was founded by about 100 pastors and lay people who had grown disenchanted with the policies and leadership of the World Fundamental Baptist Missionary Fellowship, an outgrowth of the Baptist Bible Union formed in Kansas City in 1923 by fundamentalist leaders from the Southern Baptist, Northern Baptist, and Canadian Baptist Conventions. The BBF elected W. E. Dowell as its first president and established offices and a three-year (now four-year with a graduate school) Baptist Bible College.

The BBF statement of faith was essentially that of the Baptist Bible Union, adopted in 1923, a variation of the New Hampshire Confession of Faith. It presents an infallible Bible, belief in the substitutionary death of Christ, his physical resurrection, and his premillennial return to earth. It advocates local church autonomy and strong pastoral leadership and maintains that the fundamental basis of fellowship is a missionary outreach. The BBF vigorously stresses evangelism and the international missions office reports 791 adult missionaries working on 86 fields throughout the world in 1992.

There are BBF-related churches in every state of the United States, with special strength in the upper South, the Great Lakes region, southern states west of the Mississippi, Kansas, and California. There are six related colleges and one graduate school or seminary.

A Committee of Forty-Five, elected by pastors and churches within the states, sits as a representative body, meeting in three subcommittees, each chaired by one of the principal officers: an administration committee chaired by the president; a missions committee chaired by a vice-president; an education committee chaired by a vice-president.

HEADQUARTERS

Baptist Bible Fellowship Missions Bldg., 720 E. Kearney St., Springfield, MO 65803 Tel. (417)862-5001 Fax (417)865-0794

Mailing Address, P.O. Box 191, Springfield, MO 65801

OFFICERS

Pres., Parker Dailey

First Vice-Pres., Jack Baskin, Western Hills Baptist Church, 700 Mars Hill Rd., NW, Kennesaw, GA 30144

Second Vice-Pres., Don Elmore, Temple Baptist Church, P.O. Box 292, Springdale, AR 72764

Sec., K. B. Murray, Millington Street Baptist Church, Box 524, Winfield, KS 67156

Treas., Billy Hamm, Mtn. States Baptist Temple, 8333 Acoma Way, Denver, CO 80221

Mission Dir., Dr. Bob Baird, P.O. Box 191, Springfield, MO 65801

PERIODICALS

Baptist Bible Tribune, The; Preacher, The

Baptist General Conference

The Baptist General Conference, rooted in the pietistic movement of Sweden during the 19th century, traces its history to Aug. 13, 1852. On that day a small group of believers at Rock Island, Ill., under the leadership of Gustaf Palmquist, organized the first Swedish Baptist Church in America. Swedish Baptist churches flourished in the upper Midwest and Northeast, and by 1879, when the first annual meeting was held in Village Creek, Iowa, 65 churches had been organized, stretching from Maine to the Dakotas and south to Kansas and Missouri.

By 1871, John Alexis Edgren, an immigrant sea captain and pastor in Chicago, had begun the first publication and a theological seminary. The Conference grew to 324 churches and nearly 26,000 members by 1902, to 40,000 in 1945, and 135,000 in 1991.

Many churches began as Sunday schools. The seminary evolved into Bethel, a four-year liberal arts college with 1,800 students, and theological seminaries in Arden Hills, Minn. and San Diego, California.

Missions and the planting of churches have been main objectives both in America and overseas. Today churches have been established in the United States, Canada and Mexico, as well as a dozen countries overseas. In 1985 the churches of Canada founded an autonomous denomination, The Baptist General Conference of Canada.

The Baptist General Conference is a member of the Baptist World Alliance, the Baptist Joint Committee on Public Affairs, and the National Association of Evangelicals. It is characterized by the balancing of a conservative doctrine with an irenic and cooperative spirit. Its basic objective is to seek the fulfillment of the Great Commission and the Great Commandment.

HEADQUARTERS

2002 S. Arlington Heights Rd., Arlington Heights, IL 60005 Tel. (708)228-0200 Fax (708)228-5376
Media Contact, Exec. Vice-Pres., C. Herbert Hage

OFFICERS

Pres. & Chief Exec. Officer, Dr. Robert S. Ricker

OTHER ORGANIZATIONS

Business & Planning, Vice-Pres., Rev. C. Herbert Hage
Bd. of Home Missions, Exec. Dir., Dr. John C. Dickau
Bd. of World Missions, Exec. Dir., Rev. Herbert Skoglund
Bd. of Regents: Bethel College & Seminary, Pres., Dr. George Brushaber, 3900 Bethel Dr., St. Paul, MN 55112

PERIODICAL

Standard, The

Baptist Missionary Association of America

A group of regular Baptist churches organized in associational capacity in May, 1950, in Little Rock, Ark., as the North American Baptist Association. The name changed in 1969 to Baptist Missionary Association of America. There are several state and numerous local associations of cooperating churches. In theology, these churches are evangelical, missionary, fundamental, and, in the main, premillennial.

HEADQUARTERS

721 Main Street, Little Rock, AR 72201 Tel. (501)376-6788
Media Contact, Dir. of Baptist News Service, James C. Blaylock, P.O. Box 97, Jacksonville, TX 75766 Tel. (903)586-2501 Fax (903)586-0378

OFFICERS

Pres., James B. Schoenrock, 611 Butler St., Springhill, LA 71075
Vice-Pres.: Grady L. Higgs, P.O. Box 84, Jacksonville, TX 75766; Stephen Howell, 4226 Hwy 15 N, Laurel, MS 39440
Rec. Sec.: Rev. Ralph Cottrell, P.O. Box 1203, Van, TX 75790; Rev. O. D. Christian, Rt. 1, Box 267, Streetman, TX 75859; G. H. Gordon, 3202 W. 7th St., Hattiesburg, MS 39401

DEPARTMENTS

Missions: Gen. Sec., Rev. F. Donald Collins, 721 Main St., Little Rock, AR 72201
Publications: Ed.-in-Chief, Rev. James L. Silvey, 1319 Magnolia, Texarkana, TX 75501
Christian Education: Bapt. Missionary Assoc. Theological Sem., Pres., Dr. Phillip R. Bryan, Seminary Heights, 1410 E. Pine St., Jacksonville, TX 75766
Baptist News Service: Dir., Rev. James C. Blaylock, P.O. Box 97, Jacksonville, TX 75766
Life Word Broadcast Ministries: Dir., Rev. George Reddin, P.O. Box 6, Conway, AR 72032
Armed Forces Chaplaincy: Exec. Dir., William Charles Pruitt, Jr., P.O. Box 912, Jacksonville, TX 75766
BMAA Dept. of Church Ministries: Bobby Tucker, P.O. Box 3376, Texarkana, TX 75504
Daniel Springs Encampment: James Speer, P.O. Box 310, Gary, TX 75643
Ministers Benefit Dept.: James A. Henry, 4001 Jefferson St., Texarkana, AR 75501

OTHER ORGANIZATIONS

Baptist Missionary Assoc. Brotherhood: Pres., Thomas Monroe, Rt. 4, Box 585, Carthage, TX 75633
National Women's Missionary Auxiliary: Pres., Mrs. James Schoenrock, 611 Butler St., Springhill, LA 71075

PERIODICALS

Advancer, The; Gleaner, The; Baptist Progress; Baptist Trumpet; Baptist Herald; Advocate, The; Midwest Missionary Baptist; Northwest Profile

Beachy Amish Mennonite Churches

This name came into use in Somerset County, Pa., in 1927 following a division in the Amish Mennonite Church of that area. Only for identification purposes was the church referred to by the Bishop's name. But as congregations in other locations joined the movement, they were automatically identified by the same name. Today 87 churches in the United States, 8 in Canada, and 17 in other countres go by that name. Total membership is 7,200, according to the 1992 Mennonite Yearbook.

Beachy Churches believe in one God eternally

existent in three persons (Father, Son, and Holy Spirit); that Jesus Christ is the one and only way to salvation; that the Bible is God's infallible Word to man, by which all men will be judged; that heaven is the eternal abode of the redeemed in Christ, and that the wicked and unbelieving will endure hell eternally.

Evangelical mission boards sponsor missions in Central and South America and one in Kenya, Africa.

Mission Interests Committee, founded in 1953 for evangelism and other Christian services, sponsors homes for handicapped youth and elderly people, mission outreaches among the Indians in Canada, and one in Europe.

HEADQUARTERS

Media Contact, Ervin N. Hershberger, Rt. 1, Box 176, Meyersdale, PA 15552 Tel. (814)662-2483

ORGANIZATIONS

Amish Mennonite Aid: Sec.-Treas., Noah J. Beachy, 9650 Iams Road, Plain City, OH 43064 Tel. (614)873-8140

Mission Interests Committee: Chairman, Gary Paul Miller, 3909 W. Illinois Ave., Hutchinson, KS 67505 Tel. (316)663-8558

Choice Books of Northern Virginia: Supervisor, Simon Schrock, 4614 Holly Ave., Fairfax, VA 22030 Tel. (703)830-2800

Calvary Bible School: HC 61, Box 202, Calico Rock, AR 72519 Tel. (703)830-2800; Sec.-Treas., Elmer Gingerich, HC 74, Box 282, Mountain View, AR 72560 Tel. (501)296-8764

PERIODICAL

Calvary Messenger, The

Berean Fundamental Church

Founded 1932 in North Platte, Neb., this body emphasizes conservative Protestant doctrines.

HEADQUARTERS

Lincoln, NE 68506 Tel. (402)483-6512

Media Contact, Sec., Rev. Frank Van Campen, P.O. Box 1136, Chadron, NE 69337 Tel. (308)432-4272

OFFICERS

Pres., Rev. Curt Lehman, 6400 South 70th St., Lincoln, NE 68516 Tel. (402)483-4840

Vice-Pres., Rev. Richard Cocker, 419 Lafayette Blvd., Cheyenne, WY 82009 Tel. (307)635-5914

Sec., Rev. A. Frank Van Campen, P.O. Box 1136, Chadron, NE 69337 Tel. (308)432-4272

Treas., Virgil Wiebe, P.O. Box 6103, Lincoln, NE 68506

Founder Advisor to the Council, Dr. Ivan E. Olsen

Exec. Advisor, Rev. Carl M. Goltz, P.O. Box 397, North Platte, NE 69103 Tel. (308)532-6723

The Bible Church of Christ, Inc.

The Bible Church of Christ was founded on March 1, 1961 by Bishop Roy Bryant, Sr. Since that time, the Church has grown to include congregations in the United States, Africa, and India. The church is trinitarian and accepts the Bible as the divinely inspired Word of God. Its doctrine includes miracles of healing and the baptism of the Holy Ghost.

HEADQUARTERS

1358 Morris Ave., Bronx, NY 10456 Tel. (718)588-2284

Media Contact, Pres., Bishop Roy Bryant, Sr.

OFFICERS

Pres., Bishop Roy Bryant, Sr., 3033 Gunther Ave., Bronx, NY 10469 Tel. (718)379-8080

Vice-Pres., Bishop Roy Bryant, Jr., 34 Tuxedo Rd., Montclair, NJ 07042 Tel. (201)746-0063

Sec., Sissieretta Bryant

Treas., Elder Artie Burney

EXECUTIVE TRUSTEE BOARD

Chpsn., Leon T. Mims

Vice-Chpsn., Evangelist Peggy Rawls, 100 W. 2nd St., Mount Vernon, NY 10550 Tel. (914)664-4602

OTHER ORGANIZATIONS

Foreign Missions: Pres., Elder Diane Cooper

Home Missions: Pres., Evangelist Eleanor Samuel

Sunday Schools: Gen. Supt., Elder Diane Cooper

Evangelism: Natl. Pres., Evangelist Gloria Gray

Youth: Pres., Deacon Tommy Robinson

Minister of Music: Leon T. Mims; Asst., Ray Brown

Minister of Education, Gloria Pratt

Prison Ministry Team: Pres., Evangelist Marvin Lowe

Presiding Elders: Delaware, Elder Roland Miflin, Diamond Acre, Dagsboro, DE 19939; North Carolina, Elder George Houston; Adm., Elder Larry Bryant, West Johnson Rd., Clinton, NC 28328; Monticello, Elder Jesse Alston, 104 Waverly Ave., Monticello, NY 12701; Mount Vernon, Elder Artie Burney, Sr., 100 W. 2nd St., Mount Vernon, NY 10550; Bronx, Elder Anita Robinson; Annex, Elder Betty Gilliard, 1069 Morris Ave., Bronx, NY 10456

Bible School: Pres., Dr. Roy Bryant, Sr.

Bookstore: Mgr., Elder Elizabeth Johnson, Tel. (718)293-1928

PERIODICAL

Voice, The

Bible Way Church of Our Lord Jesus Christ World Wide, Inc.

This body was organized in 1957 in the Pentecostal tradition for the purpose of accelerating evangelistic and foreign missionary commitment and to effect a greater degree of collective leadership than leaders found in the body in which they had previously participated.

The doctrine is the same as that of the Church of Our Lord Jesus Christ of the Apostolic Faith, Inc., of which some of the churches and clergy were formerly members.

This organization has churches and missions in Africa, England, Guyana, Trinidad, and Jamaica, and churches in 25 states in America. The Bible Way Church WW is involved in humanitarian, as well as evangelical outreach, with concerns for urban housing and education and economic development.

HEADQUARTERS

1100 New Jersey Ave., N.W., Washington, DC 20001 Tel. (202)789-0700

Media Contact, Presiding Bishop, Lawrence G. Campbell, Apostle, 141 Andes Dr., Danville, VA 24541 Tel. (804)793-9493

OFFICERS

Presiding Bishop, Bishop Lawrence G. Campbell

60

Gen. Sec., Bishop Edward Williams, 5118 Clarendon Rd., Brooklyn, NY 11226 Tel. (718)451-1238

Brethren Church (Ashland, Ohio)

It was organized by progressive-minded German Baptist Brethren in 1883. They reaffirmed the teaching of the original founder of the Brethren movement, Alexander Mack, and returned to congregational government.

HEADQUARTERS

524 College Ave., Ashland, OH 44805 Tel. (419)289-1708 Fax (419)281-0450
Media Contact, Dir. of Brethren Church Ministries, Ronald W. Waters

GENERAL ORGANIZATION

Dir. of Pastoral Ministries, Rev. David Cooksey
Dir. of Brethren Church Ministries, Rev. Ronald W. Waters
Ed. of Publications, Rev. Richard C. Winfield
Conf. Mod. (1993-1994), Rev. Russell Gordon

BOARD

The Missionary Bd., Exec. Dir., Rev. James R. Black
Dir. of Home Missions, Rev. Russell Gordon

PERIODICAL

Brethren Evangelist, The

Brethren in Christ Church

The Brethren in Christ Church was founded in Lancaster County, Pa. in about the year 1778 and was an outgrowth of the religious awakening which occurred in that area during the latter part of the 18th century. This group became known as "River Brethren" because of their original location near the Susquehanna River. The name "Brethren in Christ" was officially adopted in 1863. In theology they have accents of the Pietist, Anabaptist, Wesleyan, and Evangelical movements.

HEADQUARTERS

General Church Office, P.O. Box 290, Grantham, PA 17027 Tel. (717)697-2634 Fax (717)697-7714
Media Contact, Mod., Harvey R. Sider, Tel. (717)697-2634 Fax (717)697-7714

OFFICERS

Mod., Rev. Harvey R. Sider
Dir. of Bishops, Dr. John A. Byers
Gen. Sec., Dr. R. Donald Shafer, Fax (714)985-6117
Dir. of Finance, Harold D. Chubb

OTHER ORGANIZATIONS

Board of Administration: Mod., Rev. Harvey R. Sider
Board of Brotherhood Concerns: Chpsn., Dr. Samuel Brubaker, Peach Alley Ct., #310, 155 S. Popular St., Elizabethtown, PA 17022; Admn. Dir., Dr. R. Donald Shafer
Board for Congregational Life: Chpsn., Martha Starr, 3054 Pleasant View Dr., Manheim, PA 17545; Admn. Dir., Dr. John A. Byers, P.O. Box 547, Elizabethtown, PA 17022
Board of Directors: Chpsn., Dr. MarK Garis, 504 Swartley Road, Hatfield, PA 19440
Board for Evangelism & Church Planting: Chpsn., Douglas P. Sider, 142 Streb Cresc., Saskatoon, SK S7M 4T8; Dir. of Bishops, John A. Byers

Board for Media Ministries: Chpsn., Emerson C. Frey, Box 317, Owl Bridge Road, Millersville, PA 17551; Exec. Dir., Roger Williams, P.O. Box 189, Nappanee, IN 46550
Board for Ministry and Doctrine: Chpsn., James D. Ernst, 1865 Fruitville Pike, Lancaster, PA 17601
Board for World Missions: Chpsn., Lowell D. Mann, 8 W. Bainbridge St., Elizabethtown, PA 17022 Fax (717)653-6911; Dir., Rev. Jack McClane, P.O. Box 390, Mt. Joy, PA 17552-0390
Commission on Christian Education Lit.: Chpsn., Gwen White, 230 Philadelphia Ave., Waynesboro, PA 17268
Jacob Engle Foundation Bd. of Directors: Chpsn., Dr. Donald R. Zook, Fax (717)697-7714
Pension Fund Trustees: Chpsn., Donald R. Zook, P.O. Box 390, Mt. Joy, PA 17552
Board for Stewardship Services: Chpsn., Charles F. Frey, 259 Willow Valley Dr., Lancaster, PA 17602
Publishing House: Exec. Dir., Roger Williams, Evangel Press, P.O. Box 189, Nappannee, IN 46550

PERIODICAL

Evangelical Visitor

Buddhist Churches of America

Founded in 1899, organized in 1914 as the Buddhist Mission of North America, this body was incorporated in 1944 under the present name and represents the Jodo Shinshu Sect of Buddhism affiliated with the Hongwanji-ha Hongwanji denomination in the continental United States. It is a school of Buddhism which believes in becoming aware of the ignorant self and relying upon the infinite wisdom and compassion of Amida Buddha, which is expressed in sincere gratitude through the recitation of the Nembutsu, Namu Amida Butsu.

HEADQUARTERS

1710 Octavia St., San Francisco, CA 94109 Tel. (415)776-5600 Fax (415)771-6293

OFFICERS

Bishop Seigen H. Yamaoka
Exec. Asst. to the Bishop, Rev. Seikan Fukuma
Admn. Officer, Henry Shibata
Dir. of Buddhist Education, Rev. Carol Himaka

OTHER ORGANIZATIONS

Fed. of Buddhist Women's Assoc.
Fed. of Dharma School Teachers' League
Institute of Buddhist Studies
Young Adult Buddhist Association
Western Young Buddhist League
Affiliated U.S. Organizational Juris., Honpa Hongwanji Mission of Hawaii, 1727 Pali Hwy., Honolulu, HI 96813
Affiliated Can. Organizational Juris., Buddhist Churches of Canada, 220 Jackson Ave., Vancouver, BC V6A 3B3

Bulgarian Eastern Orthodox Church

Bulgarian immigration to the United States and Canada started around the turn of the century, and the first Bulgarian Orthodox church was built in 1907 in Madison, Ill. In 1938, the Holy Synod of the Bulgarian E. O. Church established the diocese in New York as an Episcopate, and Bishop Andrey was sent as diocesan Bishop. In 1947, the diocese was officially incorporated in New York and Bishop Andrey became the first elected Metropolitan.

In 1969 the Bulgarian Eastern Orthodox Church was divided into the Diocese of New York (incorporated Bulgarian Eastern Orthodox Church—Diocese of America, North and South, and Australia) and the Diocese of Akron (incorporated American Bulgarian Eastern Orthodox Diocese of Akron, Ohio). In 1989 both Dioceses were united into one Bulgarian Eastern-Orthodox Diocese in the USA, Canada and Australia.

HEADQUARTERS

Holy Metropolia, 550 A West 50th St., New York, NY 10019 Tel. (212)246-4608
Media Contact: Metropolitan Joseph

OFFICER

His Eminence Metropolitan Joseph

Christ Catholic Church

The church is a catholic communion established in 1968 to minister to the growing number of people seeking an experiential relationship with God, and who desire to make a total commitment of their lives to God. The church is catholic in faith and tradition and its orders are recognized as valid by catholics of every tradition.

HEADQUARTERS

5165 Palmer Ave., Niagara Falls, ON L2G 1Y4
Media Contact, Suffragen Bishop, Most Rev. Karl Pruter, P.O. Box 98, Highlandville, MO 65669 Tel. (417)587-3951

OFFICERS

Archbishop, The Most Rev. Donald W. Mullan, Tel. (416)354-2329

PERIODICAL

St. Willibrord Journal

Christadelphians

The Christadelphians are a body of people who believe the Bible to be the divinely inspired word of God, written by "Holy men who spoke as they were moved by the Holy Spirit" (II Peter 1: 21); in the return of Christ to earth to establish the Kingdom of God; the resurrection of those dead, at the return of Christ, who come into relation to Christ in conformity with his instructions, to be judged as to worthiness for eternal life; in opposition to war; spiritual rebirth requiring belief and immersion in the name of Jesus; and in a godly walk in this life.

The denomination was organized in 1844 by a medical doctor, John Thomas, who came to the United States from England in 1832, having survived a near shipwreck in a violent storm. This experience affected him profoundly, and he vowed to devote his life to a search for the truth of God and a future hope from the Bible.

HEADQUARTERS

Media Contact, Trustee, Norman D. Zilmer, Christadelphian Action Society, 1000 Mohawk Dr., Elgin, IL 60120-3148 Tel. (708)741-5253

LEADERS

Co-Ministers: Norman Fadelle, 815 Chippewa Dr., Elgin, IL 60120-4016; Norman D. Zilmer, 1000 Mohawk Dr., Elgin, IL 60120-3148

PERIODICALS

Christadelphian Tidings; Christadelphian Watchman; Christadelphian Advocate

The Christian and Missionary Alliance

An evangelical and evangelistic church begun in 1887 when Dr. Albert B. Simpson founded two organizations, The Christian Alliance (a fellowship of Christians dedicated to the experiencing of the deeper Christian life) and the Evangelical Missionary Alliance (a missionary sending organization) were merged in 1897 to become The Christian and Missionary Alliance. The denomination stresses the sufficiency of Jesus—Savior, Sanctifier, Healer, and Coming King—and has earned a worldwide reputation for its missionary accomplishments. The Canadian districts became autonomous in 1981 and formed The Christian and Missionary Alliance in Canada.

HEADQUARTERS

Media Contact, Asst. to the President for Comm. and Funding, Rev. Gordon McAlister, P.O. Box 35000, Colorado Springs, CO 80935-3500 Tel. (719)599-5999 Fax (719)593-8692

OFFICERS

Pres., Rev. D. L. Rambo
Vice-Pres., Rev. P. F. Bubna
Sec., R. H. Mangham
Vice-Pres. for Fin./Treas., Mr. D. A. Wheeland
Vice-Pres. for Church Ministries, Rev. R. W. Bailey
Vice-Pres. for Overseas Ministries, P. N. Nanfelt
Vice-Pres. for Gen. Services, Rev. J. A. Davey

BOARD OF MANAGERS

Chpsn., Rev. P. F. Bubna
Vice-Chpsn., Rev. G. M. Cathey

EXECUTIVE ADMINISTRATION

Admn. Staff: Pres., D. L. Rambo
Division of Finance: Vice-Pres./Treas., D. A. Wheeland; Payroll Mgr., L. L. Keeports

EXECUTIVE ADMINISTRATION

Division of Church Ministries: Vice-Pres., R. W. Bailey
Division of Overseas Ministries: Vice-Pres., P. N. Nanfelt
Division of General Services: Vice-Pres., J. A. Davey

DISTRICT SUPERINTENDENTS

Central: Rev. Howard D. Bowers, 1218 High St., Wadsworth, OH 44281 Tel. (216)336-2911
Central Pacific: Rev. D. Duane Adamson, 3824 Buell St., Suite A, Oakland, CA 94619 Tel. (510)530-5410 Fax (510)530-1396
Eastern: Rev. Leon W. Young, 1 Sherwood Dr., Mechanicsburg, PA 17055 Tel. (717)766-0261 Fax (717)766-0486
Great Lakes: Rev. Dahl B. Seckinger, 2250 Huron Pkwy, Ann Arbor, MI 48104 Tel. (313)677-8555 Fax (313)677-0087
Metropolitan: Rev. Paul B. Hazlett, 349 Watchung Ave., N. Plainfield, NJ 07060 Tel. (908)668-8421 Fax (908)757-6299
Mid-Atlantic: Rev. C. E. Mock, 7100 Roslyn Ave., Rockville, MD 20855 Tel. (301)258-0035 Fax (301)258-1021
Midwest: Rev. Gerald R. Mapstone, 260 Glen Ellyn Rd., Bloomingdale, IL 60108 Tel. (708)893-1355 Fax (708)893-1027
New England: Rev. Cornelius W. Clarke, 34 Central St., S. Easton, MA 02375 Tel. (508)238-3820

Northeastern: Rev. Woodford C. Stemple, Jr., 6275 Pillmore Dr., Rome, NY 13440 Tel. (315)336-4720

Northwestern: Rev. Gary M. Benedict, 1813 N. Lexington Ave., St. Paul, MN 55113 Tel. (612)489-1391 Fax (612)489-8535

Ohio Valley: Rev. Keith M. Bailey, LLD, 4050 Executive Park Dr., Ste. 402, Cincinnati, OH 45241 Tel. (513)733-4833

Pacific Northwest: Rev. R. Harold Mangham, DD, P.O. Box 1030, Canby, OR 97013 Tel. (503)226-2238 Fax (503)263-8052

Puerto Rico: Rev. Jorge Cuevas, P.O. Box 51394, Levittown, PR 00950 Tel. (809)261-0101 Fax (809)261-0107

Rocky Mountain: Rev. Harvey A. Town, LLD, 1215 24th W., Ste. 210, Billings, MT 59102 Tel. (406)656-4233 Fax (406)656-5502

South Atlantic: Rev. Gordon G. Copeland, 3421-B St. Vardell Ln., Charlotte, NC 28217 Tel. (704)523-9456

South Pacific: Rev. Bill J. Vaughn, 9055 Haven Ave., Ste. 107, Rancho Cucamonga, CA 91730 Tel. (909)945-9244 Fax (714)948-0794

Southeastern: Rev. Harry J. Arnold, P.O. Box 720430, Orlando, FL 32872 Tel. (407)823-9662 Fax (407)823-9668

Southern: Rev. Garfield G. Powell, 8420 Division Ave., Birmingham, AL 35206 Tel. (205)836-7048

Southwestern: Rev. Loren G. Calkins, DMin., 5600 E. Loop 820 S., Fort Worth, TX 76129 Tel. (817)561-0879

Western: Rev. Anthony G. Bollback, 1301 S. 119th St., Omaha, NE 68144 Tel. (402)330-1888 Fax (402)330-7213

Western Great Lakes: Rev. John W. Fogal, W6107 Aerotech Dr., Appleton, WI 54915 Tel. (414)734-1123

Western Pennsylvania: Rev. D. Paul McGarvey, P.O. Box 429, Punxsutawney, PA 15767 Tel. (814)938-6920 Fax (814)938-7528

INTERCULTURAL MINISTRIES DISTRICTS

Cambodian: Supt., Rev. Joseph S. Kong, 1616 S. Palmetto Ave., Ontario, CA 91762 Tel. (909)988-9434

Dega: c/o Rev. A. E. Hall, P.O. Box 35000, Colorado Springs, CO 80935

Haitian: Acting Dir., Rev. Paul V. Lehman, 21 College Ave., Nyack, NY 10960 Tel. (914)353-7305

Hmong: Supt., Rev. Timothy Teng Vang, P.O. Box 219, Brighton, CO 80601 Tel. (303)659-1538 Fax (303)659-2171

Jewish: Missionary, Rev. Abraham Sandler, 9820 Woodfern Rd., Philadelphia, PA 19115 Tel. (215)676-5122

Korean: Supt., Rev. Gil Kim, 2175 Lemoine Ave., Rm. 304, Fort Lee, NJ 07024 Tel. (201)461-5755

Lao: Dir., Mr. Sisouphanh Ratthahao, 459 Addison St., Elgin, IL 60120 Tel. (708)741-3871

Native American: Dir., Rev. Stephen Wood, 5664 Corinth Dr., Colorado Springs, CO 80918 Tel. (719)531-7823

Spanish Central: Supt., Rev. Kenneth N. Brisco, 260 Glen Ellyn Rd., Bloomingdale, IL 60108 Tel. (708)924-7171 Fax (708)893-1027

Spanish Eastern: Supt., Rev. Carlos Santiago, 6220 S. Orange Blossom Trl., Ste. 136, Orlando, FL 32809 Tel. (407)855-5942

Spanish Western: Dir., Rev. Angel V. Ortiz, 334 Springtree Pl., Escondido, CA 92026-1417 Tel. (619)489-4835

Vietnamese: Supt., Rev. Tai Anh Nguyen, 1681 W. Broadway, Anaheim, CA 92802 Tel. (714)491-8007

NATIONAL ASSOCIATIONS

Black Ministries Consultation: c/o Div. of Church Ministries, P.O. Box 35000, Colorado Springs, CO 80935

Chinese Association of the C&MA: c/o Rev. Peter Chu, 14209 Secluded La., Gaithersburg, MD 20878 Tel. (301)294-8067

Filipino Association of the C&MA: c/o Rev. Fred M. Valdez, 4144 Jerry Ave., Baldwin Park, CA 91706 Tel. (818)962-1959

PERIODICAL

Alliance Life

Christian Brethren (also known as Plymouth Brethren)

An orthodox and evangelical movement which began in the British Isles in the 1820s and is now worldwide. Congregations are usually called "assemblies." The name Plymouth Brethren was given by others because the group in Plymouth, England, was a large congregation. In recent years the term Christian Brethren has replaced Plymouth Brethren for the "open" branch of the movement in Canada and British Commonwealth countries, and to some extent in the United States.

The unwillingness to establish a denominational structure makes the autonomy of local congregations an important feature of the movement. Other features are weekly observance of the Lord's Supper and adherence to the doctrinal position of conservative, evangelical Christianity.

In the 1840s the movement divided. The "exclusive" branch, led by John Darby, stressed the interdependency of congregations. Since disciplinary decisions were held to be binding on all assemblies, exclusives had sub-divided into seven or eight main groups by the end of the century. Since 1925 a trend toward reunification has reduced that number to three or four. United States congregations number approximately 300, with an estimated 19,000 members.

The "open" branch of the movement, stressing evangelism and foreign missions, now has about 850 U.S. congregations, with an estimated 79,000 members. Following the leadership of George Muller in rejecting the "exclusive" principle of binding discipline, this branch has escaped large-scale division.

HEADQUARTERS

Media Contact, Ed. Asst., Naomi Bauman, P.O. Box 190, Wheaton, IL 60189 Tel. (708)653-6573 Fax (708)653-6595

CORRESPONDENT

Interest Ministries, Pres., Bruce R. McNicol, P.O. Box 190, Wheaton, IL 60189 Tel. (708)653-6573 Fax (708)653-6595

OTHER ORGANIZATIONS

Christian Missions in Many Lands, Box 13, Spring Lake, NJ 07762

Stewards Foundation, 218 W. Willow, Wheaton, IL 60187

International Teams, Box 203, Prospect Heights, IL 60070

Emmaus Bible College, 2570 Asbury Rd., Dubuque, IA 52001

The Partnership International, P.O. Box 5218, Glendale Heights, IL 60139 Tel. (708)653-3034

Stewards Canada, 9 Horner Ct., Richmond Hill, ON L4C 4Y8

Stewards Ministries, 1655 N. Arlington Hts. Rd., Arlington Hts., IL 60004

Vision Ontario, P.O. Box 28032, Waterloo, ON N2L 6J8

PERIODICAL

Interest

Christian Catholic Church (Evangelical-Protestant)

This church was founded by the Rev. John Alexander Dowie on Feb. 22, 1896 at Chicago, Ill. In 1901 the church opened the city of Zion, Ill., as its home and headquarters. Theologically, the church is rooted in evangelical orthodoxy. The Scriptures are accepted as the rule of faith and practice. Other doctrines call for belief in the necessity of repentance for sin and personal trust in Christ for salvation, baptism by triune immersion, and tithing as a practical method of Christian stewardship. The church teaches the Second Coming of Christ.

The Christian Catholic Church is a denominational member of The National Association of Evangelicals. It has work in 8 other nations in addition to the United States. Branch ministries are found in Michigan City, Ind.; Phoenix, Ariz.; Tonalea, Ariz.; and Lindenhurst, Ill.

HEADQUARTERS

2500 Dowie Memorial Dr., Zion, IL 60099 Tel. (708)746-1411 Fax (708)746-1452

Media Contact, Senior Pastor & Gen. Overseer

OFFICER

Gen. Overseer, Roger W. Ottersen

PERIODICAL

Leaves of Healing

Christian Church (Disciples of Christ)

Born on the American frontier in the early 1800s as a movement to unify Christians, this body drew its major inspiration from Thomas and Alexander Campbell in western Pennsylvania and Barton W. Stone in Kentucky. Developing separately, the "Disciples," under Alexander Campbell, and the "Christians," led by Stone, united in 1832 in Lexington, Ky.

The Christian Church (Disciples of Christ) is marked by informality, openness, individualism and diversity. The Disciples claim no official doctrine or dogma. Membership is granted after a simple statement of belief in Jesus Christ and baptism by immersion—although most congregations accept transfers baptized by other forms in other denominations. The Lord's Supper—generally called Communion—is open to Christians of all persuasions. The practice is weekly Communion, although no church law insists upon it.

Thoroughly ecumenical, the Disciples helped organize the National and World Councils of Churches. The church is a member of the Consultation on Church Union. The Disciples and the United Church of Christ have declared themselves to be in "full communion" through the General Assembly and General Synod of the two churches. Official theological conversations have been going on since 1967 directly with the Roman Catholic Church, and since 1987 with the Russian Orthodox Church.

Disciples have vigorously supported world and national programs of education, agricultural assistance, urban reconciliation, care of mentally retarded, family planning, and aid to victims of war and calamity. Operating ecumenically, Disciples personnel or funds work in more than 100 countries outside North America.

Three levels of church polity (general, regional, and congregational) operate as equals, managing their own finances, property, and program, with strong but voluntary ties to one another. Local congregations own their property and control their budgets and program. A General Assembly meets every two years and has voting representation from each congregation.

HEADQUARTERS

222 S. Downey Ave., P.O. Box 1986, Indianapolis, IN 46206-1986 Tel. (317)353-1491 Fax (800)458-3318

Media Contact, Dir. of News & Information, Cliff Willis

OFFICERS

Gen. Minister & Pres., C. William Nichols

Mod., Marilyn J. Moffett, RR 1, Box 252, Waynetown, IN 47990

1st Vice-Mod., Mary E. Jacobs, 1651 Oakhaven Pl., Tucson, AZ 85746

2nd Vice-Mod., Michael Saenz, 4427 Tamworth Rd., Fort Worth, TX 76116

GENERAL OFFICERS

Gen. Minister & Pres., C. William Nichols

Dep. Gen. Min./Vice-Pres. for Communication, Claudia E. Grant

Dep. Gen. Min./Vice-Pres. for Admn., Donald B. Manworren

Dep. Gen. Min./Vice-Pres. for Inclusive Ministries, John R. Foulkes

ADMINISTRATIVE UNITS

Board of Church Extension: Pres., Harold R. Watkins, 110 S. Downey Ave., Box 7030, Indianapolis, IN 46207-7030 Tel. (317)356-6333

Christian Bd. of Pub. (Chalice Press): Pres., James C. Suggs, Box 179, 1316 Convention Plaza Dr., St. Louis, MO 63166-0179 Tel. (314)231-8500 Fax (314)231-8524

Christian Church Foundation: Pres., James P. Johnson

Church Finance Council, Inc.: Pres., Robert K. Welsh

Council on Christian Unity: Pres., Paul A. Crow, Jr.

Disciples of Christ Historical Society: Pres., James M. Seale, 1101 19th Ave. S., Nashville, TN 37212-2196 Tel. (615)327-1444

Division of Higher Education: Pres., James I. Spainhower, 11780 Borman Dr., Ste. 100, St. Louis, MO 63146-4159 Tel. (314)991-3000 Fax (314)993-9018

Division of Homeland Ministries: Pres., Ann Updegraff Spleth

Division of Overseas Ministries: Pres., William J. Nottingham

National Benevolent Association: Pres., Richard R. Lance, 11780 Borman Dr., Ste. 200, St. Louis, MO 63146-4157 Tel. (314)993-9000 Fax (314)993-9018

Pension Fund: Pres., Lester D. Palmer, 200 Barrister Bldg., 155 E. Market St., Indianapolis, IN 46204-3215 Tel. (317)634-4504 Fax (317)634-4071

Alabama-Northwest Florida: Regional Minister, Carl R. Flock, 1336 Montgomery Hwy. S., Birmingham, AL 35216-2799 Tel. (205)823-5647

Arizona: Regional Minister, Gail F. Davis, 4423 N. 24th St., Ste 700, Phoenix, AZ 85016-5544 Tel. (602)468-3815

Arkansas: Exec. Minister, W. Chris Hobgood, 6100 Queensboro Dr., P.O. Box 191057, Little Rock, AR 72219-1057 Tel. (501)562-6053

California North-Nevada: Regional Minister/Pres., Richard Lauer, 111-A Fairmount Ave., Oakland, CA 94611-5918 Tel. (510)839-3550

Canada: Exec. Minister, Robert W. Steffer, 128 Woolwich St., Ste. 202, P.O. Box 64, Guelph, ON N1H 6J6 Tel. (519)823-5190

Capital Area: Regional Minister, Richard L. Taylor, 8901 Connecticut Ave., Chevy Chase, MD 20815-6700 Tel. (301)654-7794

Central Rocky Mountain Region: Exec. Regional Minister, William E. Crowl, ABS Building, 7000 N. Broadway, Ste. 400, Denver, CO 80221-2994 Tel. (303)427-1403

Florida: Regional Minister, Jimmie L. Gentle, 924 N. Magnolia, Ste. 248, Orlando, FL 32803 Tel. (407)843-4652

Georgia: Regional Minister, David L. Alexander, 2370 Vineville Ave., Macon, GA 31204-3163 Tel. (912)743-8649

Idaho-South: Regional Minister, Larry Crist, 4900 No. Five Mile Rd., Boise, ID 83704-1826 Tel. (208)322-0538

Illinois-Wisconsin: Regional Minister/Pres., Nathan S. Smith, 1011 N. Main St., Bloomington, IL 61701-1797 Tel. (309)828-6293

Indiana: Regional Minister, C. Edward Weisheimer, 1100 W. 42nd St., Indianapolis, IN 46208-3375 Tel. (317)926-6051

Kansas: Regional Minister/Pres., Ralph L. Smith, 2914 S.W. MacVicar Ave., Topeka, KS 66611-1787 Tel. (913)266-2914

Kansas City (Greater): Regional Minister/Pres., David C. Downing, 5700 Broadmoor, Ste 408, Mission, KS 66202-2405 Tel. (913)432-1414

Kentucky: Gen. Minister, A. Guy Waldrop, 1125 Red Mile Rd., Lexington, KY 40504-2660 Tel. (606)233-1391

Louisiana: Regional Minister, Bill R. Boswell, 3524 Holloway Prairie Rd., Pineville, LA 71360-9998 Tel. (318)443-0304

Michigan: Regional Minister, Morris Finch, Jr., 2820 Covington Ct., Lansing, MI 48912-4830 Tel. (517)372-3220

Mid-America Region: Regional Minister, Stephen V. Cranford, Hwy. 54 W., Box 104298, Jefferson City, MO 65110-4298 Tel. (314)636-8149

Mississippi: Regional Minister, William E. McKnight, 1619 N. West St., Jackson, MS 39202 Tel. (601)352-6774

Montana: Regional Minister, James E. Kimsey, Jr., 1019 Central Ave., Great Falls, MT 59401-3784 Tel. (406)452-7404

Nebraska: Regional Minister, N. Dwain Acker, 1268 S. 20th St., Lincoln, NE 68502-1699 Tel. (402)476-0359

North Carolina: Regional Minister, ——, 509 NE Lee St., Box 1568, Wilson, NC 27894 Tel. (919)291-4047

Northeastern Region: Regional Minister, Charles F. Lamb, 1272 Delaware Ave., Buffalo, NY 14209-1531 Tel. (716)882-4793

Northwest Region: Regional Minister/Pres., Robert Clarke Brock, 6558-35th Ave. SW, Seattle, WA 98126-2899 Tel. (206)938-1008

Ohio: Regional Pastor/Pres., Howard M. Ratcliff, 38007 Butternut Ridge Rd., P.O. Box 299, Elyria, OH 44036-0299 Tel. (216)458-5112

Oklahoma: Exec. Regional Minister, Eugene N. Frazier, 301 N.W. 36th St., Oklahoma City, OK 73118-8699 Tel. (405)528-3577

Oregon: Regional Minister, Mark K. Reid, 0245 S.W. Bancroft St., Suite F, Portland, OR 97201-4267 Tel. (503)226-7648

Pacific Southwest Region: Acting Regional Minister, John D. Wolfersberger, 1755 N. Park Ave., Pomona, CA 91768 Tel. (714)620-5503

Pennsylvania: Regional Minister, Dwight L. French, 670 Rodi Rd., Pittsburgh, PA 15235-4524 Tel. (412)731-7000

South Carolina: Regional Minister, ——, 1098 E. Montague Ave., North Charleston, SC 29406 Tel. (803)554-6886

Southwest Region: Regional Minister, M. Margaret Harrison, 3209 S. University Dr., Fort Worth, TX 76109-2239 Tel. (817)926-4687

Tennessee: Regional Minister/Pres., Richard L. Hamm, 3700 Richland Ave., Nashville, TN 37205-2499 Tel. (615)269-3409

Upper Midwest Region: Regional Minister/Pres., William L. Miller, Jr., 3300 University Ave., Box 1024, Des Moines, IA 50311 Tel. (515)255-3168

Utah: Exec. Regional Minister, William E. Crowl, ABS Building, 7000 N. Broadway, Ste. 400, Denver, CO 80221-2994 Tel. (303)427-1403

Virginia: Regional Minister, R. Woods Kent, 518 Brevard St., Lynchburg, VA 24501 Tel. (804)846-3400

West Virginia: Regional Minister, William B. Allen, Rt. 5, Box 167, Parkersburg, WV 26101-9576 Tel. (304)428-1681

PERIODICALS

Disciple, The; Vanguard; Mid-Stream: An Ecumenical Journal

Christian Church of North America, General Council

Originally known as the Italian Christian Church, its first General Council was held in 1927 at Niagara Falls, N.Y. This body was incorporated in 1948 at Pittsburgh, Pa., and is described as Pentecostal but does not engage in the "the excesses tolerated or practiced among some churches using the same name." The movement recognizes two ordinances—baptism and the Lord's Supper. Its moral code is conservative and its teaching is orthodox. Members are exhorted to pursue a life of personal holiness, setting an example to others. A conservative position is held in regard to marriage and divorce. The governmental form is, by and large, congregational. District and National officiaries, however, are referred to as Presbyteries led by Overseers.

The group functions in cooperative fellowship with the Italian Pentecostal Church of Canada and the Evangelical Christian Churches—Assemblies of God in Italy. It is an affiliate member of the Pentecostal Fellowship of North America and of the National Association of Evangelicals.

HEADQUARTERS

1294 Rutledge Rd., Transfer, PA 16154-9005 Tel. (412)962-3501 Fax (412)962-1766

Media Contact, Gen. Sec., Rev. R. Allen Noyd, 16 Rosedale Ave., Greenville, PA 16125

US RELIGIOUS BODIES

Executive Bd., Gen. Overseer, Rev. David Farina, 41 Sherbrooke Rd., Trenton, NJ 08638

Exec. Vice-Pres., Rev. Andrew Farina, 3 Alhambra Pl., Greenville, PA 16125

Asst. Gen. Overseers: Rev. James Demola, P.O. Box 157, Mullica Hill, NJ 08062; Rev. Anthony Freni, 10 Elkway Ave., Norwood, MA 02062; Rev. Charles Gay, 26 Delafield Dr., Albany, NY 12205; Rev. Michael Marino, 25595 Chardon Rd., Richmond Heights, OH 44143; Rev. Raymond Patronelli, 6203 Kelly Rd., Plant City, FL 33565

Gen. Sec.-Treas., Rev. R. Allen Noyd, 16 Rosedale Ave., Greenville, PA 16125

DEPARTMENTS

Benevolence, Rev. Eugene DeMarco, 155 Scott St., New Brighton, PA 15066

Church Growth and Media Ministries, Rev. Carmine Reigle, P.O. Box 644, Niles, OH 44446

Finance, Rev. R. Allen Noyd, 16 Rosedale Ave., Greenville, PA 16125

Faith, Order and Credentials, Rev. Andrew Farina, 3 Alhambra Pl., Greenville, PA 16125

Missions, Rev. John DelTurco, P.O. Box 1198, Hermitage, PA 16148

Publications and Promotion, Rev. John Tedesco, 1188 Heron Rd., Cherry Hill, NJ 08003

Youth, Education and Sunday School, Rev. Lou Fortunato, Jr., 248 Curry Pl., Youngstown, OH 44504

PERIODICAL

Vista

Christian Churches and Churches of Christ

The fellowship, whose churches were always strictly congregational in polity, has its origin in the American movement to "restore the New Testament church in doctrine, ordinances and life" initiated by Thomas and Alexander Campbell, Walter Scott and Barton W. Stone in the early 19th century.

CONVENTIONS

North American Christian Convention: Dir., Rod Huron, 4210 Bridgetown Rd., Box 11326, Cincinnati, OH 45211 Tel. (513)598-6222; NACC Mailing Address, Box 39456, Cincinnati, OH 45239 Tel. (513)385-2470

National Missionary Convention, Coord., Walter Birney, Box 11, Copeland, KS 67837 Tel. (513)668-5250

Eastern Christian Convention, 5300 Norbeck Rd., Rockville, MD 10853

PERIODICALS

Christian Standard; Restoration Herald; Directory of the Ministry; Horizons; Lookout, The

The Christian Congregation, Inc.

The Christian Congregation is a denominational evangelistic association that originated in 1798 and was active on the frontier in areas adjacent to the Ohio River. The church was an unincorporated organization until 1887. At that time a group of ministers who desired closer cooperation formally constituted the church. The charter was revised in 1898 and again in 1970.

Governmental polity basically is congregational. Local units are semi-autonomous. Doctrinal positions, strongly biblical, are essentially universalist in the sense that ethical principles, which motivate us to creative activism, transcend national boundaries and racial barriers. A central tenet, John 13: 34-35, translates to such respect for sanctity of life that abortions on demand, capital punishment, and all warfare are vigorously opposed. All wars are considered unjust and obsolete as a means of resolving disputes.

Early leaders were John Chapman, John L. Puckett, and Isaac V. Smith. Bishop O. J. Read was chief administrative and ecclesiastic officer for 40 years until 1961. Rev. Dr. Ora Wilbert Eads has been general superintendent since 1961. Ministerial affiliation for independent clergymen is provided.

HEADQUARTERS

804 W. Hemlock St., LaFollette, TN 37766

Media Contact, Gen. Supt., Rev. Ora W. Eads, D.D., Tel. (615)562-8511

OFFICER

Gen. Supt., Rev. Ora Wilbert Eads, D.D.

Christian Methodist Episcopal Church

In 1870 the General Conference of the Methodist Episcopal Church, South, approved the request of its colored membership for the formation of their conferences into a separate ecclesiastical body, which became the Colored Methodist Episcopal Church.

At its General Conference in Memphis, Tenn., May 1954, it was overwhelmingly voted to change the name of the Colored Methodist Episcopal Church to the Christian Methodist Episcopal Church. This became the official name on Jan. 3, 1956.

HEADQUARTERS

First Memphis Plaza, 4466 Elvis Presley Blvd., Memphis, TN 38116

Media Contact, Exec. Sec., Dr. W. Clyde Williams, 201 Ashby St., N.W., Ste. 312, Atlanta, GA 30314 Tel. (404)522-2736 Fax (901)345-0541

OFFICERS

Exec. Sec., Dr. W. Clyde Williams, 201 Ashby St., NW, Suite 312, Atlanta, GA 30314 Tel. (404)522-2736

Sec. Gen. Conf., Rev. Edgar L. Wade, P.O. Box 3403, Memphis, TN 38103

OTHER ORGANIZATIONS

Christian Education: Gen. Sec., Dr. Ronald M. Cunningham, 4466 Elvis Presley Blvd., Ste. 214, Box 193, Memphis, TN 38116-7100 Tel. (901)345-0580

Lay Ministry: Gen. Sec., Dr. I. Carlton Faulk, 1222 Rose St., Berkeley, CA 94702 Tel. (415)655-4106

Evangelism, Missions & Human Concerns: Gen. Sec., Rev. Raymond F. Williams, 909 Shanon Bradley Rd., Gastonia, NC 28052 Tel. (704)867-8119

Finance: Sec., Mr. Joseph C. Neal, Jr., P.O. Box 75085, Los Angeles, CA 90075 Tel. (213)233-5050

Publications: Gen. Sec., Rev. Lonnie L. Napier, P.O. Box 2018, Memphis, TN 38101 Tel. (901)345-0580

Personnel Services: Gen. Sec., Dr. N. Charles Thomas, P.O. Box 74, Memphis, TN 39101 Tel. (901)345-0580

Women's Missionary Council: Pres., Dr. Sylvia M. Faulk, 623 San Fernando Ave., Berkeley, CA 94707 Tel. (415)526-5536

First District: Bishop William H. Graves, 564 Frank Ave., Memphis, TN 38101 Tel. (901)947-6180

Second District: Bishop Othal H. Lakey, 6322 Elwynne Dr., Cincinnati, OH 45236 Tel. (513)984-6825

Third District: Bishop Dotcy I. Isom, Jr., 11470 Northway Dr., St. Louis, MO 63136 Tel. (314)381-3111

Fourth District: Bishop Marshall Gilmore, 109 Holcomb Dr., Shreveport, LA 71103 Tel. (318)222-6284

Fifth District: Bishop Richard O. Bass, 308 10th Ave. W., Birmingham, AL 35204 Tel. (205)252-3541

Sixth District: Bishop Joseph C. Coles, Jr., 2780 Collier Dr., Atlanta, GA 30018 Tel. (404)794-0096

Seventh District: Bishop Oree Broomfield, Sr., 6524 16th St., N.W., Washington, DC 20012 Tel. (202)723-2660

Eighth District: Bishop C. D. Coleman, Sr., 2330 Sutter St., Dallas, TX 75216 Tel. (214)942-5781

Ninth District: Bishop E. Lynn Brown, P.O. Box 11276, Los Angeles, CA 90011 Tel. (213)216-9278

Tenth District: Bishop Nathaniel L. Linsey, P.O. Box 170127, Atlanta, GA 30317

Retired: Bishop Henry C. Bunton, 853 East Dempster Ave., Memphis, TN 38106; Bishop Chester A. Kirkendoll, 10 Hurtland, Jackson, TN 38305

PERIODICALS

Christian Index, The; Missionary Messenger, The

Christian Nation Church U.S.A.

Organized in 1895, at Marion, Ohio, as a group of "equality evangelists" who later formed the Christian Nation Church, this church is Wesleyan and Arminian in doctrine, emphasizes the premillenial coming of Christ, governs semi-congregationally and emphasizes evangelism. It was reincorporated as Christian Nation Church U.S.A., 1961.

HEADQUARTERS

Media Contact, Gen. Overseer, Rev. W. Harvey Monjar, 2642 Wildwood Ct., Lake Orion, MI 48360

OFFICERS

Gen. Overseer, Rev. Harvey Monjar

Asst. Overseer, Rev. Ronald Justice, 11245 State Rt. 669 NE, Rosedale, OH 43777 Tel. (614)982-7827

Exec. Sec., Rev. Carl M. Eisenhart, 10303 Murdock-Cozaddale Rd., Goshen, OH 45122 Tel. (513)677-8274

Clerk, Rev. Clarence E. Ratcliff, Rt. 5, Box 454, Toccoa, GA 30577 Tel. (706)886-9538

Christian Reformed Church in North America

The Christian Reformed Church represents the historic faith of Protestantism. Founded in the United States in 1857, it asserts its belief in the Bible as the inspired Word of God, and is creedally united in the Belgic Confession (1561), the Heidel-berg Catechism (1563), and the Canons of Dort (1618-19). (For total statistics for this body see also those listed under the Christian Reformed Church in North America under the Religious Bodies in Canada.)

HEADQUARTERS

2850 Kalamazoo Ave., SE, Grand Rapids, MI 49560

Media Contact, Gen. Sec., Leonard J. Hofman, Tel. (616)246-0744 Fax (616)246-0834

OFFICERS

Gen. Sec., Rev. Leonard J. Hofman

Exec. Dir. of Ministries, Dr. Peter Borgdorff

Financial Coord., Harry Vander Meer

OTHER ORGANIZATIONS

The Back to God Hour: Dir. of Ministries, Dr. Joel H. Nederhood, International Headquarters, 6555 W. College Dr., Palos Heights, IL 60463

Christian Reformed Home Missions: Dir., Rev. John A. Rozeboom

Christian Reformed World Missions, US: Dir., Rev. William Van Tol

Christian Ref. World Missions, Canada: Dir., Albert Karsten, 3475 Mainway, P.O. Box 5070, Burlington, ON L7R 3Y8

Christian Reformed World Relief, US: Dir., John De Haan

Christian Reformed World Relief, Canada: Dir., Ray Elgersma, 3475 Mainway, P.O. Box 5070, Burlington, ON L7R 3Y8

CRC Publications: Dir., Gary Mulder

Ministers' Pension Fund: Admn., Dr. Ray Vander Weele

PERIODICAL

Banner, The

Christian Union

Organized in 1864 in Columbus, Ohio, Christian Union stresses the oneness of the Church with Christ as its only head. The Bible is the only rule of faith and practice, and good fruits the only condition of fellowship. Each local church governs itself.

HEADQUARTERS

P.O. Box 27, Greenfield, OH 45123 Tel. (513)981-2897

OFFICERS

Pres., Dr. Joseph Harr, Rt. 1 Box 132, Grover Hill, OH 45849 Tel. (419)587-3226

Vice-Pres., Rev. Harold McElwee, P.O. Box 132, Milo, IA 50166 Tel. (419)822-4261

Sec., Rev. Joseph Cunningham, 1005 N. 5th St., Greenfield, OH 45123 Tel. (513)981-3476

Asst. Sec., Rev. Earl Mitchell, 17500 Hidden Valley Rd., Independence, MO 64057 Tel. (816)373-3416

Treas., Rev. Lawrence Rhoads, 902 N.E. Main St., West Union, OH 45693 Tel. (513)544-2950

Church of Christ

Joseph Smith and five others organized the Church of Christ April 6, 1830, at Fayette, N.Y. In 1864 this body was directed by revelation through Granville Hedrick to return in 1867 to Independence, Mo. to the "consecrated land" dedicated by Joseph Smith. They did so and purchased the temple lot dedicated in 1831.

Temple Lot, P.O. Box 472, Independence, MO 64051 Tel. (816)833-3995
Media Contact, Gen. Church Rep., William A. Sheldon

OFFICERS

Gen. Church Rep., Apostle William A. Sheldon
Gen. Bus. Mgr., Bishop Alvin Harris
Gen. Recorder, Isaac Brockman

PERIODICAL

Zion's Advocate

Church of Christ, Scientist

The Christian Science Church was founded by New England religious leader Mary Baker Eddy in 1879 "to commemorate the word and works of our Master (Christ Jesus), which should reinstate primitive Christianity and its lost element of healing." In 1892 the church was reorganized and established as The First Church of Christ, Scientist, in Boston, also called The Mother Church, with local branch churches around the world, of which there are nearly 2,700 in 68 countries today.

The church is administered by a five-member board of directors in Boston. Local churches govern themselves democratically. Since the church has no clergy, services are conducted by laypersons elected to serve as Readers. There are also about 3,000 Christian Science practitioners who devote their full time to healing through prayer.

Organizations within the church include the Board of Education, the Board of Lectureship, the Committee on Publication and the Publishing Society.

HEADQUARTERS

The First Church of Christ, Scientist, 175 Huntington Ave., Boston, MA 02115
Media Contact, Mgr., Comm. on Publication, M. Victor Westberg, Tel. (617)450-3301 Fax (617)450-3325

OFFICERS

Bd. of Dirs.: Chpsn., Virginia S. Harris; Richard C. Bergenheim; Olga M. Chaffee; Al M. Carnesciali; John Lewis Selover
Pres., Jill Gooding
Treas., John Lewis Selover
Clk., Olga M. Chaffee
First Reader, Howard E. Johnson
Second Reader, Margaret Rogers

PERIODICALS

Christian Science Monitor, The; Christian Science Journal, The; Christian Science Sentinel; Herald of Christian Science, The; World Monitor; Christian Science Quarterly

Church of Daniel's Band

A body Methodistic in form and evangelistic in spirit was organized in Michigan in 1893.

HEADQUARTERS

Media Contact, Sec.-Treas., Rev. Wesley J. Hoggard, 2960 Croll Rd., Beaverton, MI 48612 Tel. (517)435-3649

OFFICERS

Pres., Rev. Jim Seaman, Adams St., Coleman, MI 48618 Tel. (517)465-6059
Vice-Pres., Rev. Wesley A. Hoggard, 605 N. 5th St., Coleman, MI 48618

Sec.-Treas., Rev. Wesley J. Hoggard, 2960 Croll Rd., Beaverton, MI 48612

The Church of God

Bishop A. J. Tomlinson, who served as General Overseer, 1903 to 1943, and from which many groups of the Pentecostal and Holiness Movement stemmed inaugurated the Church of God. Bishop Homer A. Tomlinson served as General Overseer, 1943 to 1968. The Church of God is episcopal in administration, evangelical in doctrines of justification by faith and sanctification as a second work of grace, and of the baptism of the Holy Ghost, speaking with other tongues, and miracles of healing. Bishop Voy M. Bullen has been the General Overseer since 1968.

HEADQUARTERS

Box 13036, 1207 Willow Brook, Apt. #2, Huntsville, AL 35802 Tel. (205)881-9629
Media Contact, Gen. Overseer, Voy M. Bullen

OFFICERS

Gen. Overseer & Bishop, Voy M. Bullen
Gen. Sec.-Treas., Marie Powell
Bus. Mgr., ———

CHURCH AUXILIARIES

Assembly Band Movement, Gen. Sec., Bishop Bill Kinslaw
Women's Missionary Band, Gen. Sec., Maxine McKenzie
Theocratic Bands, Gen. Sec., Rev. Ted Carr
Victory Leader's Band, Youth, Gen. Sec., Rev. Linda Russell
Admn. for Highway & Hedge Campaign, Earnest Hoover
Sunday School, Gen. Sec., Judy Foskey

PERIODICAL

Church of God Quarterly; COG Newsletter, The

Church of God (Anderson, Ind.)

The Church of God (Anderson, Ind.) began in 1881 when Daniel S. Warner and several associates in northern Indiana felt constrained to forsake all denominational hierarchies and formal creeds, trusting solely in the Holy Spirit as their overseer and the Bible as their statement of belief. Warner and those of similar persuasion saw themselves at the forefront of a movement to restore unity and holiness to the church, not to establish another denomination, but to promote primary allegiance to Jesus Christ so as to transcend (and even obliterate) denominational loyalties.

Deeply influenced by Wesleyan theology and Pietism, the Church of God has emphasized conversion, holiness, and attention to the Bible. Worship services tend to be informal, accentuating expository preaching and robust singing.

There is no formal membership. Persons are assumed to be members on the basis of witness to a conversion experience and evidence that supports such witness. The absence of formal membership is also consistent with the church's understanding of how Christian unity is to be achieved—that is, by preferring the label Christian before all others.

The Church of God is congregational in its government. Each local congregation is autonomous and may call any recognized Church of God minister to be its pastor and may retain him or her as long as is mutually pleasing. Ministers are ordained and disciplined by state or provincial assemblies made up predominantly (but not usually exclusively) of ministers. National program boards serve the church through coordination and resource materials.

There are Church of God congregations in 81 foreign countries, most of which are resourced by one or more missionaries. There are slightly more Church of God adherents overseas than in North America. The heaviest concentration is in Kenya.

HEADQUARTERS

Box 2420, Anderson, IN 46018 Tel. (317)642-0256

Media Contact, Gen. Sec., Leadership Council, Edward L. Foggs

LEADERSHIP COUNCIL

Gen. Sec., Edward L. Foggs
Assoc. Gen. Sec., David L. Lawson
Church Service, Exec. Dir., Keith Huttenlocker
World Service, Exec. Dir., James Williams

OTHER ORGANIZATIONS

Bd. of Christian Education, Exec. Dir., Sherrill D. Hayes, Box 2458, Anderson, IN 46018
Bd. of Church Extension & Home Missions, Pres., J. Perry Grubbs, Box 2069, Anderson, IN 46018
Foreign Missionary Bd., Pres., Norman S. Patton, Box 2498, Anderson, IN 46018
Women of the Church of God, Exec. Sec.-Treas., Doris Dale, Box 2328, Anderson, IN 46018
Bd. of Pensions, Exec. Sec.-Treas., Harold A. Conrad, Box 2299, Anderson, IN 46018
Mass Communications Bd., Sec.-Treas., Dwight L. Dye, Box 2007, Anderson, IN 46018
Warner Press, Inc., Pres., Robert G. Rist, Box 2499, Anderson, IN 46018

PERIODICALS

Vital Christianity; Church of God Missions

Church of God by Faith, Inc.

Founded 1914, in Jacksonville Heights, Fla., by Elder John Bright. This body believes the word of God as interpreted by Jesus Christ to be the only hope of salvation, and Jesus Christ the only mediator for people.

HEADQUARTERS

3220 Haines St., P.O. Box 3746, Jacksonville, FL 32206 Tel. (904)353-5111 Fax (904)355-8582
Media Contact, Ofc. Mgr., Sarah E. Lundy

OFFICERS

Bishop Emeritus, W. W. Matthews, P.O. Box 907, Ozark, AL 36360
Bishop James E. McKnight, P.O. Box 121, Gainesville, FL 32601
Treas., Elder Theodore Brown, 93 Girard Pl., Newark, NJ 07108
Ruling Elders: Elder John Robinson, 300 Essex Dr., Ft. Pierce, FL 33450; Elder D. C. Rourk, 107 Chestnut Hill Dr., Rochester, NY 14617
Exec. Sec., Elder George Matthews, 8834 Camphor Dr., Jacksonville, FL 32208

Church of God (Cleveland, Tenn.)

America's oldest Pentecostal Church began in 1886 as an outgrowth of the holiness revival under the name Christian Union. Reorganized in 1902 as the Holiness Church, in 1907 the church adopted the name Church of God. Its doctrine is fundamental and Pentecostal; it maintains a centralized form of government and an evangelistic and missionary program.

HEADQUARTERS

P.O. Box 2430, Cleveland, TN 37320 Tel. (615)472-3361 Fax (615)478-7052
Media Contact, Dir. of Publ. Relations, Michael L. Baker, Tel. (615)478-7112 Fax (615)478-7066

EXECUTIVES

Gen. Overseer, R. Lamar Vest
Asst. Gen. Overseers: Robert White; John D. Nichols; Ray H. Hughes
Gen. Sec.-Treas., Robert E. Fisher

DEPARTMENTS

Black Evangelism, Dir., Joseph E. Jackson
Business & Records, Dir., Julian B. Robinson
Evangelism & Home Missions, Dir., Bill F. Sheeks
Ladies Ministries, Pres., Mrs. Iris Vest
Lay Ministries, Dir., Leonard Albert
Media Ministries, Dir., Robert E. Fisher
Ministerial Dev., Exec. Dir., Robert E. Fisher
Pension & Legal Services, Dir., O. Wayne Chambers
Publications, Dir., Donald T. Pemberton
Public Relations, Dir., Michael L. Baker
Stewardship, Dir., Al Taylor
World Missions, Dir., Roland Vaughan
Youth & C. E., Dir., T. David Sustar
Benevolence, Dir., B. J. Moffett
Computer Info. Serv., Dir., Timothy D. O'Neal
Cross-Cultural Min., Dir., Billy J. Rayburn
Hispanic Min., Dir., Esdras Betancourt
Insurance, Dir., ——-
Ministerial Care, Dir., Sam Crisp
Ministry to the Military, Dir., John D. Nichols
Music Min., Dir., Delton Alford

PERIODICAL

Evangel

Church of God General Conference (Oregon, IL and Morrow, GA)

This church is the outgrowth of several independent local groups of similar faith. Some were in existence as early as 1800, and others date their beginnings to the arrival of British immigrants around 1847. Many local churches carried the name Church of God of the Abrahamic Faith.

State and district conferences of these groups were formed as an expression of mutual cooperation. A national organization was instituted at Philadelphia in 1888. Because of strong convictions on the questions of congregational rights and authority, however, it ceased to function until 1921, when the present General Conference was formed at Waterloo, Iowa.

The Bible is accepted as the supreme standard of faith. Adventist in viewpoint, the second (premillenial) coming of Christ is strongly emphasized. The church teaches that the kingdom of God will be literal, beginning in Jerusalem at the time of the return of Christ and extending to all nations. Emphasis is placed on the oneness of God and the Sonship of Christ, that Jesus did not pre-exist prior to his birth in Bethlehem, and that the Holy Spirit is the power and influence of God. Membership is dependent on faith, repentance, and baptism (for the remission of sins) by immersion.

With a congregational church government, the General Conference exists primarily as a means of mutual cooperation and for the development of yearly projects and enterprises.

The headquarters and Bible College were moved to Morrow Ga. in 1991.

P.O. Box 100, Oregon, IL 61601 Tel. (815)732-7991

P.O. Box 100,000, Morrow, GA 30260 Tel. (404)362-0052 Fax (404)362-9307

Media Contact, Pres., David Krogh, Georgia Ofc.

OFFICERS

Chpsn., Pastor Scott Ross, 7606 Jaynes St., Omaha, NE 68134

Vice-Chpsn., Dr. William D. Lawrence, 32 E. Marshall, Phoenix, AZ 85012

Pres., David Krogh, Georgia Ofc.

Sec., Pastor Gary Burnham, 14419 Turin Lane, Centreville, VA 22020

Treas., Pastor Stephen Bolhous, 9 Pancake Lane, Forthill, ON L0S 1E2

OTHER ORGANIZATIONS

Bus. Adm., Controller, Harry McMinn, Georgia Ofc.

Publishing Dept., Ed., Hollis Partlowe, Illinois Ofc.

Atlanta Bible College, Pres., David Krogh, Georgia Ofc.

PERIODICALS

Restitution Herald, The; Church of God Progress Journal

The Church Of God In Christ

The Church of God in Christ was founded in 1907 in Memphis, Tenn., and was organized by Bishop Charles Harrison Mason, a former Baptist minister who pioneered the embryonic stages of the Holiness movement beginning in 1895 in Mississippi.

Its founder organized four major departments between 1910-1916: the Women's Department, the Sunday School, Young Peoples Willing Workers, and Home and Foreign Mission.

The Church is trinitarian, and teaches the infallibility of scripture, the need for regeneration and subsequent baptism of the Holy Ghost. It emphasizes holiness as God's standard for Christian conduct. It recognizes as ordinances Holy Communion, Water Baptism, and Feet Washing. Its governmental structure is basically episcopal with the General Assembly being the Legislative body.

HEADQUARTERS

Mason Temple, 939 Mason St., Memphis, TN 38126

World Headquarters, 272 S. Main St., Memphis, TN 38103 Tel. (901)578-3800

Mailing Address, P.O. Box 320, Memphis, TN 38101

The Mother Church, Pentecostal Institutional, 229 S. Danny Thomas Blvd., Memphis, TN 38126 Tel. (901)527-9202

GENERAL OFFICES

Office of the Presiding Bishop: Presiding Bishop, Rt. Rev. L. H. Ford, Tel. (901)578-3838; Exec. Sec., Elder A. Z. Hall, Jr.

Office of the General Secretary: Gen. Sec., Bishop W. W. Hamilton, (901)521-1163

Office of the Financial Secretary: Sec., Dr. S. Y. Burnett, Tel. (901)744-0710

Office of the Board of Trustees: Chmn., Dr. Roger L. Jones

Office of the Clergy Bureau: Dir., Elder Samuel Smith, Tel. (901)523-7045

Office of Supt. of National Properties: Supt., Bishop W. L. Porter, Tel. (901)774-0710

Board of Publications: Chmn., Bishop Norman Quick, Tel. (901)578-3841; Headquarters Rep., Dr. David Hall

Publishing House: Mgr., Mr. Hughea Terry, Tel. (901)578-3842

Dept. of Missions: Pres., Bishop Carlis L. Moody, Tel. (901)578-3876; Exec. Sec., Elder Jesse W. Denny

Dept. of Women: Pres.-Gen. Supervisor, Dr. Mattie McGlothen, Tel. (901)578-3834; Exec. Sec., Mrs. Elizabeth C. Moore

Dept. of Evangelism: Pres., Dr. Edward L. Battles, 4310 Steeplechase Trail, Arlington, TX 76016 Tel. (817)429-7166

Dept. of Music: Pres., Mrs. Mattie Moss Clark, 18203 Sorrento, Detroit, MI 48235

Dept. of Youth (Youth Congress): Pres., Bishop C. H. Brewer, 260 Roydon Rd., New Haven, CT 06511

Dept. of Sunday Schools: Gen. Supt., Bishop Cleveland W. Williams, 270 Division St., Derby, CT 06418

United National Auxiliaries Convention: UNAC-5, Chmn., Bishop F. E. Perry, Jr.

Church of God in Christ Book Store: Mgr., Mrs. Geraldine Miller, 272 S. Main St., Memphis, TN 38103 Tel. (901)578-3803

Charles Harrison Mason Foundation: Exec. Dir., Elder O. T. Massey, 272 S. Main St., Memphis, TN 38103 Tel. (901)578-3803; Bd. of Dir., Chmn., Bishop P. A. Brooks

Dept. of Finance: Chief Financial Officer, Mrs. Sylvia H. Law

Fine Arts Dept.: Dir., Mrs. Sara J. Powell

BISHOPS IN THE U.S.A.

Alabama: First, Chester A. Ashworth, 2901 Snavely Ave., Birmingham, AL 35211; Second, W. S. Harris, 3005 Melrose Pl., N.W., Huntsville, AL 35810

Alaska: Charles D. Williams, 2212 Vanderbilt Cir., Anchorage, AK 99504

Arizona: Felton King, P.O. Box 3791, Phoenix, AZ 84030

Arkansas: First, L. T. Walker, 2315 Chester St., Little Rock, AR 72206; Second, D. L. Lindsey, 401 W. 23rd St., North Little Rock, AR 72114

California: North-Central, G. R. Ross, 815 Calmar Ave., Oakland, CA 94610; Northern, B. R. Stewart, 734 12th Ave., San Francisco, CA 94118; Northeast, L. B. Johnson, 3121 Patridge Ave., Oakland, CA 94605; Evangel, E. E. Cleveland, 31313 Braeburn Ct., Haywood, CA 96045; Northwest, Bishop W. W. Hamilton, 14145 Mountain Quail Rd., Salinas, CA 93906; Southern #1, C. E. Blake, 1731 Wellington Rd., Los Angeles, CA 90019; Southern #2, George McKinney, 5848 Arboles, San Diego, CA 92120; Southern Metropolitan, Bishop B. J. Crouch, 12418 Gain St., Pacoima, CA 91331; Southwest, B. R. Benbow, 504 Rexford Dr., Beverly Hills, CA 90210; Valley, Warren S. Wilson, 1435 Modoc St., Fresno, CA 93706

Colorado: Colorado, Frank Johnson, 12231 E. Arkansas Pl., Aurora, CO 80014

Connecticut: First, Charles H. Brewer, Jr., 180 Osborne St., New Haven, CT 06515; Second, H. Bordeaux, 135 Westwood Rd., New Haven, CT 06511

Delaware: Lieutenant T. Blackshear, Sr., 17 S. Booth Dr., Penn Acres, New Castle, DE 19720

District of Columbia: Bishop W. Crudup, 5101 Martin Dr., Oxon Hill, MD 20745

Florida: Central, Calvin D. Kensey, 9462 August Dr., Jacksonville, FL 32208; Eastern, Jacob Cohen, 3120 N. W. 48th Terr., Miami, FL 33142; Southwestern, W. E. Davis, 2008 33rd Ave., Tampa, FL 33610; Western, M. L. Sconiers, P.O. Box 5472, Orlando, FL 32805

Georgia: Central & Southeast, J. D. Husband, P.O. Box 824, Atlanta, GA 30301; Southeast, Andrew Hunter, Rt. 4, Box 328, St. Simons Island, GA 31502; Northern, J. Howard Dell, 1717 Havilon Dr., S.W., Atlanta, GA 30311; Southern, C. J. Hicks, 1894 Madden Ave., Macon, GA 31204

Hawaii: First, ——; Second, W. H. Reed, 1223 W. 80th St., Los Angeles, CA 90044

Idaho: Nathaniel Jones, 630 Chateau, Barstow, CA 92311

Illinois: First, L. H. Ford, 9401 M. L. King Dr., Chicago, IL 60619; Fifth, B. E. Goodwin, 286 E. 16th St., Chicago Heights, IL 60411; Sixth, W. Haven Bonner, 1039 Bonner Ave., Aurora, IL 60505; Central, T. T. Rose, 1000 Dr. Taylor Rose Sq., Springfield, IL 62703; Northern, Cody Marshall, 8836 Blackstone, Chicago, IL 60637; Southeast, L. E. Moore, 7840 Contour Dr., St. Louis, MO 63121; Southern, J. Cobb, 323-30th St., Cairo, IL 62914

Indiana: First, Milton L. Hall, 1404 Delphos, Kokomo, IN 46901; Second, Oscar Freeman, 1760 Taft St., Gary, IN 46404; Indiana Northern, J. T. Dupree, 1231 Hayden St., Fort Wayne, IN 40806

Iowa: Hurley Bassett, 1730 4th Ave., S.E., Cedar Rapids, IA 52403

Kansas: Central, I. B. Brown, 1635 Hudson Blvd., Topeka, KS 66607; East, William H. McDonald, 1627 N. 78th St., Kansas City, KS 66112; Southwest, J. L. Gilkey, 2403 Shadybrook, Wichita, KS 67214

Kentucky: First, Bishop M. Sykes, P.O. Box 682, Union City, TN 38621

Louisiana: Eastern, #1, Bishop J. E. Gordon, 6610 Chenault Dr., Marrero, LA 70072; Eastern #2, Bishop J. A. Thompson, 2180 Holiday, New Orleans, LA 70114; Eastern #3, Bishop H. E. Quillen, 1913 Lasley St., Bogalusa, LA 70427; Western, Roy L. H. Winbush, 235 Diamond Dr., Lafayette, LA 70501

Maine: Bishop B. W. Grayson, 1237 Eastern Pkwy., Brooklyn, NY 11213

Maryland: Central, S. L. Butts, P.O. Box 4504, Upper Marboro, MD 20775; Eastern Shore, James L. Eure, 635 West Main St., Salisbury, MD 21801; Greater, David Spann, 5023 Gwynn Oak Ave., Baltimore, MD 21207

Massachusetts: First, L. C. Young, 19 Almont St., Mattanpan, MA 02126; Second & New Hampshire, C. W. Williams, 270 Division St., Derby, CT 06418; West, Bryant Robinson, Sr., 1424 Plumtree Rd., Springfield, MA 01119

Michigan: Great Lakes, C. L. Anderson, 20485 Mendota, Detroit, MI 48221; North Central, Herbert J. Williams, 1600 Cedar St., Saginaw, MI 48601; Northeast, P. A. Brooks, II, 30945 Wendbrook Lane, Birmingham, MI 48010; Southwest, First, W. L. Harris, 1834 Outer Dr., Detroit, MI 48234; Second, Earl J. Wright, 18655 Autumn La., Southfield, MI 48076; Third, Rodger L. Jones, 1118 River Forest, Flint, MI 48594; Fourth, N. W. Wells, 530 Sue Lane, Muskegon, MI 49442

Minnesota: Bishop S. N. Frazier, 4309 Park Ave. So., Minneapolis, MN 55409

Mississippi: Northern, T. T. Scott, 1066 Barnes Ave., Clarksdale, MS 38614; Southern #1, Theodore Roosevelt Davis, 1704 Topp Ave., Jackson, MS 39204; Southern #2, Bishop R. Nance, 803 Fayard St., Biloxi, MS 39503

Missouri: Eastern #1, R. J. Ward, 4724 Palm Ave., St. Louis, MO 63115; Eastern #2, W. W. Sanders, 8167 Garner La., Berkeley, MO 63134; Western, E. Harris Moore, 405 E. 64th Terr., Kansas City, MO 64131

Montana: Bishop C. L. Moody, 2413 Lee St., Evanston, IL 60202

Nebraska: Eastern, Monte J. Bradford, 3901 Ramelle Dr., Council Bluff, IA 51501; Northeastern, B. T. McDaniels, 1106 N. 31st St., Omaha, NE 68103

Nevada: E. N. Webb, 1941 Goldhill, Las Vegas, NV 89106

New Jersey: First, Esau Courtney, 12 Clover Hill Cir., Trenton, NJ 08538; Third, Chandler David Owens, 14 Van Velsor Pl., Newark, NJ 07112

New Mexico: W. C. Griffin, 3322 Montclaire, Albuquerque, NM 87110

New York: Eastern #1, Bishop Ithiel Clemmons, 190-08 104th Ave., Hollis, NY 11412; Eastern #2, Bishop Frank White, 67 The Boulevard, Amityville, NY 11701; Eastern #3, Bishop D. W. Grayson, 1233 Eastern Pkwy., Brooklyn, NY 11213; Eastern #4, Bishop C. L. Sexton, 153 McDougal St., Brooklyn, NY 11233; Western #1, LeRoy R. Anderson, 265 Ranch Trail, W., Amherst, NY 14221; Western #2, Charles H. McCoy, 168 Brunswick Blvd., Buffalo, NY 14208

North Carolina: Greater, L. B. Davenport, P.O. Box 156, Plymouth, NC 28803; Second, J. Howard Sherman, Sr., P.O. Box 329, Charlotte, NC 28201

North Dakota: Mission Dept., Carlis L. Moody, 272 S. Main St., Memphis, TN 38103

Ohio: Northern, Bishop William James, 3758 Chippendale Ct., Toledo, OH 44320; Robert S. Fields, 419 Crandell Ave., Youngstown, OH 44504; Northwest, Robert L. Chapman, 3194 E. 18th St., Cleveland, OH 44120; Northern, Bishop Warren Miller, 3618 Beacon Dr., Cleveland, OH 44122; Southern, Floyde E. Perry, Jr., 3716 Rolliston Rd., Shaker Hts., OH 44120

Oklahoma: Northwest, J. A. Young, P.O. Box 844, Lawton, OK 73501; Southeast, Bishop F. D. Lawson, P.O. Box 581, Stillwater, OK 74076

Oregon: First, Bishop A. R. Hopkins, 1705 N.E. Dekum, Portland, OR 97211; Second, J. C. Foster, 2716 N.E. 9th Ave., Portland, OR 97212

Pennsylvania: Commonwealth, O. T. Jones, Jr., 363 N. 60th St., Philadelphia, PA 19139; Eastern, DeWitt A. Burton, 1400 Wistar Dr., Wyncote, PA 19095; Western, Gordon E. Vaughn, 6437 Stanton Ave., Pittsburgh, PA 15206

Rhode Island: Norman Quick, 1031 E. 215th St., Brooklyn, NY 11221

South Carolina: Johnnie Johnson, 679 Liberty Hall Rd., Goose Creek, SC 29445

South Dakota: Carlis L. Moody, 2413 Lee St., Evanston, IL 60202

Tennessee: Headquarters, F. Douglas Macklin, 1230 Tipton, Memphis, TN 38071; Second, H. J. Bell, P.O. Box 6118, Knoxville, TN 37914; Central, W. L. Porter, 1235 East Parkway, S., Memphis, TN 38114

Texas: Eastern, J. E. Lee, 742 Calcutta Dr., Dallas, TX 75241; Northeast, J. Neauell Haynes, 6743 Talbot, Dallas, TX 75216; Northwest, W. H. Watson, 1301 47th St., Lubbock, TX 79412; South Central, Nathan H. Henderson, 15622 Rockhouse Rd., Houston, TX 77060; Southeast #1, Robert E. Woodard, 2614 Wichita, Houston, TX 77004; Southeast #2, A. LaDell Thomas, 4401 McArthur Dr., Waco, TX 76708; South-

east, R. E. Ranger, 6604 Sabrosa Ct., W., Fort
Worth, TX 76110; Southwest, T. D. Iglehart, 325
Terrell Rd., San Antonio, TX 78209
Utah: Nathaniel Jones, c/o Mission Dept., 630
Chateau Rd., Barstow, CA 92311
Vermont: Frank Clemons, Sr., 1323 Carroll St.,
Brooklyn, NY 11216
Virginia: First, Ted Thomas, Sr., 4145 Sunkist Rd.,
Chesapeake, VA 23321; Second, Samuel L.
Green, Jr., 2416 Orcutt Ave., Newport News, VA
23607; Third, Levi E. Willis, 5110 Nichal Ct.,
Norfolk, VA 23508
Washington: T. L. Westbrook, 1256 176th St.,
Spanaway, WA 98402
West Virginia: Northern, Bishop G. F. Walker,
P.O. Box 1467, Princeton, VA 24740; Southern,
St. Claire Y. Burnett, P.O. Box 245, Altamonte
Springs, FL 32715
Wisconsin: First, Dennis Flakes, 3420 N. 1st St.,
Milwaukee, WI 53212; Northwest, P. J. Hender-
son, 1312 W. Burleigh, Milwaukee, WI 53206;
Third, J. C. Williams, 4232 N. 24th Pl., Milwau-
kee, WI 53209
Wyoming: A. W. Martin, 2453 N. Fountain St.,
Wichita, KS 67220

PERIODICALS

Whole Truth; Sunday School Literature;
Y.P.W.W. Topics; Pentecostal Interpreter, The;
Voice of Missions, The

Church of God in Christ, International

Organized in 1969 in Kansas City, Mo., by 14
bishops of the Church of God in Christ of Memphis,
Tenn. The doctrine is the same, but the separation
came because of disagreement over polity and
governmental authority. The Church is Wesleyan
in theology (two works of grace) but stresses the
experience of full baptism of the Holy Ghost with
the initial evidence of speaking with other tongues
as the spirit gives utterance.

HEADQUARTERS

170 Adelphi St., Brooklyn, NY 11205 Tel.
(718)625-9175
Media Contact, Natl. Sec., Rev. Sis. Sharon R.
Dunn

OFFICERS

Presiding Bishop, The Most Rev. Carl E. Williams,
Sr.
Vice-Presiding Bishop, Rt. Rev. J. P. Lucas, 90
Holland St., Newark, NJ 07103
Sec.-Gen., Rev. William A. Hines
Women's Dept., Natl. Supervisor, Dr. Louise Nor-
ris, 360 Colorado Ave., Bridgeport, CT 06605
Youth Dept., Pres., Evangelist Joyce Taylor, 137-
17 135th Ave., S., Ozone Park, NY 11420
Music Dept., Pres., Rev. Carl E. Williams, Jr.
Bd. of Bishops, Chpsn., Bishop J. C. White, 360
Colorado Ave., Bridgeport, CT 06605
Natl. Dir. of Public Relations, Rev. William A.
Hines, 187 St. Marks Ave., #1-R, Brooklyn, NY
11238

Church of God in Christ (Mennonite)

The Church of God in Christ (Mennonite) was
organized in 1859 by the evangelist-reformer John
Holdeman, in Ohio. The church unites with the
faith of the Waldenses, Anabaptists, and other such
groups. Emphasis is placed on obedience to the
teachings of the Bible, including the doctrine of the

new birth and spiritual life, noninvolvement in
government or the military, a head-covering for the
women, beards for the men, and separation from
the world shown by simplicity in clothing, homes,
possessions, and life-style. The church has a
worldwide membership of about 15,000, most of
them in the United States and Canada.

HEADQUARTERS

P.O. Box 313, 420 N. Wedel Ave., Moundridge,
KS 67107 Tel. (316)345-2532 Fax (316)345-
2582
Media Contact, Dale Koehn, P.O. Box 230, Moundridge, KS 67107 Tel. (316)345-2532 Fax
(316)345-2582

PERIODICAL

Messenger of Truth

Church of God, Mountain Assembly, Inc.

The church was formed in 1895 and organized in
1906 by J. H. Parks, S. N. Bryant, Tom Moses, and
Andrew Silcox.

HEADQUARTERS

110 S. Florence Ave., P.O. Box 157, Jellico, TN
37762 Tel. (615)784-8260
Media Contact, Gen. Sec.-Treas., Rev. James Kilgore

OFFICERS

Gen. Overseer, Rev. Jasper Walden
Asst. Gen. Overseer/World Missions Dir., Rev.
Cecil Johnson
Gen. Sec.-Treas., Rev. James Kilgore, Box 157,
Jellico, TN 37762
Youth Ministries & Camp Dir., Rev. Rick Mass-
ingill

PERIODICAL

Gospel Herald, The

Church of God of Prophecy

The Church of God of Prophecy is one of the
churches that grew out of the work of A. J. Tomlinson in the first half of this century. It was named in
1952, but historically shares the traditions of the
holiness classical pentecostal church, the Church
of God (Cleveland, Tenn.).

At the death of A. J. Tomlinson in 1943, M. A.
Tomlinson was named overseer and served until
1990. He emphasized unity and fellowship that is
not limited socially, racially or nationally. The
present general overseer, Billy D. Murray, Sr. is
committed to promoting Christian unity and moving forward with world-wide evangelism.

The official teachings include special emphasis
on sanctification, the doctrine of Spirit-baptism,
and belief that tongues-speech is an initial evidence. The church teaches an imminence-oriented
eschatology that involves a premillennial return of
the risen Jesus which itself will be preceded by a
series of events; a call for the sanctity of the home
which includes denial of a multiple marriage;
practice of water baptism by immersion, the Lord's
Supper and washing of the saints' feet; total abstinence from intoxicating beverages and tobacco; a
concern for moderation in all dimensions of life; an
appreciation for various gifts of the Holy Spirit,
with special attention given to divine healing.

The Church is racially integrated on all levels and
various leadership positions are occupied by
women. The Church's history includes a strong
emphasis on youth ministries, national and inter-

national missions and various parochial educational ministries.

HEADQUARTERS
P.O. Box 2910, Cleveland, TN 37320-2910
Media Contact, Perry Gillum, Tel. (615)559-5336
Fax (615)559-5117

OFFICERS
Gen. Overseer, Bishop Billy D. Murray, Sr.
Gen. Overseer, Emeritus, Bishop Milton A. Tomlinson
Admn. Asst., Perry Gillum
Admn. Asst., E. L. Jones
Admn. Asst., Jose A. Reyes, Sr.
Admn. Committee, Billy Murray, Perry Gillum, E.L. Jones, Elwood Matthes, Jose A. Reyes, Sr., Jerlena Riley, and Adrian Varlack

GENERAL STAFF
Center for Biblical Leadership, (Ed. Dept.), Oswill Williams
Communications Business Mgr., Thomas Duncan
Communications Minister (English), D. Elwood Matthews
Communications Minister (Spanish), Jose A. Reyes, Sr.
Evangelism Director, D. Elwood Matthews
Financial Director, Jerlena Riley
General Office Mgr./Personnel Dir., Perry Gillum
Ministerial Aid Director, E. L. Jones
Women's Ministries, Elva Howard
World Language Director, Henry O'Neal
World Missions Director, Adrian Varlack
Youth & Children's Ministries, William M. Wilson

PERIODICALS
White Wing Messenger; Victory Leader (Youth Magazine)

The Church of God (Seventh Day), Denver, Colo.

The Church of God (Seventh Day) began in southwestern Michigan in 1858, when a group of Sabbath-Keepers led by Gilbert Cranmer refused to give endorsement to the visions and writings of Ellen G. White, a principal in the formation of the Seventh-Day Adventist Church. Another branch of Sabbath-keepers, which developed near Cedar Rapids, Iowa, in 1860, joined the Michigan church in 1863 to publish a paper called *The Hope of Israel*, the predecessor to the *Bible Advocate*, the church's present publication. As membership grew and spread into Missouri and Nebraska, it organized the General Conference of the Church of God in 1884. The words (Seventh Day) were added to its name in 1923. The headquarters of the church was in Stanberry, Mo., from 1888 until 1950, when it moved to Denver.

The church observes the seventh day as the Sabbath; believes in the imminent, personal, and visible return of Jesus; that the dead are in an unconscious state awaiting to be resurrected, the righteous to immortality and the wicked to extinction by fire; and that the earth will be the eternal abode of the righteous. It observes two ordinances: baptism by immersion and an annual Communion service accompanied by foot washing.

HEADQUARTERS
330 W. 152nd Ave., P.O. Box 33677, Denver, CO 80233 Tel. (303)452-7973 Fax (303)452-0657
Media Contact, Pres., Calvin Burrell

OFFICERS
Chpsn., Calvin Burrell
Sec.-Treas., Jayne Kuryluk
Spring Vale Academy, Director, Clark Caswell
Youth Agency, Dir., John & Ruth Tivald
Bible Advocate Press, Dir., LeRoy Dais
Women's Assoc., Pres., Mrs. Emogene Coulter
Summit School of Theology, Dir., Jerry Griffin
Missions Abroad, Dir., Victor Burford

Church of God (Which He Purchased with His Own Blood)

This body was organized in 1953 in Oklahoma City, Okla. by William Jordan Fizer after his excommunication from the Church of the Living God (C.W.F.F.) over doctrinal disagreements relating to the Lord's Supper. The first annual convention was held in Oklahoma City, Nov. 19-21, 1954.

The church believes that water is not the element to be used in the Lord's Supper, observed every Sunday, but rather grape juice or wine and unleavened bread.

Its doctrine holds that the Holy Ghost is given to those who obey the Lord. Feet washing is observed as an act of humility and not the condition of salvation. Baptism must be administered in the name of the Father, Son, and Holy Ghost. The Church of God believes it is the Body of Christ, and because of scriptural doctrine and practice, that it is the church organized by Jesus Christ. The members are urged to lead consecrated lives unspotted from the world. Tobacco and strong drinks are condemned. Divine healing is an article of faith, but not to the exclusion of doctors.

HEADQUARTERS
1628 N.E. 50th, Oklahoma City, OK 73111 Tel. (405)427-8264
Media Contact, Chief Bishop, William J. Fizer, 1907 N.E. Grand Blvd., Oklahoma City, OK 73111 Tel. (405)427-2166

OFFICERS
Chief Bishop, William J. Fizer
Gen. Sec.-Treas., Alsie Mae Fizer
Vice-Chief Bishops, George Hill, 1109 N.W. 74, Lawton, OK 73505 Tel. (405)536-4941
Vice-Chief Bishops, Bishop Thomas R. Smith, P.O. Box 27431, Tuscon, AZ 85726 Tel. (602)624-0138
Overseers: J. W. Johnson, Rt. 1, Box 214, Choctaw, OK 73020; M. Roberson, Rt. 2, Box 214, Mounds, OK 74047; Supt. of Sunday Schools, DeWayne Cobb, 1011 Baker St., Ft. Worth, TX 76104; Thomas R. Smith, P.O. Box 27431, Tucson, AZ 85726 Tel. (602)624-0138

The Church of Illumination

Organized in 1908 for the express purpose of establishing congregations at large, offering a spiritual, esoteric, philosophic interpretation of the vital biblical teachings, thereby satisfying the inner spiritual needs of those seeking spiritual truth, yet permitting them to remain in, or return to, their former church membership.

HEADQUARTERS
Beverly Hall, 5966 Clymer Rd., Quakertown, PA 18951 Tel. (800)779-3796
Media Contact, Director General, Gerald E. Poesnecker, P.O. Box 220, Quakertown, PA 18951 Tel. (215)536-7048 Fax (215)529-9034

US RELIGIOUS BODIES

Dir.-General, Gerald E. Poesnecker, P.O. Box 220, Quakertown, PA 18951

The Church of Jesus Christ (Bickertonites)

Organized 1862 at Green Oak, Pa., by William Bickerton, who obeyed the Restored Gospel under Sidney Rigdon's following in 1845.

HEADQUARTERS

Sixth & Lincoln Sts., Monongahela, PA 15063 Tel. (412)258-3066
Media Contact, Executive Secretary, Paul Palmieri, 319 Pine Drive, Aliquippa, PA 15001 Tel. (412)378-4264 Fax (412)378-2806
Media Contact, John Manes, 319 Pine Drive, Aliquippa, PA 15001 Tel. (412)378-4264

OFFICERS

Pres., Dominic Thomas, 6010 Barrie, Dearborn, MI 48126
First Counselor, Paul Palmieri, 319 Pine Drive, Aliquippa, PA 15001
Second Counselor, Robert Watson Star, Rt. 5, Box 36, Gallup, NM 87301
Exec. Sec., John Manes, 2007 Cutter Drive, McKees Rocks, PA 15136 Tel. (412)771-4513

PERIODICAL

Gospel News, The

The Church of Jesus Christ of Latter-day Saints

Organized April 6, 1830, at Fayette, N.Y., by Joseph Smith. Members believe Joseph Smith was divinely directed to restore the gospel to the earth, and that through him the keys to the Aaronic and Melchizedek priesthoods and temple work also were restored. In addition to the Bible, members believe the Book of Mormon (a record of the Lord's dealings with His people on the American continent 600 B.C. - 421 A.D.) to be scripture. Membership is worldwide, approaching nine million in 1992.

In addition to the First Presidency, the governing bodies of the church include the Quorum of the Twelve Apostles, the Presidency of the Seventy, the First Quorum of the Seventy, the Second Quorum of the Seventy and the Presiding Bishopric.

HEADQUARTERS

50 East North Temple St., Salt Lake City, UT 84150 Tel. (801)240-1000 Fax (801)240-1167
Media Contact, Dir., Media Relations, Don LeFevre, Tel. (801)240-4377 Fax (801)240-1167

OFFICERS

Pres., Ezra Taft Benson
1st Counselor, Gordon B. Hinckley
2nd Counselor, Thomas S. Monson
Council of the Twelve Apostles: Pres., Howard W. Hunter; Boyd K. Packer; Marvin J. Ashton; L. Tom Perry; David B. Haight; James E. Faust; Neal A. Maxwell; Russell M. Nelson; Dallin H. Oaks; M. Russell Ballard; Joseph B. Wirthlin; Richard G. Scott

AUXILIARY ORGANIZATIONS

Sunday Schools, Gen. Pres., Merlin R. Lybbert
Relief Society, Gen. Pres., Elaine Jack
Young Women, Gen. Pres., Janette C. Hales
Young Men, Gen. Pres., Jack H. Goaslind
Primary, Gen. Pres., Michaelene P. Grassli

Ensign, The

Church of the Brethren

German pietists-anabaptists founded the Church of the Brethren in 1708 under Alexander Mack, Schwarzenau, Germany. They entered the colonies in 1719 and settled at Germantown, Pa. They have no other creed than the New Testament, hold to principles of nonviolence, temperance, and volunteerism, and emphasize religion in life.

HEADQUARTERS

Church of the Brethren General Offices, 1451 Dundee Ave., Elgin, IL 60120 Tel. (708)742-5100 Fax (708)742-6103
New Windsor Service Center, P.O. Box 188, New Windsor, MD 21776 Tel. (301)635-6464 Fax (301)635-8789
Washington Office, 110 Maryland Ave. NE, Box 50, Washington, DC 20002 Tel. (202)546-3202 Fax (202)544-5852
Media Contact, Dir. of Interpretation, Howard Royer, Elgin Ofc.

OFFICERS

Mod., Charles L. Boyer
Mod.-Elect, Earl K. Ziegler
Sec., Anne M. Myers

GENERAL BOARD STAFF

Office of General Secretary: Gen. Sec., Donald E. Miller

ADMINISTRATIVE COUNCIL

Treasurer's Office: Treas., Darryl K. Deardorff
General Services Commission: Assoc. Gen. Sec./Exec. of Comm., Dale E. Minnich
Parish Ministries Commission: Assoc. Gen. Sec./Exec. of Commission, Glenn F. Timmons
World Ministries Commission: Assoc. Gen. Sec./Exec. of Commission, Joan G. Deeter
Annual Conference: Mgr., Duane Steiner; Treas., Darryl K. Deardorff
Brethren Benefit Trust: Exec. Sec., Wilfred E. Nolen

PERIODICAL

Messenger

Church of the Living God (Motto: Christian Workers for Fellowship)

William Christian was born a slave in Mississippi on Nov. 10, 1856 and grew up uneducated. In 1875, he united with the Missionary Baptist Church and began to preach. In 1888, he left the Baptist Church and began what was known as Christian Friendship Work. Believing himself to have been inspired by the Spirit of God, through divine revelation and close study of the Scriptures, he was led to the truth that the Bible refers to the church as The Church of the Living God (I Tim. 3: 15).

At Caine Creek, near Wrightsville, Ark., in April 1889, Christian became founder and organizer of The Church of the Living God, the first black church in America without Anglo-Saxon roots or not begun by white missionaries.

The church believes in the infallibility of the Scriptures, is Trinitarian, and believes there are three sacraments ordained by Christ: baptism (by immersion), the Lord's Supper (unleavened bread and water), and foot washing.

The Church of the Living God, C.W.F.F., believes in holiness as a gift of God subsequent to the New Birth and manifested only by a changed life acceptable to the Lord.

HEADQUARTERS

430 Forest Ave., Cincinnati, OH 45229 Tel. (513)569-5660
Media Contact, Chief Bishop, W. E. Crumes

OFFICERS

Executive Board: Chief Bishop, W. E. Crumes; Vice-Chief Bishop, Alonza Ponder, 5609 N. Terry, Oklahoma City, OK 73111; Exec. Sec., Bishop C. A. Lewis, 1360 N. Boston, Tulsa, OK 73111; Gen. Sec., Elder Milton S. Herring, Los Angeles, CA; Gen. Treas., Elder Harry Hendricks, Milwaukee, WI; Bishop E. L. Bowie, 2037 N.E. 18th St., Oklahoma City, OK 73111; Chaplain, Bishop E. A. Morgan, 735 S. Oakland Dr., Decatur, IL 62525; Bishop L. A. Crawford, 3711 Biglow, Dallas, TX 74216; Bishop A. R. Powell, 8557 S. Wabash, Chicago, IL 60619; Bishop Jeff Ruffin, Phoenix, AZ; Aux. Bishop, R. S. Morgan, 4508 N. Indiana, Oklahoma City, OK 73118; Overseer, S. E. Shannon, 1034 S. King Hwy., St. Louis, MO 63110

NATIONAL DEPARTMENTS

Convention Planning Committee
Young People's Progressive Union
Christian Education Dept.
Sunday School Dept.
Natl. Evangelist Bd.
Natl. Nurses Guild
Natl. Women's Work Dept.
Natl. Music Dept.
Gen. Sec.'s Ofc.

Church of the Lutheran Brethren of America

The Church of the Lutheran Brethren of America was organized in December 1900. Five independent Lutheran congregations met together in Milwaukee, Wisc., and adopted a constitution patterned very closely to that of the Lutheran Free Church of Norway.

The spiritual awakening in the Midwest during the 1890s crystallized into convictions that led to the formation of a new church body. Chief among the concerns were church membership practices, observance of Holy Communion, confirmation practices and local church government.

The Church of the Lutheran Brethren practices a simple order of worship with the sermon as the primary part of the worship service. It believes that personal profession of faith is the primary criterion for membership in the congregation. The Communion service is reserved for those who profess faith in Christ as savior. Each congregation is autonomous and the synod serves the congregations in advisory and cooperative capacities.

The synod supports a world mission program in Cameroon, Chad, Japan and Taiwan. Approximately 40 percent of the synodical budget is earmarked for world missions. A growing home mission ministry is planting new congregations in the United States and Canada. Affiliate organizations operate several retirement/nursing homes, conference and retreat centers.

HEADQUARTERS

1007 Westside Dr., Box 655, Fergus Falls, MN 56538 Tel. (218)739-3336 Fax (218)739-5514
Media Contact, Pres., Rev. Robert Overgaard

OFFICERS

Pres., Rev. Robert M. Overgaard
Vice-Pres., Rev. David Rinden
Sec., Rev. Richard Vettrus, 707 Crestview Dr., West Union, IA 52175
Exec. Dir. of Finance, Mr. Bradley Martinson
Lutheran Brethren Schools, Pres., Rev. Joel Egge, Lutheran Brethren Schools, Box 317, Fergus Falls, MN 56538
World Missions, Exec. Dir., Rev. Jarle Olson
Home Missions, Exec. Dir., Rev. John Westby
Church Services, Exec. Dir., Rev. David Rinden
Youth Ministries, Exec. Dir., Rev. Warren Larson

PERIODICAL

Faith & Fellowship Press

Church of the Lutheran Confession

The Church of the Lutheran Confession held its constituting convention in Watertown, S.D., in August of 1960. The Church of the Lutheran Confession was born as a result of the people and congregations who came to their own individual convictions, based on Scripture, and were moved to withdraw from church bodies that made up what was then known as the Synodical Conference, over the issue of unionism. Following such passages as I Corinthians 1: 10 and Romans 16: 17-18, the Church of the Lutheran Confession holds the conviction that agreement with the doctrines of Scripture is essential and necessary before exercise of church fellowship is appropriate.

Members of the Church of the Lutheran Confession uncompromisingly believe the Holy Scriptures to be verbally inspired and therefore inerrant. They subscribe to the historic Lutheran Confessions as found in the Book of Concord of 1580 because they are a correct exposition of Scripture.

The Church of the Lutheran Confession exists to proclaim, preserve, and spread the saving truth of the gospel of Jesus Christ, so that the redeemed of God may learn to know Jesus Christ as their Lord and Savior, and to follow him through this life to the life to come.

HEADQUARTERS

460 75th Ave., NE, Minneapolis, MN 55432 Tel. (612)784-8784
Media Contact, Pres., Daniel Fleischer

OFFICERS

Pres., Rev. Daniel Fleischer
Vice-Pres., Rev. Elton Hallauer, 608 1st St., Hancock, MN 56244
Mod., Prof. Ronald Roehl, 515 Ingram Dr. W., Eau Claire, WI 54701
Sec., Rev. Paul Nolting, 626 N. Indian Landing Rd., Rochester, NY 14625
Treas., Lowell Moen, 3455 Jill Ave., Eau Claire, WI 54701
Archivist-Historian, John Lau
Statistician, Harvey Callies

PERIODICALS

Lutheran Spokesman, The; Church of the Lutheran Confession Directory; Journal of Theology

Church of the Nazarene

The origins of the Church of the Nazarene are in the broader holiness movement which arose soon after the American Civil War. It is the result of the merging of three independent holiness groups already in existence in the United States. The Association of Pentecostal Churches in America, located principally in New York and New England, joined at Chicago in 1907 with a California body called the Church of the Nazarene. This united body was called the Pentecostal Church of the Nazarene. The southern group, known as the Holiness Church of Christ, united with this Pentecostal Church of the Nazarene at Pilot Point, Texas, in 1908. In 1919, the word Pentecostal was dropped from the name. Principal leaders in the organization were Phineas Bresee, founder of the church in the West; William Howard Hoople and H. F. Reynolds from the East; and C. B. Jernigan in the southern group. The first Church of the Nazarene in Canada was organized in November 1902 by Dr. H. F. Reynolds, in Oxford, Nova Scotia.

The Church of the Nazarene is distinctive in its emphasis on the doctrine of entire sanctification on the proclamation of Christian Holiness. It stresses the importance of a devout and holy life and a positive witness before the world by the power of the Holy Spirit. The church feels that caring is a way of life.

Nazarene government is representative, a studied compromise between episcopacy and congregationalism. Quadrennially, the various districts elect delegates to a general assembly, at which six general superintendents are elected.

The international denomination has 10 liberal arts colleges, two graduate seminaries, 16 seminaries, and 24 Bible colleges. The church maintains missionaries in 105 countries. World services include medical, education, and religious ministries. Books, periodicals, and other Christian literature are published at the Nazarene Publishing House.

The church is a member of the Christian Holiness Association and the National Association of Evangelicals.

HEADQUARTERS

6401 The Paseo, Kansas City, MO 64131 Tel. (816)333-7000 Fax (816)333-1748
Media Contact, Gen. Sec., Dr. Jack Stone, Tel. (816)333-7000, Ext. 2366

OFFICERS

Gen. Supts.: Eugene L. Stowe; Jerald Johnson; John A. Knight; Raymond Hurn; William J. Prince; Donald D. Owens
Gen. Sec., Jack Stone
Gen. Treas., Norman O. Miller

OTHER ORGANIZATIONS

General Bd.: Sec., Jack Stone; Treas., Norman O. Miller
Church Growth Div., Dir., Bill Sullivan
Chaplaincy Min., Dir., Curt Bowers
Church Ext. Min., Dir., Mike Estep
Evangelism Min., Dir., Bill Sullivan
Pastoral Min., Dir., Wilbur Brannon
Communications Div., Dir., Paul Skiles
Media Services, Dir., David Anderson
Publications Intl., Dir., Ray Hendrix
Fin. Div., Dir., D. Moody Gunter
Planned Giving, Dir., Martin Butler
Pensions & Benefits Services, Dir., Dean Wessels
Stewardship Services, Dir., D. Moody Gunter
Sunday School Min. Div., Dir., Phil Riley
Adult Min., Dir., Randy Cloud
Children's Min., Dir., Miriam Hall
NYI Min., Dir., Fred Fullerton
World Mission Div., Dir., Robert H. Scott
Missionary Min., Dir., John Smee
Fin. Services, Dir., Dennis Berard

Nazarene World Missionary Soc., Dir., Nina Gunter
Int'l. Bd. of Educ., Ed. Commissioner, Stephen Nease

PERIODICALS

Herald of Holiness; World Mission; Preacher's Magazine; Teens Today

Church of Our Lord Jesus Christ of the Apostolic Faith, Inc.

This church as an organized body was founded by Bishop R. C. Lawson in Columbus, Ohio, and moved to New York City in 1919. It is founded upon the teachings of the Apostles and Prophets, Jesus Christ being its chief cornerstone.

HEADQUARTERS

2081 Adam Clayton Powell Jr. Blvd., New York, NY 10027 Tel. (212)866-1700
Media Contact, Exec. Sec., Bishop T. E. Woolfolk, P.O. Box 119, Oxford, NC 27565 Tel. (919)693-9449 Fax (919)693-6115

OFFICERS

Board of Apostles: Pres., Bishop William L. Bonner; Chief Apostle, Bishop J. P. Steadman; Bishop Frank S. Solomon; Bishop Henry A. Ross, Sr.; Bishop Matthew A. Norwood; Bishop Gentle L. Groover; Bishop Wilbur L. Jones
Bd. of Bishops, Chmn., Bishop James I. Clark, Jr.
Bd. of Presbyters, Pres., Elder Michael A. Dixon
Exec. Secretariat, Sec., Bishop T. E. Woolfolk
Natl. Rec. Sec., Bishop Fred Rubin, Sr. (J.B.)
Natl. Fin. Sec., Bishop Clarence Groover
Natl. Corr. Sec., Bishop Raymond J. Keith, Jr. (J.B.)
Natl Treas., Bishop Thomas J. Richardson (H.B.)

Churches of Christ

Churches of Christ are autonomous congregations, whose members appeal to the Bible alone to determine matters of faith and practice. There are no central offices or officers. Publications and institutions related to the churches are either under local congregational control or independent of any one congregation.

Churches of Christ shared a common fellowship in the 19th century with the Christian Churches/Churches of Christ and the Christian Church (Disciples of Christ). Fellowship was gradually estranged following the Civil War due to theistic evolution, higher critical theories, and centralization of church-wide activities through a missionary society.

Members of Churches of Christ believe in the inspiration of the Scriptures, the divinity of Jesus Christ, and immersion into Christ for the remission of sins. The New Testament pattern is followed in worship and church organization.

HEADQUARTERS

Media Contact, Ed., Gospel Advocate, Dr. F. Furman Kearley, P.O. Box 167, Monahans, TX 79756-0167

PERIODICALS

Action; Christian Bible Teacher; Christian Chronicle; Christian Echo, The; Firm Foundation; Gospel Advocate; Guardian of Truth; Power for Today; Restoration Quarterly; 21st Century Christian; Upreach; Rocky Mountain Christian; Gospel Tidings

Churches of Christ in Christian Union

Organized in 1909 at Washington Court House, Ohio, as the Churches of Christ in Christian Union, this body believes in the new birth and the baptism of the Holy Spirit for believers. It is Wesleyan, with an evangelistic and missionary emphasis.

The Reformed Methodist Church merged in September, 1952, with Churches of Christ in Christian Union.

HEADQUARTERS

1426 Lancaster Pike, Box 30, Circleville, OH 43113 Tel. (614)474-8856 Fax (614)477-7766
Media Contact, Gen. Supt., Daniel L. Tipton

OFFICERS

Gen. Supt., Dr. Daniel Tipton
Asst. Gen. Supt., Rev. David Dean
Gen. Treas., Beverly R. Salley
Gen. Bd. of Trustees: Chpsn., Dr. Daniel Tipton; Vice-Chpsn., Rev. David Dean
District Superintendents: West Central District, Rev. Ron Reese; South Central District, Rev. Jack Norman; Northeast District, Rev. Art Penird, Rt. 2, P.O. Box 790, Port Crane, NY 13833

Churches of God, General Conference

The Churches of God, General Conference had its beginnings in Harrisburg, Pa., in 1825.

John Winebrenner, recognized founder of the Church of God movement, was an ordained minister of the German Reformed Church. His experience-centered form of Christianity, particularly the "new measures" he used to promote it, his close connection with the local Methodists, his "experience and conference meetings" in the church, and his "social prayer meetings" in parishioners' homes resulted in differences of opinion and the establishment of new congregations. Extensive revivals, camp meetings, and mission endeavors led to the organization of additional congregations across central Pennsylvania and westward through Ohio, Indiana, Illinois, and Iowa.

In 1830 the first system of cooperation between local churches was initiated as an "eldership" in eastern Pennsylvania. The organization of other elderships followed. General Eldership was organized in 1845, and in 1974 the official name of the denomination was changed from General Eldership of the Churches of God in North America to its present name.

The Churches of God, General Conference, is composed of 16 conferences in the United States. The polity of the church is presbyterial in form. The church has mission ministries in the southwest among native Americans and is extensively involved in church planting and whole life ministries in Bangladesh, Haiti, and India.

The General Conference convenes in business session triennially. An Administrative Council composed of 16 regional representatives is responsible for the administration and ministries of the church between sessions of the General Conference.

HEADQUARTERS

Legal Headquarters, United Church Center, Rm. 200, 900 S. Arlington Ave., Harrisburg, PA 17109 Tel. (717)652-0255

Administrative Offices, General Conf. Dir., Dr. David E. Draper, 700 E. Melrose Ave., P.O. Box 926, Findlay, OH 45839 Tel. (419)424-1961
Media Contact, Exec. Sec., Roberta G. Bakies, P.O. Box 926, Findlay, OH 45840 Tel. (419)424-1961 Fax (419)424-3343

OFFICERS

Pres., Pastor George Reser, 506 N. Main St., Columbia City, IN 46725 Tel. (219)248-2482
Journalizing Sec., Dr. C. Darrell Prichard, 700 E. Melrose Ave., P.O. Box 1132, Findlay, OH 45839 Tel. (419)423-7694
Treas., Mr. Robert E. Stephenson, 700 E. Melrose Ave., P.O. Box 926, Findlay, OH 45839 Tel. (419)424-1961

DEPARTMENTS

Church Publications, Mrs. Linda M. Draper
Cross-Cultural Ministries, Mr. Travis C. Perry
Pensions, Dr. Royal P. Kear
Curriculum, Rev. Marilyn Rayle Kern
Church Renewal, Pastor Jim G. Martin
Planting, ———-
Youth & Family Life, ———-
Fin., Mr. Robert E. Stephenson

PERIODICALS

Church Advocate, The; Workman, The; Gem, The

Community Churches, International Council of

This body is a fellowship of locally autonomous, ecumenically minded, congregationally governed, non-creedal Churches. The Council came into being in 1950 as the union of two former councils of community churches, one formed of black churches known as the Biennial Council of Community Churches, and the other of white churches known as the National Council of Community Churches.

HEADQUARTERS

7808 College Dr., 2 SE, Palos Heights, IL 60463 Tel. (708)361-2600

OFFICERS

Pres., Larry McClellan
Vice-Pres.: Orsey Malone; Ronald Miller
Sec., Abraham Wright
Treas., Martha Nolan
Exec. Dir., Jeffrey R. Newhall

OTHER ORGANIZATIONS

Commission on Church Relations
Commission on Ecumenical Relations
Commission on Clergy Relations
Commission on Laity Relations
Commission on Faith & Order
Commission on Social Concerns
Commission on Missions
Commission on Informational Services
Women's Christian Fellowship, Pres., Mozella Weston
Samaritans (Men's Fellowship), Pres., Louis Oatis
Young Adult Fellowship, Pres., Michelle Kiah
Youth Fellowship, Pres., Dara Wilson

PERIODICALS

Christian Community, The; Pastor's Journal, The

Congregational Christian Churches, National Association

This association was organized in 1955 in Detroit, Mich., by delegates from Congregational

Christian Churches committed to continuing the Congregational way of faith and order in church life. Participation by member churches is voluntary.

HEADQUARTERS

P.O. Box 1620, Oak Creek, WI 53154 Tel. (414)764-1620 Fax (414)764-0319
Media Contact, Exec. Sec., Michael S. Robertson, 8473 So. Howell Ave., Oak Creek, WI 53154 Tel. (414)764-1620 Fax (414)764-0319

OFFICERS

Mod., Karl Schimpf
Exec. Sec., Michael S. Robertson, 8473 South Howell Ave., Oak Creek, WI 53154
Assoc. Exec. Secs.: Rev. Dr. Michael Halcomb; Rev. Dr. Harry W. Clark

PERIODICAL

Congregationalist, The

Congregational Holiness Church

This body was organized in 1921 and embraces the doctrine of Holiness and Pentecost. It carries on mission work in Mexico, Honduras, Costa Rica, Cuba, Brazil, Guatemala, India, Nicaragua and El Salvador.

HEADQUARTERS

3888 Fayetteville Hwy., Griffin, GA 30223 Tel. (404)228-4833 Fax (404)228-1177
Media Contact, Gen. Supt., Bishop L. G. Howard

EXECUTIVE BOARD

Gen. Supt., Bishop L. G. Howard
1st Asst. Gen. Supt., Rev. William L. Lewis
2nd Asst. Gen. Supt., Rev. Wayne Hicks
Gen. Sec., Rev. Kenneth Law
Gen. Treas., Rev. Ronald Wilson

PERIODICAL

Gospel Messenger, The

Conservative Baptist Association of America

The Conservative Baptist Association of America was organized May 17, 1947, at Atlantic City, N.J. The Old and New Testaments are regarded as the divinely inspired Word of God and are therefore infallible and of supreme authority. Each local church is independent and autonomous, and free from ecclesiastical or political authority.

CBA provides wide-ranging support to its affiliate churches and individuals. CBA offers personnel to assist churches in areas such as growth, conflict resolution and financial analysis. The association supports its clergy with medical insurance programs, retirement planning, referrals for new places of ministry and spiritual counseling. The Conservative Baptist Women's Ministries assists women in the church to be effective in their personal growth and leadership.

Each June or July there is a national meeting giving members an opportunity for fellowship, inspiration and motivation.

HEADQUARTERS

25W560 Geneva Rd., P.O. Box 66, Wheaton, IL 60189 Tel. (708)653-5350 Fax (708)653-5387
Media Contact, Dir. of Comm., Rev. Walter Fricke

OTHER ORGANIZATIONS

Conservative Baptist For. Mission Soc., Gen. Dir., Dr. Warren W. Webster, Box 5, Wheaton, IL 60189
Conservative Baptist Home Mission Soc., Gen. Dir., Dr. Jack Estep, Box 828, Wheaton, IL 60189
Conservative Baptist Higher Edu. Council, Dr. Paul Bordem, Denver Conservative Baptist Seminary, P.O. Box 10,000, Denver, CO 80210

PERIODICALS

Spectrum; Front Line

Conservative Congregational Christian Conference

In the 1930s, evangelicals within the Congregational Christian Churches felt a definite need for fellowship and service. By 1945, this loose association crystallized in the Conservative Congregational Christian Fellowship, concerned to maintain a faithful, biblical witness.

In 1948 in Chicago, the Conservative Congregational Christian Conference was established to provide a continuing fellowship for evangelical churches and ministers on the national level. In recent years, many churches have joined the Conference from backgrounds other than Congregational. These Community or Bible Churches are truly congregational in polity and thoroughly evangelical in conviction. The CCCC welcomes all evangelical churches that are, in fact, congregational. The CCCC believes in the necessity of a regenerate membership, the authority of the Holy Scriptures, the Lordship of Jesus Christ, the autonomy of the local church, and the universal fellowship of all Christians.

The Conservative Congregational Christian Conference is a member of the World Evangelical Congregational Fellowship (formed in 1986 in London, England) and the National Association of Evangelicals.

HEADQUARTERS

7582 Currell Blvd., Ste. #108, St. Paul, MN 55125 Tel. (612)739-1474
Media Contact, Conf. Min., Rev. Clifford R. Christensen

OFFICERS

Pres., Mr. William V. Nygren, 583 Sterling, Maplewood, MN 55119
Vice-Pres., Rev. Don Ehler, 620 High Ave., Hillsboro, WI 54634
Conf. Min., Rev. Clifford R. Christensen, 57 Kipling St., St. Paul, MN 55519
Controller, Mr. Leslie Pierce, 5220 E. 105th St. S., Tulsa, OK 74137
Treas., Mr. John D. Nygren, 579 Sterling St., Maplewood, MN 55119
Rec. Sec., Rev. Larry E. Scovil, 317 W. 40th St., Scottsbluff, NE 69361
Editor, Mrs. Wanda Evans, 4072 Clifton Ridge, Highland, MI 48357
Historian, Rev. Milton Reimer, P.O. Box 4456, Lynchburgg, VA 24502

PERIODICAL

Foresee

Conservative Lutheran Association

The Conservative Lutheran Association (CLA) was originally named Lutheran's Alert National

(LAN) when it was founded in 1965 by 10 conservative Lutheran pastors and laymen meeting in Cedar Rapids, Iowa. Its purpose was to help preserve from erosion the basic doctrines of Christian theology, including the inerrancy of Holy Scripture. The group grew to a worldwide constituency, similarly concerned over maintaining the doctrinal integrity of the Bible and the Lutheran Confessions.

HEADQUARTERS

3504 N. Pearl St., P.O. Box 7186, Tacoma, WA 98407 Tel. (800)228-4650 Fax (206)759-1790
Media Contact, Pres., The Rev. Dr. R. H. Redal

OFFICERS

Pres., The Rev. R. H. Redal, 409 N. Tacoma Ave., Tacoma, WA 98403
Vice-Pres., The Rev. Pomeroy Moore, 420 Fernhill Lane, Anaheim, CA 92807
Sec., The Rev. Clyde Grier, El Campo, TX
Treas., Mr. Wayne Brooks, Tacoma, WA
Faith Seminary, Dean, The Rev. Dr. Michael J. Adams

Coptic Orthodox Church

This body is part of the ancient Coptic Orthodox Church of Egypt which is currently headed by His Holiness Pope Shenouda III, 116th Successor to St. Mark the Apostle. In the United States many parishes have been organized, consisting of Egyptian immigrants to the United States. Copts exist outside of Egypt in Ethiopia, Europe, Asia, Australia, Canada and the United States. In all, the world Coptic community is estimated at 27 million. The church is in full communion with the other members of the Oriental Orthodox Church family, The Syrian Orthodox Church, Armenian Orthodox Church, Ethiopian Orthodox Church, and the Syrian Orthodox Church in India.

CORRESPONDENT

Archpriest, V. Rev. Fr. Gabriel Avdelsayed, Ph.D., 427 West Side Ave., Jersey City, NJ 07304 Tel. (201)333-0004 Fax (201)333-0502

Cumberland Presbyterian Church

The Cumberland Presbyterian Church was organized in Dickson County, Tenn., on Feb. 4, 1810. It was an outgrowth of the Great Revival of 1800 on the Kentucky and Tennessee frontier. The founders were Finis Ewing, Samuel King, and Samuel McAdow, ministers in the Presbyterian Church who rejected the doctrine of election and reprobation as taught in the Westminster Confession of Faith.

By 1813, the Cumberland Presbytery had grown to encompass three presbyteries, which constituted a synod. This synod met at the Beech Church in Sumner County, Tenn., and formulated a "Brief Statement," which set forth the points in which Cumberland Presbyterians dissented from the Westminster Confession.

1. That there are no eternal reprobates;
2. That Christ died not for a part only, but for all mankind;
3. That all those dying in infancy are saved through Christ and the sanctification of the Spirit;
4. That the Spirit of God operates on the world, or as coextensively as Christ has made atonement, in such a manner as to leave all men inexcusable.

From its birth in 1810, the Cumberland Presbyterian Church grew to a membership of 200,000 at the turn of the century. In 1906 the church voted to merge with the then-Presbyterian Church. Those who dissented from the merger became the nucleus of the continuing Cumberland Presbyterian Church.

HEADQUARTERS

Media Contact, Stated Clerk, Rev. Robert D. Prosser, 1978 Union Ave., Memphis, TN 38104 Tel. (901)276-4572 Fax (901)276-4578

OFFICERS

Mod., Dr. John D. Hall, Rt. 5 Box 613, Scottsboro, AL 35678
Stated Clk., Rev. Robert Prosser, 1978 Union Ave., Memphis, TN 38104
General Assembly Exec. Comm., Chpsn., Rev. Terrell D. Maynard, 8828 Highway 119, Alabaster, AL 35007

INSTITUTIONS

Cumberland Presbyterian Children's Home, Exec. Dir., Dr. Marvin E. Leslie, Drawer G, Denton, TX 76202 Tel. (817)382-5112 Fax (817)387-0821
Cumberland Presbyterian Center, 1978 Union Ave., Memphis, TN 38104 Tel. (901)276-4572 Fax (901)276-4578

BOARDS

Bd. of Christian Education, Exec. Dir., Mrs. Claudette Pickle, 1978 Union Ave., Memphis, TN 38104
Bd. of Missions, Exec. Dir., Rev. Jack Barker, 1978 Union Ave., Memphis, TN 38104
Bd. of Finance, Exec. Sec., Rev. Richard Magrill, 1978 Union Ave., Memphis, TN 38104

PERIODICALS

Cumberland Presbyterian, The; Missionary Messenger, The

Cumberland Presbyterian Church in America

This church, originally known as the Colored Cumberland Presbyterian Church, was formed in May 1874. In May 1869, at the General Assembly meeting in Murfreesboro, Tenn., Moses Weir of the black delegation sucessfully appealed for help in organizing a separate African church so that: blacks could learn self-reliance and independence; they could have more financial assistance; they could minister more effectively among blacks; and they could worship close to the altar, not in the balconies. He requested that the Cumberland Presbyterian Church organize blacks into presbyteries and synods; develop schools to train black clergy; grant loans to assist blacks to secure hymnbooks, Bibles, and church buildings; and establish a separate General Assembly.

In 1874 the first General Assembly of the Colored Cumberland Presbyterian Church met in Nashville. The moderator was Rev. P. Price and the stated clerk was Elder John Humphrey.

The General Assembly, the national governing body, is organized around its three program boards and agencies: Finance, Publication and Christian Education, and Missions and Evangelism.

The church has four synods (Alabama, Kentucky, Tennessee, and Texas), 15 presbyteries, and 153 congregations. The CPC extends as far north as Cleveland, Ohio and Chicago; as far west as Marshalltown, Iowa, and Dallas, Tex.; and as far south as Selma, Ala.

HEADQUARTERS
Media Contact, Stated Clerk, Rev. Dr. R. Stanley Wood, 226 Church St., Huntsville, AL 35801 Tel. (205)536-7481 Fax (205)536-7482

OFFICERS
Mod., Rev. Joel P. Rice, 6951 Clearglenn, Dallas, TX 75232
Stated Clk., Rev. Dr. R. Stanley Wood, 226 Church St., Huntsville, AL 35801 Tel. (205)536-7481

SYNODS
Alabama, Stated Clk., Arthur Hinton, 511 10th Ave. N.W., Aliceville, AL 35442
Kentucky, Stated Clk., Mary Martha Daniels, 8548 Rhodes Ave., Chicago, IL 60619
Tennessee, Stated Clk., Elder Clarence Norman, 145 Jones St., Huntington, TN 38334
Texas, Stated Clk., Arthur King, 2435 Kristen, Dallas, TX 75216

PERIODICAL
Cumberland Flag, The

Duck River (and Kindred) Associations of Baptists

This is a group of Baptist associations found in Tennessee, Alabama, Georgia, Kentucky.

OFFICERS
Duck River Assoc., Mod., Elder Wayne L. Smith, Rt. 1, Box 429, Lynchburg, TN 37352
Clk., Elder Marvin Davenport, Rt. 1, Auburntown, TN 37016
General Assoc., Mod., Elder Charles Bell, Rt. 1, Box 385A, Valley Head, TN 35989 Tel. (205)635-6539

Elim Fellowship

The Elim Fellowship, a Pentecostal Body established in 1947, is an outgrowth of the Elim Missionary Assemblies, which was formed in 1933.

It is an association of churches, ministers and missionaries seeking to serve the whole Body of Christ. It is of Pentecostal conviction and charismatic orientation, providing ministerial credentials and counsel and encouraging fellowship among local churches. Elim Fellowship sponsors leadership seminars at home and abroad, and serves as a transdenominational agency sending long-term, short-term, and tent-making missionaries to work with national movements.

HEADQUARTERS
7245 College St., Lima, NY 14485 Tel. (716)582-2790 Fax (716)624-1229
Media Contact, Gen. Sec., Chester Gretz

OFFICERS
Gen. Overseer, L. Dayton Reynolds
Asst. Gen. Overseer, Bernard J. Evans, 3727 Snowden Hill Rd., New Hartford, NY 13413 Tel. (315)736-0966
Gen. Sec., Chester Gretz
Acting Gen. Treas., Kenneth Beukema, 7284 McDonald Dr., Lima, NY 14485 Tel. (716)624-1059

PERIODICAL
Elim Herald

Episcopal Church

The Episcopal Church entered the colonies with the earliest settlers (Jamestown, Va., 1607) as the

THE YEAR IN IMAGES

Religious News Service Photo

Anglican leader visits U.S.

Archbishop of Canterbury George Carey in 1992 made his first U.S. visit since becoming leader of the worldwide Anglican church in 1991. He also visited the World Council of Churches on June 2-3, assuring WCC officials that the Anglican church is not going to withdraw from the council, in spite of criticisms of the council following the seventh assembly in Australia in 1991.

Church of England. After the American Revolution, it became autonomous in 1789 as The Protestant Episcopal Church in the United States of America. (The Episcopal Church became the official alternate name in 1967.) Samuel Seabury of Connecticut was elected the first bishop and consecrated in Aberdeen by bishops of the Scottish Episcopal Church in 1784.

In organizing as an independent body, The Episcopal Church created a bicameral legislature, the General Convention, modeled after the new U.S. Congress. It comprises a House of Bishops and a House of Clerical and Lay Deputies and meets every three years. A 38-member Executive Council, which meets three times a year, is the interim governing body. An elected presiding bishop serves as Primate and Chief Pastor.

After severe setbacks in the years immediately following the Revolution because of its association with the British Crown and the fact that a number of its clergy and members were Loyalists, the church soon established its own identity and sense of mission. It sent missionaries into the newly settled territories of the United States, establishing dioceses from coast to coast, and also undertook substantial missionary work in Africa, Latin America and the Far East. Today, the overseas dioceses are developing into independent provinces of the Anglican Communion, the worldwide fellowship of churches in communion with the Church of England and the Archbishop of Canterbury.

The beliefs and practices of The Episcopal

Church, like those of other Anglican churches, are both Catholic and Reformed, with bishops in the apostolic succession and the historic creeds of Christendom regarded as essential elements of faith and order, along with the primary authority of Holy Scripture and the two chief sacraments of Baptism and Eucharist.

EPISCOPAL CHURCH CENTER
815 Second Ave., New York, NY 10017 Tel. (212)867-8400 Fax (212)949-8059
Media Contact, News Dir., James Solheim

OFFICERS
Presiding Bishop & Primate, The Most Rev. Edmond L. Browning
House of Deputies: Pres., Mrs. Pamela Chinnis, Jr., Box 164668, Little Rock, AR 72216
Treas., Mrs. Ellen Cooke
Sec., The Rev. Donald A. Nickerson, Jr.

OFFICE OF THE PRESIDING BISHOP
Presiding Bishop, The Most Rev. Edmond L. Browning
Deputy for Admn., The Rev. Richard Chang
Information Officer, Barbara Braver
Exec. Dir., Office of Pastoral Dev., The Rt. Rev. Harold Hopkins, Jr.
Suffragan Bishop for the Armed Forces, The Rt. Rev. Charles L. Keyser, Jr.
Suffragan Bishop for American Churches in Europe, ——-
Prof. Ministry Dev., The Rev. John Docker

ADMINISTRATION AND FINANCIAL GROUP
Treas. and Senior Exec., Mrs. Ellen Cooke
Asst. Treas., J. Thompson Hiller
Business Systems, Barbara Keller Bunten
Contracts and Services, Robert E. Brown
Episcopal Parish Services, James Vest
Human Resources, John Colon

PROGRAM GROUP
Senior Exec., Diane Porter

ADVOCACY, WITNESS AND JUSTICE
Exec., Diane Porter
Asiamerica Ministry, The Rev. Winston Ching
Hispanic Ministry, The Rev. Herbert Arrunategui
Jubilee Ministry, Ntsiki Kabane-Langford
Native American Ministry, Owanah Anderson
Peace and Justice Ministry, The Rev. Brian Grieves
Rural and Small Town Ministry, The Rev. Allen Brown
Washington Office, The Rev. Robert Brooks and Dr. Betty Coats
Episcopal Migration Ministry, The Rev. Burgess Carr
AIDS Ministry, The Rev. Randolph Frew

COMMUNICATION
Exec., Sonia Francis
Electronic Media, The Rev. Clement Lee
Publications, Frank Tedeschi
News Dir., James Solheim
Episcopal Life, Jerrold Hames
Interpretation, John Ratti
Art Dir., Rochelle Arthur

EDUCATION, EVANGELISM & MINISTRY DEV.
Exec., The Rev. David Perry

Children's Ministry, The Rev. Howard Williams
Youth Ministry, The Rev. Sheryl Kujawa
Evangelism, The Rev. A. Wayne Schwab
Liturgy and Music, The Rev. Clayton Morris
Adult Education, Leadership Dev., The Rev. Linda Grenz

PARTNERSHIPS
Exec., The Rev. Patrick Mauney
Ecumenical Officer, The Rev. William Norgren
Mission Personnel, Dorothy Gist
Africa, R. Nathaniel Porter
East Asia, Pacific and Middle East, The Rev. Mark Harris
Latin America and the Caribbean, The Rev. Ricardo Potter
Women in Mission and Ministry, Ann Smith

PLANNING AND DEVELOPMENT GROUP
Senior Exec. & Deputy for PBFWR, Barry Menuez
Exec., The Rev. Bill Carradine
Development, Timothy Holder
Grants Dir., Nancy Marvel
Planning Officer, Vernon Hazelwood
Stewardship, Laura Wright
Planned Giving, Frederick Osborn

RELATED AGENCIES
Church Pension Group, Alan Blanshard
Episcopal Church Foundation, William Andersen
Archives, Mark Duffy

BISHOPS IN THE U.S.A.
C, Coadjutor; S, Suffragan; A Assistant
Address: Right Reverend
Headquarters Staff: Presiding Bishop & Primate, The Most Rev. Edmond L. Browning; Pastoral Dev., Rt. Rev. Harold Hopkins; S. Bishop for Chaplaincies to Military\Prisons\Hosp., Rt. Rev. Charles L. Keyser, Jr.
Alabama: Robert O. Miller, 521 N. 20th St., Birmingham, AL 35203
Alaska: Steve Charleston, Box 441, Fairbanks, AK 99707
Albany: David S. Ball, 62 S. Swan St., Albany, NY 12210
Arizona: Joseph T. Heistand; C, Robert Shahan, P.O. Box 13647, Phoenix, AZ 85002
Arkansas: Herbert Donovan, Jr., 300 W. 17th St., P.O. Box 6120, Little Rock, AR 72206
Atlanta: Frank Kellog Allan, 2744 Peachtree Rd. N.W., Atlanta, GA 30305
Bethlehem: J. Mark Dyer, 333 Wyandotte St., Bethelehem, PA 18015
California: William E. Swing, 1055 Taylor St., San Francisco, CA 94108
Central Florida: John H. Howe, 324 N. Interlachen Ave., Box 790, Winter Park, FL 32789
Central Gulf Coast: Charles F. Duvall, P.O. Box 8547, Mobile, AL 36608
Central New York: David B. Joslin, 310 Montgomery St., Syracuse, NY 13203
Central Pennsylvania: Charlie F. McNutt, P.O. Box W, Harrisburg, PA 17108
Chicago: Frank T. Griswold, III; S, William Wiedrich, 65 E. Huron St., Chicago, IL 60611
Colorado: William J. Winterrond, P.O. Box M, Capitol Hill Sta., Denver, CO 80218
Connecticut: Arthur E. Walmsley; S, Clarence N. Coleridge; S, Jeffrey William Rowthorn, 1335 Asylum Ave., Hartford, CT 06105
Dallas: ——-, 1630 Garrett St., Dallas, TX 75206
Delaware: Calvin C. Tennis, 2020 Tatnall St., Wilmington, DE 19802

East Carolina: B. Sidney Sanders, P.O. Box 1336, Kinston, NC 28501

East Tennessee: William E. Sanders; C, Robert Tharp, Box 3807, Knoxville, TN 37917

Eastern Oregon: Rustin R. Kimsey, P.O. Box 620, The Dalles, OR 97058

Easton: Elliot L. Sorge, P.O. Box 1027, Easton, MD 21601

Eau Claire: William C. Wantland, 510 S. Farwell St., Eau Claire, WI 54701

El Camino Real: Richard Shimpfky, P.O. Box 1093, Monterey, CA 93940

Florida: Frank S. Cerveny, 325 Market St., Jacksonville, FL 32202

Fond du Lac: William L. Stevens, P.O. Box 149, Fond du Lac, WI 54935

Fort Worth: Clarence Cullam Pope, Jr., 3572 Southwest Loop 820, Fort Worth, TX 76133

Georgia: Harry W. Shipps, 611 East Bay St., Savannah, GA 31401

Hawaii: Donald P. Hart, Queen Emma Square, Honolulu, HI 93813

Idaho: John S. Thornton, IV, Box 936, Boise, ID

Indianapolis: Edward W. Jones, 1100 W. 42nd St., Indianapolis, IN 46208

Iowa: C. Christopher Epting, 225 37th St., Des Moines, IA 50312

Kansas: William E. Smalley, Bethany Place, Topeka, KS 66612

Kentucky: David B. Reed, 421 S. 2nd St., Louisville, KY 40202

Lexington: Don A. Wimberly, 530 Sayre Ave., Lexington, KY 40508

Long Island: Orris G. Walker

Los Angeles: Federick H. Borsch; S, Chester Talton, 1220 W. 4th St., Los Angeles, CA 90017

Louisiana: James Barrow Brown, P.O. Box 15719, New Orleans, LA 70175

Maine: Edward C. Chalfant, 143 State St., Portland, ME 04101

Maryland: A. Theodore Eastman; S, Charles L. Longest, 105 W. Monument St., Baltimore, MD 21230

Massachusetts: David Elliott Johnson; S, Barbara Harris, 138 Tremont St., Boston, MA 02111

Michigan: R. Stewart Wood; S, Harry Irving Mayson, 4800 Woodward Ave., Detroit, MI 48201

Milwaukee: Roger J. White, 804 E. Juneau Ave., Milwaukee, WI 53202

Minnesota: Robert M. Anderson; S, Sanford Hampton, 309 Clinton Ave., Minneapolis, MN 55403

Mississippi: Duncan M. Gray, Jr.; C, Alfred Marble, Jr., P.O. Box 1636, Jackson, MS 39205

Missouri: Hays Rockwell, 1210 Locust St., St. Louis, MO 63103

Montana: Charles I. Jones, 515 North Park Ave., Helena, MT 59601

Newark: John Shelby Spong

Nebraska: James E. Krotz, 200 N. 62nd St., Omaha, NE 68132

Nevada: Stewart C. Zabriski, 2930 W. 7th St., Reno, NV 89503

New Hampshire: Douglas E. Theuner, 63 Green St., Concord, NH 03301

New Jersey: G. P. Mellick Belshaw

New York: Richard F. Grein; S, Walter D. Dennis, 1047 Amsterdam Ave., New York, NY 10025

Newark: John Shelby Spong; S, Jack McKelvey, 24 Rector St., Newark, NJ 07102

North Carolina: Robert W. Estill; Frank Harris Vest, Jr., (S), 201 St. Alban's, P.O. Box 17025, Raleigh, NC 27609

North Dakota: Andrew H. Fairfield, 809 8th Ave. S., Fargo, ND 58102

Northern California: Jerry A. Lamb, 1322 27th St., P.O. Box 131268, Sacramento, CA 95816

Northern Indiana: Frank C. Gray, 117 N. Lafayette Blvd., South Bend, IN 46601

Northern Michigan: Thomas K. Ray, 131 E. Ridge St., Marquette, MI 49855

Northwest Texas: Sam Byron Hulsey, 1802 Broadway, P.O. Box 1067, Lubbock, TX 79408 Tel. (806)763-1370

Northwestern Pennsylvania: Robert D. Rowley, 145 W. 6th St., Erie, PA 16501

Ohio: James R. Moodey; Arthur B. Williams, (S), 2230 Euclid Ave., Cleveland, OH 44115

Oklahoma: Robert M. Moody, P.O. Box 1098; William J. Cox, (A)

Olympia: Vincent W. Warner, 1551 Tenth Ave. East, Seattle, WA 98102

Oregon: Robert Louis Ladehoff, P.O. Box 467, Portland, OR 97034

Pennsylvania: Allan C. Bartlett; Franklin D. Turner, (S), 1700 Market St., Ste. 1600, Philadelphia, PA 19103

Pittsburgh: Alden M. Hathaway, 325 Oliver Ave., Pittsburgh, PA 15222

Quincy: Edward H. MacBurney, 3601 N. North St., Peoria, IL 61604

Rhode Island: George Hunt, 275 N. Main St., Providence, RI 02903

Rio Grande: Terence Kelshaw, 4304 Carlisle NE, Albuquerque, NM 87107

Rochester: William G. Burrill, Jr., 935 East Ave., Rochester, NY 14607

San Diego: Gethin B. Hughes, St. Paul's Church, 2728 6th Ave., San Diego, CA 92103

San Joaquin: David Schofield, 4159 East Dakota, Fresno, CA 93726

South Carolina: Edward L. Salmon; G. Edward Haynesworth, (A), 1020 King St., Drawer 2127, Charleston, SC 29403

South Dakota: ———, 200 W. 18th St., P.O. Box 517, Sioux Falls, SD 57101

Southeast Florida: Calvin O. Schofield, Jr., 525 NE 15 St., Miami, FL 33132

Southern Ohio: Herbert Thompson, Jr., 412 Sycamore St., Cincinnati, OH 45202

Southern Virginia: Frank H. Vest, 600 Talbot Hill Rd., Norfolk, VA 23505

Southwest Florida: Rogers S. Harris, Box 20899, St. Petersburg, FL 33742

Southwestern Virginia: A. Heath Light, P.O. Box 2068, Roanoke, VA 24009

Spokane: Frank J. Terry, 245 E. 13th Ave., Spokane, WA 99202

Springfield: Donald M. Hultstrand, 821 S. 2nd St., Springfield, IL 62704

Tennessee: ———, Box 3807, Knoxville, TN 37917

Texas: Maurice M. Benitez; A, Anselmo Carroll, 520 San Jacinto St., Houston, TX 77002

Upper South Carolina: William A. Beckhan, P.O. Box 1789, Columbia, SC 29202

Utah: George E. Bates, 231 E. First St. South, Salt Lake City, UT 84111

Vermont: Daniel L. Swenson, Rock Point, Burlington, VT 05401

Virginia: Peter J. Lee; S, David H. Lewis, Jr., 110 W. Franklin St., Richmond, VA 23220

Washington: Ronald Haines; S, Jane H. Dixon, Mt. St. Alban, Washington, DC 20016

West Missouri: John Buchanan, 415 W. 13th St., P.O. Box 23216, Kansas City, MO 64141

West Tennessee: Alex D. Dickson, 692 Poplar Ave., Memphis, TN 38105

West Texas: John H. McNaughton; S, Earl N. MacArthur, P.O. Box 6885, San Antonio, TX 78209

West Virginia: Robert P. Atkinson; S, William Franklin Carr, 1608 Virginia St. E., Charleston, WV 25311

Western Kansas: John F. Ashby, 142 S. 8th St., P.O. Box 1383, Salina, KS 67401

Western Louisiana: Robert J. Hargrove, P.O. Box 4046, Alexandria, LA 71301

Western Massachusetts: ——, 37 Chestnut St., Springfield, MA 01103

Western Michigan: Edward L. Lee, Jr., 2600 Vincent Ave., Kalamazoo, MI 49001

Western New York: David C. Bowman, 1114 Delaware Ave., Buffalo, NY 14209

Western North Carolina: William G. Weinhauer, P.O. Box 368, Black Mountain, NC 28711

Wyoming: Bob Gordon Jones, 104 W. 4th St., Box 1007, Laramie, WY 82070

Am. Churches in Europe—Jurisdiction: ——, The American Cathedral, 23 Avenue Georges V, 75008, Paris, France

Navajoland Area Mission: Steven Plummer, P.O. Box 720, Farmington, NM 47401

PERIODICALS

Anglican & Episcopal History; Anglican Theol. Review; Living Church, The; Cathedral Age; Episcopal Church Annual, The; Forward Day by Day; Episcopal Life

The Estonian Evangelical Lutheran Church

For information on the Estonian Evangelical Lutheran Church (EELC), please see the listing in Chapter 4, "Religious Bodies in Canada."

Ethical Culture Movement

The American Ethical Union is a federation of Ethical Culture/Ethical Humanist Societies. Ethical Culture, founded in 1876 in New York by Felix Adler, is a humanistic religious and educational movement, based on the primacy of ethics, the belief in intrinsic worth of every human being and the faith in the capacity of human beings to act in their personal relationships and in the larger community to help create a better world.

HEADQUARTERS

2 West 64th St., New York, NY 10023 Tel. (212)873-6500

OFFICERS

Pres., Annabelle Glasser
Vice-Pres., Hank Gassner
Treas., Sophie Meyer
Sec., Stephanie Dohner
Admn., Margaretha E. Jones
Dir. Religious Educ./Growth & Development, Joy McConnell
Washington Ethical Action Ofc., Herb Blinder

ORGANIZATIONS

Natl. Leaders' Council, Chpsn., Joseph Chuman
Natl. Service Conference: Co-Pres., Jean S. Kotkin; Rose Walker
Intl. Humanist & Ethical Union: Reps., Dr. Matthew Ies Spetter; Joseph Chuman
Youth of Ethical Societies (YES), Youth Rep., Daniella Ballou

The Evangelical Church

The Evangelical Church was born June 4, 1968 in Portland, Ore., when 46 congregations and about 80 ministers, under the leadership of V. A. Ballantyne and George Millen, met in an organizing session. Within two weeks a group of about 20 churches and 30 ministers from the Evangelical United Brethren and Methodist churches in Montana and North Dakota became a part of the new church. Richard Kienitz and Robert Strutz were the superintendents.

Under the leadership of Superintendent Robert Trosen, the former Holiness Methodist Church became a part of the Evangelical Church in 1969, bringing its membership and a flourishing mission field in Bolivia. The Wesleyan Covenant Church joined in 1977, with its missionary work in Mexico, in Brownsville, Texas, and among the Navahos in New Mexico.

The Evangelical Church in Canada, where T. J. Jesske was superintendent, became an autonomous organization on June 5, 1970. In 1982, after years of discussions with the Evangelical Church of North America, a founding General Convention was held at Billings, Mont., where the two churches united. There are nearly 200 congregations, with the denominational office in Salem, Ore.

The following guide the life, program and devotion of this church: faithful, biblical, and sensible preaching and teaching of those truths proclaimed by scholars of the Wesleyan-Arminian viewpoint; an itinerant system which reckons with the rights of individuals and the desires of the congregation; local ownership of all church properties and assets.

The church is affiliated with the Christian Holiness Association, the National Association of Evangelicals, Wycliffe Bible Translators, World Gospel Mission and OMS International. The denomination has more than 200 missionaries.

HEADQUARTERS

Media Contact, Gen. Supt., John F. Sills, 3000 Market St., NE, Ste. 528, Salem, OR 97301 Tel. (503)371-4818 Fax (503)375-9646

OFFICERS

Gen. Supt., Rev. John F. Sills
Dir. of Missions, Rev. Duane Erickson

PERIODICALS

The Evangelical Advocate; Share; The Challenge

The Evangelical Congregational Church

This denomination had its beginning in the movement known as the Evangelical Association, organized by Jacob Albright in the early nineteenth century. In 1891 a division occurred in the Evangelical Association, which resulted in the organization of the United Evangelical Church in 1894. An attempt to heal this division was made in 1922, but a portion of the United Evangelical Church was not satisfied with the plan of merger and remained apart, taking the above name in 1928. This denomination is Arminian in doctrine, evangelistic in spirit, and Methodistic in church government, with congregational ownership of local church property.

Congregations are located from New Jersey to Illinois. A denominational center is located in Myerstown, Pa., as well as a retirement village and a seminary. Three summer youth camps and four camp meetings continue evangelistic outreach. A worldwide missions movement includes conferences in North East India, Liberia, Mexico and Japan. The denomination is a member of National Association of Evangelicals.

HEADQUARTERS

Evangelical Congregational Church Center, 100 W. Park Ave., P.O. Box 186, Myerstown, PA 17067 Fax (717)866-7581
Media Contact, Bishop, Rev. Richard W. Kohl, Tel. (717)-866-7581

OFFICERS

Presiding Bishop, Rev. Richard W. Kohl
1st Vice-Chpsn., Rev. Robert W. Daneker, Sr., 122 S. Emerson St., Allentown, PA 18104
Sec., Rev. Robert J. Stahl, RD 2, Box 1468, Schuylkill Haven, PA 17972
Asst. Sec.: Rev. Gregory Dimick, Hatfield, PA; Rev. Richard Reigle, Dixon, IL
Treas., Martha Metz
E.C.C. Retirement Village, Supt., Rev. Franklin H. Schock, Fax (717)866-6448
Evangelical School of Theology, Pres., Dr. Ray A. Seilhamer, Fax (717)866-4667

OTHER ORGANIZATIONS

Administrative Council, Chpsn., Bishop Richard W. Kohl
Div. of Evangelism & Spiritual Care, Chpsn., Bishop Richard W. Kohl
Div. of Church Ministries, Chpsn., Rev. Keith R. Miller
Div. of Church Services, Chpsn., Rev. Keith R. Miller
Div. of Missions, Chpsn., Rev. David G. Hornberger
Div. of Christian Ed., Chpsn., Dr. Donald Metz
Bd. of Pensions, Pres., Mr. Homer Luckenbill, Jr., Pine Grove, PA

PERIODICAL

Doors and Windows

The Evangelical Covenant Church

The Evangelical Covenant Church has its roots in historical Christianity as it emerged in the Protestant Reformation, in the biblical instruction of the Lutheran State Church of Sweden, and in the great spiritual awakenings of the 19th century.

The Covenant Church adheres to the affirmations of the Protestant Reformation regarding the Holy Scriptures, the Old and the New Testament as the Word of God and the only perfect rule for faith, doctrine, and conduct. It has traditionally valued the historic confessions of the Christian church, particularly the Apostles' Creed, while at the same time it has emphasized the sovereignty of the Word over all creedal interpretations. It has especially cherished the pietistic restatement of the doctrine of justification by faith as basic to its dual task of evangelism and Christian nurture, the New Testament emphasis upon personal faith in Jesus Christ, the reality of a fellowship of believers which recognizes but transcends theological differences, and the belief in baptism and the Lord's Supper as divinely ordained sacraments of the church.

While the denomination has traditionally practiced the baptism of infants, in conformity with its principle of freedom it has given room to divergent views. The principle of personal freedom, so highly esteemed by the Covenant, is to be distinguished from the individualism that disregards the centrality of the Word of God and the mutual responsibilities and disciplines of the spiritual community.

HEADQUARTERS

5101 N. Francisco Ave., Chicago, IL 60625 Tel. (312)784-3000 Fax (312)784-4366
Media Contact, Pres., Paul E. Larsen

OFFICERS

Pres., Dr. Paul E. Larsen
Vice-Pres., Rev. Timothy C. Ek
Sec., John R. Hunt
Treas., Dean A. Lundgren

ADMINISTRATIVE BOARDS

Bd. of Christian Educ. & Discipleship: Chpsn., Rev. Stanley Olsen; Exec. Sec., Rev. Evelyn M. R. Johnson
Bd. of Church Growth & Evangelism: Chpsn., Rev. Phillip K. Brockett; Exec. Sec., Dr. James E. Persson
Bd. of Covenant Women Ministries: Chpsn., Ms. Linda Stromberg; Exec. Sec., Rev. Deirdre M. Banks
Bd. of Human Resources: Chpsn., Sheldon Peterson
Bd. of the Ministry: Chpsn., Rev. Wendell E. Danielson; Exec. Sec., Rev. Donald A. Njaa
Bd. of Pensions: Chpsn., James E. Burk; Dir. of Pensions, John R. Hunt
Bd. of Publication: Chpsn., Robert K. DeVries; Exec. Sec., Rev. James R. Hawkinson
Bd. of World Mission: Chpsn., Robert H. Jones; Exec. Sec., Rev. Raymond L. Dahlberg
Bd. of Benevolence: Chpsn., William R. Ahlem, Jr.; Pres. of Covenant Benevolent Institutions, Rolland S. Carlson, 5145 N. California Ave., Chicago, IL 60625

PERIODICALS

Covenant Companion; Covenant Quarterly; Covenant Home Altar

The Evangelical Free Church of America

In October 1884, 27 representatives from Swedish churches met in Boone, Iowa, to establish the Swedish Evangelical Free Church. In the fall of that same year, two Norwegian-Danish groups began worship and fellowship (in Boston and in Tacoma) and by 1912 had established the Norwegian-Danish Evangelical Free Church Association. These two denominations, representing 275 congregations, came together at a merger conference in 1950.

The Evangelical Free Church is an association of local, autonomous churches across the United States and Canada, blended together around common principles, policies, and practices. A 12-point statement addresses the major doctrines, but also provides for differences of understanding on minor issues of faith and practice.

Overseas outreach includes 450 missionaries serving in 18 countries.

HEADQUARTERS

901 East 78th St., Minneapolis, MN 55420-1300 Tel. (612)854-1300 Fax (612)853-8488
Media Contact, Ex. Vice Pr., Rev. William Hamel

OFFICERS

Pres., Dr. Paul Cedar
Exec. Vice-Pres., Rev. William Hamel
Mod., Mr. Kenneth Larson, 3060 Centerville Rd., Little Canada, MN 55117

Vice-Mod., Rev. Joseph Bubar, Jr., RR 4, 3936 CTH "B", LaCrosse, WI 54601
Sec., Mrs. Betty Stattine, 2713 Abbott Ave. N., Minneapolis, MN 55422
Vice-Sec., Rev. William S. Wick, 92 South Main, Northfield, VT 05663
Treas., Mr. Robert Peterson, 901 E. 78th St., Minneapolis, MN 55420-1300
Exec. Dir., Evangelical Free Church Mission, Dr. Ben Swatsky
Exec. Dir. of Church Ministries, Rev. Bill Hull

PERIODICALS
Evangelical Beacon; Pursuit

Evangelical Friends International—North America Region

The organization restructured from Evangelical Friends Alliance in 1990 to become international-ized for the benefit of its world-wide contacts. The North America Region continues to function within the United States as EFA formerly did. The organization represents one corporate step of de-nominational unity, brought about as a result of several movements of spiritual renewal within the Society of Friends. These movements are: (1) the general evangelical renewal within Christianity, (2) the new scholarly recognition of the evangeli-cal nature of 17th-century Quakerism, and (3) EFA, which was formed in 1965.

The EFA is conservative in theology and makes use of local pastors. Sunday morning worship includes singing, Scripture reading, a period of open worship—usually—and a sermon by the pas-tor.

HEADQUARTERS
393 S. Vaughn Way, Aurora, CO 80012 Tel. (303)363-0116 Fax (303)363-0116
Media Contact, Regional Dir., Stanley Perisho

YEARLY MEETINGS
Evangelical Friends Church, Eastern Region, Ron Johnson, 5350 Broadmoor Cir., N.W., Canton, OH 44709 Tel. (216)493-1660 Fax (216)493-0852
Rocky Mountain YM, John Brawner, 3350 Reed St., Wheat Ridge, CO 80033 Tel. (303)238-5200 Fax (303)766-9609
Mid-America YM, Roscoe Townsend, 2018 Ma-ple, Wichita, KS 67213 Tel. (316)267-0391 Fax (316)263-1092
Northwest YM, Mark Ankeny, 200 N. Meridian St., Newberg, OR 97132 Tel. (503)538-9419 Fax (503)538-7033
Alaska YM, P.O. Box 687, Kotebue, AK 99752 Tel. (907)442-3906

Evangelical Lutheran Church in America

The Evangelical Lutheran Church in America (ELCA) was organized April 30-May 3, 1987, in Columbus, Ohio, bringing together the 2.3 mil-lion-member American Lutheran Church, the 2.9 million-member Lutheran Church in America, and the 100,000-member Association of Evangelical Lutheran Churches.

The ELCA is, through its predecessors, the old-est of the major U.S. Lutheran churches. In the mid-17th century, a Dutch Lutheran congregation was formed in New Amsterdam (now New York). Most of the oldest congregations were the result of early 18th-century German and Scandinavian im-migration to Delaware, Pennsylvania, the Hudson and Mohawk River Valleys in New York, and the Piedmont region of the Carolinas.

The first Lutheran association of congregations, the Pennsylvania Ministerium, was organized in 1748 under Henry Melchior Muhlenberg, known as the patriarch of American Lutheranism.

In 1820, a national federation of synods, the General Synod, was formed. A split in 1867 re-sulted in a second major body, the General Council. Earlier, as a result of the Civil War, southern synods had broken away to form the United Synod in the South. These three bodies were reunited in 1918 as the United Lutheran Church in America.

In 1960, the American Lutheran Church (ALC) was created through a merger of an earlier Ameri-can Lutheran Church, which was formed in 1930 by four synods that traced their roots primarily to German immigration; the Evangelical Lutheran Church, which dated from 1917 through churches chiefly of Norwegian ethnic heritage; and the United Evangelical Lutheran Church in America, which arose from Danish immigration. On Feb. 1, 1963, the Lutheran Free Church merged with the ALC.

In 1962, the Lutheran Church in America (LCA) was formed by a merger of the United Lutheran Church with the Augustana Lutheran Church, founded in 1860 by Swedish immigrants; the American Evangelical Lutheran Church, founded in 1872 by Danish immigrants; and the Finnish Lutheran Church or Suomi Synod, founded in 1891 by Finnish immigrants.

The Association of Evangelical Lutheran Churches arose in 1976 from a doctrinal split with the Lutheran Church-Missouri Synod.

The ELCA, through its predecessor church bod-ies, was a founding member of the Lutheran World Federation, the World Council of Churches, and the National Council of the Churches of Christ in the USA.

The church is divided into 65 geographical areas, or synods. These 65 synods, in turn, are grouped into nine regions for mission, joint programs, and service.

HEADQUARTERS
8765 W. Higgins Rd., Chicago, IL 60631 Tel. (312)380-2700
Media Contact, Dir. for News, Carolyn J. Lewis, Tel. (312)380-2957 Fax (312)380-1465

OFFICERS
Bishop, The Rev. Dr. Herbert W. Chilstrom
Sec., The Rev. Dr. Lowell G. Almen
Treas., Richard L. McAuliffe
Vice-Pres., Kathy J. Magnus
Exec. for Admn., Rev. Dr. Robert N. Bacher

DIVISIONS
Div. for Congregational Min.: Exec. Dir., Revs. Mark R. & Mary Ann Moller-Gunderson; Bd. Chpsn., Jim Myers; Lutheran Youth Organiza-tion, Pres., Tim Seitz
Div. for Higher Educ. & Schools: Exec. Dir., Rev. Dr. W. Robert Sorensen; Bd. Chpsn., Rev. Stephen P. Bauman
Div. for Global Mission: Exec. Dir., Rev. Dr. Mark W. Thomsen; Bd. Chpsn., Marjorie J. Carlson
Div. for Ministry: Exec. Dir., Rev. Dr. Joseph M. Wagner; Bd. Chpsn., Marybeth A. Peterson
Div. for Outreach: Exec. Dir., Rev. Dr. Malcolm L. Minnick, Jr.; Bd. Chpsn., Susan C. Barnard

Div. for Church in Society: Exec. Dir., Rev. Charles S. Miller; Chpsn., Ingrid Christiansen

COMMISSIONS

Comm. for Multicultural Ministries: Exec. Dir., Rev. Fred E.N. Rajan; Chpsn., Rev. Dr. Edmond Yee

Comm. for Women: Exec. Dir., Joanne Chadwick; Chpsn., Audrey R. Mortensen

CHURCHWIDE UNITS

Conference of Bishops: Dir., Rev. Dr. Thomas L. Blevins; Chpsn., Rev. Dr. Kenneth H. Sauer

ELCA Foundation: Exec. Dir., Rev. Dr. Harvey A. Stegemoeller; Bd. Chpsn., William R. Halling

ELCA Publishing House: Exec. Dir., Gary J. N. Aamodt; Bd. Chpsn., Rev. Dr. George H. Anderson

ELCA Bd. of Pensions: Exec. Dir., John G. Kapanke; Bd. Chpsn, Mildred M. Berg

Women of the ELCA: Exec. Dir., Charlotte E. Fiechter; Bd. Chpsn., Gwenn Carr

DEPARTMENTS

Dept. for Communication, Dir., Rev. Eric C. Shafer

Dept. for Ecumenical Affairs, Dir., Rev. Dr. William G. Rusch

Dept. for Human Resources, Dr., Rev. A. C. Stein

Dept. for Research & Evaluation, Dir., Kenneth W. Inskeep

Dept. for Synodical Relations, Dir., Rev. Dr. Thomas L. Blevins

SYNODICAL BISHOPS

Region 1

Alaska, Rev. Donald D. Parsons, 1836 W. Northern Lights Blvd., Anchorage, AK 99517-3342 Tel. (907)272-8899

Northwest Washington, Rev. Dr. Lowell E. Knutson, 5519 Pinney Ave. N, Seattle, WA 98103-5899 Tel. (206)783-9292

Southwestern Washington, Rev. David C. Wold, 420 121st St., S., Tacoma, WA 98444-5218 Tel. (206)535-8300

Eastern Washington-Idaho, Rev. Robert M. Keller, 314 South Spruce St., Ste. A, Spokane, WA 99204-1098 Tel. (509)838-9871

Oregon, Rev. Paul R. Swanson, 2801 N. Gantenbein Ave., Portland, OR 97227-1674 Tel. (503)280-4191

Montana, Rev. Dr. Mark R. Ramseth, 2415 13th Ave. S., Great Falls, MT 59405 Tel. (406)453-1461

Regional Coord., Ronald Coen, Region 1, 766-B John St., Seattle, WA 98109-5186 Tel. (206)624-0093

Region 2

Sierra Pacific, Rev. Lyle G. Miller, 401 Roland Way, #215, Oakland, CA 94621-2011 Tel. (510)430-0500

Southern California (West), Rev. J. Roger Anderson, 1340 S. Bonnie Brae St., Los Angeles, CA 90006-5416 Tel. (213)387-8183

Pacifica, Rev. Robert L. Miller, 23655 Via Del Rio, Ste. B, Yorba Linda, CA 92687-2718 Tel. (714)692-2791

Grand Canyon, Rev. Dr. Howard E. Wennes, 4423 N. 24th St., Ste. 400, Phoenix, AZ 85016-5544 Tel. (602)957-3223

Rocky Mountain, Rev. Dr. Wayne E. Weissenbuehler, ABS Bldg., #101, 7000 Broadway, Denver, CO 80211 Tel. (303)427-7553

THE YEAR IN IMAGES

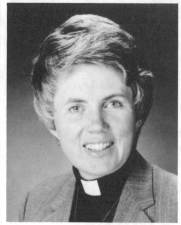

Religious News Service Photo

Lutherans elect first woman bishop

The Rev. April Larson, 42, became the first woman to be named a Lutheran bishop in the United States. On June 12, she was elected bishop of the LaCrosse Area Synod of the Evangelical Lutheran Church in America. She is one of 65 bishops in the 5.25-million-member ELCA.

Regional Coord., Rev. James E. Miley, Region 2, 2700 Chandler, Ste. A6, Las Vegas, NV 89120-4029 Tel. (702)798-3980

Region 3

Western North Dakota, Rev. Robert D. Lynne, 721 Memorial Way, P.O. Box 370, Bismarck, ND 58502-3070 Tel. (701)223-5312

Eastern North Dakota, Rev. Richard J. Foss, 1703 32nd Ave., S., Fargo, ND 58103-5936 Tel. (701)232-3381

South Dakota, Rev. Norman D. Eitrheim, Augustana College, Sioux Falls, SD 57197 Tel. (605)336-4011

Northwestern Minnesota, Rev. Dr. Arthur V. Rimmereid, P.O. Box 678, Moorhead, MN 56561-0678 Tel. (218)299-3019

Northeastern Minnesota, Rev. Roger L. Munson, 3900 London Rd., Duluth, MN 55804 Tel. (218)525-1947

Southwestern Minnesota, Rev. Charles D. Anderson, 175 E. Bridge St., P.O. Box 277, Redwood Falls, MN 56283 Tel. (507)637-3904

Minneapolis Area, Rev. David W. Olson, 122 W. Franklin Ave., Rm. 600, Minneapolis, MN 55404-2474 Tel. (612)870-3610

Saint Paul Area, Rev. Lowell O. Erdahl, 105 W. University Ave., St. Paul, MN 55103-2094 Tel. (612)224-4313

Southeastern Minnesota, Rev. Glenn W. Nycklemoe, Assisi Heights, 1001-14 St. NW, P.O. Box 4900, Rochester, MN 55903-4900 Tel. (507)280-9457

Regional Coord., Ms. Shirley A. Teig, Region 3, Brockman Hall, 2481 Como Ave., W. St. Paul, MN 55108 Tel. (612)649-0454

Region 4

Nebraska, Rev. Dr. Richard N. Jessen, 4980 S. 118th St., Ste. D, Omaha, NE 68137-2220 Tel. (402)896-5311

Central States, Rev. Dr. Charles H. Maahs, 6400 Glenwood, Ste. 210, Shawnee Mission, KS 66202 Tel. (913)362-0733

Arkansas-Oklahoma, Rev. Dr. Robert H. Studtmann, 4803 S. Lewis Ave., Tulsa, OK 74105-5199 Tel. (918)747-8517

Northern Texas-Northern Louisiana, Rev. Mark B. Herbener, 1230 Riverbend Dr., Ste. 105, P.O. Box 560587, Dallas, TX 75356-0587 Tel. (214)637-6865

Southwestern Texas, Rev. Henry Schulte, Jr., 1800 Northeast Loop 410, Ste. 202, P.O. Box 171270, San Antonio, TX 78217-8270 Tel. (210)824-0068

Southeastern Texas-Southern Louisiana, Rev. Paul J. Blom, 12707 N. Freeway, #580, Houston, TX 77060-1239 Tel. (713)873-5665

Regional Coord., Rev. Roger J. Gieschen, Region 4, 6901 W. 63rd St., Rm. 205, Overland Park, KS 66202 Tel. (913)831-3727

Region 5

Metropolitan Chicago, Rev. Sherman G. Hicks, 18 S. Michigan Ave., Rm. 605, Chicago, IL 60603-3283 Tel. (312)346-3150

Northern Illinois, Rev. Ronald K. Hasley, 103 W. State St., Rockford, IL 61101-1105 Tel. (815)964-9934

Central/Southern Illinois, Rev. Dr. John P. Kaitschuk, 1201 Veterans Pkwy., Ste. D, Springfield, IL 62704-6321 Tel. (217)546-7915

Southeastern Iowa, Rev. Dr. Paul M. Werger, 2635 Northgate Dr., P.O. Box 3167, Iowa City, IA 52244-3167 Tel. (319)388-1273

Western Iowa, Rev. Curtis H. Miller, 318 E. Fifth St., P.O. Box 1145, Storm Lake, IA 50588-2312 Tel. (712)732-4968

Northeastern Iowa, Rev. Steven L. Ullestad, 201-20th St. SW, P.O. Box 804, Waverly, IA 50677-0804 Tel. (319)352-1414

Northern Great Lakes, Rev. Dale R. Skogman, 1029 N. Third St., Marquette, MI 49855 Tel. (906)228-2300

Northwest Synod of Wisconsin, Rev. Gerhard I. Knutson, 12 W. Marshall St., P.O. Box 730, Rice Lake, WI 54868-0730 Tel. (715)234-3373

East-Central Synod of Wisconsin, Rev. Dr. Robert H. Herder, 3003B N. Richmond St., Appleton, WI 54911 Tel. (414)734-5381

Greater Milwaukee, Rev. Peter Rogness, 1212 S. Layton Blvd., Milwaukee, WI 53215-1653 Tel. (414)671-1212

South-Central Synod of Wisconsin, Rev. Dr. Jon S. Enslin, 2705 Packers Ave., Madison, WI 53704-3085 Tel. (608)249-4848

LaCrosse Area, Rev. April C. O. Larson, 2350 S. Ave., LaCrosse, WI 54601 Tel. (608)788-5000

Regional Coord., Rev. Edward F. Weiskotten, Region 5, 333 Wartburg Pl., Dubuque, IA 52003-7797 Tel. (319)589-0312

Region 6

Southeast Michigan, Rev. J. Philip Wahl, 19711 Greenfield Rd., Detroit, MI 48235 Tel. (313)837-3522

North/West Lower Michigan, Rev. Dr. Reginald H. Holle, 801 S. Waverly Rd., Ste. 201, Lansing, MI 48917 Tel. (517)321-5066

Indiana-Kentucky, Rev. Dr. Ralph A. Kempski, 9102 N. Meridian St., Ste. 405, Indianapolis, IN 46260-1809 Tel. (317)846-4026

Northwestern Ohio, Rev. James A. Rave, 621 Bright Rd., Findlay, OH 45840-6987 Tel. (419)423-3664

Northeastern Ohio, Rev. Dr. Robert W. Kelley, 282 W. Bowery, 3rd Fl., Akron, OH 44307-2598 Tel. (216)253-1500

Southern Ohio, Rev. Dr. Kenneth H. Sauer, 57 E. Main St., Columbus, OH 43215-7102 Tel. (614)464-3532

Regional Coord., Rev. Hermann J. Kuhlmann, 6100 Channingway Blvd., Ste. 503, Columbus, OH 43232 Tel. (614)759-9090

Region 7

New Jersey, Rev. E. Leroy Riley, Jr., 1930 State Hwy. 33, Trenton, NJ 08690-1714 Tel. (609)586-6800

New England, Rev. Robert L. Isaksen, 90 Madison St., Ste. 303, Worcester, MA 01608-2030 Tel. (508)791-1530

Metropolitan New York, Rev. James E. Sudbrock, 360 Park Ave., S., 7th Floor, New York, NY 10016-8803 Tel. (212)532-6350

Upstate New York, Rev. Dr. Lee M. Miller, 3049 E. Genesee St., Syracuse, NY 13224 Tel. (315)446-2502

Northeastern Pennsylvania, Rev. Dr. Harold S. Weiss, 4865 Hamilton Blvd., Wescosville, PA 18106-9705 Tel. (215)395-6891

Southeastern Pennsylvania, Rev. Michael G. Merkel, 4700 Wissahickon Ave., Philadelphia, PA 19144 Tel. (215)438-0600

Slovak Zion, Rev. Dr. Kenneth E. Zindle, 6605 MacArthur Dr., Woodridge, IL 60517 Tel. (708)810-9786

Regional Coord., Rev. George E. Handley, Region 7, Hagan Hall, 7301 Germantown Ave., Philadelphia, PA 19119 Tel. (215)248-4616

Region 8

Northwestern Pennsylvania, Rev. Paull E. Spring, Rte. 257, Salina Rd., P.O. Box 338, Seneca, PA 16346-0338 Tel. (814)677-5706

Southwestern Pennsylvania, Rev. Donald J. McCoid, 9625 Perry Hwy., Pittsburgh, PA 15237-5590 Tel. (412)367-8222

Allegheny, Rev. Gerald E. Miller, 701 Quail Ave., Altoona, PA 16602-3010 Tel. (814)942-1042

Lower Susquehanna, Rev. Dr. Guy S. Edmiston, Jr., 900 S. Arlington Ave., Rm. 208, Harrisburg, PA 17109-5031 Tel. (717)652-1852

Upper Susquehanna, Rev. Dr. A. Donald Main, Rt. 192 & Reitz Blvd., P.O. Box 36, Lewisburg, PA 17837-0036 Tel. (717)524-9778

Delaware-Maryland, Rev. Dr. George P. Mocko, 7604 York Rd., Baltimore, MD 21204-7570 Tel. (410)825-9520

Metropolitan Washington, D.C., Rev. Dr. E. Harold Jansen, 224 E. Capitol St., Washington, DC 20003-1036 Tel. (202)543-8610

West Virginia-Western Maryland, Rev. L. Alexander Black, The Atrium, Ste. 100, 503 Morgantown Avenue, Fairmont, WV 26554-4374 Tel. (304)363-4030

Regional Coord., Int. Dir., Rev. Robert L. Baughan, Jr., United Church Center, 900 S. Arlington Ave., Rm. 210, Harrisburg, PA 17109 Tel. (717)652-6001

Region 9

Virginia, Rev. Richard F. Bansemer, Roanoke College, Bittle Hall, P.O. Drawer 70, Salem, VA 24153 Tel. (703)389-1000

North Carolina, Rev. Dr. Mark W. Menees, 1988 Lutheran Synod Dr., Salisbury, NC 28144 Tel. (704)633-4861

South Carolina, Rev. Dr. James S. Aull, 1003 Richland St., P.O. Box 43, Columbia, SC 29202-0043 Tel. (803)765-0590

Southeastern, Rev. Dr. Harold C. Skillrud, 756 W. Peachtree St. NW, Atlanta, GA 30308-1188 Tel. (404)873-1977

Florida-Bahamas, Rev. Lavern G. Franzen, 3838 W. Cypress St., Tampa, FL 33607-4897 Tel. (813)876-7660

Caribbean, Rev. Rafael Malpica-Padilla, P.O. Box 14426, Barrio-Obrero Station, Santurce, PR 00916 Tel. (809)727-6015

Regional Coord., Dr. Dorothy L. Jeffcoat, Region 9, 4201 N. Main St., Columbia, SC 29203 Tel. (803)754-2879

PERIODICAL

Lutheran, The

Evangelical Lutheran Synod

The Evangelical Lutheran Synod had its beginning among the Norwegian settlers who brought with them their Lutheran heritage and established it in this country. It was organized in 1853. It was reorganized in 1918 by those who desired to adhere to these principles not only in word, but also in deed.

The Synod owns and operates Bethany Lutheran College and Bethany Lutheran Theological Seminary. It has congregations in 20 states and maintains foreign missions in Peru, Czechoslovakia, Chile, and Ukraine. It operates a seminary in Lima, Peru.

HEADQUARTERS

The Evangelical Lutheran Synod, 447 N. Division St., Mankato, MN 56001

Media Contact, Pres., Rev. George Orvick, Tel. (507)388-4868 Fax (507)625-1849

OFFICERS

Pres., Rev. George Orvick, 447 Division St., Mankato, MN 56001 Tel. (507)388-4868 Fax (507)625-1849

Sec., Rev. Alf Merseth, 106 13th St. S., Northwood, IA 50459

Treas., Mr. LeRoy W. Meyer, 1038 S. Lewis Ave., Lombard, IL 60148

OTHER ORGANIZATIONS

Lutheran Synod Book Co., Bethany Lutheran College, Mankato, MN 56001

PERIODICALS

Lutheran Sentinel; Lutheran Synod Quarterly

Evangelical Mennonite Church

The Evangelical Mennonite Church is an American denomination in the European free church tradition. It traces its heritage directly to the early Reformation period of the 16th century, to a group known as Swiss Brethren, who believed that salvation could come only by repentance for sins and faith in Jesus Christ; that baptism was only for believers; and that the church should be separate from controls of the state. Their enemies called them Anabaptists, since they insisted on rebaptizing believers who had been baptized as infants. As the Anabaptist movement spread to other countries, Menno Simons, formerly a Dutch Roman Catholic priest, became its principal leader. In time his followers were called Mennonites.

In 1693 a Mennonite minister, Jacob Amman, insisted that the church should adopt a more conservative position on dress and style of living, and should more rigidly enforce the "ban" — the church's method of disciplining disobedient members. Amman's insistence finally resulted in a division within the South German Mennonite groups; his followers became known as the Amish. Migrations to America, involving both Mennonites and Amish, took place in the 1700s and 1800s, for both religious and economic reasons.

The Evangelical Mennonite Church was formed in 1866, out of a spiritual awakening among the Amish in Indiana, and was first known as the Egly Amish, after its founder Bishop Henry Egly. A preacher in an Amish congregation in Berne, Ind., Egly underwent a spiritual experience in 1864 and began to emphasize regeneration, separation, and nonconformity to the world. His willingness to rebaptize anyone who had been baptized without repentance created a split in his church, prompting him to gather a new congregation in 1866. The conference, which has met annually since 1895, united a number of other congregations of like mind. This group became The Defenseless Mennonite Church in 1898, and has been known as the Evangelical Mennonite Church since 1948.

HEADQUARTERS

1420 Kerrway Ct., Fort Wayne, IN 46805 Tel. (219)423-3649

Media Contact, Pres., Rev. Donald W. Roth

OFFICERS

Pres., Rev. Donald W. Roth

Chpsn., Rev. Douglas R. Habegger, 1033 Lee, Morton, IL 61550

Vice-Chpsn., Rev. Roger Andrews, 11275 Eckel Junction Rd., Perrysburg, OH 43551

Sec., Jerry Lugbill, 320 Short-Buehrer Rd., Archbold, OH 43502

Treas., Alan L. Rupp, 5724 Spring Oak Ct., Ft. Wayne, IN 46845

PERIODICAL

EMC Today

Evangelical Methodist Church

Organized 1946 at Memphis, Tenn., largely as a movement of people who opposed modern liberalism and wished for a return to the historic Wesleyan position. In 1960, it merged with the Evangel Church (formerly Evangelistic Tabernacles), and with the People's Methodist Church in 1962.

HEADQUARTERS

3000 West Kellogg, Wichita, KS 67213 Tel. (316)943-3278

Media Contact, Gen. Conf. Sec.-Treas., Vernon W. Perkins, Fax (316)943-5939

OFFICERS

Gen. Supt., Rev. Clyde Zehr

Gen. Conf. Sec.-Treas., Rev. Vernon W. Perkins

Evangelical Presbyterian Church

The Evangelical Presbyterian Church (EPC), established in March 1981, is a conservative denomination of 11 geographic presbyteries — 10 in the United States, and one in Argentina. From its inception, with 12 churches, the EPC has grown to 180 churches with a membership of over 56,000.

Planted firmly within the historic Reformed tradition, evangelical in spirit, the EPC places high priority on church planting and development along with world missions. Thirty-five missionary families serve the church's mission.

Based on the truth of Scripture and adhering to the Westminster Confession of Faith plus its Book of Order, the denomination is committed to the "essentials of the faith." The historic motto "In essentials, unity; In nonessentials, liberty; In all things charity" catches the irenic spirit of the EPC, along with the Ephesians theme, "truth in love."

The Evangelical Presbyterian Church is a member of the World Alliance of Reformed Churches, National Association of Evangelicals, World Evangelical Fellowship, and the Evangelical Council for Financial Accountability. Observers annually attend the North American Presbyterian and Reformed Council (NAPARC).

HEADQUARTERS

Office of the General Assembly, 29140 Buckingham Ave., Ste. 5, Livonia, MI 48154 Tel. (313)261-2001 Fax (313)261-3282

Media Contact, Stated Clk., Dr. L. Edward Davis, 29140 Buckingham Ave., Ste. 5, Livonia, MI 48154 Tel. (313)261-2001 Fax (313)261-3282

OFFICERS

Mod., Mr. John Adamson, Second Presbyterian Church, 4055 Poplar Ave., Memphis, TN 38111

Stated Clk., Dr. L. Edward Davis

PERMANENT COMMITTEES

Committee on Admn., Chmn., Dr. William Flannagan, First Presbyterian Church, 101 E. Third Ave., Rome, GA 30161

Committee on Church Development, Chmn., Rev. Douglas Klein, Grace Chapel, 23233 Drake Rd., Farmington Hills, MI 48024

Committee on World Outreach, Chmn., Dr. Perry Mobley, Central Presbyterian Church, 7700 Davis Dr., St. Louis, MO 63105

Committee on Fraternal Relations, Chmn., Rev. Mark Brewer, Ward Presbyterian Church, 17000 Farmington Road, Livonia, MI 48154

Committee on Ministerial Vocation, Chmn., Rev. Malcolm Brown, Covenant Presbyterian Ch., P.O. Box 7269, Ann Arbor, MI 48107

Comm. on Christian Educ. & Publ., Chmn., Dr. Robert Bayley, Myrtle Grove Presbyterian Ch., 800 Piner Rd., Wilmington, NC 28409

Committee on Women's Ministries, Chmn., Ms. Susan Nash, Second Presbyterian Church, 4055 Poplar Ave., Memphis, TN 38111

Committee on Theology, Chmn., Mr. Philip Tiews, Covenant Presbyterian Church, P.O. Box 7087, Ann Arbor, MI 48107

Committee on Youth Ministries, Chmn., Rev. Rhett Payne, Grace Church (EPC), 4951 Airport Parkway #803, Dallas, TX 75248

PRESBYTERIES

Allegheny, Stated Clk., Rev. David Anderson, Perrow Presbyterian Church, 5245 Big Tyler Rd., Cross Lanes, WV 25313

Central South, Stated Clk., Rev. Michael Swain, First Presbyterian Church, P.O. Box 366, West Point, MS 39773

East, Stated Clk., Mr. Richard Bingham, 95 Prospect Ave., Maybrook, NY 12543

Far West, Stated Clk., Rev. James Brown, Jr., Santa Maria Community Church, 210 W. Fesler, Santa Maria, CA 93454

Florida, Stated Clk., Rev. Robert Garment, Trinity EPC, 5150 Oleander, Ft. Pierce, FL 34982

Mid-America, Stated Clk., Mr. Kenneth Breckner, 7500 Wydown Blvd., St. Louis, MO 64105

Mid-Atlantic, Stated Clk., Mr. Llew Fischer, 3164 Golf Colony Dr., Salem, VA 24153

Midwest, Stated Clk., Mr. Robert Sanborn

Southeast, Stated Clk., Rev. Ronald Ragon, Brainerd Presbyterian Church, 7 N. Tuxedo, Chattanooga, TN 37411

West, Stated Clk., Mr. Claude Russell, Faith Presbyterian Church, 11373 E. Alameda Ave., Aurora, CO 80012

St. Andrews, Stated Clk., Mr. Freddie Berk, Iglesia Presbiteriana San Andres, Peru 352, 1067 Buenos Aires, Argentina

Fellowship of Evangelical Bible Churches

Formerly known as Evangelical Mennonite Brethren, this body emanates from the Russian immigration of Mennonites into the United States, 1873-74. Established with the emphasis on true repentance, conversion, and a committed life to Jesus as Savior and Lord, the conference was founded in 1889 under the leadership of Isaac Peters and Aaron Wall. The founding churches were located in Mountain Lake, Minn., and in Henderson and Janzen, Neb. The conference has since grown to a fellowship of 36 churches with approximately 4,400 members in Argentina, Canada, Paraguay, and the United States.

Foreign missions have been a vital ingredient of the total ministry. Today missions constitute about 75 percent of the total annual budget, with one missionary for every 30 members in the home churches. The conference does not develop and administer foreign mission fields of its own, but actively participates with existing evangelical "faith" mission societies. The conference has representation on several mission boards and has missionaries serving under approximately 32 different agencies around the world.

The church is holding fast to the inerrancy of Scripture, the Deity of Christ, the need for spiritual regeneration of man from his sinful natural state, by faith in the death, burial, and resurrection of Jesus Christ as payment for sin. They look forward to the imminent return of Jesus Christ and retain a sense of urgency to share the gospel with those who have never heard of God's redeeming love.

HEADQUARTERS

5800 S. 14th St., Omaha, NE 68107 Tel. (402)731-4780

OFFICERS

Pres., Rev. Melvin Epp, RR 1, Wymark, SK S0N 2Y0

Vice-Pres., Mr. Stan Seifert, 2732 Springhill St., Clearbrook, BC V2T 3V9

Rec. Sec., Mr. Ruben Dyck, 7324 Jefferson St., Omaha, NE 68127

Admn. Sec., Robert L. Frey, 5800 S. 14th, Omaha, NE 68107

Commission on Churches, Chpsn., Dr. J. Paul Nyquist, 7820 Fort St., Omaha, NE 68134

Commission on Missions, Chpsn., Rev. Allan Wiebe, 1104 Day Dr., Omaha, NE 68005

Commission of Trustees, Chpsn., Mr. Neil C. J. DeRuiter, 298 Regal Ave., Winnipeg, MB R2M 0P5

Commission on Educ. & Publ., Chpsn., Mr. Joel Penner, Rte. 1, Box 55, Butterfield, MN 56120

Commission on Church Planting, Chpsn., Rev. Randy Smart, Box 1446, Winkler, MB R0G 2X0

Gospel Tidings

Fellowship of Fundamental Bible Churches

This body, until 1985, was called the Bible Protestant Church. The FFBC is a fellowship of fundamental Bible-believing local autonomous churches which believe in an inerrant and infallible Bible, is dispensational as related to the study of the Scriptures, espouses the pre-Tribulation Rapture, and is premillenial. The FFBC is evangelistic and missions-oriented. It regards itself as separatistic in areas of personal life and ecclesiastical association and believes that Baptism by immersion of believers most adequately reflects the symbolic truth of death and resurrection with Christ.

The Fellowship of Fundamental Bible Churches relates historically to the Eastern Conference of the Methodist Protestant Church, which changed its name to Bible Protestant Church at the 2nd Annual Session, held in Westville, N.J., Sept. 26-30, 1940.

HEADQUARTERS

P.O. Box 43, Glassboro, NJ 08028
Media Contact, Natl. Rep., Rev. Harold E. Haines, Tel. (609)881-5516

OFFICERS

Pres., Rev. Mark Franklin, RD 1 Box 300, Monroeville, NJ 08343 Tel. (609)881-0057
Vice-Pres., Rev. Edmund Coton, P.O. Box 31, Cassville, PA 16623 Tel. (814)448-3394
Sec., Rev. A. Glenn Doughty, 134 Delsea Dr., Westville, NJ 08093 Tel. (609)456-3791
Asst. Sec., Rev. Albert Martin, 195 East Front St., Atco, NJ 08004 Tel. (609)767-9376
Treas., Mr. William Rainey, RD 1 Box 302, Monroeville, NJ 08343 Tel. (609)881-4790
Stat. Sec., Rev. James Korth, 237 W. Main St., Moorestown, NJ 08057 Tel. (609)235-8077
Natl. Rep., Rev. Howard E. Haines, Tel. (609)881-5516

PERIODICAL

Skopeo

The Fire Baptized Holiness Church (Wesleyan)

This church came into being about 1890 as the result of definite preaching on the doctrine of holiness in some Methodist churches in southeastern Kansas. It became known as The Southeast Kansas Fire Baptized Holiness Association. The name was changed in 1945 to The Fire Baptized Holiness Church. It is entirely Wesleyan in doctrine, episcopal in church organization, and intensive in evangelistic zeal.

HEADQUARTERS

600 College Ave., Independence, KS 67301 Tel. (316)331-3049
Media Contact, Gen. Supt., Gerald Broadaway

OFFICERS

Gen. Supt., Gerald Broadaway
Gen. Sec., Wayne Knipmeyer, Box 457, South Pekin, IL 61564
Gen. Treas., Victor White, 709 N. 13th, Independence, KS 67301

PERIODICALS

Flaming Sword, The; John Three Sixteen

Free Christian Zion Church of Christ

Organized 1905, at Redemption, Ark., by a company of African-American ministers associated with various denominations, with polity in general accord with that of Methodist bodies.

HEADQUARTERS

1315 S. Hutchinson St., Nashville, AR 71852 Tel. (501)845-4933
Media Contact, Gen. Sec., Shirlie Cheatham

OFFICER

Chief Pastor, Willie Benson, Jr.

Free Lutheran Congregations, The Association of

The Association of Free Lutheran Congregations, rooted in the Scandinavian revival movements, was organized in 1962 by a Lutheran Free Church remnant which rejected merger with The American Lutheran Church. The original 42 congregations were joined by other like-minded conservative Lutherans, especially from the former Evangelical Lutheran Church and the Suomi Synod. There has been a fourfold increase in the number of congregations. Congregations subscribe to the Apostles', Nicene, and Athanasian creeds; Luther's Small Catechism; and the Unaltered Augsburg Confession. The Fundamental Principles and Rules for Work (1897), declare that the local congregation is the right form of the kingdom of God on earth, subject to no authority but the Word and the Spirit of God.

Distinctive emphases are: (1) the infallibility and inerrancy of Holy Scriptures as the Word of God; (2) congregational polity; (3) the spiritual unity of all believers, resulting in fellowship and cooperation transcending denominational lines; (4) evangelical outreach, calling all to enter a personal relationship with Jesus Christ; (5) a wholesome Lutheran pietism that proclaims the Lordship of Jesus Christ in all areas of life and results in believers becoming the salt and light in their communities; (6) a conservative stance on current social issues.

A two-year Bible school and a theological seminary are in suburban Minneapolis. Support is channeled to churches in Brazil, Mexico, and Canada.

HEADQUARTERS

3110 E. Medicine Lake Blvd., Minneapolis, MN 55441 Tel. (612)545-5631 Fax (612)545-0079
Media Contact, Pres., Rev. Robert L. Lee

OFFICERS

Pres., Rev. Robert L. Lee
Sec., Rev. Ron Knutson, Rt. 2, Box 2251, Branton, SD 57005

PERIODICAL

Lutheran Ambassador, The

Free Methodist Church of North America

The Free Methodist Church was organized in 1860 in Western New York by ministers and laymen who had called the Methodist Episcopal Church to return to what they considered the original doctrines and lifestyle of Methodism. The issues included human freedom (anti-slavery), freedom and simplicity in worship, free seats so that the poor would not be discriminated against, and freedom from secret oaths (societies) so the truth might be spoken freely at all times. They emphasized the teaching of the entire sanctification of life by means of grace through faith.

The denomination continues to be true to its founding principles. It communicates the gospel and its power to all people without discrimination through strong missionary, evangelistic, and educational programs. Six colleges, a Bible college, and numerous overseas schools train the youth of the church to serve in lay and ministerial roles.

Its members covenant to maintain simplicity in life and worship, daily devotion to Christ, and responsible stewardship of time, talent, and finance.

HEADQUARTERS

World Ministries Center: 770 N. High School Rd., Indianapolis, IN 46214 Tel. (317)244-3660 Fax (317)244-1247

Mailing Address, P.O. Box 535002, Indianapolis, IN 46253 Tel. (800)342-5531

Media Contact, Yearbook Ed., P.O. Box 535002, Indianapolis, IN 46253

OFFICERS

Bishops: Gerald E. Bates; David M. Foster; Bya'ene Akulu Ilangyi; Noah Nzeyimana; Daniel Ward; Richard D. Snyder

Gen. Conf. Sec., Melvin J. Spencer

Finance & Admn., Gen. Dir., Gary M. Kilgore

Christian Educ., Gen. Dir., Daniel L. Riemenschneider

Evangelism & Church Growth, Gen. Dir., Raymond W. Ellis

Free Methodist Publishing House, Gen. Dir., John E. Van Valin

Higher Education, Gen. Sec., Bruce L. Kline

Light & Life Magazine, Ed., Robert B. Haslam

Light & Life Men Intl., Exec. Dir., Lucien E. Behar

Free Methodist Foundation, Stanley B. Thompson

Women's Ministries Intl., Pres., Mrs. Carolyn Ellis

World Missions, Gen. Dir., M. Doane Bonney

Free Will Baptists, National Association of

This evangelical group of Arminian Baptists was organized by Paul Palmer in 1727 at Chowan, N.C. Another movement (teaching the same doctrines of free grace, free salvation, and free will) was organized June 30, 1780, in New Durham, N.H., but there was no connection with the southern organization except for a fraternal relationship.

The northern line expanded more rapidly and extended into the West and Southwest. This body merged with the Northern Baptist Convention Oct. 5, 1911, but a remnant of churches reorganized into the Cooperative General Association of Free Will Baptists Dec. 28, 1916, at Pattonsburg, Mo.

Churches in the southern line were organized into various conferences from the beginning and finally united in one General Conference in 1921.

Representatives of the Cooperative General Association and the General Conference joined Nov. 5, 1935 to form the National Association of Free Will Baptists.

HEADQUARTERS

5233 Mt. View Rd., Antioch, TN 37013-2306 Tel. (615)731-6812 Fax (615)731-0049

Mailing Address, P.O. Box 5002, Antioch, TN 37011-5002

Media Contact, Exec. Sec., Melvin Worthington

OFFICERS

Exec. Sec., Dr. Melvin Worthington

Mod., Rev. Ralph Hampton, P.O. Box 50117, Nashville, TN 37205

DENOMINATIONAL AGENCIES

Free Will Baptist Foundation, Exec. Sec., Herman Hersey

Free Will Baptist Bible College, Pres., Dr. Tom Malone

Foreign Missions Dept., Dir., Rev. R. Eugene Waddell

Home Missions Dept., Dir., Rev. Roy Thomas

Bd. of Retirement, Dir., Rev. Herman Hersey

Historical Commission, Chpsn., Mary Wisehart

Commission for Theological Integrity, Chpsn., Rev. Leroy Forlines, P.O. Box 50117, Nashville, TN 37205

Music Commission, Chpsn., Vernon Whaley, P.O. Box 50117, Nashville, TN 37205

Radio & Television Commission, Chpsn., Bob Shockey, P.O. Box 50117, Nashville, TN 37205

Sunday School & Church Training Dept., Dir., Dr. Roger Reeds

Woman's National Auxiliary Convention, Exec. Sec., Dr. Mary R. Wisehart

Master's Men Dept., Dir., Mr. James Vallance

PERIODICALS

Contact; Free Will Bible College Bulletin; Co-Laborer; Free Will Baptist Gem; Heartbeat; Mission Grams

Friends General Conference

Friends General Conference is an association of yearly meetings within the Religious Society of Friends, open to all Friends meetings which wish to be actively associated with its programs and services. It was organized in 1900, bringing together four associations, including the First-day School Conference (1868) and the Friends Union for Philanthropic Labor (1882).

Friends General Conference is primarily a service organization and has no authority over constituent meetings. A Central Committee, to which constituent yearly meetings name appointees approximately in proportion to membership, or its Executive Committee, is responsible for the direction of the FGC's year-round services.

There are seven standing program committees: Advancement & Outreach, Christian & Interfaith Relations, Long Range Conference Planning, Ministry & Nurture, Publications & Distribution, Religious Education, and Friends Meeting House Fund.

HEADQUARTERS

1216 Arch St., 2B, Philadelphia, PA 19107 Tel. (215)561-1700

Media Contact, Gen. Sec., Bruce Birchard

OFFICERS

Gen. Sec., Bruce Birchard

Clk., Tyla Ann Burger

Treas., David Miller

YEARLY MEETINGS

Philadelphia, Edwin Staudt, 1515 Cherry St., Philadelphia, PA 19102

Lake Erie, Patricia Campbell, 710 Indianola Ave., Ann Arbor, MI 48105 Tel. (313)668-8865

*New England, Elizabeth Cazden, 118 Walnut St., Manchester, NH 03014 Tel. (603)622-9835

*New York, George Rubin, 545 Rockland St., Westbury, NY 11590 Tel. (516)977-9665

*Baltimore, Miriam D. Green, 316 Rossiter Ave., Baltimore, MD 21212 Tel. (410)435-2528

*Canadian, Elaine Bishop, Box 5333, Peace River, AB T85 I9R Tel. (403)629-3745

Illinois, Jerry Nurenberg, 60255 Myrtle Rd., South Bend, IN 46614 Tel. (219)232-5729

Ohio Valley, Ellen Armontine Hodge, 4240 Cornelius Ave., Indianapolis, IN 46208 Tel. (612)879-2835

South Central, Dan O'Brien, 1007 NW 32nd St., Oklahoma City, OK 73118 Tel. (405)521-8720

*Southeastern, Ken Leibman, 4545 Highway 346, Archer, FL 32618 Tel. (904)495-9482

Northern, Jim Greenley, 1909 Vilas Ave., Madison, WI 53711 Tel. (608)251-0372

Piedmont FF, Ralph McCracken, 913 Ridgecrest Dr., Greensboro, NC 27410-3237 Tel. (919)292-8631

Southern Appalachian & Assoc., Peggy Bonnington, 408 West Coy Cir., Clarksville, TN 37043 Tel. (615)647-9284

Central Alaska, Jan Pohl, P.O. Box 22316, Juneau, AK 99802

* also affiliated with Friends United Meeting

PERIODICAL

Focus

Friends United Meeting

Friends United Meeting was organized in 1902 (originally Five Years Meeting of Friends, the name was changed in 1963) as a loose confederation of North American yearly meetings to facilitate a united Quaker witness in missions, peace work, and Christian education.

Today Friends United Meeting is comprised of 18 member yearly meetings (12 North American plus Cuba, East Africa, East Africa Yearly Meeting (South), Elgon Religious Society of Friends, Nairobi, and Jamaica yearly meetings) representing about half the Friends in the world. FUM's current work includes programs of mission and service, congregational renewal, and the publication of Christian education curriculum, books of Quaker history and religious thought, and a magazine, *Quaker Life*.

HEADQUARTERS

101 Quaker Hill Dr., Richmond, IN 47374 Tel. (317)962-7573 Fax (317)966-1293
Media Contact, Gen. Sec., Johan Maurer

OFFICERS

Presiding Clk., Sarah Wilson
Treas., John Norris
Gen. Sec., Johan Maurer

DEPARTMENTS

World Ministries Commission, Assoc. Sec., Bill Wagoner
Meeting Ministries Commission, Assoc. Sec., Mary Glenn Hadley
Quaker Hill Bookstore, Mgr., Dick Talbot
Friends United Press, Ed., Ardith Talbot

YEARLY MEETINGS

Nebraska, Dean Young, 253 S. Lorraine, Wichita, KS 67211

*New England, Elizabeth Cazden, 118 Walnut St., Manchester, NH 03104 Tel. (603)622-9835

*New York, George Rubin, 545 Rockland St., Westbury, NY 11590 Tel. (516)997-9665

*Baltimore, Miriam Green, 316 Rossiter Ave., Baltimore, MD 21212

Iowa, Louise Davis, 1644 140th St., Clemons, IA 50051

Western, Lester Paulsen, 2025 Redfern Dr., Indianapolis, IN 46227

North Carolina, Carter Pike, RR 5, Box 96, Asheboro, NC 27203

Indiana, Don Garner, 471 W 1125 S, Fairmont, IN 46928

Wilmington, Rudy Haag, P.O. Box 19, Cuba, OH 45114

Cuba, Maulio Ajo Berencen, Libertad 114, c/o Argamente & Garayalde, Holguin 80100, Holguin, Cuba

*Canadian, Elaine Bishop, Box 5333, Peace River, AB T8S 1R9

Jamaica, Angela Johnson, 4 Worthington Ave., Kingston 5, Jamaica, W.I.

*Southeastern, Ken Leibman, 15413 SW 107th St., Archer, FL 32618 Tel. (904)495-9482

Southwest, Lind Coop, 6521 Washington Ave., Whittier, CA 90601

East Africa, James Ashihunde, P.O. Box 1510, Kakamega, Kenya

East Africa (South), Joseph Kisia, P.O. Box 160, Vihiga, Kenya

Nairobi, Stanley Ndezwa, P.O. Box 377, Nakuru, Kenya

Elgon Religious Society of Friends, Elisha Wakube, P.O. Box 98, Kimilili, Kenya, East Africa

* also affiliated with Friends Gen. Conference

PERIODICAL

Quaker Life

Full Gospel Assemblies International

This Pentecostal body had its beginning in 1972 as an adjunct to an established school of biblical studies known as Full Gospel Bible Institute under the leadership of Dr. Charles E. Strauser.

HEADQUARTERS

P.O. Box 1230, Coatesville, PA 19320 Tel. (215)857-2357

OFFICERS

Pres., Dr. Charles E. Strauser
Asst., Dr. Annamae Strauser
Executive Board: Dr. C. E. Strauser; Dr. Annamae Strauser; Rev. Simeon Strauser; Carol Ann Strauser
Sec., Betty B. Stewart
Board of Directors: Rev. Harold Oswold, 340 Rand St., Rochester, NY 14611; Rev. Simeon Strauser, Box 26, Sadsburyville, PA 19369; Dr. Samuel Strauser, Box 450, Delaware Water Gap, PA 18327; Rev. Richard Hartman, 4001 Elmerton Ave., Harrisburg, PA 17109; Rev. David Alessi, P.O. Box 168, Dunkirk, NY 14048; Rev. James Scott, P.O. Box 93, Mad River, CA 95552; Rev. Marilyn Allen, 5204 A5 Kissing Camels Dr., Colorado Springs, CO 80904; Rev. Victor Fisk, 398 Gill Rd., Apollo, PA 15613

PERIODICALS

Charisma Courier, The; Pentecost Today

Full Gospel Fellowship of Churches and Ministers International

In the early 1960s, a conviction grew in the hearts of many ministers that there ought to be closer fellowship between the people of God who believed in the apostolic ministry. Also, a great number of independent churches were experiencing serious difficulties in receiving authority from the IRS to give governmentally accepted tax-exempt receipts for donations.

In September 1962, a group of ministers met in Dallas, Texas, to form a Fellowship to give expression to the essential unity of the Body of Christ under the leadership of the Holy Spirit—a unity that goes beyond individuals, churches, or organizations. This was not a movement to build another denomination, but rather an effort to join ministers and churches of like feeling across denominational lines.

To provide opportunities for fellowship and to support the objectives and goals of local and national ministries, regional conventions and an annual international convention are held.

HEADQUARTERS

4325 W. Ledbetter Dr., Dallas, TX 75233 Tel. (214)339-1200 Fax (214)337-1865
Media Contact, Exec. Dir., Dr. Chester P. Jenkins

OFFICERS

Pres., Dr. Don Arnold, P.O. Box 324, Gadsden, AL 35901
1st Vice-Pres., Dr. Ray Chamberlain, P.O. Box 986, Salisbury, MD 21801
Sec., Dr. Chester P. Jenkins
Treas., Rev. S. K. Biffle, 3833 Westerville Rd., Columbus, OH 43224
Ofc. Sec., Mrs. Anne Rasmussen, 4325 Ledbetter Dr., Dallas, TX 75233 Tel. (241)339-1200
Vice-Pres. at Large: Rev. Maurice Hart, P.O. Box 4316, Omaha, NE 68104; Rev. Don Westbrook, 3518 Rose of Sharon Rd., Durham, NC 27705

REGIONAL VICE-PRESIDENTS

Southeast, Rev. R. Richard Edgar, 5937 Franconia Rd., Alexandria, VA 22310
South Central, Rev. Robert J. Miller, P.O. Box 283, Kileen, TX 76541
Southwest, Rev. Don Shepherd, 631 Southgate Rd., Sacramento, CA 95815
Northeast, Rev. Roy C. Smith, P.O. Box 193, Shrewsbury, PA 17361
North Central, Rev. Raymond Rothwell, P.O. Box 367, Eaton, OH 45320
Northwest, Rev. Ralph Trask, 3212 Hyacinth NE, Salem, OR 97303

OFFICERS

Exec. Sec., Dr. Chester P. Jenkins
Chmn. of Evangelism, Dr. Marty Tharp
Past Pres., Dr. James Helton

PERIODICAL

Fellowship Tidings

Fundamental Methodist Church, Inc.

This group traces its origin through the Methodist Protestant Church. It withdrew from The Methodist Church and organized on Aug. 27, 1942.

HEADQUARTERS

1034 N. Broadway, Springfield, MO 65802
Media Contact, Dist. Supt., Pastor Ronnie Fieker, 425 W. Wishart, Monett, MO 65708 Tel. (417)235-3168

OFFICERS

Treas., Mr. Everett Etheridge, 3844 W. Dover, Springfield, MO 65802 Tel. (417)865-4438

Sec., Mrs. Betty Nicholson, Rt. 2, Box 397, Ash Grove, MO 65604 Tel. (417)672-2268
Dist. Supt., Rev. Ronnie Fieker, 804 13th, Monett, MO 65708 Tel. (417)235-3168

General Association of Regular Baptist Churches

Founded in May, 1932, in Chicago, by a group of churches which had withdrawn from the Northern Baptist Convention (now the American Baptist Churches in the U.S.A.) because of doctrinal differences. Its Confession of Faith, which it requires all churches to subscribe to, is essentially the old, historic New Hampshire Confession of Faith with a premillennial ending applied to the last article.

HEADQUARTERS

1300 N. Meacham Rd., Schaumburg, IL 60173 Tel. (708)843-1600 Fax (708)843-3757

OFFICERS

Chpsn., Dr. David Nettleton
Vice-Chpsn., Dr. Daniel E. Galatt
Treas., Vernon Miller
Sec., Dr. John Greening
Natl. Rep., Dr. Paul Tassell

PERIODICAL

Baptist Bulletin

General Baptists (General Association of)

Similar in doctrine to those General Baptists organized in England in the early 17th century, the first General Baptist churches were organized on the Midwest frontier following the Second Great Awakening. The first church was established by the Rev. Benoni Stinson, in 1823 at Evansville, Ind.

Stinson's major theological emphasis was general atonement — "Christ tasted death for every man." The group also allows for the possibility of apostasy. It practices open Communion and believer's baptism by immersion.

Called "liberal" Baptists because of their emphasis on the freedom of man, General Baptists organized a General Association in 1870 and invited other "liberal" Baptists (e.g., "free will" and Separate Baptists) to participate.

The policy-setting body is composed of delegates from local General Baptist churches and associations. Each local church is autonomous but belongs to an association. The group currently consists of more than 60 associations in 16 states, as well as several associations in the Philippines, Guam, Saipan, Jamaica, and India. Ministers and deacons are ordained by a presbytery.

A number of boards continue a variety of missions, schools, and other support ministries. General Baptists belong to the Baptist World Alliance and the North American Baptist Fellowship, and the National Association of Evangelicals.

HEADQUARTERS

100 Stinson Dr., Poplar Bluff, MO 63901 Tel. (314)785-7746 Fax (314)785-0564
Media Contact, Exec. Dir., Rev. Dwight Chapman

OFFICERS

Mod., Rev. John Sloan, P.O. Box 6473, Evansdale, IN 47714
Clk., Rev. Franklin Dumond, 1717 N. Main, Mt. Vernon, IN 47620
Exec. Dir., Rev. Dwight Chapman

Gen. Bd., Sec., Rev. Franklin Dumond, 1717 N. Main, Mt. Vernon, IN 47620

Foreign Missions Bd., Exec. Dir., Rev. Charles Carr

Bd. of Christian Educ. & Publication, Exec. Dir., Rev. Sam Ramdial

Home Mission Bd., Exec. Dir., Dr. Leland Duncan

Ministerial Services Bd., Exec. Dir., Rev. Gary Watson

Brotherhood Bd., Pres., Mr. Eithal Davis, 2731 Apache, Bowling Green, KY 42101

Women's Mission Bd., Exec. Dir., Mrs. Sandra Trivitt

Stewardship Dir., Rev. Ron D. Black

Nursing Home Admn., Ms. Wanda Britt, Rt. #2, Box 230, Campbell, MO 63933

College Bd., Pres., Dr. James Murray, Oakland City College, P.O. Box 235, Oakland City, IN 47660

Publishing House, Stinson Press, Rev. Wayne Foust, 400 Stinson Dr., Poplar Bluff, MO 63901

PERIODICALS

General Baptist Messenger; Capsule; Voice; The Wave

General Church of the New Jerusalem

The General Church of the New Jerusalem is the result of a reorganization in 1897 of the General Church of The Advent of the Lord. It stresses the full acceptance of the doctrines contained in the theological writings of Emanuel Swedenborg.

HEADQUARTERS

Bryn Athyn, PA 19009 Tel. (215)947-4200

Media Contact, Ed., Church Journal, Donald L. Rose, Box 743, Bryn Athyn, PA 19009 Tel. (215)947-6811 Fax (215)947-3078

OFFICERS

Presiding Bishop, Rt. Rev. P. M. Buss
Sec., Mr. Boyd Asplundh
Treas., Neil M. Buss

PERIODICAL

New Church Life

General Conference of the Evangelical Baptist Church, Inc.

This denomination is an Arminian, Wesleyan, premillennial group whose form of government is congregational.

It was organized in 1935, and was formerly known as the Church of the Full Gospel, Inc.

HEADQUARTERS

1601 E. Rose St., Goldsboro, NC 27530 Tel. (919)734-2482

OFFICERS

Pres., Rev. David J. Crawford, 101 William Dr., Goldsboro, NC 27530 Tel. (919)734-2482

1st Vice-Pres., Dr. Harry E. Jones, 3741 Sunset Ave., Westridge Village, Apt. B-1, Rocky Mount, NC 27801 Tel. (919)443-1239

2nd Vice-Pres., Rev. George C. Wallace, 909 W. Walnut St., Chanute, KS 66720 Tel. (316)431-0706

Sec.-Treas., Mrs. Evelyn Crawford, 101 William Dr., Goldsboro, NC 27530 Tel. (919)734-2482

Dir. of Evangelism, Rev. B. L. Proctor, Rt. 3, Box 442, Nashville, NC 27856 Tel. (919)459-2063

Dir. of Women's Work, ——-

Dir. of Youth Work, Rev. Ralph Jarrell, P.O. Box 1112, Burgaw, NC 28425 Tel. (919)259-9329

General Six Principle Baptists

This Baptist group, organized in Rhode Island in 1653, draws its name from Hebrews 6: 1-2.

OFFICERS

Rhode Island Conference: Pres., Rev. Edgar S. Kirk, 350 Davisville Rd., North Kingstown, RI 02852 Tel. (401)884-2750; Clk., Miss Sylvia Stoner, RR 1, Box 170, Wyoming, RI 02898

Pennsylvania Association: Pres., Elder Daniel E. Carpenetti, RR 1, Box 1750, Nicholson, PA 18446-9470 Tel. (717)942-6578; Clk., Mrs. Eleanor Warner, RR 1, Box 1778, Nicholson, PA 18446-9275

Grace Brethren Churches, Fellowship of

A division occurred in the Church of the Brethren in 1882 on the question of the legislative authority of the annual meeting. It resulted in the establishment of this body under a legal charter requiring congregational government.

HEADQUARTERS

Media Contact, Fellowship Coord., Rev. Charles Ashman, P.O. Box 386, Winona Lake, IN 46590 Tel. (219)269-1269

OFFICERS

Mod., William Snell, 1210 W. 100 South, Warsaw, IN 46580

Mod.-Elect, Robert Fetterhoff, 912 Douglas Dr., Wooster, OH 44691

Fellowship Coord., Charles Ashman, P.O. Box 386, Winona Lake, IN 46590 Tel. (219)267-5566

Sec., John Snow, P.O. Box 6, Portis, KS 67474

Treas., Steve Poppenfoose, R. 1, Box 425A, Warsaw, IN 46580

OTHER BOARDS

Grace Brethren Foreign Missions, Exec. Dir., Rev. Tom Julien, P.O. Box 588, Winona Lake, IN 46590

Grace Brethren Home Missions, Exec. Dir., Larry Chamberlain, P.O. Box 587, Winona Lake, IN 46590

Grace Schools, Pres., Dr. John Davis, 200 Seminary Dr., Winona Lake, IN 46590 Tel. (210)372-5100

Brethren Missionary Herald Co., Pub. & Gen. Mgr., Charles Turner, P.O. Box 544, Winona Lake, IN 46590

Women's Missionary Council, Pres., Mrs. Geneva Ixman, 2244 Fernwood Dr., Colorado Springs, CO 80910

CE National, Exec. Dir., Rev. Ed Lewis, P.O. Box 365, Winona Lake, IN 46590

Grace Brethren Men & Boys, Exec. Dir., Rev. Ed Jackson, c/o Grace Brethren Church of Columbus, 6675 Worthington-Galena Rd., Worthington, OH 43085

Brethren Evangelistic Ministries, Dir., Ron Thompson, 3580 Robin Hood Cir., Roanoke, VA 24019

Brethren Navajo Ministries, Dir., Steve Galegor, Counselor, NM 87018

Grace Village Retirement Community, Exec. Dir., Scott Pucket, P.O. Box 337, Winona Lake, IN 46590

Brethren Missionary Herald

Grace Gospel Fellowship

The Grace Gospel Fellowship was organized in 1944 by a group of pastors who held to a dispensational interpretation of Scripture. Most had ministries in the Midwest. Two prominent leaders were J. C. O'Hair of Chicago and Charles Baker of Milwaukee. Subsequent to 1945, a Bible Institute was founded (now Grace Bible College of Grand Rapids, Mich.), and a previously organized foreign mission (now Grace Ministries International of Grand Rapids) affiliated with the group. Churches have now been established in most sections of the country.

The body has remained a fellowship, each church being autonomous in polity. All support for its college, mission, and headquarters is on a contributory basis.

The binding force of the Fellowship has been the members' doctrinal position. They believe in the Deity and Saviorship of Jesus Christ and subscribe to the inerrant authority of Scripture. Their method of biblical interpretation is dispensational, with emphasis on the distinctive revelation to and the ministry of the apostle Paul.

HEADQUARTERS

Media Contact, Pres., Roger G. Anderson, 2125 Martindale SW, P.O. Box 9432, Grand Rapids, MI 49509 Tel. (616)245-0100 Fax (616)241-2542

OFFICERS

Pres., Roger G. Anderson

OTHER ORGANIZATIONS

Grace Bible College, Pres., Rev. Bruce Kemper, 1011 Aldon St. SW, Grand Rapids, MI 49509
Grace Ministries Intl., Exec. Dir., Dr. Samuel Vinton, 2125 Martindale Ave. SW, Grand Rapids, MI 49509
Missionary Literature Distributors, Dir., Mrs. Betty Strelow, 7514 Humbert Rd., Godfrey, IL 62305
Prison Mission Association, Gen. Dir., Mr. Vern Bigelow, P.O. Box 1587, Port Orchard, WA 98366-0140
Grace Publications Inc., Exec. Dir., Roger Anderson, 2125 Martindale Ave. SW, Grand Rapids, MI 49509
Bible Doctrines to Live By, Exec. Dir., Lee Homoki, P.O. Box 2351, Grand Rapids, MI 49501

PERIODICAL

Truth

Greek Orthodox Archdiocese of North and South America

The Greek Orthodox Archdiocese of North and South America is under the jurisdiction of the Ecumenical Patriarchate of Constantinople, in Istanbul.

It was chartered in 1922 by the State of New York and has parishes in the United States, Canada, Central and South America. The first Greek Orthodox Church was founded in New Orleans in 1864.

HEADQUARTERS

8-10 E. 79th St., New York, NY 10021 Tel. (212)570-3500 Fax (212)861-2183
Media Contact, News Media Liaison, Jim Golding, Tel. (212)628-2590 Fax (212)570-4005

ARCHDIOCESAN COUNCIL

Chpsn., Archbishop Iakovos
Vice-Chpsn., Metropolitan Silas of New Jersey
Pres., Andrew A. Athens, Chicago, IL
1st Vice-Pres., George Chimples, Cleveland, OH
2nd Vice-Pres., Elenie K. Huszagh
Sec., Basil C. Foussianes, Detroit, MI
Treas., Peter Dion, New York, NY
Theodore Prounis, New York, NY

SYNOD OF BISHOPS

Chpsn., His Eminence Archbishop Iakovos
His Excellency Metropolitan Silas of New Jersey, 8 East 79th St., New York, NY 10021
His Grace Bishop Iakovos of Chicago, Forty East Burton Pl., Chicago, IL 60610
His Grace Bishop Timothy of Detroit, 19504 Renfrew, Detroit, MI 48211
His Grace Bishop Sotirios of Toronto, 40 Donlands Ave., Toronto, ON M4J 3N6
His Grace Bishop Anthony of San Francisco, 372 Santa Clara Ave., San Francisco, CA 94127
His Grace Bishop Maximos of Pittsburgh, 5201 Ellsworth Ave., Pittsburgh, PA 15232
His Grace Bishop Gennadios of Buenos Aires, Avenida Figueroa Alcorta 3187, Buenos Aires, Argentina
His Grace Bishop Methodios of Boston, 162 Goddard Ave., Brookline, MA 02146
Assistant Bishops to Archbishop Iakovos: His Grace Bishop Philotheos of Meloa; His Grace Bishop Philip of Daphnousia, 2801 Buford St., Ste. 365, Atlanta, GA; His Grace Bishop Isaiah of Aspendos, Chancellor; His Grace Bishop Alexios of Troas, Chorepiscopos of Astoria, 27-09 Crescent St., Astoria, NY 11102

ARCHDIOCESAN DEPARTMENTS

Rel. Educ., 50 Goddard Ave., Brookline, MA 02146
Go Telecom, 27-09 Crescent St., Astoria, NY 11102
Archives Logos, Mission Center, P.O. Box 4319, St. Augustine, FL 32085
Youth Ministry & Camping
Economic Development
Church & Society
Ecumenical Ofc.
Stewardship
Registry
Ionian Village
Communications

ORGANIZATIONS

Ladies Philoptochos Society, 345 E. 74th St., New York, NY 10021
Greek Orthodox Young Adult League (GOYAL)
Order of St. Andrew the Apostle
Archdiocesan Presbyters' Council
National Sisterhood of Presbyteres
Natl. Forum of Greek Orthodox Church Musicians, 1700 N. Walnut St., Bloomington, IN 47401

PERIODICAL

Orthodox Observer, The

The Holiness Church of God, Inc.

Established at Madison, N.C., in 1920; this church was incorporated in 1928 at Winston-Salem, N.C.

HEADQUARTERS

Winston-Salem, NC

Pres., Bishop B. McKinney, 602 E. Elm St., Graham, NC 27253
Vice-Bishop, Melvin Charley, 140-39 172nd St., Springfield Gardens, NY 11434
Gen. Sec., Mrs. Nina B. Hash, Box 541, Galax, VA 24333
Northern Area of N.E. Dist., Overseer, Melvin Charley, 140-39 172nd St., Springfield Gardens, NY 11434
So. Dist., Overseer, Bishop T. R. Rice, 1439 Sedgefield Dr., Winston-Salem, NC 27105 Tel. (919)227-4755
Va. & W. Va. Area of N.W. Dist., Overseer, Elder Arnie Joyce, Thorpe, WV 24888
North Carolina Area of N.W. Dist., Overseer, James Himes, 3661 Barkwood Dr., Winston-Salem, NC 27105

Holy Ukrainian Autocephalic Orthodox Church in Exile

Organized in a parish in New York in 1951. The laymen and clergy who organized it came from among the Ukrainians who settled in the Western Hemisphere after World War II. In 1954 two bishops, immigrants from Europe, met with clergy and laymen and formally organized the religious body.

HEADQUARTERS

103 Evergreen St., W. Babylon, NY 11704

OFFICERS

Admn., Rt. Rev. Serhij K. Pastukhiv, Tel. (516)669-7402

House of God, Which is the Church of the Living God, the Pillar and Ground of the Truth, Inc.

This body, founded by Mary L. Tate in 1919, is episcopally organized.

OFFICER

Bishop, Raymond W. White, 6107 Cobbs Creek Pkwy., Philadelphia, PA 19143 Tel. (215)748-6338

Hungarian Reformed Church in America

A Hungarian Reformed Church was organized in New York in 1904 in connection with the Reformed Church of Hungary. In 1922, the Church in Hungary transferred most of its congregations in the United States to the Reformed Church in the U.S. Some, however, preferred to continue as an autonomous, self-supporting American denomination, and these formed the Free Magyar Reformed Church in America. This group changed its name in 1958 to Hungarian Reformed Church in America.

This church is a member of the World Alliance of Reformed Churches, Presbyterian and Congregational, the World Council of Churches and the National Council of Churches of Christ. It is deeply involved in the Roman Catholic, Presbyterian Reformed Consultation, of which Dr. Andrew Harsanyi was co-chairman for 12 years.

HEADQUARTERS

Bishop's Office, P.O. Box D, Hopatcong, NJ 07843 Tel. (201)398-2764

Media Contact, Bishop, Dr. Andrew Harsanyi, Tel. (210)398-2764

OFFICERS

Bishop, Rt. Rev. Dr. Andrew Harsanyi
Chief Lay-Curator, Prof. Stephen Szabo, 464 Forest Ave., Paramus, NJ 07652
Gen. Sec. (Clergy), Rt. Rev. Paul A. Mezö, 8 Dunthorne Ct., Scarborough, ON M1B 2S9
Gen Sec. (Lay), Zoltan Ambrus, 3358 Maple Dr., Melvindale, MI 48122
Eastern Classis, Dean (Senior of the Deans, Chair in Bishop's absence), The V. Rev. Stefan M. Torok, 331 Kirkland Pl., Perth Amboy, NJ 08861
New York Classis, Dean, The V. Rev. Alex Forro, 13 Grove St., Poughkeepsie, NY 12601
Western Classis, Dean, The V. Rev. Andor Demeter, 3921 W. Christy Dr., Phoenix, AZ 85029

PERIODICAL

Magyar Egyhaz

Hutterian Brethren

Small groups of Hutterites derive their names from Jacob Hutter, a 16th-century Anabaptist who advocated communal ownership of property and was burned as a heretic in Austria in 1536.

Many believers are of German descent and still use their native tongue at home and in church. Much of the denominational literature is produced in German and English. "Colonies" share property, practice non-resistance, dress differently, refuse to participate in politics, and operate their own schools. There are 375 colonies with 40,000 members in North America.

Each congregation conducts its own youth work through Sunday school. Until age 15, children attend German school after attending public school. All youth, ages 15 to 20 must attend Sunday school. They are baptized upon confession of faith, around age 20.

HEADQUARTERS

Media Contact, Correspondent, Rev. Paul S. Gross, Rt. 1, Box 6E, Reardon, WA 99029 Tel. (509)299-5400 Fax (509)299-3099

OFFICERS

Vice-Pres., Rev. Joseph Hofer, P.O. Box 159, Sunburst, MT 59482 Tel. (406)937-3045
Hutterite Bishop, Rev. John Wipf, P.O. Box 1509, Rosetown, SK S0L 2V0 Tel. (306)882-3112

Independent Fundamental Churches of America

Organized 1930 at Cicero, Ill., by representatives of the American Council of Undenominational Churches and representatives of various independent churches. The founding churches and members had separated themselves from various denominational affiliations. The IFCA provides an advance movement among independent churches and ministers to unite in a close fellowship and cooperation, in defense of the fundamental teachings of Scripture and in the proclamation of the gospel of God's grace.

HEADQUARTERS

3520 Fairlanes, Grandville, MI 49468 Tel. (616)531-1840 Fax (616)531-1814
Mailing Address, P.O. Box 810, Grandville, MI 49418

Natl. Exec. Dir., Dr. Richard Gregory, 2684 Meadow Ridge Dr., Byron Center, MI 49315 Tel. (616)878-1285

Pres., Dr. Elwood Chipchase, 3645 South 57th Ct., Cicero, IL 60650 Tel. (708)656-6857

1st Vice-Pres., Rev. Donald Fredericks, 3224 North Patterson Blvd., Flagstaff, AZ 86004-2009 Tel. (602)526-1493

2nd Vice-Pres., Dr. Robert Graves, 3615 Chanate Rd., Santa Rosa, CA 95404 Tel. (707)528-0864

PERIODICAL

Voice, The

International Church of the Foursquare Gospel

Founded by Aimee Semple McPherson in 1927, the International Church of the Foursquare Gospel proclaims the message of Jesus Christ the Savior, Healer, Baptizer with the Holy Spirit and Soon-coming King. Headquartered in Los Angeles, this evangelistic missionary body of believers consists of nearly 1,568 churches in the United States and Canada.

The International Church of the Foursquare Gospel is incorporated in the state of California is governed by a Board of Directors who direct its corporate affairs. A Foursquare Cabinet, consisting of the Corporate Officers, Board of Directors, District Supervisors of the various districts of the Foursquare Church in the United States, and other elected or appointed members, serves in an advisory capacity to the President and the Board of Directors.

Each local Foursquare Church is a subordinate unit of the International Church of the Foursquare Gospel. The pastor of the church is appointed by the Board of Directors and is responsible for the spiritual and physical welfare of the church. To assist and advise the pastor, a church council is elected by the local church members.

Foursquare Churches seek to build strong believers through Christian education, Christian day schools, youth camping and ministry, United Foursquare Women who support and encourage Foursquare missionaries abroad, radio and television ministries, the *Foursquare World Advance Magazine* and 149 Bible Colleges worldwide.

Worldwide missions remains the focus of the Foursquare Gospel Church with nearly 25,577 churches, 17,773 national Foursquare pastors/leaders and 1,683,267 members and adherents in 72 countries around the globe. The Church is affiliated with the Pentecostal Fellowship of North America, National Association of Evangelicals, and the World Pentecostal Fellowship.

HEADQUARTERS

1910 W. Sunset Blvd., Ste. 200, Los Angeles, CA 90026 Tel. (213)484-2400 Fax (213)413-3824

Media Contact, Editor, Dr. Ron Williams

OFFICERS

Pres., Dr. John R. Holland
Pres. Emeritus, Dr. Rolf K. McPherson
Vice-Pres., Dr. Roy Hicks, Jr.
Gen. Sup., Dr. J. Eugene Kurtz
Dir. of Missions Intl., Dr. Roy Hicks, Jr.
Sec., Dr. John W. Bowers
Treas., Rev. Virginia Cravens
Exec. Sec., Rev. James Rogers
Bd. of Directors: Dr. John R. Holland; Dr. Roy Hicks; Dr. John W. Bowers; Dr. Harold Helms;

Dr. Howard P. Courtney, Sr.; Mr. Douglas L. Slaybaugh; Dr. J. Eugene Kurtz; Dr. Ron Williams; Dr. Paul Risser; Rev. Loren Edwards

District Supervisors: Eastern, Rev. Dewey Morrow; Great Lakes, Rev. Fred Parker; Midwest, Dr. Glenn Metzler; Northwest, Dr. Cliff Hanes; South Central, Dr. Sidney Westbrook; Southeast, Rev. Glenn Burris, Jr.; Southern California, Rev. Don Long; Southwest, Rev. John Watson; Western, Dr. Fred Wymore

Foursquare Cabinet: Corporate Officers, Board of Directors, District Supervisors , Rev. Charles Aldridge, Rev. Tom Ferguson, Rev. Ken Wold, Jr., Dr. Daniel Brown, Rev. David Holland

PERIODICALS

Foursquare World Advance; United Foursquare Women's Magazine

The International Pentecostal Church of Christ

At a General Conference held at London, Ohio, Aug. 10, 1976, the International Pentecostal Assemblies and the Pentecostal Church of Christ, after a two-year trial period, consolidated into one body, taking the name International Pentecostal Church of Christ.

The International Pentecostal Assemblies was the successor of the Association of Pentecostal Assemblies and the International Pentecostal Missionary Union. The other body involved in the merger, the Pentecostal Church of Christ, was founded by John Stroup of Flatwoods, Ky., on May 10, 1917, and was incorporated at Portsmouth, Ohio, in 1927. The International Pentecostal Church of Christ is an active member of the Pentecostal Fellowship of North America, as well as a member of the National Association of Evangelicals.

The priorities of the International Pentecostal Church of Christ are to be an agency of God for evangelizing the world, to be a corporate body in which people may worship God, and to be a channel of God's purpose to build a body of saints being perfected in the image of his Son.

The Annual Conference is held each year during the first full week of August in London, Ohio.

HEADQUARTERS

2245 St. Rt. 42 SW, P.O. Box 439, London, OH 43140 Tel. (614)852-0348 Fax Same

Media Contact, Gen. Overseer, Clyde M. Hughes

EXECUTIVE COMMITTEE

Gen. Overseer, Clyde M. Hughes, P.O. Box 439, London, OH 43140 Tel. (614)852-0348

Asst. Gen. Overseer, Wells T. Bloomfield, P.O. Box 439, London, OH 43140 Tel. (614)852-0448

Gen. Sec., Rev. Thomas Dooley, 3200 Dueber Ave. S.W., Canton, OH 44706 Tel. (216)484-6053

Gen. Treas., Rev. Clifford A. Edwards, P.O. Box 18145, Atlanta, GA 30316 Tel. (404)627-2681

Dir. of Global Missions, Dr. James B. Keiller, P.O. Box 18145, Atlanta, GA 30316 Tel. (404)627-2681

DISTRICT OVERSEERS

Blue Ridge District, Robert Culler, Rt. 2, Box 12, Pinnacle, NC 27043 Tel. (919)368-2540

Central District, Ervin Hargrave, 3208 Tackett St., Springfield, OH 45505 Tel. (513)399-0668

US RELIGIOUS BODIES

97

Mid-Eastern District, Earl Alexander, 103 Griggs St., Elizabeth City, NC 27909 Tel. (919)331-1786

Mountain District: Wells T. Bloomfield, P.O. Box 439, London, OH 43140 Tel. (614)852-0448; Member-at-Large, Jerry L. Castle, Rt. 276, Box 377, Paintsville, KY 41240 Tel. (606)789-5598

New River District, Calvin Weikel, Rt. 2, Box 300, Ronceverte, WV 24970 Tel. (304)647-4301

North Central District, Larry Austin, 8495 Smith Rd., Perrinton, MI 48871 Tel. (517)236-0587

North Eastern District, Thomas Dillow, P.O. Box 7, Millville, WV 25432 Tel. (304)725-0587

South Eastern District: Clifford Edwards, 892 Berne St. SE, Atlanta, GA Tel. (404)627-2681; Member-at-Large, Samuel Chand, P.O. Box 18145, Atlanta, GA 30316 Tel. (404)627-2681

Tri-State, J. W. Ferguson, 9724 US Rt. 60, Ashland, KY 41102 Tel. (606)928-6651

Gen. Pres. of Pentecostal Ambassadors, Asa Lowe, 3153 Old Carolina Rd., Virginia Beach, VA 23457 Tel. (404)421-3773

IPCC Loan Committee, Chmn., Cecil McCarty, 3113 Penrose Ave., Springfield, OH 45505 Tel. (513)324-2748

Locust Grove Rest Home, Dir., Frank Myers, Rt. 3, Box 175, Harpers Ferry, WV 25425 Tel. (304)535-6355

Ladies Auxiliary, Gen. Pres., Janice Boyce, 121 W. Hunters Trail, Elizabeth City, NC 27909 Tel. (919)338-3003

Men's Fellowship, Gen. Pres., Maynard Bingamon, 4369 Wolford Rd., Xenia, OH 45385 Tel. (513)675-2325

PERIODICAL

Bridegroom's Messenger, The

International Pentecostal Holiness Church

This body grew out of the National Holiness Association movement of the last century, with roots in Methodism. Beginning in the South and Midwest, the church represents the merger of the Fire-Baptized Holiness Church founded by B. H. Irwin in Iowa in 1895; the Pentecostal Holiness Church founded by A. B. Crumpler in Goldsboro, N.C., in 1898; and the Tabernacle Pentecostal Church founded by N. J. Holmes in 1898.

All three bodies joined the ranks of the pentecostal movement as a result of the Azusa Street revival in Los Angeles in 1906 and a 1907 pentecostal revival in Dunn, N.C., conducted by G. B. Cashwell, who had visited Azusa Street. In 1911 the Fire-Baptized and Pentecostal Holiness bodies merged in Falcon, N.C., to form the present church; the Tabernacle Pentecostal Church was added in 1915 in Canon, Ga.

The church stresses the new birth, the Wesleyan experience of entire sanctification, the pentecostal baptism in the Holy Spirit, evidenced by speaking in tongues, divine healing and the premillennial second coming of Christ.

HEADQUARTERS

P.O. Box 12609, Oklahoma City, OK 73157 Tel. (405)787-7110 Fax (405)789-3957
Media Contact, Admn. Asst., Rick Hurst

OFFICERS

Gen. Supt., Bishop B. E. Underwood
Vice Chpsn./Asst. Gen. Supt., Rev. Jesse Simmons
Asst. Gen. Supt., Rev. James Leggett
Gen. Sec.-Treas., Rev. Jack Goodson

OTHER ORGANIZATIONS

The Publishing House (Advocate Press), Gen. Admn., Greg Hearn, Franklin Springs, GA 30639

Christian Education Dept., Gen. Dir., Rev. Doyle Marley

Gen. Woman's Ministries, Pres., Mrs. Doris Moore

Gen. Men's Fellowship, Natl. Dir., Col. Jack Kelley, P.O. Box 53307, Fayetteville, NC 28305

PERIODICALS

Pentecostal Holiness Advocate, The; Helping Hand; Sunday School Literature; Witness; Worldrama

Israelite House of David

The Israelite House of David, commonly called House of David, was established in 1903 in Benton Harbor, Mich., by Brother Benjamin, the founder and leader, after he had preached the Life of the Body without going to the grave, while traveling for seven years throughout a number of mid-American states.

This denomination is a Christian Association following Jesus' teachings (I Tim. 1: 16) and the first born among many brethren (Rom. 8: 29). The House of David is an Apostolic order (Acts 2 & 4). Refer to Deuteronomy 7: 6-7. They believe Brother Benjamin to have been the voice of the seventh angel referred to in Revelation 10: 7; Malachi 3: 1; Job 33: 23-25. His writings seek to explain the way for the elect to receive the Life of the Body (Hosea 13: 14; Is. 38: 18; I Thess. 5: 23; Matt. 7: 14; Titus 1: 2; II Tim. 1: 10; John 10: 10, 27, 28).

The church expects to gather the 12 tribes of Israel (Jer. 31: 1; Ezek. 20: 34, 34: 13, 14; Hosea 1: 11), which will be carried over into the millennium day of rest, 1,000 years (Rev. 20: 1, 2 and 21: 2, 4; Isa. 11: 6-9, 35: 1, 55: 13, 54: 13). Israel will be gathered from both Jew and Gentile.

The church uses the King James version of the Bible and the Apocrypha.

HEADQUARTERS

P.O. Box 1067, Benton Harbor, MI 49023 Tel. (616)926-6695 Fax (616)429-5594
Media Contact, Pillar & Sec., H. Thomas Dewhirst

OFFICERS

Chpsn. of Bd., Lloyd H. Dalager
Pillar & Sec., H. Thomas Dewhirst

PERIODICAL

Shiloh's Messenger of Wisdom

Jehovah's Witnesses

The modern history of Jehovah's Witnesses began when, in the early 1870s, Charles Taze Russell was the prime mover in a Bible study in Allegheny City, Pa. In July 1879, the first issue of *Zion's Watch Tower and Herald of Christ's Presence* appeared. (Now called *The Watchtower* with a circulation of 15,570,000 in 111 languages.) By 1880 scores of congregations had spread into nearby states. In 1884 Zion's Watch Tower Tract Society was incorporated, later changed to Watch Tower Bible and Tract Society. Many witnessed from house to house, offering biblical literature.

By 1909, the international Society's headquarters moved to the present location in Brooklyn, N.Y. By 1913, printed sermons were in four languages in 3,000 newspapers in the United States, Canada, and Europe. Books, booklets, and tracts had been distributed by the hundreds of millions.

Russell died in 1916 and was succeeded by Joseph F. Rutherford and N.H. Knorr in 1942. The magazine *Golden Age* was introduced (now called *Awake!* with a circulation of 13,110,000 in 67 languages). In 1931 the name Jehovah's Witnesses, based on Isaiah 43: 10-12, was adopted.

During the 1930s and 1940s Jehovah's Witnesses fought many court cases, in the interest of preserving freedom of speech, press, assembly, and worship. They have won a total of 43 cases before the Supreme Court. Professor C. S. Braden stated, "In their struggle they have done much to secure those rights for every minority group in America."

In 1942, Jehovah's Witnesses instituted a concerted program of training for all Jehovah's Witnesses. The Watchtower Bible School of Gilead was established in 1943 for training missionaries. Through these missionaries, the word has expanded today to include 211 countries. The Witnesses now number more than 4.2 million throughout the world. President F. W. Franz and a small group of fellow administrators oversee the work, organized under 93 branches.

Jehovah's Witnesses believe in one almighty God, Jehovah, creator of heaven and earth; that Christ is God's Son, the first of God's creations and subject to Jehovah; that Christ's human life was paid as a ransom for obedient humans; and that Jehovah has assigned him a Kingdom, a government for which all Christians pray and through which Christ will cleanse the earth of wickedness and rule it in righteousness and peace. The book of Revelation assigns 144,000 individuals "who have been bought from the earth," to rule with him (14: 1-5). These people from all nations, along with the resurrected dead, will work to transform the earth into a global Edenic paradise. Jehovah's Witnesses are commissioned to preach from house to house during these last days. When this has been accomplished Jesus says "the end will come" and will be followed by the righteous rule of his kingdom (Matt. 24: 14).

HEADQUARTERS

25 Columbia Heights, Brooklyn, NY 11201 Tel. (718)625-3600

OFFICER

Pres., Frederick W. Franz

PERIODICAL

Awake!

Jewish Organizations

Jews arrived in the colonies before 1650. The first Congregation is recorded in 1654, in New York City, the Shearith Israel (Remnant of Israel).

CONGREGATIONAL AND RABBINICAL

Fed. of Reconst. Congs. & Havurot: Pres., Roger Price, Church Road & Greenwood Ave., Wyncote, PA 19095 Tel. (215)887-1988

*Union of Am. Hebrew Congs. (Reform), Pres., Rabbi Alexander M. Schindler; Bd., Chpsn., 838 Fifth Ave., New York, NY 10021 Tel. (212)249-0100

*United Synagogue of Am. (Conservative), Pres., Alan Tichnor, 155 Fifth Ave., New York, NY 10010 Tel. (212)533-7800

*Union of Orthodox Jewish Congs. of Am., Pres., Sheldon Rudoff, 333 - 7th Ave., New York, NY 10001 Tel. (212)563-4000

*Central Conf. of Am. Rabbis (Reform), Pres., Rabbi Samuel E. Kariff, 192 Lexington Ave., New York, NY 10016 Tel. (212)684-4990

Rabbinical Alliance of Am. (Orthodox), Pres., Rabbi Abraham B. Hecht, 3 W. 16th St., 4th Fl., New York, NY 10011 Tel. (212)242-6420

*The Rabbinical Assembly (Conservative), Pres., Rabbi Irwin Groner, 3080 Broadway, New York, NY 10027 Tel. (212)678-8060

*Rabbinical Council of Am. Inc. (Ortho.), Pres., Rabbi Max N. Schreier, 275 Seventh Ave., New York, NY 10001 Tel. (212)807-7888

Reconstructionist Rabbinical Assn., Pres., Rabbi Sandy Sasso, Church Rd. & Greenwood Ave., Wyncote, PA 19095 Tel. (215)576-0800

Union of Orthodox Rabbis of US & Canada, Dir., Rabbi Hersh M. Ginsberg, 235 E. Broadway, New York, NY 10002 Tel. (212)964-6337

*Synagogue Council of America, Pres., Rabbi Joel H. Zaiman, 327 Lexington Ave., New York, NY 10016 Tel. (212)686-8670

*Synagogue Council of Am. coordinates

EDUCATIONAL AND SOCIAL SERVICE

The American Council for Judaism, Dir., Allan C. Brownfield, P.O. Box 9009, Alexandria, VA 22304 Tel. (703)836-2546

American Jewish Committee, Pres., Sholom D. Comay, 165 E. 56th St., New York, NY 10022 Tel. (212)751-4000 Fax (212)319-0975

American Jewish Congress, Pres., Robert L. Lifton, 15 E. 84th St., New York, NY 10028 Tel. (212)879-4500

American Jewish Historical Society, Pres., Phil David Fine, 2 Thornton Rd., Waltham, MA 02154 Tel. (617)891-8110 Fax (617) 899-9208

Am. Jewish Joint Distribution Comm., Pres., Sylvia Hassenfeld, 711 Third Ave., New York, NY 10017 Tel. (212)687-6200

Anti-Defamation League of B'nai B'rith, Chpsn., Burton S. Levinson, 823 United Nations Plaza, New York, NY 10017 Tel. (212)490-2525

B'nai B'rith Hillel Foundations Inc., Chpsn. B'nai B'rith Hillel Committee, David Bittker, 1640 Rhode Island Ave. NW, Washington, DC 20036 Tel. (202)857-6560

Conf. of Pres. of Major Am. Jewish Org., Chpsn., Seymour D. Reich, 515 Park Ave, New York, NY 10022 Tel. (212)752-1616

Council for Jewish Education, Pres., Reuven Yalon, 426 W. 58th St., New York, NY 10019 Tel. (212)713-0290

Council of Jewish Federations, Pres., Mandell Berman, 730 Broadway, New York, NY 10003 Tel. (212)475-5000

Hadassah: Women's Zionist Org. of Am, Natl. Pres., Carmela E. Kalmanson, 50 W. 58th St., New York, NY 10019 Tel. (212)355-7900

HIAS Inc. (Hebrew Immigrant Aid Society), Pres., Ben Zion Leuchter, 200 Park Ave. S., New York, NY 10003 Tel. (212)674-6800

Jewish Publication Society, Pres., Edward E. Elson, 1930 Chestnut St., Philadelphia, PA 19103 Tel. (215)564-5925

Jewish Reconstructionist Foundation, Pres., Rabbi Elliot Skiddell, Church Rd. & Greenwood Ave., Wycote, PA 19095 Tel. (215)887-1988

JWB (National Jewish Welfare Bd.), Pres., Donald R. Mintz, 15 E 26th St., New York, NY 10010 Tel. (212)532-4949

Jewish War Veterans of the U S of A Inc., Natl. Exec. Dir., Steven Shaw, 1811 R St., Washington, DC 20009 Tel. (202)265-6280

Natl. Fed. of Temple Brotherhoods, Pres., Richard D. Karfunkle, 838 Fifth Ave., New York, NY 10021 Tel. (212)570-0707

Natl. Federation of Temple Sisterhoods, Pres., Judith Hertz, 838 Fifth Ave., New York, NY 10021 Tel. (212)249-0100

Natl. Jewish Comm. Rel. Adv. Council, Chpsn., Arden E. Shenker, 443 Park Ave. S., 11th Fl., New York, NY 10016 Tel. (212)684-6950

United Jewish Appeal, Natl. Chmn., Morton A. Kornreich, 99 Park Ave., Ste. 300, New York, NY 10016 Tel. (212)818-9100

Women's Branch, Pres., ——, 156 Fifth Ave., New York, NY 10010 Tel. (212)929-8857

Women's League for Conservative Judaism, Pres., Evelyn Auerbach, 48 E. 74th St., New York, NY 10021 Tel. (212)628-1600

Zionist Organization of America, Pres., Sidney Silverman, 4 E. 34th St., New York, NY 10016 Tel. (212)481-1500

PERIODICALS

Tradition: A Journal of Orthodox Jewish Thought; Conservative Judaism; Reform Judaism; American Jewish History; Jewish Action; United Synagogue Review; Journal of Reform Judaism; Reconstructionist, The; Jewish Education; Judaism; Reform Judaism

Kodesh Church of Immanuel

Founded 1929 and incorporated in April 1930 by Rev. Frank Russell Killingsworth and 120 laymen, some of whom were former members of the African Methodist Episcopal Zion Church. On Jan. 22, 1934, the Christian Tabernacle Union, a body of fundamental believers with headquarters in Pittsburgh, merged with the Kodesh Church of Immanuel.

The Hebrew word "Kodesh" means "sanctified, holy"; and Immanuel is a title of the Messiah which means "God with us." The church is composed of a sanctified, Spirit-filled constituency, an interracial body of believers whose teachings are Wesleyan and Arminian.

HEADQUARTERS

2601 Centre Ave., Pittsburgh, PA 15219
Media Contact, Supv. Elder, Dr. Kenneth O. Barbour, 932 Logan Rd., Bethel Park, PA 15102 Tel. (412)833-1351

OFFICERS

Supervising Elder, Dr. Kenneth O. Barbour

OTHER ORGANIZATIONS

Church Extension Bd., Chmn., Mrs. Thelma P. Holmes, 2516 Graham Blvd., Pittsburgh, PA 15235

Foreign Mission Bd., Pres., Mrs. E. Lucille Lockhart, Roosevelt Arms, Apt. #1211, 609 Penn Ave., Pittsburgh, PA 15222

Young People's Societies, Gen. Pres., Mrs. Lutitia Clipper, 615 Twin Oaks Dr., Pittsburg, PA 15235

Harty Bible School, President, Dr. Kenneth O. Barbour, 932 Logan Rd., Bethel Park, PA 15102

Sunday Schools, Gen. Supt., Miss Dolores Laremore, 6220 Carpenter St., Philadelphia, PA 19143

Korean Presbyterian Church in America, General Assembly of the

This body came into official existence in the United States in 1976 and is currently an ethnic church, using the Korean language.

HEADQUARTERS

1251 Crenshaw Blvd., Los Angeles, CA 90019 Tel. (213)857-0361. Fax (213)857-0361
Media Contact, Gen. Sec., Rev. Nicholas C. Chun

OFFICERS

Mod., Rev. Yong Ju Kim, 344 Hoffman Ave., New Milford, NJ 07646 Tel. (201)967-1497

Vice-Mod., Rev. Do Seuk Kim, 907 N. Alexandria Ave., Los Angeles, CA 90029 Tel. (213)662-1838

Stated Clk., Rev. In Chul Kim, 44 Holsworthy Cress., Thornhill, ON L3T 4C6 Tel. (416)764-7905

Treas., Eld. Kwang Mo Lee, 47-37 45th St. 2M, Woodside, NY 11377 Tel. (718)361-1699

STAFF

Intl. Mission Cmte., Chpsn., Rev. Hee Min Park, 4529 Frederick Ave., La Crescenta, CA 91214 Tel. (818)248-1496
Gen. Sec., Rev. Nicholas C. Chun

The Latvian Evangelical Lutheran Church in America

This body was organized into a denomination on Aug. 22, 1975, after having existed as the Federation of Latvian Evangelical Lutheran Churches in America since 1955. This church is a regional constituent part of the Lutheran Church of Latvia in Exile, a member of the Lutheran World Federation and the World Council of Churches.

The Latvian Evangelical Lutheran Church in America works to foster religious life, traditions and customs in its congregations in harmony with the Holy Scriptures, the Apostles', Nicean and Athanasian Creeds, the unaltered Augsburg Confession, Martin Luther's Small and Large Catechisms and other documents of the Book of Concord.

The LELCA is ordered by its Synod (General Assembly), executive board, auditing committee, and district conferences.

HEADQUARTERS

6551 West Montrose Ave., Chicago, IL 60634 Tel. (312)725-3820 Fax (312)725-3835
Media Contact, Pres., Rev. Vilis Varsbergs

OFFICERS

Pres., Dean Vilis Varsbergs
Vice-Pres., Rev. Maris Kirsons, 171 Erskin Ave. #1101, Toronto, ON M4P 1Y8 Tel. (416)486-3910

2nd Vice-Pres., Aivrs Ronis, 449 S. 40th St., Lincoln, NE 68510 Tel. (402)489-2776

Sec., Ansis Abele, 25182 Northrup Dr., Laguna Beach, CA 92653 Tel. (714)830-9712

Treas., Mr. Alfreds Trautmanis, 103 Rose St., Freeport, NY 11520 Tel. (516)623-2646

PERIODICAL

Cela Biedrs

The Liberal Catholic Church—Province of the United States of America

Founded Feb. 13, 1916 as a reorganization of the Old Catholic Church in Great Britain, the Rt. Rev. James I. Wedgwood being the first Presiding Bishop. The first ordination of a Priest in the United States was Fr. Charles Hampton, later a

Bishop. The first Regionary Bishop for the American Province was the Rt. Rev. Irving S. Cooper (1919-1935).

HEADQUARTERS
Media Contact, Pres., Rt. Rev. Lawrence J. Smith, 9740 S. Avers Ave., Evergreen Park, IL 60642 Tel. (708)424-6548

OFFICERS
Pres. & Regionary Bishop, The Rt. Rev. Lawrence J. Smith

Vice-Pres., Rev. Alfred Strauss, 10606 Parrot Ave., Apt. A, Downey, CA 90241 Tel. (310)861-7569

Sec. (Provincial), Rev. Lloyd Worley, 1232 24th Avenue Ct., Greeley, CO 80631 Tel. (303)356-3002

Provost, The V. Rev. Wm. Holme, P.O. Box 7042, Rochester, MN 55903

Treas., Rev. Lloyd Worley

BISHOPS
Regionary Bishop for the American Province, The Rt. Rev. Lawrence J. Smith

Aux. Bishops of the American Province: Rt. Rev. Dr. Robert S. McGinnis, Jr., 2204 Armond Blvd., Destrehan, LA 70065; Rt. Rev. Joseph L. Tisch, P.O. Box 1117, Melbourne, FL 32901; Rt. Rev. Dr. Hein VanBeusekom, 12 Krotona Hill, Ojai, CA 93023

PERIODICAL
Ubique: American Province

Liberty Baptist Fellowship
The Liberty Baptist Fellowship consists of independent Baptist churches and pastors organized for the purpose of planting indigenous local New Testament churches in North America. The Fellowship is in general accord with the doctrines and philosophy of the Independent Baptist movement.

HEADQUARTERS
Candler's Mountain Rd., Lynchburg, VA 24506 Tel. (804)582-2061

Media Contact, Exec. Dir., Dr. Kenneth Chapman, P.O. Box 368, Madison Heights, VA 24572 Tel. (804)582-2603

OFFICERS
Exec. Comm.: Natl. Chmn., Jerry Falwell; Exec. Dir., Harry Dean; Exec. Sec., Kenneth Chapman

Natl. Comm.: Pres., Lamarr Mooneyham

The Lutheran Church—Missouri Synod
The Lutheran Church—Missouri Synod, which began in the state of Missouri in 1847, has more than 6,000 congregations in the United States and works in various capacities in 42 other countries. It has 2.6 million members worldwide, and is the second-largest Lutheran denomination in North America.

Christian education for all ages offers an array of weekday, Sunday school and Bible-class opportunities. The North American congregations operate the largest elementary and secondary school systems of any Protestant denomination in the nation, and eight colleges, two universities and two seminaries in the United States enroll 11,195 students.

Traditional beliefs concerning the authority and interpretation of Scripture are important. In the late 1960s, a controversy developed, but following a decade of soul-searching that resulted in the walk-out of most faculty members and students from one seminary and the eventual departure of slightly more than 100,000 members, little evidence of the controversy remains.

The synod is known for mass-media outreach through "The Lutheran Hour" on radio, "This Is The Life" dramas on television, and the products of Concordia Publishing House, the third-largest Protestant publisher, whose Arch Books children's series has sold more than 55 million copies.

An extensive Braille volunteer network of more than 1,000 volunteers in 40 work centers makes devotional materials for the blind; 54 of the 85 deaf congregations affiliated with U.S. denominations are LCMS; and many denominations use the Bible lessons prepared for developmentally disabled persons.

The involvement of women is high, though they do not occupy clergy positions. Serving as teachers, deaconesses, and social workers, women comprise approximately 48 percent of total professional workers.

The members' responsibility for congregational leadership is a distinctive characteristic of the synod, a word that means "walking together." Practice holds that the pastor is the equipper of the saints. Power is vested in voters' assemblies, generally comprised of adults of voting age. Synod decision making is given to the delegates at national and regional conventions, where the franchise is equally divided between lay and pastoral representatives.

HEADQUARTERS
The Lutheran Church—Missouri Synod, International Center, 1333 S. Kirkwood Rd., St. Louis, MO 63122

Media Contact, Dir., News & Information, Rev. David Mahsman, Tel. (314)965-9000 Fax (314)822-8307

OFFICERS
Pres., Dr. A.L. Barry
1st Vice-Pres., Dr. August T. Mennicke
2nd Vice-Pres., Dr. Robert King
3rd Vice-Pres., Dr. Eugene Bunkowske
4th Vice-Pres., Dr. Robert C. Sauer
5th Vice-Pres., Dr. Walter A. Maier
Sec., Dr. Walter L. Rosin
Treas., Dr. Norman Sell
Admn. Officer of Bd. of Dir., Dr. John P. Schuelke
Dir. of Personnel, Mr. Gary Mittendorf
Bd. of Directors: Dr. Karl L. Barth, Milwaukee, WI; Rev. Richard L. Thompson, Billings, MT; Donald Brosz, Laramie, WY; John L. Daniel, Emmaus, PA; Ernest Garbe, Dietirich, IL; Oscar H. Hanson, Lafayette, CA; Mr. Robert W. Hirsch, Yankton, SC; Dr. Florence Montz, Bismarck, ND; Dr. Harold M. Olsen, Springfield, IL; Mr. Lester W. Schultz, Russellville, AR; Mr. Gilbert E. LaHaine, Lansing, MI; Dr. Donald Snyder, Henrietta, NY

BOARDS AND COMMISSIONS
Communication Services, Exec. Dir., Rev. Paul Devantier
Evangelism Services, Exec. Dir., Rev. Lyle Muller
Mission Services, Exec. Dir., Dr. Glenn O'Shoney
Parish Services, Exec. Dir., Dr. H. James Boldt
Higher Education Services, Exec. Dir., Dr. William F. Meyer
Youth Services, Exec. Dir., Mr. LeRoy Wilke
Human Care Ministries, Exec. Dir., Rev. Richard L. Krenzke
Worker Benefit Plans, Admn., Mr. Earl E. Haake

Lutheran Church Ext. Fund-Missouri Synod, Pres., Mr. Arthur C. Haake

Min. to the Armed Forces Standing Comm., Exec. Dir., Rev. James Shaw

Dept. of Stewardship, Acting Dir., Rev. John Meyer

ORGANIZATIONS

Concordia Publishing House, Pres./CEO, John Gerber, 3558 S. Jefferson Ave., St. Louis, MO 63118

Concordia Historical Institute, Dir., Dr. August R. Suelflow, Concordia Seminary, 801 De Mun Ave., St. Louis, MO 63105

Intl. Lutheran Laymen's League, Exec. Dir., Mr. Laurence E. Lumpe, 2185 Hampton Ave., St. Louis, MO 63110

KFUO Radio, Exec. Dir., Rev. Paul Devantier, 85 Founders Ln., St. Louis, MO 73105

Intl. Lutheran Women's Missionary League, Pres., Mrs. Ida Mall, 3558 S. Jefferson Ave., St. Louis, MO 63118

PERIODICALS

Lutheran Witness, The; Reporter

Lutheran Churches, The American Association of

This church body was constituted on Nov. 7, 1987. The AALC was formed by laity and pastors of the former American Lutheran Church in America who held to a high view of Scripture (inerrancy and infallibility). This church body also emphasizes the primacy of evangelism and world missions and the authority and autonomy of the local congregation.

Congregations of the AALC are distributed throughout the continental United States from Long Island, N.Y., to Los Angeles. The primary decision-making body is the General Convention, to which each congregation has proportionate representation.

HEADQUARTERS

The AALC National Office, P.O. Box 17097, Minneapolis, MN 55417 Tel. (612)884-7784

Mailing Address, P.O. Box 17097, Minneapolis, MN 55417

The AALC Regional Office, 214 South St., Waterloo, IA 50701

OFFICERS

Presiding Pastor, Dr. Daune R. Lindberg, P.O. Box 416, Waterloo, IA 50701 Tel. (319)232-3971

Asst. Presiding Pastor, Rev. Donald C. Thorson, P.O. Box 775, Chippewa Falls, WI 54729

Sec., Rev. Thomas V. Aadland, 2415 Ensign St., Duluth, MN 55811 Tel. (218)722-7931

Treas., Rev. James E. Minor, 341 S. Hamline Ave., St. Paul, MN 55105

Admn. Coord., Mr. Gene Quist, 11 Norman Ridge Dr., Bloomington, MN 55437

PERIODICAL

Evangel, The

Mennonite Brethren Churches, The Conference of

A small group, requesting that closer attention be given to prayer, Bible study, and a consistent lifestyle, withdrew from the larger Mennonite Church in the Ukraine in 1860. Anabaptist in origin, the group was influenced by Lutheran pietists and Baptist teachings, and adopted a quasi-Congregational form of church government. In 1874 and years following, small groups of these German-speaking Mennonites left Russia, settled in Kansas, and then spread to the Midwest west of the Missisppi and into Canada. Some years later the movement spread to California and the West Coast. In 1960, the Krimmer Mennonite Brethren Conference merged with this body.

Today the General Conference of Mennonite Brethren Churches conducts services in many European languages as well as in Vietnamese, Mandarin, and Hindi. It works with other denominations in missionary and development projects in 25 countries outside North America.

HEADQUARTERS

4812 East Butler Avenue, Fresno, CA 93727

Media Contact, Exec. Sec., Marvin Hein, 4812 E. Butler Ave., Fresno, CA 93727 Tel. (209)251-8681 Fax (209)251-1432

OFFICERS

Mod., Edmund Janzen, 4935 E. Heaton, Fresno, CA 93727

Asst. Mod., Harry Heidebrecht, 2285 Clearbrook Rd., Clearbrook, BC V2T 2X4

Sec., Roland Reimer, 1631 N. Callahan, Wichita, KS 67212

Exec. Sec., Marvin Hein, 4812 E. Butler Ave., Fresno, CA 93727

PERIODICAL

Christian Leader

Mennonite Church

The Mennonite Church in North America traces its beginnings to the Protestant Reformation. Conrad Grebel, Georg Blaurock, and a small band of radical believers felt that Martin Luther and Ulrich Zwingli had not gone far enough in their break with Roman Catholic tradition and a return to New Testament discipleship. They baptized one another in Zurich, Switzerland, on Jan. 21, 1525. First nicknamed Anabaptists (Rebaptizers) by their opponents, they preferred the term Brothers and Sisters in Christ. They later took their name from the Dutch priest Menno Simons, who joined the movement in 1536.

The Mennonites' refusal to conform to majesterial decrees, including bearing of arms and the swearing of oaths, attracted fierce animosity. Thousands were martyred for their beliefs in nearly a century of persecution. They moved to many places, including the United States and Canada, where some arrived as early as 1683. Between 4,000 and 5,000 Mennonites settled in southeastern Pennsylvania between 1717 and 1756 in the first major migration from Europe. Caught between warring factions of America's struggle for independence, many moved west to Ohio, Indiana, Iowa, and to upper Canada (now Ontario).

North American Mennonites began their first home mission program in Chicago, Ill., in 1893 and their first overseas mission program in India in 1899. Since the 1920s the church has established extensive emergency relief and development services in conjunction with its mission program.

Mennonites hold that the Word of God is central and that new life in Christ is available to all who believe. Adult "Believer's" baptism is practiced, symbolizing a conscious decision to follow Christ. Mennonites take seriously Christ's command to witness in word and deed. They regard faith and works as two sides of the same coin. They stress that Christians need the support of a faith community for encouragement and growth. In times of crisis their "mutual aid" network makes time, money, and goods available to those in need. They view Jesus' teachings as directly applicable to their lives. Following the Prince of Peace, Mennonites generally refuse to serve in the military or to use violent resistance.

This is the largest body of Mennonites in North America. The Mennonite Church is a member of the Mennonite and Brethren in Christ World Conference — a fellowship of 171 bodies in 60 countries around the world with a membership of 850,000. The denomination is also a member of Mennonite Central Committee with offices in Akron, Pennsylvania and Winnipeg, Manitoba, a world-wide relief and service agency representing 12 North American churches and bodies. Individuals and program agencies participate in a variety of ecumenical activities at various levels of church life.

HEADQUARTERS
421 S. Second St., Ste. 600, Elkhart, IN 46516 Tel. (219)294-7131
Media Contact, Churchwide Communications Dir., John Bender, Fax (219)293-3977

OFFICERS
Mod., David W. Mann

OTHER ORGANIZATIONS
Gen. Bd., Gen. Sec., James M. Lapp
Historical Cmte., Dir., Levi Miller, 1700 S. Main, Goshen, IN 46526 Tel. (219)535-7477
Council on Faith, Life & Strategy, Staff, Miriam Book
Bd. of Congregational Min., Exec. Sec., Everett Thomas, Box 1245, Elkhart, IN 46515 Tel. (219)294-7523
Bd. of Educ., Exec. Sec., Albert Meyer, Box 1142, Elkhart, IN 46515 Tel. (219)294-7523
Bd. of Missions, Pres., Paul M. Gingrich, Box 370, Elkhart, IN 46515 Tel. (219)294-7523
Mutual Aid Bd., Pres., Howard Brenneman, 1110 North Main, P.O. Box 483, Goshen, IN 46526 Tel. (219)533-9511
Mennonite Publication Bd., Publisher, J. Robert Ramer, 616 Walnut Ave., Scottdale, PA 15683 Tel. (412)887-8500

PERIODICALS
Gospel Herald; Christian Living; Rejoice!; Mennonite Historical Bulletin; Mennonite Yearbook; Mennonite Quarterly Review; With; Purpose; On the Line; Sharing; Story Friends; Voice

Mennonite Church, The General Conference

The General Conference Mennonite Church was formed in 1860, uniting Mennonites throughout the United States who were interested in doing missionary work together. Today 60,000 Christians in 363 congregations try to follow the way of Jesus in their daily lives.

The conference consists of people of many ethnic backgrounds — Swiss and German, Russian and Dutch, Black, Hispanic, Chinese, Vietnamese, and Laotian. Some native Americans in both Canada and the United States also relate to the conference.

The basic belief and practice of the conference come from the life and teachings of Jesus Christ, the early church of the New Testament, and the Anabaptists of the 16th-century Reformation. Thus the conference seeks to be evangelical,

guided by the Bible, led by the Holy Spirit, and supported by a praying, discerning community of believers in congregations and fellowships. Peace, or shalom, is at the very heart of members, who seek to be peacemakers in everyday life.

The goals of the conference for the next three to six years are to evangelize, teach and practice biblical principles, train and develop leaders, and work for Christian unity.

HEADQUARTERS
722 Main, Newton, KS 67114 Tel. (316)283-5100 Fax (316)283-0454
Media Contact, Communications Dir., David Linscheid

OFFICERS
Mod., Darrell Fast, 328 E. 2nd St., Newton, KS 67114
Asst. Mod., Bernie Wiebe, 46 Belair Rd., Winnipeg, MB R3T 0S2
Sec., Anita Penner, 33304 Century Cres., Abbotsford, BC V2S 5V5
Gen. Sec., Vern Preheim

OTHER ORGANIZATIONS
Commission on Home Ministries, Exec., Lois Barrett
Commission on Overseas Mission, Exec. Sec., Erwin Rempel
Women in Mission, Coord., Susan Jantzen
Commission on Education, Exec. Sec., Norma Johnson
Div. of General Services, Bus. Mgr., Ted Stuckey
Div. of General Services, Planned Giving Dir., Gary Franz
Div. of General Services, Communications Dir., David Linscheid
Mennonite Men, Coord., Heinz Janzen
Faith & Life Press, Mgr., Dietrich Rempel
Committee on Ministry, Dir. of Ministerial Leadership, John A. Esau

PERIODICALS
Being In Touch; Builder; Mennonite, The; Window to Mission

The Metropolitan Church Association, Inc.

Organized after a revival movement in Chicago in 1894 as the Metropolitan Holiness Church, It was chartered as the Metropolitan Church Association in 1899. It has Wesleyan theology.

HEADQUARTERS
323 Broad St., Lake Geneva, WI 53147 Tel. (414)248-6786
Media Contact, Pres., Rev. Warren W. Bitzer

OFFICERS
Pres., Rev. Warren W. Bitzer
Vice-Pres. & Sec., Elbert L. Ison
Treas., Gertrude J. Puckhaber

PERIODICAL
Burning Bush, The

Metropolitan Community Churches, Universal Fellowship of

Founded Oct. 6, 1968 by the Rev. Troy D. Perry in Los Angeles, with a particular but not exclusive outreach to the gay community. Since that time, the Fellowship has grown to include congregations throughout the world.

103

The group is trinitarian and accepts the Bible as the divinely inspired Word of God. The Fellowship has two sacraments: baptism and holy communion, as well as a number of traditionally recognized rites such as ordination.

This Fellowship acknowledges "the Holy Scriptures interpreted by the Holy Spirit in conscience and faith, as its guide in faith, discipline, and government." The government of this Fellowship is vested in its General Council (consisting of Elders and District Coordinators), clergy and church delegates, who exert the right of control in all of its affairs, subject to the provisions of its Articles of Incorporation and By-Laws."

HEADQUARTERS

5300 Santa Monica Blvd. #304, Los Angeles, CA 90029 Tel. (213)464-5100 Fax (213)464-2123
Media Contact, PR Rep., Rev. Kittridge Cherry

OFFICERS

Mod., Rev. Elder Troy D. Perry
Vice-Mod., Rev. Elder Freda Smith, P.O. Box 20125, Sacramento, CA 95820
Treas., Rev. Elder Donald Eastman
Clk., Elder Larry Rodriguez
Rev. Elder Nancy L. Wilson
Rev. Elder Willem Hein, P.O. Box 392, Elsternwick, VIC 3185, Australia
Rev. Elder Jean A. White, 2A Sistova Rd., Balham, London SW12 9QT England
Dir. of Admn., Mr. Ravi Verma

DISTRICT COORDINATORS

Australian District, Rev. Greg Smith, 109 Maiala Rd., Cooks Gap, Mudgee, NSW 2850, Australia
Eastern Canadian District, Ms. Lydia Segal, 50 Cosburn Ave. #802, Toronto, ON M4K 2G5
European North Sea District, Rev. Hong Tan, 72 Fleet Rd., Hampstead, London NW3 2QT England
Great Lakes District, Judy Dale, 1300 Ambridge Dr., Louisville, KY 40207 Tel. (502)897-3821
Gulf Lower Atlantic District, Mr. Jay Neely, P.O. Box 8356, Atlanta, GA 30306
Mid-Central District, Rev. Bonnie Daniel, 1364 Collins Ave., Topeka, KS 66604
Mid-Atlantic District, R. Adam DeBaugh, P.O. Box 7864, Gaithersburg, MD 20898
Northeast District, Rev. Jeff Pulling, P.O. Box 340529, Hartford, CT 06134
Northwest District, Rev. Thomas Bigelow, P.O. Box 20489, Seattle, WA 98102
South Central District, Clarke Friesen, P.O. Box 262822, Houston, TX 77207
Southeast District, Rev. Judy Davenport, Jacksonville, FL
Southwest District, Rev. Don Pederson, 10913 Fruitland Dr., #117, Studio City, CA 91604
Western Canadian District, Rev. Bev Baptiste, 3531-33rd Ave., Edmonton, AB T6L 4N6

OTHER COMMISSIONS & COMMITTEES

Excel International, Exec. Dir., Brenda Blizzard, 4921 NE 187th, Seattle, WA 98155
World Church Extension, Exec. Sec., Rev. Elder Jean White, 2A Sistova Rd., Balham, London SW12 9QT England
Faith Fellowship & Order, Chpsn., Rev. Steven Torrence, 1215 Petronia St., Key West, FL 33040
Dept. of People of Color, Dir., Bernard Barbour, c/o UFMCC
Commission on the Laity, Chpsn., JoNee Shelton, 3029 Royal Street, New Orleans, LA 70117

Clergy Credentials & Concerns, Chpsn., Rev. Candace Shultis, 415 M St. N.W., Washington, DC 20001
Bd. of Pensions: Pres., Leon Hampton, 6219 Edison Dr., Alexandria, VA 22310; Admn., Lois Luneburg, P.O. Box 107, Arnold, CA 95223
Ecumenical Witness & Ministry: Chief Officer, Rev. Elder Nancy Wilson, 5879 Washington Blvd., Culver City, CA 90232
UFMCC AIDS Ministry: Exec Dir., Rev. Elder Donald Eastman, c/o UFMCC; Field Dir., Rev. Steve Pieters, c/o UFMCC

PERIODICALS

Keeping in Touch; Alert

The Missionary Church

The Missionary Church was formed in 1969 through a merger of the United Missionary Church (organized in 1883) and the Missionary Church Association (founded in 1898). It is evangelical and conservative with a strong emphasis on missionary work and church planting.

There are three levels of church government with local, district, and general conferences. There are 10 church districts in the United States. The general conference meets every two years. The denomination operates one college in the United States.

HEADQUARTERS

3811 Vanguard Dr., P.O. Box 9127, Ft. Wayne, IN 46899-9127 Tel. (219)747-2027 Fax (219)747-5331
Publishing Headquarters, Bethel Publishing Co., 1819 S. Main St., Elkhart, IN 46516 Tel. (219)293-8585
Media Contact, Pres., Dr. John P. Moran

OFFICERS

Pres., Dr. John Moran
Vice-Pres., Rev. William Hossler
Sec., Rev. Dave Engbrecht
Treas., Mr. Milt Gerber
Asst. to the Pres., Rev. Bob Ransom
Overseas Ministries (World Partners): Dir., Rev. Charles Carpenter; Dir. of Mission Ministries, Rev. David Mann
Services Dir., Mr. David von Gunten
Bethel Publishing Co., Exec. Dir., Rev. Richard Oltz
Stewardship, Dir., Rev. Ken Stucky
Youth Dir., Mr. Eric Liechty
Children's Dir., Dr. Neil McFarlane
Adult Dir., Dr. Duane Beals
Missionary Men Intl., Pres., Mr. Carl White
Missionary Women Intl., Pres., Mrs. Opal Speicher
Investment Foundation, Mr. Bob Henschen

PERIODICALS

Emphasis on Faith and Living; Ministry Today; World Partners; Priority

Moravian Church in America (Unitas Fratrum)

In 1735 German Moravian missionaries of the pre-Reformation faith of Jan Hus came to Georgia, in 1740 to Pennsylvania, and in 1753 to North Carolina. They established the American Moravian Church, which is broadly evangelical, ecumenical, liturgical, with an episcopacy as a spiritual office and in form of government "conferential."

See Provincial addresses
Media Contact, Editor, *The Moravian*, The Rev.
Hermann I. Weinlick, P.O. Box 1245, Bethlehem, PA 18016-1245 Tel. (215)867-7566 Fax
(215)866-9223

NORTHERN PROVINCE
1021 Center St., P.O. Box 1245, Bethlehem, PA
18016-1245 Tel. (215)867-7566 Fax (215)866-
9223

OFFICERS
Provincial Elders' Conference, Pres., Rev. Dr.
Gordon L. Sommers
Provincial Elders' Conference, Vice-Pres./Sec.
(Eastern Dist.), The Rev. David L. Wickmann
Provincial Elders' Conference, Vice-Pres. (West-
ern Dist.), Rev. R. Burke Johnson, P.O. Box 386,
Sun Prairie, WI 53590 Fax (608)825-6610
Provincial Elders' Conference, Treas., John F.
Ziegler, 1021 Center St., P.O. Box 1245, Bethle-
hem, PA 18016

SOUTHERN PROVINCE
459 S. Church St., Winston-Salem, NC 27108 Tel.
(919)725-5811 Fax (919)725-1893

OFFICERS
Provincial Elders' Conference, Pres., Rev. Dr.
Graham H. Rights
Provincial Elders' Conference, Vice-Pres., The
Rev. William H. McElveen
Provincial Elders' Conference, Sec., Richard R.
Bovender
Provincial Elders' Conference, Treas., Ronald R.
Hendrix, Drawer O, Salem Station, Winston-
Salem, NC 27108

ALASKA PROVINCE
P.O. Box 545, Bethel, AK 99559

OFFICERS
Pres., The Rev. John P. Andrew
Vice-Pres., The Rev. David Paul
Sec., Ferdinand Sharp
Treas., Juanita Asicksik
Dir. of Theological Education, Rev. Dr. Kurt H.
Vitt

PERIODICAL
Moravian, The

Muslims
Islam now claims approximately 6 million adherents in the United States. Some of them are
immigrants, who represent almost every part of the
world. Others are Americans who converted to
Islam. These are apart from those who come to
America temporarily as Muslim diplomats, students, and those who work in international institutions such as the World Bank, the International
Monetary Fund, and the United Nations.
Muslims are found in nearly every American
town. Their number increases in large industrial
and commercial cities in the East and Midwest, but
there are also large numbers of Muslims in some
areas on the West Coast.
Many Islamic organizations exist in the United
States under such titles as Islamic Society, Islamic
Center, or Muslim Mosque. The aim is to provide
a group in a locality with a place of worship and of
meeting for other religious, social, and educational
purposes. These societies and organizations are
not regarded as religious sects or divisions. All the
groups hold the same beliefs, aspire to practice the
same rituals: namely, prayers, fasting, almsgiving,
and pilgrimage to Makkah. Black organizations
may mix civil rights aspirations with Islamic objectives and may, therefore, follow a rigid discipline for their members.
The main Islamic organizations are the Islamic
centers which are found in all 300 large cities. Their
objectives are cultural, religious, and educational;
and each one has a mosque or a prayer hall.
The regional and national groups listed below
were started with the objective of helping local
groups coordinate their work, and promote closer
unity among them. Prominent among these is: The
Islamic Center of Washington, 2551 Massachusetts Ave. NW, Washington, DC 20008. Tel.
(202)332-8343.

REGIONAL AND NATIONAL GROUPS
American Muslim Council, Exec. Dir., Ab-
durahman Alamoudi, 1212 New York Ave., NW,
Ste. 525, Washington, DC 20005 Tel. (202)789-
2262 Fax (202)789-2550
Council of Masajid (Mosques) in the USA, Pres.,
Dawud Assad, 99 Woodview Dr., Old Bridge, NJ
08857 Tel. (908)679-8617 Fax (908)679-1216
Fed. of Islamic Assoc. in US & Canada, Sec. Gen.,
Nihad Hamid, 25351 Five Mile Rd., Redford
Township, MI 48239 Tel. (313)535-0014
Islamic Society of North America, Pres., Dr. Syed
Imtiaz Ahmad, P.O. Box 38, Plainfield, IN
46168 Tel. (317)839-8157
Council of Muslim Communities of Canada, Dir.,
Dr. Mir Iqbal Ali, 1250 Ramsey View Ct., Ste.
504, Sudbury, ON P3E 2E7 Tel. (705)522-2948
Muslim World League: Dir., Sahal Al-Matrafi,
1655 N. Fort Myer Dr., Ste. 700, Arlington, VA
22209 Tel. (703)351-5296 Fax (703)351-5241;
Assoc. Dir., Dawud Assad

PERIODICAL
Majallat Al-Masjid

National Missionary Baptist Convention of America
The National Missionary Baptist Convention of
America was organized as a separate entity from
the National Baptist Convention of America, Inc.,
in 1988, after a dispute over control of the convention's publishing efforts. The new organization
intended to remain committed to the National
Baptist Sunday Church School and Baptist Training Union Congress and the National Baptist Publishing Board.
The purpose of the National Missionary Baptist
Convention of America is to serve as an agency of
Christian education, church extension, and missionary efforts. It seeks to maintain and safeguard
full religious liberty and engage in social and
economic development.

HEADQUARTERS
719 Crosby St., San Diego, CA 92113 Tel.
(619)233-6487

OFFICERS
Pres., Dr. S.M. Lockridge
Vice pres., at-large, Dr. E.S. Branch
Vice pres., ecumenical affairs, Dr. F. Benjamin
Davis
Vice pres., auxiliaries, Dr. Harvey Leggett
Vice-pres., boards, Dr. S.M. Wright
Pres., National Baptist Publishing Bd., Dr. T.B.
Boyd, III

Gen. Sec., Dr. S.J. Gilbert, Sr, 902 W. 8th St., Houston, TX 77007 Te. (713)869-9171 Fax (713)869-0902.
Corresp. Sec., Dr. H.J. Johnson
Treas., Dr. W.N. Daniel
Recording Sec., Dr. M.V. Wade

National Baptist Convention of America

The National Baptist Convention of America, Incorporated, was organized in 1880 following a dispute over control of the publishing board in which another Convention was organized. Membership of the churches is largely African-American.

HEADQUARTERS

Media Contact, Liaison Officer, Dr. Richard A. Rollins, 777 S.R.L. Thornton Fwy., Ste. 205, Dallas, TX 75203 Tel. (214)946-8913 Fax (214)946-9619

OFFICERS

Pres., Dr. E. Edward Jones
1st Vice-Pres., Dr. Albert E. Chew
2nd Vice-Pres., Dr. Wallace Hartsfield
3rd Vice-Pres., Rev. Stephen J. Thurston
4th Vice-Pres., Rev. H. T. Rhim
Gen. Recording Sec., Dr. Clarence C. Pennywell
1st Asst. Sec., Dr. Louis W. Smith
2nd Asst. Sec., Rev. T. E. Gainous
3rd Asst. Sec., Dr. W. A. Johnson
4th Asst. Sec., Dr. L. Z. Blankenship
Corresponding Sec., Dr. E. E. Stafford
Treas., Rev. F. N. Williams
Hist., Dr. Marvin C. Griffin
Statistician, Rev. Clyde Kelly
Auditor, Rev. J. Carlton Allen
Liaison Officer, Dr. Richard A. Rollins
Public Relations Dir., Rev. Joe R. Gant
Dir. of Music, Mrs. Jessie M. Berry
Youth Dir., Dr. Benjamin J. Maxon, Jr.
Social Justice Commission, Rev. Mac Charles Jones
Commission on Orthodoxy, Rev. F. D. Sampson
Commission on Chaplaincy, Rev. J. William Dailey
Lantern Editor, Rev. L. A. Williams

BOARDS AND AUXILIARIES

Education Bd.: Chpsn., Dr. J. B. Adams; Exec. Sec., Rev. Wm. "Bill" Brent
Christian Education Bd.: Chpsn., Rev. Gusta Booker; Exec. Sec., Rev. Timothy Winters; Rev. George Brooks
Evangelical Bd.: Chpsn., Rev. Earl A. Pleasant; Sec./Treas., Rev. Hayward Wiggins
Foreign Mission Bd.: Chpsn., Rev. Asa W. Sampson
Foreign Missions Bd.: Exec. Sec., Rev. Isadore Edwards
Home Mission Bd.: Chpsn., Rev. Luke W. Mingo
Benevolent Bd.: Sec./Treas., Rev. J. D. Williams; Chpsn., Dr. C. B. T. Smith; Sec./Treas., Rev. N. S. Sanders
Publishing Bd.: Chpsn., Rev. H. T. Rhim; Dr. Frank Pinkard
Congress of Christian Workers: Pres., Dr. Robert H. Wilson
Senior Women's Auxiliary: Pres., Mrs. Evelyn Reed
Junior Women's Auxiliary: Pres., Ms. Deborah Johnson
Matrons: Pres., Mrs. Susan Turner

Nurses: Pres., Mrs. Della H. Bryson
Ushers: Pres., Mrs. Frankie A. Carter

BOARDS AND AUXILIARIES

Brotherhood: Pres., Mr. Cornelius Lee
Men of Christian Action—Young Men: Pres., Mr. Al Curtis Green
Youth Convention: Pres., Mr. Darwan Lazard

PERIODICAL

NBCA Lantern

National Baptist Convention, U.S.A., Inc.

The older and parent convention of black Baptists, this body is to be distinguished from the National Baptist Convention of America.

HEADQUARTERS

1700 Baptist World Center Dr., Nashville, TN 37207 Tel. (615)228-6292 Fax (615)226-5935

OFFICERS

Pres., Dr. T. J. Jemison, 356 East Boulevard, Baton Rouge, LA 70802 Tel. (504) 383-5401
Gen. Sec., Dr. W. Franklyn Richardson, 52 South 6th Ave., Mt. Vernon, NY 10550 Tel. (914) 664-2676
Vice-Pres.-at-large, Dr. C. A. W. Clark, 3110 Bonnie View Rd., Dallas, TX 75216 Tel. (214)375-6982
Treas., Dr. Isaac Green, 3068 Iowa St., Pittsburgh, PA 15219 Tel. (412)556-1437
Vice-Pres.: Dr. David Matthews, P.O. Box 627, Indianola, MS; Dr. P. J. James, 1104 E. Cherry St., Blytheville, AZ 72315; Dr. Henry L. Lyons; Dr. E. Victor Hill, 1300-08 East 50th St., Los Angeles, CA 90011; Dr. Allen Stanley, 2165 Fifth Ave., Troy, NY 12182
Asst. Sec.: Dr. B. J. Whipper, Sr., 15 Ninth St., Charleston, SC 29403; Rev. Otis B. Smith, P.O. Box 544, Tuscaloosa, AL 35404; Dr. Roger P. Derricotte, 539 Roseville Ave., Newark, NJ 07107; Dr. McKinley Dukes, 4223 S. Benton, Kansas City, MO 64130
Stat., Rev. H. L. Harvey, Jr., 3212 Reading Rd., Cincinnati, OH 45229
Hist., Dr. Clarence Wagner, 500 Myrtle St., Gainesville, GA 30501 Tel. (404)536-8474

OFFICERS OF BOARDS

Foreign Mission Bd., Sec., Dr. William J. Harvey, 701 S. 19th St. Philadelphia, PA 19146
Home Mission Bd., Exec. Sec., Dr. Jerry Moore, 1612 Buchanan St. N.W., Washington, DC 20011
Sunday School Publishing Bd., Exec. Dir., Mrs. C. N. Adkins, 330 Charlotte Ave., Nashville, TN 37201
Education Bd., Chpsn., Dr. J. Parrish Wilson, 114 S. 22nd St., Saginaw, MI 48601
Evangelism Bd., Dr. Manuel Scott, 2600 S. Marsalis Ave., Dallas, TX 75216
Laymen's Movement, Pres., Mr. Walter Cade, 1421 North 13th St., Kansas City, KS 66102
Woman's Auxiliary Convention, Pres., Mrs. Mary O. Ross, 584 Arden Pk., Detroit, MI 48202
Congress of Christian Education, Dr. A. Lincoln James, Sr., 5302 S. Michigan Ave., Chicago, IL 60615 Tel. (312)723-3488

PERIODICAL

National Baptist Voice

National Organization of the New Apostolic Church of North America

This body is a variant of the Catholic Apostolic Church, which began in England in 1830. The New Apostolic Church distinguished itself from the parent body in 1863 by recognizing a succession of Apostles.

HEADQUARTERS

3753 N. Troy St., Chicago, IL 60618

Media Contact, Sec. & Treas., Ellen E. Eckhardt, Tel. (312)539-3652 Fax (312)478-6691

OFFICERS

Pres., Rev. Michael Kraus, 267 Lincoln Rd., Waterloo, ON

First Vice-Pres., Rev. John W. Fendt, 36 Colony La., Manhasset, NY 11030

Second Vice-Pres., Rev. Erwin Wagner, 330 Arlene Pl., Waterloo, ON

Treas. & Sec., Ellen E. Eckhardt, 6380 N. Indian Rd., Chicago, IL 60646

Asst. Sec., Rev. William K. Schmeerbauch, 5516 Pine Wood Forest, St. Louis, MO 63128

PERIODICAL

Our Family

National Primitive Baptist Convention, Inc.

Throughout the years of slavery and the Civil War, the Negro population of the South worshipped with the white population in their various churches. At the time of emancipation, their white brethren helped them to establish their own churches, granting them letters of fellowship, ordaining their deacons and ministers, and helping them in other ways.

The doctrine and polity of this body are quite similar to that of white Primitive Baptists, except that they are "opposed to all forms of church organization"; yet there are local associations and a national convention, organized in 1907.

Each church is independent and receives and controls its own membership. This body was formerly known as Colored Primitive Baptists.

HEADQUARTERS

P.O. Box 2355, Tallahassee, FL

OFFICERS

Natl. Convention, Pres., Elder F. L. Livingston, 1334 Carson St., Dallas, TX 75216 Tel. (214)946-4650

Natl. Convention, Sec. Bd. of Dirs., Elder M. G. Miles, 1525 S. Bronough St., Tallahassee, FL 32301 Tel. (904)222-4753

Natl. Church School Training Union, Pres., Elder W.D. Judge, 1718 West Grand Ave., Orlando, FL 32805

Natl. Ushers Congress, Pres. & Sec., Bro. Carl Batts, 21213 Garden View Dr., Maple Heights, OH 44137

Publishing Bd., Chpsn., Elder T. W. Samuels, 6433 Hidden Forest Dr., Charlotte, NC 28206

Women's Congress, Pres., Mrs. Lillian J. Brantley, 1795 N.W. 58th St., Miami, FL 33142

Natl. Laymen's Council, Pres., George W. Brown, 405 E. 26th St., Patterson, NJ 07514

Natl. Youth Congress, Pres., Levy Freeman, 3920 Gardenside Dr. NW, Huntsville, AL 35810

National Spiritualist Association of Churches

This organization is made up of believers that Spiritualism is a science, philosophy, and religion based upon the demonstrated facts of communication between this world and the next.

HEADQUARTERS

Media Contact, Sec., Rev. Sharon L. Snowman, 13 Cottage Row, Lily Dale, NY 14752 Tel. (716)595-2000 Fax (716)595-2020

OFFICERS

Pres., Rev. Joseph H. Merrill, 13 Cleveland Ave., Lily Dale, NY 14752

Vice-Pres., Rev. Brenda Wittich, 3903 Connecticut St., St. Louis, MO 63116

Sec., Rev. Sharon L. Lynch, P.O. Box 217, Lily Dale, NY 14752 Tel. (716)595-2000 Fax (716)595-2020

Treas., Rev. Alfred A. Conner, 293 Jersey St., San Francisco, CA 94114

OTHER ORGANIZATIONS

Bureau of Educ., Supt., Rev. Joseph Sax, Morris Pratt Institute, 11811 Watertown Plank Rd., Milwaukee, WI 53226

Bureau of Public Relations, Rev. Brenda Wittich, 3903 Connecticut St., St. Louis, MO 63116

The Stow Memorial Foundation, Sec., Rev. Sharon L. Snowman, P.O. Box 217, Lily Dale, NY 14752 Tel. (716)595-2000 Fax (716)595-2020

Spiritualist Benevolent Society, Inc., P.O. Box 217, Lily Dale, NY 14752

PERIODICAL

National Spiritualist Summit, The

Netherlands Reformed Congregations

The Netherlands Reformed Congregations organized denominationally in 1907. In the Netherlands, the so-called Churches Under the Cross (established in 1839, after breaking away from the 1834 Secession congregations) and the so-called Ledeboerian churches (established in 1841 under the leadership of the Rev. Ledeboer, who seceded from the Reformed State Church), united in 1907 under the leadership of the then 25-year-old Rev. G. H. Kersten, to form the Netherlands Reformed Congregations. Many of the North American congregations left the Christian Reformed Church to join the Netherlands Reformed Congregations after the Kuyperian presupposed regeneration doctrine began making inroads.

All Netherlands Reformed Congregations, office-bearers, and members subscribe to three Reformed Forms of Unity: The Belgic Confession of Faith (by DeBres), the Heidelberg Catechism (by Ursinus and Olevianus), and the Canons of Dort. Both the Belgic Confession and the Canons of Dort are read regularly at worship services, and the Heidelberg Catechism is preached weekly, except on church feast days.

HEADQUARTERS

Media Contact, Synodical Clk., Dr. Joel R. Beeke, 2115 Romence Ave., N.E., Grand Rapids, MI 49503 Tel. (616)459-6565 Fax (616)459-7709

OFFICERS

Clk. of Synod, Dr. Joel R. Beeke, 2115 Romence Ave. N.E., Grand Rapids, MI 49503

Netherlands Reformed Book and Publishing, 1020 N. Main Ave., Sioux Center, IA 51250

PERIODICALS
Banner of Truth, The; Paul

North American Baptist Conference

The North American Baptist Conference began through immigrants from Germany. The first church was organized by the Rev. Konrad Fleischmann in Philadelphia in 1843. In 1865 delegates of the churches met in Wilmot, Ont., and organized the North American Baptist Conference. Today only a few churches still use the German language, mostly in a bilingual setting.

The Conference meets in general session once every three years for fellowship, inspiration and to conduct the business of the Conference through elected delegates from the local churches. The General Council, composed of representatives of the various Associations and Conference organizations and departments, meets annually to determine the annual budget and programs for the Conference and its departments and agencies. The General Council also makes recommendations to the Triennial Conference on policies, long-range plans and election of certain personnel, boards and committees.

Approximately 80 missionaries serve in Cameroon, Nigeria, West Africa, Japan, Brazil, Eastern Europe, Mexico, and the Philippines, as well as among various ethnic groups throughout the United States and Canada.

Nine homes for the aged are affiliated with the Conference and 10 camps are operated on the association level.

HEADQUARTERS
1 S. 210 Summit Ave., Oakbrook Terrace, IL 60181 Tel. (708)495-2000 Fax (708)495-3301
Media Contact, Development Dir., Rev. Lewis Petrie

OFFICERS
Mod., Mr. Richard Russell
Vice-Mod., Rev. Ron Norman
Exec. Dir., Dr. John Binder
Treas., Mr. Jackie Loewer

OTHER ORGANIZATIONS
Missions Dept., Dir., Rev. Herman Effa
Church Min. Dept., Dir., Dr. Ronald Mayforth
Management Services Dept., Dir., Mr. Ron Salzman
Area Ministries, Dir., Dr. Ronald Mayforth
Church Extension Investors Fund, Dir., Mr. Robert Mayforth

PERIODICAL
Baptist Herald

North American Old Roman Catholic Church

This church can be traced back to the early 1700s to the Ultrajectine Tradition when the church in Holland experienced a truly catholic reform. The Church came to the United States and Mexico in its present form in the early part of this century.

English and Latin pre-Vatican II masses are celebrated. The Baltimore Catechism is used. The Pontificale Romanum is used for consecration and other episcopal and liturgical functions. This church recognizes the authority of the See of St. Peter. The sacraments and holy orders of the Old Roman Catholic Church are universally accepted .

HEADQUARTERS
4200 N. Kedvale Ave., Chicago, IL 60641 Tel. (312)685-0461
Media Contact, Presiding Archbishop, Most Rev. Theodore J. Rematt, SGS

OFFICERS
Archbishop, Most Rev. Theodore J. Rematt

PERIODICAL
North American Catholic, The

North American Old Roman Catholic Church (Archdiocese of New York)

This body is identical with the Roman Catholic Church in faith, but differs from it in discipline and worship. The Mass is offered with the appropriate rite either in Latin or in the vernacular. All other sacraments are taken from the Roman Pontifical. This jurisdiction allows for married clergy.

PRIMATIAL HEADQUARTERS
Box 021647 GPO, Brooklyn, NY 11202-0036 Tel. (718)855-0600
Media Contact, Chancellor, Rev. Albert J. Berube

OFFICERS
Primate, The Most Rev. Herve L. Quessy
Chancellor, Bishop-Elect Albert J. Berube

OFFICERS-DIOCESE OF NEW YORK
Ordinary, Bishop-Elect Albert J. Berube

OFFICERS -DIOCESE OF MONTREAL & FRENCH CANADA
Ordinary, Most Rev. Herve L. Quessy

Old German Baptist Brethren

This group separated from the Church of the Brethren (formerly German Baptist Brethren) in 1881 as a protest against a liberalizing tendency.

HEADQUARTERS
Media Contact, Vindicator Ofc. Ed., Elder Keith Skiles, 1876 Beamsville-Union City Rd., Union City, OH Tel. (513)968-3877

OFFICERS
Foreman, Elder Clement Skiles, Rt. 1, Box 140, Bringhurst, IN 46913 Tel. (219)967-3367
Reading Clk., Elder Herman Shuman, Rt. 4, Box 301, Pendleton, IN 46064
Writing Clk., Elder Carl Bowman, 4065 State Rt. 48, Covington, OH 45318 Tel. (513)473-2729

PERIODICAL
Vindicator, The

Old Order Amish Church

The congregations of this Old Order Amish group have no annual conference. They worship in private homes. They adhere to the older forms of worship and attire. This body has bishops, ministers, and deacons.

HEADQUARTERS
Media Contact, LeRoy Beachy, Beachy Amish Menn. Church, 4324 SR 39, Millersburg, OH 44654 Tel. (216)893-2883

Der Neue Amerikanische Calendar, c/o Raber's Book Store, 2467 C R 600, Baltic, OH 43804

Old Order (Wisler) Mennonite Church

This body arose from a separation of Mennonites dated 1870, under Jacob Wisler, in opposition to what were thought to be innovations.

The group is in the Eastern United States and Canada. Each state, or district, has its own organization and holds a yearly conference.

HEADQUARTERS

Media Contact, Amos B. Hoover, 376 N. Muddy Creek Rd., Denver, PA 17517 Tel. (215)484-4849

Open Bible Standard Churches, Inc.

Open Bible Standard Churches originated from two revival movements: Bible Standard Conference, founded in Eugene, Ore., under the leadership of Fred L. Hornshuh, in 1919, and Open Bible Evangelistic Association, founded in Des Moines, Iowa, under the leadership of John R. Richey, in 1932.

Similar in doctrine and government, the two groups amalgamated on July 26, 1935, as "Open Bible Standard Churches, Inc.," with headquarters in Des Moines, Iowa.

The original group of 210 ministers has enlarged to incorporate over 1,579 ministers and 850 churches in 32 countries. The first missionary left for India in 1926. The church now ministers in Asia, Africa, South America, Europe, Canada, Mexico, and the Caribbean Islands.

Historical roots of the parent groups reach back to the outpouring of the Holy Spirit in 1906 at Azusa Street Mission in Los Angeles, and to the full gospel movement in the Midwest. Both groups were organized under the impetus of pentecostal revival. Simple faith, freedom from fanaticism, emphasis on evangelism and missions, and free fellowship with other groups were characteristics of the growing organizations.

The highest governing body of Open Bible Standard Churches meets biennially and is composed of all ministers and one voting delegate per 100 members from each church. A National Board of Directors, elected by the national and regional conferences, conducts the business of the organization. Official Bible College is Eugene Bible College in Oregon.

Open Bible Standard Churches is a charter member of the National Association of Evangelicals and of the Pentecostal Fellowship of North America. It is a member of the Pentecostal World Conference.

HEADQUARTERS

2020 Bell Ave., Des Moines, IA 50315 Tel. (515)288-6761 Fax (515)288-2510
Media Contact, Pres., Ray E. Smith

OFFICERS

Pres., Ray E. Smith
Sec.-Treas., Patrick L. Bowlin
Dir. of Intl. Min., Paul V. Canfield
Dir. of Christian Education, Randall A. Bach

PERIODICALS

Message of the Open Bible; World Vision; Outreach Magazine

The (Original) Church of God, Inc.

This body was organized in 1886 as the first church in the United States to take the name "The Church of God." In 1917 a difference of opinion led this particular group to include the word (Original) in its name. It is a holiness body and believes in the whole Bible, rightly divided, using the New Testament as its rule and government.

HEADQUARTERS

P.O. Box 3086, Chattanooga, TN 37404 Tel. (615)629-4505

OFFICERS

Gen. Overseer, Rev. Johnny Albertson
Asst. Gen. Overseer, Rev. Alton Evans
Sec.-Treas., Michael B. Mitchell

PERIODICAL

Messenger, The

The Orthodox Church in America

The Russian Orthodox Greek Catholic Church of America entered Alaska in 1794 before its purchase by the United States in 1867. Its canonical status of independence (autocephaly) was granted by its Mother Church, the Russian Orthodox Church, on April 10, 1970, and it is now known as The Orthodox Church in America.

HEADQUARTERS

P.O. Box 675, Syosset, NY 11791 Tel. (516)922-0550 Fax (516) 922-0954
Media Contact, Dir. of Communications, Rev. Gregory Havrilak

OFFICERS

Primate: The Most Blessed Theodosius, Archbishop of Washington, Metropolitan of All America & Canada
Chancellor, V. Rev. Robert S. Kondratick, Fax (516)922-0954

SYNOD

Chpsn., His Beatitude Theodosius
Archbishop of New York, The Most Rev. Peter, 33 Hewitt Ave., Bronxville, NY 10708
Archbishop of Pittsburgh & Western PA, The Most Rev. Kyrill, P.O. Box R, Wexford, PA 15090
Bishop of Dallas, The Rt. Rev. Dmitri, 4112 Throckmorton, Dallas, TX 75219
Bishop of Philadelphia, The Rt. Rev. Herman, St. Tikhon's Monastery, South Canaan, PA 18459
Bishop of Sitka, The Rt. Rev. Gregory, St. Michael's Cathedral, Box 697, Sitka, AK 99835
Bishop of Detroit, The Rt. Rev. Nathaniel, 2522 Grey Tower Rd., Jackson, MI 49201
Bishop of Hartford, The Rt. Rev. Job, 6 Clark Rd., Cumberland, RI 02864
Bishop of San Francisco, The Rt. Rev. Tikhon, 649 North Robinson St., Los Angeles, CA 90026
Bishop of Ottawa and Canada, The Rt. Rev. Seraphim, RR 5, Box 179, Spencerville, ON K0E 1X0 Tel. (613)925-5226
Auxiliary Bishop, Titular Bishop of Bethesda, The Rt. Rev. Mark, 9511 Sun Pointe Dr., Boynton Beach, FL 33437

PERIODICAL

The Orthodox Church

US RELIGIOUS BODIES

The Orthodox Presbyterian Church

On June 11, 1936, certain ministers, elders, and lay members of the Presbyterian Church in the U.S.A. withdrew from that body to form a new denomination. Under the leadership of the late Rev. J. Gresham Machen, noted conservative New Testament scholar, the new church determined to continue to uphold the Westminster Confession of Faith as traditionally understood by Presbyterians, and to engage in proclamation of the gospel at home and abroad.

The church has grown modestly over the years and suffered early defections, most notably one in 1937 that resulted in the formation of the Bible Presbyterian Church under the leadership of Dr. Carl McIntire. It now has congregations throughout the states of the continental United States.

The denomination is a member of the North American Presbyterian and Reformed Council.

HEADQUARTERS
303 Horsham Rd., Ste. G, Horsham, PA 19044 Tel. (215)956-0123 Fax (215)957-6286
Media Contact, Stated Clerk, The Rev. Donald J. Duff

OFFICERS
Mod., Rev. Stephen L. Phillips, 42 Beresford Rd., Rochester, NY 14610-1903 Tel. (716)482-6398
Stated Clk., Rev. Donald J. Duff

PERIODICAL
New Horizons in the Orthodox Pres. Ch.

Pentecostal Assemblies of the World, Inc.

This organization is an interracial Pentecostal holiness of the Apostolic Faith, believing in repentance, baptism in Jesus' Name, and being filled with the Holy Ghost, with the evidence of speaking in tongues. It originated in the early part of the century in the Middle West has spread throughout the country.

HEADQUARTERS
3939 Meadows Dr., Indianapolis, IN 46205 Tel. (317)547-9541
Media Contact, Admin., John E. Hampton, Fax (317)543-0512

OFFICERS
Presiding Bishop, Paul A. Bowers
Asst. Presiding Bishop, David Ellis
Gen. Sec, Suffragan Bishop Richard Young
Gen. Treas., Elder James Loving
Asst. Treas., Suffragan Bishop Willie Ellis

PERIODICAL
Christian Outlook

Pentecostal Church of God

Growing out of the pentecostal revivals at the turn of the century, the Pentecostal Church of God was organized in Chicago on Dec. 30, 1919, as the Pentecostal Assemblies of the U.S.A. The name was changed to Pentecostal Church of God in 1922, in 1934 was changed again to The Pentecostal Church of God of America, Inc., and finally to Pentecostal Church of God (Incorporated) in 1979.

The International Headquarters was moved from Chicago to Ottumwa, Iowa, in 1927, then to Kansas City, Mo., in 1933, and finally to Joplin, Mo., in 1951.

The denomination is evangelical and pentecostal in doctrine and practice. Active membership in the National Association of Evangelicals and the Pentecostal Fellowship of North America is maintained.

Doctrinally, the church is Trinitarian and teaches the absolute inerrancy of the Scripture from Genesis to Revelation. Among its cardinal beliefs are the doctrines of salvation, which includes regeneration; divine healing, as provided for in the atonement; the baptism in the Holy Ghost, with the initial physical evidence of speaking in tongues; and the premillennial second coming of Christ.

HEADQUARTERS
4901 Pennsylvania, P.O. Box 850, Joplin, MO 64802 Tel. (417)624-7050 Fax (417)624-7102
Media Contact, Gen. Sec., Dr. Ronald R. Minor

OFFICERS
Gen. Supt., Dr. James D. Gee
Gen. Sec., Dr. Ronald R. Minor

OTHER GENERAL EXECUTIVES
Dir. of World Missions, Rev. Charles R. Mosier
Dir. of Indian Missions, Dr. C. Don Burke
Gen. PYPA Pres., Rev. R. Edward Vansell
Dir. of Christian Ed., Dr. Aaron M. Wilson
Dir. of Home Missions/Evangelism, Dr. H. O. (Pat) Wilson

ASSISTANT GENERAL SUPERINTENDENTS
Northwestern Division, Rev. Robert L. McGee
Southwestern Division, Dr. Norman D. Fortenberry
North Central Division, Rev. Billy G. Jennings
South Central Division, Rev. E. L. Redding
Northeastern Division, Rev. Thomas E. Branham
Southeastern Division, Rev. James F. Richter

OTHER DEPARTMENTAL OFFICERS
Bus. Mgr., Rev. George Gilmore
Gen. PLA Dir., Mrs. Diana L. Gee
Sunday School Curriculum Ed., Ms. Billie Blevins, Messenger Publishing House, 4901 Pennsylvania, Joplin, MO 64802

PERIODICAL
Pentecostal Messenger, The

Pentecostal Fire-Baptized Holiness Church

Organized in 1918, this group consolidated with Pentecostal Free Will Baptists in 1919. It maintains rigid discipline over members.

HEADQUARTERS
Dry Fork, VA 24549 Tel. (804)724-4879
Media Contact, Gen. Mod., Steve E. Johnson, Rt. 2, Box 203, Dry Fork, VA 24549 Tel. (804)724-4879

OFFICERS
Gen. Treas., Kenwin N. Johnson, P.O. Box 1528, Laurinburg, NC 28352 Tel. (919)276-1295
Gen. Sec., W. H. Preskitt, Sr., Rt. 1, Box 169, Wetumpka, AL 36092 Tel. (205)567-6565
Gen. Mod., Steve E. Johnson, Rt. 2, Box 203, Dry Fork, VA 24549 Tel. (804)724-4879
Gen. Supt. Mission Bd., Jerry Powell, Rt. 1, Box 384, Chadourn, NC 28431

The Pentecostal Free Will Baptist Church, Inc.

The Cape Fear Conference of Free Will Baptists, organized in 1855, merged in 1959 with The Wilmington Conference and The New River Conference of Free Will Baptists and was renamed the Pentecostal Free Will Baptist Church, Inc. The doctrines include regeneration, sanctification, the Pentecostal baptism of the Holy Ghost, the Second Coming of Christ, and divine healing.

HEADQUARTERS

P.O. Box 1568, Dunn, NC 28335 Tel. (919)892-4161
Media Contact, Genl. Supt., Don Sauls

OFFICERS

Gen. Supt., Dr. Don Sauls
Asst. Gen. Supt., Dr. W. L. Ellis
Gen. Sec., Rev. J. T. Hammond
Gen. Treas., Dr. W. L. Ellis
World Witness Dir., Rev. David Taylor
Christian Ed. Dir., Rev. J. T. Hammond
Gen. Services Dir., Chuch Hardison
Ministerial Council Dir., Rev. Preston Heath
Ladies' Auxiliary Dir., Mrs. Dolly Davis
Heritage Bible College, Pres., Dr. W. L. Ellis
Crusader Youth Camp, Dir., Rev. J. T. Hammond

OTHER ORGANIZATIONS

Heritage Bible College, P.O. Box 1628, Dunn, NC 28335 Tel. (919)892-4268
Crusader Youth Camp
Mutual Benefit Assoc.
Blessings Bookstore, 1006 W. Cumberland St., Dunn, NC 28334 Tel. (919)892-2401
Cape Fear Christian Academy, Rt 1 Box 139, Erwin, NC 28339 Tel. (919)897-5423

PERIODICAL

Messenger, The

Pillar of Fire

The Pillar of Fire was founded by Alma Bridwell White in Denver on Dec. 29, 1901 as the Pentecostal Union. In 1917, the name was changed to Pillar of Fire. Alma White was born in Kentucky in 1862 and taught school in Montana where she met her husband, Kent White, a Methodist minister, who was a University student in Denver.

Because of Alma White's evangelistic endeavors, she was frowned upon by her superiors, which eventually necessitated her withdrawing from Methodist Church supervision. She was ordained as Bishop and her work spread to many states, to England, and since her decease to Liberia, West Africa, Malawi, East Africa, Yugoslavia, Spain, India, and the Philippines.

The Pillar of Fire organization has a college and two seminaries stressing Biblical studies. It operates eight schools for young people. The church continues to keep in mind the founder's goals and purposes.

HEADQUARTERS

Zarephath, NJ 08890 Tel. (201)356-0102
Western Headquarters, 1302 Sherman St., Denver, CO 80203 Tel. (303)427-5462
Media Contact, 1st Vice Pres., Robert B. Dallenbach, 3455 W. 83 Ave., Westminster, CO 80030 Tel. (303)427-5462 Fax (303)429-0910

OFFICERS

Pres. & Gen. Supt., Bishop Donald J. Wolfram
1st Vice-Pres. & Asst. Supt., Bishop Robert B. Dallenbach
2nd Vice-Pres./Sec.-Treas., Lois R. Stewart
Trustees: Kenneth Cope; Elsworth N. Bradford; S. Rea Crawford; June Blue

PERIODICAL

Pillar of Fire

Polish National Catholic Church of America

After a number of attempts to resolve differences regarding the role of the laity in parish administration in the Roman Catholic Church in Scranton, Pa., this Church was organized in 1897. With the consecration to the episcopacy of the Most Rev. F. Hodur, this Church became a member of the Old Catholic Union of Utrecht in 1907.

HEADQUARTERS

Office of the Prime Bishop, 1002 Pittston Ave., Scranton, PA 18505 Tel. (717)346-9131
Media Contact, Prime Bishop, Most Rev. John F. Swantek, Fax (717)346-2188

OFFICERS

Prime Bishop, Most Rev. John F. Swantek, 115 Lake Scranton Rd., Scranton, PA 18505
Bishop of the Central Diocese, Rt. Rev. Anthony M. Rysz, 529 E. Locust St., Scranton, PA 18505
Bishop of the Eastern Diocese, Rt. Rev. Thomas J. Gnat, 166 Pearl St., Manchester, NH 03104
Bishop of the Buffalo-Pittsburgh Diocese, Rt. Rev. Thaddeus S. Peplowski, 182 Sobieski St., Buffalo, NY 14212
Bishop of Western Diocese, Rt. Rev. Joseph K. Zawistowski, 2019 W. Charleston St., Chicago, IL 60647
Bishop of the Canadian Diocese, ——
Ecumenical Officer, V. Rev. Stanley Skrzypek, 206 Main Street, New York Mills, NY 13416 Tel. (315)736-9757

PERIODICALS

God's Field; Polka

Presbyterian Church in America

The Presbyterian Church in America has a strong commitment to evangelism, missionary work at home and abroad and to Christian education.

Organized in December 1973, this church was first known as the National Presbyterian Church but changed its name in 1974 to Presbyterian Church in America (PCA).

The PCA made a firm commitment on the doctrinal standards which had been significant in presbyterianism since 1645, namely the Westminster Confession of Faith and Catechisms. These doctrinal standards express the distinctives of the Calvinistic or Reformed tradition.

The PCA maintains the historic polity of Presbyterian governance, namely rule by presbyters (or elders) and the graded courts which are the session governing the local church, the presbytery for regional matters and the general assembly at the national level. It has taken seriously the position of the parity of elders, making a distinction between the two classes of elders, teaching and ruling.

In 1982, the Reformed Presbyterian Church, Evangelical Synod (RPCES) joined the PCA. It brought with it a tradition that had antecedents in Colonial America. It also included Covenant College in Lookout Mountain, Ga., and Covenant Theological Seminary in St. Louis, both of which are national denominational institutions of the PCA.

HEADQUARTERS

1852 Century Pl., Atlanta, GA 30345 Tel. (404)320-3366 Fax (404)320-7219

Media Contact, Ed., Rev. Robert G. Sweet, Tel. (404)320-3388 Fax (404)320-7964

OFFICERS

Mod., Dr. W. Wilson Benton, St. Louis, MO

Stated Clk., Dr. Paul R. Gilchrist, 1852 Century Pl., Ste. 190, Atlanta, GA 30345 Tel. (404)320-3366

PERMANENT COMMITTEES

Admn., Dr. Paul R. Gilchrist, 1852 Century Pl., Ste. 190, Atlanta, GA 30345 Tel. (404)320-3366 Fax (404)320-7219

Christian Educ. & Publ., Dr. Charles Dunahoo, Tel. (404)320-3388

Mission to North America, Rev. Terry Gyger, 1852 Century Pl., Ste. 205, Atlanta, GA 30345

Mission to the World, Rev. John E. Kyle, 1852 Century Pl., Ste. 201, Atlanta, GA 30345

PERIODICAL

Messenger, The

Presbyterian Church (U.S.A.)

The Presbyterian Church (U.S.A.) was organized June 10, 1983, when the Presbyterian Church in the United States and the United Presbyterian Church in the United States of America united in Atlanta. The union healed a major division which began with the Civil War when Presbyterians in the South withdrew from the Presbyterian Church in the United States of America to form the Presbyterian Church in the Confederate States.

The United Presbyterian Church in the United States of America had been created by the 1958 union of the Presbyterian Church in the United States of America and the United Presbyterian Church of North America. Of those two uniting bodies, the Presbyterian Church in the U.S.A. dated from the first Presbytery organized in Philadelphia, about 1706. The United Presbyterian Church of North America was formed in 1858, when the Associate Reformed Presbyterian Church and the Associate Presbyterian Church united.

Strongly ecumenical in outlook, the Presbyterian Church (U.S.A.) is the result of at least 10 different denominational mergers over the last 250 years. A Structural Design for Mission, adopted by the General Assembly meeting in June 1986, has been implemented, and the Presbyterian Church (U.S.A.) dedicated its new headquarters in Louisville, Ky. in 1988.

HEADQUARTERS

100 Witherspoon St., Louisville, KY 40202 Tel. (502)569-5000 Fax (502)569-5018

Media Contact, Mgr., Ofc. of News Service, Marj Carpenter, Tel. (502)569-5418 Fax (502)569-8073

OFFICERS

Mod., John Fife

Stated Clk., James E. Andrews

Assoc. Stated Clk., Catherine M. Phillippe

THE OFFICE OF THE GENERAL ASSEMBLY

Tel. (502)569-5360 Fax (502)569-8005

Stated Clk., James E. Andrews

Dept. of the Stated Clerk, Dir., Juanita H. Granady

Dept. of Administration, Dir., J. Scott Schaefer

Dept. of Constitutional Services, Dir., C. Fred Jenkins

Dept. of Governing Body, Ecumenical & Agency Rel., Dir., Gene Turner

Dept. of Assembly Services, Dir., Catherine M. Phillippe

Mgr. for Assembly Arrangements, Kerry Clements

Dept. of Hist., Philadelphia: 425 Lombard St., Philadelphia, PA 19147 Tel. (215)627-1852 Fax (215)627-0509; Dir., Frederick J. Heuser, Jr

Dept. of Hist., Montreat: Montreat, P.O. Box 847, Montreat, NC 28757 Tel. (704)669-7061; Deputy Dir. of Prog., Michelle Francis

GENERAL ASSEMBLY COUNCIL

Office of the Exec. Dir., James Brown, Fax (502)569-8080

UNITS

CHURCH VOCATIONS: Dir., Edgar W. Ward

EDUCATION AND CONGREGATIONAL NURTURE: Dir., Donald Brown; Publisher/Director, Robert McIntyre

EVANGELISM AND CHURCH DEVELOPMENT MIN.: Dir., Andrea Pfaff

GLOBAL MISSION MINISTRY: Dir., Clifton Kirkpatrick

RACIAL ETHNIC MINISTRIES: Dir., James Foster Reese

SOCIAL JUSTICE AND PEACEMAKING: Dir., Belle Miller McMaster

STEWARDSHIP AND COMMUNICATION DEV. MIN.: Dir., John Coffin

THE BICENTENNIAL FUND: Dir., Richard M. Ferguson

THEOLOGY AND WORSHIP MINISTRY: Dir., George Telford, Jr.

WOMEN'S MINISTRY: Dir., Mary Ann Lundy

SUPPORT SERVICES: Dir., Robert T. Mehrhoff

CENTRAL TREASURY CORPORATION: Pres./Treas., G. A. Goff

COMMITTEES

COMMITTEE ON SOCIAL WITNESS POLICY: Dir., Kenneth G. Y. Grant

COMMITTEE ON HIGHER EDUCATION: Dir., Duncan S. Ferguson

COMMITTEE ON THEOLOGICAL EDUCATION: Dir., Joyce Tucker

PRESBYTERIAN CHURCH (U.S.A.) FOUNDATION

Ofc., 200 E. Twelfth St., Jeffersonville, IN 47130 Tel. (812)288-8841 Fax (502)569-5980

Chair of the Bd., Frank Deming

Pres., ——

SYNOD EXECUTIVES

Alaska-Northwest, David C. Meekhof, 233 6th Ave. N., Ste. 100, Seattle, WA 98109-5000 Tel. (206)448-6403

Covenant, H. Davis Yeuell, 6172 Bush Blvd., Ste. 3000, Columbus, OH 43229-2564 Tel. (614)436-3310

Lakes & Prairies, Rev. Robert T. Cuthill, 8012 Cedar Ave. S., Bloomington, MN 55425-1204 Tel. (612)854-0144

Lincoln Trails, Rev. Verne E. Sindlinger, 1100 W. 42nd St., Indianapolis, IN 46208-3381 Tel. (317)923-3681

Living Waters, Rev. J. Harold Jackson, P.O. Box 290275, Nashville, TN 37229-0275 Tel. (615)370-4008

Mid-America, Rev. John L. Williams, 6400 Glenwood, Ste. 111, Overland Park, KS 66202-4072 Tel. (913)384-3020

Mid-Atlantic, Carroll D. Jenkins, P.O. Box 27026, Richmond, VA 23261-7026 Tel. (804)342-0016

Northeast, ——— ,3049 E. Genesee St., Syracuse, NY 13224-1644 Tel. (315)446-5990

Pacific, Rev. Philip H. Young, P.O. Box 1810, San Anselmo, CA 94960-7091 Tel. (415)258-0333

Puerto Rico, Rev. Harry Fred Del Valle, Medical Center Plaza, Oficina 216, Mayaguez, PR 00708 Tel. (809)832-8375

Rocky Mountains, Ramona McKee, 7000 N. Broadway, Suite 410, Denver, CO 80221-2475 Tel. (303)428-0523

South Atlantic, Rev. John Niles Bartholomew, Interstate North Office Center, 435 Clark Rd., Ste. 404, Jacksonville, FL 32218-5574 Tel. (904)764-5644

Southern California, Hawaii, Rev. Rafael J. Aragon, 1501 Wilshire Blvd., Los Angeles, CA 90017-2293 Tel. (213)483-3840

Southwest, Rev. Gary Skinner, 4423 N. 24th St., Ste. 800, Phoenix, AZ 85016-5544 Tel. (602)468-3800

Sun, Rev. William J. Fogelman, 920 S. 135 E, Denton, TX 76205-7898 Tel. (817)382-9656

Trinity, Rev. Thomas M. Johnston, Jr., 3040 Market St., Camp Hill, PA 17011-4599 Tel. (717)737-0421

PERIODICALS

American Presbyterians: Journal of Presbyterian History; Church & Society Magazine; Horizons; Monday Morning; Presbyterian Survey; These Days

Primitive Advent Christian Church

This body split from the Advent Christian Church. All its churches are in West Virginia. The Primitive Advent Christian Church believes that the Bible is the only rule of faith and practice and that Christian character is the only test of fellowship and communion. The church agrees with Christian fidelity and meekness; exercises mutual watch and care; counsels, admonishes, or reproves as duty may require; and receives the same from each other as becomes the household of faith. Primitive Advent Christians do not believe in taking up arms against in case of war.

The church believes that three ordinances are set forth by the Bible to be observed by the Christian church: (1) baptism by immersion; (2) the Lord's Supper, by partaking of unleavened bread and wine; (3) feet washing, to be observed by the saints' washing of one another's feet.

HEADQUARTERS

Media Contact, Sec.-Treas., Hugh W. Good, 395 Frame Rd., Elkview, WV 25071 Tel. (304)965-1550

OFFICERS

Pres., Roger Hammons, 273 Frame Rd., Elkview, WV 25071 Tel. (304)965-6247

Vice-Pres., Herbert Newhouse, 7632 Hughart Dr., Sissionville, WV 25320 Tel. (304)984-9277

Sec. & Treas., Hugh W. Good, 395 Frame Rd., Elkview, WV 25071 Tel. (304)965-1550

Primitive Baptists

This large group of Baptists, located throughout the United States, opposes all centralization and modern missionary societies. They preach Salvation by Grace alone.

HEADQUARTERS

Cayce Publ. Co., S. Second St., P.O. Box 38, Thornton, AR 71766 Tel. (501)352-3694

OFFICER

Elder W.H. Cayce

PERIODICALS

Baptist Witness; Christian Baptist, The; Christian Pathway, The; Primitive Baptist; For the Poor

Primitive Methodist Church in the U.S.A.

Hugh Bourne and William Clowes, local preachers in the Wesleyan Church in England, organized a daylong meeting at Mow Cop in Staffordshire on May 31, 1807, after Lorenzo Dow, a Methodist preacher from America, told them of American camp meetings. Thousands attended and many were converted but the church, founded by the open-air preacher John Wesley, refused to accept the converts and reprimanded the preachers.

After waiting for two years for a favorable action by the Wesleyan Society, Bourne and Clowes established The Society of the Primitive Methodists. This was not a schism, Bourne said, for "we did not take one from them ... it now appeared to be the will of God that we ... should form classes and take upon us the care of churches in the fear of God." Primitive Methodist missionaries were sent to New York in 1829. An American conference was established in 1840.

Missionary efforts reach into Guatemala, Spain, and other countries. The denomination joins in federation with the Evangelical Congregational Church and the United Brethren in Christ Church, and is a member of the National Association of Evangelicals.

The church believes the Bible is the only true rule of faith and practice, the inspired Word of God. It believes in one Triune God, the Deity of Jesus Christ, the Deity and personality of the Holy Spirit, the innocence of Adam and Eve, the Fall of the human race, the necessity of repentance, justification by faith of all who believe, regeneration witnessed by the Holy Spirit, sanctification by the Holy Spirit, the second coming of the Lord Jesus Christ, the resurrection of the dead and conscious future existence of all men, and future judgments and eternal rewards and punishments.

HEADQUARTERS

Media Contact, Exec. Dir., Rev. William H. Fudge, 1045 Laurel Run Rd., Wilkes-Barre, PA 18702 Tel. (717)472-3436 Fax (717)472-9283

OFFICERS

Pres., Dr. K. Gene Carroll, 223 Austin Ave., Wilkes-Barre, PA 18702

Vice-Pres., Rev. John D. Sargent, 750 Madison St., Platteville, WI 53818

Exec. Dir., Rev. William H. Fudge, 1045 Laurel Run Rd., Wilkes-Barre, PA 18702 Fax (717)472-9283

Treas., Mr. Raymond Baldwin, 11012 Langton Arms Ct., Oakton, VA 22124

Gen. Sec., Rev. Reginald H. Thomas, 110 Pittston Blvd., Wilkes-Barre, PA 18702 Tel. (717)823-3425

Progressive National Baptist Convention, Inc.

This body held its organizational meeting in Cincinnati, November 1961. Subsequent regional sessions were followed by the first annual session in Philadelphia in 1962.

HEADQUARTERS

601 50th Street, N.E., Washington, DC 20019 Tel. (202)396-0558 Fax (202)398-4998
Media Contact, Gen. Sec., Rev. Tyrone S. Pitts

OFFICERS

Pres., Dr. Charles G. Adams, Hartford Memorial Baptist Church, 18900 James Couzens Hwy., Detroit, MI 48235
Gen. Sec., Rev. Tyrone S. Pitts, 601 50th St., NE, Washington, DC 20019 Tel. (202)396-0558 Fax (202)398-4998

OTHER ORGANIZATIONS

Dept. of Christian Education, Exec. Dir., Ms. Brenda D. Tribett, 601 50th St., NE, Washington, DC 20019
Women's Dept., Mrs. Earl C. Bryant, 537 Woolfolk St., Macon, GA 31201
Home Mission Bd., Exec. Dir., Rev. Archie LeMone, 601 50th St., NE, Washington, DC 20019
Congress of Christian Education, Pres., Dr. Thomas H. Peoples, Jr., Pleasant Green Missionary Baptist Church, 540 W. Maxwell St., Lexington, KY 40508
Baptist Global Mission Bureau, Dr. Ronald K. Hill, 161-163 60th St., Philadelphia, PA 19139

The Protes'tant Conference (Lutheran), Inc.

The Conference came into being in 1927 as the result of expulsions of pastors and teachers from the Wisconsin Evangelical Lutheran Synod (WELS). The underlying cause which ignited the suspensions was a rebellion against what was labeled The Wauwatosa Theology, so named after the location of the Wisconsin Synod seminary at that time and the fresh approach to Scripture study there by the faculty. This approach sought to overcome the habits of dogmatism. Chiefly responsible for this renewal was Professor John Philipp Koehler.

The Conference was formed as the result of these suspensions, which were to be followed by other suspensions. To give testimony to the issues at operation in this controversy and in particular to bear witness to the grace of the Wauwatosa Theology, the Conference has published *Faith-Life* since 1928. The congregations are chiefly in Wisconsin. The Conference has no official officers. Chief in influence have been Professor J. P. Koehler (1859-1951); his son Karl Koehler (1885-1948), who was the chief architect of *Faith-Life* with its Policy and Purpose; and Paul Hensel (1888-1977) who displayed the Wauwatosa Theology.

OFFICERS

Recording Sec., Pastor Gerald Hinz, P.O. Box 86, Shiocton, WI 54170 Tel. (414)986-3918
Fin. Sec.-Treas., Michael Meler, 1023 Colan Blvd., Rice Lake, WI 54868

PERIODICAL

Faith-Life

Protestant Reformed Churches in America

The Protestant Reformed Churches in America were organized in 1926 as a result of doctrinal disagreement relating to such matters as world conformity, problems of higher criticism and God's grace that pervaded the Christian Reformed Church in the early 1920s.

After the passage of the formula on Three Points of Common Grace by the Synod of the Christian Reformed Church in 1924, and during the resulting storm of controversy, three clergy and those in their congregations who agreed with them, were expelled from the Christian Reformed Church. These clergy were Herman Hoeksema of the Eastern Ave. Christian Reformed Church in Grand Rapids, Mich., George Ophoff, pastor of the Hope congregation in Riverbend, Mich., and Henry Danhof in Kalamazoo, Mich.

In March 1925, the consistories of these congregations signed an Act of Agreement and adopted the temporary name of "Protesting Christian Reformed Churches." The break was made final following the Synod of the Christian Reformed Church of 1926.

The Protestant Reformed Churches in America hold to the doctrinal tenets of Calvinism, the Belgic Confession, the Heidelberg Catechism and the Canons of Dordrecht.

HEADQUARTERS

16515 South Park Ave., South Holland, IL 60473 Tel. (708)333-1314
Media Contact, Stat. Clk., Rev. M. Joostens, 2016 Tekonsha, S.E., Grand Rapids, MI 49506 Tel. (616)247-0638

OFFICER

Stat. Clk., Rev. M. Joostens

Reformed Church in America

The Reformed Church in America was established in 1628 by the earliest settlers of New York. It is the oldest Protestant denomination with a continuous ministry in North America. Until 1867 it was known as the Reformed Protestant Dutch Church.

The first ordained minister, Domine Jonas Michaelius, arrived in New Amsterdam from The Netherlands in 1628. Throughout the colonial period, the Reformed Church lived under the authority of the Classis of Amsterdam. Its churches were clustered in New York and New Jersey. Under the leadership of Rev. John Livingston, it became a denomination independent of the authority of the Classis of Amsterdam in 1776. Its geographical base was broadened in the 19th century by the immigration of Reformed Dutch and German settlers in the midwestern United States. The Reformed Church now spans the United States and Canada.

The Reformed Church accepts as its standards of faith the Heidelberg Catechism, Belgic Confession, and Canons of Dort. It has a rich heritage of world mission activity. It claims to be loyal to reformed tradition which emphasizes obedience to God in all aspects of life.

Although the Reformed Church in America has worked in close cooperation with other churches, it has never entered into merger with any other denomination. It is a member of the World Alliance of Reformed Churches, the World Council of Churches, and the National Council of the Churches of Christ in the United States of America.

114

THE YEAR IN IMAGES

Religious News Service Photo

Woman leads RCA

For the first time in its 364 years, the Reformed Church in America elected a woman as presiding officer. Beth Marcus, of Holland, Mich., became president of the General Synod on June 19. She served 33 years on the staff, retiring in 1986.

HEADQUARTERS

475 Riverside Dr., Rm. 1811, New York, NY 10115 Tel. (212)870-2841 Fax (212)870-2499
Media Contact, Dir., Promotion, Communication, Development, E. Wayne Antworth, Tel. (212)870-2954

OFFICERS AND STAFF OF GENERAL SYNOD

Pres., Beth E. Marcus
Gen. Sec., Edwin G. Mulder

OTHER ORGANIZATIONS

Bd. of Direction, Pres., Gerald Verbridge
Bd. of Pensions: Pres., Louis E. Lotz; Sec., Edwin G. Mulder
General Program Council: Mod., Steven Stan, 475 Riverside Dr., Rm. 1812, New York, NY 10115; Sec. for Program, Eugene P. Heideman
Ofc. of Human Resources, Coord., Alvin J. Poppen
Ofc. of Finance, Treas., Wayne D. Kramer
Ofc. of Promotion, Comm., & Dev., Dir., E. Wayne Antworth
Reformed Church Women, Exec. Dir., Diana Paulsen
African-American Council, Exec. Dir., John David Cato
Council for Hispanic Ministries, Natl. Sec., Johnny Alicea-Baez
American Indian Council, Interim Sec., Kenneth W. Mallory
Council for Pacific/Asian-American Min., Natl. Sec., Ella White

PERIODICAL

Church Herald, The

Reformed Church in the United States

Lacking pastors, early German Reformed immigrants to the American colonies were led in worship by "readers." One reader, schoolmaster John Philip Boehm, organized the first congregations near Philadelphia in 1725. A Swiss pastor, Michael Schlatter, was sent by the Dutch Reformed Church in 1746. Strong ties with the Netherlands existed until the formation of the Synod of the Reformed High German Church in 1793.

The Eureka Classis, organized in North and South Dakota in 1910 and strongly influenced by the writings of H. Kohlbruegge, P. Geyser and J. Stark, refused to become part of the 1934 merger of the Reformed Church with the Evangelical Synod of North America, holding that it sacrificed the Reformed heritage. (The merged Evangelical and Reformed Church became part of the United Church of Christ in 1957.) Under the leadership of pastors W. Grossmann and W. J. Krieger, the Eureka Classis in 1942 incorporated as the continuing Reformed Church in the United States.

The growing Eureka Classis dissolved in 1986 to form a Synod with four regional classes. An heir to the Reformation theology of Zwingli and Calvin, the Heidelberg Catechism of 1563 is used as the confessional standard of the church. The Bible is strictly held to be the inerrant, infallible Word of God.

The RCUS supports Westminster Theological Seminary in Philadelphia and Escondido, Calif.; Dordt College and Mid-America Reformed Seminary in Iowa. The RCUS is the official sponsor to the Reformed Confessing Church of Zaire.

OFFICERS

Pres., Rev. Vernon Pollema, 235 James Street, Shafter, CA 93263
Vice-Pres., Rev. Paul Treick, 1515 Carlton Ave., Modesto, CA 95350 Tel. (209)526-0637
Stated Clk., Rev. Frank Walker, 927 E. Graceway Dr., Napoleon, OH 43545 Tel. (419)599-2266
Treas., Mr. Clayton Greimon, RR 3, Garner, IA 50438

PERIODICAL

Reformed Herald

Reformed Episcopal Church

The Reformed Episcopal Church was founded Dec. 2, 1873, in New York City by Bishop George D. Cummins, an assistant bishop in the Protestant Episcopal Church from 1866 until 1873. Cummins and other evangelical Episcopalians viewed with alarm the influence of the Oxford Movement in the Protestant Episcopal Church, for the interest it stimulated in Roman Catholic ritual and doctrine and for intolerance it bred toward evangelical Protestant doctrine.

Throughout the late 1860s, evangelicals and ritualists clashed over ceremonies and vestments, exchanges of pulpits with clergy of other denominations, the meaning of critical passages in the Book of Common Prayer, interpretation of the sacraments, and validity of the Apostolic Succession.

In October, 1873, other bishops publicly attacked Cummins in the church newspapers for participating in an ecumenical Communion service sponsored by the Evangelical Alliance. Cummins resigned and drafted a call to Episcopalians to organize a new Episcopal Church for the "purpose of restoring the old paths of their fathers." On

Dec. 2, 1873, a *Declaration of Principles* was adopted and Dr. Charles E. Cheney was elected bishop to serve with Cummins. The Second General Council, meeting in May 1874 in New York City, approved a *Constitution and Canons* and a slightly amended version of the *Book of Common Prayer*. In 1875, the Third General Council adopted a set of *Thirty-Five Articles*.

Cummins died in 1876. The church had grown to nine jurisdictions in the United States and Canada at that time. Substantial growth ceased after 1900. The church now comprises three synods (New York-Philadelphia, Chicago, Charleston-Atlanta-Charlotte) and a missionary jurisdiction of the West. The Reformed Episcopal Church is a member of the National Association of Evangelicals.

OFFICERS

Pres. & Presiding Bishop, Rev. Franklin H. Sellers, Sr., 1629 W. 99th St., Chicago, IL 60643

Vice-Pres., Bishop Sanco K. Rembert, P.O. Box 20068, Charleston, SC 29413

Sec., Rev. Willie J. Hill, Jr., 271 W. Tulpehocken St., Philadelphia, PA 19144

Treas., Mr. William B. Schimpf, 67 Westaway Lane, Warrington, PA 18976

OTHER ORGANIZATIONS

Bd. of Foreign Missions: Pres., Dr. William J. Hollman, Jr., 319 E. 50th St., New York, NY 10022

Bd. of Natl. Church Extension: Pres., Rev. George B. Fincke, 901 Church Rd., Oreland, PA 19075

Trustees Sustentation Fund: Pres., Mr. E. Earl Shisler, Jr., RD #2, Perkasie, PA 18944

Publication Society: Pres., Rev. Richard K. Barnard, 8027 Inwood Rd., Dallas, TX 75209

The Reapers: Pres., Mrs. Nancy Fleischer, RR #1, Box 500, Pipersville, PA 18947

BISHOPS

William H.S. Jerdan, Jr., 414 W. 2nd South St., Summerville, SC 29483

Sanco K. Rembert, P.O. Box 20068, Charleston, SC 29413

Franklin H. Sellers, Sr., 1629 W. 99th St., Chicago, IL 60643

Leonard W. Riches, Sr., RD 1, Box 501, Smithown Rd., Pipersville, PA 18947

Daniel G. Cox, 9 Hilltop Pl., Catonsville, MD 21228

Royal U. Grote, Jr., 19 Heather Ct., New Providence, NJ 07974

James C. West, Sr., 91 Anson St., Charleston, SC 29401

Robert H. Booth, 1222 Haworth St., Philadelphia, PA 19124

PERIODICAL

Episcopal Recorder

Reformed Mennonite Church

A small group of people who were organized into church fellowship by John Herr and others. They adhere to the doctrine and principles of love as taught in the New Testament and practiced by true Christians in all ages since the church was established on the day of Pentecost.

HEADQUARTERS

Lancaster County only, Reformed Mennonite Church, 602 Strasburg Pike, Lancaster, PA 17602

Media Contact, Bishop, Glenn M. Gross, Tel. (717)697-4623

OFFICER

Bishop Glenn M. Gross, 906 Grantham Rd., Mechanicsburg, PA 17055

Reformed Methodist Union Episcopal Church

The Reformed Methodist Union Episcopal church was formed after a group of ministers withdrew from the African Methodist Episcopal Church following a dispute over the election of ministerial delegates to the General Conference.

These ministers organized the Reformed Methodist Union church during a four-day meeting beginning on Jan. 22, 1885 at Hills Chapel (now known as Mt. Hermon RMUE church), in Charleston, S.C. The Rev. William E. Johnson was elected president of the new church. Following the death of Rev. Johnson in 1896, it was decided that the church would conform to regular American Methodism (the Episcopacy). The first Bishop, Edward Russell Middleton, was elected, and "Episcopal" was added to the name of the church. Bishop Middleton was consecrated on Dec. 5, 1896, by Bishop P. F. Stephens of the Reformed Episcopal Church.

HEADQUARTERS

Charleston, SC 29407

OFFICERS

Bishop, Rt. Rev. Leroy Gethers, 1136 Brody Ave., Charleston, SC 29407 Tel. (803) 766-3534

Asst. Bishop, Rt.Rev. Gary M. DeVoe, Jr

Gen. Sec., Rev. Willie Oliver, 3-8857

Treas., Rev. Rufus German

Sec. of Education, Rev. William Polite

Sec. of Books Concerns, Rev. Thomas Watson, Jr

Sec. of Pension Fund, Rev. Joseph Powell

Sec. of Sunday School Union, Rev. Hercules Champaigne

Sec. of Mission, Rev. Jerry M. DeBoer

Reformed Presbyterian Church of North America

Also known as the Church of the Covenanters, its origin dates back to the Reformation days of Scotland when the Covenanters signed their "Covenants" in resistance to the king and the Roman Church in the enforcement of state church practices. The Church in America has signed two "Covenants" in particular, those of 1871 and 1954.

HEADQUARTERS

Media Contact, Dir. of Publ. & Youth Min., James C. Pennington, 7408 Penn Ave., Pittsburgh, PA 15208 Tel. (412)241-0436 Fax (412)731-8861

OFFICERS

Mod., Rev. Raymond P. Joseph, Jr., 26580 Evergreen Rd., Southfield, MI 48076 Tel. (313)356-3932

Stated Clk., Louis D. Hutmire, 7408 Penn Ave., Pittsburgh, PA 15208 Tel. (412)731-1177

PERIODICAL

Covenanter Witness, The

Reformed Zion Union Apostolic Church

This group was organized in 1869, at Boydton, Va., by Elder James R. Howell of New York, a minister of the A.M.E. Zion Church; with doctrines of the Methodist Episcopal Church.

Sec., Deacon James C. Feggins, 416 South Hill Ave., South Hill, VA 23970 Tel. (804)447-3374

Religious Society of Friends (Conservative)

These Friends mark their present identity from separations occurring by regions at different times from 1845 to 1904. They hold to a minimum of organizational structure. Their meetings for worship, which are unprogrammed and based on silent, expectant waiting upon the Lord, demonstrate the belief that all individuals may commune directly with God and may share equally in vocal ministry.

They continue to stress the importance of the Living Christ and the experience of the Holy Spirit working with power in the lives of individuals who obey it.

YEARLY MEETINGS

North Carolina YM, George Stabler, 788 W. 52nd St., Norfolk, VA 23508

Iowa YM, Martha Davis and Bill Deutsch, 678 38th St., Des Moines, IA 50312

Ohio YM, Susan S. Smith, RD #4 Box 288, Harrisonburg, VA 22801

Religious Society of Friends (Unaffiliated Meetings)

Though all groups of Friends acknowledge the same historical roots, 19th-century divisions in theology and experience led to some of the current organizational groupings. Many newer yearly meetings, often marked by spontaneity, variety, and experimentation and hoping for renewed Quaker unity, have chosen not to identify with past divisions by affiliating in traditional ways with the larger organizations within the Society. Some of these unaffiliated groups have begun within the past 25 years.

HEADQUARTERS

Friends World Committee for Consultation, Section of the Americas, 1506 Race St., Philadelphia, PA 19102 Tel. (215)241-7250

Media Contact, Exec. Sec., Asia Bennett

UNAFFILIATED YEARLY MEETINGS

Amigos Central de Bolivia, Casilla 11070, La Paz, Bolivia

Amigos de Santidad de Bolivia, Casilla 992, La Paz, Bolivia

Central Yearly Meeting, 109 West Berry St., Alexandria, IN 46001

Iglesia Evangelica Amigos, Apartado 235, Santa Rosa de Capan, Honduras

Iglesia Nacional Evangelica de Los Amigos-Bolivia, Casilla 8385, La Paz, Bolivia

Iglesia Nacional Evangelica de Los Amigos-Peru, Apartado 369, Puno, Peru

Intermountain Yearly Meeting, 1720 Linden Ave., Boulder, CO 80304

North Pacific Yearly Meeting, 3311 N.W. Polk, Corvallis, OR 97330

Pacific Yearly Meeting, 808 Melba Rd., Encinitas, CA 92024

Reunion Gen. de Mexico, 5y6 Matamoros, Ciudad Victoria, Tamaulipas, Mexico

El Salvador Yearly Meeting, Calle Roosevelt, Km. 4.5, #60, Soyapango, San Salvador, El Salvador

Guatemala Yearly Meeting, Apartado 8, Chiquimula, Guatemala

Newsletter, FWCC of the Americas

Reorganized Church of Jesus Christ of Latter Day Saints

Founded April 6, 1830, by Joseph Smith, Jr., and reorganized under the leadership of the founder's son, Joseph Smith III, in 1860. The Church, with headquarters in Independence, Mo., is established in 36 countries in addition to the United States and Canada. A biennial world conference is held in Independence, Mo. The current president is Wallace B. Smith, great-grandson of the original founder. The church has a world-wide membership of approximately 245,000.

HEADQUARTERS

World Headquarters, P.O. Box 1059, Independence, MO 64051 Tel. (816)833-1000 Fax (816)521-3097

Media Contact, Publ. Rel. Commissioner, Stephanie Kelley

OFFICERS

First Presidency: Wallace B. Smith; Counselor, Howard S. Sheehy, Jr.; Counselor, W. Grant McMurray

Council of 12 Apostles, Pres., Geoffrey F. Spencer

Presiding Bishopric: Presiding Bishop, Norman E. Swails; Counselor, Larry R. Norris; Counselor, Dennis D. Piepergerdes

Presiding Evangelist, Paul W. Booth

World Church Sec., A. Bruce Lindgren

Public Relations, Stephanie Kelley

PERIODICALS

Saints Herald; Restoration Witness

The Roman Catholic Church

The Roman Catholic Church, the largest single body of Christians in the United States, is under the spiritual leadership of His Holiness the Pope. Its establishment in America dates back to the priests who accompanied Columbus on his second voyage to the New World. A settlement, later discontinued, was made at St. Augustine, Fla. The continuous history of this Church in the Colonies began at St. Mary's in Maryland, in 1634.

(The following information has been furnished by the editor of The Official Catholic Directory, published by P. J. Kenedy & Sons, 3004 Glenview Rd., Wilmette, IL 60091. Reference to this complete volume will provide additional information.)

INTERNATIONAL ORGANIZATION

His Holiness the Pope, Bishop of Rome, Vicar of Jesus Christ, Supreme Pontiff of the Catholic Church.

Pope John Paul II, Karol Wojtyla (born May 18, 1920; installed Oct. 22, 1978)

APOSTOLIC PRO NUNCIO TO THE UNITED STATES

Archbishop Agostino Cacciavillan, 3339 Massachusetts Ave., N.W., Washington, DC 20008. Tel. (202)333-7121

U.S. ORGANIZATION

National Conference of Catholic Bishops, 3211 Fourth St., Washington, DC 20017. Tel. (202)541-3000; Fax (202)541-3088

The National Conference of Catholic Bishops (NCCB) is a canonical entity operating in accordance with the Vatican II Decree, Christus Dominus. Its purpose is to foster the Church's mission to

Religious News Service Photo

Clashes over abortion

A Catholic nun holds rosary beads over her head as she is led away from a confrontation in Buffalo. Pro-life Operation Rescue was protesting at an abortion clinic, while pro-choice advocates tried to keep the clinic open. The U.S. presidential campaign, with pro-choice Bill Clinton and pro-life George Bush, intensified the abortion debate.

mankind by providing the Bishops of this country with an opportunity to exchange views and insights of prudence and experience and to exercise in a joint manner their pastoral office.

Pres., Archbishop Daniel Pilarczyk
Vice-Pres., Archbishop William H. Keeler
Treas., Archbishop Daniel Kucera
Sec., Bishop Raymond W. Lessard

GENERAL SECRETARIAT

Gen. Sec., Rev. Msgr. Robert N. Lynch
Assoc. Gen. Sec., Francis X. Doyle, Sr. Sharon A. Euart, R.S.M.
Sec. for Communication, Richard Daw

COMMITTEES

Ecumenical and Interreligious Affairs (Ecumenism): Chmn., Archbishop J. Francis Stafford
Secretariat: Exec. Dir., Rev. John Hotchkin
Assoc. Dir., Bro. Jeffrey Gros
Liturgy:
Chmn., Bishop Joseph Delaney
Secretariat: Dir., Rev. Ronald Krisman, Assoc. Dir., Rev. Msgr. Alan Detscher; Rev. Kenneth F. Jenkins
Priestly Formation: Chpsn., Bishop James P. Keleher
Staff: Exec. Dir., Rev. Howard Bleichner, S.S.
Permanent Diaconate:
Chmn., Archbishop Patrick F. Flores
Secretariat: Exec. Dir., Deacon Constantino J. Ferriola, Jr.
Priestly Life and Ministry:
Chmn., Bishop Donald W. Wuerl
Secretariat: Exec. Dir., Rev. David E. Brinkmoeller

Pro-Life Activities:
Chmn., John Cardinal O'Connor
Secretariat: Dir., Rev. John W. Gouldrick, C.M.
United States Catholic Conference, 3211 Fourth St., Washington, DC 20017, Tel. (202)541-3000
The United States Catholic Conference (USCC) is a civil entity which assists the American Catholic Bishops in their service to the Church in this country by uniting the people of God where voluntary, collective action on a broad diocesan level is needed. The USCC provides an organization structure and the resources needed to insure coordination, cooperation, and assistance in the public, educational, and social concerns of the church at the national, regional, state, interdiocesan, and, as appropriate, diocesan levels.

OFFICERS

Pres., Archbishop Daniel E. Pilarczyk
Vice-Pres., Archbishop William H. Keeler
Treas., Archbishop Daniel Kucera
Sec., Bishop Raymond W. Lessard

GENERAL SECRETARIAT

Gen. Sec., Rev. Robert Lynch
Assoc. Gen. Sec., Rev. Donald Heintschel, Francis X. Doyle, Jr., Sr. Sharon A. Euart, R.S.M.
Sec. for Communications, Richard W. Daw

STAFF OFFICES

Finance, Dir., Sister Frances A. Mlocek, I.H.M.
Accounting, Kenneth Korotky
Human Resources, Dir., Thomas Meehan
Office of Publishing and Promotion Services, Dir., Dan Juday
General Counsel, Mark E. Chopko
Government Liaison, Dir., Frank Monahan

Research, Dir., Rev. Eugene Hemrick

COMMITTEES AND DEPARTMENTS

Communication: Chmn., Edward J. O'Donnell; Sec., Richard W. Daw; National Catholic News Services, Thomas N. Lorsung, Dir. & Ed.-in-Chief; Film and Broadcasting, Henry Herx, Dir.

Education: Chpsn., Archbishop Francis Shulte

Social Development and World Peace: Chmn., Bishop Joseph M. Sullivan; Sec., John Carr; Domestic Social Development, Sharon Daly; Health and Welfare Issues, Rev. Fred Kammer; Rural Energy and Food Issues, Walter Grazer; Urban and Economic Issues, Thomas Schellabarger; International Justice and Peace, Robert Hennemeyer; Latin American Affairs, Thomas Quigley; African and Western European Affairs, Robert A. Dumas, Sr.; Political and Military Affairs and Human Rights, Dr. Gerard F. Powers

RELATED ORGANIZATIONS

Campaign for Human Development: Nat'l. Chmn., Bishop Joseph A. Fiorenza; Exec. Dir., Catholic Relief Services, 209 W. Fayette St., Baltimore, MD 21201 Tel. (301)625-2220. Exec. Dir., Lawrence Pezzulo

U.S.CATHOLIC BISHOPS' NATIONAL ADVISORY COUNCIL

Chmn., Elizabeth Habergerger

NATIONAL ORGANIZATIONS

Catholic Charities, -USA Exec. Dir., Rev. Thomas J. Harvey, 1319 F St., N.W., Washington, DC 20004

Conference of Major Religious Superiors of Men, Men's Institutes of the United States, Inc., Exec. Dir., Rev. Roland Faley, TOR, 8808 Cameron St., Silver Spring, MD 20910. Tel. (301)588-4030

Leadership Conference of Women Religious, Exec. Dir., Sr. Janet Roesener, CSJ, 8808 Cameron St., Silver Spring, MD 20910. Tel. (301)588-4955

National Catholic Educational Association, Pres., Sr. Catherine McNamee, 1077 30th St., N.W., Suite 100, Washington, DC 20007. Tel. (202)337-6232

National Council of Catholic Laity, Pres., Thomas Simmons, 5664 Midforest Ln., Cincinnati, OH 45233. Tel. (513)922-2495

National Council of Catholic Women, Pres., Beverly Medved; Exec. Adm., Annette Kane, 1275 K. St., NW, Washington, DC 20005. Tel. (202)682-0334

National Office for Black Catholics, The Paulist Center, 3025 4th St., N.E., Washington, D.C. 20017. Tel. (202)635-1778

CATHOLIC ORGANIZATIONS WITH INDIVIDUAL I.R.S. RULINGS

Canon Law Society of America, Exec. Coord., Rev. Edward Pfnausch, Catholic University, Washington, DC 20064. Tel. (202)269-3491

National Institute for the Word of God, Exec. Dir., Rev. John Burke, O.P., 487 Michigan Ave., NE, Washington, DC 20017. Tel. (202)529-0001

ARCHDIOCESES AND DIOCESES

There follows an alphabetical listing of Archdioceses and Dioceses of The Roman Catholic Church. Each Archdiocese or Diocese contains the following information in sequence: Name of incumbent Bishop; name of Auxiliary Bishop or Bishops, and the Chancellor or Vicar General of the Archdiocese or Diocese, or just the address and

telephone number of the chancery office.

Cardinals are addressed as "His Eminence" and Archbishops and Bishops as "Most Reverend."

Albany, Bishop Howard J. Hubbard; Chancellor, Rev. Randall P. Patterson. Chancery Office, Pastoral Center, 40 N. Main Ave., Albany, NY 12203; Tel. (518)453-6611. Fax (518)453-6793

Diocese of Alexandria, Bishop Sam G. Jacobs; Chancellor, Rev. Msgr. Joseph M. Susi. Office, 4400 Coliseum Blvd., P.O.Box 7417, Alexandria, LA 71306. Tel. (318)445-2401

Allentown, Bishop Thomas J. Welsh; Chancellor, Rev. Joseph M. Whalen. Chancery Office, 202 N. 17th St., P.O. Box F, Allentown, PA 18105. Tel. (215)437-0755

Altoona-Johnstown, Bishop Joseph V. Adamec; Chancellor, Rev. Msgr. George B. Flinn. Chancery Office, Box 126, Logan Blvd., Hollidaysburg, PA 16648. Tel. (814)695-5579. Fax(814)695-8894

Amarillo, Bishop Leroy T. Matthiesen; Chancellor, Rev. Allen F. Bruening, OSF. Chancery Office,1800 N. Spring St., P.O. Box 5644, Amarillo, TX 79117.Tel.(806)383-2243

Archdiocese of Anchorage, Archbishop Francis T. Hurley; Chancery Office, 225 Cordova St., P.O. Box 102239, Anchorage, AK 99510. Tel. (907)258-7898. Fax (905)279-3885

Arlington, Bishop John Richard Keating; Chancellor, Rev. Msgr. William T. Reinecke. Chancery, Ste. 704, 200 N. Glebe Rd., Arlington, VA 22203. Tel. (703)841-2500. Fax (703)524-5028

Archdiocese of Atlanta, Archbishop James P. Lyke, OFM; Vicar General, Edward J. Dillon. Chancery Office, 680 West Peachtree St., N.W., Atlanta, GA 30308. Tel. (404)888-7802. Fax (404)885-7494

Austin, Bishop John E. McCarthy; Vicar General, Rev. Msgr. Edward C. Matocha. Chancery Office, N. Congress and 16th, P.O. Box 13327, Capital Sta., Austin, TX 78711. Tel.(512)476-4888. Fax (512)469-9537

Baker, Bishop Thomas J. Connolly; Chancellor, Rev. Charles T. Grant. Chancery Office,911 S.E. Armour, Bend, OR 97702; P.O. Box 5999, Bend, OR 97708. Tel. (503)388-4004.

Archdiocese of Baltimore, Archbishop William H. Keeler; Auxiliary Bishops: Bishop William C. Newman, Bishop P. Francis Murphy, Bishop John H. Ricard; Chancellor, W. Francis Malooly. Chancery Office, 320 Cathedral St., Baltimore, MD 21201.Tel. (301)547-5446.

Baton Rouge, Bishop Stanley J. Ott; Chancellor, Rev. Msgr. Robert Berggreen. Chancery Office, 1800 S. Acadian Thruway, P.O. Box 2028, Baton Rouge, LA 70821. Tel. (504)387-0561. Fax (504)336-8789

Beaumont, Bishop Bernard J. Ganter; Chancellor Rev. Bennie J. Patillo. Chancery Office, 703 Archie St., P.O. Box 3948, Beaumont, TX 77704, Tel. (409)838-0451

Belleville, Bishop James P. Keleher; Chancellor, Rev. Msgr. Bernard O. Sullivan. Chancery Office, 222 S. Third St., Belleville, IL 62220. Tel. (618)277-8181. Fax (618)277-0387

Biloxi, Bishop Joseph L. Howze; Chancellor, Rev. Msgr. Andrew Murray. Chancery Office, 120 Reynoir St., P.O. Box 1189, Biloxi, MS 39533. Tel. (601)374-0222. Fax (601)435-7949

Birmingham, Bishop Raymond J. Boland; Chancellor, Rev. Paul L. Rohling. Chancery Office, 8131 Fourth Ave. South, P.O. Box 12047, Birmingham, AL 35202. Tel.(205)833-0175. Fax (205)836-1910

Bismarck, Bishop John F. Kinney, Chancellor, Sr. Joanne Graham, OSB. Chancery Office, 420 Raymond St., Box 1575, Bismarck, ND 58502. Tel. (701)223-1347

Boise, Bishop Tod D. Brown;Chancellor, Deacon James Bowen; Chancery Office, Box 769, 303 Federal Way, Boise, ID 83701. Tel.(208)342-1311. Fax (208)342-0224

Archdiocese of Boston, Archbishop Bernard Cardinal Law; Auxiliary Bishops: Bishop Daniel A. Hart, Bishop John P. Boles, Bishop Alfred C. Hughes, Bishop John J. Mulcahy, Bishop John R. McNamara, Bishop Lawrence J. Riley, Bishop Roberto O. Gonzales, OFM. Chancellor, Gerald T. Reilly. Chancery Office, 2121 Commonwealth Ave., Brighton, MA 02135. Tel. (617)254-0100. Fax (617)787-8144, 783-5642

Bridgeport, Bishop Edward M. Egan; Chancellor, Rev. Msgr. Thomas J. Driscoll. Chancery Office, 238 Jewett Ave., Bridgeport, CT 06606. Tel. (203)372-4301. Fax (203)371-8698

Brooklyn, Bishop Thomas V. Daily; Auxiliary Bishops: Bishop Joseph M. Sullivan, Bishop Rene A. Valero, Chancellor, Rev. Msgr. Otto L. Garcia. Chancery Office, 75 Greene Ave., Box C, Brooklyn, NY 11202. Tel. (718)638-5500. Fax (718)399-5934

Brownsville, Bishop Enrique San Pedro; Chancellor, Sr. Esther Dunegan.Chancery Office, P.O. Box 2279, Brownsville, TX 78522. Tel.(512)542-2501. (512)542-6751

Buffalo, Bishop Edward D. Head; Auxiliary Bishop Edward M. Grosz; Chancellor, Rev. Msgr. Robert J. Cunningham. Chancery Office, 795 Main St., Buffalo, NY 14203. Tel. (716)847-5500. Fax (716)847-5557

Burlington, (Vacant See); Chancellor, Rev. Jay C. Haskin. Chancery Office, 351 North Ave., Burlington, VT 05401. Tel. (802)658-6110. Fax (802)658-0436

Camden, Bishop James T. McHugh; Auxiliary Bishop James L. Schad; Chancellor, Rev. Msgr. Joseph W. Pokusa. Chancery Office, 1845 Haddon Ave., P.O. Box 709, Camden, NJ 08101. Tel. (609)756-7900. Fax (609)963-2655

Charleston, Bishop David B. Thompson; Vicar General, Rev. Msgr. Thomas R. Duffy; Chancellor for Administration, Miss Cleo C. Cantey. Chancery Office, 119 Broad St., P.O. Box 818, Charleston, SC 29402. Tel. (803)723-3488. Fax (803)724-6387

Charlotte, Bishop John F. Donoghue; Chancellor, Rev. John T. McSweeney. Chancery Office, P.O. Box 36776, Charlotte, NC 28236. Tel. (704)377-6871

Cheyenne, Bishop Joseph H. Hart; Chancellor, Rev. Carl Beavers. Chancery Office, 2121 Capitol Ave., Box 426, Cheyenne, WY 82003. Tel. (307)638-1530. Fax (307)637-7936

Archdiocese of Chicago, Archbishop Joseph Cardinal Bernardin; Auxiliary Bishops: Bishop Alfred L. Abramowicz, Bishop Wilton D. Gregory; Bishop Timothy J. Lyne, Bishop Placido Rodriquez, C.M.F., Bishop Thad J. Jakubowski; Bishop John R. Gorman; Chancellor, Rev. Robert L. Kealy. Chancery Office, P.O. Box 1979, Chicago, IL 60690. Chancery Office, 155 E. Superior Ave., P.O. Box 1979, Chicago, IL 60611. Tel. (312)751- 7999

Archdiocese of Cincinnati, Archbishop Daniel E. Pilarczyk; Auxiliary Bishop James H.Garland. Chancellor, Rev. R. Daniel Conlon. Chancery Office, 100 E. 8th St., Cincinnati, OH 45202. Tel. (513) 421-3131. Fax (513)381-2242

Cleveland, Bishop Anthony M. Pilla; Auxiliary Bishops: Bishop A. Edward Pevec, Bishop A. James Quinn; Chancellor, Rev. Ralph E. Wiatrowski. Chancery Office, 350 Chancery Bldg., Cathedral Square, 1027 Superior Ave., Cleveland, OH 44114. Tel. (216)696-6525. Fax (216)696-3226

Colorado Springs, Bishop Richard C. Hanifen; Chancellor, Rev. George V. Fagan, Chancery Office, 29 West Kiowa St., Colorado Springs, CO 80903. Tel. (719)636-2345

Columbus, Bishop James A. Griffin; Chancellor, Rev. Joseph M. Hendricks. Chancery Office, 198 E. Broad St., Columbus, OH 43215. Tel. (614)224-2251. Fax (614)224-6306

Corpus Christi, Bishop Rene H. Gracida; Chancellor, Deacon Roy M. Grassedonio. Chancery Office, 620 Lipan St., Corpus Christi, TX 78401. Tel. (512)882-6191. Fax (512)882-1018

Covington, Bishop William A. Hughes; Chancellor, Rev. Roger L. Kriege. Chancery Office, The Catholic Center, P.O. Box 18548, Erlanger, KY 41018. Tel. (606)283-6210. Fax (606)283-6334

Crookston, Bishop Victor Balke; Chancellor, Very Rev. Michael Patnode. Chancery Office, 1200 Memorial Dr., P.O. Box 610, Crookston, MN 56716. Tel. (218)281-4533. Fax (218)281-3328

Dallas, Bishop Charles V. Grahmann; Chancellor, Rev. Msgr. Raphael Kamel. Chancery Office, 3915 Lemmon Ave., P.O. Box 190507, Dallas, TX 75219. Tel. (214)528-2240. Fax (214)526-1743

Davenport, Bishop Gerald Francis O'Keefe; Chancellor, Rev. Msgr. Leo Feeney. Chancery Office, 2706 N. Gaines St., Davenport, IA 52804. Tel. (319)324-1911. Fax (319)324-5842

Archdiocese of Denver, Archbishop J. Francis Stafford; Chancellor, Sr. Rosemary Wilcox. Chancery Office, 200 Josephine St., Denver, CO 80206. Tel. (303)388-4411. Fax (303)388-0517

Des Moines, Bishop William H. Bullock; Chancellor, Lawrence Breheny. Chancery Office, 818 5th Ave., P.O. Box 1816, Des Moines, IA 50306. Tel. (515)243-7653. Fax (515)283-1982

Archdiocese of Detroit, Archbishop Adam J. Maida; Auxiliary Bishops: Bishop Moses B. Anderson, S.S.E., Bishop Thomas J. Gumbleton, Bishop Dale J. Melczek, Bishop Walter J. Schoenherr; Chancellor, Rev. John P. Zenz. Chancery Office, 1234 Washington Blvd., Detroit, MI 48226. Tel. (313)237-5816. Fax (313)965-3989

Dodge City, Bishop Stanley G. Schlarman; Chancellor, Rev. David H., Kraus. Chancery Office, 910 Central Ave., P.O. Box 849, Dodge City, KS 67801. Tel. (316)227-3131. Fax (316)227-1570

Archdiocese of Dubuque, Archbishop Daniel W. Kucera; Auxiliary Bishop William E. Franklin; Chancellor, Sr. Mary Kevin Gallagher, BVM, P.O. Box 479, Dubuque, IA 52001. Tel. (319)556-2580. Fax (319)588-0557

Duluth, Bishop Roger L. Schwietz; Chancellor, Edward N. Peters. Chancery Office, 2803 E. 4th St., Duluth, MN 55812. Tel.(218)727-6861. Fax (218)724-1056

El Paso, Bishop Raymundo J. Pena; Chancellor, Very Rev. John Telles. Chancery Office, 499 St. Matthews, El Paso, TX 79907. Tel.(915)595-5038. Fax (915)595-5095

Erie, Bishop Donald W. Trautman; Chancellor, Rev. Msgr. Lawrence E. Brandt. Chancery Office, P.O. Box 10397, Erie, PA 16514. Tel. (814)825-3333. Fax (814)825-4363

Evansville, Bishop Gerald A. Gettelfinger; Chancellor, Sr. Louise Bond. Chancery Office, 4200 N. Kentucky Ave., Evansville, IN 47711. Tel. (812)424-5536. Fax (812)421-1334

Fairbanks, Bishop Michael Kaniecki, S.J.; Chancellor, Sr. Eileen Brown. Tel. (907)456-6753. Chancery Office, 1316 Peger Rd., Fairbanks, AK 99709. Tel. (907)474-0753.

Fall River, Bishop Sean P. O'Malley, OFM; Chancellor, Rev. Msgr. John J. Oliveira. Chancery Office, 47 Underwood St., Box 2577, Fall River, MA 02722. Tel. (508)675-1311. Fax (508)679-9220

Fargo, Bishop James S. Sullivan; Chancellor, Rev. James A. Leith. Chancery Office, 1310 Broadway, P.O. Box 1750, Fargo, ND 58107. Tel. (701)235-6429. (701)235-6429

Fort Wayne-South Bend, Bishop John M. D'Arcy; Auxiliary Bishop John R. Sheets. Vicar General-Chancellor, James J. Wolf, Rev. Msgr. J. William Lester. Chancery Office, 1103 S. Calhoun St., P.O. Box 390. Fort Wayne, IN 46801. Tel. (219)422-4611. Fax (219)423-3382

Fort Worth, Bishop Joseph D. Delaney; Chancellor, Rev. Robert W. Wilson. Chancery Office, 800 W. Loop 820 South, Fort Worth TX 76108. Tel. (817)560-3300

Fresno, Bishop John T. Steinbock; Chancellor, Rev. Raymond C. Dreiling. Chancery Office, P.O. Box 1668, 1550 N. Fresno St., Fresno, CA 93717. Tel. (209)237-5125

Gallup, Bishop Donald Pelotte, SSS; Chancellor, Br. Duane Torisky. Chancery Office, 711 S. Puerco Dr., P.O. Box 1338, Gallup, NM 87301. Tel. (505)863-4406

Galveston-Houston, Bishop Joseph A. Fiorenza; Auxiliary Bishops: Bishop Curtis J. Guillory, SVD; Chancellor, Rev. Msgr. Daniel Scheel. Chancery Office, 1700 San Jacinto St., Houston, TX 77002. Tel. (713)659-5461. Fax (713)759-9151

Gary, Bishop Norbert F. Gaughan; Chancellor, Rev. Richard A. Emerson. Chancery Office, 9292 Broadway, Merrillville, IN 46410 Tel. (219)769-9292. Fax (219)738-9034

Gaylord, Bishop Patrick R. Cooney; Vicar Gen., Raymond C. Mulka. Chancery Office, 1665 West M-32, Seton Bldg., Gaylord, MI 49735. Tel. (517)732-5147. Fax (517)732-1706

Grand Island, Bishop Lawrence J. McNamara; Chancellor, Rev. Richard L. Piontkowski. Chancery Office, 311 W. 17th St., P.O. Box 996, Grand Island, NE 68802. Tel.(308)382-6565

Grand Rapids, Bishop Robert J. Rose; Auxiliary Bishop, Bishop Joseph McKinney; Chancellor, Sr. Patrice Konwinski. Chancery Office, 660 Burton St. S.E., Grand Rapids, MI 49507. Tel. (616)243-0491. Fax (616)243-4910

Great Falls-Billings, Bishop Anthony M. Milone; Chancellor, Rev. Martin J. Burke. Chancery Office, 121 23rd St. S., P.O. Box 1399, Great Falls, MT 59403. Tel. (406)727-6683. Fax (406)454-3480

Green Bay, Bishop Robert J. Banks; Auxiliary Bishop Robert F. Morneau; Chancellor, Sr. Ann F. Rehrauer, OSF. Chancery Office, Box 20366, Green Bay, WI 54305. Tel. (414)435-4406. Fax (414)435-1330

Greensburg, Bishop Anthony G. Bosco; Chancellor, Rev. Lawrence T. Persico. Chancery Office, 723 E. Pittsburgh St., Greensburg, PA 15601. Tel. (412)837-0901

Harrisburg, Bishop Nicholas C. Dattilo; Chancellor, Carol Houghton. Chancery Office, P.O. Box 2153, 4800 Union Deposit Rd., Harrisburg, PA 17105. Tel. (717)657-4804

Archdiocese of Hartford, Archbishop Daniel A. Cronin; Auxiliary Bishops Peter A. Rosazza, Bishop Paul S. Loverde. Chancellor, Sr. Helen Margaret Feeney, C.S.J., Chancery Office, 134 Farmington Ave., Hartford, CT 06105. Tel. (203)527-4201. Fax (203)525-2037

Helena, Bishop Elden F. Curtiss; Chancellor, Rev. John W. Robertson. Chancery Office, 515 N. Ewing, P.O. Box 1729, Helena, MT 59624. Tel. (406)442-5820. Fax (406)442-5191

Honolulu, Bishop Joseph A. Ferrario; Chancellor, Sr. Grace Dorothy Lim, JCL. Chancery Office, 1184 Bishop St., Honolulu, HI 96813. Tel. (808)533-1791. Fax (808)521-8428

Houma-Thibodaux, Bishop Warren L. Boudreaux; Chancellor, Rev. Msgr. James B. Songy. Chancery Office, P.O. Box 9077, Houma, LA 70361. Tel. (504)868-7720. Fax (504)868-7727

Archdiocese of Indianapolis, Archbishop Daniel M. Buechlein, OSB; Chancellor, Susan L. Magnant. Chancery Office, 1400 N. Meridian St., P.O. Box 1410, Indianapolis, IN 46206. Tel.(317)236-1405. Fax (317)236-1406

Jackson, Bishop William R. Houck; Vicar General-Chancellor, Rev. Francis J. Cosgrove. Chancery Office, 237 E. Amite St., P.O. Box 2248, Jackson, MS 39225. Tel. (601)969-1880. Fax (601)960-8455

Jefferson City, Bishop Michael F. McAuliffe; Chancellor, Sr. Mary Margaret Johanning. Chancery Office, 605 Clark Ave., P.O. Box 417, Jefferson City, MO 65102. Tel. (314)635-9127. Fax (314)635-2286

Joliet, Bishop Joseph L. Imesch; Auxiliary Bishop Roger L. Kaffer; Chancellor, Sr. Judith Davies. Chancery Office, 425 Summit St., Joliet, IL 60435. Tel. (815)722-6606. Fax (815)722-6602

Juneau, Bishop Michael H. Kenny; Vicar General, Rev. Msgr. James F. Miller. Chancery Office, 419 6th St., Juneau, AK 99801. Tel. (907)586-2227

Kalamazoo, Bishop Paul V. Donovan; Chancellor, Rev. Msgr. Dell F. Stewart. Chancery Office, P.O. Box 949, 215 N. Westnedge Ave., Kalamazoo, MI 49005. Tel. (616)349-8714. Fax (616)349-6440

Archdiocese of Kansas City in Kansas, Archbishop Ignatius J. Strecker; Auxiliary Bishop Marion F. Forst; Chancellor, Rev. William T. Curtin. Chancery Office, 12615 Parallel, KS 66109, Tel. (913)721-1570

Kansas City-St. Joseph, Bishop John J. Sullivan; Chancellor, Rev. Richard F. Carney. Chancery Office, P.O. Box 419037, Kansas City, MO 64141. Tel. (816)756-1850. Fax (816)756-0878

Knoxville, Bishop Anthony J. O'Connell; Vicar General/Chancellor, Rev. Xavier Mankel. Chancery Office, 417 Erin Drive, Knoxville, TN 37919. Tel. (615)584-3307.

La Crosse, Bishop John J. Paul; Chancellor, Rev. Michael J. Gorman, Chancery Office. 3710 East Ave., La Crosse, WI 54602. Tel.(608)788-7700. Fax (608)788-8413

Lafayette in Indiana, Bishop William L. Higi; Chancellor, Rev. Robert L. Sell. Chancery Office, P.O. Box 260, 610 Lingle Ave., Lafayette, IN 47902. Tel. (317)742-0275

Lafayette (Louisiana), Bishop Harry J. Flynn; Chancellor, Sr. Joanna Valoni, SSND. Chancery Office, Diocesan Office Bldg., 1408 Carmel Ave., Lafayette, LA 70501. Tel. (318)261-5500

Lake Charles, Bishop Jude Speyrer; Chancellor Deacon George Stearns. Chancery Office, 414 Iris St., P.O. Box 3223, Lake Charles, LA 70602. Tel. (318)439-7404. Fax (318)439-7413

Lansing, Bishop Kenneth J. Povish; Chancellor, Rev. James Murray. Chancery Office, 300 W. Ottawa, Lansing, MI 48933. Tel. (517)342-2440. Fax (517)342-2515

Las Cruces, Bishop Ricardo Ramirez, CSB; Chancellor, Sr. Mary Ellen Quinn. Chancery Office, P.O. Box 16318, Las Cruces, NM 88004. Tel. (505)523-7577. Fax (505)524-3874

Lexington, Bishop James K. Williams; Chancellor, Sr. Mary Kevan Seibert; Chancery Office, P.O. Box 12350. Erlanger, KY 41018. Tel. (606)283-6200. Fax (606)254-6284

Lincoln, Fabian W. Bruskewitz; Chancellor, Rev. Msgr. Thomas M. Kealy. Chancery Office, 3400 Sheridan Blvd., P.O. Box 80328, Lincoln, NE 68501. Tel. (402)488-0921

Little Rock, Bishop Andrew J. McDonald; Chancellor, Francis I. Malone. Chancery Office, 2415 N. Tyler St., P.O. Box 7239, Little Rock, AR 72217. Tel. (501)664-0340

Archdiocese of Los Angeles, Archbishop Roger M. Mahony; Auxiliary Bishops: Bishop Juan Arzube, Bishop John J. Ward, Bishop Carl Fisher, SSJ, Bishop Armando Ochoa, Bishop Stephen E. Blaire; Chancellor, Bishop Stephen E. Blaire. Chancery Office, 1531 W. Ninth St., Los Angeles, CA 90015. Tel. (213)251-3200. Fax (213)251-2607

Archdiocese of Louisville, Archbishop Thomas C. Kelly, OP; Chancellor, Very Rev. Bernard J. Breen. P.O. Box 1073, Louisville, KY 40201. Chancery Office, 212 E. College St., Louisville, KY 40201.Tel. (502)585-3291

Lubbock, Bishop Michael Sheehan; Chancellor, Sr. Elena Gonzalez, RSM. Chancery Office. 4620 4th St., P.O. Box 98700, Lubbock, TX 79499-8700. Tel. (806)792-3943

Madison, (Vacant See); Auxiliary Bishop George O.Wirz; Chancellor, Rev. Joseph P.Higgins. Chancery Office, 15 E. Wilson St., Box 111, Madison, WI 53701. Tel. (608)256-2677

Manchester, Bishop Leo Edward O'Neil; Chancellor Rev. Msgr. Francis J. Christian. Chancery Office, 153 Ash St., P.O. Box 310, Manchester, NH 03105. Tel. (603)669-3100 Fax (603)669-0377

Marquette, Bishop Mark F. Schmitt; Chancellor, Rev. Peter Oberto.Chancery Office, 444 S. Fourth St., P.O. Box 550, Marquette, MI 49855. Tel. (906)225-1141. Fax (906)225-0437

Memphis, (Vacant See); Chancellor, Rev. J. Peter Sartain. Chancery Office, 1325 Jefferson Ave., P.O. Box 41679, Memphis, TN 38174. Tel. (901)722-4737. Fax (901)722-4769

Metuchen, Bishop Edward Hughes; Chancellor, Sr. M. Michaelita Wiechetek, CSSF. Chancery Office, P.O. Box 191, Metuchen, NJ 08840. Tel. (201)283-3800. Fax (908)283-2012

Archdiocese of Miami, Archbishop Edward A. McCarthy; Auxiliary Bishop Agustin A. Roman; Chancellor, Very Rev. Gerard T. LaCerra. Chancery Office, 9401 Biscayne Blvd., Miami Shores, FL 33138. Tel. (305)757-6241. Fax (305)754-1797.

Archdiocese for the Military Services, Bishop Joseph T. Dimino; Auxiliary Bishops: Bishop Francis X. Roque, Bishop John G. Nolan, Bishop Joseph J. Madera, Bishop John J. Glynn; Chancellor, Bishop John Glynn. Chancery Office, 962 Wayne Ave., Silver Spring, MD 20910. Tel. (301)495-4100. Fax (301)589-3774

Archdiocese of Milwaukee, Archbishop Rembert G. Weakland, OSB; Auxiliary Bishop Richard J. Sklba; Chancellor, Rev. Ralph C. Gross. Chancery Office, 3501 S. Lake Dr., P.O. Box 07912, Milwaukee, WI 53207. Tel. (414)769-3340. Fax (414)769-3408

Archdiocese of Mobile, Archbishop Oscar H. Lipscomb; Chancellor, Very Rev. G. Warren Wall. Chancery Office, 400 Government St., P.O. Box 1966, Mobile, AL 36633. Tel.(205)433-2241. Fax (205)434-1588

Monterey, Bishop Sylvester D. Ryan; Chancellor, Rev. Msgr. D. Declan Murphy. Chancery Office, 580 Fremont St., P.O. Box 2048, Monterey, CA 93940. Tel. (408)373-4345. Fax (408)373-1175

Nashville, Bishop James D. Niedergeses; Chancellor, Rev. J. Patrick Connor. Chancery Office, 2400 21st Ave., S., Nashville, TN 37212. Tel. (615)383-6393. Fax (615)292-8411

Archdiocese of Newark, Archbishop Theodore E. McCarrick; Auxiliary Bishops: Bishop David Arias, OAR, Bishop Joseph Francis, SVD, Bishop Robert F. Garner, Bishop Dominic A. Marconi, Bishop Michael A. Salterelli; Chancellor, Sr. Thomas Mary Salerno, . Chancery Office, 31 Mulberry St., Newark, NJ 07102. Tel. (201)596-4000. Fax (201)596-3763

Archdiocese of New Orleans, Archbishop Francis B. Schulte; Auxiliary Bishops: Bishop Nicholas D'Antonio, OFM, DD; Bishop Robert W. Muench; Chancellor, Rev. Msgr. Earl C. Woods. Chancery Office, 7887 Walmsley Ave., New Orleans, LA 70125. Tel. (504)861-9521. Fax (504)866-2906

Melkite Diocese of Newton, Bishop Ignatius Ghattas; Auxiliary Bishops: Bishop John A. Elya, Bishop Nicholas J. Samra. Chancellor, Very Rev. James E. King. Chancery Office, 19 Dartmouth St., West Newton, MA 02165. Tel. (617)969-8957. Fax (617)969-4115

New Ulm, Bishop Raymond A. Lucker; Chancellor, Rev. Dennis C. Labat. Chancery Office, 1400 Sixth North St., New Ulm, MN 56073. Tel. (507)359-2966

Archdiocese of New York, Archbishop John Cardinal O'Connor; Auxiliary Bishops: Bishop Patrick V. Ahern, Bishop Francis Garmendia, Bishop James P. Mahoney, Bishop Emerson J. Moore, Bishop Austin B. Vaughan, Bishop Anthony F. Mestice, Bishop William J. McCormack, Bishop Patrick J. Sheridan. Chancellor, Rev. Msgr. Henry Mansell. Chancery Office, 1011 First Ave., New York, NY 10022. Tel. (212)371-1000. Fax (212)319-8265

Norwich, Bishop Daniel P. Reilly; Chancellor, Rev. Robert L. Brown. Chancery Office, 201 Broadway, P.O. Box 587, Norwich, CT 06360. Tel. (203)887-9294. Fax (203)886-1670

122

Oakland, Bishop John S. Cummins; Chancellor, Rev. Raymond Breton. Chancery Office, 2900 Lakeshore Ave., Oakland, CA 94610. Tel. (415)893-4711. Fax (415)893-0945

Ogdensburg, Bishop Stanislaus J. Brzana; Chancellor, Rev. Robert H. Aucoin. Chancery Office, Box 369, 622 Washington St., Ogdensburg, NY 13669. Tel. (315)393-2920

Archdiocese of Oklahoma City, Archbishop Charles A. Salatka; Chancellor, Rev. John A. Steichen. Chancery Office, 7501 Northwest Expressway, P.O. Box 32180, Oklahoma City, OK 73123. Tel. (405)721-5651. Fax(405)721-5210

Archdiocese of Omaha, Archbishop Daniel E. Sheehan; Chancellor, Rev. Eldon J. McKamy. Chancery Office, 100 N. 62nd St., Omaha, NE 68132. Tel. (402)558-3100

Orange, Bishop Norman F. McFarland; Auxiliary Bishop Michael P. Driscoll; Chancellor, Rev. John Urell. Chancery Office, 2811 Villa Real Dr., Orange, CA 92667. Tel. (714)974-7120

Orlando, Bishop Norbert M. Dorsey; Chancellor, Sr. Lucy Vazquez.Chancery Office, 421 E. Robinson, P.O. Box 1800, Orlando, FL 32802. Tel. (305)425-3556. Fax (407)649-7846

Owensboro, Bishop John J. McRaith; Chancellor, Sr. Joseph Angela Boone. Chancery Office, 600 Locust St., Owensboro, KY 42301. Tel. (502)683-1545. Fax (502)683-6883

Palm Beach, Bishop J. Keith Symons; Chancellor, Rev. Charles Hawkins. Chancery Office, 9995 N. Military Trail, Bldg. C #201, Palm Beach Gardens, FL 33410. Tel. (407)775-9500. Fax (407)775-9556

Byzantine Eparchy of Parma, Bishop Andrew Pataki; Chancellor, Rev. Emil Masich. Chancery Office, 1900 Carlton Rd., Parma, OH 44134. Tel. (216)741-8773. Fax (216)741-9356

Byzantine Diocese of Passaic, Bishop Michael J. Dudick; Chancellor, Rev. Msgr. Raymond Misulich. Chancery Office, 445 Lackawanna Ave., West Paterson, NJ 07424. Tel. (201)890-7777. Fax (201)890-7175

Paterson, Bishop Frank J. Rodimer; Chancellor, Rev. Msgr. Herbert K. Tillyer. Chancery Office, 777 Valley Rd., Clifton, NJ 07013. Tel. (201)777-8818. Fax (201)777-8976

Pensacola-Tallahassee, Bishop John M. Smith; Chancellor, Rev. Msgr. James Amos. Chancery Office, 11 N. "B" St., Pensacola, FL 32501. Tel. (904)432-1515. Fax (904)469-8176

Peoria, Bishop John J. Myers; Chancellor, Rev. James F. Campbell. Chancery Office, P.O. Box 1406, 607 NE Madison Ave., Peoria, IL 61655. Tel. (309)671-1550. Fax (309)671-5079

Archdiocese of Philadelphia, Archbishop Anthony Cardinal Bevilacqua;Auxiliary Bishops: Bishop Louis A. DeSimone, Bishop Martin N. Lohmuller; Chancellor, Rev. Msgr. Joseph A. Pepe. Chancery Office, 222 N. 17th St. Philadelphia, PA 19103. Tel. (215)587-4538. Fax (215)587-4545

Archdiocese of Philadelphia, Ukraine, Archbishop Stephen Sulyk; Auxiliary Bishop Walter Paska; Chancellor, Sr. Thomas Hrynewich, SSMI. Chancery Office, 827 N. Franklin St., Philadelphia, PA 19123. Tel. (215)627-0143. Fax (215)627-0377

Phoenix, Bishop Thomas J. O'Brien; Chancellor, Rev. Timothy R. Davern. Chancery Office, 400 E. Monroe St., Phoenix, AZ 85004.Tel. (602)257-0030. Fax (602)258-3425

Pittsburgh, Bishop Donald W. Wuerl; Auxiliary Bishop: Bishop John B. McDowell, Bishop William J. Winter. Chancellor, Rev. Lawrence A. DiNardo. Chancery Office, 111 Blvd. of Allies, Pittsburgh, PA 15222. Tel. (412)456-3000

Archdiocese of Pittsburgh, Byzantine Rite, Archbishop Thomas V. Dolinay;Auxiliary Bishop John M. Bilock; Chancellor, Rev. Msgr. Raymond Balta. Chancery Office, 54 Riverview Ave., Pittsburgh, PA 15214. Tel.(412)322-7300. Fax (412)322-9935

Portland, Bishop Joseph J. Gerry; Auxiliary Bishop Amedee Proulx; Co-Chancellors, Rev. Michael J. Henchal, Rev. Rita-Mae Bissonnette. Chancery Office, 510 Ocean Ave., P.O. Box 6750, Portland, ME 04101-6750. Tel.(207)773-6471. Fax (207)773-0182

Archdiocese of Portland in Oregon, Archbishop William J. Levada; Auxiliary Bishops: Bishop Kenneth Steiner, Bishop Paul Waldschmidt, CSC; Chancellor, Mary Jo Tully. Chancery Office, 2838 E. Burnside St., Portland, OR 97214-1895. Tel. (503)234-5334. Fax (503)234-2545

Providence, Bishop Louis E. Gelineau; Auxiliary Bishop Kenneth A. Angell; Chancellor, Rev. Msgr. William I. Varsanyi. Chancery Office, 1 Cathedral Square, Providence, RI 02903-3695. Tel. (401)278-4500. Fax (401)278-4548

Pueblo, Bishop Arthur N. Tafoya; Chancellor, Rev. Edward H. Nunez. Chancery Office, 1001 N. Grand Ave., Pueblo, CO 81003. Tel.(303)544-9861

Raleigh, Bishop F. Joseph Gossman; Chancellor, Rev. Joseph G. Vetter. Chancery Office, 300 Cardinal Gibbons Dr., Raleigh, NC 27606. Tel. (919)821-9700. Fax (919)821-9705

Rapid City, Bishop Charles J. Chaput, OFM Cap.; Chancellor, Sr. M. Celine Erk. Chancery Office, 606 Cathedral Dr., P.O. Box 678, Rapid City, SD 57709. Tel. (605)343-3541. Fax (605)345-7985

Reno-Las Vegas, Bishop Daniel F. Walsh; Chancellor, Rev. Anthony Vercellone, Jr. Chancery Office, 515 Court St., Reno, NV 89501. Tel. (702)329-9274. Fax(702)873-4946

Richmond, Bishop Walter F. Sullivan; Auxiliary Bishop David E. Foley; Chancellor, Bishop David E. Foley. Chancery Office, 811 Cathedral Pl., Ste. C, Richmond, VA 23220-4898. Tel. (804)359-5661. Fax ((804)358-9159

Rochester, Bishop Matthew H. Clark; Chancellor, (Vacant). Chancery Office, 1150 Buffalo Rd., Rochester, NY 14624-1890. Tel. (716)328-3210. Fax (716)328-3149

Rockford, Bishop Arthur J. O'Neill; Chancellor, Very Rev. Charles W. McNamee. Chancery Office, 1245 N. Court St., Rockford, IL 61103 Tel. (815)962-3709. Fax (815)968-2824

Rockville Centre, Bishop John R. McGann; Auxiliary Bishops: Bishop James J. Daly, Bishop Alfred J. Markiewicz, Bishop Emil A. Wcela, Bishop John C.Dunne; Chancellor, Rev. Msgr. John A. Alesandro. Chancery Office, 50 N. Park Ave. Rockville Centre, NY 11570. Tel. (516)678-5800. Fax (516)678-1786

Sacramento, Bishop Francis A. Quinn; Chancellor, Sr. Bridget Mary Flynn, SM. Chancery Office, 1119 K St., P.O. Box 1706, Sacramento, CA 95812-1706. Tel. (916)443-1996. Fax (916)4436-4990

Saginaw, Bishop Kenneth E. Untener; Chancellor, Rev. Msgr. Thomas P. Schroeder. Chancery Office, 5800 Weiss St., Saginaw, MI 48603. Tel. (517)799-7910

St. Augustine, Bishop John J. Snyder; Chancellor, Rev. Msgr. Eugene C. Kohls. Chancery Office, 11625 Old St. Augustine Road, P.O. Box 24000, Jacksonville, FL 32241. Tel.(904)262-3200. Fax (904)262-0698

St. Cloud, Bishop Jerome Hanus, OSB; Chancellor, Rev. Severin Schwieters. Chancery Office, P.O. Box 1248, 214 Third Ave. S., St.Cloud, MN 56302. Tel. (612)251-2340

St. Josaphat in Parma, Ukrainian Bishop Robert M. Moskal; Chancellor, Rev. Msgr. Thomas A. Sayuk. Chancery Office 5720 State Rd., P.O. Box 347180, Parma, OH 44134. Tel. (216)888-1522. Fax (216)888-3477

Archdiocese of St. Louis, Archbishop John L. May; Auxiliary Bishops: Bishop Charles R. Koester, Bishop Edward J. O'Donnell, Bishop J. Terry Steib, Bishop Paul A. Zipfel; Chancellor, Rev. George J. Lucas. Chancery Office, 4445 Lindell Blvd., St. Louis, MO 63108. Tel. (314)533-1887. Fax (314)533-1887(Station 212)

St. Maron of Brooklyn, Bishop Francis M. Zayek; Auxiliary Bishop John G. Chedid; Chancellor, Rev. John D. Faris. Chancery Office, 8120 15th Ave.,Brooklyn, NY 11228. Tel. (718)259-9200. Fax (718)259-8968

St. Nicholas in Chicago for Ukrainians, Bishop Innocent Lotocky, OSBM; Chancellor, Sonia Ann Peczeniuk. Chancery Office, 2245 W. Rice St., Chicago, IL 60622. Tel. (312)276-5080. Fax (312)276-6799

Archdiocese of St. Paul and Minneapolis, Archbishop John R. Roach; Auxiliary Bishops: Bishop Robert J. Carlson, Bishop Joseph J. Charron, Bishop Lawrence H. Welsh; Chancellor, Rev. Thomas V. Vowell. Chancery Office, 226 Summit Ave., St. Paul, MN 55102. Tel. (612)291-4400. Fax (612)290-1629

St. Petersburg, Bishop John C. Favalora; Chancellor, Very Rev. Robert Sherman. Chancery Office, 6363 9th Ave. N., P.O. Box 40200. St. Petersburg, FL 33743. Tel. (813)344-1611. Fax (813)345-2143

Salina, Bishop George K. Fitzsimons; Chancellor, Rev. Msgr. James E. Hake. Chancery Office, 103 N. 9th, P.O. Box 980, Salina, KS 67402. Tel. (913)827-8746. Fax (913)827-8746

Salt Lake City, Bishop William K. Weigand; Chancellor, Deacon Silvio Mayo. Chancery Office, 27 C. St., Salt Lake City, UT 84103. Tel. (801)328-8641. Fax (801)328-9680

San Angelo, Bishop Michael Pfeifer, OMI; Chancellor, Rev. Msgr. Larry J. Droll. Chancery Office, 804 Ford, Box 1829, San Angelo, TX 76902. Tel. (915)653-2466.

Archdiocese of San Antonio, Archbishop Patrick F. Flores; Auxiliary Bishops: Bishop Bernard F. Popp; Chancellor, Rev. Msgr. Patrick J. Murray, Chancery Office, 2718 W. Woodlawn Ave., P.O. Box 28410, San Antonio, TX 78228. Tel.(512)734-2620. Fax (512)734-2774

San Bernardino, Bishop Phillip F. Straling; Chancellor, Sr. Maura Feeley; Auxiliary Bishop Gerald R. Barnes. Chancery Office, 1450 North D St., San Bernardino, CA 92405 Tel. (714)384-8200. Fax (714)884-4890

San Diego, Bishop Robert Brom; Auxiliary Bishop: Bishop Gilbert E. Chavez; Chancellor, Rev. Msgr. Daniel J. Dillabough. Chancery Office, Alcala Park, P.O. Box 85728, San Diego, CA 92186-5728. Tel.(619)574-6300. Fax (619)574-0962

Archdiocese of San Francisco, Archbishop John R. Quinn; Auxiliary Bishops: Bishop Carlos A. Sevilla, Bishop Patrick J. McGrath. Chancellor, Sr. Mary B. Flaherty, RSCJ. Chancery Office, 445 Church St., San Francisco, CA 94114. Tel. (415)565-3600. Fax (415)565-3633

San Jose, Bishop Pierre DuMaine; Chancellor, Sr. Patricia Marie Mulpeters, Chancery Office, 841 Lenzen Ave., San Jose, CA 95126-2700. Tel. (408)925-0181

Archdiocese of Santa Fe, Archbishop Robert F. Sanchez; Chancellor, Rev. Richard Olona. Chancery Office, 4000 St. Joseph Place, N.W. Albuquerque, NM 87120. Tel. (505)831-8100

Santa Rosa, Bishop Patrick G. Zieman; Chancellor, Rev. Msgr. James E. Pulskamp. Chancery Office, 547 "B" St., P.O. Box 1297, Santa Rosa, CA 95402. Tel. (707)545-7610. Fax (707)542-9702

Savannah, Bishop Raymond W. Lessard; Chancellor, Rev. Jeremiah J. McCarthy. Chancery Office, 601 E. Liberty St., Savannah, GA 31401-5196. Tel. (912)238-2320 Fax (912)238-2335

Scranton, Bishop James C. Timlin; Auxiliary Bishop Francis X. DiLorenzo; Chancellor, Rev. Neil J. Van Loon. Chancery Office, 300 Wyoming Ave., Scranton, PA 18503. Tel. (717)346-8910

Archdiocese of Seattle, Archbishop Thomas J. Murphy; Chancellor, Very Rev. George L. Thomas. Chancery Office, 910 Marion St., Seattle, WA 98104. Tel. (206)382-4560. Fax (206)382-4840

Shreveport, Bishop William B. Friend; Chancellor, Sr. Margaret Daues, CSJ, 2500 Line Ave., Shreveport, LA 71104. Tel. (318)222- 2006. Fax (318)222-2080

Sioux City, Bishop Lawrence D.Soens; Chancellor, Rev. Kevin C. McCoy. Chancery Office, 1821 Jackson St., P.O. Box 3379, Sioux City, IA 51102. Tel. (712)255-7933

Sioux Falls, Bishop Paul V. Dudley; Chancellor, Rev. Gregory Tschakert. Chancery Office, 609 W. 5th St., Box 5033, Sioux Falls, SD 57117. Tel. (605)334-9861. Fax (605)334-2092

Spokane, Bishop William Skylstad; Chancellor, Rev. Mark Pautler. Chancery Office, 1023 W. Riverside Ave., P.O. Box 1453, Spokane, WA 99201. Tel. (509)456-7100

Springfield-Cape Girardeau, Bishop John J. Leibrecht; Chancellor, Rev. Msgr. Thomas E. Reidy. Chancery Office, 601 South Jefferson, Springfield, MO 65806-3107. Tel. (417)866-0841. Fax (417)866-1140

Springfield in Illinois, Bishop Daniel L. Ryan; Vicar Gen., Rev. John Renken. Chancery Office, 1615 W. Washington, P.O. Box 3187, Springfield, IL 62708. Tel. (217)698-8500. Fax (217)698-8620

Springfield in Massachusetts, Bishop John A. Marshall; Auxiliary Bishop Thomas L. Dupre, Chancellor, Bishop Thomas L. Dupre. Chancery Office, 76 Elliot St., P.O. Box 1730, Springfield, MA 01101. Tel. (413) 732-3175. Fax (413)737-2337

Stamford, Ukrainian Byzantine, Bishop Basil H. Losten; Chancellor, Rt. Rev. Mitred Matthew Berko. Chancery Office, 161 Glenbrook Rd., Stamford, CT 06902-3092. Tel. (203)324-7698. Fax (203)967-9948

Steubenville, Bishop Gilbert I. Sheldon; Chancellor, Linda A. Nichols. Chancery Office, 422 Washington St., P.O. Box 969, Steubenville, OH 43952. Tel. (614)282-3631. Fax (614)282-3327

Stockton, Bishop Donald W. Montrose; Chancellor, Rev. Richard J. Ryan. Chancery Office, 1105 N. Lincoln St., P.O. Box 4237, Stockton, CA 95204-0237. Tel. (209)466-0636. Fax (209)941-9722

Superior, Bishop Raphael M. Fliss; Chancellor, Rev. James F. Tobolski. Chancery Office, 1201 Hughitt Ave., Box 969, Superior, WI 54880. Tel. (715)392-2937

Syracuse, Bishop Joseph T. O'Keefe; Auxiliary Bishop Thomas J. Costello; Co-Chancellors, Rev. David W. Barry, Rev. Richard M. Kopp. Chancery Office, 240 E. Onandaga St., P.O. Box 511, Syracuse, NY 13201. Tel. (315)422-7203. Fax (315)478-4619

Toledo, Bishop James R. Hoffman; Auxiliary Bishop Robert W. Donnelly. Chancery Office, 1933 Spielbush, P.O. Box 985, Toledo, OH 43624. Tel. (419)244-6711. Fax (419)244-4791

Trenton, Bishop John C. Reiss; Auxiliary Bishop Edward U. Kmiec; Chancellor, Rev. Msgr. William F. Fitzgerald. Chancery Office, 701 Lawrenceville Road, P.O. Box 5309, Trenton, NJ 08638. Tel. (609)882-7125. Fax (609)771-6793

Tucson, Bishop Manuel D. Moreno; Chancellor, Rev. John F. Allt. Chancery Office, 192 S. Stone Ave., Box 31, Tucson, AZ 85702. Tel. (602)792-3410

Tulsa, Bishop Eusebius J. Beltran. Chancellor, Rev. Patrick J. Gaalaas. Chancery Office, 820 S. Boulder St., P.O. Box 2009, Tulsa, OK 74101. Tel. (918)587-3115

Tyler, Bishop Edmond Carmody; Vicar General, Rev. Msgr. Milam J. Joseph. Chancery Office, 1920 Sybil Lane, Tyler, TX 75703. Tel.(214)534-1077. Fax (903)534-1370

Van Nuys Eparchy, Byzantine Rite, Bishop George M. Kuzma; Chancellor, Rev. Msgr. Michael Moran. Chancery Office, 18024 Parthenia St., Northridge, CA 91325. Tel. (818)701-6114. Fax (818)701-6116

Venice, Bishop John J. Nevins; Chancellor, Very Rev. Jerome A. Carosella. Chancery Office, 1000 Pinebrook Rd., P.O. Box 2006, Venice, FL 34284. Tel. (813)484-9543. Fax (813)484-1121

Victoria, Bishop David E. Fellhauer; Chancellor, Rev. Msgr. Thomas C. McLaughlin. Chancery Office, 1505 E. Mesquite Lane, P.O. Box 4708, Victoria, TX 77903. Tel. (512)573-0828. Fax (512)573-5725

Archdiocese of Washington, Archbishop James Cardinal Hickey; Auxiliary Bishops: Bishop Alvaro Corrada, SJ; Bishop Leonard J. Oliver; Bishop William C. Curlin; Chancellor, Rev. William J. Kane. Chancery Office, 5001 Eastern Ave., P.O. Box 29260, NW, Washington, DC 20017. Tel.(301)853-3800. Fax (301)853-3246

Wheeling-Charleston, Bishop Bernard W. Schmitt; Chancellor, Rev. Robert C. Nash. Chancery Office, 1300 Byron St., P.O. Box 230, Wheeling, WV 26003. Tel. (304)233-0880. Fax (304)233-0890

Wichita, Bishop Eugene J. Gerber; Chancellor, Rev. Robert E. Hemberger. Chancery Office, 424 N. Broadway, Wichita, KS 67202. Tel. (316)269-3900

Wilmington, Bishop Robert E. Mulvee; Auxiliary Bishop James C. Burke, OP; Chancellor, Rev. Msgr. Joseph F. Rebman. Chancery Office, P.O. Box 2030, 1925 Delaware Ave., Ste 1A, Wilmington, DE 19899. Tel. (302)573-3100. Fax (302)573-3128

Winona, Bishop John G. Vlazny; Chancellor, Rev. Edward F. McGrath. Chancery Office, 55 W. Sanborn, P.O. Box 588, Winona, MN 55987. Tel. (507)454-4643. Fax (507)454-8106

Worcester, Bishop Timothy J. Harrington; Auxiliary Bishop George E. Rueger. Chancery Office, 49 Elm St., Worcester, MA 01609. Tel. (617)791-7171. Fax (508)753-7180

Yakima, Bishop Francis E. George; Vicar General, Very Rev. Perron J. Auve. Chancery Office, 5301-A Tieton Dr., Yakima, WA 98908. Tel. (509)965-7117

Youngstown, Bishop James W. Malone; Auxiliary Bishop Benedict C. Franzetta; Chancellor, Rev. Robert J. Siffrin. Chancery Office, 144 W. Wood St., Youngstown, OH 44503. Tel. (216)744-8451

The Romanian Orthodox Church in America

The Romanian Orthodox Church in America is an autonomous Archdiocese chartered under the name of "Romanian Orthodox Archdiocese in America."

The diocese was founded in 1929 and approved by the Holy Synod of the Romanian Orthodox Church in Romania in 1934. The Holy Synod of the Romanian Orthodox Church of July 12, 1950, granted it ecclesiastical autonomy in America, continuing to hold only dogmatical and canonical ties with the Holy Synod and the Romanian Orthodox Patriarchate of Romania.

In 1951, approximately 40 parishes with their clergy from the United States and Canada separated from this church. In 1960, they joined the Russian Orthodox Greek Catholic Metropolia, now called the Orthodox Church in America, which reordained for these parishes a bishop with the title "Bishop of Detroit and Michigan."

The Holy Synod of the Romanian Orthodox Church, on June 11, 1973, elevated the Bishop of Romanian Orthodox Missionary Episcopate in America to the rank of Archbishop.

HEADQUARTERS

19959 Riopelle, Detroit, MI 48203 Tel. (313)893-8390

Media Contact, Archdiocesan Dean & Secretary, V. Rev. Fr. Nicholas Apostola, 44 Midland St., Worcester, MA 01602-4217 Tel. (508)799-0040 Fax (508)756-9866

OFFICERS

Archbishop, His Eminence the Most Rev. Archbishop Victorin (Ursache), 19959 Riopelle St., Detroit, MI 48203 Tel. (313)893-8390

Vicar, V. Rev. Archim. Dr. Vasile Vasilachi, 45-03 48th Ave., Woodside, Queens, NY 11377 Tel. (718)784-4453

Inter-Church Relations, Dir., Rev. Fr. Nicholas Apostola, 14 Hammond St., Worcester, MA 01610 Tel. (617)799-0040

Sec., V. Archim. Rev. Felix Dubneae, 19959 Riopelle St., Detroit, MI 48203 Tel. (313)892-2402

PERIODICALS

Credinta—The Faith; Calendarul Credinta

The Romanian Orthodox Episcopate of America

This body of Eastern Orthodox Christians of Romanian descent was organized in 1929 as an autonomous Diocese under the jurisdiction of the Romanian Patriarchate. In 1951 it severed all relations with the Orthodox Church of Romania. Now under the canonical jurisdiction of the autocephalous Orthodox Church in America, it enjoys full administrative autonomy and is headed by its own Bishop.

HEADQUARTERS

P.O.Box 309, Grass Lake, MI 49240 Tel. (517)522-4800 Fax (517)522-5907
Media Contact, Ed./Sec., Dept. of Publications, David Oancea, P.O. Box 185, Grass Lake, MI 49240-0185 Tel. (517)522-3656 Fax (517)522-5907

OFFICERS

Ruling Bishop, His Grace Bishop Nathaniel (Popp)
The Council of the Episcopate: Sec., Very Rev. Laurence Lazar, 18430 W. Nine Mile Rd., Southfield, MI 48075; Treas., Rev. Fr. Leonte Copacia, 5993 Wilmington Dr., Shelby Twp., MI 48316

OTHER ORGANIZATIONS

The American Romanian Orthodox Youth, Pres., David Maxim, 3633 22nd St., Wyandotte, MI 48192
Assoc. of Romanian Orthodox Ladies' Aux., Pres., Mrs. Pauline Trutza, 1466 Waterbury Ave., Lakewood, OH 44107
Orthodox Brotherhood U.S.A., Pres., George Aldea, 824 Mt. Vernon Blvd., Royal Oak, MI 48073
Orthodox Brotherhood of Canada, Pres., Thrisia Pana, #510 - 2243 Hamilton St., Regina, SK S4P 4B6

Russian Orthodox Church in the U.S.A., Patriarchal Parishes of the

This group of parishes is under the direct jurisdiction of the Patriarch of Moscow and All Russia, His Holiness Aleksy II, in the person of a Vicar Bishop, His Grace Paul, Bishop of Zaraisk.

HEADQUARTERS

St. Nicholas Cathedral, 15 E. 97th St., New York, NY 10029 Tel. (212)831-6294 Fax (212)427-5003
Media Contact, Office of the Bishop

PERIODICAL

One Church

The Russian Orthodox Church Outside of Russia

This group was organized in 1920 to unite in one body of dioceses the missions and parishes of the Russian Orthodox Church outside of Russia. The governing body, set up in Constantinople, was sponsored by the Ecumenical Patriarchate. In November 1950, it came to the United States. The Russian Orthodox Church Outside of Russia emphasizes being true to the old traditions of the Russian Church. It is not in communion with the Moscow Patriarchate.

HEADQUARTERS

75 E. 93rd St., New York, NY 10128 Tel. (212)534-1601 Fax (212)534-1798

Media Contact, Dep. Sec., Bishop Hilarion

COUNCIL OF BISHOPS

Synod, His Eminence Metropolitan Vitaly
Sec., Archbishop Laurus of Syracuse and Trinity
Dep. Sec., Hilarion, Bishop of Manhattan, Tel. (212)722-6577
Dir. of Public & Foreign Relations Dept., Archbishop Laurus of Syracuse and Trinity

The Salvation Army

The Salvation Army, founded in 1865 by William Booth (1829-1912) in London, England, and introduced into America in 1880, is an international religious and charitable movement organized and operated on a paramilitary pattern and is a branch of the Christian church. To carry out its purposes, The Salvation Army has established a widely diversified program of religious and social welfare services which are designed to meet the needs of children, youth, and adults in all age groups.

HEADQUARTERS

615 Slaters La., Alexandria, VA 22313 Tel. (703)684-5500 Fax (703)684-5538
Media Contact, Natl. Commications Dir., Col. Leon R. Ferraez, Tel. (703)684-5521 Fax (703)684-5538

OFFICERS

Natl. Commander, Commissioner James Osborne
Natl. Chief Sec., Commissioner Kenneth Hood
Natl. Communications Dept., Dir., Colonel Leon R. Ferraez

TERRITORIAL ORGANIZATIONS

Eastern Territory: 440 W. Nyack Rd., P.O. Box C-635, West Nyack, NY 10994 Tel. (914)623-4700 Fax (914)620-7466; Territorial Commander, Commissioner Robert E. Thomson
Central Territory: 10 W. Algonquin Rd., Des Plains, IL 60016 Tel. (708)294-2000 Fax (708)294-2299; Territorial Commander, Commissioner Harold E. Shoults
Western Territory: 30840 Hawthorne Blvd., Ranchos Palos Verdes, CA 90274 Tel. (310)541-4721 Fax (310)544-1674; Territorial Commander, Commissioner Paul A. Rader
Southern Territory: 1424 Northeast Expressway, Atlanta, GA 30329 Tel. (404)728-1300 Fax (404)728-1331; Territorial Commander, Commissioner Kenneth L. Hodder

PERIODICAL

War Cry, The

The Schwenkfelder Church

The Schwenkfelders are the spiritual descendants of the Silesian nobleman Caspar Schwenkfeld von Ossig (1489-1561), a scholar, reformer, preacher, and prolific writer who endeavored to aid in the cause of the Protestant Reformation. A contemporary of Martin Luther, John Calvin, Ulrich Zwingli, and Phillip Melanchthon, Schwenkfeld sought no following, formulated no creed, and did not attempt to organize a church based on his beliefs. He labored for liberty of religious belief — a fellowship of all believers, for one united Christian church — the ecumenical church.

He and his cobelievers supported a movement known as the Reformation by the Middle Way. Persecuted by state churches, ultimately 180 Schwenkfelders exiled from Silesia emigrated to Pennsylvania. They landed at Philadelphia Sept.

22, 1734. In 1882, the Society of Schwenkfelders, the forerunner of the present Schwenkfelder Church, was formed. The church was incorporated in 1909.

The General Conference of the Schwenkfelder Church is a voluntary association for the Schwenkfelder Churches at Palm, Worcester, Lansdale, Norristown, and Philadelphia, Pa.

They practice adult baptism and dedication of children, and observe the Lord's Supper regularly with open Communion. In theology, they are Christo-centric; in polity, congregational; in missions, world-minded; in ecclesiastical organization, ecumenical.

The ministry is recruited from graduates of colleges, universities, and accredited theological seminaries. The churches take leadership in ecumenical concerns through ministerial associations, community service and action groups, councils of Christian education, and other agencies.

HEADQUARTERS
1 Seminary St., Pennsburg, PA 18073 Tel. (215)679-3103

OFFICERS
Mod., Kenneth D. Slough, Jr., 197 N. Whitehall Rd., Norristown, PA 19403
Sec., Frances Witte, Central Schwenkfelder Church, Worcester, PA 19490
Treas., Ellis W. Kriebel, 523 Meetinghouse Rd., Harleysville, PA 19438

PERIODICAL
Schwenkfeldian, The

Separate Baptists in Christ
A group of Baptists found in Indiana, Ohio, Kentucky, Tennessee, Virginia, West Virginia, Florida and North Carolina, dating back to an association formed in 1758 in North Carolina and Virginia.

Today this group consists of approximately 100 churches. They believe in the infallibility of the Bible, the divine ordinances of the Lord's Supper, feetwashing, baptism, and that those who endureth to the end shall be saved.

At the 1991 General Association, an additional article of doctrine was adopted. "We believe that at Christ's return in the clouds of heaven all Christians will meet the Lord in the air, and time shall be no more," thus leaving no time for a literal one thousand year reign. Two of the sister associations which were members of the General Association withdrew in protest of the adoption of the new article. There are now seven sister associations comprising the General Association of Separate Baptists.

HEADQUARTERS
Media Contact, Clk., Rev. Mark Polston, 787 Kitchen Rd., Mooresville, IN 46158 Tel. (317)834-0286

OFFICERS
Mod., Rev. Jim Goff, 1020 Gagel Ave., Louisville, KY 40216
Asst. Mod., Rev. Jimmy Polston, 785 Kitchen Rd., Mooresville, IN 46158 Tel. (317)831-6745
Clk., Rev. Mark Polston
Asst. Clk., Bro. Randy Polston, 3105 N. Elmhurst Dr., Indianapolis, IN 46226 Tel. (317)549-3782

Serbian Orthodox Church in the U.S.A. and Canada
The Serbian Orthodox Church is an organic part of the Eastern Orthodox Church. As a local church it received its autocephaly from Constantinople in 1219 A.D. The Patriarchal seat of the church today is in Belgrade, Yugoslavia.

In 1921, a Serbian Orthodox Diocese in the United States of America and Canada was organized. In 1963, it was reorganized into three dioceses, and in 1983 a fourth diocese was created for the Canadian part of the church. The Serbian Orthodox Church in the USA and Canada received its administrative autonomy in 1982. The Serbian Orthodox Church is in absolute doctrinal unity with all other local Orthodox Churches.

HEADQUARTERS
St. Sava Monastery, P.O. Box 519, Libertyville, IL 60048 Tel. (708)362-2440

BISHOPS
Metropolitan of Midwestern America, Administrator, Most Rev. Metropolitan Christopher, Tel. (708)367-0698
Administrator of Canada, Bishop of Milesevo Georgije, 5A Stockbridge Ave., Toronto, ON M8Z 4M6 Tel. (416)231-4009
Diocese of Western America, Metropolitan Christopher, Administrator, 2541 Crestline Terr., Alhambra, CA 91803 Tel. (818)264-6825
Bishop of Eastern America, Rt. Rev. Bishop Mitrophan, P.O. Box 368, Sewickley, PA 15143 Tel. (412)741-5686

OTHER ORGANIZATIONS
Brotherhood of Serbian Orth. Clergy in U.S.A. & Canada, Pres., V. Rev. Branko Skaljac, Lorain, OH
Federation of Circles of Serbian Sisters
Serbian Singing Federation

PERIODICALS
Path of Orthodoxy (Eng.), The; Path of Orthodoxy (Serbian), The

Seventh-day Adventist Church
The Seventh-day Adventist Church grew out of a worldwide religious revival in the mid-19th century. People of many religious persuasions believed Bible prophecies indicated that the second coming or advent of Christ was imminent.

When Christ did not come in the 1840s, a group of these disappointed Adventists in the United States continued their Bible studies and concluded they had misinterpreted prophetic events and that the second coming of Christ was still in the future. This same group of Adventists later accepted the teaching of the seventh-day Sabbath and became known as Seventh-day Adventists. The denomination organized formally in 1863.

The church was largely confined to North America until 1874, when its first missionary was sent to Europe. Today over 34,000 congregations meet in 201 countries. Membership exceeds 6 million and increases between six and seven percent each year.

In addition to a mission program, the church has the largest worldwide Protestant parochial school system with more than 5,400 schools with more than 750,000 students on elementary through college and university levels.

The Adventist Development and Relief Agency (ADRA) helps victims of war and natural disasters, and many local congregations have community

THE YEAR IN IMAGES

Religious News Service photo

Baptist Baby Boomers

Two Southern Baptists overcame incumbents who appealed to the religious right and "family values" in the U.S. presidential race. Arkansas Gov. Bill Clinton and Sen. Al Gore of Tennessee won the White House for Democrats for the first time in 12 years, defeating President George Bush and Vice President Dan Quayle, and billionaire businessman Ross Perot.

service facilities to help those in need close to home.

The church also has a worldwide publishing ministry with more than 50 printing facilities producing magazines and other publications in over 180 languages and dialects. In the United States and Canada, the church sponsors a variety of radio and television programs, including "Christian Lifestyle Magazine," "It Is Written," "Breath of Life," "Ayer, Hoy, y Mañana," "Voice of Prophecy," and "La Voz de la Esperanza."

The North American Division of Seventh-day Adventist includes 180 Conferences which are grouped together into 9 organized Union Conferences. The various Conferences work under the general direction of these Union Conferences.

HEADQUARTERS

12501 Old Columbia Pike, Silver Spring, MD 20904-6600 Tel. (301)680-6000

WORLD-WIDE OFFICERS

Pres., Robert S. Folkenberg
Sec., G. Ralph Thompson
Treas., Donald F. Gilbert

WORLD-WIDE DEPARTMENTS

Church Ministries, Dir., Israel Leito
Communication, Dir., Shirley Burton
Education, Dir., Humberto M. Rasi
Health & Temperance, Dir., Albert S. Whiting
Ministerial Assoc., Sec., James A. Cress
Public Affairs & Religious Liberty, Dir., B. B. Beach
Publishing, Dir., Ronald E. Appenzeller

NORTH AMERICAN OFFICERS

Pres., Alfred C. McClure
Vice Pres.: Robert L. Dale; Manuel Vasquez

Admn. Asst. to Pres., Gary B. Patterson
Sec., Harold W. Baptiste
Assoc. Sec., Rosa T. Banks
Treas., George H. Crumley
Assoc. Treas.: Donald R. Pierson
Treas.: Meade C. VanPuttern

NORTH AMERICAN ORGANIZATIONS

Atlantic Union Conf.: P.O. Box 1189, South Lancaster, MA 01561-1189; Pres., David L. Taylor
Canada: Seventh-day Adventist Church in Canada (see Ch. 4)
Columbia Union Conf.: 5427 Twin Knolls Rd., Columbia, MD 21045; Pres., Ron M. Wisbey
Lake Union Conf.: P.O. Box C, Berrien Springs, MI 49103; Pres., R. H. Carter
Mid-America Union Conf.: P.O. Box 6128, Lincoln, NE 68506; Pres., Joel O. Tompkins
North Pacific Union Conf.: P.O. Box 16677, Portland, OR 97216; Pres., Bruce Johnston
Pacific Union Conf.: P.O. Box 5005, Westlake Village, CA 91359; Pres., Thomas J. Mostert, Jr
Southern Union Conf.: P.O. Box 849, Decatur, GA 30031; Pres., M. D. Gordon
Southwestern Union Conf.: P.O. Box 4000, Burleson, TX 76097; Pres., Cyril Miller

PERIODICALS

Celebration!; Adventist Review; Christian Record; Cornerstone Connections; Guide; Insight and Insight/Out; Journal of Adventist Education; Liberty; Listen; Message; Ministry; Mission, Adult and Junior-Teen; Our Little Friend; Primary Treasure; Shabbat Shalom; Signs of the Times; Vibrant Life; Youth Ministry Accent

Seventh Day Baptist General Conference, USA and Canada

Seventh Day Baptists emerged during the English Reformation, organizing their first churches in the mid-1600s. The first Seventh Day Baptists of record in America were Stephen and Anne Mumford, who emigrated from England in 1664. Beginning in 1665 several members of the First Baptist Church at Newport, R.I., began observing the seventh day Sabbath, or Saturday. In 1671, five members, together with the Mumfords, formed the first Seventh Day Baptist Church in America at Newport.

Beginning about 1700, other Seventh Day Baptist churches were established in New Jersey and Pennsylvania. From these three centers, the denomination grew and expanded westward. They founded the Seventh Day Baptist General Conference in 1802.

The organization of the denomination reflects an interest home and foreign missions, publications, and education. Women have encouraged to participate. From the earliest years, religious freedom has been championed for all, and the separation of church and state advocated.

Seventh Day Baptists are members of the Baptist World Alliance. The Seventh Day Baptist World Federation has 17 member conferences in six continents.

HEADQUARTERS

Seventh Day Baptist Center, 3120 Kennedy Rd., P.O. Box 1678, Janesville, WI 53547-1678 Tel. (608)752-5055 Fax (608)752-7711
Media Contact, Gen. Services Admn., Calvin Babcock

OTHER ORGANIZATIONS

Seventh Day Baptist Missionary Society, Exec. Vice-Pres., Mr. Kirk Looper, 119 Main St., Westerly, RI 02891
Seventh Day Bapt. Bd. of Christian Ed., Exec. Dir., Rev. Ernest K. Bee, Jr., Box 115, Alfred Station, NY 14803
Women's Soc. of the Gen. Conference, Pres., Mrs. Donna Bond, RFD 1, Box 426, Bridgeton, NJ 08302
American Sabbath Tract & Comm. Council, Dir. of Communications, Rev. Kevin Butler, 3120 Kennedy Rd., P.O. Box 1678, Janesville, WI 53547
Seventh Day Baptist Historical Society, Historian, Don A. Sanford, 3120 Kennedy Rd., P.O. Box 1678, Janesville, WI 53547
Seventh Day Bapt. Center on Min., Dir. of Pastoral Services, Rev. Rodney L. Henry, 3120 Kennedy Rd., P.O. Box 1678, Janesville, WI 53547

PERIODICAL

Sabbath Recorder

Social Brethren

Organized 1867 among members of various evangelical bodies; its confession of faith has nine articles.

OFFICERS

General Assembly, Mod., Rev. Earl Vaughn, RR #2, Flora, IL 62839 Tel. (618)662-4373
Union Association, Mod., Rev. Herbert Tarleton, 420 S. Mill, Harrisburg, IL 62946 Tel. (618)252-7196
Illinois Association, Mod., Rev. Norman Cozart, Rt. 1, Stonefort, IL 62987

Midwestern Association, Mod., Rev. Edward Darnell, 53 E. Newport, Pontiac, MI 48055 Tel. (313)335-9125

Southern Baptist Convention

The Southern Baptist Convention was organized on May 10, 1845, in Augusta, GA.

Cooperating Baptist churches are located in all 50 states, the District of Columbia, Puerto Rico, American Samoa, and the Virgin Islands. The members of the churches work together through 1,208 district associations and 39 state conventions and/or fellowships. The Southern Baptist Convention has an Executive Committee and 20 national agencies — four boards, six seminaries, seven commissions, a foundation and two associated organizations.

The purpose of the Southern Baptist Convention is "to provide a general organization for Baptists in the United States and its territories for the promotion of Christian missions at home and abroad and any other objects such as Christian education, benevolent enterprises, and social services which it may deem proper and advisable for the furtherance of the Kingdom of God". (Constitution, Article II)

The Convention exists in order to help the churches lead people to God through Jesus Christ. From the beginning, there has been a mission desire to share the Gospel with the peoples of the world. The Cooperative Program is the basic channel of mission support. In addition, the Lottie Moon Christmas Offering for Foreign Missions and the Annie Armstrong Easter Offering for Home Missions support Southern Baptists' world mission programs.

In 1992, there were 3,918 foreign missionaries serving in 126 foreign countries and 4,922 home missionaries serving within the United States.

In 1987, the Southern Baptist Convention adopted themes and goals for the major denominational emphasis of Bold Mission Thrust for 1990-2000. Bold Mission Thrust is an effort to enable every person in the world to have opportunity to hear and to respond to the Gospel of Christ by the year 2000.

HEADQUARTERS

901 Commerce St., Ste. 750, Nashville, TN 37203 Tel. (615)244-2355
Media Contact, Vice-Pres. for Convention Relations, Mark Coppenger, Tel. (615)244-2355 Fax (615)742-8919

OFFICERS

Pres., H. Edwin Young, Second Baptist Church, 6400 Woodway, Houston, TX 77057
Recording Sec., David W. Atchison, P.O. Box 1543, Brentwood, TN 37027
Executive Committee: Pres., Morris M. Chapman; Exec. Vice-Pres., Ernest E. Mosley; Vice-Pres., Business & Finance, Richard Rosenbaum; Vice-Pres., Convention Relations, Mark Coppenger; Vice-Pres., Convention News, Herb V. Hollinger

GENERAL BOARDS AND COMMISSIONS

Foreign Mission Board: Pres., ——, Box 6767, Richmond, VA 23230
Home Mission Board: Pres., Larry L. Lewis, 1350 Spring St., NW, Atlanta, GA 30367 Tel. (404)898-7700
Annuity Board: Pres., Paul W. Powell, P.O. Box 2190, Dallas, TX 75221 Tel. (214)720-0511

Sunday School Board: Pres., James T. Draper, Jr., 127 Ninth Ave., N., Nashville, TN 37234 Tel. (615)251-2000

Brotherhood Commission: Pres., James D. Williams, 1548 Poplar Ave., Memphis, TN 38104 Tel. (901)272-2461

SB Commis. on the Am. Bapt. Theol. Sem.: Exec. Sec.-Treas., Arthur L. Walker, Jr.; Pres. of the Seminary, Odell McGlothian, Sr.

Christian Life Commission: Exec. Dir., Richard D. Land, 901 Commerce St., Nashville, TN 37203 Tel. (615)244-2495

Education Commission: Exec. Sec.-Treas., Arthur L. Walker, Jr., 901 Commerce St., Nashville, TN 37203 Tel. (615)244-2362

Historical Commission: Exec. Dir., Treas., Lynn E. May, Jr., 901 Commerce Street, Nashville, TN 37203 Tel. (615)244-0344

The Radio & TV Commission: Pres., Jack Johnson, 6350 West Freeway, Ft. Worth, TX 76150 Tel. (817)737-4011

Stewardship Commission: Pres., A. R. Fagan, 901 Commerce St., Nashville, TN 37203 Tel. (615)244-2303

STATE CONVENTIONS

Alabama, Troy L. Morrison, 2001 E. South Blvd., Montgomery, AL 36198 Tel. (205)288-2460

Alaska, Bill G. Duncan, 1750 O'Malley Rd., Anchorage, AK 99516 Tel. (907)344-9627

Arizona, Dan C. Stringer, 4520 N. Central Ave., Ste. 550, Phoenix, AZ 85013 Tel. (602)264-9421

Arkansas, Don Moore, P.O. Box 552, Little Rock, AR 72203 Tel. (501)376-4791

California, C. B. Hogue, 678 E. Shaw Ave., Fresno, CA 93710 Tel. (209)229-9533

Colorado, Charles Sharp, 7393 So. Alton Way, Englewood, CO 80112 Tel. (303)771-2480

District of Columbia, W. Jere Allen, 1628 16th St. NW, Washington, DC 20009 Tel. (202)265-1526

Florida, John Sullivan, 1230 Hendricks Ave., Jacksonville, FL 32207 Tel. (904)396-2351

Georgia, James N. Griffith, 2930 Flowers Rd., S, Atlanta, GA 30341 Tel. (404)455-0404

Hawaii, O. W. Efurd, 2042 Vancouver Dr., Honolulu, HI 96822 Tel. (808)946-9581

Illinois, Maurice Swinford, P.O. Box 19247, Springfield, IL 62794 Tel. (217)786-2600

Indiana, Charles Sullivan, 900 N. High School Rd., Indianapolis, IN 46224 Tel. (317)241-9317

Kansas-Nebraska, R. Rex Lindsay, 5410 W. Seventh St., Topeka, KS 66606 Tel. (913)273-4880

Kentucky, William W. Marshall, P.O. Box 43433, Middletown, KY 40243 Tel. (502)245-4101

Louisiana, Mark Short, Box 311, Alexandria, LA 71301 Tel. (318)448-3402

Maryland-Delaware, Kenneth Lyle, 10255 S. Columbia Rd., Columbia, MD 21064 Tel. (301)290-5290

Michigan, Robert Wilson, 15635 W. 12 Mile Rd., Southfield, MI 48076 Tel. (313)557-4200

Minnesota-Wisconsin, Otha Winningham, 519 16th St. SE, Rochester, MN 55904 Tel. (507)282-3636

Mississippi, William W. Causey, P.O. Box 530, Jackson, MS 39205 Tel. (601)968-3800

Missouri, Donald V. Wideman, 400 E. High, Jefferson City, MO 65101 Tel. (314)635-7931

Nevada, David Meacham, 406 California Ave., Reno, NV 89509 Tel. (702)786-0406

New England, ———, Box 688, 5 Oak Ave., Northboro, MA 01532 Tel. (508)393-6013

New Mexico, Claude Cone, P.O. Box 485, Albuquerque, NM 87103 Tel. (505)247-0586

New York, R. Quinn Pugh, 6538 Collamer Dr., East Syracuse, NY 13057 Tel. (315)475-6173

North Carolina, Roy J. Smith, 205 Convention Dr., Cary, NC 27511 Tel. (919)467-5100

Ohio, Acting Exec. Dir., Orville H. Griffin, 1680 E. Broad St., Columbus, OH 43203 Tel. (614)258-8491

Northwest Baptist Convention, Cecil Sims, 1033 N.E. 6th Ave., Portland, OR 97232 Tel. (503)238-4545

Oklahoma, William G. Tanner, 3800 N. May Ave., Oklahoma City, OK 73112 Tel. (405)942-3800

Pennsylvania-South Jersey, 4620 Fritchey St., Harrisburg, PA 17109 Tel. (717)652-5856

South Carolina, B. Carlisle Driggers, 907 Richland St., Columbia, SC 29201 Tel. (803)765-0030

Tennessee, D. L. Lowrie, P.O. Box 728, Brentwood, TN 37024 Tel. (615)373-2255

Texas, William M. Pinson, Jr., 333 N. Washington, Dallas, TX 75246 Tel. (214)828-5100

Utah-Idaho, Sec., C. Clyde Billingsley, P.O. Box 1039, Sandy, UT 84091 Tel. (801)255-3565

Virginia, Reginald M. McDonough, P.O. Box 8568, Richmond, VA 23226 Tel. (804)672-2100

West Virginia, Don R. Mathis, Number One Mission Way, Scott Depot, WV 25560 Tel. (304)757-0944

Wyoming, John W. Thomason, Box 3074, Casper, WY 82602 Tel. (307)472-4087

FELLOWSHIPS

Dakota Southern Baptist Fellowship, Dewey W. Hickey, P.O. Box 7187, Bismark, ND 58502 Tel. (701)255-3765

Iowa Southern Baptist Fellowship, O. Wyndell Jones, Westview #27, 2400 86th St., Des Moines, IA 50322 Tel. (515)278-1516

Montana Southern Baptist Fellowship, James Nelson, P.O. Box 99, Billings, MT 59103 Tel. (406)252-7537

Canadian Convention of Southern Baptists, Allen Schmidt, Postal Bag 300, Cochrane, AL T0L 0W0 Tel. (403)932-5688

PERIODICALS

Western Recorder; Biblical Recorder; Word and Way; WSBC Horizons; Capital Baptist; Baptist True Union; Commission, The; Baptist Program; Baptist and Reflector; Religious Herald; MissionsUSA; Contempo; Baptist Message

Southern Methodist Church

Organized in 1939, this body is composed of congregations desirous of continuing in true Biblical Methodism and preserving the fundamental doctrines and beliefs of the Methodist Episcopal Church, South. These congregations declined to be a party to the merger of the Methodist Episcopal Church, The Methodist Episcopal Church, South, and the Methodist Protestant Church into The Methodist Church.

HEADQUARTERS

P.O. Drawer A, Orangeburg, SC 29116-0039 Tel. (803)536-1378

Media Contact, Pres., Rev. Dr. Richard G. Blank, Fax (803)534-7827

OFFICERS

Pres., Rev. Dr. Richard G. Blank

Admn. Asst. to Pres., Philip A. Rorabaugh

Vice-Presidents: The Carolinas-Virginia Conf., Rev. E. Legrand Adams, Rt. 2, Box 1050, Laurens, SC 29360; Alabama-Florida-Georgia Conf., Rev. John Courson, RD2, Box 280, Madison, FL 32340; Mid-South Conf., Rev. Bedford F. Landers, 1307 Walnut St., Waynesboro, MS 39367; South-Western Conf., Rev. Dr. Arthur P. Meacham, 5910 Youree Dr., Ste. C, Shreveport, LA 71105

Gen. Conf., Treas., Rev. Philip A. Rorabaugh

PERIODICAL

The Southern Methodist

Sovereign Grace Baptists

The Sovereign Grace Baptists are a contemporary movement which began its stirrings in the mid-1950s when some pastors in traditional Baptist churches returned to a Calvinist-theological perspective.

The first "Sovereign Grace" conference was held in Ashland, Ky., in 1954 and since then, conferences of this sort have been sponsored by various local churches on the West Coast, Southern and Northern states, and Canada. This movement is a spontaneous phenomenon concerning reformation at the local church level. Consequently, there is no interest in establishing a Reformed Baptist "Convention" or "Denomination." Each local church is to administer the keys to the kingdom.

Most Sovereign Grace Baptists formally or informally relate to the "First London" (1646), "Second London" (1689), or "Philadelphia" (1742) Confessions.

There is a wide variety of local church government in this movement. Many Calvinist Baptists have a plurality of elders in each assembly. Other Sovereign Grace Baptists, however, prefer to function with one pastor and several deacons.

Membership procedures vary from church to church but all would require a credible profession of faith in Christ, and proper Baptism as a basis for membership.

Calvinistic Baptists financially support gospel efforts (missionaries, pastors of small churches at home and abroad, literature publication and distribution, radio programs, etc.) in various parts of the world.

HEADQUARTERS

Media Contact, Corres., Jon Zens, P.O. Box 548, St. Croix Falls, WI 54024 Tel. (715)755-3560 Fax (612)465-5101

The Swedenborgian Church

Founded in North America in 1792 as the Church of the New Jerusalem, the Swedenborgian Church was organized as a national body in 1817 and incorporated in Illinois in 1861. Its biblically-based theology is derived from the spiritual, or mystical, experiences and exhaustive biblical studies of the Swedish scientist and philosopher Emanuel Swedenborg (1688-1772).

The church centers its worship and teachings on the historical life and the risen and glorified present reality of the Lord Jesus Christ. It looks with an ecumenical vision toward the establishment of the kingdom of God in the form of a universal Church, active in the lives of all people of good will who desire and strive for freedom, peace, and justice for all. It is a member of the NCCC and active in many local councils of churches.

With churches and groups throughout the United States and Canada, the denomination's central administrative offices and its seminary — Swedenborg School of Religion — are located in Newton, Mass. Affiliated churches are found in Africa, Asia, Australia, Canada, Europe, the United King-

dom, Japan, and South America. Many philosophers and writers have acknowledged their appreciation of Swedenborg's teachings.

HEADQUARTERS

48 Sargent St., Newton, MA 02158 Tel. (617)969-4240 Fax (617)964-3258

Media Contact, Central Ofc. Mgr., Martha Bauer

OFFICERS

Pres., Rev. Edwin G. Capon, 170 Virginia St., St. Paul, MN 55102

Vice-Pres., Mrs. Elizabeth S. Young, 3715 Via Palomino, Palos Verdes Estates, CA 90274

Rec. Sec., Mrs. Gloria L. Toot, 10280 Gentlewind Dr., Montgomery, OH 45242

Treas., John C. Perry, RFD 2, Box 2341A, Brunswick, ME 04011

Ofc. Mgr., Mrs. Martha Bauer

PERIODICALS

Messenger, The; Our Daily Bread

Syrian Orthodox Church of Antioch (Archdiocese of the United States and Canada)

An archdiocese in North America of the Syrian Orthodox Church of Antioch, the church traces its origin to the Patriarchate established in Antioch by St. Peter the Apostle. It is under the supreme ecclesiastical jurisdiction of His Holiness the Syrian Orthodox Patriarch of Antioch and All the East, now residing in Damascus, Syria. The Syrian Orthodox Church — composed of several archdioceses, numerous parishes, schools and seminaries - professes the faith of the first three Ecumenical Councils of Nicaea, Constantinople, and Ephesus, and numbers faithful in the Middle East, India, the Americas, Europe and Australia.

The first Syrian Orthodox faithful came to North America during the late 1800s, and by 1907 the first Syrian Orthodox priest was ordained to tend to the community's spiritual needs. In 1949, His Eminence Archbishop Mar Athanasius Y. Samuel came to America and was soon appointed Patriarchal Vicar.

There are 24 official archdiocesan parishes in the United States, located in California, Georgia, Illinois, Maryland, Massachusetts, Michigan, New Jersey, New York, Oklahoma, Oregon, Pennsylvania, Rhode Island and Texas. In Canada, there are five official parishes: three in the Province of Ontario and two in the Province of Quebec.

HEADQUARTERS

Archdiocese of the U.S. and Canada, 49 Kipp Ave., Lodi, NJ 07644 Tel. (201)778-0638 Fax (201)773-7506

Media Contact, Archdiocesan Gen. Sec., V. Rev. Chorepiscopus John Meno, 45 Fairmount Ave., Hackensack, NJ 07061 Tel. (201)646-9443 Fax (201)773-7506

OFFICERS

Primate, Archbishop Mar Athanasius Y. Samuel

Archdiocesan Gen. Sec., V. Rev. Chorepiscopus John Meno

PERIODICAL

The Syrian Antiochian Perspective

US RELIGIOUS BODIES

131

Triumph the Church and Kingdom of God in Christ Inc. (International)

This church was given through the wisdom and knowledge of God to the Late Apostle Elias Dempsey Smith, on Oct. 20, 1897, in Issaquena County, Miss., while he was pastor of a Methodist church.

The Triumph Church, as this body is more commonly known, was founded in 1902, its doors opened in 1904, and confirmed in Birmingham, Ala., with 225 members in 1915. It was incorporated in Washington, DC, in 1918 and currently operates in 31 states and overseas. The General Church is divided into 18 districts, including the Africa District.

Triumphant doctrine and philosophy is based on the principles of life, truth, and knowledge; God in man, and being expressed through man; manifested wisdom; complete and full understanding; and constant new revelations. Its concepts and methods of teaching "the second coming of Christ" are based on these and all other attributes of goodness.

Triumphians emphasize that God is the God of the living, and not the God of the dead.

HEADQUARTERS

213 Farrington Ave. S.E., Atlanta, GA 30315

OFFICERS

Chief Bishop, Rt. Rev. A. J. Scott, 1323 N.E. 36th St., Savannah, GA 31404 Tel. (912)236-2877

Asst. Chief Apostle, Bishop C. W. Drummond, 7114 Idlewild, Pittsburgh, PA 15208 Tel. (412)731-2286

Gen. Bd of Trustees, Chmn., Bishop Leon Simon, 1028 59th St., Oakland, CA 94608 Tel. (415)652-9576

Gen. Treas., Bishop Hosea Lewis, 1713 Needlewood Ln., Orlando, FL 32818 Tel. (407)295-5488

Gen. Rec. Sec., Bishop Zephaniah Swindle, Box 1927, Shelbyville, TX 75973 Tel. (409)598-3082

True Orthodox Ch. of Greece (Synod of Metropolitan Cyprian), American Exarchate

The American Exarchate of the True (Old Calendar) Orthodox Church of Greece adheres to the tenets of the Eastern Orthodox Church, which considers itself the legitimate heir of the historical Apostolic Church.

When the Orthodox Church of Greece, the official state church, adopted the New or Gregorian Calendar in 1924, many felt that this breach with tradition compromised the church's festal calendar, based on the Old or Julian calendar, and its unity with world Orthodoxy. In 1935, three State Church Bishops returned to the Old Calendar and established a Synod in Resistance, The True Orthodox Church of Greece. When the last of these Bishops died, the Russian Orthodox Church Abroad consecrated a new hierarchy for the Greek Old Calendarists and, in 1969, declared them a sister church.

In the face of persecution by the state church, some Old Calendarists denied the validity of the Mother Church of Greece and formed into two synods, now under the direction of Archbishop Chrysostomos of Athens and Archbishop Andreas of Athens. A moderate faction under Metropolitan

Cyprian of Oropos and Fili does not maintain communion with what it considers the ailing Mother Church of Greece, but recognizes its validity and seeks a restoration of unity by a return to the Julian Calendar and traditional ecclesiastical polity by the state church. About 2 million Orthodox Greeks belong to the Old Calendar Church.

The first Old Calendarist communities in the United States were formed in the 1930s. The Exarchate under Metropolitan Cyprian was established in 1986. Placing emphasis on clergy education, youth programs, and recognition of the Old Calendarist minority in American Orthodoxy, the Exarchate has encouraged the establishment of monastic communities and missions. Cordial contacts with the New Calendarist and other Orthodox communities are encouraged. A center for theological training and Patristic studies has been established at the Exarchate headquarters in Etna, Calif.

HEADQUARTERS

St. Gregory Palamas Monastery, P.O. Box 398, Etna, CA 96027 Tel. (916)467-3228 Fax (916)467-3996

Media Contact, His Eminence Bishop Chrysostomos

OFFICERS

Synodal Exarch in America, His Eminence Bishop Chrysostomos

Asst. to the Exarch, His Grace Bishop Auxentios

Dean of Exarchate, The Rev. James P. Thornton, P.O. Box 2833, Garden Grove, CA 92642

PERIODICAL

Orthodox Tradition

Ukrainian Orthodox Church of America (Ecumenical Patriarchate)

This body was organized in the United States in 1928, when the first convention was held. In 1932, Dr. Joseph Zuk was consecrated as first Bishop. His successor was the Most Rev. Bishop Bohdan, Primate, who was consecrated by the order of the Ecumenical Patriarchate of Constantinople in 1937, in New York City. He was succeeded by the Most Rev. Metropolitan Andrei Kuschak, consecrated by the blessing of Ecumenical Patriarch by Archbishop Iakovos, Metropolitan Germanos and Bishop Silas of Greek-Orthodox Church, in 1967. His successor is Bishop Vsevolod, ordained in 1987 by Archbishop Iakovos, Metropolitan Silas and Bishops Philip and Athenagoras.

HEADQUARTERS

Ukrainian Orthodox Church of America, 90-34 139th St., Jamaica, NY 11435 Tel. (718)297-2407 Fax (718)291-8308

Media Contact, Primate, Bishop Vsevolod

OFFICERS

Primate, Rt. Rev. Bishop Vsevolod

Administrator for Canada, Rev. Michael Pawlyshyn

Chancellor, Rev. W. Czekaluk

PERIODICAL

Ukrainian Orthodox Herald

Ukrainian Orthodox Church of the U.S.A.

The church was formally organized in United States in 1919. Archbishop John Theodorovich arrived from Ukraine in 1924.

HEADQUARTERS

P.O. Box 495, South Bound Brook, NJ 08880 Tel. (908)356-0090 Fax (908)356-5556

OFFICERS

Patriarch: His Holiness Patriarch Mstyslav I; Archbishop Constantine Buggan, 15157 Waterman Dr., S., Holland, IL 60473; Archbishop Antony, 4 Von Steuben Lane, South Bound Brook, NJ 08880

Consistory: Pres., V. Rev. William Diakiw; Vice-Pres., V. Rev. Nestor Kowal; Sec., Rev. Frank Estocin; Treas., V. Rev. Taras Chubenko

Unitarian Universalist Association

The Unitarian Universalist Association is the consolidated body of the former American Unitarian Association and the Universalist Church of America. The Unitarian movement arose in congregationalism in the 18th century, producing the American Unitarian Association in 1825. In 1865 a national conference was organized.

The philosophy of Universalism originated with the doctrine of universal salvation in the first century, and was brought to America in the 18th century. Universalists were first formally organized in 1793. In May, 1961, the Unitarian and Universalist bodies were consolidated to become the Unitarian Universalist Association. The movement is noncreedal. The UUA has observer status with the National Council of Churches.

HEADQUARTERS

25 Beacon St., Boston, MA 02108 Tel. (617)742-2100

Media Contact, Dir. of Publ. Info., Deborah Weiner, Fax (617)367-3237

OFFICERS

Pres., Rev. William F. Schulz
Exec. Vice-Pres., Kathleen C. Montgomery
Mod., Natalie W. Gulbrandsen
Sec., Ralph Robins
Treas., David E. Provost
Financial Advisor, Arnold W. Bradburd

OTHER ORGANIZATIONS

Beacon Press, Dir., Wendy Strothman
Unitarian Universalist Ministers' Assoc., Pres., Rev. Leon Hopper
Unitarian Universalist Women's Fed., Pres., Kay Aler-Maida
Young Religious Unitarian Universalists, Contact, Rev. Jory Agate
Unitarian Universalist Serv. Comm., Inc., Exec. Dir., Dr. Richard Scobie, 78 Beacon St., Boston, MA 02108
Unitarian Universalist Hist. Society, Pres., Rev. Janet Bowering
Church of the Larger Fellowship, Rev. Scott Alexander

PERIODICAL

World, The

United Brethren in Christ

The Church of the United Brethren in Christ began with Philip William Otterbein and Martin Boehm, who were leaders in the revivalistic movement in Pennsylvania and Maryland during the late 1760s, which continued into the early 1800s.

On Sept. 25, 1800, they and others associated with them formed a society under the name of United Brethren in Christ. Subsequent conferences adopted a Confession of Faith in 1815 and a constitution in 1841. The Church of the United Brethren in Christ adheres to the original constitution as amended in 1957, 1961 and 1977.

HEADQUARTERS

302 Lake St., Huntington, IN 46750 Tel. (219)356-2312 Fax (219)356-4730

Media Contact, Chmn., Bd. of Bishops, Dr. C. Ray Miller

OFFICERS

Bishops: Chpsn., C. Ray Miller; Clarence A. Kopp, Jr.; Jerry Datema
Gen. Treas./Office Mgr., Marda J. Hoffman
Dept. of Education, Dir., Dr. G. Blair Dowden
Dept. of Church Services, Dir., Rev. Paul Hirschy

PERIODICAL

UB

United Christian Church

The United Christian Church originated about 1864. There were some ministers and laymen in the United Brethren in Christ Church who disagreed with the position and practice of the church on infant baptism, voluntary bearing of arms and belonging to oath-bound secret combinations. This group developed into United Christian Church, organized at a conference held in Campbelltown, Pa., on May 9, 1877. The principal founders of the denomination were George Hoffman, John Stamn, and Thomas Lesher. Before they were organized, they were called Hoffmanites.

The United Christian Church has district conferences, a yearly general conference, a general board of trustees, a mission board, a board of directors of the United Christian Church Home, a campmeeting board, a young peoples board, and has local organized congregations.

It believes in the Holy Trinity, the inspired Holy Scriptures with the doctrines they teach, and practices the ordinances of Baptism, Holy Communion, and Foot Washing.

It welcomes all into its fold who are born again, believe in Jesus Christ as Savior and Lord, and who have received the Holy Spirit.

HEADQUARTERS

c/o John P. Ludwig, Jr., 523 W. Walnut St., Cleona, PA 17042 Tel. (717)273-9629

Media Contact, Presiding Elder, John P. Ludwig, Jr.

OFFICERS

Mod. & Presiding Elder, Elder John P. Ludwig, Jr.
Conf. Sec., Elder David W. Heagy, RD 4, Box 100, Lebanon, PA 17042

OTHER ORGANIZATIONS

Mission Board: Pres., Elder John P. Ludwig, Jr.; Sec., Elder Walter Knight, Jr., Rt. #3, Box 98, Palmyra, PA 17078; Treas., Elder Henry C. Heagy, 2080 S. White Oak St., Lebanon, PA 17042

United Church of Christ

The United Church of Christ was constituted on June 25, 1957 by representatives of the Congregational Christian Churches and of the Evangelical and Reformed Church, in Cleveland, Ohio.

The Preamble to the Constitution states: "The United Church of Christ acknowledges as its sole head, Jesus Christ ... It acknowledges as kindred in Christ all who share in this confession. It looks to the Word of God in the Scriptures, and to the presence and power of the Holy Spirit ... It claims ... the faith of the historic Church expressed in the ancient creeds and reclaimed in the basic insights of the Protestant Reformers. It affirms the responsibility of the Church in each generation to make this faith its own in ... worship, in honesty of thought and expression, and in purity of heart before God. ... it recognizes two sacraments: Baptism and the Lord's Supper."

The creation of the United Church of Christ brought together four unique traditions:

(1) Groundwork for the Congregational Way was laid by Calvinist Puritans and Separatists during the late 16th-early 16th centuries, then achieved prominence among English Protestants during the civil war of the 1640s. Opposition to state control prompted followers to emigrate to the United States, where they helped colonize New England in the 17th century. Congregationalists have been self-consciously a denomination from the mid-19th century.

(2) The Christian Churches, an 18th-century American restorationist movement emphasized Christ as the only head of the church, the New Testament as their only rule of faith, and "Christian" as their sole name. This loosely organized denomination found in the Congregational Churches a like disposition. In 1931, the two bodies formally united as the Congregational Christian Churches.

(3) The German Reformed Church comprised an irenic aspect of the Protestant Reformation, as a second generation of Reformers drew on the insights of Zwingli, Luther and Calvin to formulate the Heidelberg Catechism of 1563. People of the German Reformed Church began immigrating to the New World early in the 18th century, the heaviest concentration in Pennsylvania. Formal organization of the American denomination was completed in 1793. The church spread across the country. In the Mercersburg Movement, a strong emphasis on evangelical catholicity and Christian unity was eveloped.

(4) In 19th-century in Germany, Enlightenment criticism and Pietist inwardness decreased long-standing conflicts between religious groups. In Prussia, a royal proclamation merged Lutheran and Reformed people into one United Evangelical Church (1817). Members of this new church way migrated to America. The Evangelicals settled in large numbers in Missouri and Illinois, emphasizing pietistic devotion and unionism; in 1840 they formed the German Evangelical Church Society in the West. After union with other Evangelical church associations, in 1877 it took the name of the German Evangelical Synod of North America.

On June 25, 1934, this Synod and the Reformed Church in the U.S. (formerly the German Reformed Church) united to form the Evangelical and Reformed Church. They blended the Reformed tradition's passion for the unity of the church and the Evangelical tradition's commitment to the liberty of conscience inherent in the gospel.

HEADQUARTERS

700 Prospect Ave., Cleveland, OH 44115 Tel. (216)736-2100 Fax (216)736-2120

Media Contact, UCC-Sec., Edith A. Guffey, Tel. (216)736-2110

OFFICERS

Pres., Rev. Paul H. Sherry

Sec., Ms. Edith A. Guffey

Dir. of Finance & Treas., Rev. Doris R. Powell

Exec. Assoc. to the Pres., Ms. Bernice Powell Jackson

Asst. to Pres. For Ecumenical Conerns, Rev. John H. Thomas

Asst. to Pres., Ms. Marilyn Dubasak

Affirmative Action Officer, Rev. Hollis Wilson

Chpsn. Exec. Council, The Honorable Denise Page Hood

Vice-Chpsn., Mr. Terry L. White

Mod., Rev. David R. Ruhe (NEB)

Asst. Mod., Ms. Lilia L. Enriquez (CAL. S)

Asst. Mod., Mr. William A. Malaski, Sr. (ND)

ORGANIZATIONS

UNITED CHURCH BOARD FOR WORLD MIN.: 475 Riverside Dr., New York, NY 10115 Tel. (212)870-2637; 14 Beacon St., Boston, MA 02018; Exec. Vice-Pres., Rev. Scott S. Libbey; Planning, Correlation & Admn. Unit, Gen. Sec., Rev. Scott S. Libbey; Mission Program Unit, Gen. Sec., Rev. Daniel F. Romero; Support Services Unit, Acting Treas., Mr. Bruce Foresman

UNITED CHURCH BOARD FOR HOMELAND MIN.: Tel. (216)736-3800 Fax (216)736-3803; Office of Exec. Vice-Pres., Exec. Vice-Pres., Rev. Thomas E. Dipko; Gen. Sec., Rev. Robert P. Noble, Jr.; Office of the Treasurer, Treas., Rev. Robert P. Noble, Jr.; Div. of Evangelism & Local Church Dev., Gen. Sec., Rev. Robert L. Burt; Div. of Education & Publication, Gen. Sec., Rev. Ansley Coe Throckmorton; Div. of American Missionary Association, Co-Gen. Secs., Rev. B. Ann Eichhorn; Rev. L. William Eichhorn

COMMISSION FOR RACIAL JUSTICE: Ofc. for Urban & Natl. Racial Justice, 5113 Georgia Ave. NW, Washington, DC 20011 Tel. (202)291-1593; Ofc. for Constituency Dev./Rural Racial Justice, Franklinton Center, P.O. Box 187, Enfield, NC 27823 Tel. (919)437-1723; Ofc. for Ecumenical Racial Justice, 475 Riverside Dr., Room 1948, New York, NY 10115 Tel. (212)870-2077; Exec. Dir., Rev. Benjamin F. Chavis, Jr.

COUNCIL FOR AMERICAN INDIAN MINISTRY: 122 W. Franklin Ave., Rm. 304, Minneapolis, MN 55405 Tel. (612)870-3679; Exec. Dir., Rev. Armin L. Schmidt

COUNCIL FOR HEALTH & HUMAN SERVICE MINS.: Tel. (216)736-2250; Exec. Dir., Bryan Sickbert

COORD. CENTER FOR WOMEN IN CHURCH & SOC.: Tel. (216)736-2150; Exec. Dir., Rev. Mary Sue Gast

OFFICE FOR CHURCH IN SOCIETY: 110 Maryland Ave. NE, Washington, DC 20002; Exec. Dir., Ms. Valerie E. Russell (OH); Dir., Washington Ofc., Rev. Jay E. Lintner

OFFICE FOR CHURCH LIFE AND LEADERSHIP: Exec. Dir., Rev. William A. Hulteen, Jr. (OH)

OFFICE OF COMMUNICATION: Tel. (216)736-2222 Fax (216)736-2223; 475 Riverside Dr., 16th Fl., New York, NY 10115 Tel. (212)870-2137; Dir., Dr. Beverly J. Chain

STEWARDSHIP COUNCIL: 1400 N. Seventh St., St. Louis, MO 63106; 409 Prospect St., Box 304, New Haven, CT 06511; 475 Riverside Dr., 16th Fl., New York, NY 10115; Exec. Dir., Rev. George W. Otto

COMMISSION ON DEVELOPMENT: Dir. Planned Giving, Rev. Donald G. Stoner

HISTORICAL COUNCIL: Office of Archivist, Phillip Schaff Library, Lancaster Theological Seminary, 555 W. James St., Lancaster, PA 17603

PENSION BOARDS: 475 Riverside Dr., New York, NY 10115; Exec. Vice-Pres., Dr. John Ordway

UNITED CHURCH FOUNDATION, INC.: 475 Riverside Dr., New York, NY 10115; Financial Vice-Pres. & Treas., Donald G. Hart

CONFERENCES

Western Region

California, Northern, Rev. David J. Jamieson, 20 Woodside Ave., San Francisco, CA 94127

California, Southern, Rev. Davida Foy Crabtree, 466 E. Walnut St., Pasadena, CA 91101

Hawaii, Rev. Norman Jackson, 15 Craigside Pl., Honolulu, HI 96817

Montana-Northern Wyoming, Rev. John M. Schaeffer, 2016 Alderson Ave., Billings, MT 59102

Central Pacific, Rev. Donald J. Sevetson, 0245 SW Bancroft St., Ste. E, Portland, OR 97201

Rocky Mountain, Rev. Clyde H. Miller, Jr., 7000 Broadway, Ste. 420, ABS Bldg., Denver, CO 80221

Southwest, Rev. Carole G. Keim, 4423 N. 24th St., Ste. 600, Phoenix, AZ 85016

Washington-North Idaho, Rev. Lynne S. Fitch, 720 14th Ave. E., Seattle, WA 98102

Washington-North Idaho, Rev. David J. Brown, 12 N. Chelan, Wenatchee, WA 98801

West Central Region

Iowa, Rev. Donald A. Gall, 600 42nd St., Des Moines, IA 50312

Kansas-Oklahoma, Rev. John H. Krueger, 1248 Fabrique, Wichita, KS 67218

Minnesota, Rev. Jeffrey N. Stinehelfer, 122 W. Franklin Ave., Rm. 323, Minneapolis, MN 55404

Missouri, A. Gayle Engel (Interim), 461 E. Lockwood Ave., St. Louis, MO 63119

Nebraska, Rev. Clarence M. Higgins, Jr., 825 M St., Lincoln, NE 68508

North Dakota, Rev. Jack J. Seville, Jr., 227 W. Broadway, Bismarck, ND 58501

South Dakota, Rev. Ed Mehlhaff, Ste. B, 801 E. 41st St., Sioux Falls, SD 57105

Great Lakes Region

Illinois, Rev. W. Sterling Cary, 1840 Westchester Blvd., Ste. 200, P.O. Box 7208, Westchester, IL 60154

Illinois South, Rev. Martha Ann Baumer, Box 325 Broadway, Highland, IL 62249

Indiana-Kentucky, Rev. Ralph C. Quellhorst, 1100 W. 42nd St., Indianapolis, IN 46208

Michigan, Rev. Marwood E. Rettig, P.O. Box 1006, East Lansing, MI 48826

Ohio, Rev. Carlton N. Weber, 4041 N. High St., Ste. 301, Columbus, OH 43214

Wisconsin, Rev. Frederick R. Trost, 2719 Marshall Ct., Madison, WI 53705

Southern Region

Florida, Rev. Charles L. Burns, Jr., 222 E. Welbourne Ave., Winter Park, FL 32789

South Central, Rev. James Tomasek, Jr., 6633 E. Hwy. 290, #200, Austin, TX 78723-1157

Southeast, Rev. Roger Knight, P.O. Box 29883, Atlanta, GA 30359

Southern, Rev. Rollin O. Russell, 217 N. Main St., Box 658, Graham, NC 27253

Middle Atlantic Region

Central Atlantic, Rev. John R. Deckenback, 916 S. Rolling Rd., Baltimore, MD 21228

New York, Rev. William Briggs, The Church Center, Rm. 260, 3049 E. Genesee St., Syracuse, NY 13224

Penn Central, Rev. Lyle J. Weible, The United Church Center, Rm. 126, 900 S. Arlington Ave., Harrisburg, PA 17109

Penn Northeast, Rev. Donald E. Overlock, 431 Delaware Ave., P.O. Box 177, Palmerton, PA 18071

Penn Southeast, Rev. Ronald G. Kurtz, 505 Second Ave., P.O. Box 400, Collegeville, PA 19426

Penn West, Rev. Paul L. Westcoat, Jr., 320 South Maple Ave., Greensburg, PA 15601

Puerto Rico, Rev. Jaime Rivera-Solero, Box 5427, Hato Rey, PR 00919

New England Region

Connecticut, Rev. David Y. Hirano, 125 Sherman St., Hartford, CT 06105

Maine, Rev. Otto E. Sommer, 68 Main St., P.O. Box 966, Yarmouth, ME 04096

Massachusetts, Rev. Bennie E. Whiten, Jr., P.O. Box 2246, Salem & Badger Rds., Framingham, MA 01701

New Hampshire, Rev. Robert D. Witham, 314 S. Main, P.O. Box 465, Concord, NH 03302

Rhode Island, Rev. H. Dahler Hayes, 56 Walcott St., Pawtucket, RI 02860

Vermont, Rev. D. Curtis Minter, 285 Maple St., Burlington, VT 05401

Nongeographic

Calvin Synod, Rev. Zoltan D. Szucs, 3036 Globe Ave., Lorain, OH 44055

PERIODICAL

United Church News

United Holy Church of America, Inc.

The United Holy Church of America, Inc. is an outgrowth of the great revival that began with the outpouring of the Holy Ghost on the Day of Pentecost. The church is built upon the foundation of the Apostles and Prophets, Jesus Christ being the cornerstone.

During a revival of repentence, regeneration, and holiness of heart and life that swept through the South and West, the United Holy Church was born. The founding fathers had no desire to establish a denomination, but were pushed out of organized churches because of this experience of holiness and testimony of the Spirit-filled life.

On the first Sunday in May 1886, in Method, N.C., what is today known as the United Holy Church of America, Inc. was born. The church was incorporated on Sept. 25, 1918.

Baptism by immersion, the Lord's Supper, and feet washing are observed. The premillennial teaching of the Second Coming of Christ, Divine healing, justification by faith, sanctification as a second work of grace, and Spirit baptism are accepted.

5104 Dunstan Rd., Greensboro, NC 27405 Tel. (919)621-0669

Mailing Address, Bishop Thomas E. Talley, P.O. Box 1035, Portsmouth, VA 23705

Media Contact, General Recording Sec., Rev. A. Thomas Godfrey, P.O. Box 7940, Chicago, IL 60680 Tel. (312)849-2525

OFFICERS

Gen. Pres., Bishop Thomas E. Talley, P.O. Box 1035, Portsmouth, VA 23705 Tel. (804)399-3644

1st Vice-Pres., Bishop Odell McCollum, 3206 Blueridge Rd., Columbus, OH 43219 Tel. (614)475-4713

2nd Vice-Pres., Bishop Elijah Williams, 901 Briarwood St., Reidsville, NC 27320 Tel. (919)349-7275

Gen. Rec. Sec., Rev. A. Thomas Godfrey, P.O. Box 7940, Chicago, IL 60680 Tel. (312)849-2525

Asst. Rec. Sec., Mrs. Beatrice S. Faison, 224 Wenz Rd., Toledo, OH 43615 Tel. (419)531-1859

Gen. Fin. Sec., Mrs. Vera Perkins-Hughes, 3425 Rosedale Rd., Cleveland Hts., OH 44112 Tel. (216)851-7448

Gen. Asst. Fin. Sec., Mrs. Bertha Williams, 4749 Shaw Dr., Wilmington, NC 28405 Tel. (919)395-4462

Gen. Corres. Sec., Mrs. Gloria Rainey, 198 Easton South/102, Laurel, MD 20707 Tel. (301)725-6982

Gen. Treas., Ms. Louis Bagley, 8779 Wales Dr., Cincinnati, OH 45249 Tel. (513)247-0588

Gen Pres. Missionary Dept., Rev. Mrs. Ardelia M. Corbett, 519 Madera Dr., Youngstown, OH 44504 Tel. (216)744-3284

Gen. Supt. Bible Church School, Mr. Robert L. Rollins, 1628 Avondale Ave., Toledo, OH 43607 Tel. (419)246-4046

Gen. Pres. Y.P.H.A., Elder James W. Brooks, Rt. 3 Box 105, Pittsboro, NC 27312 Tel. (919)542-5357

Gen. Educ. Dept., Elder Franklin R. Freeman, 2805 Collingwood Blvd., Toledo, OH 43610 Tel. (419)244-4498

Gen. Usher's Dept., Mrs. Sherly Hughes, 1491 E. 191st St., Apt. H-604, Euclid, OH 44117 Tel. (216)383-0038

Gen. Statistician, Ms. Sheila Y. Holt-Williams, 3914 N. 20th St., Milwaukee, WI 53206 Tel. (414)445-4467

Music Dept., Gen. Chair, Mrs. Rosie Johnson, 2009 Forest Dale Dr., Silver Spring, MD 20932

PRESIDENTS OF CONVOCATIONAL DISTRICTS

Barbados, New England & Northern Dist., Bishop Joseph T. Bowens, 825 Fairoak Ave., Chillum, MD 20783

Bermuda Dist., Bishop Norris N. Dickenson, P.O. Box Cr32, 27 Old Road, Crawl CR BX, Bermuda, CR01

Central Western Dist., Bishop Bose Bradford, 6279 Natural Bridge, Pine Lawn, MO 63121 Tel. (314)355-1598

Haiti Dist., Bishop Cannier Guillaume, 108 Bas Fort National, Port-au-Prince, Haiti, West Indies

Florida/Georgia Dist., Bishop Elijah Williams, 901 Briarwood St., Reidsville, NC 27320 Tel. (919)349-7275

Northwestern Dist., Bishop Odell McCollum, 3206 BlueRidge Rd., Columbus, OH 43219

Southern Dist./W. North Carolina Dist., Bishop Jesse Jones, 608 Cecil St., Durham, NC 27707 Tel. (919)682-8249

Virginia Dist., Bishop Thomas E. Talley, 2710 Magnolia St., Portsmouth, VA 23705

West Virginia Dist., Bishop Alvester McConnell, Rte. 3, Box 263, Bluefield, WV 24701 Tel. (304)248-8046

Western Dist., Bishop M. D. Borden, 8655 Melody Land, Macedonia, OH 44056 Tel. (216)468-0270

PERIODICAL

Holiness Union, The

The United Methodist Church

The United Methodist Church was formed April 23, 1968, in Dallas by the union of The Methodist Church and The Evangelical United Brethren Church. The two churches shared a common historical and spiritual heritage. The Methodist Church resulted in 1939 from the unification of three branches of Methodism — the Methodist Episcopal Church; the Methodist Episcopal Church, South; and the Methodist Protestant Church.

The Methodist movement began in 18th-century England under the preaching of John Wesley, but the Christmas Conference of 1784 in Baltimore is regarded as the date on which the organized Methodist Church was founded as an ecclesiastical organization. It was there that Francis Asbury was elected the first bishop in this country.

The Evangelical United Brethren Church was formed in 1946 with the merger of the Evangelical Church and the Church of the United Brethren in Christ, both of which had their beginnings in Pennsylvania in the evangelistic movement of the 18th and early 19th centuries. Philip William Otterbein and Jacob Albright were early leaders of this movement among the German-speaking settlers of the Middle Colonies.

HEADQUARTERS

Media Contact, Dir., United Methodist News Service, Thomas S. McAnally, P.O. Box 320, Nashville, TN 37202 Tel. (615)742-5470 Fax (615)742-5469

OFFICERS

Gen. Conference, Sec., Carolyn M. Marshall, 204 N. Newlin St., Veedersburg, IN 47987

Council of Bishops: Pres., Bishop C. P. Minnick, Jr., P.O. Box 10955, Raleigh, NC 27605 Tel. (919)832-9560; Sec., Bishop Melvin G. Talbert, P.O. Box 467, San Francisco, CA 94101 Tel. (415)474-3101

BISHOPS AND CONFERENCE COUNCIL DIRECTORS

North Central Jurisdiction

Central Illinois: Bishop David L. Lawson, Tel. (217)544-4604; Larry J. Lawler, P.O. Box 515, Bloomington, IL 61702 Tel. (309)828-5092

Detroit: Bishop Donald A. Ott, Tel. (313)559-7000; Theodore E. Doane, 21700 Northwestern Hwy., Southfield, MI 48075 Tel. (313)559-7000

East Ohio: Bishop Edwin C. Boulton, Tel. (216)499-8471; Judith A. Olin, 8800 Cleveland Ave. NW, North Canton, OH 44720 Tel. (216)499-3972

Iowa: Bishop Charles W. Jordan, Tel. (515)283-1991; Don Mendenhall, 1019 Chestnut St., Des Moines, IA 50309 Tel. (515)283-1991

Minnesota: Bishop Sharon Brown Christopher, Tel. (612)870-3648; Delton Kraueger, 122 W. Franklin Ave., Room 400, Minneapolis, MN 55404 Tel. (612)870-0058

North Dakota: Bishop William B. Lewis, Tel. (701)232-2241; Ray Wagner, 2410 12th St. N., Fargo, ND 58102 Tel. (701)232-2241

North Indiana: Bishop Woodie W. White, Tel. (317)924-1321; Louis E. Haskell, P.O. Box 869, Marion, IN 46952 Tel. (317)664-5138

Northern Illinois: Bishop R. Sheldon Duecker, Tel. (312)380-5060; Bonnie Ogie-Kristianson, 8765 W. Higgins Rd., Ste. 650, Chicago, IL 60631 Tel. (312)380-5060

South Dakota: Bishop William B. Lewis, Tel. (701)232-2241; Richard Fisher, P.O. Box 460, Mitchell, SD 57301 Tel. (605)996-6552

South Indiana: Bishop Woodie W. White, Tel. (317)924-1321; Robert Coleman, Box 5008, Bloomington, IN 47402 Tel. (812)336-0186

Southern Illinois: Bishop David J. Lawson, Tel. (217)544-4604; William Frazier, 1919 Broadway, Mt. Vernon, IL 62864 Tel. (618)242-4070

West Michigan: Bishop Donald A. Ott, Tel. (313)961-8340; David B. Nelson, P.O. Box 6287, Grand Rapids, MI 49506 Tel. (616)459-4503

West Ohio: Bishop Judith Craig, Tel. (614)228-6784; Vance Summers, 471 E. Broad St., Ste. 1106, Columbus, OH 43215 Tel. (614)228-6784

Wisconsin: Bishop Sharon Z. Rader, Tel. (608)837-8526; Bill Bross, P.O. Box 220, Sun Prairie, WI 53590 Tel. (608)837-7328

Northeastern Jurisdiction

Baltimore-Washington: Bishop Joseph H. Yeakel, Tel. (301)587-9226; Marcus Matthews, 5124 Greenwich Ave., Baltimore, MD 21229 Tel. (301)233-7300

Central Pennsylvania: Bishop Felton E. May, Tel. (717)652-6705; Bruce Fisher, 900 S. Arlington Ave., #112, Harrisburg, PA 17109 Tel. (717)652-0460

Eastern Pennsylvania: Bishop Susan M. Morrison, Tel. (215)666-9090; Robert Daughtery, P.O. Box 820, P.O. Box 820, Valley Forge, PA 19482 Tel. (215)666-9090

Maine: Bishop F. Herbert Skeete, Tel. (617)536-7764; Lorna Grace Stuart, P.O. Box 277, Winthrop, ME 04364 Tel. (207)377-2912

New Hampshire: Bishop F. Herbert Skeete, Tel. (617)536-7764; Philip M. Polhemus, 722A, Route 3A, Concord, NH 03301 Tel. (603)225-6312

New York: Bishop Forrest C. Stith, Tel. (914)997-1570; Wilson Boots, 252 Bryant Ave., White Plains, NY 10605 Tel. (914)997-1570

North Central New York: Bishop Hae-Jong Kim, Tel. (315)446-6731; Garrie F. Stevens, P.O. Box 1515, Cicero, NY 13039 Tel. (315)699-5506

Northern New Jersey: Bishop Neil Irons, Tel. (609)737-3940; Barrie T. Smith, P.O. Box 546, Madison, NJ 07940 Tel. (201)377-3800

Peninsula-Delaware: Bishop Susan M. Morrison, Tel. (212)666-9090; Harvey Manchester, 139 N. State St., Dover, DE 19901 Tel. (302)674-2626

Southern New England: Bishop F. Herbert Skeete, Tel. (617)536-7764; Donald J. Rudalevige, 566 Commonwealth Ave., Boston, MA 02115 Tel. (617)266-3900

Southern New Jersey: Bishop Neil Irons, Tel. (609)737-3940; George T. Wang, 1995 E. Marlton Pike, Cherry Hill, NJ 08003 Tel. (609)424-1701

Troy: Bishop William B. Grove, Tel. (518)425-0386; James M. Perry, P.O. Box 560, Saratoga Springs, NY 12866 Tel. (518)584-8214

West Virginia: Bishop S. Clifton Ives, Tel. ((304)344-8330; Thomas E. Dunlap, Sr., P.O. Box 2313, Charleston, WV 25328 Tel. (304)344-8331

Western New York: Bishop Hae-Jong Kim, Tel. (315)446-6731; J. Fay Cleveland, 8499 Main St., Buffalo, NY 14221 Tel. (716)633-8558

Western Pennsylvania: Bishop George W. Bashore, Tel. (412)776-2300; John Ross Thompson, 1204 Freedom Rd., Mars, PA 16046 Tel. (412)776-2300

Wyoming: Bishop William B. Grove, Tel. (518)425-0386; Charles F. Gommer, Jr., 1700 Monroe St., Endicott, NY 13760 Tel. (607)757-0608

South Central Jurisdiction

Exec. Dir.: L. Ray Branton, 5646 Milton St., #240, Dallas, TX 75228 Tel. (214)692-9081

Central Texas: Bishop Joe A. Wilson, Tel. (817)877-5222; Michael Patison, 464 Bailey, Ft. Worth, TX 76107 Tel. (817)877-5222

Kansas East: Bishop A. F. Mutti, Tel. (913)272-0587; H. Sharon Howell, P.O. Box 4187, Topeka, KS 66604 Tel. (913)272-9111

Kansas West: Bishop A. F. Mutti, Tel. (913)272-0587; Wayne D. Findley, Sr., 9440 E. Boston, #150, Wichita, KS 67207 Tel. (316)684-0266

Little Rock: Bishop Richard B. Wilke, Tel. (501)374-6679; Jay Lofton, 715 Center St., Ste. 202, Little Rock, AR 72201 Tel. (501)374-5027

Louisiana: Bishop William B. Oden, Tel. (504)346-1646; Donald C. Cottrill, 527 North Blvd., Baton Rouge, LA 70802 Tel. (504)346-1646

Missouri East: Bishop Ann B. Sherer, Tel. (314)891-1207; Duane Van Giesen, 870 Woods Mill Rd., #400, Ballwin, MO 63011 Tel. (314)891-1207

Missouri West: Bishop Ann B. Sherer, Jr., Tel. (314)891-1207; Keith T. Berry, 1512 Van Brunt Blvd., Kansas City, MO 64127 Tel. (816)241-7650

Nebraska: Bishop Joel L. Martinez, Tel. (402)464-5994; Richard D. Turner, P.O. Box 4553, Lincoln, NE 68504 Tel. (402)464-5994

New Mexico: Bishop Alfred L. Norris, Tel. (505)883-5418; Milton Chester, 8100 Mountain Rd. NE, Albuquerque, NM 87110 Tel. (505)255-8786

North Arkansas: Bishop Richard B. Wilke, Tel. (501)374-6679; Jim Beal, 715 Center St., Little Rock, AR 72201 Tel. (501)753-8946

North Texas: Bishop Bruce Blake; Gary E. Mueller, P.O. Box 516069, Dallas, TX 75251 Tel. (214)490-3438

Northwest Texas: Bishop Alfred L. Norris, Tel. (505)883-5418; Louise Schock, 1415 Ave. M, Lubbock, TX 79401 Tel. (806)762-0201

Oklahoma: Bishop Dan E. Solomon, Tel. (405)525-2252; David Severe, 2420 N. Blackwelder, Oklahoma City, OK 73106 Tel. (405)525-2252

Oklahoma Indian Missionary: Bishop Dan E. Solomon, Tel. (405)525-2252; Becky Thompson, 147 Delaware Ave., Tulsa, OK 74110 Tel. (405)632-2006

Rio Grande: Bishop Raymond Owen, Tel. (512)432-0401; Arturo Mariscal, Jr., P.O. Box 28098, San Antonio, TX 78284 Tel. (512)432-2534

Religious News Service Photo

Homosexuals, the church, the military

Episcopalians, Presbyterians, and United Methodists had historic discussions on homosexuality, then the issue came to the forefront in January 1993 when President Bill Clinton said he would end the U.S. ban on gays in the military. Here, the United Methodist gay caucus protested when the denomination reaffirmed its stand against homosexuality.

Southwest Texas: Bishop Raymond Owen, Tel. (512)432-0401; Harry G. Kahl, P.O. Box 28098, San Antonio, TX 78284 Tel. (512)432-4680

Texas: Bishop J. Woodrow Hearn, Tel. (713)528-6881; Asbury Lenox, 5215 S. Main St., Houston, TX 77002 Tel. (713)521-9383

Southeastern Jurisdiction

Exec. Sec.: Reginald Ponder, P.O. Box 67, Lake Junaluska, NC 28745 Tel. (704)452-2881

Alabama-West Florida: Bishop William W. Morris, Tel. (205)277-1787; William Calhoun, P.O. Box 700, Andalusia, AL 36420 Tel. (205)222-3127

Florida: Bishop H. Hasbrock Hughes, Jr., Tel. (813)688-4427; Robert Bledsoe, P.O. Box 3767, Lakeland, FL 33802 Tel. (813)688-5563

Holston: Bishop Clay F. Lee, Tel. (615)525-1809; Gordon C. Goodgame, P.O. Box 1178, Johnson City, TN 37601 Tel. (615)928-2156

Kentucky: Bishop Robert C. Morgan, Tel. (502)893-6715; Larry B. Gardner, P.O. Box 55107, Lexington, KY 40555 Tel. (606)254-7388

Louisville: Bishop Robert C. Morgan, Tel. (502)893-6715; Rhoda Peters, 1115 S. Fourth St., Louisville, KY 40203 Tel. (502)584-3838

Memphis: Bishop Kenneth L. Carder, Tel. (615)327-3462; James H. Holmes, St., 575 Lambuth Blvd., Jackson, TN 38301 Tel. (901)427-8589

Mississippi: Bishop M. L. Meadows, Jr., Tel. (601)948-4561; Jack Loflin, P.O. Box 1147, Jackson, MS 39215 Tel. (601)354-0515

North Alabama: Bishop Robert E. Fannin, Tel. (205)879-8665; C. Phillip Huckaby, 898 Arkadelphia Rd., Birmingham, AL 35204 Tel. (205)251-9279

North Carolina: Bishop C. P. Minnick, Jr., Tel. (919)832-9560; G. Robert McKenzie, Jr., P.O. Box 10955, Raleigh, NC 27605 Tel. (919)832-9560

North Georgia: Bishop J. Lloyd Knox, Tel. (404)659-0002; Robert Bridges, 159 Ralph McGill Blvd. NE, Atlanta, GA 30365 Tel. (404)659-0002

Red Bird Missionary: Bishop Robert C. Morgan, Tel. (502)893-6715; Ruth Wiertzema, Queendale Ctr., Box 3, Beverly, KY 40913 Tel. (606)598-5915

South Carolina: Bishop Joseph B. Bethea, Tel. (803)786-9486; Lemuel C. Carter, 4908 Colonial Dr., Ste. 101, Columbia, SC 29203 Tel. (803)754-0297

South Georgia: Bishop Richard C. Looney, Tel. (404)659-0002; William E. McTier, Jr., P.O. Box 408, St. Simons Island, GA 31522 Tel. (912)638-8626

Tennessee: Bishop Kenneth L. Carder, Tel. (615)327-3462; Thomas C. Cloyd, P.O. Box 120607, Nashville, TN 37212 Tel. (615)329-1177

Virginia: Bishop Thomas B. Stockton, Tel. (804)359-9451; Lee B. Sheaffer, P.O. 11367, Richmond, VA 23230 Tel. (804)359-9451

Western North Carolina: Bishop L. Bevel Jones, Tel. (704)535-2260; Harold K. Bales, P.O. Box 18005, PO Box 18005, Charlotte, NC 28218 Tel. (704)535-2260

Western Jurisdiction

Alaska Missionary: Bishop William W. Dew, Jr., Tel. (503)226-7931; James Campbell, Box 182, Willow, AK 99508 Tel. (907)333-5050

California-Nevada: Bishop Melvin G. Talbert, Tel. (415)474-3101; James H. Corson, P.O. Box 420467, San Francisco, CA 9414201 Tel. (415)474-3101

California-Pacific: Bishop Roy I. Sano, Tel. (818)568-7300; J. Delton Pickering, P.O. Box 6006, Pasadena, CA 91102 Tel. (818)568-7300

Desert Southwest: Bishop Elias Galvin, Tel. (602)496-9446; Lawrence A. Hinshaw, 2933 E. Indian School Rd., #402, Phoenix, AZ 85016 Tel. (602)496-9446

Oregon-Idaho: Bishop William A. Dew, Jr., Tel. (503)226-7931; —— 1505 SW 18th Ave., Portland, OR 97201 Tel. (503)226-7931

Pacific Northwest: Bishop Calvin D. McConnell, Tel. (206)728-7462; W. F. Summerour, 2112 Third Ave., Ste. 300, Seattle, WA 98121 Tel. (206)728-7462

Rocky Mountain: Bishop Mary Ann Swenson, Tel. (303)733-3736; Janet Forbes, 2200 S. University Blvd., Denver, CO 80210 Tel. (303)733-3736

Yellowstone: Bishop Mary Ann Swenson, Tel. (303)733-3736; Gary Keene, 335 Broadwater Ave., Billings, MT 59101 Tel. (406)256-1385

OTHER ORGANIZATIONS

Judicial Council: Pres., Tom Matheny; Sec., Wayne Coffin, 2420 N. Blackwelder, Oklahoma City, OK 73106

Council on Finance & Administration: Pres., Bishop Forrest C. Stith, 1200 Davis St., Evanston, IL 60201 Tel. (708)869-3345; Gen. Sec., Clifford Droke

Council on Ministries: Pres., Bishop William W. Dew, Jr., 601 W. Riverview Ave., Dayton, OH 45406 Tel. (513)227-9400; Gen. Sec., C. David Lundquist

Comm. on Communication/UM Communications: Pres., Bishop L. Bevel Jones, III, P.O. Box 320, 810 12th Ave. S., Nashville, TN 37202 Tel. (615)742-5400; Gen. Sec., Roger Burgess

Board of Church & Society: Pres., Bishop Joseph H. Yeakel, 100 Maryland Ave. NE, Washington, DC 20002 Tel. (202)488-5600; Gen. Sec., Thom W.W. Fassett; U.N. Office, Coordinator Robert McClean, 777 U.N. Plaza, New York, NY 10017 Tel. (212)682-3633

Board of Discipleship: Pres., Bishop David J. Lawson, P.O. Box 840, (1908 Grand Ave. & 1001 19th Ave. S.), Nashville, TN 37202 Tel. (615)340-7200; Gen. Sec., Ezra Earl Jones

The Upper Room: World Editor, Janice T. Grana

Board of Global Ministries: Pres., Bishop F. Herbert Skeete, 475 Riverside Dr., New York, NY 10115 Tel. (212)870-3600; Gen. Sec., Randolph Nugent

Board of Higher Education & Ministry: Pres., ishop Calvin McConnell, P.O. Box 871, (1001 Nineteenth Ave. S), Nashville, TN 37202 Tel. (615)340-7000; Gen. Sec., Roger Ireson

Board of Pensions: Pres., Bishop Clay Lee, 1200 Davis St., Evanston, IL 60201 Tel. (708)869-4550; Gen. Sec., James F. Parker

Board of Publications: Chpsn., William Deel

The United Methodist Publishing House: Pres. & Publisher, Robert K. Feaster, P.O. Box 801, 201 Eighth Ave. S, Nashville, TN 37202 Tel. (615)749-6000

Commission on Archives & History: Pres., Bishop Emilio De Carvalho, P.O. Box 127, Madison, NJ 07940 Tel. (201)822-2787; Gen. Sec., Charles Yrigoyen

Comm. Christian Unity/Interrel. Concerns: Pres., Bishop William Boyd Grove, 475 Riverside Dr., Rm. 1300, New York, NY 10115 Tel. (212)749-3553; Gen. Sec., Bruce Robbins

Commission on Religion & Race: Pres., Bishop Joseph B. Bethea, 100 Maryland Ave. NE, Washington, DC 20002 Tel. (202)547-4270; Gen. Sec., Barbara R. Thompson

Commission on the Status & Role of Women: Pres., Bishop Ann B. Sherer, 1200 Davis St., Evanston, IL 60201 Tel. (312)869-7330; Gen. Secs., Cecelia Long, Stephanie Hixson

Worship/Music & Other Arts: Int. Exec. Sec., Bill Weisser, 228 W. Edenton St., Raleigh, NC 27603 Tel. (919)832-0160; Pres., Sara Collins

PERIODICALS

Mature Years; El Interprete; New World Outlook; Newscope; Interpreter; Methodist History; Christian Social Action; Pockets; Response; World Parish; Quarterly Review

United Pentecostal Church International

The United Pentecostal Church International came into being through the merger of two oneness Pentecostal organizations — the Pentecostal Church, Inc., and the Pentecostal Assemblies of Jesus Christ. The first of these was known as the Pentecostal Ministerial Alliance from its inception in 1925 until 1932. The second was formed in 1931 by a merger of the Apostolic Church of Jesus Christ with the Pentecostal Assemblies of the World.

The church contends that the Bible teaches that there is one God who manifested himself as the Father in creation, in the Son in redemption, and as the Holy Spirit in regeneration; that Jesus is the name of this absolute deity and that water baptism should be administered in his name, not in the titles Father, Son, and Holy Ghost (Acts 2: 38, 8: 16, and 19: 6).

The Fundamental Doctrine of the United Pentecostal Church International, as stated in its *Articles of Faith*, is "the Bible standard of full salvation, which is repentance, baptism in water by immersion in the name of the Lord Jesus Christ for the remission of sins, and the baptism of the Holy Ghost with the initial sign of speaking with other tongues as the Spirit gives utterance."

Further doctrinal teachings concern of a life of holiness and separation, the operation of the gifts of the Spirit within the church, the second coming of the Lord, and the church's obligation to take the gospel to the whole world.

HEADQUARTERS

8855 Dunn Rd., Hazelwood, MO 63042 Tel. (314)837-7300 Fax (314)837-4503

Media Contact, Gen. Sec.-Treas., Rev. C. M. Becton

OFFICERS

Gen. Supt., Rev. Nathaniel A. Urshan

Asst. Gen. Supts.: Rev. James Kilgore, Box 15175, Houston, TX 77020; Jesse Williams, P.O. Box 64277, Fayetteville, NC 28306

Gen. Sec.-Treas., Rev. C. M. Becton

Dir. of Foreign Missions, Rev. Harry Scism

Gen. Dir. of Home Missions, Rev. Jack E. Yonts

Editor-in-Chief, Rev. J. L. Hall

Gen. Sunday School Dir., Rev. E. J. McClintock

Pentecostal Publishing House, Mgr., Rev. Marvin Curry
Youth Division (Pentecostal Conquerors), Pres., Jerry Jones, Hazelwood, MO 63042
Ladies Auxiliary, Pres., Vera Kinzie, 4840 Elm Pl., Toledo, OH 43608
Harvestime Radio Broadcast, Dir., Rev. J. Hugh Rose, 698 Kerr Ave., Cadiz, OH 43907
Stewardship Dept., Contact Church Division, Hazelwood, MO 63042
Education Division, Supt., Rev. Arless Glass, 4502 Aztec, Pasadena, TX 77504
Public Relations Division, Contact Church Division, Hazelwood, MO 63042
Historical Society & Archives

PERIODICALS
Pentecostal Herald, The; Global Witness, The; Outreach, The; Homelife; Conqueror; Reflections; Forward

United Zion Church
A branch of the Brethren in Christ which settled in Lancaster County, Pa., it was organized under the leadership of Matthias Brinser in 1855.

HEADQUARTERS
United Zion Home, 722 Furnace Hills Pk, Lititz, PA 17543
Media Contact, Bishop, Luke G. Showalter, 181 Hurst Dr, Ephrata, PA 17522 Tel. (717)733-8392

OFFICERS
Gen. Conf. Mod., Bishop Luke Showalter, 181 Hurst Dr., Ephrata, PA 17522 Tel. (717)733-8392
Asst. Mod., Rev. Leon Eberly, 615 N. Ridge Rd., Reinholds, PA 17569 Tel. (215)484-2614
Gen. Conf. Sec., Mr. Dale O. Martin, 173 Denver Rd., Denver, PA 17517 Tel. (215)267-6293
Gen. Conf. Treas., Kenneth Kleinfelter, 919 Sycamore Lane, Lebanon, PA 17042

PERIODICAL
Zion's Herald

Unity of the Brethren
Czech and Moravian immigrants in Texas (beginning about 1855) established congregations which grew into an Evangelical Union in 1903, and with the accession of other Brethren in Texas, into the Evangelical Unity of the Czech-Moravian Brethren in North America. In 1959, it shortened the name to the original name used in 1457, the Unity of the Brethren (Unitas Fratrum, or Jednota Bratrska).

HEADQUARTERS
3829 Sandstone, San Angelo, TX 76904
Media Contact, Sec. of Exec. Committee, Dorothy E. Kocian, 107 S. Barbara, Waco, TX 76705 Tel. (817)799-5331 Fax (817)799-6277

OFFICERS
Pres., Rev. Tommy Tallas
1st Vice Pres., Rev. W. John Baletka, P.O. Box 614, Caldwell, TX 77836
Sec., Dorothy Kocian, 107 S. Barbara, Waco, TX 76705 Tel. (817)799-5331
Fin. Sec., Roy Vajdak, 920 Malone, Houston, TX 77007

Treas., Ron Sulak, 1217 Christine, Troy, TX 76579

Bd. of Christian Educ., Chmn., Rev. Dick Stone, 403 S. Main St., Caldwell, TX 77836
Brethren Youth Fellowship, Pres., Melynda Tomasek, Route 1, Box 101A, Georgetown, TX 78626
Young Adult Fellowship, Pres., Joyce Koslovsky, 921 Erath Dr., Temple, TX 76501
Christian Sisters Union, Pres., Mrs. Ruth Paul, Route 2,, Caldwell, TX 77836
Sunday School Union, Pres., Mrs. Dorothy Kocian, 107 S. Barbara, Waco, TX 76705

PERIODICAL
Brethren Journal

Vedanta Societies
Followers of the Vedas, the scriptures of the Indo-Aryans, doctrines expounded by Swami Vivekanada at the Parliament of Religions, Chicago, 1893. There are 13 such Centers in the United States and one in Canada. All are under the spiritual guidance of the Ramakrishna Mission, organized by Swami Vivekananda in India.

HEADQUARTERS
34 W. 71st St., New York, NY 10023 Tel. (212)877-9197

Volunteers of America
Volunteers of America, founded in 1896 by Ballington and Maud Booth, provides spiritual and material aid for those in need in more than 300 communities across the United States. As one of the nation's largest multipurpose human-service agencies, VOA offers more than 400 programs for the elderly, families, youth, alcoholics, drug abusers, offenders, and the disabled.

HEADQUARTERS
3813 N. Causeway Blvd., Metairie, LA 70002 Tel. (504)837-2652 Fax (504)837-4200
Media Contact, Dir. of Publ. Relations, Arthur Smith

OFFICERS
Chpsn., Walter Faster
Pres., J. Clint Cheveallier
Vice-Pres.: Alex Brodrick; David Cheveallier; Thomas Clark; Charles Gould; James Hogie; Margaret Ratcliff; John Hood

The Wesleyan Church
The Wesleyan Church was formed on June 26, 1968, through the union of the Wesleyan Methodist Church of America (1843) and the Pilgrim Holiness Church (1897). Headquarters was established at Marion, Ind., and relocated to Indianapolis in 1987.

The Wesleyan movement centers around the beliefs, based on Scripture, that the atonement in Christ provides for the regeneration of sinners and the entire sanctification of believers. John Wesley led a revival of these beliefs in the 18th century.

When a group of New England ministers led by Orange Scott began to crusade for the abolition of slavery, with which many Methodist ministers and members had become involved, the bishops and others sought to silence them. This led to a series of withdrawals from the Methodist Episcopal Church. In 1843, the organization of the Wesleyan Methodist Connection of America was organized.

Scott, Jotham Horton, LaRoy Sunderland, Luther Lee, and Lucius C. Matlack were prominent leaders in the new denomination.

As the holiness revival swept across many denominations in the last half of the 19th century, holiness replaced social reform as the major tenet of the Connection. In 1947 the name was changed from Connection to Church and a central supervisory authority was set up.

The Pilgrim Holiness Church was one of many independent holiness churches which came into existence as a result of the holiness revival. Led by Martin Wells Knapp and Seth C. Rees, the International Holiness Union and Prayer League was inaugurated in 1897 in Cincinnati. Its purpose was to promote worldwide holiness evangelism and the Union had a strong missionary emphasis from the beginning. It developed into a church by 1913.

The Wesleyan Church is now spread across most of the United States and Canada and 37 other countries. The Wesleyan World Fellowship was organized in 1972 to unite Wesleyan mission bodies developing into mature churches. The Wesleyan Church is a member of the Christian Holiness Association, the National Association of Evangelicals, and the World Methodist Council.

HEADQUARTERS

P.O. Box 50434, Indianapolis, IN 46250 Tel. (317)842-0444

OFFICERS

Gen. Supts.: Dr. Earle L. Wilson; Dr. Lee M. Haines; Dr. H. C. Wilson
Gen. Sec., Dr. Ronald R. Brannon
Gen. Treas., Mr. Daniel D. Busby
Gen. Director of Communications, Dr. Norman G. Wilson
Gen. Publisher, Rev. Nathan Birky
Evangelism & Church Growth, Gen. Dir., Dr. B. Marlin Mull
World Missions, Gen. Dir., Rev. Donald L. Bray
Local Church Educ., Gen. Dir., Dr. Keith Drury
Youth, Gen. Dir., Rev. Thomas E. Armiger
Education & the Ministry, Gen. Dir., Dr. Kenneth R. Heer
Estate Planning, Gen. Dir., Rev. Howard B. Castle
Wesleyan Pension Fund, Gen. Dir., Mr. Bobby L. Temple
Wesleyan Investment Foundation, Gen. Dir., Dr. John A. Dunn

PERIODICALS

Wesleyan Woman; Wesleyan Advocate, The; Wesleyan World

Wesleyan Holiness Association of Churches

This body was founded Aug. 4, 1959 near Muncie, Ind. by a group of ministers and laymen who were drawn together for the purpose of spreading and conserving sweet, radical, scriptural holiness. These men came from various church bodies. This group is Wesleyan in doctrine and standards.

HEADQUARTERS

108 Carter Ave., Dayton, OH 45405

OFFICERS

Gen. Supt., Rev. J. Stevan Manley, Tel. (513)278-3770

Asst. Gen. Supt., Rev. Jack W. Dulin, Rt. 2, Box 309, Milton, KY 40045 Tel. (502)268-5826
Gen. Sec.-Treas., Rev. Robert W. Wilson, 10880 State Rt. 170, Negley, OH Tel. (216)385-0416
Gen. Youth Pres., Rev. John Brewer, 504 W. Tyrell St., St. Louis, MI 48880 Tel. (517)681-2591

PERIODICAL

Eleventh Hour Messenger

Wisconsin Evangelical Lutheran Synod

Organized in 1850 at Milwaukee, Wisc. by three pastors sent to America by a German mission society, the Wisconsin Evangelical Lutheran Synod still reflects its origins, although it has now has congregations in 50 states and three Canadian provinces.

The Wisconsin Synod federated with the Michigan and Minnesota Synods in 1892 in order to more effectively carry on education and mission enterprises. A merger of these three Synods followed in 1917 to give the Wisconsin Evangelical Lutheran Synod its present form.

Although at its organization in 1850 the Synod turned away from conservative Lutheran theology, today it is ranked as one of the most conservative Lutheran bodies in the United States. The Synod confesses that the Bible is the verbally inspired, infallible Word of God and subscribes without reservation to the confessional writings of the Lutheran Church. Its interchurch relations are determined by a firm commitment to the principle that unity of doctrine and practice are the prerequisites of pulpit and altar fellowship and ecclesial cooperation. It does not hold membership in ecumenical organizations.

HEADQUARTERS

2929 N. Mayfair Rd., Milwaukee, WI 53222 Tel. (414)771-9357 Fax (414)771-3708
Publ. Rel. Dir., Rev. James P. Schaefer, 2929 N. Mayfair Rd., Milwaukee, WI 53222 Tel. (414)771-9357 Fax (414)771-3708

OFFICERS

Pres., Rev. Carl H. Mischke
1st Vice-Pres., Rev. Richard E. Lauersdorf, 105 Aztalan Ct., Jefferson, WI 53549
2nd Vice-Pres., Rev. Robert J. Zink, S68 W14329 Gaulke Ct., Muskego, WI 53150
Sec., Rev. David Worgull, 1201 W. Tulsa, Chandler, AZ 85224

OTHER ORGANIZATIONS

Bd. of Trustees, Admn., Mr. Clair V. Ochs
Bd. for Worker Trng., Admn., Rev. Wayne Borgwardt
Bd. for Parish Services, Admn., Rev. Wayne Mueller
Bd. for Home Missions, Admn., Rev. Harold J. Hagedorn
Bd. for World Missions, Admn., Rev. Duane K. Tomhave

PERIODICALS

Wisconsin Lutheran Quarterly; Northwestern Lutheran; Lutheran Educator, The

RELIGIOUS BODIES IN THE UNITED STATES ARRANGED BY FAMILIES

The following list of religious bodies appearing in the Directory Section of this yearbook shows the "families," or related clusters into which American religious bodies can be grouped. For example, there are many communions that can be grouped under the heading "Baptist" for historical and theological reasons. It is not to be assumed, however, that all denominations under one family heading are similar in belief or practice. Often, any similarity is purely coincidental. The family clusters tend to represent historical factors more often than theological or practical ones. The family categories provided one of the major pitfalls of church statistics because of the tendency to combine the statistics by "families" for analytical and comparative purposes. Such combined totals are almost meaningless, although often used as variables for sociological analysis.

Religious bodies not grouped under family headings appear alphabetically and are not indented in the following list.

Adventist Bodies

Advent Christian Church
Church of God General Conference (Oregon, IL.)
Primitive Advent Christian Church
Seventh-day Adventists

Amana Church Society
American Evangelical Christian Churches
American Rescue Workers
Apostolic Christian Church (Nazarene)
Apostolic Christian Churches of America
The Anglican Orthodox Church
Bahá'í Faith

Baptist Bodies

American Baptist Association
American Baptist Churches in the U.S.A.
Baptist Bible Fellowship International
Baptist General Conference
Baptist Missionary Association of America
Conservative Baptist Association of America
Duck River (and Kindred) Associations of Baptists
Free Will Baptists, National Association of
General Association of Regular Baptist Churches
General Baptists (General Association of)
General Conference of the Evangelical Baptist Church, Inc.
General Six-Principle Baptists
Liberty Baptist Fellowship
National Baptist Convention of America
National Baptist Convention, U.S.A., Inc.
National Missionary Baptist Convention of America
National Primitive Baptist Convention, Inc.
North American Baptist Conference
Primitive Baptists
Progressive National Baptist Convention, Inc.
Separate Baptists in Christ
Seventh Day Baptist General Conference, USA and Canada
Southern Baptist Convention
Sovereign Grace Baptists

Berean Fundamental Church

Brethren (German Baptists)

Brethren Church (Ashland, Ohio)
Church of the Brethren
Grace Brethren Churches, Fellowship of
Old German Baptist Brethren

Brethren, River

Brethren in Christ Church
United Zion Church

Buddhist Churches of America
Christadelphians
The Christian and Missionary Alliance
Christian Brethren (also known as Plymouth Brethren)
Christian Catholic Church (Evangelical-Protestant)
The Christian Congregation, Inc.
Christian Nation Church U.S.A.
Christian Union
Church of Christ, Scientist
Church of Daniel's Band
The Church of Illumination
Church of the Living God (Motto: Christian Workers for Fellowship)
Church of the Nazarene
Churches of Christ in Christian Union

Churches of Christ-Christian Churches

Christian Church (Disciples of Christ)
Christian Churches and Churches of Christ
Churches of Christ

Churches Of God

Church of God (Anderson, Ind.)
Church of God by Faith, Inc.
The Church of God (Seventh Day), Denver, Colo.,
Church of God (Which He Purchased With His Own Blood)
Churches of God, General Conference

Churches of the New Jerusalem

General Church of the New Jerusalem
The Swedenborgian Church

Community Churches, International Council of
Congregational Christian Churches, National Association of
Conservative Congregational Christian Conference

Eastern Churches

Albanian Orthodox Archdiocese in America
Albanian Orthodox Diocese of America
The American Carpatho-Russian Orthodox Greek Catholic Church

The Antiochian Orthodox Christian Archdiocese of North America
Apostolic Catholic Assyrian Church of the East, North American Dioceses
Armenian Apostolic Church of America
Armenian Church of America, Diocese of the
Bulgarian Eastern Orthodox Church
Coptic Orthodox Church
Greek Orthodox Archdiocese of North and South America
Holy Ukrainian Autocephalic Orthodox Church in Exile
The Orthodox Church in America
Romanian Orthodox Church in America
The Romanian Orthodox Episcopate of America
Russian Orthodox Church in the U.S.A., Patriarchal Parishes of the
The Russian Orthodox Church Outside Russia
Serbian Orthodox Church in the U.S.A. and Canada
Syrian Orthodox Church of Antioch (Archdiocese of the United States and Canada)
True Orthodox Church of Greece (Synod of Metropolitan Cyprian), American Exarchate
Ukrainian Orthodox Church of the U.S.A.
Ukrainian Orthodox Church in America (Ecumenical Patriarchate)

The Episcopal Church
Ethical Culture Movement
The Evangelical Church
Evangelical Congregational Church
The Evangelical Covenant Church
The Evangelical Free Church of America
Fellowship of Fundamental Bible Churches
The Fire Baptized Holiness Church (Wesleyan)
Free Christian Zion Church of Christ

Friends

Evangelical Friends International—North America Region
Friends General Conference
Friends United Meeting
Religious Society of Friends (Conservative)
Religious Society of Friends (Unaffiliated Meetings)

Grace Gospel Fellowship
The Holiness Church of God, Inc.
House of God, Which is the Church of the Living God, the Pillar and Ground of the Truth, Inc.
Independent Fundamental Churches of America
Israelite House of David
Jehovah's Witnesses
Jewish Organizations
Kodesh Church of Immanuel

Latter Day Saints

Church of Christ
The Church of Jesus Christ (Bickertonites)
The Church of Jesus Christ of Latter-day Saints
Reorganized Church of Jesus Christ of Latter Day Saints

The Liberal Catholic Church-Province of the United States of America

Lutherans

Apostolic Lutheran Church of America
Church of the Lutheran Brethren of America
Church of the Lutheran Confession
Conservative Lutheran Association
Estonian Evangelical Lutheran Church
Evangelical Lutheran Church in America
Evangelical Lutheran Synod
Free Lutheran Congregations, The Association of
Latvian Evangelical Lutheran Church in America
The Lutheran Church—Missouri Synod
Lutheran Churches, The American Association of
The Protes'tant Conference (Lutheran), Inc.
Wisconsin Evangelical Lutheran Synod

Mennonite Bodies

Beachy Amish Mennonite Churches
Church of God in Christ (Mennonite)
Evangelical Mennonite Church
Fellowship of Evangelical Bible Churches
Mennonite Brethren Churches, The Conference of
Hutterian Brethren
Mennonite Church
Mennonite Church, The General Conference
Old Order Amish Church
Old Order (Wisler) Mennonite Church
Reformed Mennonite Church

Methodist Bodies

African Methodist Episcopal Church
African Methodist Episcopal Zion Church
Allegheny Wesleyan Methodist Connection (Original Allegheny Conference)
Christian Methodist Episcopal Church
Evangelical Methodist Church
Free Methodist Church of North America
Fundamental Methodist Church, Inc.
Primitive Methodist Church in the U.S.A.
Reformed Methodist Union Episcopal Church
Reformed Zion Union Apostolic Church
Southern Methodist Church
The United Methodist Church
The Wesleyan Church

The Metropolitan Church Association, Inc.
Metropolitan Community Churches, Universal Fellowship of
The Missionary Church

Moravian Bodies

Moravian Church in America (Unitas Fratrum)
Unity of the Brethren

National Organization of the New Apostolic Church of North America
Muslims
National Spiritualist Association of Churches
North American Old Roman Catholic Church (Archdiocese of New York)

Old Catholic Churches

Christ Catholic Church
North American Old Roman Catholic Church

Pentecostal Bodies

Apostolic Faith Mission of Portland, Oregon
Apostolic Faith Mission Church of God
Apostolic Overcoming Holy Church of God, Inc.
Assemblies of God
Assemblies of God International Fellowship (Independent/Not Affiliated)
The Bible Church of Christ, Inc.
Bible Way Church of Our Lord Jesus Christ, World Wide, Inc.
Christian Church of North America, General Council
The Church of God
Church of God (Cleveland, Tenn.)
The Church of God in Christ
Church of God in Christ, International
The Church of God of Prophecy
The Church of God, Mountain Assembly, Inc.
Church of Our Lord Jesus Chrost of the Apostolic Faith, Inc.
Congregational Holiness Church
Elim Fellowship
Full Gospel Assemblies International
Full Gospel Fellowship of Churches and Ministers International
International Church of the Foursquare Gospel
The International Pentecostal Church of Christ
International Pentecostal Holiness Church
Open Bible Standard Churches, Inc.
The (Original) Church of God, Inc.
Pentecostal Assemblies of the World, Inc.
Pentecostal Church of God
Pentecostal Fire-Baptized Holiness Church
Pentecostal Free Will Baptist Church, Inc.
United Holy Church of America, Inc.
United Pentecostal Church International

Pillar of Fire
Polish National Catholic Church of America

Presbyterian Bodies

Associate Reformed Presbyterian Church (General Synod)
Cumberland Presbyterian Church
Cumberland Presbyterian Church in America
Evangelical Presbyterian Church
Korean Presbyterian Church in America, General Assembly of the
The Orthodox Presbyterian Church
Presbyterian Church in America
Presbyterian Church (U.S.A.)
Reformed Presbyterian Church of North America

Reformed Bodies

Christian Reformed Church in North America
Hungarian Reformed Church in America
Netherlands Reformed Congregations
Protestant Reformed Churches in America
Reformed Church in America
Reformed Church in the United States
United Church of Christ

Reformed Episcopal Church
The Roman Catholic Church
The Salvation Army
The Schwenkfelder Church
Social Brethren
Triumph the Church and Kingdom of God in Christ Inc. (International)
Unitarian Universalist Association

United Brethren Bodies

United Brethren in Christ
United Christian Church

Vedanta Societies
Volunteers of America
Wesleyan Holiness Association of Churches

4. RELIGIOUS BODIES IN CANADA

A large number of Canadian religious bodies were organized by immigrants from Europe and elsewhere, and a smaller number sprang up originally on Canadian soil. In the case of Canada, moreover, many denominations that overlap the U.S.-Canada border have headquarters in the United States.

What follows is, first, an alphabetical directory of religious bodies in Canada that have supplied information. The second section is an alphabetical list, with addresses and other information, of bodies known to exist in Canada that have not yet supplied complete directory information. This second section is titled "Other Religious Bodies in Canada." A final section lists denominations according to denominational families.

Complete statistics for Canadian denominations are found in the table "Canadian Current Statistics" in the statistical section of the *Yearbook*. Addresses for periodicals are found in the listing of Canadian Religious Periodicals. Information about finances for some of the denominations is in the Church Finance section.

The Anglican Church of Canada

Anglicanism came to Canada with the early explorers such as Martin Frobisher and Henry Hudson. Continuous services began in Newfoundland about 1700 and in Nova Scotia in 1710. The first Bishop, Charles Inglis, was appointed to Nova Scotia in 1787. The numerical strength of Anglicanism was increased by the coming of American Loyalists and by massive immigration both after the Napoleonic wars and in the later 19th and early 20th centuries.

The Anglican Church of Canada has enjoyed self-government for over a century and is an autonomous member of the worldwide Anglican Communion. The General Synod, which normally meets triennially, consists of the Archbishops, Bishops, and elected clerical and lay representatives of the 30 dioceses. Each of the Ecclesiastical Provinces—Canada, Ontario, Rupert's Land, and British Columbia—is organized under a Metropolitan and has its own Provincial Synod and Executive Council. Each diocese has its own Diocesan Synod.

HEADQUARTERS

600 Jarvis St., Toronto, ON M4Y 2J6 Tel. (416)924-9192 Fax (416)968-7983

Media Contact, Dir., Communications, Mr. Douglas Tindal, 600 Jarvis St., Toronto, ON M4Y 2J6 Tel. (416)924-9192 Fax (416)968-7983

GENERAL SYNOD OFFICERS

Primate of the Anglican Church of Canada, Most Rev. M. G. Peers, 600 Jarvis St., Toronto, ON M4Y 2J6

Prolocutor, Mrs. Amy Newell, RR #1, Fitzroy Harbor, ON K0A 1X0

Gen. Sec., Ven. D. J. Woeller, 600 Jarvis St., Toronto

Treas., Gen. Synod, John R. Ligertwood

Exec. Dir. of Program, Ms. Suzanne Lawson

DEPARTMENTS AND DIVISIONS

Anglican Book Centre, Dir. & Publ., Rev. M. J. Lloyd

Missionary Society, Exec. Sec., Rev. J. S. Barton

Dir. of World Mission, Rev. J. S. Barton

Div. of Pensions, Dir., Mrs. J. Mason

Dir. of Admn. & Fin., Mr. J. R. Ligertwood

Dir. of Communications, Mr. D. Tindal

Dir. of Ministries in Church & Society, Rev. P. Elliott

METROPOLITANS (ARCHBISHOPS)

Ecclesiastical Province of: Canada, The Most Rev. Stewart Payne, 25 Main Street, Corner Brook, NF A2H 1C2 Tel. (709)639-8712 Fax (709)639-1636; Rupert's Land, The Most Rev. Walter Jones, 935 Nesbitt Bay, Winnipeg, MB R3T 1W6 Tel. (204)453-6130 Fax (204)452-3915; British Columbia, The Most Rev. Douglas Hambidge, 302-814 Richards Street, Vancouver, BC V6B 3A7 Tel. (604)684-6306 Fax (604)684-7017; Ontario, The Most Rev. Edwin K. Lackey, 71 Bronson Ave., Ottawa, ON K1R 6G6 Tel. (613)232-7124 Fax (613)232-7088

DIOCESAN BISHOPS

Algoma: The Rt. Rev. L. Peterson, 619 Wellington St. E, Box 1168, Sault Ste. Marie, ON P6A 5N7 Tel. (705)256-5061 Fax (705)946-1860

Arctic: The Rt. Rev. J. C. R. Williams, 1055 Avenue Rd., Toronto, ON M5N 2C8 Tel. (416)481-2263 Fax (416)487-4948

Athabasca: The Right Rev. John R. Clarke, P.O. Box 6868, Peace River, AB T8S 1S6 Tel. (403)624-2767 Fax (403)624-2365

Brandon: The Rt. Rev. Malcolm Harding, 341-13th St., Brandon, MB R7A 4P8 Tel. (204)727-7550 Fax (204)727-4135

British Columbia: The Rt. Rev. Barry Jenks, 912 Vancouver St., Victoria, BC V8V 3V7 Tel. (604)386-7781 Fax (604)386-4013

Caledonia: The Rt. Rev. J. E. Hannen, Box 278, Prince Rupert, BC V8J 3P6 Tel. (604)624-6013 Fax (604)624-4299

Calgary: The Rt. Rev. J. B. Curtis, 3015 Glencoe Rd. SW, Calgary, AB T2S 2L9 Tel. (403)243-3673 Fax (403)243-2182

Cariboo: The Right Rev. James D. Cruickshank, 5-618 Tranquille Rd., Ste. 5, Kamloops, BC V2B 3H6 Tel. (604)376-0112 Fax (604)376-1984

Central Newfoundland: The Rt. Rev. Donald F. Harvey, 34 Fraser Rd., Gander, NF A1V 2E8 Tel. (709)256-2372 Fax (709)256-2396

Eastern Newfoundland and Labrador: The Rt. Rev. M. Mate, 19 King's Bridge Rd., St. John's, NF A1C 3K4 Tel. (709)576-6697 Fax (709)576-7122

Edmonton: The Rt. Rev. K. Genge, 10033 - 84 Ave., Edmonton, AB T6E 2G6 Tel. (403)439-7344 Fax (403)439-6549

Fredericton: The Rt. Rev. G. C. Lemmon, 115 Church St., Fredericton, NB E3B 4C8 Tel. (506)459-1801 Fax (506)459-8475

Huron: The Rt. Rev. P. R. O'Driscoll, 4-220 Dundas St., London, ON N6A 1H3 Tel. (519)434-6893 Fax (519)673-4151

Keewatin: The Rt. Rev. T. W. R. Collings, 915 Ottawa St., Keewatin, ON P0X 1C0 Tel. (807)547-3353 Fax (807)547-3356

Kootenay: The Rt. Rev. D. P. Crawley, 201-1636 Pandosy St., Kelowna, BC V1Y 7P2 Tel. (604)762-3306 Fax (604)762-4150

Montréal: The Rt. Rev. A. S. Hutchison, 1444 Union Ave., Montréal, QC H3A 2B8 Tel. (514)843-6577 Fax (514)843-6344

Moosonee: The Rt. Rev. C. J. Lawrence, Box 841, Schumacher, ON P0N 1G0 Tel. (705)360-1129 Fax (705)360-1120

New Westminster: Archbishop, The Most Rev. D. W. Hambidge, 302-814 Richards St., Vancouver, BC V6B 3A7 Tel. (604)684-6306 Fax (604)684-7017

Niagara: The Right Rev. Walter Asbil, 67 Victoria Ave. S, Hamilton, ON L8N 2S8 Tel. (416)527-1278 Fax (416)527-1281

Nova Scotia: The Rt. Rev. A. G. Peters, 5732 College St., Halifax, NS B3H 1X3 Tel. (902)420-0717 Fax (902)425-0717

Ontario: The Rt. Rev. Peter Mason, 90 Johnson St., Kingston, ON K7L 1X7 Tel. (613)544-4774 Fax (613)547-3745

Ottawa: Archbishop, The Most Rev. E. K. Lackey, 71 Bronson Ave., Ottawa, ON K1R 6G6 Tel. (613)232-7124 Fax (613)232-7088

Qu'Appelle: The Rt. Rev. E. Bays, 1501 College Ave., Regina, SK S4P 1B8 Tel. (306)522-1608 Fax (306)352-6808

Québec: The Rt. Rev. A. B. Stavert, 36 rue des Jardins, Québec, QC G1R 4L5 Tel. (418)692-3858 Fax (418)692-3876

Rupert's Land: Archbishop, The Most Rev. W. Jones, 935 Nesbitt Bay, Winnipeg, MB R3T 1W6 Tel. (204)453-6130 Fax (204)452-3915

Saskatchewan: The Rt. Rev. T. O. Morgan, Box 1088, Prince Albert, SK S6V 5S6 Tel. (306)763-2455 Fax (306)764-5172

Saskatoon: The Rt. Rev. R. A. Wood, Box 1965, Saskatoon, SK S7K 3S5 Tel. (306)244-5651

Toronto: The Most Rev. T. Finlay, 135 Adelaide St. East, Toronto, ON M5C 1L8 Tel. (416)363-6021 Fax (416)363-3683

Western Newfoundland: Archbishop, The Most Rev. S. S. Payne, 25 Main St., Corner Brook, NF A2H 1C2 Tel. (709)639-8712 Fax (709)639-1636

Yukon: The Rt. Rev. R. C. Ferris, Box 4247, Whitehorse, YT Y1A 3T3 Tel. (403)667-7746 Fax (403)667-6125

PERIODICALS

Anglican Journal/Journal Anglican; Rupert's Land News; Anglican Montréal Anglican; Saskatchewan Anglican

The Antiochian Orthodox Christian Archdiocese of North America

The approximately 100,000 members of the Antiochian Orthodox community in Canada are under the jurisdiction of the Antiochian Orthodox Christian Archdiocese of North America with headquarters in Englewood, N.J. There are churches in Edmonton, Winnipeg, Halifax, London, Ottawa, Toronto, Windsor, Montréal, and Saskatoon.

HEADQUARTERS

Metropolitan Philip Saliba, 358 Mountain Rd., Englewood, NJ 07631 Tel. (201)871-1355 Fax (201)871-7954

Media Contact, Vicar, The Very Rev. George S. Corey, 52 78th St., Brooklyn, NY 11209 Tel. (718)748-7940 Fax (201)871-7954

PERIODICAL

Word, The

Apostolic Christian Church (Nazarene)

This church was formed in Canada as a result of immigration from various European countries. The body began as a movement originated by the Rev. S. H. Froehlich, a Swiss pastor, whose followers are still found in Switzerland and Central Europe.

HEADQUARTERS

Apostolic Christian Church Foundation, 1135 Sholey Rd., Richmond, VA 23231 Tel. (804)222-1943

OFFICER

Exec. Dir., James Hodges

The Apostolic Church in Canada

The Apostolic Church in Canada is affiliated with the worldwide organization of the Apostolic Church with headquarters in Great Britain. A product of the Welsh Revival (1904 to 1908), its Canadian beginnings originated in Nova Scotia in 1927. Today its main centers are in Nova Scotia, Ontario, and Québec. This church is evangelical, fundamental, and Pentecostal, with special emphasis on the ministry gifts listed in Ephesians 4: 11-12.

HEADQUARTERS

27 Castlefield Ave., Toronto, ON M4R 1G3

Media Contact, Natl. Sec., Rev. John Kristensen, 388 Gerald St., La Salle, QC H8P 2A5 Tel. (514)366-8356

OFFICERS

Pres., Rev. D. S. Morris, 685 Park St. S., Peterborough, ON K9J 3S9 Tel. (705)743-3418

Natl. Sec., Rev. John Kristensen, 388 Gerald St., Ville LaSalle, QC H8P 2A5

Apostolic Church of Pentecost of Canada Inc.

This body was founded in 1921 at Winnipeg, Manitoba, by Pastor Frank Small. Doctrines include belief in eternal salvation by the grace of God, baptism of the Holy Spirit with the evidence of speaking in tongues, water baptism by immersion in the name of the Lord Jesus Christ.

HEADQUARTERS

105-807 Manning Rd. N.E., Calgary, AB T2E 7M8

Media Contact, Clk./Admn., Leonard Larsen, Tel. (403)273-5777 Fax (403)273-8102

OFFICERS

Mod., Rev. G. Killam

Clk., Leonard K. Larsen

PERIODICAL

A.C.O.P. Messenger

The Armenian Church of North America, Diocese of Canada

The Canadian branch of the ancient Church of Armenia founded in A.D. 301 by St. Gregory the Illuminator. It was established in Canada at St. Catherines, Ontario, in 1930. The diocesan organization is under the jurisdiction of the Holy See of Etchmiadzin, Armenia. The Diocese has churches in St. Catherine, Hamilton, Toronto, Scarborough, Ottawa, Vancouver, Mississauga, and Montréal.

HEADQUARTERS

Diocesan Offices: Primate, Canadian Diocese, Rt. Rev. Hovnan Derderian, 615 Stuart Ave., Outremont, QC H2V 3H2 Tel. (514)276-9479 Fax (514)276-9960

PERIODICALS

Nor Serount; Pourastan

Armenian Evangelical Church

Founded in 1960 by immigrant Armenian evangelical families from the Middle East, this body is conservative doctrinally, with an evangelical, biblical emphasis. The polity of churches within the group differ with congregationalism being dominant, but there are Presbyterian Armenian Evangelical churches as well. Most of the local churches have joined main-line denominations. All of the Armenian Evangelical (Congregational or Presbyterian) local churches in the United States and Canada have joined with the Armenian Evangelical Union of North America.

HEADQUARTERS

Media Contact, Chief Editor, Rev. Yessayi Sarmazian, 42 Glenforest Rd., Toronto, ON M4N 1Z8 Tel. (416)489-3188 Fax (416)485-4336

A.E.U.N.A. OFFICERS

Min. to the Union, Rev. Karl Avakian, 1789 E. Frederick Ave., Fresno, CA 93720

OFFICERS

Min., Rev. Yessayi Sarmazian, 42 Glenforest Rd., Toronto, ON M4N 1Z8 Tel. (416)489-3188

PERIODICAL

Canada Armenian Press

Associated Gospel Churches

The Associated Gospel Churches (A.G.C.) body traces its historical roots to the early years of the 20th century, which were marked by the growth of liberal theology in many established denominations. Individuals and whole congregations, seeking to uphold the final authority of the Scriptures in all matters of faith and conduct, withdrew from those denominations and established churches with an evangelical ministry under the inspired Word of God. These churches defended the belief that "all Scripture is given by inspiration of God" and also declared that the Holy Spirit "gave the identical words of sacred writings of holy men of old, chosen by Him to be the channel of His revelation to man."

In 1922, four churches of similar background in Ontario banded together in fellowship for counsel and cooperation. Known as The Christian Workers' Church in Canada, the group consisted of the Gospel Tabernacle, Hamilton; the Winona Gospel Tabernacle; the Missionary Tabernacle, Toronto; and West Hamilton Gospel Mission. The principal organizers were Dr. P. W. Philpott of Hamilton and H. E. Irwin, K. C., of Toronto.

In 1925 the name was changed to Associated Gospel Churches under a new Dominion Charter. Since that time the A.G.C. has grown steadily.

HEADQUARTERS

3430 South Service Rd., Burlington, ON L7N 3T9 Tel. (416)634-8184 Fax (416)634-6283
Media Contact, Pres., D. G. Hamilton

PERIODICAL

Advance

Association of Regular Baptist Churches (Canada)

Organized in 1957 by a group of churches for the purpose of mutual cooperation in missionary activities. The Association believes the Bible to be God's word, stands for historic Baptist principles, and opposes modern ecumenism.

HEADQUARTERS

130 Gerrard St. E., Toronto, ON M5A 3T4 Tel. (416)925-3261
Media Contact, Sec., Rev. W. P. Bauman, Tel. (416)925-3263 Fax (416)925-8305

PERIODICAL

Gospel Witness, The

Bahá'í Faith

Bahá'ís are followers of Bahá'u'lláh (1817-1892) whose religion teaches the essential oneness of all the great religions and promotes the oneness of mankind and racial unity.

The Bahá'í administrative order consists of nine-member elected institutions called spiritual assemblies, which function at the local and national level. The international administrative institution, the Universal House of Justice, is located in Haifa, Israel, at the Bahá'í World Centre, the spiritual headquarters of the Bahá'í community and the burial place of its founders.

In Canada, the Bahá'í Faith is administered by the National Spiritual Assembly. This body was incorporated by Act of Parliament in 1949. There are approximately 1,650 Bahá'í communities in Canada, of which 400 elect local Spiritual Assemblies.

HEADQUARTERS

Bahá'í National Centre of Canada, 7200 Leslie St., Thornhill, ON L3T 6L8 Tel. (416)889-8168 Fax (416)889-8184
Media Contact, Dir., Dept. of Public Affairs, Mrs. Brit-Karina Regan

Baptist General Conference of Canada

Founded in Canada by missionaries from the United States. Originally a Swedish body, but no longer an ethnic body. The BGC-Canada includes people of many nationalities and is conservative and evangelical in doctrine and practice.

HEADQUARTERS

4306-97 St., Edmonton, AB T6E 5R9 Tel. (403)438-9127 Fax (403)435-2478
Media Contact, Exec. Dir., Rev. Abe Funk

PERIODICAL

BGC Canada News

The Central Canada Baptist Conference

Central Baptist Conference, originally a Scandinavian group, is one of three districts of the Baptist General Conference of Canada. In 1907, churches from Winnipeg—Grant Memorial, Teulon, Kenora, Port Arthur, Sprague, Erickson, and Midale—organized under the leadership of Fred Palmberg. Immigration from Sweden declined, and in 1947 only nine churches remained. In 1948 the group dropped the Swedish language, withdrew from the Baptist Union, city churches were started, and today CCBC has 37 functioning churches.

An evangelical Baptist association holding to the inerrancy of the Bible, CCBC seeks to reach Central Canada for Christ by establishing local gospel-preaching churches.

CCBC offers pastoral aid to new churches, recommendations as to pastoral supply, counsel, and fellowship. It encourages contributions to the CCBC and BGC of Canada budgets, the purchase of CCBC Serial Notes, support of the Conference BATT program (contributions to special needs of churches), and other projects to assist needy churches and pastors.

HEADQUARTERS

Box 135, Stonewall, MB R0C 2Z0 Tel. (204)467-2169

Baptist General Conference of Alberta

HEADQUARTERS

10727-114 St., Edmonton, AB T5H 3K1 Tel. (403)438-9126

PERIODICAL

Alberta Alert, The

British Columbia Baptist Conference

British Columbia Baptist Conference is a district of the Baptist General Conference of Canada, with roots in Sweden, where Christians began to read the Bible in their homes. One convert, F.O. Nilsson, saw the significance of baptism subsequent to a personal commitment to Christ; he went to Hamburg, Germany, where he was baptized in the Elbe River by Rev. John Oncken. When Nilsson returned to Sweden, five of his converts were baptized in the North Sea and, with him, formed the first Swedish Baptist Church. Nilsson was imprisoned by the local government for violation of state church regulations and later, when exiled from Sweden, went to the United States. As Swedish Baptists emigrated to the United States to escape persecution, they formed churches in Illinois, Iowa, Minnesota, and Wisconsin and carried on aggressive evangelism among other immigrating Swedes. In 1879 they formed the Swedish Baptist General Conference of America, later named The Baptist General Conference.

HEADQUARTERS

7600 Glover Rd., Langley, BC V3A 6H4 Tel. (604)888-2246 Fax (604)888-1905
Media Contact, Dist. Exec. Min., Rev. Walter W. Wieser

PERIODICAL

B.C. Conference Call

The Bible Holiness Movement

The Bible Holiness Movement, organized in 1949 as an outgrowth of the city mission work of the late Pastor William James Elijah Wakefield, an early-day Salvation Army officer, has been headed since its inception by his son, Evangelist Wesley H. Wakefield, its bishop-general.

It derives its emphasis on the original Methodist faith of salvation and scriptural holiness from the late Bishop R. C. Horner. It adheres to the common evangelical faith in the Bible, the Deity, and the atonement of Christ, and stresses a personal experience of salvation for the repentant sinner, of being wholly sanctified for the believer, and of the fullness of the Holy Spirit for effective witness.

Membership involves a life of Christian love, evangelistic and social activism, and the disciplines of simplicity and separation, including total abstinence from liquor and tobacco, nonattendance at popular amusements, and no membership in secret societies. Divorce and remarriage are forbidden. Similar to Wesley's Methodism, members are, under some circumstances, allowed to retain membership in other evangelical church fellowships. Interchurch affiliations are maintained with a number of Wesleyan-Arminian Holiness denominations.

Year-round evangelistic outreach is maintained through open-air meetings, visitation, literature, and other media. Noninstitutional welfare work, including addiction counseling, is conducted among minorities. There is direct overseas famine relief, civil rights action, environment protection, and antinuclearism. The movement sponsors a permanent committee on religious freedom and an active promotion of Christian racial equality.

The movement has a world outreach with branches in the United States, India, Nigeria, Philippines, Ghana, Liberia, Cameroon, Kenya, Zambia, South Korea, and Haiti. It ministers to 89 countries in 42 languages through literature, radio, and audiocassetes.

HEADQUARTERS

Box 223, Postal Stn. A, Vancouver, BC V6C 2M3 Tel. (604)498-3895
Media Contact, Bishop-General, Evangelist Wesley H. Wakefield, P.O. Box 223, Postal Station A, Vancouver, BC V6C 2M3 Tel. (604)498-3895

PERIODICAL

Hallelujah

Brethren in Christ Church, Canadian Conference

The Brethren in Christ, formerly known as Tunkers in Canada, arose out of a religious awakening in Lancaster County, Pa. late in the 18th century. Representatives of the new denomination reached Ontario in 1788 and established the church in the southern part of the present province. Presently the conference has congregations in Ontario, Alberta, Québec, and Saskatchewan. In theology they have accents of the Pietist, Anabaptist, Wesleyan, and Evangelical movements.

HEADQUARTERS

Brethren in Christ Church, Gen. Ofc., P.O. Box 290, Grantham, PA 12027 Tel. (717)697-2634 Fax (717)697-7714
Canadian Headquarters, Bishop's Ofc., 2619 Niagara Pkwy., Ft. Erie, ON L2A 5M4 Tel. (416)871-9991
Media Contact, Mod., Harvey R. Sider, Brethren in Christ Church Gen. Ofc.

PERIODICAL

Evangelical Visitor

British Methodist Episcopal Church of Canada

The British Methodist Episcopal Church was organized in 1856 in Chatham, Ontario and incorporated in 1913. It has congregations across the Province of Ontario.

HEADQUARTERS

460 Shaw St., Toronto, ON M6G 3L3 Tel. (416)534-3831

Media Contact, Editor, Rev. Jean Markham, 1413-145 Hillcrest, Mississauga, ON L5B 3Z1

Buddhist Churches of Canada

Founded at Vancouver, British Columbia in 1904. The first minister was the Rev. Senju Sasaki. This body is the Mahayana division of Buddhism, and its sectarian belief is the Pure Land School based on the Three Canonical Scriptures with emphasis on pure faith.

HEADQUARTERS

220 Jackson Ave., Vancouver, BC V6A 3B3 Tel. (604)244-1101

Canadian and American Reformed Churches

The Canadian and American Reformed Churches accept the Bible as the infallible Word of God, as summarized in The Belgic Confession of Faith (1561), The Heidelberg Cathechism(1563), and The Canons of Dordt (1618-1619). The denomination was founded in Canada in 1950 and American congregations have been formed since 1955.

HEADQUARTERS

Synod: P.O. Box 62053, Burlington, ON L7R 4K2

Canadian Reformed Churches: Ebenezer Canadian Reformed Church, P. O. Box 62053, Burlington Mall Postal Outlet, Burlington, ON L7R 4K2

American Reformed Churches: American Reformed Church, Rev. P. Kingma, 3167-68th St. S.E., Caledonia, MI 46316

Media Contact, Rev. G. Nederveen, 3089 Woodward Ave., Burlington, ON L7N 2M3 Tel. (416)681-9837 Fax (416)681-9837

PERIODICALS

Reformed Perspective: A Magazine for the Christian Fam.; Yearbook - Canadian and American Reformed Churches; In Holy Array; Mission News; Evangel: The Good News of Jesus Christ; Clarion: The Canadian Reformed Magazine

Canadian Baptist Federation

The Canadian Baptist Federation has four federated member bodies: (1) Baptist Convention of Ontario and Québec, (2) Baptist Union of Western Canada, (3) the United Baptist Convention of the Atlantic Provinces, (4) Union d'Églises Baptistes Françaises au Canada (French Baptist Union). Its main purpose is to act as a coordinating agency for the four groups.

HEADQUARTERS

7185 Millcreek Dr., Mississauga, ON L5N 5R4 Tel. (416)826-0191 Fax (416)826-3441

Media Contact, Gen. Sec.-Treas., Dr. Richard C. Coffin

PERIODICAL

Enterprise

Baptist Convention of Ontario and Québec

The Baptist Convention of Ontario and Québec is a family of 372 churches in Ontario and Québec, united for mutual support and encouragement and united in missions in Canada and the world.

The Convention was formally organized in 1888. It has two educational institutions—McMaster University, founded in 1887 and the Baptist Leadership Education Centre at Whitby. The Convention works through the all-Canada missionary agency, Canadian Baptist International Ministries. The churches also support the Sharing Way, the relief and development arm of the Canadian Baptist Federation.

HEADQUARTERS

217 St. George St., Toronto, ON M5R 2M2 Tel. (416)922-5163 Fax (416)922-3254

Media Contact, Exec. Min., Rev. John Wilton

PERIODICAL

Canadian Baptist, The

Baptist Union of Western Canada

HEADQUARTERS

202, 838-11th Ave. S.W., Calgary, AB T2R 0E5 Tel. (403)234-9044 Fax (403)269-6755

Media Contact, Exec. Min., Rev. William Cram

PERIODICAL

Tidings

United Baptist Convention of the Atlantic Provinces

The United Baptist Convention of the Atlantic Provinces is the largest Baptist Convention in Canada. Through the Canadian Baptist Federation, it is a member of the Baptist World Alliance.

Work in Canada began in the Atlantic Provinces in the 1700s when Baptists from New England began to migrate into the area. The Rev. Ebenezer Moulton organized a Baptist Church in Horton (now Wolfville, Nova Scotia) in 1763. The present church in Wolfville was formed in 1778 and is Canada's oldest continuing Baptist church. The United Baptist Convention was formed in 1905 when Calvinistic and Free Baptist churches merged; thus the name United Baptist is often used.

The first Baptist Association in Canada met in Nova Scotia in 1800. Today there are 21 Associations (usually comprised of one or two counties) within the convention. Through the Canadian Baptist Overseas Mission Board they support more than 100 missionaries in Kenya, Zaire, Brazil, Bolivia, Indonesia, and Sri Lanka. They have an active program of evangelism, Christian education, and church planting. They own and operate two colleges: Atlantic Baptist College in Moncton, New Brunswick, and Acadia Divinity College in Wolfville, Nova Scotia, which provides training for those entering the ministry and overseas missions. The convention operates six senior citizens' homes and a Christian bookstore.

HEADQUARTERS

1655 Manawagonish Rd., Saint John, NB E2M 3Y2 Tel. (506)635-1922 Fax (506)635-0366

Media Contact, Dir. of Communications, Rev. Douglas Hapeman

PERIODICAL

Atlantic Baptist, The

Union d'Eglises Baptistes Françaises au Canada

Baptist churches in French Canada first came into being through the labors of two missionaries from Switzerland, Rev. Louis Roussy and Mme. Henriette Feller, who arrived in Canada in 1835. The earliest church was organized in Grande Ligne (now St.-Blaise), Québec in 1838.

By 1900 there were 7 churches in the province of Québec and 13 French-language Baptist churches in the New England states. The leadership was totally French Canadian.

By 1960, the process of Americanization had caused the disappearance of the French Baptist churches. During the 1960s Québec as a society, began rapidly changing in all its facets: education, politics, social values and structures. Mission, evangelism and church growth once again flourished. In 1969, in response to the new conditions, the Grande Ligne Mission passed control of its work to the newly formed Union of French Baptist Churches in Canada, which then included 8 churches. By 1990 the French Canadian Baptist movement had grown to include 25 congregations.

The Union d'Églises Baptistes Françaises au Canada is a member body of the Canadian Baptist Federation and thus is affiliated with the Baptist World Alliance.

HEADQUARTERS
2285 avenue Papineau, Montréal, QC H2K 4J5 Tel. (514)526-6643
Media Contact, Sec. Gen., John S. Gilmour

PERIODICAL
Trait D'Union, Le

Canadian Convention of Southern Baptists

The Canadian Convention of Southern Baptists was formed at the Annual Meeting, May 7-9, 1985, in Kelowna, British Columbia. It was formerly known as the Canadian Baptist Conference, founded in Kamloops, British Columbia, in 1959 by pastors of existing churches.

HEADQUARTERS
Postal Bag 300, Cochrane, AB T0L 0W0 Tel. (403)932-5688 Fax (403)932-4937
Media Contact, Exec. Dir.-Treas., Rev. Allen Schmidt

PERIODICAL
Baptist Horizon, The

Canadian Yearly Meeting of the Religious Society of Friends

Founded in Canada as an offshoot of the Quaker movement in Great Britain and colonial America. Genesee Yearly Meeting, founded 1834, Canada Yearly Meeting (Orthodox), founded in 1867, and Canada Yearly Meeting, founded in 1881, united in 1955 to form the Canadian Yearly Meeting. The Canadian Yearly Meeting is affiliated with the Friends United Meeting and the Friends General Conference. It is also a member of Friends World Committee for Consultation.

HEADQUARTERS
91A Fourth Ave., Ottawa, ON K1S 2L1 Tel. (613)235-8553 Fax (613)235-8553
Media Contact, Gen. Sec.-Treas., Anne Thomas

PERIODICAL
Canadian Friend, The

Christ Catholic Church

HEADQUARTERS
5165 Palmer Ave., Niagara Falls, ON L2E 3T9 Tel. (416)354-2329 Fax (416)354-9934

PERIODICALS
Entre-nous; Relations

Christian and Missionary Alliance in Canada

A Canadian movement, dedicated to the teaching of Jesus Christ the Saviour, Sanctifier, Healer and Coming King, commenced in Toronto in 1887 under the leadership of the Rev. John Salmon. Two years later, the movement united with The Christian Alliance of New York, founded by Rev. A. B. Simpson, becoming the Dominion Auxiliary of the Christian Alliance, Toronto, under the presidency of the Hon. William H. Howland. Its four founding branches were Toronto, Hamilton, Montréal, and Québec. By Dec. 31, 1991, there were 336 churches across Canada, with 1054 official workers, including a worldwide missionary force of 253.

In 1980, the Christian and Missionary Alliance in Canada became autonomous. Its General Assembly is held every two years.

HEADQUARTERS
Natl. Office, #510-105 Gordon Baker Rd., North York, ON M2H 3P8 Tel. (416)492-8775 Fax (416)492-7708
Media Contact, Dir. of Communications, Myrna McCombs

DISTRICT SUPERINTENDENTS
Canadian Pacific: Rev. Gordon R. Fowler
Western Canadian: Rev. Arnold Downey
Canadian Midwest: Rev. Arnold Reimer
Eastern and Central: Rev. Robert J. Gould
St. Lawrence: Rev. Jesse D. Jespersen

Christian Brethren (Also known as Plymouth Brethren)

This orthodox and evangelical movement, which began in the British Isles in the 1820s, is now worldwide. For more detail on the history and theology, see "Religious Bodies in the United States" section of the *Yearbook*.

In the 1840s the movement divided. The "exclusive" branch, led by John Darby, stressed the interdependence of congregations. Canadian congregations number approximately 150, with an inclusive membership estimated at 11,000. The "open" branch of the movement, stressing evangelism and foreign missions, followed the leadership of George Muller in rejecting the "Exclusive" principle of binding discipline, and has escaped large-scale division.

Canadian congregations number approximately 450, with an inclusive membership estimated at 41,000. There are 250 "commended" full-time ministers, not including foreign missionaries.

HEADQUARTERS
For Québec, Christian Brethren Church in the Province of Québec, Norman R. Buchanan, Sec., 222 Alexander St., Sherbrooke, QC J1H 4S7 Tel. (819)562-9198
Correspondent for North America, Interest Ministries, Bruce R. McNichol, Pres., P.O. Box 190, Wheaton, IL 60189 Tel. (708)653-6573 Fax (708)653-6595

Media Contact, Editorial Asst., Naomi Bauman, P.O. Box 190, Wheaton, IL 60189 Tel. (708)653-6573 Fax (708)653-6595

OTHER ORGANIZATIONS

Missionary Service Committee, Exec. Dir., Claude Loney, 1562A Danforth Ave., Toronto, ON M4J 1N4 Tel. (416)469-2012

Vision Ontario, Dir., Gord Martin, P.O. Box 28032, Waterloo, ON N2L 6J8 Tel. (519)725-1212 Fax (519)725-9421

PERIODICAL

News of Québec

Christian Church (Disciples of Christ) in Canada

Disciples have been in Canada since 1810 but were organized nationally in 1922 when the All-Canada Committee was formed. It seeks to serve the Canadian context as part of the whole Christian Church (Disciples of Christ) in the United States and Canada.

HEADQUARTERS

128 Woolwich St., #202, Guelph, ON N1H 3V2 Tel. (519)823-5190

Media Contact, Exec. Minister, Robert W. Steffer

PERIODICAL

Canadian Disciple

Christian Churches and Churches of Christ in Canada

This fellowship, dedicated to the "restoration of the New Testament Church in doctrine, ordinances and life," has been operating in Canada since 1820. There is no general organization. Each church within the fellowship is completely independent. For detailed information see: *Directory of the Ministry, Christian Churches and Churches of Christ*, 1525 Cherry Rd., Springfield, IL 62704, U.S.A., telephone (217)546-7338.

Christian Reformed Church in North America

The Christian Reformed Church in North America represents the historic faith of Protestantism and is creedally united in the Belgic Confession (1561), the Heidelberg Catechism (1563), and the Canons of Dort (1618-19). The denomination was founded in the U.S. in 1857. Canadian congregations have been formed since 1908.

HEADQUARTERS

United States Office: 2850 Kalamazoo Ave., S.E., Grand Rapids, MI 49560 Tel. (616)246-0744 Fax (616)246-0834

Canadian Office: 3475 Mainway, P.O. Box 5070, Burlington, ON L7R 3Y8 Tel. (416)336-2920 Fax (416)336-8344

Media Contact, Gen. Sec., Leonard J. Hofman, U.S. Office

PERIODICAL

The Banner

Church of God (Anderson, Ind.)

This body is one of the largest of the groups which have taken the name "Church of God." Its headquarters are at Anderson, Ind. It originated about 1880 and emphasizes Christian unity.

HEADQUARTERS

Western Canada Assembly, Chpsn., Jack Wagner, 4717 56th St., Camrose, AB T4V 2C4 Tel. (403)672-0772 Fax (403)672-6888

Eastern Canada Assembly, Chpsn., Rev. John Campbell, 48 Leaside Dr., Welland, ON L3C 6B2

Media Contact for Western Canada, Interim Admn., Lloyd W.E. Moritz

PERIODICAL

Gospel Contact, The

Church of God (Cleveland, Tenn.)

This body began in the United States in 1886 as the outgrowth of the holiness revival under the name Christian Union, and in 1902 it was reorganized as the Holiness Church. In 1907, the church adopted the name Church of God. Its doctrine is fundamental and Pentecostal, and it maintains a centralized form of government and an evangelistic and missionary program.

The first church in Canada was established in 1919 in Scotland Farm, Manitoba. Paul H. Walker became the first overseer of Canada in 1931.

HEADQUARTERS

Intl. Offices: 2490 Keith St., NW, Cleveland, TN 37311 Tel. (615)472-3361

Media Contact, Dir. of Publ. Relations, Michael L. Baker, P.O. Box 2430, Cleveland, TN 37320-2430 Tel. (615)472-7112 Fax (615)478-7066

OFFICERS

Exec. Office in Canada: Rev. Paul Clawson, P.O. Box 2036, Bramalea, ON L6T 3S3 Tel. (416)793-2213

Western Canada: Rev. Philip F. Siggelkow, Box 54055, 2640 52 St., NE, Calgary, AB T1Y 6S6 Tel. (403)293-8817 Fax (403)293-8832

Church of God in Christ (Mennonite)

The Church of God in Christ, Mennonite, was organized by the evangelist-reformer John Holdeman, in Ohio. The church unites with the faith of the Waldenses, Anabaptists, and other such groups throughout history. Emphasis is placed on obedience to the teachings of the Bible, including the doctrine of the new birth and spiritual life, noninvolvement in government or the military, a headcovering for women, beards for men, and separation from the world shown by simplicity in clothing, homes, possessions, and lifestyle. The church has a worldwide membership of about 15,000, largely concentrated in the United States and Canada.

HEADQUARTERS

P.O. Box 313, 420 N. Wedel Ave., Moundridge, KS 67107 Tel. (316)345-2532 Fax (316)345-2582

The Church of God of Prophecy in Canada

In the late 19th century, men seeking God's eternal plan as they followed the Reformation spirit began to delve further for scriptural light concerning Christ and his church. On June 13, 1903, A.J. Tomlinson and several others joined them. Under Tomlinson's leadership, the church enjoyed tremendous growth. It is now operating in all 50 states of the United States. In 1911, the first missionary effort was launched in the Bahamas; today the church is represented in 91 countries and territories around the world. In 1923, two churches emerged. Those that opposed Tomlinson's leadership are known today in Canada as the New Testament Church of God, Tomlinson's followers as the Church of God of Prophecy.

In Canada, the first Church of God of Prophecy congregation was organized in Swan River, Manitoba, in 1937. Churches are now established in British Columbia, Manitoba, Alberta, Saskatchewan, Ontario, and Québec.

The church accepts the whole Bible rightly divided, with the New Testament as the rule of faith and practice, government, and discipline. The membership upholds the Bible as the inspired Word of God and believes that its truths are known by illumination of the Holy Spirit. The Trinity is recognized as one supreme God in three persons—Father, Son, and Holy Ghost. Jesus Christ, the virgin-born Son of God, lived a sinless life, fulfilled his ministry on earth, was crucified, resurrected, and later ascended to the right hand of God.

HEADQUARTERS

Canadian Headquarters: 1st Line East, RR #2, Brampton, ON L6V 1A1 Tel. (416)843-2379
World Headquarters: Bible Place, Cleveland, TN 37311
Media Contact, Natl. Overseer, Bishop Wade H. Phillips, P.O. Box 457, Brampton, ON L6V 1A1 Tel. (416)843-2379

BOARD OF DIRECTORS

Pres., Bishop Wade H. Phillips
Vice Pres., Bishop Vernon Van Deventer
Sec., John Anderson
Members: Bishop Billy D. Murray; Bishop Adrian Varlack; Bishop A. R. Morrison; Bishop Leroy V. Greenaway

PERIODICAL

Canadian Trumpeter Canada-West

The Church of Jesus Christ of Latter-day Saints in Canada

This body has no central headquarters in Canada, only stake and mission offices. Elders H. Burke Peterson, Hugh W. Pinnock and F. Enzio Busche of the Quorum of the Seventy oversee the Church's activities in Canada. They reside in Salt Lake City, Utah. All General Authorities may be reached at the headquarters. [See U. S. Directory, "Religious Bodies in the United States" in this edition for further details.] In Canada, there are 34 stakes, 6 missions, 8 districts, and 380 wards/branches (congregations).

HEADQUARTERS

50 East North Temple St., Salt Lake City, UT 84150
Media Contact, Public Affairs Dir., William and Donna Smart, 91 Scenic Millway, North York, ON M2L 1S9 Tel. (416)441-0452 Fax (416)441-0457

Church of the Lutheran Brethren

Organized in Milwaukee, Wisc., in 1900, it adheres to the Lutheran Confessions and accepts into membership those who profess a personal faith in Jesus Christ. It practices congregational autonomy and conducts its services in a nonliturgical

pattern. The synod has an advisory rather than ruling function on the congregational level, but in the cooperative efforts of all congregations (Education, American and World Missions, Publications, and Youth Ministries) it exercises a ruling function.

HEADQUARTERS

1007 Westside Dr., P.O. Box 655, Fergus Falls, MN 56538 Tel. (218)739-3336 Fax (218)739-5514
Media Contact, Pres., Rev. Robert Overgaard

PERIODICAL

Faith and Fellowship

Church of the Nazarene

The first Church of the Nazarene in Canada was organized in November, 1902, by Dr. H. F. Reynolds. It was in Oxford, Nova Scotia. The Church of the Nazarene is Wesleyan Arminian in theology, representative in church government, and warmly evangelistic.

HEADQUARTERS

73800-19 St., N.E., Calgary, AB T2E 6V2
Media Contact, Gen. Sec., Dr. Jack Stone, 6401 The Paseo, Kansas City, MO 64131 Tel. (816)333-7000 Fax (816)361-4983

Churches of Christ in Canada

Churches of Christ are autonomous congregations, whose members appeal to the Bible alone to determine matters of faith and practice. There are no central offices or officers. Publications and institutions related to the churches are either under local congregational control or independent of any one congregation.

Churches of Christ shared a common fellowship in the 19th century with the Christian Churches/Churches of Christ and the Christian Church (Disciples of Christ). Fellowship was broken after the introduction of instrumental music in worship and centralization of church-wide activities through a missionary society. Churches of Christ began in Canada soon after 1800, largely in the middle provinces. The few pioneer congregations were greatly strengthened in the mid-1800s, growing in size and number.

Members of Churches of Christ believe in the inspiration of the Scriptures, the divinity of Jesus Christ, and immersion into Christ for the remission of sins. The New Testament pattern is followed in worship and church organization.

HEADQUARTERS

Media Contact, Man. Ed., Gospel Herald, Eugene C. Perry, 4904 King St., Beansville, ON L0R 1B6 Tel. (416)563-7503

PERIODICALS

Gospel Herald; Good News West

Conference of Mennonites in Canada

The Conference of Mennonites in Canada began in 1902 as an organized fellowship of Mennonite immigrants from Russia clustered in southern Manitoba and around Rosthern, Saskatchewan. The first annual sessions were held in July, 1903. Its members hold to traditional Christian beliefs, believer's baptism, and congregational polity. They emphasize practical Christianity: opposition to war, service to others, and personal ethics.

Further immigration from Russia in the 1920s and 1940s increased the group which is now located in all provinces from New Brunswick to British Columbia. This conference is affiliated with the General Conference Mennonite Church whose offices are at Newton, Kan.

HEADQUARTERS

600 Shaftesbury Blvd., Winnipeg, MB R3P 0M4 Tel. (204)888-6781 Fax (204)831-5675
Media Contact, Gen. Sec., Helmut Harder

PERIODICALS

Mennonite, The; Mennonite Reporter

Congregational Christian Churches in Canada

This body originated in the early 18th century when devout Christians within several denominations in the northern and eastern United States, dissatisfied with sectarian controversy, broke away from their own denominations and took the simple title "Christians." First organized in 1821 at Keswick, Ontario, the Congregational Christian Churches in Canada was incorporated on Dec. 4, 1989, as a national organization. In doctrine the body is evangelical, being governed by the Bible as the final authority in faith and practice. It believes that Christian character must be expressed in daily living; it aims at the unity of all true believers in Christ that others may believe in Him and be saved. In church polity, the body is democratic and autonomous. It is also a member of The World Evangelical Congregational Fellowship.

HEADQUARTERS

P.O. Box 4688, Brantford, ON N3T 6H2 Tel. (519)751-0606
Media Contact, Pres., Rev. John Tweedie, 48 Sky Acres Dr., Brantford, ON N3R 1P3 Tel. (519)759-4692

The Coptic Church in Canada

The Coptic Church in North America was begun in Canada in 1964 and was registered in the province of Ontario in 1965. The Coptic Church has spread since then to a number of locations in North America.

The governing body of each local church is an elected Board of Deacons. The Diocesan Council is the national governing body and meets at least once a year.

Elim Fellowship of Evangelical Churches and Ministers

The Elim Fellowship of Evangelical Churches and Ministers, a Pentecostal body, was established in 1984 as a sister organization of Elim Fellowship in the United States

This is an association of churches, ministers, and missionaries seeking to serve the whole body of Christ. It is Pentecostal and has a charismatic orientation.

HEADQUARTERS

30 Amelia St., Paris, ON N3L 3V5 Tel. (519)442-3288 Fax (519)442-1487
Bus. Mgr., Larry Jones
Sec., Debbie Jones

The Estonian Evangelical Lutheran Church

The Estonian Evangelical Lutheran Church (EELC) was founded in 1917 in Estonia and reorganized in Sweden in 1944. The teachings of the EELC are based on the Old and New Testaments, explained through the Apostolic, Nicean and Athanasian confessions, the unaltered Confession of Augsburg and other teachings found in the Book of Concord.

HEADQUARTERS

383 Jarvis St., Toronto, ON M5B 2C7 Tel. (416)925-5465
Media Contact, Archbishop, Rev. Udo Petersoo

Evangelical Baptist Churches in Canada, The Fellowship of

Founded in 1953 by the merging of the Union of Regular Baptist Churches of Ontario and Québec with the Fellowship of Independent Baptist Churches of Canada.

HEADQUARTERS

679 Southgate Dr., Guelph, ON N1G 4S2 Tel. (519)821-4830 Fax (519)821-9829
Media Contact, Pres., Rev. Terry Cuthbert

PERIODICALS

B.C. Fellowship Baptist; Evangelical Baptist; Intercom

The Evangelical Church in Canada

Founded early in the 19th century by Jacob Albright and William Otterbein in Pennsylvania as the Evangelical Church, this body became known later as the Evangelical United Brethren Church, which in the United States became a part of The United Methodist Church in 1968. This Canadian body is Methodist in organization and Arminian, Wesleyan, and Methodist in doctrine. It was incorporated in 1928 by Dominion Charter as The Northwest Canada Conference Evangelical Church. In 1970, this Canadian Conference was granted autonomy and became a separate denomination. In 1982 The Evangelical Church in Canada joined with The Evangelical Church of North America.

HEADQUARTERS

Evangelical Church Ofc. Bldg., 2801 13th Ave., S.E., Medicine Hat, AB T1A 3R1 Tel. (403)527-4101 Fax (403)526-8404
Media Contact, A. W. Riegel

PERIODICAL

Northwest Canada Echoes

The Evangelical Covenant Church of Canada

A Canadian denomination organized in Canada at Winnipeg in 1904 which is affiliated with the Evangelical Covenant Church of America and with the International Federation of Free Evangelical Churches, which includes churches in 11 European countries.

This body believes in the one triune God as confessed in the Apostles' Creed, that salvation is received through faith in Christ as Saviour, that the Bible is the authoritative guide in all matters of faith and practice. Christian Baptism and the Lord's Supper are accepted as divinely ordained sacraments of the church. As descendants of the 19th century northern European pietistic awakening, the group believes in the need of a personal experience of commitment to Christ, the development of a virtuous life, and the urgency of spreading the gospel to the "ends of the world."

HEADQUARTERS

245 21st St. E., Prince Albert, SK S6V 1L9 Tel. (306)922-3449 Fax (306)922-5414
Media Contact, Superintendent, Rev. Jerome Johnson

PERIODICAL

Covenant Messenger, The

Evangelical Free Church of Canada

The Evangelical Free Churches in Canada celebrated 50 years of Free Church work under the American Evangelical Free Church by becoming incorporated as a Canadian organization on March 21, 1967. On July 8, 1984, the Evangelical Free Church of Canada was given its autonomy as a self-governing Canadian denomination.

HEADQUARTERS

#200, 20316-56 Ave., Langley, BC V3A 3Y7

PERIODICAL

The Beacon

Evangelical Lutheran Church in Canada

The Evangelical Lutheran Church in Canada was organized in 1985 through a merger of The Evangelical Lutheran Church of Canada (ELCC) and the Lutheran Church in America—Canada Section.

The merger is a result of an invitation issued in 1972 by the ELCC to the Lutheran Church in America—Canada Section and the Lutheran Church—Canada (LC-MS). Three-way merger discussions took place until 1978 when it was decided that only a two-way merger was possible. The ELCC was the Canada District of the ALC until autonomy in 1967.

The Lutheran Church in Canada traces its history back more than 200 years. Congregations were organized by German Lutherans in Halifax and Lunenburg County in Nova Scotia in 1749. German Lutherans, including many United Empire Loyalists, also settled in large numbers along the St. Lawrence and in Upper Canada. In the late 19th century, immigrants arrived from Scandinavia, Germany, and central European countries, many via the United States. The Lutheran synods in the United States have provided the pastoral support and help for the Canadian church.

HEADQUARTERS

1512 St. James St., Winnipeg, MB R3H 0L2 Tel. (204)786-6707 Fax (204)783-7548
Media Contact, Bishop, Rev. Donald W. Sjoberg

DIVISIONS AND OFFICES

Div. for Canadian Mission, Exec. Dir., Rev. James A. Chell
Div. for Church & Society, Exec. Dir., Rev. Dr. Kenneth C. Kuhn
Div. for College & Univ. Services, Exec. Dir., Rev. Dr. Lawrence Denef
Div. for Parish Life, Exec. Dir.
Div. for Theological Educ. & Leadership, Exec. Dir., Rev. Dr. Lawrence Denef

Div. for World Mission, Exec. Dir., Rev. Peter E. Mathiasen
Ofc. for Communication, ——
Dept. of Fin. & Admn., Dir., Joan E. Nolting
Ofc. for Resource Dev., Exec. Dir., Rev. Richard Husfloen
Evangelical Lutheran Women, Pres., Marquise Sopher
Exec. Dir., Diane Doth Rehbein

SYNODS

Alberta and the Territories: Bishop, Rev. J. Robert Jacobson, 10014-81 Ave., Edmonton, AB T6E 1W8 Tel. (403)439-2636 Fax (403)433-6623
Eastern: Bishop, Rev. Dr. William D. Huras, 50 Queen St. N., Kitchener, ON N2H 6P4 Tel. (519)743-1461 Fax (519)743-4291
British Columbia: Bishop, Rev. Dr. Marlin Aadland, 80-10th Ave., E., New Westminster, BC V3L 4R5 Tel. (604)524-1318 Fax (604)524-9255
Manitoba/Northwestern Ontario: Bishop, Rev. Dr. G. W. Luetkehoelter, 201-3657 Roblin Blvd., Winnipeg, MB R3G 0E2 Tel. (204)889-3760 Fax (204)869-0272
Saskatchewan: Bishop, Rev. Telmor G. Sartison, Bessborough Towers, Rm. 707, 601 Spadina Cres. E., Saskatoon, SK S7K 3G8 Tel. (306)244-2474 Fax (306)664-8677

PERIODICALS

Canada Lutheran; Esprit

The Evangelical Mennonite Conference

The Evangelical Mennonite Conference came about as the result of a renewal movement among a small group of Mennonites in Southern Russia in 1812. Klaas Reimer, a Mennonite minister, had become concerned about the apparent decline of spiritual life in the church, lack of discipline, and the church's backing of the Russian government in the Napoleonic War. Around 1812, Reimer and several others began separate worship services, emphasizing a more strict discipline and separation from the world. By 1814, they were organized as a separate group, called the Kleinegemeinde (small church).

Increasing pressure from the Russian government, particularly in the area of military conscription, finally led to a migration (1874 to 1875) of the entire group to North America. Fifty families settled in Manitoba, and 36 families settled in Nebraska. Ties between the two segments gradually weakened, and eventually the U.S. group gave up its EMC identity.

The conference has passed through numerous difficult times and survived several schisms and migrations. Beginning in the 1940s, a growing vision for missions and concern for others fostered a new vitality and growth, reaching people from a variety of cultural backgrounds. Thirty-two of the 51 congregations are in Manitoba. In 1991 its membership passed 6,000. The conference has some 150 mission workers in 23 countries of the world.

HEADQUARTERS

Box 1268, 440 Main St., Steinbach, MB R0A 2A0 Tel. (204)326-6401 Fax (204)326-1613
Media Contact, Conf. Sec., Don Thiessen

PERIODICAL

Messenger, The

Evangelical Mennonite Mission Conference

Founded in 1936 as the Rudnerweider Mennonite Church in Southern Manitoba and organized as the Evangelical Mennonite Mission Conference in 1959. It was incorporated in 1962. The Annual Conference meeting is held in July.

HEADQUARTERS

526 McMillan Ave., Winnipeg, MB R3L 0N5 Tel. (204)477-1213 Fax (204)477-1214
Media Contact, Mod., Leonard Sawatzky, Box 2126, Steinbach, MB R0A 2A0 Tel. (204)326-3315 Fax (204)326-2759

OTHER ORGANIZATIONS

Missions Dir.: Mr. Lawrence Giesbrecht, Box 927, Altona, MB R0G 0B0 Tel. (204)324-6179
The Gospel Message: Box 1622, Saskatoon, SK S7K 3R8 Tel. (306)242-5001 Fax (306)242-6115; 210-401-33rd St. W., Saskatoon, SK S7L 0V5 Tel. (306)242-5001; Radio Pastor, Rev. Ed Martens; Radio Admn., Ernest Friessen
Aylmer Bible School: Principal, Abe Harms, Box 246, Aylmer, ON N5H 2R9 Tel. (519)773-5095

PERIODICAL

EMMC Recorder

Foursquare Gospel Church of Canada

The Western Canada District was formed in 1964 with the Rev. Roy Hicks as supervisor. Prior to 1964 it had been a part of the Northwest District of the International Church of the Foursquare Gospel with headquarters in Portland, Ore.

A Provincial Society, The Church of the Foursquare Gospel of Western Canada, was formed in 1976; a Federal corporation, the Foursquare Gospel Church of Canada was incorporated in 1981, and a national church formed.

HEADQUARTERS

#200 - 3965 Kingsway, Burnaby, BC V5H 1Y7
Media Contact, Pres. & Gen. Supervisor, Timothy J. Peterson, Tel. (604)439-9567 Fax (604)439-1451

PERIODICALS

News & Views; Canadian Foursquare Challenge

Free Methodist Church in Canada

The Free Methodist Church was founded in New York in 1860 and expanded to Canada in 1880. It is Methodist in doctrine, evangelical in ministry, and emphasizes the teaching of holiness of life through faith in Jesus Christ.

The Free Methodist Church in Canada was incorporated in 1927 after the establishment of a Canadian Executive Board. In 1959 the Holiness Movement Church merged with the Free Methodist Church. Full autonomy for the Canadian church was realized in 1990 with the formation of a Canadian General Conference. Mississauga, Ontario, continues to be the location of the Canadian Headquarters.

The Free Methodist Church ministers in 28 countries through its World Ministries Center in Indianapolis, Indiana. Aldersgate College in Moose Jaw, Saskatchewan, is the church's Canadian college.

HEADQUARTERS

4315 Village Centre Ct., Mississauga, ON L4Z 1S2 Tel. (416)848-2600

PERIODICAL

Free Methodist Herald, The

Free Will Baptists

As revival fires burned throughout New England in the mid- and late 1700s, Benjamin Randall proclaimed his doctrine of Free Will to large crowds of seekers. In due time, a number of Randall's converts moved to Nova Scotia. One such believer was Asa McGray, who was to become instrumental in the establishment of several Free Baptist churches. Local congregations were organized in New Brunswick. After several years of numerical and geographic gains, disagreements surfaced over the question of music, Sunday school, church offerings, salaried clergy, and other issues. Adherents of the more progressive element decided to form their own fellowship. Led by George Orser, they became known as Free Christian Baptists.

The new group faithfully adhered to the truths and doctrines which embodied the theological basis of Free Will Baptists. Largely through Archibald Hatfield, contact was made with Free Will Baptists in the United States in the 1960s. The association was officially welcomed into the Free Will Baptist family in July 1981, by the National Association.

HEADQUARTERS

RR #5, Box 355, Hartland, NB E0J 1N0 Tel. (506)375-4032
Media Contact, Promotional Sec., Rev. Fred D. Hanson, Tel. (506)375-6735 Fax (506)375-8473

PERIODICAL

Gospel Standard, The

General Church of the New Jerusalem

The Church of the New Jerusalem is founded on the Writings of Emanuel Swedenborg (1688-1772). These were first brought to Ontario in 1835 by Christian Enslin.

HEADQUARTERS

40 Chapel Hill Dr., Kitchener, ON N2G 3W5 Tel. (519)748-5802
Media Contact, Exec. Vice-Pres., Rev. Louis D. Synnestvedt

PERIODICALS

New Church Life; New Church Canadian

Greek Orthodox Diocese of Toronto (Canada)

Greek Orthodox Christians in Canada under the jurisdiction of the Ecumenical Patriarchate of Constantinople (Istanbul).

HEADQUARTERS

27 Teddington Park Ave., Toronto, ON M4N 2C4 Tel. (416)322-5055
Media Contact, Sec. to the Bishop, Fr. Stavros Moscitos, Tel. (416)485-5929

Independent Assemblies of God—Canada

This fellowship of churches has been operating in Canada for over 25 years. It is a branch of the Pentecostal Church in Sweden. Each church within the fellowship is completely independent.

HEADQUARTERS

1211 Lancaster St., London, ON N5V 2L4 Tel. (519)451-1751

Media Contact, Gen. Sec., Rev. Harry Wuerch

PERIODICAL

Mantle, The

Independent Holiness Church

The former Holiness Movement of Canada merged with the Free Methodist Church in 1958. Some churches remained independent of this merger and they formed the Independent Holiness Church in 1960, in Kingston, Ontario. The doctrines are Methodist and Wesleyan. The General Conference is every three years, next meeting in 1992.

HEADQUARTERS

Rev. R. E. Votary, Box 194, Sydenham, ON K0H 2T0 Tel. (613)376-3114

Media Contact, Gen. Sec., Dwayne Reaney, 5025 River Rd. RR #1, Manotick, ON K4M 1B2 Tel. (613)692-3237

The Italian Pentecostal Church of Canada

This body had its beginnings in Hamilton, Ontario, in 1912 when a few people of an Italian Presbyterian Church banded themselves together for prayer and received a Pentecostal experience of the baptism in the Holy Spirit. Since 1912, there has been a close association with the teachings and practices of the Pentecostal Assemblies of Canada.

The work spread to Toronto, then to Montrèal, where it also flourished. In 1959, the church was incorporated in the province of Quèbec. The early leaders of this body were the Rev. Luigi Ippolito and the Rev. Ferdinand Zaffuto. The churches carry on their ministry in both the English and Italian languages.

HEADQUARTERS

6724 Fabre St., Montréal, QC H2G 2Z6 Tel. (514)593-1944

Media Contact, Gen. Sec., Rev. John Della Foresta, 6550 Maurice Duplesis, Montréal North, QC H1G 6K9 Tel. (514)323-3087

PERIODICAL

Voce Evangelica/Evangel Voice

Jehovah's Witnesses

For details on Jehovah's Witnesses see the directory in this edition "Religious Bodies in the United States."

HEADQUARTERS

25 Columbia Heights, Brooklyn, NY 11201 Tel. (718)625-3600

Canadian Branch Office: Box 4100, Halton Hills, ON L7G 4Y4

Jewish Organizations in Canada

Jews are spread from coast to coast, with organized communities ranging from Saint John's, Newfoundland, to Victoria, British Columbia. The largest concentrations are in Montréal (some 95,000) and in Toronto (approximately 104,000).

The history of the Jewish Community began in 1760 with the conquest of Québec by the British during the Seven Years War, although a few Jews had come north to Halifax from the Atlantic Colonies as early as 1752. The Colony of Lower Canada (new Québec) had the first considerable settlement, and it was there that, in 1768, a synagogue was organized, cemeteries established, rabbis were invited to officiate, and the community won its battles for official legal status and civic equality.

The first synagogue, Shearith Israel of Montréal, was affiliated with the Spanish-Portuguese Congregation in London and follows its rite to the present day. In 1846, the east European tradition was formally established, and in 1882 the Reform Temple Emanu-El was organized. In mid-19th century the Toronto and Hamilton communities established facilities for worship and for interment of the dead.

After 1880, a large number of immigrants from eastern Europe came to Canada and the present-day community took shape. Its social history parallels that of the United States, with its story of immigrant reception and settlement, industrial life in the garment industries in large cities, the implantation of synagogues in the Russian tradition, and slow integration and development of the community.

In 1919, the Canadian Jewish community united in the Canadian Jewish Congress (CJC) for a short duration. It was revived in 1934 in the face of the internal threat of anti-semitism and the worldwide problems of Jewry. The Canadian Jewish Congress became a unique nationwide institution which arranged for the reception of over 40,000 immigrants in the years following World War II. The Canadian Jewish Congress fought anti-semitism, coordinated development of a school system and voiced concerns of the Jewish community.

The CJC is active through the National Religious Department, which speaks for the varied religious institutions of the community and participates in their behalf in the tripartite commission. The commission unites Jews, Catholics and Protestants in a common program to make the voice of the community of faith heard in the nation, and to strengthen the friendship between the adherents of the Judeao-Christian revelation. In addition, a Committee of Dialogue brings together Jews, Protestants, and Catholics, for understanding in the particular context of French Canada.

A census by the Religious Department of the Canadian Jewish Congress indicates 53 of the synagogues are Orthodox, 43 are Conservative, 14 are Reform and two are Reconstructionist.

Note: The Congregational and Rabbinical Organizations pertaining to Canada are the same as those for the United States and are listed in "Religious Bodies in the United States," under "Jewish Organizations."

HEADQUARTERS

Media Contact, Dir., Communications, Jack Samuel, 3101 Bathurst St. #400, Toronto, ON M6A 2A6 Tel. (416)789-3351 Fax (416)789-9436

EDUC. & SOCIAL SERVICE ORGANIZATIONS

Canada-Israel Securities, Ltd.: State of Israel Bonds, 3101 Bathurst St. #400, Toronto, ON M6A 2A6 Tel. (416)789-3351 Fax (416)789-9436

State of Israel Bonds: Chmn., Melvyn A. Dobrin; Natl. Exec. Dir., Charles Diamond

Canadian Foundation for Jewish Culture: 4600 Bathurst St., Willowdale, ON M2R 3V2 Tel. (416)635-2883; Pres., Mira Koschitzky; Exec. Sec., Edmond Y. Lipsitz

Canadian Jewish Congress: 1590 Ave. Docteur Penfield, Montréal, QC H3G 1C5 Tel. (514)931-7531; Pres., Les Scheininger; Exec. Vice-Pres, Alan Rose

Canadian ORT (Rehab. through Training): 5165 Sherbrooke St. W., Ste. 208, Montréal, QU H4A 1T6 Tel. (514)481-2787; Pres., Bernard Gross; Exec. Dir., Mac Silver

Canadian Sephardi Federation: 210 Wilson Ave., Toronto, ON M5M 3B1 Tel. (416)483-8968; Pres., Maurice Benzacar; Sec., Laeticia Benabou

Canadian Zionist Federation: 5250 Decarie Blvd., Ste. 500, Montréal, QC H3X 2H9 Tel. (514)486-9526; Pres., David J. Azrieli

Hadassah-WIZO Organization of Canada: 1310 Greene Ave., Ste. 900, Montréal, QC H3Z 2B8 Tel. (514)937-9431; Natl. Pres., Naomi Frankenberg; Vice-Pres., Lily Frank

Jewish Immigrant Aid Services of Canada: 5151 Cote St. Catherine Rd., 220 Montréal, QC H3W 1M6 Tel. (514)342-9351; Pres., Sheldon Sper; Exec. Dir., Susan Davis

Jewish Natl. Fund of Canada: 1980 Sherbrooke St. W., Ste. 500, Montréal, QC H3H 1E8 Tel. (514)934-0313; Pres., Neriy J. Bloomfeld; Exec. Vice-Pres., Morris Zilka

Labor Zionist Movement of Canada: 7005 Kildare Rd., Ste. 10, Cote St. Luc, QC H3W 1C1 Tel. (514)484-1789; Pres., David Kofsky; Chmn. Toronto City Committee, Harry Weinstock; Chmn. Montréal City Committee, Harry Froimovitch

Natl. Council of Jewish Women of Canada: 1110 Finch Ave. W., #518, Downsview, ON M3J 2T2 Tel. (416)665-8251

Natl. Council of Jewish Women of Canad: Pres., Gloria Strom

Natl. Council of Jewish Women of Canada: Exec. Dir., Eleanor Appleby

Natl. Joint Community Relations Comm.: Canadian Jewish Congress, 4600 Bathurst St., Willowdale, M2R 3V2 Tel. (416)635-2883; Chpsn., Joseph L. Wilder; Exec. Dir., Manuel Prtuschi

JEWISH WELFARE FUNDS, COMMUNITY COUNCILS

Calgary, Alberta: Calgary Jewish Community Council, 1607 90th Ave., SW, Calgary, AB T2V 4V7 Tel. (403)253-8600; Pres., Hal Joffe; Exec. Dir., Drew Stauffenberg

Edmonton, Alberta: Jewish Federation of Edmonton, 7500-156th St., Edmonton, AB T5R 1X3 Tel. (403)481-3463; Pres., Shelly Maerov; Exec. Dir., Sidney Indig

Hamilton, Ontario: Jewish Fund of Hamilton Wentworth & Area, P.O. Box 7258, 1030 Lower Lion Club Rd., Ancaster, ON L9G 3N6 Tel. (416)648-0605 Fax (416)648-8388; Pres., Gerald Swaye, Q.C.; Exec. Dir., Mark Silverberg

London, Ontario: London Jewish Community Council, 536 Huron St., London, ON N5Y 4J5 Tel. (519)673-1161; Pres., Gloria Gilbert; Exec. Dir., Gerald Enchin

Montréal, Québec: Allied Jewish Services, 5151 Cote St. Catherine Rd., Montréal, QC H3W 1M6 Tel. (514)735-3541 Fax (514)735-8972; Pres., Maxine Sigman; Vice-Pres., John Fishel

Ottawa, Ontario: Jewish Community Council of Ottawa, 151 Chapel St., Ottawa, ON K1N 7Y2 Tel. (613)232-7306 Fax (613)563-4593; Pres., Dr. Eli Rabin; Exec. Dir., Gerry Koffman

Toronto, Ontario: Toronto Jewish Congress, 4600 Bathurst St., Willowdale, ON M2R 3V2 Tel. (416)635-2883 Fax (416)635-1408; Pres., Charles S. Diamond; Exec. Dir., Steven Ain

Vancouver, British Columbia: Jewish Federation of Greater Vancouver, 950 W. 41st Ave., Vancouver, BC V5Z 2N7 Tel. (604)266-7115; Pres., Daniel U. Pekarsky; Exec. Dir., Steve Drysdale

Windsor, Ontario: Jewish Community Council, 1641 Ouellette Ave., Windsor, ON N8X 1K9 Tel. (519)973-1772 Fax (519)973-1774; Pres., Alan R. Orman; Exec. Dir., Allen Juris

Winnipeg, Manitoba: Winnipeg Jewish Community Council, 370 Hargrave, St., Winnipeg, MB R3B 2K1 Tel. (204)943-0406 Fax (204)956-0609; Pres., Sidney Halpern; Exec. Dir., Robert Freedman

PERIODICALS

Bulletin du Congres Juif Canadien; Canadian Jewish Herald; Canadian Jewish News; Canadian Jewish Outlook; Canadian Zionist; Jewish Post and News; Jewish Standard; Jewish Western Bulletin; Journal of Psychology and Judaism; Ottawa Jewish Bulletin & Review; Undzer Veg; Windsor Jewish Federation Bulletin

The Latvian Evangelical Lutheran Church in America

This body was organized into a denomination on Aug. 22, 1975, after having existed as the Federation of Latvian Evangelical Lutheran Churches in America since 1955. This church is a regional constituent part of the Lutheran Church of Latvia in Exile, a member of the Lutheran World Federation and the World Council of Churches.

The Latvian Evangelical Lutheran Church in America works to foster religious life, tradition and customs in its congregations in harmony with the Holy Scriptures, the Apostles', Nicene, and Athanasian Creeds, the unaltered Augsburg Confession, Martin Luther's Small and Large Catechisms and other documents of the Book of Concord.

The LELCA is ordered by its Synod, executive board, auditing committee, and district conferences.

HEADQUARTERS

6551 W. Montrose Ave., Chicago, IL 60634-1499 Tel. (312)725-3820 Fax (312)725-3835
Media Contact, Pres., Rev. Vilis Varsbergs

PERIODICAL

Cela Biedrs

Lutheran Church—Canada

Established in 1959 at Edmonton, Alberta, as a federation of Canadian districts of the Lutheran Church, Missouri Synod; constituted in 1988, at Winnipeg, Manitoba, as an autonomous church.

The church confesses the Bible as both inspired and infallible, the only source and norm of doctrine and life, and subscribes without reservation to the Lutheran Confessions as contained in the Book of Concord of 1580.

Alberta-British Columbia, District Pres., Rev. H. Ruf, 7100 Ada Blvd., Edmonton, AB T5B 4E4 Tel. (403)474-0063 Fax (403)477-9829

Central, District Pres., Dr. R. Holm, 1927 Grant Dr., Regina, SK S4S 4V6 Tel. (306)586-4434 Fax (306)586-0656

200-1625 Dublin Ave., Winnipeg, MB R3H 0W3 Tel. (204)772-0676 Fax (204)772-1090

East, District Pres., Dr. R. Winger, 275 Lawrence Ave., Kitchener, ON N2M 1Y3 Tel. (519)578-6500 Fax (519)578-3369

Media Contact, Pres., Dr. Edwin Lehman

PERIODICALS

Update; Canadian Lutheran

Mennonite Brethren Churches, Canadian Conference of

The conference was incorporated Nov. 22, 1945.

HEADQUARTERS

3-169 Riverton Ave., Winnipeg, MB R2L 2E5 Tel. (204)669-6575 Fax (204)654-1865

Media Contact, Conf. Min., Ike Bergen

PERIODICALS

College Newsletter; Mennonite Brethren Herald; Mennonitische Rundschau; IdeaBank; Lien, Le

Metropolitan Community Churches, Universal Fellowship

The Universal Fellowship of Metropolitan Community Churches is a Christian church which directs a special ministry within, and on behalf of, the gay and lesbian community. Involvement, however, is not exclusively limited to gays and lesbians; U.F.M.C.C. tries to stress its openness to all people and does not call itself a "gay church."

Founded in 1968 in Los Angeles by the Rev. Troy Perry, the U.F.M.C.C. has 250 member congregations worldwide. Thirteen congregations are in Canada, in Victoria, Vancouver, Edmonton, Calgary, Windsor, London, Kitchner, Toronto, Oshawa, Kingston, and Ottawa.

Theologically, the Metropolitan Community Churches stand within the mainstream of Christian doctrine, being "ecumenical" or "interdenominational" in stance (albeit a "denomination" in their own right).

The Metropolitan Community Churches are characterized by their belief that a)the love of God is a gift, freely offered to all people, regardless of "sexual orientation" and that b)no incompatibility exists between human sexuality and the Christian faith.

The Metropolitan Community Churches in Canada were founded in Toronto in 1973 by the Rev. Robert Wolfe.

The Missionary Church of Canada

This denomination in Canada is affiliated with the worldwide body of the Missionary Church. Historically part of the Anabaptist, Mennonite movement, it changed its name to the United Missionary Church in 1947 and in 1969 it merged with the Missionary Church Association of Fort Wayne, Indiana. It is an evangelical, missionary church and became an autonomous national church in Canada in 1987.

Media Contact, Asst. to the Pres., Mr. Murray Bennett, 89 Centre Ave., North York, ON M2M 2L7 Tel. (416)223-3019 Fax (416)229-4017

Moravian Church in America, Northern Province, Canadian District of the

The work in Canada is under the general oversight and rules of the Moravian Church, Northern Province, general offices for which are located in Bethlehem, PA.

HEADQUARTERS

1021 Center St., P.O. Box 1245, Bethlehem, PA 18016-1245

Media Contact, Ed., *The Moravian*, The Rev. Hermann I. Weinlick

PERIODICAL

Moravian, The

Muslims

The Muslim community in Canada is gathered together by Islamic societies and Muslim Mosques. These societies and other organizations are not regarded as religious sects or divisions. Their multiplication arises from the needs of each group in a given area, long distances between groups, and the absence in Islam of organized hierarchy. All the groups hold the same beliefs, aspire to practice the same rituals; namely prayers, fasting, almsgiving, and pilgrimage to Makkah Almukarramah (Mecca).

HEADQUARTERS

Federation of Islamic Associations in the US and Can., 25351 Five Mile Rd., Redford Twp., MI 48239 Tel. (313)535-0014 Fax (313)535-0015

REGIONAL AND NATIONAL GROUPS

Fed. of Islamic Assn. in the US & Can., Sec. Gen., Nihad Hamed, Fax (313)534-1474

Islamic Society of North America, P.O. Box 38, Plainfield, IN 46168 Tel. (317)839-8157

Council of Muslim Communities of Canada, Dir., Dr. Mir Iqbal Ali, 1250 Ramsey View Ct., Ste. 504, Sudbury, ON P3E 2E7 Tel. (705)522-2948

Council of Masajid (Mosques) in the USA, Sec. Gen., Dawud A. Assad, 99 Woodview Dr., Old Bridge, NJ 08857 Tel. (908)679-8617

PERIODICALS

Islamic Horizons, The; Majallat Al-Masjid

Netherlands Reformed Congregations of North America

The Netherlands Reformed Congregations, presently numbering 162 congregations in the Netherlands (90,000 members), 25 congregations in North America (10,000 members), and a handful of congregations in various other countries, organized denominationally in 1907. The so-called Churches Under the Cross (established in 1839 after breaking away from the 1834 secession congregations) and the so-called Ledeboerian churches (established in 1841 under the leadership of Rev. Ledeboer who seceded from the Reformed state church), united in 1907 under the leadership of the then 25-year-old Rev. G. H. Kersten to form the Netherlands Reformed Congregations (Gereformeerde Gemeenten).

Many of the North American congregations left

158

the Christian Reformed Church to join the Netherlands Reformed Congregations after the Kuyperian presupposed regeneration doctrine began making serious inroads into that denomination.

All Netherlands Reformed congregations, office bearers, and members subscribe to three Reformed Forms of Unity: the Belgic Confession of Faith (by DeBres), the Heidelberg Catechism and the Canons of Dordt. The Belgic Confession and Canons of Dordt are read regularly at worship services, and the Heidelberg Catechism is preached weekly except on church feast days.

The NRC stresses the traditional Reformed doctrines of grace, such as the sovereignty of God, responsibility of humankind, the necessity of the new birth, and the experience of God's sanctifying grace.

HEADQUARTERS

Media Contact, Clk. of Synod, Dr. Joel R. Becker, 2115 Romence NE, Grand Rapids, MI 49503 Tel. (616)459-6565 Fax (616)459-7709

PERIODICALS

Banner of Truth; Paul; Insight Into

North American Baptist Conference

Churches belonging to this conference emanated from German Baptist immigrants of more than a century ago. Although scattered across Canada and the U.S., they are bound together by a common heritage, a strong spiritual unity, a Bible-centered faith, and a deep interest in missions.

Note: The details of general organization, officers, and periodicals of this body will be found in the North American Baptist Conference directory in the "Religious Bodies in the United States" section of this Yearbook.

HEADQUARTERS

1 S. 210 Summit Ave., Oakbrook Terrace, IL 60181 Tel. (708)495-2000 Fax (708)495-3301
Media Contact, Dev. Dept. Dir., Dr. Lewis Petrie

PERIODICAL

Baptist Herald

Old Order Amish Church

This is the most conservative branch of the Mennonite Church and direct descendants of Swiss Brethren (Anabaptists) who emerged from the Reformation in Switzerland in 1525. The Amish, followers of Bishop Jacob Ammann, became a distinct group in 1693. They began migrating to North America about 1720; all of them still reside in the United States or Canada. They first migrated to Ontario in 1824 directly from Bavaria, Germany and also from Pennsylvania and Alsace-Lorraine. Since 1953 some Amish have migrated to Ontario from Ohio, Indiana, and Iowa.

No membership figures are kept by this group, and no central headquarters. Each congregation is served by a bishop, two ministers, and a deacon, all of whom are chosen from among the male members by lot for life.

PERIODICALS

Blackboard Bulletin; Budget, The; Diary, The; Die Botschaft; Family Life; Herold der Wahrheit; Young Companion

The Open Bible Standard Churches of Canada

This is the Canadian branch of the Open Bible Standard Churches, Inc., USA of Des Moines, Iowa. It is an evangelical, full gospel denomination emphasizing evangelism, missions, and the message of the Open Bible. The Canadian Branch was chartered Jan. 7, 1982.

HEADQUARTERS

62 Overlea Blvd., Toronto, ON M4H 1N9 Tel. (416)429-3882
Media Contact, Gen. Overseer, C. Russell Archer, P.O. Box 518, Vandalia, OH 45377-0518 Tel. (513)898-2864

Orthodox Church in America (Canada Section)

The Archdiocese of Canada of the Orthodox Church in America was established in 1926. First organized by St. Tikhon, martyr Patriarch of Moscow, previously Archbishop of North America, it is part of the Russian Metropolia and its successor, the autocephaleous Orthodox Church in America.

The Archdiocesan Council meets twice yearly, the General Assembly of the Archdiocese takes place every three years. The next Assembly will be held in July 1993.

HEADQUARTERS

P.O. Box 179, Spencerville, ON K0E 1X0 Tel. (613)925-5226 Fax (613)925-1521

ARCHDIOCESAN COUNCIL

Clergy Members: V. Rev. Nicolas Boldireff; V. Rev. Orest Olekshy; Rev. Lawrence Farley; Rev. Hieromonk Irenee (Rochon); Protodeacon Cyprian Hutcheon
Lay Members: Audrey Ewanchuk; Peter Ferst; Nicholas Ignatieff; Euthymius Katsikas; Constance Kucharczyk; Rhoda Zion
Ex Officio: Chancellor; Treas.; Eastern Sec.; Western Sec.

REPRESENTATIVES TO METROPOLITAN COUNCIL

V. Rev. John Tkachuk
Jim Blizman

The Pentecostal Assemblies of Canada

This body is incorporated under the Dominion Charter of 1919 and is also recognized in the Province of Québec as an ecclesiastical corporation. Its beginnings are to be found in the revivals at the turn of the century, and most of the first Canadian Pentecostal leaders came from a religious background rooted in the Holiness movements.

The original incorporation of 1919 was implemented among churches of eastern Canada only. In the same year, a conference was called in Moose Jaw, Saskatchewan, to which the late Rev. J. M. Welch, general superintendent of the then-organized Assemblies of God in the U.S., was invited. The churches of Manitoba and Saskatchewan were organized as the Western District Council of the Assemblies of God. They were joined later by Alberta and British Columbia. In 1921, a conference was held in Montréal, to which the general chairman of the Assemblies of God was invited. Eastern Canada also became a district of the Assemblies of God, joining Eastern and Western

THE YEAR IN IMAGES

Religious News Service Photo

Pilgrimmage of Trust

Brother Roger, founder of Taize, sits among children in Dayton, Ohio, during the Pilgrimmage of Trust on Earth, five days of worship, study, and prayer. It was the first U.S. pilgrimmage ever for the France-based ecumenical community, with its message of healing and peace.

Canada as two districts in a single organizational union.

In 1920, at Kitchener, Ontario, eastern and western churches agreed to dissolve the Canadian District of the Assemblies of God and unite under the name The Pentecostal Assemblies of Canada.

Today, The Pentecostal Assemblies of Canada operate throughout the nation, and religious services are conducted in more than 27 languages, in more than 200 ethnic churches. There are 109 native churches.

HEADQUARTERS

6745 Century Ave., Mississauga, ON L5N 6P7 Tel. (416)542-7400 Fax (416)542-7313
Media Contact, Gen. Supt., Rev. James M. MacKnight

DISTRICT SUPERINTENDENTS

British Columbia: Rev. Lester E. Markham, 5641 176 A St., Surrey, BC V3S 4G8 Tel. (604)576-9421 Fax (604)576-1499
Alberta: Rev. John A. Keys, 10585-111 St., #101, Edmonton, AB T5H 3E8 Tel. (403)426-0084 Fax (403)420-1318
Saskatchewan: Rev. L. Calvin King, 119-C Cardinal Cres., Saskatoon, SK S7L 6H5 Tel. (306)652-6088
Manitoba: Rev. Gordon V. Peters, #201, 3303 Portage Ave., Winnipeg, MB R3K 0W7 Tel. (204)885-2125 Fax (204)888-6319

Western Ontario: Rev. W. D. Morrow, #100, 3410 S. Service Rd., Burlington, ON L7M 3T2 Tel. (416)637-5566 Fax (416)637-7558
Eastern Ontario and Québec: Rev. E. Stewart Hunter, Box 1600, Belleville, ON K8N 5J3 Tel. (613)968-3422 Fax (613)968-8715
Maritime Provinces: Rev. David C. Slauenwhite, Box 1184, Truro, NS B2N 5H1 Tel. (902)895-4212 Fax (902)897-0705

CONFERENCES

German Conference: Rev. Horst Doberstein, P.O. Box 2310, Stn. B, St. Catharines, ON L2M 7M7
French Conference: Rev. Raymond Lemaire, 4975 Sir Wilfred Laurier Blvd., St. Hubert, QC J3Y 7R6
Slavic Conferences: Eastern District, Rev. Walter Senko, RR 1, Wilsonville, ON N0E 1Z0; Western District, Rev. Michael Brandebura, 4108-134 Ave., Edmonton, AB T5A 3M2
Finnish Conference: Rev. A. Wirkkala, 1920 Argyle Dr., Vancouver, BC V5P 2A8

PERIODICAL

Pentecostal Testimony

Pentecostal Assemblies of Newfoundland

This body began in 1910 and held its first assembly at the Bethesda Pentecostal Mission at St. John's. It was incorporated in 1925 as the Bethesda Pentecostal Assemblies and changed its name in 1930 to the Pentecostal Assemblies of Newfoundland.

HEADQUARTERS

57 Thorburn Rd., St. John's, NF A1B 3N4 Tel. (709)753-6314 Fax (709)753-4945
Media Contact, Gen. Sec.-Treas., Clarence Buckle, P.O. Box 8895, Station A, St. John's, NF A1B 3T2 Tel. (709)753-6314 Fax (709)753-4945

DEPARTMENTS

Youth & Sunday School, Dir., Robert H. Dewling, 26 Wicklow St., St. John's, NF A1B 3H2
Literature, Gen. Mgr., Calvin T. Andrews, 28 Royal Oak Dr., St. John's, NF A1G 1S3
Women's Ministries, Dir., Mrs. Sylvia Purchase, Box 64, R.R. #3, Botwood, NF A0H 1E0
Men's Fellowship, Dir., Gordon W. Young, 7 Stamp's Lane, St. John's, NF A1E 3C9

PERIODICAL

Good Tidings

Pentecostal Holiness Church of Canada

The first General Conference convened in May, 1971 in Toronto. Prior to this, the Canadian churches were under the leadership of the Pentecostal Holiness Church in the U.S.A. The General Conference meets every four years. The next meeting is in 1994.

HEADQUARTERS

Box 442, Waterloo, ON N2J 4A9 Tel. (519)746-1310

Polish National Catholic Church of Canada

This Diocese was created at the XII General Synod of the Polish National Catholic Church of America in October, 1967. Formerly, the Canadian parishes were a part of the Western Diocese and Buffalo-Pittsburgh Diocese of the Polish National Catholic Church in America.

HEADQUARTERS

186 Cowan Ave., Toronto, ON M6K 2N6 Tel. (416)537-1706

Media Contact, Bishop, The Rt. Rev. Joseph Nieminski, 296 Mill Rd. #F-5, Etobicoke, ON M9C 4X8 Tel. (416)626-1095

Presbyterian Church in America (Canadian Section)

Canadian congregations of the Reformed Presbyterian Church, Evangelical Synod, became a part of the Presbyterian Church in America when the RPCES joined PCA in June 1982. Some of the churches were in predecessor bodies of the RPCES, which was the product of a 1965 merger of the Reformed Presbyterian Church in North America, General Synod, and the Evangelical Presbyterian Church. Others came into existence later as a part of the home missions work of RPCES. Congregations are located in six provinces, and the PCA is continuing church extension work in Canada. The denomination is committed to world evangelization and to a continuation of historic Presbyterianism. Its officers are required to subscribe to the Reformed faith as set forth in the Westminster Confession of Faith and Catechisms.

HEADQUARTERS

Media Contact, Correspondent, Doug Codling, Faith Reformed Presbyterian Church, 2581 E. 45th St., Vancouver, BC V5R 3B9 Tel. (604)438-8755

PERIODICAL

Coast to Coast

The Presbyterian Church in Canada

This is the nonconcurring portion of the Presbyterian Church in Canada that did not become a part of The United Church of Canada in 1925.

HEADQUARTERS

50 Wynford Dr., Don Mills, ON M3C 1J7 Tel. (416)441-1111 Fax (416)441-2825

Media Contact, Principal Clk., Rev. Thomas Gemmell, 50 Wynford Drive, Don Mills, ON M3C 1J7 Tel. (416)441-1111 Fax (416)441-2825

PERIODICALS

Presbyterian Record; Glad Tidings; Vie Chrétienne, La

Reformed Church in Canada

The Canadian branch of the Reformed Church in America consists of 36 churches organized under the Council of the Reformed Church in Canada and within the classis of Ontario (20 churches), Cascades (15 churches), Lake Erie (one church). The Reformed Church in America was established in 1628 by the earliest Dutch settlers in America as the Reformed Protestant Dutch Church. It is evangelical in theology and presbyterian in government.

HEADQUARTERS

Gen. Sec., Rev. Edwin G. Mulder, 475 Riverside Dr., New York, NY 10115 Tel. (212)870-2841 Fax (212)870-2499

Council of the Reformed Church in Canada, Exec. Sec., Rev. Dr. Jonathan N. Gerstner, Reformed Church Center, RR #4, Cambridge, ON N1R 5S5 Tel. (519)622-1777

Media Contact, Dir., Promotion, Comm., & Dev., Rev. E. Wayne Antworth, 475 Riverside Drive, New York, NY 10115 Tel. (212)870-2954 Fax (212)870-2499

Reformed Doukhobors, Christian Community and Brotherhood of

Doukhobors were founded in the late 17th century in Russia. Their doctrine is the *Living Book*, which is based on traditional songs and chants and on contents of the Bible. The *Living Book* is memorized by each generation.

HEADQUARTERS

Site 8, Comp. 52, RR 1, Crescent Valley, BC V0G 1H0

Media Contact, Sonya Sapriken

The Reformed Episcopal Church

The Reformed Episcopal Church is a separate entity. It was established in Canada by an act of incorporation given royal assent on June 2, 1886. It maintains the founding principles of episcopacy (in historic succession from the apostles), Anglican liturgy, Reformed doctrine and evangelical zeal, and in its practice, continues to recognize the validity of certain nonepiscopal orders of evangelical ministry.

HEADQUARTERS

628 Royal Ave., New Westminster, BC V3M 1J2

Media Contact, Sec., Mrs. B. Gamble, #5-4603 Evergreen La., Ladner, BC V4K 2W7

Reinland Mennonite Church

This group was founded in 1958 when 10 ministers and approximately 600 members separated from the Sommerfelder Mennonite Church. In 1968, four ministers and about 200 members migrated to Bolivia. The church has work in six communities in Manitoba and one in Ontario.

HEADQUARTERS

Bishop William H. Friesen, P.O. Box 96, Rosenfeld, MB R0G 1X0 Tel. (204)324-6339

Media Contact, Decon, Henry Wiebe, Box 2587, Winkler, MB R6W 4C3 Tel. (204)325-8487

Reorganized Church of Jesus Christ of Latter Day Saints

Founded April 6, 1830, by Joseph Smith, Jr., the church was reorganized under the leadership of the founder's son, Joseph Smith III, in 1860. The Church is established in 38 countries including the United States and Canada, with nearly a quarter of a million members. A biennial world conference is held in Independence, Missouri. The current president is Wallace B. Smith, greatgrandson of the founder.

HEADQUARTERS

World Headquarters Complex: The Auditorium, The Temple, P.O. Box 1059, Independence, MO 64051 Tel. (816)833-1000 Fax (816)521-3095

Ontario Regional Ofc.: 390 Speedvale Ave. E., Guelph, ON N1E 1N5

Media Contact, Public Relations Coordinator, Stephanie Kelley, World Headquarters

CANADIAN REGIONS AND DISTRICTS

North. Plains & Prairie Provinces Region: Regional Admn., Alvin Mogg, 119 MacEwan Pack Heights NW, Calgary, AB T3K 3W6

No. Plains & Prairie Provinces Region: Alberta District, G Ivan Miller, #31 135 Jerry Potts Blvd. West, Lethbridge, AB T1K 6H2; Saskatchewan District, Charles J. Lester, 629 East Place, Saskatoon, SK S7J 2Z1

Pacific Northwest Region: Regional Admn., Raymond Peter, P.O. Box 18469, 4820 Morgan, Seattle, WA 98118; British Columbia District, Dennis L. McKelvie, 207-25 Richmond St., New Westminster, BC V3L 5P9

Ontario Region: Regional Admn., Donald H. Comer, 390 Speedvale Ave. E., Guelph, ON N1E 1N5; Chatham District, David R. Wood, 127 Mount Pleasant, Wallaceburg, ON N8A 5A3; Grand River District, Douglas A. Robinson, 7 Kennedy Drive, Breslau, ON N0B 1M0; London District, John H. German, 354 Erie St., Port Stanley, ON N0L 2A0; Northern Ontario District, Donald Arrowsmith, 917 Woodbine Ave., Sudbury, ON P3A 2L8; Ottawa District, Roy A. Young, RR #4, Odessa, ON K0H 2H0; Owen Sound District, Robin M. Duff, P.O. Box 52, Owen Sound, ON N1K 5P1; Toronto Metropole, Larry D. Windland, 8142 Islington Ave. N., Woodridge, ON L4L 1B7

The Roman Catholic Church in Canada

The largest single body of Christians in Canada, the Roman Catholic Church is under the spiritual leadership of His Holiness the Pope. Catholicism in Canada dates back to 1534, when the first Mass was celebrated on the Gaspé Peninsula on July 7, by a priest accompanying Jacques Cartier. Catholicism had been implanted earlier by fishermen and sailors from Europe. Priests came to Acadia as early as 1604. Traces of a regular colony go back to 1608 when Champlain settled in Québec City. The Recollets (1615), followed by the Jesuits (1625) and the Sulpicians (1657), began the missions among the native population. The first official Roman document relative to the Canadian missions dates from March 20, 1618. Bishop Fran(ois de Montmorency-Laval, the first bishop, arrived in Québec in 1659. The church developed in the East, but not until 1818 did systematic missionary work begin in western Canada.

In the latter 1700s, English-speaking Roman Catholics, mainly from Ireland and Scotland, began to arrive in Canada's Atlantic provinces. After 1815 Irish Catholics settled in large numbers in what is now Ontario. The Irish potato famine of 1847 greatly increased that population in all parts of eastern Canada.

By the 1850s the Catholic Church in both English- and French-speaking Canada had begun to erect new dioceses and found many religious communities. These communities did educational, medical, and charitable work among their own people as well as among Canada's native peoples. By the 1890s large numbers of non-English and non-French-speaking Catholics had settled in Canada, especially in the Western provinces. In the 20th century the pastoral horizons have continued to expand to meet the needs of what has now become a very multiracial church.

HEADQUARTERS

Media Contact, Dir. of Information, Mr. Dennis Gruending, 90 Parent St., Ottawa, ON K1N 7B1

CANADIAN ORGANIZATION

Canadian Conference of Catholic Bishops: (Conférence des évêques cath. du Canada), 90 Parent Ave., Ottawa, ON K1N 7B1 Tel. (613)236-9461 Fax (613)236-8117

EXECUTIVE COMMITTEE

National Level

Pres., Most Rev. Marcel A. J. Gervais, Archbishop of Ottawa

Vice-Pres., Mgr. Jean-Guy Hamelin, (Rouyn-Noranda)

Co-Treas.: Most Rev., Mgr. Jean-Louis Plouffe, (Sault Ste. Marie); Most Rev. Francis J. Spence, (Kingston)

EPISCOPAL COMMISSIONS

National Level

Social Affairs, Most Rev. J. Faber MacDonald

Canon Law—Inter-rite, Most Rev. Charles A. Halpin

Relations with Assoc. of Priests, Religious, & Laity, Most Rev. Jacques Berthelet

Missions, Most Rev. Jean-Guy Couture

Ecumenism, Most Rev. Donat Chiasson

Theology, Msgr. Brendan O'Brien

Sector Level

Comm. sociales, Msgr. Louis-de-Gonzaque Langevin

Social Comm., Most Rev. John A. O'Mara

Education Chrétien, Msgr. Jean Gratton

Christian Education, Most Rev. Frederick B. Henry

Liturgie, Msgr. Raymond Saint-Gelais

Liturgy, Most Rev. Raymond J. Lahey

OFFICES

Secteur français

Office des Missions, Dir., Père Lucien Casterman, O.M.I.

Office des communications sociales, Dir., Abbé Lucien Labelle, 4005, rue de Bellechasse, Montréal, QC H1X 1J6 Tel. (514)729-6391 Fax (514)729-7375

Office national de liturgie, coordonnateur, M. l'abbé Paul Boily, 3530, rue Adam, Montréal, QC H1W 1Y8 Tel. (514)522-4930

Service incroyance et foi, Dir., Père Gilles Langevin, s.j., 7400, boulevard Saint-Laurent, Montréal, QC H2R 2Y1 Tel. (514)948-3186

Centre canadien d'oecuménisme, Rev. Thomas Ryan, C.S.P., 2065 ouest, rue Sherbrooke, Montréal, QC H3H 1G6 Tel. (514)937-9176 Fax (514)935-5497

Services des relations publiques, Dir., M. Jacques Binet

Service des Editions, Dir., Mlle Claire Dubé

English Sector

Natl. Liturgical Ofc., Dir., Rev. John Hibbard

Natl. Ofc. of Religious Educ., Dir., Mrs. Bernadette Tourangeau

Ofc. for Missions, Dir., Fr. Lucien Casterman, O.M.I.

Public Information Ofc., Dir., Mr. Dennis Gruending

Social Affairs, Dir., Mr. Tony Clarke

REGIONAL EPISCOPAL ASSEMBLIES

Atlantic Episcopal Assembly: Pres., Msgr. Gérard Dionne; Vice-Pres., Most Rev. J. Edward Troy, C.S.C.; Sec., Rev. Guy Léger, C.S.C., Site 1 Boîte 389, R.R. 1, St. Joseph, NB E0A 2Y0 Tel. (506)758-2531 Fax (506)758-1187

Assemblée des évêques du Que: Prés., Mgr. Bernard Hubert; Vice-Pres., Mgr. Maurice Couture;

Sécretaire général, L'abbé Clément Vigneault; Secrétariat, 1225 Boulevard Saint Joseph est, Montréal, QC H2J 1L7 Tel. (514)274-4323 Fax (514)274-4383

Ontario Conference of Catholic Bishops: Pres., Most Rev. John O'Mara; Vice-Pres., Msgr. Eugéne LaRocque; Sec., Rev. Angus J. Macdougall, S.J.; Secretariat, 67 Bond St., Ste. 304, Toronto, ON M5B 1X5 Tel. (416)368-1804 Fax (416)368-6687

Western Catholic Conference: Pres., Msgr. Antoine Hacault; Vice-Pres., Most Rev. Maxim Hermaniuk; Sec., Msgr. Peter Sutton, 108-1st St., West, P.O. Box 270, Le Pas, MB R9A 1K4 Tel. (204)623-6152 Fax (204)623-6121

MILITARY ORDINARIATE

Ordinaire aux forces canadiennes: Msgr. André Vallée, p.m.é., National Defense Headquarters, Ottawa, ON K1A 0k2 Tel. (613)992-1261

Canadian Religious Conference: Sec. Gen., Sr. Henriette Laliberte, C.S.C., 324 Laurier Ave. East, Ottawa, ON K1N 6P6 Tel. (613)236-0824 Fax (613)236-0825

LATIN RITE

Alexandria-Cornwall: Msgr. Eugéne P. LaRocque, Centre diocésain, 220 Chemin Montréal, C. P. 1388, Cornwall, ON K6H 5V4 Tel. (613)933-1138

Amos: Evêché, Msgr. Gérard Drainville, 450, Principale Nord, Amos, QC J9T 2M1 Tel. (819)732-6515

Antigonish: Bishop Colin Campbell, Chancery Office, 155 Main St., P.O. Box 1330, Antigonish, NS B2G 2L7 Tel. (902)863-4818

Baie-Comeau: Evêché, Msgr. Pierre Morissette, 639 Rue de Bretagne, Baie-Comeau, QC G5C 1X2 Tel. (418)589-5744

Bathurst: Evêché, Msgr. André Richard, 645, avenue Murray, C.P. 460, Bathurst, NB E2A 3Z4 Tel. (506)546-3493

Calgary: Bishop Paul J. O'Byrne, Bishop's Office, 1916 Second St. S.W., Calgary, AB T2S 1S3 Tel. (403)228-4501

Charlottetown: Most Rev. Joseph Vernon Fougère, D.D., P.O. Box 907, Charlottetown, PE C1A 7L9 Tel. (902)368-8005

Chicoutimi: Evêché, Msgr. Jean-Guy Couture, 602 est, rue Racine, C.P. 278, Chicoutimi, QC G7H 6J6 Tel. (418)543-0783

Churchill-Baie D'Hudson: Evêché, Msgr. Reynald Rouleau, O.M.I., C.P. 10, Churchill, MB R0B 0E0 Tel. (204)675-2541

Archdiocese of Edmonton: Archbishop, Joseph N. MacNeil, Archdiocesan Office, 8421-101st Ave., Edmonton, AB T6A 0L1 Tel. (403)469-1010

Edmundson: Evêché, Msgr. Gérard Dionne, Centre diocésain, Edmundston, NB E3V 3K1 Tel. (506)735-5578

Gaspé: Evêché, —— C.P. 440, Gaspé, QC G0C 1R0 Tel. (418)368-2274

Gatineau-Hull: Archévêché, Msgr. Roger Ebacher, 180, boulevard Mont-Bleu, Hull, QC J8X 3J5 Tel. (819)771-8391

Grand Falls: Bishop, Joseph Faber MacDonald, Chancery Office, P.O. Box 397, Grand Falls, NF A2A 2J8 Tel. (709)489-4019

Gravelbourg: Secrétariat, Msgr. Noel Delaquis, C.P. 690, Gravelbourg, SK S0H 1X0 Tel. (306)648-2615

Archidiocèse de Grouard-McLennan: Archévêché, Msgr. Henri Légaré, C.P. 388, McLennan, AB T0H 2L0 Tel. (403)324-3002

Archdiocese of Halifax: Archbishop, Austin E. Burke, Archbishop's Residence, 6541 Coburg Rd., P.O. Box 1527, Halifax, NS B3J 2Y3 Tel. (902)429-9388

Hamilton: Bishop, Bishop Anthony Tonnos, 700 King St. W., Hamilton, ON L8P 1C7 Tel. (416)528-7988

Hearst: Evêché, Msgr. Roger A. Despatie, 76, 7 rue C.P. 1330, Hearst, ON P0L 1N0 Tel. (705)362-4903

Joliette: Evêché, Msgr. Gilles Lussier, 2 rue St.-Charles Borromée, Nord. C.P. 470, Joliette, QC J6E 6H6 Tel. (514)753-7596

Kamloops: Bishop, Lawrence Sabatini, Bishop's Residence, 635A Tranquille Rd., Kamloops, BC V2B 3H5 Tel. (604)376-3351

Archidiocèse de Keewatin-LePas: Archbishop, Peter-Alfred Sutton, Résidence, 108 1st St. W., C.P. 270, Le Pas, MB R9A 1K4 Tel. (204)623-3529

Archdiocese of Kingston: Archbishop, Francis J. Spence, 390 Palace Rd., Kingston, ON K7L 4X3 Tel. (613)548-4461

Labrador City-Schefferville: Evêché, Msgr. Henri Goudreault, 318 Ave. Elizabeth, Labrador City, Labrador, NF A2V 2K7 Tel. (709)944-2046

London: Bishop, John M. Sherlock, Chancery Office, 1070 Waterloo St., London, ON N6A 3Y2 Tel. (519)433-0658

Mackenzie-Fort Smith (T.No.O.): Evêché, Msgr. Denis Croteau, 5117, 52 rue, Bag 8900, Fort Smith, T.N.O, X1A 1T7 Tel. (403)920-2129

Archidiocèse de Moncton: Archévêché, Msgr. Donat Chiasson, C.P. 248, Moncton, NB E1C 8K9 Tel. (506)857-9531

Mont-Laurier: Evêché, Msgr. Jean Gratton, 435 rue de la Madone, C.P. 1290, Mont Laurier, QC J9L 1S1 Tel. (819)623-5530

Archidiocèse de Montréal: Archévêché, Msgr. Jean-Claude Turcotte, 2000 ouest rue Sherbrooke, Montréal, QC H3H 1G4 Tel. (514)931-7311

Monsonee: Msgr. Vincent Cadieux, Résidence, C.P. 40, Moosonee, ON P0L 1Y0 Tel. (705)336-2908

Abbatia Mullius of Muenster: Rt. Rev. Peter Novecosky, OSB, Abbot's Residence, St. Peter's Abbey, Muenster, SK S0K 2Y0 Tel. (306)682-5521

Nelson: Bishop Peter Mallon, Chancery Office, 813 Ward St., Nelson, BC V1L 1T4 Tel. (604)352-6921

Nicolet: Evêché, Msgr. Raymond Saint-Gelais, C.P. 820, Nicolet, QC J0G 1E0 Tel. (819)293-4234

Archidiocèse D'Ottawa: Chancellerie, Msgr. Marcel Gervais, 1247, avenue Kilborn, Ottawa, ON K1H 6K9 Tel. (613)738-5025

Pembroke: Bishop, J. R. Windle, Bishop's Residence, 188 Renfrew St., P.O. Box 7, Pembroke, ON K8A 6X1 Tel. (613)732-3895

Peterborough: Bishop, James L. Doyle, Bishop's Residence, 350 Hunter St. W., Peterborough, ON K9J 6Y8 Tel. (705)745-5123

Prince-Albert: Evêché, Msgr. Blaise Morand, 1415-ouest, 4e Ave. West, Prince-Albert, SK S6V 5H1 Tel. (306)922-4747

Prince-George: —— , Chancery Office, 2935 Highway 16 West, P.O. Box 7000, Prince George, BC V2N 3Z2 Tel. (604)964-4424

Archidiocèse de Québec: Archévêché, Msgr. Maurice Couture, 2 rue Port Dauphin, C.P. 459, Québec, QC G1R 4R6 Tel. (418)692-3935

Archdiocese of Regina: Archbishop, Charles A. Halpin, Chancery Office, 455 Broad St. North, Regina, SK S4R 2X8 Tel. (306)352-1651

Archidiocèse de Rimouski: Archévêché, Msgr. Bertrand Blanchet, 34 ouest, rue de L'évêché, ouest C.P. 730, Rimouski, QC G5L 7C7 Tel. (418)723-3320

Rouyn-Moranda: Evêché, Msgr. Jean-Guy Hamelin, 515 avenue Cuddihy, C.P. 1060, Rouyn-Noranda, QC J9X 5W9 Tel. (819)764-4660

Ste-Anne de la Pocatière: Evêché, Msgr. André Gaumond, C.P. 430 La Pocatière, Pocatière, QC G0R 1Z0 Tel. (418)856-1811

Archidiocèse de Saint-Boniface: Archévêché, Msgr. Antoine Hacault, 151 ave de la Cathédrale, St-Boniface, MB R2H 0H6 Tel. (204)237-9851

St. Catharine's: Bishop, Thomas B. Fulton, Bishop's Residence, 122 Riverdale Ave., St. Catharines, ON L2R 4C2 Tel. (416)684-0154

St. George's: Bishop, Raymond J. Lahey, Bishop's Residence, 16 Hammond Dr., Corner Brook, NF A2H 2W2 Tel. (709)639-7073

Saint Hyacinthe: Evêché, Msgr. Louis-de-Gonzaque Langevin, 1900 ouest Girouard, C. P. 190, Saint-Hyacinthe, QC J2S 7B4 Tel. (514)773-8581

Saint-Jean-de-Longueuil: Evêché, Msgr. Bernard Hubert, 740 boul. Ste-Foy, C.P. 40, Longueuil, QC J4K 4X8 Tel. (514)679-1100

Saint-Jérome: Evêché, Msgr. Charles Valois, 355 rue St-Georges, C.P. 580, Saint-Jér‰ome, QC J7Z 5V3 Tel. (514)432-9741

Saint John: Bishop, J. Edward Troy, Chancery Office, 1 Bayard Dr., Saint John, NB E2L 3L5 Tel. (506)632-9222

Archdiocese of St. John's: Archbishop, James H. MacDonald, Archbishop's Residence, P.O. Box 37, Basilica Residence, St. John's, NF A1C 5H5 Tel. (709)726-3660

Saint-Paul: Evêché, Msgr. Raymond Roy, 4410 51e Ave., St-Paul, AB T0A 3A2 Tel. (403)645-3277

Saskatoon: Bishop, James P. Mahoney, Chancery Office, 106 - 5th Ave. N., Saskatoon, SK S7K 2N7 Tel. (306)242-1500

Sault Ste. Marie: Bishop, Jean-Louis Plouffe, Bishop's Residence, 480 McIntyre St., W., P.O. Box 510, North Bay, ON P1B 8J1 Tel. (705)476-1300

Archidiocèse de Sherbrooke: Archévêché, Msgr. Jean-Marie Fortier, 130 rue de la Cathedrale, C.P. 430, Sherbrooke, QC J1H 5K1 Tel. (819)563-9934

Thunder Bay: Bishop, John A. O'Mara, Bishop's Residence, P.O. Box 756, Thunder Bay, ON P7C 4W6 Tel. (807)622-8144

Timmins: Most Rev. Gilles Cazabon, O.M.I., 65, avenue Jubilee est, Timmins, ON P4N 5W4 Tel. (705)267-6224

Archdiocese of Toronto: Archbishop, Aloysius M. Ambrozic, Chancery Office, 355 Church St., Toronto, ON M5B 1Z8 Tel. (416)977-1500

Trois-Rivièrés: Evêché, Msgr. Laurent Noel, 362 rue Bonaventure, C.P. 879, Trois-Rivièrès, QC G9A 5J9 Tel. (819)374-9847

Valleyfield: Evêché, Msgr. Robert Lebel, 11 rue de l'Eglise, Valleyfield, QC J6T 1J5 Tel. (514)373-8122

Archdiocese of Vancouver: Archbishop, Adam Exner, Chancery Office, 150 Robson St., Vancouver, BC V6B 2A7 Tel. (604)683-0281

Victoria: Bishop, Remi J. De Roo, Bishop's Office, 1 - 4044 Nelthorpe St., Victoria, BC V8X 2A1 Tel. (604)479-1331

Whitehorse (Yukon): Bishop, Thomas Lobsinger, O.M.I. Bishop's Residence, 5119 5th Ave., Whitehorse, YT Y1A 1L5 Tel. (403)667-2052

Archdiocese of Winnipeg: Most Rev. Leonard J. Wall, 1495 Pembina Hwy., Winnipeg, ON R3T 2C6 Tel. (204)452-2227

Yarmouth: ——, 53 rue Park, Yarmouth, NS B5A 4B2 Tel. (902)742-7163

EASTERN RITES

Eparchy of Edmonton Eparch: Most Rev. Myron Daciuk, V Eparch's Residence, 6240 Ada Blvd., Edmonton, AB T5W 4P1 Tel. (403)479-0381

Eparchy of New Westminster: Eparch, —— Eparch's Residence, 502 5th Ave., New Westminster, BC V3L 1S2 Tel. (604)521-8015

Eparchy of Saskatoon: Eparch, Most Rev. Basil Filevich, Eparch's Residence, 866 Saskatchewan. Crescent East, Saskatoon, SK S7N 0L4 Tel. (306)653-0138

Ukrainian Eparchy of Toronto: Eparch, Most Rev. Isidore Borecky, Eparch's Residence, 61 Glen Edyth Dr., Toronto, ON M4V 2V8 Tel. (416)924-2381

Ukrainian Archeparchy of Winnipeg: Archeparchy, Most Rev. Maxim Hermaniuk, Archiparch's Residence, 235 Scotia St., Winnipeg, MB R2V 1V7 Tel. (204)339-7457

Toronto, Ontario Eparchy: Eparch, Most Rev. Michael Rusnak, Chancery Office, 223 Carlton Rd., Unionville, ON L3R 3M2 Tel. (416)477-4867

Montréal (Qué) Archéparchie: Pour Les Grecs-Melkites, Archéparque, Msgr. Michel Hakim, Chancelerie: 34 Maplewood, Montréal, QC H2V 2M1 Tel. (514)272-6430

Archéparchie de Montréal: Archéparque, Msgr. Georges Abi-Saber, 12475, rue Grenet, Montréal, QC H4J 2K4 Tel. (514)331-2807

Romanian Orthodox Church in America (Canadian Parishes)

The first Romanian Orthodox immigrants in Canada called for Orthodox priests from their native country of Romania. Between 1902 and 1914, they organized the first Romanian parish communities and built Orthodox churches in different cities and farming regions of western Canada (Alberta, Saskatchewan, Manitoba) as well as in the eastern part (Ontario and Québec).

In 1929, the Romanian Orthodox parishes from Canada joined with those of the United States in a Congress held in Detroit, Mich., and asked the Holy Synod of the Romanian Orthodox Church of Romania to establish a Romanian Orthodox Missionary Episcopate in America. The first Bishop, Policarp (Morushca), was elected and consecrated by the Holy Synod of the Romanian Orthodox Church and came to the United States in 1935. He established his headquarters in Detroit with jurisdiction over all the Romanian Orthodox parishes in the United States and Canada.

In 1950, the Romanian Orthodox Church in America (i.e. the Romanian Orthodox Missionary Episcopate in America) was granted administrative autonomy by the Holy Synod of the Romanian Orthodox Church of Romania, and only doctrinal and canonical ties remain with this latter body.

In 1974 the Holy Synod of the Romanian Orthodox Church of Romania recognized and approved the elevation of the Episcopate to the rank of Archdiocese.

HEADQUARTERS

Canadian Office: St. Demetrios Romanian Orthodox Church, 103 Furby St., Winnipeg, MB R3C 2A4 Tel. (204)775-6472

Media Contact, The Romanian Orthodox Archdiocese in America and Canada, Most Rev. Archbishop Victorin, 19959 Riopelle St., Detroit, MI 48203. Tel. (313)893-8390

PERIODICALS

Calendarul Credinta (Yearbook with Church Directory); Credinta—The Faith

The Romanian Orthodox Episcopate of America (Jackson, MI)

This body of Eastern Orthodox Christians of Romanian descent was organized in 1929 as an autonomous Diocese under the jurisdiction of the Romanian Patriarchate. In 1951, it severed all relations with the Orthodox Church of Romania. Now under the canonical jurisdiction of the autocephalous Orthodox Church in America, it enjoys full administrative autonomy and is headed by its own bishop.

HEADQUARTERS

2522 Grey Tower Rd., Jackson, MI 49201 Tel. (517)522-4800 Fax (517)522-5907

Media Contact, Ed./Sec., David Oancea, P.O. Box 185, Grass Lake, MI 49240-0185 Tel. (517)522-4800 Fax (517)522-5907

OTHER ORGANIZATIONS

The American Romanian Orthodox Youth: Pres., Emily Lipovan, 3451 West Blvd., Cleveland, OH 44111

Assoc. of Romanian Orthodox Ladies Auxs.: Pauline Trutza, 1446 Waterbury Ave., Lakewood, OH 44107

Orthodox Brotherhood of Canada: Pres., Thrisia Pana, #510-2243 Hamilton St., Regina, SK S4P 4B6

Orthodox Brotherhood, USA: Pres., George Aldea, 824 Mt. Vernon Blvd., Royal Oak, MI 48073

PERIODICAL

Solia/The Herald

Russian Orthodox Church in Canada, Patriarchal Parishes of the

Diocese of Canada of the former Exarchate of North and South America of the Russian Orthodox Church. Originally founded in 1897 by the Russian Orthodox Archdiocese in North America.

HEADQUARTERS

St. Barbara's Russian Orthodox Cathedral, 10105 96th St., Edmonton, AB T5H 2G3

Media Contact, Sec.-Treas., Victor Lopushinsky, #303 9566-101 Ave., Edmonton, AB T5H 0B4 Tel. (403)455-9071

The Salvation Army in Canada

The Salvation Army, an evangelical branch of the Christian Church, is an international movement founded in 1865 in London, England. The ministry of Salvationists, consisting of clergy (officers) and laity, comes from a commitment to Jesus Christ and is revealed in practical service, regardless of race, color, creed, sex, or age.

The goals of The Salvation Army are to preach the gospel, disseminate Christian truths, instill Christian values, enrich family life, and improve the quality of all life.

To attain these goals, The Salvation Army operates local congregations, provides counseling, supplies basic human needs, and undertakes spiritual and moral rehabilitation of any needy people who come within its influence.

A quasi-military system of government was set up in 1878, by General William Booth, founder (1829-1912). Converts from England started Salvation Army work in London, Ontario, in 1882. Two years later, Canada was recognized as a Territorial Command, and since 1933 it has included Bermuda. An act to incorporate the Governing Council of The Salvation Army in Canada received royal assent on May 19, 1909.

HEADQUARTERS

Salvation Square, P.O. Box 4021, Postal Sta. A, Toronto, ON M5W 2B1 Tel. (416)598-2071

Media Contact, Asst. Public Rel. Sec. for Comm. & Spec. Events, Major Gary Venables, P.O. Box 4021, Stn. A, Toronto, ON M5W 2B1 Tel. (416)340-2162 Fax (416)598-1672

PERIODICALS

War Cry, The; En Evant!; Young Soldier, The; Edge, The; Sally Ann; Ministry to Women Sketch, The; Horizons

Serbian Orthodox Church in the U.S.A. and Canada, Diocese of Canada

The Serbian Orthodox Church is an organic part of the Eastern Orthodox Church. As a local church it received its autocephaly from Constantinople in A.D. 1219. The Patriarchal seat of the church today is in Belgrade, Yugoslavia. In 1921, a Serbian Orthodox Diocese in the United States of America and Canada was organized. In 1963, it was reorganized into three dioceses, and in 1983 a fourth diocese was created for the Canadian part of the church. The Serbian Orthodox Church is in absolute doctrinal unity with all other local Orthodox Churches.

HEADQUARTERS

5a Stockbridge Ave., Toronto, ON M8Z 4M6 Tel. (416)231-4409

Seventh-day Adventist Church in Canada

The Seventh-day Adventist Church in Canada is part of the worldwide Seventh-day Adventist Church with headquarters in Washington, D.C. (See "Religious Bodies in the United States" section of this *Yearbook* for a fuller description.) The Seventh-day Adventist Church in Canada was organized in 1901 and reorganized in 1932.

HEADQUARTERS

1148 King St., E., Oshawa, ON L1H 1H8 Tel. (416)433-0011 Fax (416)433-0982

Media Contact, Sec. to the Pres., Orville Parchment

DEPARTMENTS

Under Treas., Brian Christenson
Asst. Treas., Clareleen Ivany
Computer Services, Brian Ford
Communications, ——
Acting. Coord. of Ministries, Claude Sabot
Education, Jan Saliba

Ministerial Assoc., ———
Public Affairs/Religious Liberty Trust, Karnik Doukmetzian
Publishing, George Dronen

PERIODICAL

Canadian Adventist Messenger

Sikh

Sikhism was born in the northwestern part of the Indo-Pakistan sub-continent in Punjab province about 500 years ago. Guru Nanak, founder of the religion, was born in 1469. He was followed by nine successor Gurus. The Guruship was then bestowed on the Sikh Holy Book, popularly known as the Guru Granth. The Granth contains writings of the Sikh Gurus and some Hindu and Muslim saints and was compiled by the fifth Guru, Arjan Dev. For the Sikhs, the Granth is the only object of worship. It contains, mostly, hymns of praise of God, the Formless One.

Sikhs started migrating from India more than 50 years ago. A number of them settled on the West coast of North America, in British Columbia and California. More recently, a sizable group has settled in the eastern part of the continent as well, particularly in Ontario, New York and Michigan. Sikhs are found in all major cities of the United States and Canada.

When Sikhs settle, they soon establish a Gurdwara, or Sikh temple, for worship and social gathering. Gurdwaras are found, among other places, in Toronto, Vancouver, Victoria, and Yuba City, Calif. At other places, they meet for worship in schools and community centers.

The First Sikh Conference was held on March 24-25, 1979 in Toronto. This is the first step in establishing a federation of all the Sikh Associations in Canada, and, if possible, in the United States as well. A Sikh Heritage Conference was held Sept. 19-21, 1981 in Toronto.

There are approximately 200,000 Sikhs in North America.

HEADQUARTERS

Media Contact, The Sikh Foundation, Mr. Kawal Kohli or Mary Singh, Royal Bank Plaza, North Tower, Ste. 1200, Toronto, ON M5J 2J3 Tel. (416)360-2148. Fax (416)484-1410

Syrian Orthodox Church of Antioch (Archdiocese of the United States and Canada)

An archdiocese of the Syrian Orthodox Church of Antioch in North America, the Syrian Orthodox Church professes the faith of the first three ecumenical councils of Nicaea, Constantinople, and Ephesus and numbers faithful in the Middle East, India, the Americas, Europe and Australia. It traces its origin to the Patriarchate established in Antioch by St. Peter the Apostle and is under the supreme ecclesiastical jurisdiction of His Holiness the Syrian Orthodox Patriarch of Antioch and All the East, now residing in Damascus, Syria.

The Archdiocese of the Syrian Orthodox Church in the U.S. and Canada was formally established in 1957. The first Syrian Orthodox faithful came to Canada in the 1890s and formed the first Canadian parish in Sherbrooke, Québec. Today five official parishes of the Archdiocese exist in Canada—two in Québec and three in Ontario. There is also an official congregation in Calgary, Alberta.

HEADQUARTERS

Archdiocese of the U.S. and Canada, 49 Kipp Ave., Lodi, NJ 07644 Tel. (201)778-0638 Fax (201)773-7506
Media Contact, Archdiocesan Gen. Sec., Very Rev. Chorepiscopus John Meno, 45 Fairmount Ave., Hackensack, NJ 07601 Tel. (201)646-9443 Fax (201)773-7506

Ukrainian Orthodox Church of Canada

Toward the end of the 19th century many Ukrainian immigrants settled in Canada—1991 marked the centenary of this immigration. In 1918, these pioneers established the Ukrainian Orthodox Church of Canada, today the largest Ukrainian Orthodox Church beyond the borders of Ukraine.

HEADQUARTERS

Consistory of the Ukrainian Orthodox Church of Canada, 9 St. John's Ave., Winnipeg, MB R2W 1G8 Tel. (204)586-3093 Fax (204)582-5241
Media Contact, V. Rev. Dr. Ihor Kutash, 6270-12th Ave., Montréal, QC H1X 3A5 Tel. (514)727-2236 Fax (514)728-9834

Union of Spiritual Communities of Christ (Orthodox Doukhobors in Canada)

Groups of Canadians of Russian origin living in the western provinces of Canada, their beginnings in Russia are unknown. The name "Doukhobors," or "Spirit Wrestlers," was given in derision by the Russian Orthodox clergy in Russia as far back as 1785. Victims of decades of persecution in Russia, about 7,500 Doukhobors arrived in Canada in 1899.

The teaching of the Doukhobors is penetrated with the Gospel spirit of love. Worshiping God in the spirit they affirm that the outward church and all that is performed in it and concerns it has no importance for them; the church is where two or three are gathered together, united in the name of Christ. Their teaching is founded on tradition, which they call the "Book of Life," because it lives in their memory and hearts. In this book are sacred songs or chants, partly composed independently, partly formed out of the contents of the Bible, and these are committed to memory by each succeeding generation. Doukhobors observe complete pacifism and non-violence.

The Doukhobors were reorganized in 1938 by their leader, Peter P. Verigin, shortly before his death, into the Union of Spiritual Communities of Christ, commonly called Orthodox Doukhobors. It is headed by a democratically elected Executive Committee which executes the will and protects the interests of the people.

At least 99 percent of the Doukhobors are law-abiding, pay taxes, and "do not burn or bomb or parade in the nude" as they say a fanatical offshoot called the ("Sons of Freedom") does.

HEADQUARTERS

USCC Central Office, Box 760, Grand Forks, BC V0H 1H0 Tel. (604)442-8252

PERIODICAL

Iskra

Unitarian Universalist Association

Three of the 23 districts of the Unitarian Universalist Association are located partly or wholly in Canada, as are 40 of the 1,020 congregations. Conseil Unitaire Canadien handles matters of particular concern to Canadian churches and fellowships. See "Religious Bodies in the United States" section of this *Yearbook* for a fuller description of the history and theology.

HEADQUARTERS

Headquarters: 25 Beacon St., Boston, MA 02108 Tel. (617)742-2100 Fax (617)367-3237

Conseil Unitaire Canadien: 600 Eglinton Ave. East, Toronto, ON M4P 1P3 Fax (416)489-4121

Media Contact, Dir. of Public Rel. & Marketing, Deborah Weiner, Fax (617)523-4123

United Brethren Church in Canada

Founded in 1767 in Lancaster County, Pa., missionaries came to Canada about 1850. The first class was held in Kitchener in 1855, and the first building was erected in Port Elgin in 1867.

The Church of the United Brethren in Christ had its beginning with Philip William Otterbein and Martin Boehm, who were leaders in the revivalistic movement in Pennsylvania and Maryland during the late 1760s.

HEADQUARTERS

302 Lake St., Huntington, IN 46750

PERIODICAL

United Brethren, The

The United Church of Canada

The United Church of Canada was formed on June 10, 1925, through the union of the Methodist Church, Canada; the Congregational Union of Canada; the Council of Local Union Churches; and 70 percent of the Presbyterian Church in Canada. The union culminated years of negotiation between the churches, all of which had integral associations with the development and history of the nation.

In fulfillment of its mandate to be a uniting as well as a United Church, the denomination has been enriched by other unions during its history. The Wesleyan Methodist Church of Bermuda joined in 1930. On Jan. 1, 1968, the Canada Conference of the Evangelical United Brethren became part of The United Church of Canada. At various times, congregations of other Christian communions have also become congregations of the United Church.

The United Church of Canada is a full member of the World Methodist Council, the World Alliance of Reformed Churches (Presbyterian and Congregational), and the Canadian and World Councils of Churches.

The United Church is the largest Protestant denomination in Canada.

National Offices

The United Church House, 85 St. Clair Ave. E., Toronto, ON M4T 1M8 Tel. (416)925-5931 Fax (416)925-3394

Media Contact, Publicist, Mary-Frances Denis

CONFERENCE EXECUTIVE SECRETARIES

Alberta and Northwest: Rev. William F. A. Phipps, 9911-48 Ave., Edmonton, AB T6E 5V6 Tel. (403)435-3995 Fax (403)434-0597

All Native Circle: Speaker, —— 18-399 Berry St., Winnipeg, MB R3J 1N6 Tel. (204)831-0740 Fax (204)837-9703

Bay of Quinte: Rev. David M. Iverson, 218 Barrie St., Kingston, ON K7L 3K3 Tel. (613)549-2503 Fax (613)549-1050

British Columbia: Rev. Dr. Gordon C. How, 1955 W. 4th Ave., Vancouver, BC V6J 1M7 Tel. (604)734-0434 Fax (604)734-7024

Hamilton: K. Virginia Coleman, Box 100, Carlisle, ON L0R 1H0 Tel. (416)659-3343 Fax (416)659-7766

London: Rev. W. Peter Scott, 359 Windermere Rd., London, ON N6G 2K3 Tel. (519)672-1930 Fax (519)439-2800

Manitoba and Northwestern Ontario: H. Dianne Cooper, 120 Maryland St., Winnipeg, MB R3G 1L1 Tel. (204)786-8911 Fax (204)774-0159

Manitou: Rev. J. Stewart Bell, 1402 Regina St., North Bay, ON P1B 2L5 Tel. (705)474-3350 Fax (705)497-3597

Maritime: Rev. Robert H. Mills, Box 1560, Sackville, NS E0A 3C0 Tel. (506)536-1334 Fax (506)536-2900

Montréal and Ottawa: Rev. Tadashi Mitsui, 225-50 Ave., Lachine, QC H8T 2T7 Tel. (514)634-7015 Fax (514)634-2489

Newfoundland and Labrador: Rev. Boyd L. Hiscock, 320 Elizabeth Ave., St. John's, NF A1B 1T9 Tel. (709)754-0386 Fax (709)754-8336

Saskatchewan: Rev. Wilbert R. Wall, 418 A. McDonald St., Regina, SK S4N 6E1 Tel. (306)721-3311 Fax (306)721-3171

Toronto: Dr. Helga Kutz-Harder, Rm. 404, 85 St. Clair Ave., E., Toronto, ON M4T 1L8 Tel. (416)967-1880 Fax (416)925-3394

PERIODICALS

United Church Observer; Mandate; Exchange; Worldwind/Worldview; Aujourd'hui Credo

United Pentecostal Church in Canada

This body, which is affiliated with the United Pentecostal Church, International with headquarters in Hazelwood, Mo., accepts the Bible standard of full salvation, which is repentance, baptism by immersion in the name of the Lord Jesus Christ for the remission of sins, and the baptism of the Holy Ghost, with the initial signs of speaking in tongues as the Spirit gives utterance. Other tenets of faith include the Oneness of God in Christ, holiness, divine healing, and the second coming of Jesus Christ.

HEADQUARTERS

United Pentecostal Church Intl., 8855 Dunn Rd., Hazelwood, MO 63042 Tel. (314)837-7300 Fax (314)837-4503

Media Contact, Gen. Sec./Treas., Rev. C. M. Becton

DISTRICT SUPERINTENDENTS

Atlantic: Rev. R. A. Beesley, Box 965, Sussex, NB E0E 1P0

British Columbia: Rev. Paul V. Reynolds, 13447-112th Ave., Surrey, BC V3R 2E7

Canadian Plains: Rev. Johnny King, 1840 38th St., SE, Calgary, AB T2B 0Z3

167

Central Canadian: Rev. Clifford Heaslip, 4215 Roblin Blvd., Winnipeg, MB R3R 0E8

Nova Scotia-Newfoundland: Rev. John D. Mean, P.O. Box 2183, D.E.P.S., Dartmouth, NS B2W 3Y2

Ontario: Rev. Carl H. Stephenson, 63 Castlegrove Blvd., Don Mills, ON M3A 1L3

PERIODICAL

Pentecostal Herald, The

The Wesleyan Church of Canada

The Canadian portion of The Wesleyan Church which consists of the Atlantic and Central Canada districts. The Central Canada District of the former Wesleyan Methodist Church of America was organized at Winchester, Ontario, in 1889 and the Atlantic District was founded in 1888 as the Alliance of the Reformed Baptist Church, which merged with the Wesleyan Methodist Church in July, 1966.

The Wesleyan Methodist Church and the Pilgrim Holiness Church merged in June, 1968, to become The Wesleyan Church. The doctrine is evangelical and Arminian and stresses holiness beliefs. For more details, consult the U.S. listing .

HEADQUARTERS

The Wesleyan Church Intl. Center, P.O. Box 50434, Indianapolis, IN 46250-0434

Media Contact, Dist. Supt., Central Canada, Rev. S. Allan Summers, 3 Applewood Dr. Ste. 102, Belleville, ON K8P 4E3 Tel. (613)966-7527 Fax (613)968-6190

DISTRICT SUPERINTENDENTS

Central Canada: Rev. S. Allan Summers

Atlantic: Rev. Ray Barnwall, P.O. Box 20, 41 Summit Ave., Sussex, NB E0E 1P0 Tel. (506)433-1007

PERIODICALS

Atlantic Wesleyan; Central Canada Clarion; Wesleyan Advocate, The

RELIGIOUS BODIES IN CANADA
ARRANGED BY FAMILIES

The following list of religious bodies appearing in preceding directory, "Religious Bodies in Canada," including "Other Religious Bodies in Canada," shows the "families" or related clusters into which Canadian religious bodies can be grouped. For example, there are many bodies that can be grouped under the heading "Baptist" for historical and theological reasons. It is not to be assumed, however, that all denominations under one family heading are necessarily similar in belief or practice. Often any similarity is purely coincidental since ethnicity, theological divergence, and even political and personality factors have shaped the directions denominational groups have taken.

Family categories provide one of the major pitfalls of church statistics because of the tendency to combine statistics by "families" for analytical and comparative purposes. Such combined totals are almost meaningless, although often used as variables for sociological analysis.

Religious bodies not grouped under family headings appear alphabetically and are not indented in the following list.

The Anglican Church of Canada
Apostolic Christian Church (Nazarene)
Armenian Evangelical Church
Associated Gospel Churches
Bahá'í Faith

Baptist Bodies

The Association of Regular Baptist Churches
   (Canada)
Baptist General Conference of Canada
   The Central Canada Baptist Conference
   Baptist General Conference of Alberta
   British Columbia Baptist Conference
Canadian Baptist Federation
   Baptist Convention of Ontario and Québec
   Baptist Union of Western Canada
   Union d'Églises Baptistes Françaises au
      Canada
   United Baptist Convention of the Atlantic
      Provinces
Canadian Convention of Southern Baptists
Evangelical Baptist Churches in Canada, The
   Fellowship of
Free Will Baptists
North American Baptist Conference

Bible Holiness Movement
Brethren in Christ Church, Canadian Conference
Buddhist Churches of Canada
The Canadian Yearly Meeting of the Religious Society of Friends
Christadelphians in Canada
The Christian and Missionary Alliance in Canada
Christian Brethren (aka Plymouth Brethren)
Christian Science in Canada
Church of God, (Anderson, Ind.)
Church of the Nazarene

Churches of Christ—Christian Churches

Christian Church (Disciples of Christ) in Canada
Christian Churches and Churches of Christ in Canada
Churches of Christ in Canada
Congregational Christian Churches in Canada

Doukhobors

Reformed Doukhobors, Christian Community and Brotherhood of
Union of Spiritual Communities of Christ (Orthodox Doukhobors in Canada)

Eastern Churches

The Antiochian Orthodox Christian Archdiocese of North America
The Armenian Church of North America, Diocese of Canada
The Coptic Church in Canada
Greek Orthodox Diocese of Toronto (Canada)
Orthodox Church in America (Canada Section)
Romanian Orthodox Church in America (Canadian Parishes)
The Romanian Orthodox Episcopate of America (Jackson, MI)
Russian Orthodox Church in Canada, Patriarchal Parishes of the
Serbian Orthodox Church in the U.S.A. and Canada, Diocese of Canada
Syrian Orthodox Church of Antioch (Archdiocese of the United States and Canada)
Ukrainian Orthodox Church of Canada

The Evangelical Covenant Church of Canada
Evangelical Free Church of Canada
General Church of the New Jerusalem
Independent Holiness Church
Jehovah's Witnesses
Jewish Organizations in Canada

Latter Day Saints

The Church of Jesus Christ of Latter-day Saints in Canada
Reorganized Church of Jesus Christ of Latter Day Saints

Lutherans

Church of the Lutheran Brethren
The Estonian Evangelical Lutheran Church
The Evangelical Lutheran Church in Canada
The Latvian Evangelical Lutheran Church in America
Lutheran Church—Canada

Mennonite Bodies

Church of God in Christ, Mennonite
Conference of Mennonites in Canada
The Evangelical Mennonite Conference
Evangelical Mennonite Mission Conference
Mennonite Brethren Churches, Canadian Conference of
Old Order Amish Church
Reinland Mennonite Church

169

Methodist Bodies

British Methodist Episcopal Church of Canada
The Evangelical Church in Canada
Free Methodist Church in Canada
The Wesleyan Church of Canada

Metropolitan Community Churches, Universal Fellowship
The Missionary Church of Canada
Moravian Church in America, Northern Province, Canadian Province of the
Muslims
The Old Catholic Church of Canada

Pentecostal Bodies

The Apostolic Church in Canada
Apostolic Church of Pentecost of Canada, Inc.
Church of God (Cleveland, Tenn.)
The Church of God of Prophecy in Canada
Elim Felowship of Evangelical Churches and Ministers
Foursquare Gospel Church of Canada
Independent Assemblies of God—Canada
The Italian Pentecostal Church of Canada
The Open Bible Standard Churches of Canada

The Pentecostal Assemblies of Canada
Pentecostal Assemblies of Newfoundland
Pentecostal Holiness Church of Canada
United Pentecostal Church in Canada

Polish National Catholic Church of Canada

Presbyterian Bodies

Presbyterian Church in America (Canadian Section)
The Presbyterian Church in Canada

Reformed Bodies

Canadian and American Reformed Churches
Christian Reformed Church in North America
Netherlands Reformed Congregations of North America
Reformed Church in Canada
The United Church of Canada
The Reformed Episcopal Church
The Roman Catholic Church in Canada
The Salvation Army in Canada
Seventh-day Adventist Church in Canada
Sikh
Unitarian Universalist Association
United Brethren Church in Canada

5. UNITED STATES REGIONAL AND LOCAL ECUMENICAL AGENCIES

One of the many ways Christians and Christian churches relate to one another locally and regionally is through ecumenical agencies. The membership in these ecumenical organizations is diverse. Historically, councils of churches were formed primarily by Protestants, but many local and regional organizations now include Orthodox and Roman Catholics. Many are made up of congregations or judicatory units of churches. Some have a membership-base of individuals. Others foster cooperation between ministerial groups, community ministries, coalitions, or church agencies. While Councils of Churches is a term still commonly used to describe this form of cooperation, other terms such as "conference of churches," "ecumenical councils," "churches united," "metropolitan ministries," are coming into use.

An increasing number of ecumenical agencies have been exploring ways to strengthen the interreligious aspect of life in the context of religious pluralism in the United States today. Some organizations in this listing are interfaith agencies primarily through the inclusion of Jewish congregations in their membership. Other organizations are considering ways to nurture partnership with a broader base of religious groups in their communities, especially in the areas of public policy and interreligious dialogue.

This list does not include all local and regional ecumenical and interfaith instrumentalities in existence today. For information about other groups contact the Ecumenical Networks Working Groups of the National Council of Churches of Christ in the U.S.A.

The terms regional and local are sometimes relative, making identification somewhat ambiguous. Regional councils may cover sections of large states or cross state borders. Local councils may be made up of several counties, towns, or clusters of congregations. State councils or state-level ecumenical contacts exist in 45 of the 50 states.

REGIONAL

Appalachian Ministries Educational Resource Center (AMERC)
518 Second Ave., South Charleston, WV 25303
Exec. Dir., Rev. Dr. Mary Lee Daughtery
Chair, AMERC Bd., Dr. Richard Reid, O.F.M.
Office Admin., Ruby Provance
Major activities: Education and Training for Seminarians; Small-town and Rural Churches in Appalachia; Travel Seminar; Intensive Summer Term; Scholarships

The Commission on Religion in Appalachia, Inc. (AMERC)
864 Weisgarber Rd., NW, P.O. Box 37950-2910, Knoxville, TN 37909
Media Contact, Exec. Coord., Jim Sessions
Exec. Coord., Jim Sessions
Admin. Sec., Linda Selfridge
Financial Sec., Pearl Jones
Stewardship Coord., Jim Rugh
Coord. Appalachian Dev. Proj. Committee, Gaye Evans
Prgm. Chpsn. Appalachian Dev Proj. Comm., Jean Stone
Prgm. Chpsn. Appalachian Dev. Proj. Comm., Marty Zinn
Coord., Coop. Congregational Dev., Tena Willemsma
Prgm. Chpsn. Coop. Cong. Dev., Gladys Campbell
Coord. Volunteer Prog., John MacLean
Coord. Volunteer Prog., Chickie MacLean
Prog. Chpsn. Volunteer Prog., Dory Campbell
Consultant, Northn Appalachian Comm., Douglas Macneal
Prog. Chpsn. Northern App. Comm., Ron Evans
Communications Consultant, Jamie Harris
Tennessee Industrial Renewal Netwk. on Assgn. from CORA, Bill Troy

Major activities: Ecumenical Work among 17 Communions, 10 State Councils of Churches in 13-State Region

INTERFAITH IMPACT for Justice and Peace
110 Maryland Ave., NE, Washington, DC 20002
Media Contact, Communications Coord., Robert Greenwood
Executive Dir., James M. Bell
Major activities: Legislative Update (1-800-424-7290 in D.C. 543-2803); Justice for Women & Families; Civil, Human & Voting Rights; International Peace; Domestic Poverty & Human Needs; Economic Policy & Sustainable Development; Environment, Energy & Agriculture; Health Care

National Farm Worker Ministry
1337 W. Ohio, Chicago, IL 60622
Media Contact, Exec. Dir., Sr. Patricia Drydyk
Exec. Dir., Sr. Patricia Drydyk
Major activities: UFW Table Grape Boycott; Farm Labor Organizing Committee Support; Witness for Farm Worker Justice Delegation; Grape Free Zone Campaign; Support of Boycott of Chateau Ste. Michelle Wines; Educational Workshops, Presentations and Publications

North American Interfaith Network (NAIN)
Media Contact, Sec., Robert Greenwood, Fax (202)547-8107
Co-chair, Elizabeth Esperson, Thanks-Giving Square, P.O. Box 1770, Dallas, TX 75221
Co-Chair, Dr. Jamsheed Maualwala, Dept. of Anthropology, University of Toronto, Toronto, ON M55 1A1
Major activities: Interfaith Directory; Interfaith Conferences; Interfaith Networking

171

ALABAMA

Greater Birmingham Ministries
1205 N. 25th St., Birmingham, AL 35234-3197
Exec. Dir., ——
Co-Chair, Economic Justice: ; Hattie Belle Lester; Scott Douglas
Chair, Direct Services, Janine Hagan
Chair, Faith in Community, Peggy Miller
Chair, Finance & Fund-Raising, Dick Sales
Pres., Richard Johnson
Sec., Della Huber
Treas., Chris Hamlin
Major activities: Direct Service Ministries (Food, Utilities, Rent, and Nutrition Education, Shelter); Alabama Arise (Statewide legislative network focusing on low income issues); Economic Justice Issues (Low Income Housing and Advocacy, Health Care, Community Development, Jobs Creation); Faith in Community Ministries (Interchurch Forum, Interpreting and Organizing, Bible Study)

Interfaith Mission Service
411-B Holmes Ave., Huntsville, AL 35801
Exec. Min., Rev. Robert Loshuertos
Pres., Karen Neir
Major activities: Food Pantry and Emergency Funds; Interfaith Dialogue; Harvest of Food; Ministry Development; Clergy Luncheon; Workshops; Evaluation of Member Ministries; Response to Community Needs; Information and Referral; Police Department Chaplains; Interfaith Understanding

ALASKA

Alaska Christian Conference
3031 LaTouche, Anchorage, AK 99508
Media Contact, Pres., Rev. Wesley Veatch
Pres., Rev. Wesley Veatch
Vice-Pres., Mrs. Betty Taylor, 1307 Grenac Rd., Fairbanks, AK 99701
Sec., Rev. David Fison, 6800 O'Malley Rd., Anchorage, AK 99516
Treas., Mary Kron, 9650 Arlene Dr., Anchorage, AK 99515
Major activities: Legislative & Social Concerns; Resources and Continuing Education; New Ecumenical Ministries; Communication; Alcoholism (Education & Prevention); Family Violence (Education & Prevention); Native Issues; Ecumenical/Theological Dialogue; HIV/AIDS Education and Ministry; Criminal Justice

ARIZONA

Arizona Ecumenical Council
4423 N. 24th St., Ste. 750, Phoenix, AZ 85016
Media Contact, Pres., Dr. Carl Wallen
Admn., Dr. Arlo Nau
Pres., Dr. Carl Wallen, 525 E. Alameda Dr., Tempe, AZ 85282
Major activities: Donohoe Ecumenical Forum Series; Political Action Team; Legislative Workshop; Arizona Ecumenical Indian Concerns Committee; Mexican/American Border Issues; VISN-TV; AZ Volunteer Organizations; Disaster Relief

ARKANSAS

Arkansas Interfaith Conference
16th & Louisiana, P.O. Box 164073, Little Rock, AR 72216
Media Contact, Conf. Exec., Mimi Dortch
Conf. Exec., Mimi Dortch
Pres., Rev. Bryan Fulwider, P.O. Box 6594, Sherwood, AR 72116
Sec., Joy Greer, 6904 Burton, Little Rock, AR 72204
Treas., Mr. Jim Davis, Box 7239, Little Rock, AR 72217
Major activities: Task Force on Hunger; Institutional Ministry; Interfaith Executives' Advisory Council; TV Awareness; Drug Abuse, Interfaith Relations; Church Women United; IMPACT; AIDS Task Force; Public Schools Committee; Our House-Shelter; Governor's Task Force on Education; Statewide Fair Trial Committee Legislation

CALIFORNIA

California Council of Churches, Office for State Affairs
1300 N. St., Sacramento, CA 95814
Media Contact, Exec. Dir., Patricia Whitney-Wise
Exec. Dir., Patricia Whitney-Wise
Major activities: Monitoring State Legislation; Calif. IMPACT Network; Legislative Principles; Food Policy Advocacy; Family Welfare Issues; Health; Church/State Issues

Council of Churches of Contra Costa County
1543 Sunnyvale Ave., Walnut Creek, CA 94596
Media Contact, Dir., Rev. Machrina L. Blasdell
Dir., Rev. Machrina L. Blasdell
Chaplains: ; Rev. Keith Spooner; Rev. Jana L. Johnsen; Rev. Duane Woida; Rev. Harold Wright
Pres., Rev. Tim Tiffany
Treas., Mr. Bertram Sturm
Major activities: Institutional Chaplaincies, Community Education

The Council of Churches of Santa Clara County
1229 Naglee Ave., San Jose, CA 95126
Exec. Dir., Rev. Hugh Wire
Sec., ——
Affordable Housing, James McCullough
Interpretation & Dev., Paul Burks
Pres., Rev. John L. Freesemann
Assoc. Dir., Nina McCrory
Food Proj. Coord., Jo Anne Solomon
Major activities: Social Education/Action; Ecumenical and Interfaith Witness; Affordable Housing; Emergency Food Supply

The Ecumenical Council of the Pasadena Area Churches
P.O. Box 41125, Pasadena, CA 91114-8125
Exec. Dir., Donald R. Locher
Pres., Lyn Caulfield
Major activities: Christian Education; Community Worship; Community Concerns; Christian

Unity; Ethnic Ministries; Hunger; Peace; Food, Clothing Assistance for the Poor; Emergency Shelter Line

Fresno Metropolitan Ministry
1055 N. Van Ness, Ste. H, Fresno, CA 93728
Exec. Dir., Rev. Walter P. Parry
Admn. Asst., Sandy Sheldon
Pres., Carrol Cotton
Major activities: Hunger Relief Advocacy; Homelessness, Human Relations and Anti-Racism; Cross Cultural Mental Health; Health Care Advocacy; Public Education Concerns; Children's Needs; Biblical and Theological Education For Laity; Refugee Advocacy;; Ecumenical & Interfaith Celebrations & Cooperation

Interfaith Service Bureau
3720 Folsom Blvd., Sacramento, CA 95816
Media Contact, Exec. Dir., Ron Holehouse
Exec. Dir., Ron Holehouse
Pres., Rev. Lloyd Hansen
Major activities: Chaplaincy; Interfaith Food Closet Network; Clergy Concerns Committee; Religious Cable Television; Brown Bag Network (ages 60 & up); Faith in Crisis; Interfaith Hospitality Network

Marin Interfaith Council
35 Mitchell Blvd., Ste. 13, San Rafael, CA 94903
Exec. Dir., Rev. Linda Compton
Major activities: Basic Human Needs—Homelessness; Interfaith Dialogue; Education & Advocacy; Religious Leadership and Values; Interfaith Worship Services & Commemorations

Northern California Ecumenical Council
942 Market St., No. 702, San Francisco, CA 94102
Exec. Dir., Rev. Ben Fraticelli
Vice-Pres., Nancy Nielsen
Sec., Rev. Michael Cooper-White
Treas., Paul Stacy
Pres., Rev. Phillip Lawson
Adm. Asst., Juliet Twomey
Major activities: Peace with Justice; Faith and Witness; Ministry; Communications

Pacific and Asian American Center for Theology and Strategies (PACTS)
1798 Scenic Ave., Berkeley, CA 94709
Media Contact, Admin. Asst., Ruby Okazaki
Media Contact, Public Relations, Luisa Lavulo
Dir., Julia K. Estrella
Pres., Rev. Diana Akiyama
Fin. Sec., Rev. Daniel Maedjaja
Major activities: Collect and Disseminate Resource Materials; Training Conferences; Public Seminars; Women in Ministry; Human Rights; Racial and Ethnic Minority Concerns; Journal and Newsletter; Sadao Watanabe Calendars; Pacific Ecumenical Forum

Pomona Valley Council of Churches
1753 N. Park Ave., Pomona, CA 91768
Media Contact, Dir. of Development, Holly Eichinger, Fax (714)622-0484
Pres., Rev. Ricky Porter
Exec. Dir., Ms. Pat Irish

Sec., Ms. Mary Anne Parrot
Treas., Ms. Dorothy Becker
Major activities: Advocacy and Education for Social Justice; Ecumenical Celebrations; Hunger Advocacy; Emergency Food and Shelter Assistance; Farmer's Market; Affordable Housing; Transitional Housing

San Diego County Ecumenical Conference
4075 Park Bldg., San Diego, CA 92103
Media Contact, Exec. Dir., Rev. E. Vaughan Lyons
Exec. Dir., Rev. E. Vaughan Lyons
Dir. of Communication, Rev. Bernard Filmyer, S.J.
Admin., Patricia R. Munley
Pres., Rev. Glenn Allison
Treas., Joseph Ramsey
Major activities: Interfaith Shelter Network/Transitional Housing for the Homeless; Emerging Issues; Communications; Faith Order & Witness; Worship & Celebration; Ecumenical Tribute Dinner; Advent Prayer Breakfast; AIDS Chaplaincy Program; Third World Opportunies; Seafarer's Mission; "Sunday Focus" TV News; Seminars and Workshops

San Fernando Valley Interfaith Council
10824 Topanga Canyon Blvd., No. 7, Chatsworth, CA 91311
Media Contact, Exec. Dir., Barry A. Smedberg
Exec. Dir., Barry Smedberg
Pres., Rev. Allyn D. Axelton
Major activities: Seniors Multi-Purpose Centers; Nutrition & Services; Meals to Homebound; Meals on Wheels; Interfaith Reporter; Interfaith Relations; Interfaith AIDS Committee; Social Adult Day Care; Hunger/Homelessness; Volunteer Care-Givers; Clergy Gatherings; Food Pantries and Outreach; Peace and Justice; Aging; Hunger; Human Relations; Child Abuse Program; Medical Service; Homeless Program

South Coast Ecumenical Council
3326 Magnolia Ave., Long Beach, CA 90806
Media Contact, Exec. Dir., Rev. Ginny Wagener, Fax (310)595-0268
Exec. Dir., Rev. Ginny Wagener
Interfaith Action for the Aging, Cathy Trott
Centro Shalom, Olivia Herraka
Counseling Ministries, Dr. Lester Kim
Farmers' Markets, Rev. Dale Whitney
Job Center (South Bay), Michelle May
Mid-Cities Help Center, Sherrie Cheng
Pres., Ms. Bobbie Smith
Major activities: Homeless Support Services; Interfaith Action for Aging; Farmers' Markets; Hunger Projects; Lay Academy of Religion; Church Athletic Leagues; Community Action; Hunger Walks; Christian Unity Worships; Interreligious Dialogue; Justice Advocacy

Southern California Ecumenical Council
1010 S. Flower, Ste. 403, Los Angeles, CA 90015
Exec. Dir., David Brenner
Admn. Coord., Magaly Sevillano
Pres., Rev. J. Delton Pickering
Ed. Hope Publishing, Ms. Faith Sand

Religious News Service Photo

What have we created?

Churches were forced to confront justice and racism issues in the aftermath of riots in Los Angeles. The deadly riots exploded in April, following the acquittal of officers involved in the 1991 beating of African American motorist Rodney King. The National and World councils of churches held three days of talks with Los Angeles residents in June.

Dir., Interfaith Hunger Coalition, Ms. Elizabeth Riley

Dir., Interfaith Taskforce on Cent. Am., Ms. Mary Brent Wehrli

Dir., Witness for Peace, ———

Dir., Peace with Justice, Rev. Ignacio Custuera

Dir., Witness Life, Rev. Al Cowen

Dir., Faith & Order, Rev. Barbara Mudge

Dir., Ecology Task Force, Rev. Gary Herbertson

Dir., L.A.N.D., Mr. Bruce Young

Dir., Interfaith Taskforce on S.A.

Major activities: Communications Div. (ECUME-DIA, Hope Publ. House, ECUNEWS newsletter); Faith and Order (Faith and Order Comm. Celebrations Cmte.); Witness Life (Clergy and Laity Concerned, Disaster Response, Econ. Devel., Ecology Task Force, Interfaith Hunger, LAND); Peace with Justice (Southern Calif. Interfaith Task Force on Central Am.; Southern Calif. Ecumenical Task Force on South Africa; Witness for Peace

Westside Ecumenical Conference

P.O. Box 1402, Santa Monica, CA 90406

Exec. Dir., Rev. Gregory Garland

Major activities: Convalescent Hospital Visiting; Meals on Wheels; Community Religious Services; Convalescent Hospital Chaplaincy; Shelter Coordinator

COLORADO

Colorado Council of Churches

1234 Bannock St., Denver, CO 80204

Media Contact, Staff Assoc., Cynthia Buschagen

Pres., Elder Beverly Webber

Exec. Dir., Rev. Gilbert Horn

Major activities: Ecumenical Witness and Religious Dialogue; Institutional Ministries; Human Needs and Economic Issues (Includes Homelessness, Migrant Ministry, Justice in the Workplace); World Peace and Global Affairs; Communication, Media and the Arts; Interfaith Child Care Network

Interfaith Council of Boulder

3700 Baseline Rd., Boulder, CO 80303

Media Contact, Pres., Mark Peterson

President, Mark Peterson

Major activities: Interfaith Dialogue and Programs; Thanksgiving Worship Services; Food for the Hungry; Share-A-Gift; Quarterly Newsletter

CONNECTICUT

Association of Religious Communities

213 Main St., Danbury, CT 06810

Media Contact, Exec. Dir., Samuel E. Deibler, Jr.

Exec. Dir., Samuel E. Deibler, Jr.

Pres., The Rev. Dr. Mark A. Horton

Major activities: Refugee Resettlement, Family Counseling; Family Violence Prevention; Affordable Housing

The Capitol Region Conference of Churches
30 Arbor St., Hartford, CT 06106
Media Contact, Exec. Dir., Rev. Roger W. Floyd
Exec. Dir., Rev. Roger W. Floyd
Dir. Pastoral Care & Training, Rev. John Swift
Dir. Social Concerns, ——
Dir. Aging Project, Rev. Robert Feldmann
Community Organizer, Mr. Joseph Wasserman
Educ. Advocate, Ms. Annette Carter
Hartford Correctional Center Chaplain, Rev. Raymond Sailor
Broadcast Ministry Consultant, Ivor T. Hugh
Pres., Rev. Arthur Murphy
Major activities: Organizing for Peace and Justice; Aging; Legislative Action; Cooperative Broadcast Ministry; Ecumenical Cooperation; Interfaith Reconciliation; Chaplaincies; Affordable Housing; Low-Income Senior Empowerment; Anti-Racism Education

Center City Churches
170 Main St., Hartford, CT 06106
Media Contact, Exec. Dir., Paul C. Christie
Exec. Dir., Paul C. Christie
Pres., Rev. Hopeton Scott
Sec., Suzanne Jacobson
Treas., Peter Grant
Major activities: Senior Services; Family Support Center; Energy Bank; Crisis Intervention; After-School Tutoring; Summer Day Camp; Housing for Persons with AIDS; Mental Health Residence; Community Soup Kitchen

Christian Community Action
98 S. Main St., South Norwalk, CT 06854
Dir., Jacquelyn P. Miller
Major activities: Emergency Food Program; Used Furniture; Loans for Emergencies; Loans for Rent, Security, and Fuel

Christian Community Action
168 Davenport Ave., New Haven, CT 06519
Exec. Dir., The Rev. Bonita Grubbs
Major activities: Emergency Food Program; Used Furniture & Clothing; Loans for Rent, Security, & Fuel; Emergency Housing for Families; Advocacy

Christian Conference of Connecticut (CHRISCON)
60 Lorraine St., Hartford, CT 06105
Media Contact, Exec. Dir., Rev. Stephen J. Sidorak, Jr.
Exec. Dir., Rev. Stephen J. Sidorak, Jr.
Exec. Asst., Sharon Anderson
Admn. Asst., Mildred Robertson
Pres., Rev. Geroge B. Elia
Vice-Pres., Ms. Elisabeth C. Miller
Sec., Rev Walter M. Elwood
Treas., Mr. Thomas F. Sarubbi
Major activities: Communications; Institutional Ministries; Conn. Bible Society; Conn. Council on Alcohol Problems; Ecumenical Forum; Faith & Order; Social Concerns; Public Policy

Council of Churches and Synagogues of Lower Fairfield County
628 Main St., Stamford, CT 06901
Major activities: Prison Visitation; Senior Neighborhood Support Services; Ecumenical Services; Interfaith Dialogue; Food Bank; Fuel Assistance; Interfaith AIDS Ministry; Elderly Visitation Programs; Adopt-A-House; Friendship House; Homeless Planning

Council of Churches of Greater Bridgeport, Inc.
126 Washington Ave., Bridgeport, CT 06604
Media Contact, Exec. Dir., Rev. John S. Kidd, Fax (203)367-8113
Exec. Dir., Rev. John S. Kidd
Pres., Gilbert Mott
Sec., Mrs. Dorothy Allsop
Treas., Lynne Quido
Major activities: Youth in Crisis; Youth Shelter; Criminal Justice; Hospital, Nursing Home and Jail Ministries; Local Hunger; Ecumenical Relations, Prayer and Celebration; Covenantal Ministries; Homework Help

The Downtown Cooperative Ministry in New Haven
57 Olive St., New Haven, CT 06511
Media Contact, Coord., Rev. Samuel Slie
Coord., Rev. Samuel N. Slie
Co-Pres., Rev. Kate Latimer, 343 Litchfield Turnpike, Bethany, CT 06525
Co-Pres., Rev. Florestine Taylor
Treas., Murray Harrison, 264 Curtis St., Meriden, CT 06450
Major activities: Mission to Poor and Dispossessed; Criminal Justice; Elderly; Sheltering Homeless; Soup Kitchen; Low Income Housing; AIDS Residence

Manchester Area Conference of Churches
736 East Middle Tpke., P.O. Box 773, Manchester, CT 06045
Exec. Dir., Christina B. Edelwich
Dir., Dept. of Sheltering Ministries, Denise Cabrana
Dir., Dept. of Human Needs, Elizabeth Harlow
Dir., Project Reentry, Joseph M. Piescik
Pres., Rev. Dr. Bill Scott
Treas., Florence Noyes
Interim Dir., Rose Eagen Cabana
Major activities: Provision of Basic Needs (Food, Fuel, Clothing, Furniture); Emergency Aid Assistance; Emergency Shelter; Soup Kitchen; Reentry Assistance to Ex-Offenders; Pastoral Care in Local Institutions; Interfaith Day Camp; Advocacy for the Poor; Ecumenical Education and Worship

New Britain Area Conference of Churches (NEWBRACC)
19 Chestnut St., New Britain, CT 06051
Media Contact, Exec. Dir., Rev. Dr. David D. Mellon
Exec. Minister, Rev. Dr. David D. Mellon
Pastoral Care/Chaplaincy, Rev. Susan Gregory-Davis
Pastoral Care/Chaplaincy, Rev. Ron Smith, Rev. Will Baumgartner, Rev. Frank Carter

Pres., Joanne Dimauro-Staves
Treas., Jacqueline Maddy
Office Mgr., Judy Briggs
Major activities: Worship; Social Concerns; Emergency Food Bank Support; Communications-Mass Media; Hospital and Nursing Home Chaplaincy; Elderly Programming; Homelessness and Hunger Programs; Telephone Ministry; Urban Sisters Center; Thanksgiving Vouchers

Waterbury Area Council of Churches
24 Central Ave., Waterbury, CT 06702
Media Contact, Coord., Susan Girdwood
Consultant, Mrs. Virginia B. Tillson
Coordin., Susan Girdwood
Pres., Rev. Peter Marsden
Admn.Asst., Judith Juraschka
Major activities: Emergency Food Program; Emergency Fuel Program; Soup Kitchens; Ecumenical Worship; Christmas Toy Sale

DELAWARE

The Christian Council of Delaware and Maryland's Eastern Shore
1626 N. Union St., Wilmington, DE 19806
Interfaith Resource Center, Dir., Mrs. Elaine B. Stout
Pres., The Rev. Jeffrey N. Leath
Major activities: Ecumenical Work in: Public Policy; Faith and Order; Religious Education; Supporting Local Efforts

DISTRICT OF COLUMBIA

The Council of Churches of Greater Washington
5 Thomas Circle NW, Washington, DC 20005
Exec. Dir., Rev. Rodney L. Young
Asst. Dir. for Prog., City, Mr. Daniel Thompson
D.C. Communities Ministries, Rev. George N. Bolden
Prog. Coord., Hope Valley Camp, Mr. Daniel Thompson
Pres., Rev. Lincoln Dring
Major activities: Development of Group and Community Ministries; Church Development and Redevelopment; Liaison with Public Agencies; In-school Youth Employment; Summer Youth Employment; Hope Valley Camp; Institutional Ministry; Hunger Relief; Vision to Action—Community Revitalization; Health Ministries; Cluster of Store Front Churches

Interfaith Conference of Metropolitan Washington
1419 V St., NW, Washington, DC 20009
Media Contact, Exec. Dir., Rev. Dr. Clark Lobenstine, Fax (202)234-6303
Exec. Dir, Rev. Dr. Clark Lobenstine
Asst. Dir., Rev. Ruth Bersin
Ofc. Mgr., Ms. Kadija Ash
Staff Assoc., Ms. Susan Burton
Sec., Najla Robinson
Pres., Bishop J. Clinton Hoggard
1st Vice Pres., Bishop E. Harold Jansen
Vice Pres., Elder Raul McQuivey
Vice Pres., Imam Yusuf Saleem

Vice Pres., James Cardinal Hickey
Vice Pres., Dr. Amrit Kaur
Sec., Rev. Dr. Rena Karefa-Smart
Treas., Simeon Kriesberg, Esq.
Major activities: Interfaith Dialogue; Interfaith Concert; Racial and Ethnic Polarization; Drugs; AIDS; Hunger; Homelessness

FLORIDA

Christian Service Center for Central Florida, Inc.
808 West Central Blvd., Orlando, FL 32805-1809
Media Contact, Exec. Dir., Dr. Patrick J. Powers, Fax (407)849-1495
Exec. Dir., Dr. Patrick J. Powers
Assoc. Dir, Terry Laugherty
Dir. Family Emergency Services, Andrea Evans
Dir. Marriage & Family Therapy Center, Dr. Gloria Lobnitz
Dir. Daily Bread, Rev. James Blount
Dir. Alzheimers Respite, Mary Ellen Ort-Marvin
Dir. Fresh Start, Rev. Fred Robinson
Dir. of Mktg., Margaret Ruffier-Farris
Pres., Robert Bryan
Pres.-Elect, W. Marvin Hardy, III
Treas., Terry Bitner
Sec., Barbara Lehman
Major activities: Provision of Basic Needs (food, clothing, shelter); Emergency Assistance; Professional Counseling. Noon-time Meals; Sunday Church Services at Walt Disney World; Collection and Distribution of Used Clothing; Shelter for Homeless; Training for Homeless; Respite for caregivers of Alzheimers

Florida Council of Churches
924 N. Magnolia Ave., Ste. 236, Orlando, FL 32803
Exec. Dir., Walter F. Horlander
Admn. Asst., Mrs. Margarita Thompson
Staff Assoc., Refugee Services, Orlando Offc., Richard K. Walker
Staff Assoc., Refugee Services, Tallahassee Offc., Mary Jane Barabash
Staff Assoc., Disaster Response, William Nix
Staff Assoc., Program Development, ——
Assoc. for Haitian Issues, Jean Claude Picard
Major activities: Faith and Order; Education and Renewal; Evangelism and Mission; Justice and Peace Refugee Resettlement; Disaster Response; Legislation & Public Policy

GEORGIA

Christian Council of Metropolitan Atlanta
465 Boulevard, S.E., Atlanta, GA 30312
Media Contact, Exec. Dir., Dr. Robert P. Reno
Exec. Dir., Dr. Robert P. Reno
Assoc. Dir., Mr. Neal P. Ponder, Jr.
Pres., Marie Cofer
Treas., Ms. June B. Debatin
Major activities: Refugee Services; Emergency Assistance; Voluntary Service; Employment; Racism; Homeless; Ecumenical and Interreligious Events; Interchurch Ministry Planning; Persons with Handicapping Conditions; Women's Concerns; Seminary Student Internship Program

Georgia Christian Council

P.O. Box 7193, Macon, GA 31209-7193
Media Contact, Exec. Dir., Rev. F. Thomas Scholl, Jr.
Exec. Dir., Rev. F. Thomas Scholl, Jr.
Pres., Rev. Jacoba Hurst, P.O. Box 889, Tifton, GA 31793
Treas., Rev. Gordon Reinersten, 3264 Northside Pkwy. NW, Atlanta, GA 30327
Major activities: Local Ecumenical Support and Resourcing; Legislation (GRAIN); Rural Development; Racial Justice; Networking for Migrant Coalition and Aging Coalition

HAWAII

Hawaii Council of Churches

1300 Kailua Rd., B-1, Kailua, HI 96734
Media Contact, Exec. Dir., Ms. Patricia Mumford
Exec. Dir., Ms. Patricia Mumford
Major activities: Laity and Clergy Education; Ecumenical Worship; Religious Art, Music, Drama; Legislative Concerns; Interfaith TV and Radio Ministry; Social Action; AIDS Education; Advocacy for Peace with Justice and Hawaiian Self-Determination; Disaster Response

IDAHO

The Regional Council for Christian Ministry, Inc.

P.O. Box 2236, Idaho Falls, ID 83403
Exec. Sec., Wendy Schoonmaker
Major activities: Island Park Ministry; Community Food Bank; Community Observances; Community Information and Referral Service; F.I.S.H.

ILLINOIS

Churches United of the Quad City Area

630 - 9th St., Rock Island, IL 61201
Media Contact, Exec. Dir., Charles R. Landon, Jr
Exec. Dir., Charles R. Landon, Jr.
Assoc. Exec. Dir., Sheila D. Fitts
Pres., The Very Rev. John L. Hall
Treas., Clark Arons
Major activities: Jail Ministry; Hunger Projects; Minority Enablement; Criminal Justice; Radio-TV; Peace; Local Church Development

Contact Ministries of Springfield

401 E. Washington, Springfield, IL 62701
Media Contact, Exec. Dir., Ethel Butcher
Exec. Dir., Ethel Butcher
Major activities: Information; Referral and Advocacy; Ecumenical Coordination; Low Income Housing Referral; Food Pantry Coordination; Low Income Budget Counseling; 24 hours on call

Evanston Ecumenical Action Council

P.O. Box 1414, Evanston, IL 60204
Media Contact, Comm. Chmn., Robert Fickes
Exec. Dir., Michael D. Johnson
Dir. Hospitality Cntr. for the Homeless, Patricia Johnson

Pres., Charles Underwood
Treas., Ann C. Campbell
Major activities: Interchurch Communication and Education; Peace and Justice Ministries; Coordinated Social Action; Soup Kitchens; Multi-Purpose Hospitality Center for the Homeless; Worship and Renewal

Greater Chicago Broadcast Ministries

112 E. Chestnut St., Chicago, IL 60611-2014
Media Contact, Exec. Dir., Lydia Talbot
Pres., Bd. of Dir., David Hardin
Exec. Dir., Lydia Talbot
Admn. Asst., Margaret Early
Major activities: Television, Cable, Interfaith/Ecumenical Development; Social/Justice Concerns

The Hyde Park & Kenwood Interfaith Council

1448 East 53rd St., Chicago, IL 60615
Media Contact, Exec. Dir., Mr. Werner H. Heymann
Exec. Dir., Mr. Werner H. Heymann
Pres., Rev. Lawrence R. Hamilton
Treas., Ms. Barbara Krell
Major activities: Interfaith Work; Hunger Projects; Community Development

Illinois Conference of Churches

615 S. 5th St., Springfield, IL 62703
Media Contact, Gen. Sec., Rev. Dr. Carol M. Worthing, Fax (217)9307
Gen. Sec., Rev. Dr. Carol M. Worthing
Dir., IMPACT, Rev. Dr. George Ogle
Dir., Farm Worker Ministry, ——
Dir., Domestic Violence Prog., ——
Dir., Human Services Ministry, ——
Pres., Dr. David MacDonna, 1360 W. Main, Decatur, IL 62522
Treas., Rev. Daniel Holland, P.O. Box 3786, Springfield, IL 62708
Major activities: Migrant & Farm Worker Ministry; Chaplaincy in Institutions; Governmental Concerns and Illinois Impact; Ecumenical Courier; Ministry to Developmentally Disabled; Ministry with Aging; Immigration and Refugee Resettlement; Domestic Violence

Oak Park-River Forest Community of Congregations

324 N. Oak Park Ave., Oak Park, IL 60302
Media Contact, D. Laini Zinn
Exec. Sec., D. Laini Zinn
Vice-Pres., Mrs. Kathleen Lobato-Martinez
Pres., Rev. Thomas Cross
Major activities: Community Affairs; Ecumenical/Interfaith Affairs; Youth Education; Food Pantry; Senior Citizens Worship Services; Interfaith Thanksgiving Services; Good Friday Services; UNICEF Children's Fund Drive; ASSIST (Network); Blood Drive; Literacy Training; Christian Unity Week Pulpit Exchange; CROP/CWS Hunger Walkathon; Austin Community Table (feeding hungry); Work with Homeless Commission; Unemployed Task Force; Economic & Health Bridgemaking to Chicago Westside

Peoria Friendship House of Christian Service

800 N.E. Madison Ave., Peoria, IL 61603
Media Contact, Exec. Dir., Rev. Cheryl F. Dudley, Fax (309)671-5206
Exec. Dir., Rev. Cheryl F. Dudley
Dir. of Community Outreach, Ms. M. Lee Shaw
Dir. of Prog. & Spiritual Nurture, Rev. Beth Hennessey
Pres. of Board, Ms. Nora Sullivan
Major activities: Children's After-School; Teen Programs; Parenting Groups; Recreational Leagues; Senior Citizens Activities; Emergency Food/Clothing Distribution; Emergency Payments for Prescriptions, Rent, Utilities, Transportation; Community Outreach/Housing Advocacy; Economic Development; Grassroots Community Organizing; Crime Prevention; Neighborhood Empowerment

US ECUMENICAL AGENCIES

INDIANA

The Associated Churches of Fort Wayne & Allen County

602 E. Wayne St., Fort Wayne, IN 46802
Media Contact, Exec. Dir., Rev. Vernon R. Graham
Exec. Dir., Rev. Vernon R. Graham
Sec., Linda Elliot
Foodbank: ; Ellen Graham; Rev. Ed. Pease
WRE Coord., Maxine Bandemer
Prog. Development, Ellen Graham
Pres., Marilyn Rousseau, 3228 Glencairn Dr., Fort Wayne, IN 46815
Treas., Jean Streicher, 436 Downing Avenue, Fort Wayne, IN 46807
Major activities: Weekday Religious Ed.; Radio & TV; Church Clusters; Church and Society Commission; Ed. for Christian Life Division; Clergy United for Action; Faith and Order Commission; Christian Ed.; Widowed-to-Widowed; CROP; Campus Ministry; Feeding the Babies; Food Bank System; Peace Education; Welfare Reform; Endowment Development; Habitat for Humanity; Child Care Advocacy; Project 25; Ecumenical Dialogue; Feeding Children; Vincent House (Homeless); A Learning Journey (Literacy); Reaching Out in Love

Christian Ministries of Delaware County

404 E. Main, Muncie, IN 47305
Exec. Dir., Sallie Maish
Pres., Rev. Glenn Barth
Treas., Dr. J. B. Black
Major activities: Migrant Ministry; Christian Education; Feed-the-Baby Program; Youth Ministry at Detention Center; Community Church Festivals; Community Pantry; Community Assistance Fund; CROP Walk; Social Justice; Quality of Homelife

Church Community Services

1703 Benham Ave., Elkhart, IN 46516
Exec. Dir., Mary Jane Carpenter
Major activities: Advocacy for Low Income Persons; Emergency Housing, Financial Assistance; Transportation; Educational Programs; Food Pantry

The Church Federation of Greater Indianapolis

1100 W. 42nd St., Ste. 345, Indianapolis, IN 46208
Media Contact, Dir., Development, Carol Blinzinger
Exec. Dir., ——
Dir., Social Ministries, ——
Dir., Development, Carol J. Blinzinger
Dir., Communications, ——
Pres., Rev. Darin Moore
Treas., Earline Moore
Major activities: Celebrations and Unity; Ministries in Media; Ministries in Specialized Settings; Ministries in Society; Education and Training

Evansville Area Council of Churches

414 N.W. Sixth St., Evansville, IN 47708-1332
Media Contact, Exec. Dir., Joseph N. Peacock
Exec. Dir., Rev. Joseph N. Peacock
Weekday Supervisor, Ms. Linda M. Schenk
Office Mgr., Ms. Barbara Gaisser
Pres., Rev. Conrad Grosenick
Sec., The Rev. Dennis Hollinger-Laut
Fin. Chpsn., Rev. Will Jewsbury
Major activities: Christian Education; Community Responsibility & Service; Public Relations; Interpretation; Church Women United; Institutional Ministries; Interfaith Dialogue; Earth Care Ethics; Public Education Support; Disaster Preparedness

Indiana Council of Churches

1100 W. 42nd St., Rm. 225, Indianapolis, IN 46208-3383
Pres., Edith M. Jones
Vice Pres., Bishop Ralph A. Kempski
Sec., Rev. Bryon Rose
Treas., David F. Rees
Peace with Justice Facilitator, Rev. John E. Gaus
Major activities: Educational Ministries; Communications and Public Media; Social Ministries; Peace and Justice; Farmworker Ministries; Institutional Ministries; Ecumenical Concerns; Indiana Rural Justice Network; Refugee Resettlement; NAESNET; IMPACT

Indiana Interreligious Commission on Human Equality

1100 W. 42nd St., Ste. 365, Indianapolis, IN 46208
Exec. Dir., Cathy J. Cox-Overby
Pres., Dr. Hamilton F. Niff
Treas., Rev. Norman L. Morford
Major activities: Human Rights; Anti-Racism Training; Racism/Sexism Inventory; Cultural and Religious Intolerance; South Africa Consultations; Interfaith Dialogue

Interfaith Community Council

702 E. Market St., New Albany, IN 47150
Exec. Dir., Rev. Dr. George Venable Beury
Dir. of Finance, Mary Ann Sodrel
Dir., Child Dev. Center, Carol Welsh
Dir., Deaf Relay, Susan Wagner
Dir., Hedden House, Hope LaChance
Dir., RSVP, Matie Watts
Chpsn., Ms. Jane Harmon
Treas., Dick Peterson
Major activities: Child Development Center;

Emergency Assistance; Hedden House (Half Way Home for Recovering Alcoholic Women); Retired Senior Volunteer Program; New Clothing and Toy Drives; Convalescent Sitter & Mother's Aides; Senior Day College; Emergency Food Distribution; Homeless Prevention

Lafayette Urban Ministry
12 North 8th St., Lafayette, IN 47901
Media Contact, Exec. Dir., Joseph Micon, Fax (317)742-2721
Exec. Dir., Joseph Micon
Advocate Coord., Jean Stearns
Public Policy Coord., Jo Johannsan
Pres., John Dahl
Major activities: Social Justice Ministries with and among the Poor

United Religious Community of St. Joseph County
2015 Western Ave., South Bend, IN 46629
Media Contact, Exec. Dir., Dr. James J. Fisko
Exec. Dir., Dr. James J. Fisko
Pres., Robert Curtis
Coord., State Prison Visitation, Sr. Susan Kinzele, CSC
Coord. Victim Offender Reconciliation Prog. (VORP), Ruth Andrews
Coord., Volunteer Advocacy Project, Sara Goetz
Major activities: Religious Understanding; Social and Pastoral Ministries; Congregational Ministries

West Central Neighborhood Ministry
1210 Broadway, Fort Wayne, IN 46802-3304
Media Contact, Exec. Dir., Andrea S. Thomas
Exec. Dir., Andrea S. Thomas
Ofc. Mgr., Joseph L. Falk
Food Bank Coord., Doras Bailey
Youth Dir., Richard R. Rutland
Independent Living Dir., Ranelle Melton
Senior Citizens Dir., Gayle Mann
Major activities: After-school Program; Teen Drop-In Center; Church League Basketball; Summer Day Camp; Summer Overnight Camps; Information and Referral Services; Food Pantry; Nutrition Program for Senior Citizens; Senior Citizens Activities; Vocational Development for Teens/Young Adults; Developmental Services for Families, Senior Citizens, and Disabled

IOWA

Churches United
222 29th St. Drive S.E., Cedar Rapids, IA 52403
Admn. Sec., Mrs. Marcey Luxa
Pres., Rev. Lloyd Brockmeyer
Treas., Christian Davies, 3142 Grandview Ct., Iowa City, IA 52246
Major activities: Community Food Bank; LEAF (Local Emergency Assistance Fund; CROP; Cooperative Low Income Store (ONE Store); Community Information and Referral; Jail Chaplaincy; World Hunger; Nursing Home Ministry; Radio and TV Ministry; Ecumenical City-Wide Celebrations

Des Moines Area Religious Council
3816 - 36th St., Des Moines, IA 50310
Media Contact, Exec. Dir., Forrest Harms
Exec. Dir., Forrest Harms
Pres., David Bear
Treas., Bill McGill
Major activities: Outreach and Nurture; Education; Social Concerns; Mission; Worship; Emergency Food Pantry; Ministry to Widowed; Child Care Assistance

Ecumenical Ministries of Iowa (EMI)
3816 - 36th St., Ste. 202, Des Moines, IA 50310
Media Contact, Exec. Dir., Dr. James R. Ryan
Exec. Dir., Dr. James R. Ryan
Admn. Coord., Wendy E. Hanson Wagner
Office Mgr., Martha E. Jungck
Major activities: A forum dialogue related to theological faith issues and social concerns; Opportunity to develop responses to discern needs and join in common mission; Communication, Global, Justice and Unity

KANSAS

Cross-Lines Cooperative Council
736 Shawnee Ave., Kansas City, KS 66105
Exec. Dir., David Schmidt Shulman
Dir. of Programs, Rev. Robert L. Moore
Board Pres., Larry Leighton
Board Treas., Phil Woodworth
Major activities: Emergency Assistance; Family Support Advocacy; Crisis Heating/Plumbing Repair; Thrift Store; Workcamp Experiences; Adult Education (GED and Basic English Literacy Skills; School Supplies (served 550 student in August/September 1991); Christmas Store (550 families registered to shop December 1991); Institute for Poverty and Empowerment Studies (Education on poverty for the non-poor); Business Incubator (Entrepeneurial assistance for the poor)

Inter-Faith Ministries—Wichita
334 N. Topeka, Wichita, KS 67202-2410
Exec. Dir., Rev. Sam Muyskens
Ofc. Mgr., Virginia Courtright
Dir., Inter-Faith Inn (Homeless Shelter), Sandy Swank
Dir., Operation Holiday, Sally Dewey
Dev./Communic. Dir., Christina Lott
Pres., Carolyn Benefiel
Major activities: Communications; Urban Education; Inter-religious Understanding; Community Needs and Issues; Theology and Worship; Hunger; Advocacy

Kansas Ecumenical Ministries
5942 SW 29th St., Ste. D, Topeka, KS 66614-2539
Exec. Dir., Rev. Alden Hickman
Pres., Rev. Kathy Timpany
Vice-Pres., Mrs. Winnie Crapson
Sec., Rev. George Harvey
Major activities: Legislative Activities; Program Facilitation and Coordination; World Hunger; Higher Education Concerns; Interfaith Rural Life Committee; Education; Mother-to-Mother Program; Peacemaking

KENTUCKY

Fern Creek/Highview United Ministries
P.O. Box 91372, Louisvlle, KY 40291
Exec. Dir., Darla A. Bailey
Pres., Elizabeth A. Sneed
Major activities: Ecumenically supported social service agency providing services to the community, including Emergency Financial Assistance, Food/Clothes Closet, Health Aid Equipment Loans, Information/Referral, Advocacy, Monthly Blood-Pressure Checks; Holiday Programs, Adult Day-Care Program, Life Skills Training, and Intensive Care Management

Hazard-Perry County Community Ministries, Inc.
P.O. Box 1506, Hazard, KY 41702
Exec. Dir., Ms. Gerry Feamster-Martin
Chpsn., Rev. Terry Reffett
Treas., Ralph Ed Miller
Major activities: Food Pantry/Crisis Aid Program; Day Care; Summer Day Camp; After-school Program; Christmas Tree

Highlands Community Ministries
1140 Cherokee Rd., Louisville, KY 40204
Media Contact, Exec. Dir., Stan Esterle
Exec. Dir., Stan Esterle
Pres., Rev. Jack Oliver
Vice-Pres., Sandy Hoover
Sec./Treas., Larry Carr
Major activities: Welfare Assistance; Day Care; Counseling with Youth, Parents and Adults; Adult Day Care; Social Services for Elderly; Housing for Elderly and Handicapped; Ecumenical Programs; Community Classes; Activities for Children; Neighborhood and Business

Kentuckiana Interfaith Community
1115 South 4th St., Louisville, KY 40203
Media Contact, Exec. Dir., Rev. Dr. Gregory C. Wingenbach
Exec. Dir., Rev. Dr. Gregory C. Wingenbach
Pres., Rev. Deacon David Kannapell
Vice-Pres., Rev. Dr. Curtis Miller
Sec., Ms. Sara Klein Wagner
Treas., Rev. Wallace Garner
Admn. Sec., Mrs. Sue Weatherford
Major activities: Ecumenical Ministries in Kentucky and Indiana; Consensus Advocacy; Inter-Christian/Interfaith Dialogue; Interpastoral/Ministry Support; Religion & Race, Education & Racial Justice Forums; Network for Neighborhood-based Community Ministries; Community Winterhelp; LUAH/Hunger & Justice Concerns Commission; Intermedia: FAITH Channel, Radio and Cable TV, *Horizon* Newspaper; Ecumenical Research & Planning; Chaplaincy & Ministry Support; Networking with Seminaries & Religious-Affiliated Colleges

Kentucky Council of Churches
1039 Goodwin Dr., Lexington, KY 40505
Media Contact, Pres., Nancy Jo Kemper
Exec. Dir., Rev. Nancy Jo Kemper

Coord., Disaster Recovery Prog., C. Nelson Hostetter
Ed., *Intercom*, Dr. David Berg
Pres., Rev. William Brown, P.O. Box 12350, Lexington, KY 40582-2350
Major activities: Christian Unity; Hunger; Church and Government; Disaster Response; Peace Issues; Racism; Health Care Issues; Local Ecumenism; Rural Land/Farm Issues

Northern Kentucky Interfaith Commission, Inc.
601 Greenup St., Covington, KY 41011
Media Contact, Admin. Asst., Karen Yates
Exec. Dir., Rev. William C. Neuroth
Major activities: Understanding Faiths; Meeting Spiritual and Human Needs

Paducah Cooperative Ministry
1359 S. 6th St., Paducah, KY 42003
Media Contact, Dir., Jo Ann Ross
Dir., Jo Ann Ross
Chpsn., Rev. Brian Cope
Major activities: Programs for Hungry; Elderly; Poor; Prisoners; Homeless, Handicapped; and Undereducated

South East Associated Ministries (SEAM)
2125 Goldsmith Ln., Louisville, KY 40218
Exec. Dir., Mary Beth Helton
Dir., Life Skills Center, Kay Sanders
Dir., Youth Services, Tracey Frazier
Pres., Rev. Rick White
Treas., Joe Hays
Major activities: Emergency Food and Financial Assistance; Life Skills Center (Programs of Prevention and Self-Sufficiency Through Education, Empowerment, Support Groups, etc.); Juvenile Court Diversion Program; Bloodmobile; Ecumenical Education and Worship; Family Counseling

South Louisville Community Ministries
204 Seneca Trail, Louisville, KY 40214
Media Contact, Exec. Dir., J. Michael Jupin
Exec. Dir., J. Michael Jupin
Bd. Chair., Rev. Lloyd Spencer
Bd. Vice-Chair., ——
Bd. Treas., Eugene Wells
Major activities: Food, Clothing & Financial Assistance; Home Delivered Meals, Transportation, Refugee Resettlement; Ecumenical Worship; Juvenile Diversion Program; Affordable Housing; Adult Day Care

St. Matthews Area Ministries
319 Browns Ln., Louisville, KY 40207
Exec. Dir., Rev. A. David Bos
Dir., Emergency Fin. Assis., Linda Leeser
Dir., After-School Care Centers, Janet Hennessey
Dir. of Volunteers, Karen DeFazio
Major activities: After-School Care; Youth Services; Interchurch Worship and Education; Emergency Financial Assistance

LOUISIANA

Louisiana Interchurch Conference
660 N. Foster Dr., Ste. A-225, Baton Rouge, LA 70806
Media Contact, Exec. Dir., The Rev. C. Dana Krutz
Exec. Dir., The Rev. C. Dana Krutz
Pres., Bishop Marshall Gilmore
Major activities: Ministries to Aging; Prison Reform; Liason with State Agencies; Ecumenical Dialogue; Institutional Chaplains; Racism

LOUISIANA

Greater Baton Rouge Federation of Churches and Synagogues
P.O. Box 626, Baton Rouge, LA 70821
Media Contact, Exec. Dir., Rev. Jeff Day
Exec. Dir., Rev. Jeff Day
Admn. Asst., Mrs. Marion Zachary
Pres., Dr. William Staats
Vice-Pres., Mr. Richard K. Goldberger
Treas., Mr. E. Cole Thornton
Major activities: Combating Hunger; Housing (Helpers for Housing); Lay Academy of Religion (training); Interfaith Relations

Greater New Orleans Federation of Churches
4545 Magnolia St., #206, New Orleans, LA 70115
Exec. Dir., Rev. J. Richard Randels
Major activities: Radio-TV Programs; Central Business District Ministries; Regional Suburban Network; Leadership Training; Senior Citizens; Social Action; Public Information; Religious Census and Survey; Literacy; Counseling Coordination; Cable TV Channel; Emergency

MAINE

Maine Council of Churches
15 Pleasant Ave., Portland, ME 04103
Media Contact, Communications Director, Sarah Campbell
Pres., Marc Mutty
Exec. Dir., Thomas C. Ewell
Major activities: Legislative Issues; Criminal Justice; Adult Education; Environmental Issues

MARYLAND

Central Maryland Ecumenical Council
Cathedral House, 4 E. University Pkwy., Baltimore, MD 21218
Exec. Dir., The Rev. Roy W. Cole, III
Pres., The Rev. Barbara Sands
Major activities: Interchurch Communicationis and Collaboration; Information Systems; Ecumenical Relations; Urban Mission and Advocacy; Staff Judiciary Leadership Council; Commission on Dialogue; Commission on Church & Society; Commission on Admin. & Dev.; Annual Ecumenical Choral Concert; Annual Ecumenical Service

Community Ministries of Rockville
114 West Montgomery Ave., Rockville, MD 20850
Exec. Dir., Mansfield M. Kaseman
Assoc. Dir., Hune Allred
Major activities: Shelter Care; Emergency Assistance; Elderly Home Care; Affordable Housing; Political Advocacy

Community Ministry of Montgomery County
114 West Montgomery Ave., Rockville, MD 20850
Exec. Dir., Lincoln S. Dring, Jr.
Major activities: Interfaith Clothing Center; Grant Assistance Program; Manna Food Center; The Advocacy Function; Thanksgiving in February; Information and Referral Services; Friends in Action; The Thanksgiving Hunger Drive; Montgomery Habitat for Humanity

MASSACHUSETTS

Attleboro Area Council of Churches, Inc.
505 N. Main St., Attleboro, MA 02703
Media Contact, Executive Director, Carolyn L. Bronkar
Exec. Dir., Carolyn L. Bronkar
Admn. Sec., Joan H. Lindstrom
Ofc. Asst., Roberta Kohler
Hosp. Chpln., Rev. Linnea Prefontaine
Pres., Rev. Carole Baker, P.O. Box 1319, Attleboro Falls, MA 02760
Treas., David Quinlan, 20 Everett St., Plainville, MA 02762
Major activities: Hospital Chaplaincy; Radio Ministry; Personal Growth/Skill Workshops; Ecumenical Worship; Media Resource Center; Referral Center; Communications/Publications; Community Social Action; Food'n Friends Kitchens; Emergency Food and Shelter Fund; Nursing Home Volunteer Visitation Program

The Cape Cod Council of Churches, Inc.
142 Corporation Rd., Hyannis, MA 02601
Media Contact, Exec. Dir., Rev. Ellen C. Chahey
Exec. Dir., Rev. Ellen C. Chahey
Admn. Asst., Muriel L. Eggers
Pres., Rev. John H. Williams
Chaplain, Cape Cod Hospital, Rev. William Wilcox
Chaplain, Barnstable County Hospital, Elizabeth Stommel
Chaplain, Falmouth Hospital, Rev. Allen Page
Chaplain, House of Correction & Jail, Rev. Thomas Shepherd
Dir., Service Center & Thrift Shop, Joan McCurdy, P.O. Box 125, Dennisport, MA 02639
Asst. to Dir., Service Center & Thrift Shop, Merilyn Lansing
Major activities: Pastoral Care; Social Concerns; Religious Education; Emergency Distribution of Food, Clothing, Furniture; Referral and Information; Church World Service; Interfaith Relations; Media Presence; Hospital & Jail Chaplaincy

Cooperative Metropolitan Ministries

474 Centre St., Newton, MA 02158
Media Contact, Exec. Dir., Claire Kashuck
Exec. Dir., Claire Kashuck
Board Pres., Thayce Morgan
Treas., James Blanchflower
Sec., Mary Morrison
Major activities: Low Income, Elderly, Affordable Housing; Legislative Advocacy; Hunger; Networking; Volunteerism; Publications & Worksops on Elder Housing Options

Council of Churches of Greater Springfield

152 Sumner Ave., Springfield, MA 01108
Media Contact, Asst. to Dir., Sr. John Bridgid, Fax (413)733-9817
Exec. Dir., Rev. Ann Geer
Dir. of Community Min., Mr. Arthur Serota, Esq.
Dir., Nursing Home Min., Laurie Misischia
Pres., The Rev. Dr. Rolf Hedburg
Treas., Mr. Jerre Hoffman
Major activities: Christian Education Resource Center; Advocacy; Emergency Fuel Fund; Peace and Justice Division; Community Ministry; Visitor Ombudspersons to Nursing Homes; Task Force on Aging; Hospital and Jail Chaplaincies; Pastoral Service; Crisis Counseling; Christian Social Relations; Relief Collections; Ecumenical and Interfaith Relations; Ecumenical Dialogue with Roman Catholic Diocese; Mass Media; Church/Community Projects and Dialog

Greater Lawrence Council of Churches

117A S. Broadway, Lawrence, MA 01843
Major activities: Ecumenical Worship; Radio Ministry; Hospital and Nursing Home Chaplancy; ; Church Women United; Afterschool Children's Program; Educational Programs

Inter-Church Council of Greater New Bedford

412 County St., New Bedford, MA 02740
Acting Exec. Min., Rev. Dr. John Douhan
Pres., Rev. Nehemiah Boynton, III
Treas., William Reed
Major activities: Pastoral Counseling; Chaplaincy; Housing for Elderly; Urban Affairs; Parent-Child Center; Social Rehabilitation Club

Massachusetts Commission on Christian Unity

82 Luce St., Lowell, MA 01852
Media Contact, Exec. Dir., Rev. K. Gordon White
Exec. Sec., Rev. K. Gordon White
Major activities: Faith and Order Dialogue with Church Judicatories

Massachusetts Council of Churches

14 Beacon St., Rm. 416, Boston, MA 02108
Media Contact, Exec. Dir., Rev. Diane C. Kessler, Fax (617)523-2771
Exec. Dir., Rev. Diane C. Kessler
Assoc. Dir. for Public Policy, Dr. Ruy Costa
Assoc. Dir., Ecumenical Development, Rev. David A. Anderson
Major activities: Christian Unity; Education and Evangelism; Defend Social Justice & Individual Rights; Ecumenical Worship; Services and Resources for Individuals and Churches

Worcester County Ecumenical Council

25 Crescent St., Worcester, MA 01605
Media Contact, Sec., Eleanor G. Bird
Exec. Dir., Rev. Richard A. Hennigar
Program Asst., Richard Monroe
Pres., Rev. Clifford Gerber
Major activities: Clusters of Churches; Electronic Media; Economic Justice; Youth Ministries; Ecumenical Worship and Dialogue; Interfaith Activities; Nursing Home Chaplaincies; Assistance to Churches; Peace; Hunger Ministries; AIDS Pastoral Care Network; Mental Illness; Group Purchasing Consortium; Alcohol & Other Drug Abuse Prevention

MICHIGAN

ACCORD—Area Churches Together . . . Serving

312 Capital Ave., NE, Battle Creek, MI 49017
Media Contact, Exec. Dir., Patricia A. Staib
Exec. Dir., Patricia A. Staib
Pres., Rev. David Morton
Vice-Pres./Church, Rev. Charles Sandum
Vice-Pres./Admn., David Lucas
Vice-Pres./Community, Rev. Joseph Bistayi
Major activities: CROP Walk; Thanksgiving International Student Homestay; Food Closet; Christian Sports; Week of Prayer for Christian Unity; Nursing Home Vesper Services; Ecumenical Worship

Christian Communication Council of Metropolitan Detroit Churches

1300 Mutual Building, 28 W. Adams, Detroit, MI 48226
Exec. Dir., Rev. Edward Willingham
Assoc. Dir., Mrs. Angie Willingham
Media Assoc., Mrs. Tawnya Bender
Prog. Dir., Meals for Shut-ins, Mr. John Simpson
Coord., Summer Feeding Prog., Ms. Monique Lindsey
Major activities: Theological and Social Concerns; Ecumenical Worship; Educational Services; Electronic Media; Print Media; Meals for Shut-Ins; Summer Feeding Program

Grand Rapids Area Center for Ecumenism (GRACE)

38 W. Fulton, Grand Rapids, MI 49503
Media Contact, Exec. Dir., Rev. David P. Baak
Exec. Dir., Rev. David P. Baak
Prog. Dir., Ms. Betty Zylstra
Major activities: Hunger Walk; November Hunger and Shelter Awareness Week; Shelter Forum; Aging Committee; AIDS Pastoral Care Network; Clergy Interracial Forum; Annual Week of Prayer for Christian Unity; Ecumenical Eucharist and Pentecost Services, Educational Forums.; Affiliates: ACCESS (All County Churches Emergency Support System); FISH for My People (Transportation); Habitat for Humanity/GR; *Grace Notes*

Greater Flint Council of Churches

927 Church St., Flint, MI 48502
Media Contact, Pres., Barbara Spaulding-Westcott
Pres., Barbara Spaulding-Westcott
Major activities: Christian Education; Christian Unity; Christian Missions; Hospital and Nursing Home Visitors; Church in Society; American Bible Society Materials; Interfaith Dialogue; Church Teacher Exchange Sunday; Directory of Area Faiths and Clergy; Operation Brush-up; Thanksgiving & Easter Sunrise Services

The Jackson County Interfaith Council

425 Oakwood, P.O. Box 156, Clarklake, MI 49234-0156
Media Contact, Exec. Dir., Rev. Loyal H. Wiemer
Exec. Dir., Rev. Loyal H. Wiemer
Major activities: Chaplaincy at Institutions and Senior Citizens Residences; Martin L. King, Jr. Day Celebrations; Ecumenical Council Representation; Radio and TV Programs; Food Pantry; Interreligious Events; Clergy Directory

Michigan Ecumenical Forum

809 Center St., Ste. 7-B, Lansing, MI 48906
Media Contact, Coord./Exec. Dir., Rev. Stephen L. Johns-Boehme
Coord./Exec. Dir., Rev. Steven L. Johns-Boehme
Major activities: Communication and Coordination; Support and Development of Regional Ecumenical Fora; Ecumenical Studies; Fellowship and Celebration; Church and Society Issues; Continuing Education

MINNESOTA

Arrowhead Council of Churches

230 E. Skyline Pkwy., Duluth, MN 55811
Media Contact, Exec. Dir., Ava M. Calbreath, Fax (218)727-5022
Exec. Dir., Ava. M. Calbreath
Pres., Mark Frykholm
Major activities: Inter-Church Evangelism; Community Concerns; Joint Religious Legislative Coalition; Downtown Ecumenical Good Friday Service; Corrections Chaplaincy; CROP Hunger Walk; Forum for Interfaith Dialogue; Community Seminars; Children's Concerns

Community Emergency Assistance Program (CEAP)

7231 Brooklyn Blvd., Brooklyn Center, MN 55429
Exec. Dir., Edward T. Eide
Major activities: Provision of Basic Needs (Food, Clothing, Furniture); Emergency Financial Assistance for Shelter; Home Delivered Meals; Chore Services and Homemaking Assistance; Single Parent Loan Program; Volunteer Services

Greater Minneapolis Council of Churches

122 W. Franklin Ave., Ste. 218, Minneapolis, MN 55404
Media Contact, Dir. of Public Relations, Gay Gonnerman
Pres., Phyllis Sutton

Treas., Mike McCarthyExec. Dir., Rev. Dr. Gary B. Reierson
Assoc. Exec. Dir., Indian Work, Mary Ellen Dumas
Dir., Twin Cities Metropolitan Church Comm., Rev. Sally Hill
Dir., Meals on Wheels, Barbara Green
Dir., Minnesota FoodShare, Rev. Peg Chemberlin
Correctional Chaplain, Rev. Norman Menke
Correctional Chaplain, Rev. Susan Allers Hatlie
Correctional Chaplain, Rev. Thomas Van Leer
Dir., Congs. Concerned for Children, Carolyn Hendrixson
Dir., Shared Ministries Tutorial Program, Rev. Belinda Green
Dir., Metro Paint-A-Thon, Jodi Young
Dir., HandyWorks, DeLaine Brown

Dir., Emerg. Asst. Prog., Div. of Indian Work, George McCauley
Dir., Family Violence Prog., Div. of Indian Work, Don Chapin
Dir., Teen Indian Parents Prog., Div. of Indian Work, Noya Woodrich
Dir., Youth Leadership Dev. Prog., Div. of Indian Work, Margaret Thunder
Dir., Finance and Admn., Philip J. A. Hatlie
Dir., Development, Ch. Relations, and Public Relations, Gay Gonnerman
Major activities: Indian Work (Emergency Assistance, Youth Leadership, Teen Indian Parents Program, and Family Violence Program); Minnesota FoodShare; Metro Paint-A-Thon; Meals on Wheels; Shared Ministries Tutorial Program; Congregatio; Correctional Chaplaincy Program; HandyWorks; Education and Celebration;

The Joint Religious Legislative Coalition

122 West Franklin Ave., Rm. 315, Minneapolis, MN 55404
Media Contact, Executive Director, Brian Rusche
Exec. Dir., Brian Rusche
Research Dir., Jim Casebolt
Major activities: Lobbying at State Legislature; Researching Social Justice Issues and Preparing Position Statements; Organizing Grassroots Citizen's Lobby

Minnesota Council of Churches

122 W. Franklin Ave., #100, Minneapolis, MN 55404
Media Contact, Executive Director, Rev. Dr. Margaret J. Thomas, Fax (612)870-3663
Exec. Dir., Rev. Dr. Margaret J. Thomas
Dir. of Life & Work, Louis S. Schoen
Dir. of Hispanic Ministry, Carlos Mariani-Rosa
Dir. of Faith & Order, Rev. Molly M. Cox
Dir., Refugee Services, Shannon Bevans
Caseworker, Ge Cheuthang Yang
Case Mgr./Sponsor Developer, Brenda Otterson
Dir. of Indian Concerns, Mary Ann Walt
Dir. of Facilities, Cynthia Darrington-Ottinger
Dir., Twin Cities Metropolitan Church Com, Rev. Sally L. Hill
Dir., Joint Religious Legislative Coalition, Brian A. Rusche
Pres., Rev. Dean Larson
Major activities: Minnesota Church Center; Local Ecumenism; Life & Work: Hispanic Ministries, Indian Concerns; Legislative Advocacy; Refugee Services; Service to Newly Legalized/Un-

documented Persons; Sexual Exploitation within the Religious Community; State Fair Ministry; Faith & Order; Consultation on Church Union; Ecumenical Dialogue; Jewish-Christian Relations; Muslim-Christian Relations; Spirituality

St. Paul Area Council of Churches
1671 Summit Ave., St. Paul, MN 55105
Media Contact, Admin. Asst., Ella Snyder, Fax (612)646-6568
Exec. Dir., Rev. Thomas Duke
Chaplaincy, Dr. Fred A. Hueners
Ecumenical Relations, Rev. Sally Hill
Congregations Concerned for Children, Ms. Peg Wangensteen
Volunteer Care Ministries, Ms. Pat Argyros
Coop. Ministries for Children/Youth, Ms. Anita Arrington-Reynolds
Dept. of Indian Work, Ms. Sheila WhiteEagle
Pres., Rev. George Weinman
Treas., Bert Neinaber
Sec., Ms. Kay Andrews
Major activities: Chaplaincy at Detention and Corrections Authority Institutions; Police Chaplaincy; Education and Advocacy Regarding Children and Poverty; Assistance to Churches Developing Child Care Services; Ecumenical Encounters and Activities; Indian Ministries; Leadership in Forming Cooperative Ministries for Children and Youth; Parent Befriender Ministry

Twin Cities Metropolitan Church Commission
122 W. Franklin, Rm. 100, Minneapolis, MN 55404
Exec. Dir., Rev. Sally L. Hill
Pres., Rev. Tom Duke, 1673 Summet Ave., St. Paul, MN 55105
Major activities: Education; Criminal Justice Committee; Peace Education Project; Interreligious Committee on Central America; Ecumenical Decade; Churches in Solidarity with Women; US/USSR Religious Exchanges

MISSISSIPPI

Mississippi Religious Leadership Conference
P.O. Box 68123, Jackson, MS 39286-8123
Media Contact, Exec. Dir., Rev. Canon Thomas E. Tiller
Exec. Dir., Rev. Canon Thomas E. Tiller, Jr.
Chair, Rev. Rayford Woodrick
Treas., Mrs. Barbara Barnes
Co-Treasurer, Rev. Tom Clark
Major activities: Cooperation among Religious Leaders; Lay/Clergy Retreats; Social Concerns Seminars; Disaster Task Force; Advocacy for Disadvantaged

MISSOURI

Council of Churches of the Ozarks
P.O. Box 3947, Springfield, MO 65808-3947
Media Contact, Assoc. Dir., Rosanna Bradshaw
Exec. Dir., Dr. Dorsey E. Levell
Assoc. Dir., Rosanna Bradshaw

Major activities: Ministerial Alliance; Hospital Chaplains' Fellowship; Retired Sr. Volunteer Prog.; Treatment Center for Alcohol and Drug Abuse; Helping Elderly Live More Productively; Daybreak Adult Day Care Services; Ombundsman for Nursing Homes; Homesharing; Family Day Care Homes; USDA Food Program; Youth Ministry; Disaster Aid and Counseling; Homebound Shoppers; Alternatives to Incarceration; Food and Clothing Pantry; Ozarks Food Harvest; Spiritual Care Chaplains; Parenting Life Family Skills

Ecumenical Ministries
#2 St. Louis Ave., Fulton, MO 65251
Media Contact, Ofc. Mgr., Karen Luebbort
Exec. Dir., ——-
Pres., William Jessop
Major activities: Kingdom Hospice; CROP Hunger Walk; Little Brother and Sister; Older Kids Partnership; Summer Youth Day Camps; Widow to Widow Support; Christmas Bookmobile; Unity Service; Family Ministry; Inmate and Family Counseling; Criminal Justice Advocacy; AIDS Prison Counseling and Education; Community Pastor Study; BRIDGE College-to-Senior Program; Senior Center Bible Study; Older Adult Connection; Senior Advocacy and Study Seminars

Interfaith Community Services
200 Cherokee St., P.O. Box 4038, St. Joseph, MO 64504-0038
Media Contact, Exec. Dir., David G. Berger
Exec. Dir., David G. Berger
Major activities: Child Development; Neighborhood Family Services; Group Home for Girls; Retired Senior Volunteer Program; Nutrition Program; Mobile Meals; Southside Youth Program; Church and Community; Housing Development

MONTANA

Montana Association of Churches
Andrew Square, Ste. G, 100 24th St. W., Billings, MT 59102
Media Contact, Exec. Dir., Margaret E. McDonald
Exec. Dir., Margaret E. MacDonald
Admn. Asst., Larry D. Drane
Pres., Jessica Stickey, 2206 Main, Miles City, MT 59301
Treas., Don Patterson, East Lake Shore Rd., Big Fork, MT 59911
Rural Ministry Coord., Mary Lou Heiken, 935 S. 72nd St. W., Billings, MT 59106
Legislative Liaison, Harley Warner, 901 Elm, Helena, MT 59601
Campus Ministries Program Assoc., Rev. Kent Elliot, P.O. Box 389, Boulder, MT 59632
Major activities: Christian Education; Montana Religious Legislative Coalition; Christian Unity; Junior Citizen Camp; Public Information; Ministries Development; Social Ministry; Rural Ministry

NEBRASKA

Interchurch Ministries of Nebraska
215 Centennial Mall S., Rm. 411, Lincoln, NE 68508-1888
Media Contact, Exec. Sec., Rev. Daniel J. Davis, Sr.
Exec. Sec., Rev. Daniel J. Davis, Sr.
Admin. Asst., Sharon K. Kalcik
Pres., Rev. Dr. Roger Harp
Treas., Rev. "Clip" Higgins
Major activities: Interchurch Planning and Development; Comity; Indian Ministry; Rural Church Strategy; World Hunger; Refugee Resettlement Coordination; United Ministries in Higher Education; Disaster Response; Christian in Society Forum; Clergy Consultations; Farm Families Crisis Response Network; Video Technology; Interim Ministry Network; Pantry Network; Farm Mediation Services; Hispanic Ministry; the Church & Mental Illness Program; Conflict Management; Rural Health

Lincoln Interfaith Council
215 Centennial Mall South, Rm. 411, Lincoln, NE 68508
Media Contact, Exec. Dir., Rev. Dr. Norman E. Leach
Exec. Dir., Rev. Dr. Norman E. Leach
Pres., Cantor Michael Weisser
Treas., Ms. Nancy Glaesemann
Media Specialist, Mr. David Hancock
Urban Ministires, ——
Admin. Asst., Marge Daugherty
Fiscal Mgr., Sharon Kalchik
Jail Chaplain, Cantor Michael Weisser
Communities of Hope, Rev. Otto Schultz
Major activities: Media Ministry; Emergency Food Pantry; Communites of Hope; Jail Chaplaincy; Spiritual Growth; Clergy Fellowship; Clergy Connection for Non-Lincoln Patients; Prayer Breakfast; Refugee Work; Clergy Orientation; Directory of Resources; Anti-Drug & Gang Activities; Boy-Girl Scouts/Campfire/4-H Religious Awards Programs; HS Baccalaureate; UNICEF; Festival of Faith; Holocaust Memorial Observation; Dr. Martin Luther King, Jr. Observance

NEW HAMPSHIRE

New Hampshire Council of Churches
24 Warren St., P.O. Box 1107, Concord, NH 03302
Media Contact, Exec. Sec., Mr. David Lamarre-Vincent
Exec. Sec., Mr. David Lamarre-Vincent
Pres., Rev. Robert Witham
Treas., Richard Edmunds
Major activities: Ecumenical Work

NEW JERSEY

Bergen County Council of Churches
165 Burton Ave., Hasbrouck Hts., NJ 07604
Media Contact, Pres., Rev. Stephen Giordano
Exec. Sec., Neila Vander Vliet
Major activities: Ecumenical and Religious Institute; Brotherhood/Sisterhood Breakfast; Center for Food Action; Homeless Aid; Operation Santa Claus; Aging Services; Boy & Girl Scouts; Easter Dawn Services; Music; Youth; Ecumenical Representation

Council of Churches of Greater Camden
P.O. Box 1208, Merchantville, NJ 08109
Media Contact, Exec. Sec., Rev. Dr. Samuel A. Jeanes
Exec. Sec., Rev. Dr. Samuel A. Jeanes
Pres., Rev. Lawrence L. Dunn
Treas., Mr. William G. Mason
Major activities: Radio & T.V.; Hospital Chaplaincy; United Services; Good Friday Breakfast; Mayors' Prayer Breakfast; Public Affairs; Easter Sunrise Service

Metropolitan Ecumenical Ministry
525 Orange St., Newark, NJ 07107
Exec. Dir., C. Stephen Jones
Major activities: Community Advocacy (education, housing, environment); Church Mission Assistance; Community and Clergy Leadership Development

New Jersey Council of Churches
116 N. Oraton Pkwy., East Orange, NJ 07017
176 W. State St., Trenton, NJ 08608
Commission on Impact & Public Witness, Rev. Steven C. Case
Commission on Mission Planning & Strategy, Rev. Robert K. Stuhlmann
Commission on Theology & Interreligious Relations, Rev. Betty Jane Bailey
Dir., IMPACT, Ms. Joan Diefenbach
Pres., Rev. William F. Freeman
Major activities: Racial Justice; AIDS Education; Ethics Public Forums; Advocacy

Trenton Ecumenical Area Ministry (TEAM)
2 Propsect St., Trenton, NJ 08618
Media Contact, Exec. Dir., Rev. David A. Gibbons
Exec. Dir., Rev. David A. Gibbons
Chpsn., Rev. Ronald Bagnall
Hospital Chaplains: ; Rev. Leo Forsberg; Ms. Lee Carol S. Hollendonner; Rev. Jessie L. Irvin
Campus Chaplains: ; Rev. Wayne Griffith; Rev. Nancy Schulter
Sec., Ms. Tina Swan
Major activities: Racial Justice; Children & Youth Ministries; Advocacy; CROP Walk; Ecumenical Worship; Hospital Chaplaincy; Church Women United; Campus Chaplaincy; TV Program; Congregational Empowerment

NEW MEXICO

Inter-Faith Council of Santa Fe, New Mexico
818 Camino Sierra Vista, Santa Fe, NM 87501
Media Contact, Secretary, Barbara A. Robinson, Fax (505)473-5637
Pres., Hib Sabin
Chpsn., Peace with Justice Task Force, Marjorie Schuckman
Chpsn., Barbara A. Robinson

Major activities: Faith Community Assistance Center; Hunger Walk, Interfaith Dialogues/Celebrations/Visitations; Peace Projects; Understanding Hispanic Heritage; Newsletter

New Mexico Conference of Churches

124 Hermosa S.E., Albuquerque, NM 87108-2610
Media Contact, Exec. Sec., Dr. Wallace Ford
Pres., Rev. Shannon Webster, P.O. Box 1434, Roswell, NM 88202-1434
Treas., Mr. Stan Hanamoto
Exec. Sec., Dr. Wallace Ford
Major activities: State Task Forces: Peace With Justice, Poverty, Disability Concerns, Legislative Concerns/Impact, Faith and Order, AIDS, Correctional Ministries, Public Education, Eco-Justice, Ecumenical Continuing Education; Regional Task Forces: Aging, Ecumenical Worship, Refugees, Emergency Care, Alcoholism; Church's Solidarity with Women

NEW YORK

Allied Christians of Tioga

228 Main Street, Owega, NY 13827
Exec. Dir., Al Smith, Jr.
Pres., Jack Checchia
Major activities: Jail Ministry; Soup Kitchen; Food Pantry; Coordinate Special Events

Bronx Division of the Council of Churches of the City of

39 W. 190th St., P.O. Box 144, Bronx, NY 10468
Pres., Rev. Robert L. Foley, Sr.
Exec. Dir., ——
Major activities: Pastoral Care; Christian Education & Youth Ministry; Welfare & Advocacy; Substance Abuse

Brooklyn Council of Churches

125 Ft. Greene Pl, Brooklyn, NY 11217
Dir., Mr. Charles Henze
Pres., Rev. Harvey P. Jamison
Treas., Rev. Albert J. Berube
Major activities: Education Workshops; Food Pantries; Welfare Advocacy; Hospital and Nursing Home Chaplaincy; Church Women United; Legislative Concerns

Broome County Council of Churches, Inc.

81 Main St., Binghamton, NY 13905
Media Contact, Exec. Dir., Mr. William H. Stanton, Fax (607)724-9148
Exec. Dir., Mr. William H. Stanton
Admin. Asst., Ms. Joyce M. Kirby
Hospital Chaplain, Rev. LeRoy Flohr
Hospital Chaplain, Mrs. Betty Pomeroy
Jail Chaplain, Rev. Philip Singer
Aging Ministry Coord., Mrs. Dorothy Myers
CHOW Prog. Coord., Mrs. Billie L. Briggs
Pres., Mr. Ray A. Hull
Treas., Mrs. Rachel Light
Major activities: Hospital and Jail Chaplains; Youth and Aging Ministries; CHOW (Emergency Hunger Program); Christian Education; Ecumenical Worship and Fellowship; Media; Community Affairs; Peace

Buffalo Area Council of Churches

1272 Delaware Ave., Buffalo, NY 14209
Exec. Dir., Rev. Dr. G. Stanford Bratton
Coord., Church Women United, Sally Giordano
Coord., Radio/TV, Linda Velazquez
Pres., Rev. Dr. Robert Graham
Vice-Pres., Charles Banks
Vice Pres., Rev. Donald Garrett
Sec., Dolores Gibbs
Treas., Rev. Kenneth Neal
Pres. Church Women United, Bobbie Campbell
Chpsn., Admin., Emerson Barr, Jr.
Chpsn., Community Witness & Ministry, Pastor Virginia Williams
Chpsn, Ecumenical Events, Rev. Robert Leach
Chpsn., Public Policy, Rev. Julius Jackson
Spirituality & Community Building, Chpsn., Rev. Donald Garrett
Radio & TV, Chairperson, Rev. Robert Hutchinson
Major activities: Radio-TV; Social Services; Chaplains; Church Women United; Ecumenical Relations; Refugees; Public Policy; Community Development; Lay/Clergy Education; Interracial Dialogue; Police/Community Relations

Buffalo Area Metropolitan Ministries, Inc.

775 Main St., Ste. 203, Buffalo, NY 14203-1310
Exec. Dir., Rev. Dr. Charles R. White
Pres., Rev. Francis X. Mazur
Vice-Pres. for Plng. & Prog., Rev. Steven Metcalfe
Vice-Pres. for Admn. & Fin., Rev. Richard Zajac
Sec., Dr. R. Parthasarathy
Treas., Rev. Richard E. McFail
Chair, Food for All Prog., Maureen Gensler
Major activities: An association of religious communities in Western New York with Jewish, Muslim, Christian, Unitarian, Univeralist, Hindu, and Jain membership providing a united religious witness through these major activities: Shelter; Hunger; Economic Issues; Interreligious Dialogue; Interfaith AIDS Network

Capital Area Council of Churches, Inc.

646 State St., Albany, NY 12203
Media Contact, Admin. Asst., Renee Kemp
Exec. Dir., Rev. Dr. Robert C. Lamar
Admn. Asst., Renee Kemp
Pres., Rev. Dr. S. Albert Newman
Treas., Mr. Alan Spencer
Major activities: Hospital Chaplaincy; Food Pantries; CROP Walk; Jail and Nursing Home Ministries; Martin Luther King Memorial Service and Scholarship Fund; Emergency Shelter for the Homeless; Campus Ministry; Ecumenical Dialogue; Forums on Social Concerns; Community W; Peace and Justice Education; Inter-Faith Programs; Legislative Concerns; Half-Way House for Ex-Offenders; Annual Ecumenical Musical Celebration

Chautauqua County Rural Ministry

127 Central Ave., P.O. Box 362, Dunkirk, NY 14048
Media Contact, Exec. Dir., Mr. Christopher J. Owens
Exec. Dir., Mr. Christopher J. Owens
Major activities: Chautauqua County Food Bank; Collection/Distribution of Furniture, Clothing,

& Appliances; Homeless Services; Building & Refurbishing Housing; Summer Work Camps

Christians United in Mission
224 Mohawk Ave., Box 2199, Scotia, NY 12302
Prog. Dir., Mr. Ronald K. Willis
Communications Dir., Mr. Stephen Esker
Major activities: Promote Cooperation/Coordination Among Member Judicatories in Urban Ministries, Media Communications, Social Action, Criminal Justice; Emergency Food; AIDS; Homelessness

Concerned Ecumenical Ministries of West Side Buffalo
286 LaFayette Ave., Buffalo, NY 14213
Exec. Dir., Mr. Cliff Whitman
Pres., Carl Henzelman
Major activities: Community center serving aging seniors;

Cortland County Council of Churches, Inc.
7 Calvert St., Cortland, NY 13045
Media Contact, Office Mgr., Joy Niswender
Exec. Dir., Rev. Donald M. Wilcox
Major activities: College Campus Ministry; Hospital Chaplaincy; Nursing Home Ministry; Newspaper Column; Interfaith Relationships; Hunger Relief; CWS; Crop Walk; Leadership Education; Community Issues; Mental Health Chaplaincy, Grief Support

Council of Churches of Chemung County, Inc.
330 W. Church St., Elmira, NY 14901
Media Contact, Exec. Dir., Joan Geldmacher
Exec. Dir., Mrs. Joan Geldmacher
Pres., Rev. Curtis Coley
Chaplain, Lee Griffith
Major activities: CWS Clothing Collection; CROP Walk; UNICEF; Institutional Chaplaincies; Radio, Easter Dawn Service; Communications Network; Representation on Community Boards and Agencies; Meals on Wheels; Campus Ministry; Food Cupboards; Ecumenical Services; Amerasian Resettlement

Council of Churches of the City of New York
475 Riverside Dr., Rm. 439, New York, NY 10015
Media Contact, Executive Director, Rev. Patricia A. Reeberg
Exec. Dir., Rev. Patricia A. Reeberg
Pres., Bishop Norman N. Quick
First Vice-Pres., Rev. N. J. L'Heureux, Jr.
Second Vice-Pres., Rev. Robert L. Foley, Sr.
Third Vice-Pres., Rev. Edward Earl Johnson
Sec., Ms. Paule Alexander
Treas., Dr. John E. Carrington
Major activities: Radio & TV; Pastoral Care; Protestant Chapel, Kennedy International Airport; Coordination and Strategic Planning; Religious Conferences; Referral & Advocacy

Dutchess Interfaith Council
9 Vassar St., Poughkeepsie, NY 12601
Exec. Dir., Rev. Gail Burger
Pres., Timmian C. Massie

Treas., Elizabeth M. DiStefano
Major activities: County Jail Chaplaincy; Radio; CROP Hunger Walk; Interfaith Music Festival; Public Worship Events; Interfaith Dialog; Christian Unity; Interfaith Youth Evening; Oil Purchase Group; Interfaith Volunteer Caregivers Program

East Harlem Interfaith
2050 - 2nd Ave., New York, NY 10029
Exec. Dir., Claudette Spence
Bd. Chmn., Rev. Robert Lott
Major activities: Ecumenical Worship; Welfare and Hunger Advocacy; AIDS Advocacy; Community Organizing; Economic Development (Community Reinvestment)

Genesee County Churches United, Inc.
P.O. Box 547, Batavia, NY 14021
Pres., Mrs. Captain Lucy Jordan
Exec. Sec., M. Deloris Cooper
Chaplain, Rev. Arthur Dolch
Major activities: Jail Ministry.; Food Pantries; Serve Needy Families; Radio Ministry; Pulpit Exchange; Community Thanksgiving; Ecumenical Services at County Fair

Genesee-Orleans Ministry of Concern
118 S. Main St., Box 245, Albion, NY 14411
Media Contact, Exec. Dir., Marian M. Adrian, GNSH
Exec. Dir., Marian Adrian, G.N.S.H.
Advocates: ; Jeannette Winiarz; Robert Fleming
Pres., Betsy Dexheimer
Chaplains: ; Orleans County Jail, Rev. Wilford Moss; Orleans Albion Correctional Facility, Sr. Dolores O'Dowd
Major activities: Advocacy Services for the Disadvantaged, Homeless, Ill, Incarcerated, and Victims of Family Violence; Emergency Food, Shelter, Utilities, Medicines

Greater Rochester Community of Churches
17 S. Fitzhugh St., Rochester, NY 14614-1488
Media Contact, Exec. Dir., Rev. Lawrence E. Witmer
Exec. Dir., Rev. Lawrence E. Witmer
Admin. Asst., Marie E. Gibson
Fin. Admn., Ilse Kearney
Pres., Rev. J. Paul Womack
Treas., Stanley Grenn
Major activities: Mission Education & Training; Refugee Resettlement; Hospital Chaplaincies; Evangelism; Church Unity; Social Ministries; Commission on Christian-Jewish Relations

InterReligious Council of Central New York
910 Madison St., Syracuse, NY 13210
Media Contact, Development Assoc., Marianne Valone
Exec. Dir., Dorothy F. Rose
Pres., Marilyn L. Pinsky
Assoc. Dir., Rev. Dale Hindmarsh
Assoc. Dir., Rev. Robert Stoppert
Dir. of Refugee Resettlement, Nona Stewart
Dir. Senior Companion Prog., Virginia Frey
Dir. Hunger Outreach Services, Daun Burk

Dir. Project Exodus Re-entry Program, Raheem Jami

Dir., Covenant Housing, Victoria Gilbert

Interreligious Relations, Mary Keller

Bus. Mgr., Arthur A. West

Major activities: Interreligious Relations; Education, Worship; Institutional Pastoral Care; Children/Youth Ministry; Low Cost Housing Program; Community Advocacy and Planning

Jamestown Area Ministry Association

SS Peter & Paul Church, 508 Cherry St., Jamestown, NY 14701

Dir., Rev. James E. Wall

Chaplain, Rev. John Kuhlmann

Chaplain Mayville Jail, Sr. Mary Elligan

Major activities: Food Vouchers; Homeless/Needy Program; Jail Ministry

Livingston County Coalition of Churches

P.O. Box 548, Lakeville, NY 14480

Coord., Rev. Robert Booher

Pres., Rev. Richard Clough

Major activities: Hospice Program; Jail Ministry; Visitors' Center at Groveland Correctional Facility; Food Pantries; Gateways Family Service; Parents Anonymous; Alternative Sentencing Program; Coordinate Services for Aging and Rural Poor; Christian Education Learning Fair; Lecture Series and Chaplain at SUNY Geneseo

The Long Island Council of Churches

1644 Denton Green, Hempstead, NY 11550

Eastern Office, 235 Sweezy Ave., Riverhead, NY 11901

Media Contact:, Adm. Asst., Ms. Barbara McLaughlin, Fax Call for inst

Exec. Dir., Rev. Robert L. Pierce

Exec. Asst., Rev. Ruth Phillips-Huyck

Admn. Asst., Ms. Barbara McLaughlin

Int. Dir., Pastoral Care, Rev. Walter Baepler

Dir., Clinical Pastoral Educ., Rev. Kai Borner

Dir., Social Services, Mrs. Lillian Sharik

Dir., Project REAL, Mr. Stephen Gervais

Dir., Counseling Services, Rev. S. Bruce Wagner

Nassau Cnty. Ofc.: Social Services Sec., Dorothy Hughes

Suffolk Cnty. Ofc.: Family Support, Carolyn Gumbs

Food Prog., Mrs. Millie McSteen

Blood Prog. Coord., Ms. Leila Truman

Blood Prog. Coord., Ms. Audry Wolf

Coord. for Training in Caring Ministry, Ms. Barbara Mathews

Major activities: Pastoral Care in Hospitals and Jails; Clinical Pastoral Education; Emergency Aid and Food; Advocacy for Domestic and International Peace & Justice; Blood Donor Coordination; Church World Service; Inter-faith Cooperation; Media Project; Newsletter; Church Directory; Counseling Service; Community Residences for Adults with Psychiatric Disabilities (Project REAL); HIV Education Projects; Special Projects

New York State Council of Churches

362 State St., Albany, NY 12210

3049 E. Genesee St., Syracuse, NY 13224 Fax (315)446-5789

Media Contact, Assoc. for Admin. & Communications, Thila Bell

Exec. Dir., Rev. Dr. Arleon L. Kelley

Coord., New York State IMPACT, Edward J. Bloch

Pres., Rev. J. Fay Cleveland

1st Vice-Pres., Rev. Allen A. Stanley

2nd Vice-Pres., The Ven. Michael S. Kendall

Sec., Isabel Morrison

Treas., Dr. George H. DeHority

Consultant for Resource Development, Mary Lu Bowen

Assoc. for Admn. Services, Ms. Sylvenia Cochran

Assoc. for Finance & Personnel, Helen Vault

Assoc. for Admn. & Communications, Thila A. Bell

Consultant for Resource Development, George Black

Program Assoc. for Chaplaincy, Rev. Frank Snow

Progam Assoc. for Issues Research & Advocacy, Dr. Sabine O'Hara

Major activities: Public Policy and Ecumenical Ministries; Chaplaincy in State Institutions; Rural Poor and Migrants; Homeless; AIDS; Universal Health Care; Life and Law; U.S.-Canadian Border Concerns; Single Parent Families; Faith and Order; Environmental Issues; The Family, Education, Violence; Covenanting Congregations

The Niagara Council of Churches Inc.

Rainbow Blvd. at Second St., Niagara Falls, NY 14303

Exec. Dir., Caroline C. Latham

Pres., Mr. Paul Wilson, 1556 101st St., Niagara Falls, NY 14304

Treas., Mr. Edward Weber, 1306 Maple Ave., Niagara Falls, NY 14305

Major activities: Ecumenical Worship; Bible Study; Christian Ed. & Social Concerns; Church Women United; Evangelism & Mission; Institutional Min. Youth Activities; Hymn Festival; Week of Prayer for Christian Unity; CWS Projects; Audio-Visual Library; UNICEF; Food Pantries and Kitchens; Community Missions, Inc.; Political Refugees; Eco-Justice Task Force; Migrant/rural Ministries; Interfaith Coalition on Energy

Niagara County Migrant Rural Ministry

5465 Upper Mountain Rd., Lockport, NY 14094

Media Contact, Coord., Ms. Barbara Meeks

Coord., Ms. Barbara Meeks

Sec./Asst., Grayce Dietz

Seasonal Outreach Worker, Jesse Garcia, Ofelia Carmona, Deborah Hill, Sally Quiros

Major activities: Migrant Farm Worker Program; Primary Health Clinic; Assist with immigration problems and application process for social services; Emergency Food Pantry; "Rummage Room" for clothing and household goods; Monitor Housing Conditions; Assist Rural Poor; Referrals to appropriate service agencies

Queens Federation of Churches

86-17 105th St., Richmond Hill, NY 11418-1597
Exec. Dir., Rev. N. J. L'Heureux, Jr.
Exec. Asst., Kevin Murphy
York College Chaplain, Rev. Dr. Hortense Merritt
Pres., Rev. Dr. Hortense Merritt
Treas., Lloyd W. Patterson, Jr.
Major activities: Emergency Food Service; York College Campus Ministry; Blood Bank; Scouting; Christian Education Workshops; Planning and Strategy; Church Women United; Community Consultations; Seminars for Church Leaders; Directory of Churches and Synagogues; Christian Relations (Prot/RC); Chaplaincies; Public Policy Issues; N.Y.S. Interfaith Commission on Landmarking of Religious Property; Queens Interfaith Hunger Network

Rural Migrant Ministry

P.O. Box 4757, Poughkeepsie, NY 12601
Media Contact, Exec., Richart Witt
Exec., Robert Witt
Pres., Mary Sherwig
Major activities: Serving the rural poor and migrants through pastoral work and social programs; Women's Support Group; Youth Program; Men's Soccer League; Latino Committee; Organization and Advocacy with and for Rural Poor; Jail Ministry

Schenectady Inner City Ministry

5 Catherine St., Schenectady, NY 12307
Media Contact, Urban Agent, Rev. Phillip N. Grigsby
Urban Agent, Rev. Phillip N. Grigsby
Admn. Asst., Ms. Elaine MacKinnon
Emergency Food Liaison, Ms. Patricia Obrecht
Nutrition Dir., Diane Solomon
Project SAFE/Safehouse Dir., Ms. Delores Edmonds-McIntosh
Church/Community Worker, Jim Murphy
Learning Tree Nursery, Dir., Victoria Filiaci
Pres., Sr. Stella Dillon
Bethesda House, Rev. Paul Fraser
Save and Share, Nilda Colon
Major activities: Emergency Food; Advocacy; Housing; Child Care; Alternatives to Prostitution for Runaway and At-Risk Youth; Shelter for Runaway/Homeless Youth; Neighborhood and Economic Issues; Ecumenical Worship and Fellowship; Community Research; Education in Churches on Faith Responses to Social Concerns; Legislative Advocacy; Nutrition Outreach Program; Hispanic Community Ministry; Food Buying Club; Day Shelter; CROP Walk

Southeast Ecumenical Ministries

25 Westminister Rd., Rochester, NY 14607
Dir., Laura Julien
Pres., Eileen Thomas-Poehner
Major activities: Food Cupboard; Transportation of Elderly

Staten Island Council of Churches

2187 Victory Blvd., Staten Island, NY 10314
Media Contact, Exec. Sec., Mrs. Mildred J. Saderholm

Pres., Rev. Donald C. Mullen
Vice-Pres., Rev. William E. Merryman
Exec. Sec., Mrs. Mildred J. Saderholm
Major activities: Support; Christian Education; Pastoral Care; Congregational Concerns; Urban Affairs

Troy Area United Ministries

17 First St., Troy, NY 12180
Exec. Dir., Mrs. Margaret T. Stoner
Pres., Rev. James E. Robinson
Chaplain, R.P.I., Rev. Donald Stroud
Chaplain, Russell Sage College, Cheryl Donkin
Major activities: Community Dispute Settlement (mediation) Program; College Ministry; Nursing Home Ministry; CROP Walk; Homeless and Housing Concerns; Weekend Meals Program at Homeless Shelter; Community Worship Celebrations; Racial Relations; and Bias Awareness

Wainwright House Interfaith Center

260 Stuyvesant Ave., Rye, NY 10580
Exec. Dir., Kathe Rhinesmith
Major activities: Educational Program and Conference Center; Intellectual, Psychological, Physical, and Spiritual Growth

NORTH CAROLINA

Asheville-Buncombe Community Christian Ministry (ABCCM)

24 Cumberland Ave., Asheville, NC 28801
Media Contact, Exec. Dir., Rev. Scott Rogers
Exec. Dir., Rev. Scott Rogers
Pres., Mr. James A. Lee
Major activities: Crisis Ministry; Jail/Prison Ministry; Shelter Ministry; Medical Ministry

Greensboro Urban Ministry

305 West Lee St., Greensboro, NC 27406
Media Contact, Exec. Dir., Rev. Mike Aiken
Exec. Dir., Rev. Mike Aiken
Major activities: Emergency Financial Assistance; Housing; Hunger Relief; Inter-Faith and Inter-Racial Understanding; Justice Ministry; Indigent Health Care

North Carolina Council of Churches

Methodist Bldg., 1307 Glenwood Ave., Ste. 162, Raleigh, NC 27605-3258
Media Contact, Exec. Dir., Rev. S. Collins Kilburn
Exec. Dir., Rev. S. Collins Kilburn
Program Assoc., Jimmy Creech
Pres., Rev. Raymon Hunt, 2607 Century Oaks Lane, Charlotte, NC 28262
Treas., Dr. James W. Ferree, P.O. Box 11772, Winston-Salem, NC 27116
Major activities: Children and Families; Health Care Justice; Christian Unity; Equal Rights; Legislative Program; Criminal Justice; Farmworker Ministry; Peace; Rural Crisis; Racial Justice; Disaster Response; CaringProgram for Children

NORTH DAKOTA

North Dakota Conference of Churches
227 W. Broadway, Bismarck, ND 58501
Media Contact, Office Mgr., Eunice Brinckerhoff
Pres., Paula Ringuette, PBVM
Treas., Rev. Randall Phillips
Ofc. Mgr., Eunice Brinckerhoff
Major activities: Prison Chaplaincy; Rural Life Ministry; Interfaith Dialogue; BEM Study; Faith and Order

OHIO

Akron Area Association of Churches
750 Work Dr., Akron, OH 44320
Media Contact, Admin. Asst., Chloe Ann Kriska
Exec. Dir., Rev. Harry Eberts, Jr.
Pres. Bd. of Trustees, Dr. Arthur Kemp
Vice-Pres.: ; Rev. Jan Walker; Mrs. Katherine Chapman
Sec., Rev. Dan Petry
Treas., Dr. Stephen Laning
Program Dir., Elsbeth Fritz
Chr. Ed. Dir., Mrs. Kimberly Porter
Major activities: Messiah Sing; Interfaith Council; Newsletters; Resource Center; Community Worship; Training of Local Church Leadership; Radio Programs; Clergy and Lay Fellowship Breakfasts; Cable TV; Interfaith Caregivers; Neighborhood Development; Community Outreach

Alliance of Churches
470 E. Broadway, Alliance, OH 44601
Dir., Richard A. Duro
Pres., Rev. Robert Stewart
Treas., Betty Rush
Major activities: Christian Education; Community Relations & Service; Ecumenical Worship; Community Ministry; Peacemaking; Medical Transportation; Job Placement Service

Churchpeople for Change and Reconciliation
326 W. McKibben, Box 488, Lima, OH 45802
Media Contact, Exec. Dir., Richard Keller
Exec. Dir., Richard Keller
Major activities: Developing Agencies for Minorities, Poor, Alienated, and Despairing; Community Kitchens

Council of Christian Communions of Greater Cincinnati
2439 Auburn Ave., Cincinnati, OH 45219
Media Contact, Exec. Dir., Joellen W. Grady
Exec. Dir., Joellen W. Grady
Assoc. Dir. for Justice Chaplaincy, Rev. Jack Marsh
Assoc. Dir. for Educ., Sharon D. Jones
Asst. Dir. Communication, John H. Gassett
Pres., Rev. Esther Chandler
Major activities: Christian Unity & Interfaith Cooperation; Justice Chaplaincies; Police-Clergy Team; Adult and Juvenile Jail Chaplains; Religious Education; Broadcasting and Communications; Information Service; Social Concerns

Ecumenical Communication Commission of N.W. Ohio
1011 Sandusky, Ste. M, P.O. Box 351, Perrysburg, OH 43551
Dir., Ms. Margaret Hoepfl
Major activities: Electronic Media Production; Media Education

Greater Dayton Christian Council
212 Belmonte Park E., Dayton, OH 45405
Media Contact, Exec. Dir., Rev. Robert B. Peiffer, Fax (513)222-8656
Exec. Dir., Rev. Robert B. Peiffer
Coord., Volunteer Jail Chaplaincy Program, Nancy Haas
Dir., Race Relations, Angela D. Montgomery
Pres., Rev. Don Dixon
Major activities: Communications: Service to Churches and Community; Housing Advocacy; Race Relations Advocacy; Substance Abuse Prevention; Jail Chaplaincy

Inner City Renewal Society
2230 Euclid Ave., Cleveland, OH 44115
Exec. Dir., Myrtle L. Mitchell
Major activities: Friendly Town; Urban Ministries Training and Community Development Center; Drug and Alcohol Education; Juvenile Opportunity and Involvement Network (J.O.I.N.); Project Chore; Career Beginnings; AIDS Education, Scholarship; Burial Aid

Interchurch Council of Greater Cleveland
2230 Euclid Ave., Cleveland, OH 44115-2499
Media Contact, Janice Giering
Exec. Dir., Rev. Thomas Olcott
Assoc. Dir. & Dir., Church and Society, Ms. Mylion Waite
Assoc. Dir. & Dir., Communications, Ms. Janice Giering
Pres., Frank Rasmussen
Chmn. of the Assembly, Mildred McFarland
Major activities: Church and Society; Communications; Hunger; Christian Education; Legislation; Faith and Order; Public Education; Interchurch News; Tutoring; Parent-Child Books Program; Shelter for Homeless Women and Children; Radio & T.V.; Interracial Cooperation; Interfaith Cooperation; Adaopt-A-School; Women of Hope; Leadership Development; Religious Education; Center for Peace & Reconciliation—Youth and the Courts

Mahoning Valley Association of Churches
631 Wick Ave., Youngstown, OH 44502
Exec. Dir., Elsie L. Dursi
Pres., Rev. William Brewster, St. John's Epis. Ch., 323 Wick Ave., Youngstown, OH 44503
Treas., Mr. Paul Fryman, 42 Venloe Dr., Poland, OH 44514
Major activities: Communications; Christian Education; Ecumenism; Social Action; Advocacy

Metropolitan Area Church Council
760 E. Broad St., Columbus, OH 43205
Media Contact, Chpsn. of Bd., Mrs. Marilyn Shreffler
Exec. Dir., ——
Support Service Coord., Rebecca S. Trover
Chpsn. of Bd., Mrs. Marilyn Shreffler
Vice Chmn., Dr. Luther Holland
Sec., Mrs. Juanita Bridges
Treas., Robert Godwin
Major activities: Newspaper; Liaison with Community Organizations; Assembly; Week of Prayer for Christian Unity; Support for Ministerial Associations and Church Councils; Seminars for Church Leaders; Prayer Groups; CROP Walk; Social Concerns Hearings

Metropolitan Area Religious Coalition of Cincinnati
1035 Enquirer Bldg., 617 Vine St., Cincinnati, OH 45202
Media Contact, Dir., Rev. Duane Holm, Fax (513)721-4844
Dir., Rev. Duane Holm
Pres., Rabbi Samuel Joseph
Major activities: Children-At-Risk; Public Education; Food & Welfare; Housing

Ohio Council of Churches
89 E. Wilson Bridge Rd., Columbus, OH 43085-2391
Media Contact, Dir. for Public Policy, Rev. David O. McCoy
Exec. Dir., Rev. Debra L. Moody
Dir. for Ecumenical Relations, Mr. David A. Leslie
Dir. for Public Policy, Rev. David O. McCoy
Dir. for Church & Community Issues, Mr. Raymond S. Blanks
Pres., Mrs. Violet Retzer
Treas., Mrs. Catherine Childs
Vice Pres., Rev. Charles W. Loveless
Sec., Rev. Joseph J. Witmer
Major activities: Economic Justice; Minority Church Empowerment; Ecumenical Development; Public Policy Issues; Criminal Justice Issues; World Peace and Justice

Pike County Outreach Council
122 E. Second St., Waverly, OH 45690
Dir., Judy Dixon

Toledo Ecumenical Area Ministries
444 Floyd St., Toledo, OH 43620
Admn., Metro-Toledo Churches United, Nancy Lee Atkins
Exec. Dir., Toledo Campus Ministry, Rev. Glenn B. Hosman, Jr.
Exec. Dir., Toledo Metropolitan Mission, Nancy Atkins
Major activities: Ecumenical Relations; Interfaith Relations; Food Program; Campus Ministry; Social Action (Public Education; Health Care; Urban Ministry; Employment; Community Organization; Welfare Rights; Housing; Refugee Assistance; Mental Retardation; Voter Registration/Education)

Tuscarawas County Council for Church and Community
120 First Dr. SE, New Philadelphia, OH 44663
Exec. Dir., Barbara E. Lauer
Pres., Mr. Thomas L. Kane, Jr., 1221 Crater Ave., Dover, OH 44622
Treas., Mr. James Barnhouse
Office Mgr., Shirley Dinger
Major activities: Human Services; Health; Family Life; Child Abuse; Housing; Educational Programs; Emergency Assistance; Legislative Concerns; Juvenile Prevention Program; Teen Pregnancy Prevention Program; Prevention Program for High Risk Children; Bimonthly newsletter The Pilot

West Side Ecumenical Ministry
4315 Bridge Ave, Cleveland, OH 44113
Exec. Dir., Robert T. Begin
Major activities: Emergency Food Centers; Senior Meals Programs; Youth Services; Advocacy, Empowerment Programs; Church Clusters; Drug Rehabilitation Program; Head Start Centers; Theatre

OKLAHOMA

Oklahoma Conference of Churches
P.O. Box 60288, 2901 Classen Blvd., Ste. 260, Oklahoma City, OK 73146-0288
Media Contact, Exec. Dir., The Rev. Dr. William B. Moorer
Exec. Dir., The Rev. Dr. William Moorer
Pres., Rev. John A. Petuskey, 1912 S. 69th East Ave., Tulsa, OK 74112
Treas., Mrs. Ann Fent
Major activities: Christian Unity Issues; COCU Covenanting; Community Building Among Members; Farm Crisis; Ecumenical Decade with Women ; Children's Advocacy; Refugee Resettlement; Day at the Legislature

Tulsa Metropolitan Ministry
221 S. Nogales, Tulsa, OK 74127
Exec. Dir., Sr. Sylvia Schmidt, S.C.C.
Assoc. Dir., ——-
Resident Service Dir., Shanita Spencer
Dir., Day Center for the Homeless, Marcia Sharp
Dir., (Housing Outreach Services of Tulsa), Rev. Charles Boyle
Advocacy Program Director, Rev. Larry Cowan
Pres., Rev. LeRoy K. Jordan
Vice-Pres., Sylvia Tuers
Sec., Dr. Rita Cowan
Treas., Joe Unger
Major activities: Corrections Ministry; Jewish-Christian Understanding; Police-Community Relations; Shelter for the Homeless; Women's Issues; Shelter for Mentally Ill; Outreach and Advocacy for Public Housing; Spirituality and Aging; Legislative Issues; Interfaith Dialogue TV Series; Christian Issues/Justice and Peace Issues; Central America Concerns & Events; Eco-Spirituality; Environmental Concerns; Communications

OREGON

Ecumenical Ministries of Oregon

0245 S.W. Bancroft St., Ste. B, Portland, OR 97201
Exec. Dir., Rev. Rodney I. Page
Dep. Dir., Barbara J. George
Dir. of Center for Urban Education, Rodney I. Page
Dir., Legis. & Govt. Ofc., Ellen C. Lowe
Comptroller, Gary B. Logsdon
Dir., Clinical Services, Cindy Klug
Med. Dir., Neal Rendleman, M.D.
Hopewell House Dir., Judith Kenning
Alternative Break Coalition, Eric Massanari
Dir., Hope Haven, Meg Oleson, Lee Tomerlin
Dirs., Hemophilia NW: ; Larkey DeNeffe; Beth Weinstein
Drug Educ. Proj., Bob McNeil
Sophia Center, Dir., Kathryn Knoll
Alcohol & Drugs Min., Nancy Anderson
Police Chaplain, Rev. Greg Kammann
Sponsors Organized to Assist Refugees, Gary Gamer, Fax (503)284-6445
Dir., Emergency Food, Britt Olson
Dir., Folk-Time (Soc. Prog. for Mentally Ill), Susan Alperin
Dir., Job Opportunity Bank, Noreen Goplen, Fax (503)249-2857
Dir., HIV Day Center, Tina Tommaso-Jennings
Pres., The Rev. Richard Osburn
Pres.-Elect, The Rev. William Creevey
Treas., Ron Means
Major activities: Educational Ministries; Legislation; Urban Ministries; Refugees; Chaplaincy; Social Concerns; Direct Services; Jewish-Christian Relations; Farm Ministry; Alcohol and Drug Ministry; Welfare Advocacy; Faith & Order; Peace Ministries; IMPACT; Communications; AIDS Ministry; Prostitution Ministry; Farm and Rural Ministries; Racism; Religious Education; Health and Human Ministries

PENNSYLVANIA

Allegheny Valley Association of Churches

1333 Freeport Road, Natrona Heights, PA 15065
Dir., Luella H. Barrage
Pres., Rev. Dr. W. James Legge, RR #4, Box 186, Tarentum, PA 15084
Treas., Mrs. Libby Grimm, RR #2, Box 36, Tarentum, PA 15084
Major activities: Education Evangelism Workshops; Ecumenical Services; Dial-a-Devotion; Youth Activities; CROP Walk; Food Bank; Super Cupboard; Emergency Aid; Cross-on-the-Hill; AVAC Interfaith Hospitality Network for Homeless Families

Christian Associates of Southwest Pennsylvania

239 Fourth Ave., #1817, Pittsburgh, PA 15222-1769
Media Contact, Exec. Dir., Rev. Donald E. Leiter
Exec. Dir., Rev. Donald Leiter
Assoc. Exec. Dir., Rev. Bruce H. Swenson
Cable TV Co-ordinator, ———
Admn. Asst., Mrs. Barbara Irwin
Pres., Rev. Robert Rigg
Treas., Rev. David Zubik
Communications Coord., Mr. Bruce J. Randolph

Major activities: Communications; Planning; Church and Community; Leadership Development; Theological Dialogue; Evangelism/Church Growth; Racism

Christian Churches United of the Tri-County Area

900 S. Arlington Ave., Rm. 128, Harrisburg, PA 17109
Media Contact, Resource Devel. Dir., Rev. Rodger Clark
Exec. Dir., Rev. Michael Morrill
Pres., Rev. K. Joy Kaufman
Treas., Rev. Lawrence Jones
V.P., Geraldine Brown
Sec., Doris Frysinger
Asst. Dir., Kathy Cracroft
Dir., HELP, Jacqueline Rucker, 201 Locust St., Harrisburg, PA 17101 Fax (717)238-1916
Dir., La Casa, Maria Davila, 1312 Derry St., Harrisburg, PA 17104
Major activities: Volunteer Ministries to Prisons; Hospitals; Mental Health; Aging; Christian Education; HELP (Housing, Rent, Food, Medication, Transportation, Home Heating, Clothing); La Casa de Amistad (The House of Friendship) Social Services; AIDS Outreach; Prison Chaplaincy

Christians United in Beaver County

1098 Third Street, Beaver, PA 15009
Media Contact, Exec. Sec., Mrs. Lois L. Smith
Exec. Sec., Mrs. Lois L. Smith
Chaplains, Rev. Samuel Ward, Mrs. Erika Bruner, Rev. Anthony Massey, Rev. Frank Churchill, Mr. Jack Kirkpatrick
Pres., Mrs. Erika Bruner
Treas., Mr. William Young, 2903-20th St., Beaver Falls, PA 15010
Major activities: Christian Education; Evangelism; Radio; Social Action; Church Women United; United Church Men; Ecumenism; Hospital, Detention Home, and Jail Ministry

Delaware Valley Media Ministry

1501 Cherry St., Philadelphia, PA 19102
Media Contact, Exec. Dir., Ms. Nancy Nolde
Exec. Dir., Ms. Nancy Nolde
Major activities: Interfaith Communication and Television Production Agency

East End Cooperative Ministry

250 N. Highland Ave., Pittsburgh, PA 15206
Media Contact, Nancy Paul, Fax (412)362-1992
Exec. Dir., Mrs. Judith Marker
Major activities: Food Pantry; Soup Kitchen; Men's Emergency Shelter; Meals on Wheels; Casework and Supportive Services for Elderly; Information and Referral; Program for Children and Youth; Bridge Housing Program for Men and Women in Recovery and their Children

Easton Area Interfaith Council

330 Ferry St., Easton, PA 18042
Admn. Sec., Marlene Smith
Major activities: Food Bank; Hospital and Nursing Home Chaplaincy; Center for Mentally Handicapped; Homeless

Ecumenical Conference of Greater Altoona

1208 - 13th St., P.O. Box 305, Altoona, PA 16603
Exec. Dir., Mrs. Eileen Becker
Major activities: Religious Education; Workshops; Ecumenical Activities; Religious Christmas Parade; Campus Ministry; Community Concerns; Peace Forum; Religious Education for Mentally Handicapped; Inter-faith Committee

Ecumenical Urban Ministries

100 N. Bellefield at Fifth Ave., Pittsburgh, PA 15213
Exec. Dir., Rev. James C. Faltot
Pres. of EUM Bd., Dr. Walter Wiest
Major activities: Training Programs Focused on Increasing the Effectiveness of the Urban Church; Advocacy on Social Justice Matters

Greater Bethlehem Area Council of Churches

520 E. Broad St., Bethlehem, PA 18018
Media Contact, Exec. Dir., Audrey R. Bertsch
Exec. Dir., Audrey R. Bertsch
Pres., Rev. Dr. William Matz, 3138 Patterson Dr., Bethlehem, PA 18017
Treas., Mrs. Polly McClure
Major activities: Support Ministry; Institutional Ministry to Elderly and Infirm; Family Concerns; Scripture Center; Social Concerns; World Local Hunger Projects; Elderly Ministry

The Greater Reading Council of Churches

54 N. 8th St., Reading, PA 19601
Media Contact, Exec. Dir., Rev. Dr. Larry T. Nallo
Exec. Dir., Rev. Dr. Larry T. Nallo
Admn. Asst., Constance B. Fegley
Pres., Rev. Edward Ward
Rec. Sec., Rev. Thomas Ross
Treas., Mr. Lee M. LeVan
Major activities: Institutional Ministry; CWU; Social Action; Migrant Ministry; CWS; CROP Walk for Hunger; Emergency Assistance; Furniture Bank; Prison Chaplaincy; AIDS Hospice Development; Hospital Chaplaincy

Hanover Area Council of Churches

120 York St., Hanover, PA 17331
Exec. Dir., Nancy M. Hewitt
Major activities: Meals on Wheels, Provide a Lunch Program, Fresh Air Program, Clothing Bank, Hospital Chaplaincy Services Congregational & Interfaith Relations, Public Ecumenical Programs and Services, State Park Chaplaincy Services & Children's Program

Inter-Church Ministries of Erie County

252 W. 7th St., Erie, PA 16501
Media Contact, Exec. Dir., The Rev. Willis J. Merriman
Exec. Dir., Rev. Willis J. Merriman
Assoc. Dir., Rev. Deborah R. Dockstader
Adjunct Staff: ; Pastoral Counseling, Dr. David J. Sullivan; Aging Prog., Ms. Carolyn A. DiMattio
Pres., The V. Rev. John P. Downey

Treas., The Rev. Victoria Wood Parrish, 538 E. 10th St., Erie, PA 16503
Major activities: Local Ecumenism; Ministry with Aging; Social Ministry; Pastoral Counseling; Continuing Education; N.W. Pa. Conf. of Bishops and Judicatory Execs.; Institute of Pastoral Care; Theological Dialogue; AIDS Ministry and Interracial Sharing of Families Ministry

Lancaster County Council of Churches

447 E. King St., Lancaster, PA 17602
Media Contact, Publicity Chairperson, Donna Crosby
Pres., Rev. Charlotte Whiting
Interim Exec. Dir., Rev. Robert Bistline
Prison Chaplain, Rev. David F. Myer
Dir. Prescott House, Casey Jones
Asst. Admn., Kim Y. Wittel
Dir. Child Abuse, Ursula Wanner
Dir. CONTACT, Rhoda Mull
Dir., Service Ministry, Adela Dohner
Major activities: Social Ministry; Residential Ministry to Youthful Offenders; Prison Ministry; CONTACT; Advocacy; Child Abuse Prevention

Lebanon County Christian Ministries

818 Water St., P.O. Box 654, Lebanon, PA 17042
Exec. Dir., Mrs. Elizabeth F. Greer
Food & Clothing Bank Dir., Lillian Morales
H.O.P.E. Services, P. Richard Forney
Noon Meals Coord., Mrs. Glenda Wenger
Major activities: H.O.P.E. (Helping Our People in Emergencies); Food & Clothing Bank; Free Meal Program; Commodity Distribution Program; Ecumenical Events; Chaplaincy and Support Services

Lehigh County Conference of Churches

534 Chew St., Allentown, PA 18102
Media Contact, Exec. Dir., Rev. William A. Seaman
Exec. Dir., Rev. William A. Seaman
Pres., Rev. Dr. Iris Simpson
Treas., Mr. James G. Hottenstein
Major activities: Chaplaincy Program; Migrant Ministry; Social Concerns and Action; Clergy Dialogues; Drop-In-Center for De-Institutionalized Adults; Ecumenical Food Kitchen; Housing Advocacy Program; Pathways (Reference to Social Services)

Metropolitan Christian Council of Philadelphia

1501 Cherry St., Philadelphia, PA 19102
Media Contact, Assoc. Communications, Ms. Nancy L. Nolde
Exec. Dir., Rev. C. Edward Geiger
Assoc. Communications, Ms. Nancy L. Nolde
Admn. Asst., Mrs. Joan G. Shipman
Pres., Rev. Gus Roman
Vice-Pres., Rt. Rev. Allen L. Bartlett, Jr.
Treas., John A. Clark, 1 Liberty Pl., Philadelphia, PA 19103
Major activities: Congregational Clusters; Public Policy Advocacy; Communication; Interfaith Dialogue

North Hills Youth Ministry

802 McKnight Park Dr., Pittsburgh, PA 15237
Exec. Dir., Ronald B. Barnes
Major activities: Junior and Senior High School
Family and Individual Counseling; Pre-Adolescent Youth Early Intervention Counseling; Educational Programming for Churches and
Schools; Youth Advocacy

Northside Common Ministries

P.O. Box 99861, Pittsburgh, PA 15233
Media Contact, Exec. Dir., Rev. Robert J. Wilde, MSW
Exec. Dir., Rev. Robert J. Wilde, MSW
Pres., Rev. Thomas Moog
Major activities: Pleasant Valley Shelter for
Homeless Men; Advocacy around Hunger,
Housing, Poverty, and Racial Issues; Community Service Center and Pantry;

Northwest Interfaith Movement

6757 Greene St.,, Philadelphia, PA 19119
Exec. Dir., Rev. Richard R. Fernandez
Dir., Long Term Care Connection, Valerie Pogozelski
Chpsn., Dr. Phillip Welser
Dir., Northwest Child Care Resource Prog., Amy
Gendall
Dir., Neighborhood Child Care Resource Program, Amy Gendall
Major activities: Community Development &
Community Reinvestment; Older Adult Concerns; Nursing Home Program; Unemployment;
Economic Issues; Public Education; Peace; Racism; Poverty Issues

Pennsylvania Conference on Interchurch Cooperation

P.O. Box 2835, 223 North St., Harrisburg, PA
17105
900 S. Arlington Ave., Harrisburg, PA 17109
Co-Staff, Dr. Howard Fetterhoff
Co-Staff, Rev. Albert E. Myers
Co-Chairpersons, Bishop Nicholas Dattilo
Co-Chairpersons, Bishop Guy S. Edmiston, Jr.
Major activities: Theological Consultation; Social
Concerns; Inter-Church Planning; Conferences
and Seminars; Disaster Response Preparedness

The Pennsylvania Council of Churches

900 S. Arlington Ave., Ste. 100, Harrisburg, PA
17109
Media Contact, Exec. Dir., Rev. Albert E. Myers,
Fax (717)545-4765
Exec. Dir., Rev. Albert E. Myers
Asst. Exec. Dir., Soc. Min., Rev. Paul D. Gehris
Asst. Exec. Dir., Special Min., Rev. Charles E.
Dorsey
Pres., Bishop Charlie F. McNutt, Jr., 221 N. Front
St., P.O. Box 11937, Harrisburg, PA 17108
Vice-Pres., Mrs. Pattee Miller, Jr.
Sec., Rev. Jack Rothenberger
Treas., Robert Ziegler
Bus. Mgr., Janet Gollick
Major activities: Institutional Ministry; Migrant
Ministry; Truck Stop Chaplaincy; Social Ministry; Park Ministry; Inter-Church Planning and
Dialog; Conferences; Disaster Response; Trade
Association Activities; Church Education; Ethnic Cooperation

Reading Urban Ministry

134 N. Fifth St., Reading, PA 19601
Media Contact, Beth Bitler
Exec. Dir., Beth Bitler
Pres., Mark C. Potts
Vice-Pres., Rev. Lydia A. Speller
Sec., Sarah Boyd
Treas., Raymond Drain
Major activities: Community Clothing Center;
Friendly Visitor Program to Elderly; Caring
When It Counts (Emergency Intervention with
Elderly); Summer Youth Program; Family Action Support Team (For Single-Parent Families)

South Hills Interfaith Ministries

393 Vanadium Rd., Pittsburg, PA 15243
Exec. Dir., Robert Laird Brashear
Psychological Services, Mr. Don Zandier
Cmty. Services, Mr. Thomas Tompkins
Cmty. Services, Sherry Kotz
Admn. Operations Dir., Ms. Jacqueline Riebel
Interfaith Reemployment Job Advocate, Mr.
David Bates
Pres., Rev. Dan Merry
Treas., Mr. Jerry Sherman
Major activities: Basic Human Needs; Unemployment; Community Organization and Development; Inter-Faith Cooperation; Family Hospice;
Personal Growth

United Churches of Williamsport and Lycoming County

202 E. Third St., Williamsport, PA 17701
Media Contact, Exec. Dir., Mrs. Gwen Nelson
Bernstine
Exec. Dir., Mrs. Gwen Nelson Bernstine
Ofc. Sec., Mrs. Linda Winter
Pres., Msgr. William J. Fleming
Treas., Mr. Russell E. Tingue
Shepherd of the Streets, Rev. Joseph L. Walker
Dir., Ecumenism, Rev. Robert L. Driesen
Dir., Educ. Ministries, Rev. George E. Doran, Jr.,
122 S. Main St., Hughesville, PA 17737
Dir., Institutional Ministry, Rev. Wilbur L. Scranton III, 207 E. Water St., Box 504, Muncy, PA
17756
Dir., Radio-TV, Rev. Michael D. Gingerich, P.O.
Box 366, Picture Rocks, PA 11762
Dir., Social Concerns, Rev. Mark A. Santucci
Dir., Prison Ministry, Rev. John N. Mostoller
Major activities: Ecumenism; Educational Ministries; Church Women United; Church World
Service and CROP; Prison Ministry; Radio-TV;
Nursing Homes; Fuel Bank; Food Pantry; Family
Life; Shepherd of the Streets Urban Ministry;
Peace Concerns

Willkinsburg Community Ministry

710 Mulberry St., Pittsburgh, PA 15221
Media Contact, Dir., Rev. Vivian Lovingood
Dir., Rev. Vivian Lovingood
Pres. of Bd., Rev. Walter Pietschmann
Major activities: Hunger Ministry; After School
Youth Programs; Child Care for Working Parents; Summer Bible School; Teen-Moms Infant
Care; Meals on Wheels; Tape Ministry

Wyoming Valley Council of Churches

35 S. Franklin St., Wilkes-Barre, PA 18701
Exec. Dir., Rev. Lynn P. Lampman
Ofc. Sec., Mrs. Sandra Karrott
Pres., Rev. Donald Lyon
Treas., Ronald Honeywell
Major activities: Hospital and Nursing Home Chaplaincy; Church Women United; High Rise Apartment Ministry; Hospital Referral Service; Emergency Response; Food Bank; Migrant Ministry; Meals on Wheels; Dial-A-Driver; Radio and TV; Leadership Schools; Interfaith Programs; Night Chaplain Ministry; Area Hospitals; CROP Hunger Walks; Pastoral Care Ministries

York County Council of Churches

104 Lafayette St., York, PA 17403
Exec. Dir., ——
CONTACT-York Teleministry Dir., Mrs. Lois Wetzler
Pres., Dr. Florence Ames
Treas., Mr. William Anderson
Major activities: Educational Development; Spiritual Growth and Renewal; Worship and Witness; Congregational Resourcing; Outreach and Mission

RHODE ISLAND

The Rhode Island State Council of Churches

734 Hope St., Providence, RI 02906
Media Contact, Exec. Minister, Rev. James C. Miller
Exec. Minister, Rev. James C. Miller
Admn. Asst., Ms. Peggy Macnie
Pres., Mr. George Weavill, Jr.
Treas., Mr. Robert A. Mitchell
Major activities: Urban Ministries; TV; Institutional Chaplaincy; Advocacy/Justice & Service; Legislative Liaison; Faith & Order; Leadership Development; Campus Ministries

SOUTH CAROLINA

South Carolina Christian Action Council, Inc.

P.O. Box 3663, Columbia, SC 29230
Media Contact, Exec. Minister, Dr. L. Wayne Bryan
Exec. Minister, Dr. L. Wayne Bryan
Pres., Ms. Betty Park
Major activities: Advocacy and Ecumenism; Continuing Education; Interfaith Dialogue; Citizenship and Public Affairs; Publications

United Ministries

606 Pendleton St., Greenville, SC 29601
Media Contact, Exec. Dir., Rev. Beth Templeton
Exec. Dir., Rev. Beth Templeton
Pres., Rev. Bob Coon
Vice-Pres., Mr. Curt Elmore
Sec., Ms. Mack Pazdan
Treas., Mr. Bill Kellett
Major activities: Volunteer Programs; Adopt-A-House; Spend a Day; Building Wheelchair Ramps; Emergency Assistance with Rent, Utili-

ties, Medication, Heating, Food, Shelter Referrals; Homeless Programs: Place of Hope Day Shelter for Homeless; Employment Readiness; Travelers Aid; Magdalene Project; Case Management

SOUTH DAKOTA

Association of Christian Churches

1320 S. Minnesota Ave., Ste. 210, Sioux Falls, SD 57105
Media Contact, Vice Pres., Rev. Howard Carroll
Exec. Dir., ——
Pres., Rev. R. William Ingvoldstad
Ofc. Mgr., Pat Willard
Major activities: Ecumenical Forums; Continuing Education for Clergy; Legislative Information; Resourcing Local Ecumenism; Native American Issues; Ecumenical Fields Ministries; Rural Economic Development

TENNESSEE

Metropolitan Inter Faith Association (MIFA)

P.O. Box 3130, Memphis, TN 38173-0130
Media Contact, Dir., Media Relations, Dee Sandlin
Exec. Dir., Mr. Allie Prescott
Dir. of Urban Ministries, Sara Holmes
Major activities: Emergency Housing; Emergency Services (Rent, Utility, Food, Clothing Assistance); Home-Delivered Meals and Senior Support Services; Youth Services

Tennessee Association of Churches

413 Moss Creek Ct., Nashville, TN 37221
Media Contact, Exec. Dir., Dr. C. Ray Dobbins
Exec. Dir., Dr. C. Ray Dobbins
Pres., Rev. Dr. T. Wright Pillow
Major activities: Faith and Order; Christian Unity; Social Concern Ministries; Legislative Concerns

TEXAS

Austin Metropolitan Ministries

2026 Guadalupe, Ste. 226, Austin, TX 78705
Media Contact, Exec. Dir., Patrick Flood, Fax (512)472-5274
Exec. Dir., Patrick Flood
Pres., Gail Miller
Treas., Shaun P. O'Brien
Chaplain, Rev. Charles I. Fay, Travis Co. Jails
Chaplain, Rev. Tommy MacIntosh, Travis Co. Jails
Chaplain, Rev. Floyd Vick, Gardner-Betts Juvenile Home
Chaplain, Rev. Don Bobb, Program Staff
Chaplain, Rev. Valerie Bridgeman-Davis, Program Staff
Office Admn., Carole Hatfield
Major activities: Pastoral Care in Jails; Broadcast Ministry; Emergency Assistance; Older Persons Task Force; Housing Task Force; Peace and Justice Commission; Youth at Risk; AIDS Service; Commission on Racism; Interfaith Dialogues; Economy and Jobs Issues

Border Association for Refugees from Central America

P.O. Box 715, Edinburg, TX 78540
Exec. Dir, Ninfa Ochoa-Krueger
Dir. Refugee Children Serv., Kathleen Grace
Major activities: Food, Shelter, Clothing, to Central Americans; Medical and Other Emergency Aid; Legal Advocacy; Special Services to Children; Speakers on Refugee Concerns for Church Groups

Corpus Christi Metro Ministries

1919 Leopard St., P.O. Box 4899, Corpus Christi, TX 78469-4899
Media Contact, Exec. Dir., Rev. Edward B. Seeger, Fax (512)887-7900
Exec. Dir., Rev. Edward B. Seeger
Dir., Admn., Daniel D. Scott
Dir., Volunteers, Ann Schiro
Fin. Coord., Sue McCown
Dir., Loaves & Fishes, Ray Gomez
Dir., Counseling, Amie Harrell
Dir., Rustic House, Amie Harrell
Dir., Employment, Curtis Blevins
Dir., Bethany House, Mike Swearingen
Dir., Rainbow House, Judy Fuhrman
Dir., Child Abuse Prevention, Judy Fuhrman
Dir., Health Clinic, Ann Schiro
Major activities: Food Center; Shelters; Counseling; Job Readiness; Job Placement; Abuse Prevention and Intervention; Adult Day Care; Primary Health Care; Community Service Restitution

East Dallas Cooperative Parish

P.O. Box 64725, Dallas, TX 75206
Pres., David Terry
Sec., Richard Miller
Major activities: Emergency Food, Clothing, Job Bank; Pediatric Medical Clinic; Legal Clinic; Tutorial Education; Home Companion Service; Pre-School Education; Learning Center; Asian Ministry; Hispanic Ministry; Activity Center for Low Income Older Adults; Pastoral Counseling

Greater Dallas Community of Churches

2800 Swiss Ave., Dallas, TX 75204
Media Contact, Exec. Asst., Colleen Townsley Hager
Exec. Dir., Rev. Thomas H. Quigley
Assoc. Dirs., Church & Comm.: ; Rev. Holsey Hickman; John Stoesz
Dir., Community College Min., Dr. Philip del Rosario
Dev. Dir., Carole Rylander
Pres., Dr. Willie Champion
Treas., Gilbert Hernandez
Program Assoc., Child Advocacy, Rev. Carolyn Bullard-Zerweck
Major activities: Hospital Chaplaincy; Community College Ministry; Housing; Hunger; Peacemaking; Faith and Life; Jewish-Christian Relations; Racial Ethnic Justice; Child Advocacy

Interfaith Ministries for Greater Houston

3217 Montrose Blvd., Houston, TX 77006
Media Contact, Exec. Dir., Betty K. Mathis
Exec. Dir., Betty K. Mathis
Assoc. Exec. Dirs.: ; Kassie Larson; Douglass L. Simmons
Dir. of Dev., Lisa Estes
Dir., Family Connection, Larry Norton
Dir., Foster Grandparent Program, Vicki Hopkins
Dir., Hunger Coalition, Barbara McCormick
Dir., Jail Chaplaincy, Rev. Freddie Wier
Dir., Meals on Wheels, Evelyn Velasquez
Dir., Refugee Services, David Deming
Dir. Retired Sr. Volunteer Program, Candice Twyman
Dir., Senior Companion Program, Lillian Walker
Dir., Senior Services, Anne Mahaffey
Dir. Youth Victim/Witness, Pamela Hobbs
Communications Coord., James L. Maxwell
Pres., Garland D. Pohl
Treas., Everett A. Marley, Jr.
Major activities: Community Concerns: Hunger; Older Adults; Families; Youth; Child Abuse; Refugee Services; Jail Chaplaincy; Congregational and Interfaith Development

North Dallas Shared Ministries

2526 Manana #203A, Dallas, TX 75220
Exec. Dir., Rev. Matt English
Pres., Edward St. John
Major activities: Emergency Assistance; Job Counseling; Advocacy for Homeless

Northside Inter-Church Agency (NICA)

506 N.W. 15th St., Fort Worth, TX 76106
Dir., Francine Esposito Pratt

San Antonio Community of Churches

1101 W. Woodlawn, San Antonio, TX 78201
Media Contact, Exec. Dir., Dr. Kenneth Thompson
Exec. Dir., Dr. Kenneth Thompson
Pres., Mr. C. W. Granrath
Major activities: Christian Educ.; Missions; Radio-TV; Resource Center Infant Formula and Medical Prescriptions for Children of Indigent Families; Continuing Education For Clergy; Media Resource Center; Social Issues; Aging Concerns; Youth Concerns

San Antonio Urban Ministries

2002 W. Olmos Dr., San Antonio, TX 78201
Exec. Dir., Sue Kelly
Pres., Troy Warwick
Major activities: Homes for Discharged Mental Patients; After School Care for Latch Key Children; Christian Based Community Ministry; San Antonio Legalization Education Coalition

Southeast Area Churches (SEARCH)

P.O. Box 51256, Fort Worth, TX 76105
Dir., Ms. Dorothy Anderson
Major activities: Emergency Assistance; Advocacy; Information and Referral; Community Worship

Southside Area Ministries (SAM)
305 W. Broadway, Fort Worth, TX 76104
Exec. Dir., Diane Smiley
Major activities: Assisting those for whom English is a second language; Tutoring grades K-12; Mentoring Grades 6-9; Programs for Senior Citizens and Refugees

Tarrant Area Community of Churches
801 Texas St., Fort Worth, TX 76102
Pres., Rev. Dr. John Tietjen
Treas., Mr. Luther Atkinson
Acting Exec. Dir., Rev. Elizabeth F. Lamberth
Major activities: Councils; Church, Community-based, Interfaith, Pastoral Ministry; Jail Ministry; Elderly Ministry

Texas Conference of Churches
6633 Hwy. 290 East, Ste. 200, Austin, TX 78723-1157
Exec. Dir., Rev. Dr. Frank H. Dietz
Church & Society Asst., Mary Berwick
Dir., Addictions Min., Ms. Trish Merrill
Dir., Texas Regional AIDS Interfaith Network, Rev. Robert Huie
Pres., Rev. A.M. Hart
Major activities: Church and Society; Ecumenism; Christian-Jewish Relations; Domestic Violence; Peace; Disaster Response; BARCA; Texas Church World Service/CROP; Alcoholism-Addiction Education; Church Woman United In Texas; Central American Issues; Texas IM-PACT; AIDS

United Board of Missions
1701 Bluebonnet Ave., P.O. Box 3856, Port Arthur, TX 77643-3856
Media Contact, Admn. Asst., Carolyn Schwarr
Exec. Dir., Clark Moore
Pres., Rev. Gene Easterly
Major activities: Emergency Assistance (Food and Clothing, Rent and Utility, Medical, Dental, Transportation); Share a Toy at Christmas; Counseling; Back to School Clothing Assistance; Information and Referral; Hearing Aid Bank; Meals on Wheels; Super Pantr y; Energy Conservation Programs; Job Bank

UTAH

The Shared Ministry
175 W. 200 S., Ste. 3006, Salt Lake City, UT 84101
Exec. Min., Rev. Dr. Max E. Glenn
Major activities: Poverty, Hunger, and Homelessness; Legislation Concerns; Family Counseling; Peacemaking; Prison Youth and Singles Ministries

VERMONT

Vermont Ecumenical Council and Bible Society
285 Maple St., Burlington, VT 05401
Media Contact, Admin. Asst., Carolyn Carpenter
Exec. Sec., Rev. John E. Nutting
Pres., Rev. James M. MacKellar
Treas., Rev. Louis Drew, Jr.

Major activities: Christian Unity; Bible Distribution; Social Justice; Committees on Peace, Life and Work, Faith and Order, and Bible

VIRGINIA

Community Ministry of Fairfax County
1920 Association Dr., Rm. 406, Reston, VA 22091
Media Contact, Exec. Dir., Frederick S. Lowry
Exec. Dir., Rev. Frederick S. Lowry
Newsletter Ed., James Vining
Chpsn., Nancy Wormeli
Sec., Marge DeBlaay
Treas., Robert Hunt
Major activities: Ecumenical Social Ministry; Elderly; Criminal Justice; Housing; Public Education

Virginia Council of Churches, Inc.
1214 W. Graham Rd., Richmond, VA 23230-1409
Media Contact, Gen. Min., Rev. James F. McDonald
Gen. Min., Rev. James McDonald
Prog. Assoc., Rev. Judith Bennett
Dir., Migrant Head Start, Rev. Myron Miller
Dir., Refugee Resettlement, Rev. David Montanye
Coord., Weekday Rel. Ed., Ms. Evelyn W. Simmons, P.O. Box 245, Clifton Forge, VA 24422
Coord., Campus Ministry Forum, Rev. Robert Thomason, 5000 Echols Ave., Alexandria, VA 22304
Major activities: Faith and Order; Network Building & Coordination; Ecumenical Communications; Justice and Legislative Concerns; Educational Development; Rural Concerns; Refugee Resettlement; Migrant Ministries and Migrant Day Care; Disaster Coordination

WASHINGTON

Associated Ministries of Tacoma-Pierce County
1224 South "I" St., Tacoma, WA 98405
Media Contact, Exec. Dir., Rev. David T. Alger
Exec. Dir., Rev. David T. Alger, 4510 Defiance, Tacoma, WA 98407
Assoc. Dir., Janet E. Leng, 1809 N. Lexington, Tacoma, WA 98406
Pres., Virginia Gilmore
Sec., Betty Tober
Treas., Mr. Dennis Paul
Vice-Pres., Danna Clancy
Major activities: FISH/Food Banks; Hunger Awareness; Economic Justice; Christian Education; Shalom (Peacemaking) Resource Center; Social Service Program Advocacy; Communication and Networking of Churches; Housing; Paint Tacoma/Pierce Beautiful; Interfaith Task Force on Safe Streets

Associated Ministries of Thurston County
P.O. Box 895, Olympia, WA 98507
Media Contact, Exec. Dir., Ken Schwilk
Exec. Dir., Ken Schwilk
Pres., Jim Castrolang
Treas., Carroll Dick
Major activities: Church Inf. & Referral; Worship; Workshops; Social & Health Concerns;

Center for the Prevention of Sexual and Domestic Violence

1914 N. 34th St., Ste. 105, Seattle, WA 98103
Media Contact, Exec. Dir., Rev. Dr. Marie M. Fortune
Exec. Dir., Rev. Marie M. Fortune
Admin. Asst., Alex McGee
Video Project Coordinator, Jean Anton
Program Specialist, Rev. Thelma B. Burgonio-Watson
Program Assoc., Sandra Barone
Program Asst., Rebecca M. Voelkel
Devel. Assoc., Lennie Ziontz
Program Specialist, Elizabeth A. Stellas, M.Div.
Fin. & Dev. Direct, Nan Stoops
Mission Intern, Dinah Hall
Major activities: Educational Ministry; Clergy and Lay Training; Social Action.

Church Council of Greater Seattle

4759 - 15th Ave., NE, Seattle, WA 98105
Media Contact, Assoc. Dir., Alice M. Woldt
Pres.-Dir., Rev. Elaine J. W. Stanovsky
Assoc. Dir.-Urban Min., Rev. David C. Bloom
Assoc. Dir.-Admn., Alice M. Woldt
Exec. Asst., Angela W. Ford
Dir. Emerg. Feeding Prog., Arthur Lee
Dir. Friend-to-Friend, Marilyn Soderquist
Dir. Youth Service Chaplaincy, Terri Ward
Dir. Mental Health Chaplaincy, Rev. Craig Rennebohm
Dir., Native Am. Task Force, Ron Adams
Dir., The Sharehouse, Mike Buchman
Dir. Homelessness Project, Nancy Dorman
Dir., Mission for Music & Healing, Esther "Little Dove" John
Dir., Seattle Displacement Coalition, John Fox
Dir., Task Force on Aging, Mary Liz Chaffee
Dir., Public Education Task Force, Rev. Joyce Manson
Dir., Housing & Homelessness Task Force, Josephine Archuleta
Vice-Pres., Rev. Rodney Romney
Treas., Dorothy Eley
Ed., Source, Marge Lueders
Major activities: Racial Justice; Peace Action; Pastoral Ministry; Hunger; Public Education; Housing; Mental Health; Gay Rights; Aging; Latin America; Asia Pacific; South Africa; Native Americans; Jewish-Christian Relations; Ecology; Homelessness; Labor & Economic Justice; Children, Youth & Families; Race Relations; International Relations

Ecumenical Metropolitan Ministry

P.O. Box 12272, Seattle, WA 98102
Media Contact, Devel. Officer, Mel Matteson
Exec. Dir., Ruth M. Velozo
Chpsn., Rev. Henry F. Seaman
Major activities: Northwest Harvest (Hunger Response); Northwest Infants Corner (Special Nutritional Products for Infants and Babies); Northwest Caring Ministry (Individuals and Family Crisis Intervention and Advocacy); E.M.M. (Advocacy, Education, Communications Relative to Programs and Economic Justice).

North Snohomish County Association of Churches

2301 Hoyt, P.O. Box 7101, Everett, WA 98201
Media Contact, Exec. Dir., Rev. Lisa Jankanish
Exec. Dir., Rev. Lisa Jankanish
Pres., Rev. Edwin C. Coon
Major activities: Housing and Shelter; Economic Justice; Hunger; Family Life; Ecumenical and Interfaith Worship

Spokane Christian Coalition

E. 245-13th Ave., Spokane, WA 99202
Exec. Dir., Rev. John A. Olson
Pres., Rev. Jim Burford
Treas., Lula Hage
Admn. Coord. & Ed., Mary Stamp Haworth
Major activities: Greater Spokane Coalition Against Poverty; Multi-Cultural Human Relations Camp for High School Youth; Night Walk Ministry; Calling and Caring Training; Fig Tree Newspaper; Solidarity with Women Task Force; Dir. of Churches & Community Agencies; Interfaith Thanksgiving Worship; Community Easter Sunrise Service; Forums on Issues; Friend to Friend Visitation with Nursing Home Patients; Interstate Task Force on Human Relations

Washington Association of Churches

4759 - 15th Ave. N.E., Seattle, WA 98105
Exec. Min., Rev. John C. Boonstra
Dir., Legislative, Tony Lee
Dir., Immigration & Refugee Prog., Hua Hoa, 233 Sixth Ave. N., Ste. 110, Seattle, WA 98103
Pres., Bishop Calvin McConnell
Treas., Rev. David T. Alger
Major activities: Faith and Order; Poverty and Justice Advocacy; Hunger Action; Legislation; Denominational Ecumenical Coordination; Theological Formation; Leadership Development; Refugee Resettlement; Racial Justice Advocacy; Immigration; International Solidarity

WEST VIRGINIA

Greater Fairmont Council of Churches

P.O. Box 108, Fairmont, WV 26554
Exec. Sec., Nancy Hoffman
Major activities: Community Ecumenical Services; Youth and Adult Sports Leagues; CROP Walk Sponsor; Weekly Radio Broadcasts

The Greater Wheeling Council of Churches

110 Methodist Bldg., Wheeling, WV 26003
Exec. Dir., Kathy J. Burley
Hospital Notification Sec., Mrs. Ruth Fletcher
Pres., Rev. Charles Ellwood
Treas., Mrs. Naoma Boram
Major activities: Christian Education; Evangelism; Summer Vespers; Television; Institutional Ministry; Religious Film Library; Church Women United; Volunteer Pastor Care at OVMC Hospital; School of Religion; Hospital Notification; Hymn Sing in the Park; Flood Relief Network; Pentecost Celebration; Clergy Council; Easter Sunrise Service; Community Seder

West Virginia Council of Churches
1608 Virginia St. E., Charleston, WV 25311
Media Contact, Exec. Dir., Rev. James M. Kerr, Fax (304)343-3295
Exec. Dir., Rev. James M. Kerr
Pres., Bishop L. Alexander Black, ELCA Synod of WV-MD, 503 Morgantown Ave., Atrium Mall, Ste. 100, Fairmont, WV 26554
Vice-Pres., Mary Virginia DeRoo, 2006 Northwood Rd., Charleston, WV 25314
Sec., Sr. Marguerite St. Amand, 63 Elk River Rd., Clendinin, WV 25045
Treas., Rev. Richard Flowers, P.O. Box 667, Scott Depot, WV 25560
Major activities: Leisure Ministry; Disaster Response; Faith and Order; Family Concerns; Inter-Faith Relations; Peace and Justice; Government Concerns; Support Sevices Network

WISCONSIN

Center for Community Concerns
1501 Villa St., Racine, WI 53403
Exec. Dir., Mrs. Jean Mandli
Skillbank Coord., Eleanor Sorenson
Volunteer Prog. Coord., Chris Udell-Solberg
RSVP (Retired Senior Volunteer Program), Kay Larson
Admn. Asst., Bonnie Wrixton
Major activities: Advocacy; Direct Services; Research; Community Consultant; Criminal Justice; Volunteerism; Senior Citizen Services

Christian Youth Council
1715-52nd St., Kenosha, WI 53140
Exec. Dir., Ron Stevens
Sports Dir., Krisp Jensen
Outreach Dir., Linda Osborne
Pres., Floyd Wilkinson
Major activities: Leisure Time Ministry; Institutional Ministries; Ecumenical Committee; Social Concerns

Interfaith Conference of Greater Milwaukee
1442 N. Farwell Ave., Ste. 200, Milwaukee, WI 53202
Media Contact, Exec. Dir., Jack Murtaugh
Exec. Dir., Mr. Jack Murtaugh
First Vice-Chair, Bishop Peter Rogness
Second Vice-Chair, Archbishop Rembert Weakland
Sec., Rev. Paul Bodine, Jr.
Treas., Rev. Mary Ann Neevel
Prog. Coord. on Poverty Issues: Mr. Marcus White
Ofc. Admn., Mrs. Frankie Mason-McCain
Prog. Coord. for Public Educ., Mrs. Charlotte Holloman
Consultant in Communications, Rev. Robert Seater
Chpsn., Bishop Peter Rogness

Beyond Racism Program, Mrs. Charlotte Holloman
Major activities: Economic Issues; Racism; CROP Walk; Public Policy; Religion and Labor Committee; Public Education Committee; TV Programming; Peace and International Issues Committee; Annual Membership Luncheon

Madison Urban Ministry
1127 University Ave., Madison, WI 53715
Media Contact, Office/Program Mgrs., Cheryl Wade or Margaret Tanaka
Exec. Dir., Charles Pfeifer
Office/Program Mgrs., Margaret Tanaka
Office/Program Mgrs., Cheryl Wade
Admn. Asst./Community Liaison, Cynthia Adams
Major activities: Community Projects; Race Relations; Housing Coalition; Tutoring/Mentoring Network

Wisconsin Conference of Churches
1955 W. Broadway, Ste. 104, Madison, WI 53713
Media Contact, Communications Coord., Ms. Linda Spilde
Exec. Dir., Rev. John D. Fischer
Office Mgr.-Communications Coord., Ms. Linda Spilde
Assoc. Dir., Social Ministry, Ms. Bonnee Voss
Assoc. Dir., Broadcasting, Rev. Robert P. Seater, 2717 E. Hampshire, Milwaukee, WI 53211
Co-Dir., Peace & Justice Ecumenical Partnership, Jane Hammatt-Kavaloski, Rt. #3, Box 228E, Dodgeville, WI 53533
Co-Dir., Peace & Justice Ecumenical Partnership, Vincent Kavaloski, Rt. #3, Box 228E, Douglasville, WI 53533
Chaplaincy Coord., Rev. M. Charles Davis, 1221 Jackson St., Oshkosh, WI 54901
Commission on Aging Coord., Mr. A. Rowland Todd
President, Bishop Robert Herder
Treas., Mr. Chester Spangler, 625 Crandall, Madison, WI 53711
Major activities: Church and Society; Migrant Ministry; Broadcasting Ministry; Aging; IMPACT; Institutional Chaplaincy; Peace and Justice; Faith and Order; Rural Concerns Forum; American Indian Ministries Council; Park Ministry

WYOMING

Wyoming Church Coalition
P.O. Box 990, Laramie, WY 82070
Media Contact, Chair, Rev. Mike Parr
Admn. Coord., Melissa Sanders
Chair, Rev. Michael Parr, 262 N. 3rd, Lander, WY 82520-2811
Penitentiary Chaplain, Rev. Lynn Schumacher, P.O. Box 400, Rawlins, WY 82301
Major activities: Death Penalty; Empowering the Poor and Oppressed; Peace and Justice; Prison Ministry

6. CANADIAN REGIONAL AND LOCAL ECUMENICAL AGENCIES

Most of the organizations listed below are councils of churches in which churches participate officially, whether at the parish or judicatory level. They operate at either the city, metropolitan area, or county level. Parish clusters within urban areas are not included.

Canadian local ecumenical bodies operate without paid staff, with the exception of a few which have part-time staff. In most cases the name and address of the president or chairperson is listed. As these offices change from year to year, some of this information may be out of date by the time the *Yearbook of American and Canadian Churches* is published. Up-to-date information may be secured from the Canadian Council of Churches, 40 St. Clair Ave., E., Toronto, Ontario M4T 1M9.

ALBERTA

Calgary Inter-Faith Community Association
Rev. V. Hennig, 7515 7th St.SW, Calgary, AB T2V 1G1

Calgary Inter-Faith SAWDAP
Mrs. Caroline Brown, #240-15 Ave. SW, Calgary, AB T2R 0P7

Calgary Council of Churches
Stephen Kendall, Treas. 1009 - 15 Ave. SW, Calgary, AB T3R 0S5

ATLANTIC PROVINCES

Atlantic Ecumenical Council of Churches
Pres., Rev. John E. Boyd, Box 637, 90 Victoria St., Amherst, NS B4H 4B4

Pictou Council of Churches
Rev. D. J. Murphy, Sec., P.O. Box 70, Pictou, NS B0K 1H0

BRITISH COLUMBIA

Canadian Ecumenical Action
Co-ordinator, 1410 West 12th Ave., Vancouver, BC V6H 1M8

Greater Victoria Council of Churches
c/o Rev. Edwin Taylor, St. Alban's Church, 1468 Ryan St. at Balmont, Victoria, BC V8R 2X1

MANITOBA

Association of Christian Churches in Manitoba
Pres., The Rev. Cliff McMillan, 622 Tache Ave., Winnipeg, MB R2H 2B4

NEW BRUNSWICK

Moncton Area Council of Churches
Rev. Yvon Berrieau, Visitation Ministry, Grande Digue, New Brunswick EOA 1SO

First Miramichi Inter-Church Council
Pres., Ellen Robinson, Doaktown, New Brunswick E0C 1G0

NOVA SCOTIA

Bridgewater Inter-Church Council
Pres., Wilson Jones, 30 Parkdale Ave., Bridgewater, NS B4V 1L8

Cornwallis District Inter-Church Council
Pres., Mr. Tom Regan, Centreville, R.R. #2, Kings County, NS BOT 1JO

Halifax-Dartmouth Council of Churches
Mrs. Betty M. Short, 3 Virginia Ave., Dartmouth, NS B2W 2Z4

Industrial Cape Breton Council of Churches
Rev. Karen Ralph, 24 Huron Ave., Sydney Mines, NS B1S 1V2

Kentville Council of Churches
Rev. Canon S.J.P. Davies, 325-325 Main St., Kentville, NS B4N 1C5

ONTARIO

Burlington Inter-Church Council
Mr. Fred Townsend, 425 Breckenwood, Burlington, ON L7L 2J6

Christian Council - Capital Area
Fr. Peter Shonenback, 1247 Kilborn Ave., Ottawa, ON K1H 6K9

Christian Leadership Council of Downtown Toronto
Ken Bhagan, Chair, 40 Homewood Ave, #509, Toronto, ON M4Y 2K2

Ecumenical Committee
Rev. William B. Kidd, 76 Eastern Ave., Sault Ste. Marie, ON P6A 4R2

Glengarry-Prescott-Russell Christian Council
Pres., Rev. G. Labrosse, St. Eugene's, Prescott, ON K0B 1P0

Hamilton & District Christian Association
Chpsn., Rev. Dr. John A. Johnston, 147 Chedoke Ave., Hamilton, ON L8P 4P2

Ignace Council of Churches
Box 5, 205 Pine St., St. Ignace, ON P0T 1H0

Kitchener-Waterloo Council of Churches
Rev. Clarence Hauser, CR, 53 Allen St. E., Waterloo, ON N2J 1J3

London Inter-City Faith Team
David Carouthers, Chair, c/o United Church, 711 Colbourne St., London, ON N6A 3Z4

Massey Inter-Church Committee
Eva Fraser, Sec., Box 238, Massey, ON P0P 1P0

St. Catharines & Dist. Clergy Fellowship
Rev. Victor Munro, 663 Vince4 St., St. Catharines, ON L2M 3V8

Spadina-Bloor Interchurch Council
Rev. Frances Combes, Chair, c/o Bathurst St. United Church, 427 Bloor St. W, Toronto, ON M5S 1X7

Stratford & District Council of Churches
Rev. Ted Heinze, Chair, 202 Erie St., Stratford, ON N5A 2M8

Thorold Inter-Faith Council
1 Dunn St., St. Catharines, ON L2T 1P3

Thunder Bay Council of Churches
Rev. Richard Darling, 1800 Moodie St. E., Thunder Bay, ON P7E 4Z2

PRINCE EDWARD ISLAND

Summerside Christian Council
Ms. A. Kathleen Miller, P.O. Box 1551, Summerside, PE C1N 4K4

QUEBEC

Hemmingford Ecumenical Committee
c/o Catherine Priest, Box 300, Hemmingford, QC J0L 1H0

Montréal Council of Churches
Rev. Ralph Watson, 3560 Connough Ave., Montréal, QC H4B 1X3

Centre for Ecumenism/Centre d'oecuménisme
2065 Sherbrooke Ave. W, Montréal, QC H3H 1G6

The Ecumenical Group
c/o Mrs. C. Haten, 1185 Ste. Foy, St. Bruno, QC J3V 3C3

SASKATCHEWAN

Humboldt Clergy Council
Fr. Leo Hinz, OSB, Box 1989, Humboldt, SK S0K 2A0

Melville Association of Churches
Attn., Catherine Gaw, Box 878, Melville, SK S0A 2P0

Saskatoon Centre for Ecumenism
Rev. Bernard de Margerie, 1006 Broadway Ave., Saskatoon, SK S7N 1B9

Saskatoon Council of Churches
816 Spadina Cres. E, Saskatoon, SK S7K 3H4

CAN ECUMENICAL AGENCIES

7. THEOLOGICAL SEMINARIES AND BIBLE COLLEGES IN THE UNITED STATES

The following list includes theological seminaries and departments in colleges and universities in which ministerial training is given. Many denominations have additional programs. The lists of Religious Bodies in the United States should be consulted for the address of denominational headquarters.

Inclusion in or exclusion from this list implies no judgment about the quality or accreditation of any institution.

The listing includes the institution name, denominational sponsor when appropriate, location, the head of the institution, telephone number, and fax number when known.

Abilene Christian University, (Churches of Christ), ACU Station, Box 7000, Abilene, TX 79699. Royce Money. Tel. (915)674-2412. Fax (915)674-2958

Academy of the New Church (Theol. Sch.), (General Church of the New Jerusalem), 2815 Huntingdon Pk., Box 717, Bryn Athyn, PA 19009. Brian W. Keith. Tel. (215)947-4200. Fax (215)938-2616

Alaska Bible College, (Nondenominational), P.O. Box 289, Glennallen, AK 99588. Gary J. Ridley. Tel. (907)822-3201. Fax (907)822-3290

Alliance Theological Seminary, (Christian and Missionary Alliance), Alliance Theological Seminary, Nyack, NY 10960. Paul F. Bubna. Tel. (914)358-1710. Fax (914)358-2651

American Baptist College, (Natl. Bapt., USA, Inc.; So. Bapt. Conv.), 1800 Baptist World Center Dr., Nashville, TN 37207. Bernard Lafayette. Tel. (615)262-1369

American Baptist Seminary of the West, (American Baptist Churches), 2606 Dwight Way, Berkeley, CA 94704. Theodore Keaton. Tel. (510)841-1905

Anderson University School of Theology, (Church of God), Anderson University, Anderson, IN 46012-3462. James Earl Massey. Tel. (317)641-4032. Fax (317)641-3851

Andover Newton Theological School, (Amer. Bapt.; United Church of Christ), 210 Herrick Rd., Newton Centre, MA 02159. David T. Shannon. Tel. (617)964-1100. Fax (617)965-9756

Appalachian Bible College, (Independent), P.O. Box ABC, Bradley, WV 25818. Daniel L. Anderson. Tel. (304)877-6428

Aquinas Institute of Theology, (Roman Catholic), 3642 Lindell Blvd., St. Louis, MO 63108. Charles E. Bouchard. Tel. (314)658-3882. Fax (314)652-0935

Arizona College of the Bible, (Nondenominational), 2045 W. Northern Ave., Phoenix, AZ 85021. Robert W. Benton. Tel. (602)995-2670

Arlington Baptist College, 3001 W. Division, Arlington, TX 76012. Wendell Hiers. Tel. (817)461-8741

Asbury Theological Seminary, (Interdenominational), 204 N. Lexington Ave., Wilmore, KY 40390. David McKenna. Tel. (606)858-3581. Fax (606)858-3581

Ashland Theological Seminary, (Brethren Church (Ashland, OH)), 910 Center St., Ashland, OH 44805. Frederick J. Finks. Tel. (419)289-5161. Fax (419)289-5969

Assemblies of God Theological Seminary, (Assemblies of God), 1445 Boonville Ave., Springfield, MO 65802. Del Tarr. Tel. (417)862-3344. Fax (417)862-3214

Associated Mennonite Biblical Seminaries, (Mennonite and General Conf. Mennonite), 3003 Benham Ave., Elkhart, IN 46517-1999. Marlin E. Miller. Tel. (219)295-3726. Fax (219)295-0092

Atlanta Christian College, (Christian Churches/Church of Christ), 2605 Ben Hill Rd., East Point, GA 30344. James C. Donovan. Tel. (404)761-8861. Fax (404)669-2024

Austin Presbyterian Theological Seminary, (PCUSA), 100 E. 27th St., Austin, TX 78705. Jack L. Stotts. Tel. (512)472-6736. Fax (512)479-0738

Azusa Pacific University, (Interdenominational), 901 E. Alosta, P.O. Box APU, Azusa, CA 91702. Richard Felix. Tel. (818)969-3434. Fax (818)969-7180

Bangor Theological Seminary, (United Church of Christ), 300 Union St., Bangor, ME 04401. Malcolm Warford. Tel. (207)942-6781. Fax (207)942-4914

Baptist Bible College, (Baptist), 628 E. Kearney, Springfield, MO 65803. Leland Kennedy. Tel. (417)869-9811. Fax (417)831-8029

Baptist Bible College and Seminary, (Baptist), 538 Venard Rd., Clarks Summit, PA 18411. Milo Thompson. Tel. (717)587-1172. Fax (717)586-1753

Baptist Missionary Association Theological Seminary, (Baptist Missionary Assoc. of America), 1530 E. Pine St., Jacksonville, TX 75766. Philip R. Bryan. Tel. (903)586-2501. Fax (903)586-0378

Barclay College, (Friends), P.O. Box 288, Haviland, KS 67059. Robin W. Johnston. Tel. (316)862-5252. Fax (316)862-5403

Bay Ridge Christian College, (Church of God, Anderson, Ind.), P.O. Box 726, Kendleton, TX 77451. Wilfred Jordan. Tel. (409)532-3982

Berean Christian College, (Interdenominational), 6801 Millmark Ave., Long Beach, CA 90805. A. A. Bachman. Tel. (213)428-0030

Berean Christian College, (Interdenominational), 12550 Central Southwest, Albuquerque, NM 87121

Berkeley Divinity School at Yale, (Episcopalian), 363 St. Ronan St., New Haven, CT 06511. Dean Philip Turner. Tel. (203)432-6106. Fax (203)432-6110

Bethany College, (Assemblies of God), 800 Bethany Dr., Scotts Valley, CA 95066. Tom Duncan. Tel. (408)438-3800. Fax (408)438-4517

Bethany Lutheran Theological Seminary, (Evangelical Lutheran Synod), 447 N. Division St., Mankato, MN 56001. W. W. Petersen. Tel. (507)625-2977. Fax (507)625-1849

Bethany Theological Seminary, (Church of the Brethren), Butterfield and Meyers Rd., Oak Brook, IL 60521. Eugene F. Roop. Tel. (708)620-2200. Fax (708)620-9014

Bethel Theological Seminary, (Baptist General Conference), 3949 Bethel Drive, St. Paul, MN 55112. George K. Brushaber. Tel. (612)638-6230. Fax (612)638-6002

Beulah Heights Bible College, (Pentecostal), 892 Berne St. SE, Atlanta, GA 30316. James B. Keiller. Tel. (404)627-2681. Fax (404)627-5279

Biblical Theological Seminary, (Interdenominational), 200 N. Main St., Hatfield, PA 19440. David G. Dunbar. Tel. (215)368-5000. Fax (215)368-7002

Boise Bible College, (Independent), 8695 Marigold St., Boise, ID 83714. Charles A. Crane. Tel. (208)376-7731

Boston University (School of Theology), (United Methodist Church), 745 Commonwealth Ave., Boston, MA 02215. Robert C. Neville. Tel. (617)353-3050. Fax (617)353-2053

Brite Divinity School, Texas Christian University, (Christian Church, Disciples of Christ), P.O. Box 32923, TCU, Ft. Worth, TX 76129. Leo G. Perdue. Tel. (817)921-7575. Fax (817)921-7333

Calvary Bible College, (Nondenominational), 15800 Calvary Rd., Kansas City, MO 64147. Donald A. Urey. Tel. (800)326-3960

Calvin Theological Seminary, (Christian Reformed Church), 3233 Burton St. SE, Grand Rapids, MI 49546. J. A. DeJong. Tel. (616)957-6036. Fax (616)957-8621

Capital Bible Seminary/Washington Bible College, (Interdenominational), 6511 Princess Garden Pkwy., Lanham, MD 20706. John A. Sproule. Tel. (301)552-1400. Fax (301)552-2775

Catholic Theological Union, (Catholic), 5401 S. Cornell Ave., Chicago, IL 60615. Donald Senior. Tel. (312)324-8000

Catholic University of America (Theological College), (Catholic), 401 Michigan Ave. NE, Washington, DC 20017. Howard P. Bleichner. Tel. (202)319-5900. Fax (202)319-5967

Central Baptist College, (Baptist), 1501 College Ave., Conway, AR 72032. Charles Attebery. Tel. (501)329-6872. Fax (501)329-2941

Central Baptist Theological Seminary, (American Baptists), 741 N. 31st St., Kansas City, KS 66102-3964. John R. Landgraf. Tel. (913)371-5313. Fax (913)371-8110

Central Baptist Theological Seminary in Indiana, (Natl. Bapt., USA, Inc; Natl. Bapt. Conv.), 1535 Dr. A. J. Brown Ave. N, Indianapolis, IN 46202. F. Benjamin Davis. Tel. (317)636-6622

Central Bible College, (Assemblies of God), 3000 N. Grant Ave., Springfield, MO 65803. H. Maurice Lednicky. Tel. (417)833-2551. Fax (417)833-5141

Central Christian College of the Bible, (Christian Church), 911 E. Urbandale, Moberly, MO 65270. Lloyd M. Pelfrey. Tel. (816)263-3900

Central Indian Bible College, (Assemblies of God), P.O. Box 550, Mobridge, SD 57601. Howard Hodson. Tel. (605)845-7801

Central Wesleyan College, (Wesleyan Church), One Wesleyan Dr., P.O. Box 1020, Central, SC 29630. John Newby. Tel. (803)639-2453. Fax (803)639-0826

Chicago Theological Seminary, (United Church of Christ), 5757 South University Ave., Chicago, IL 60637. Kenneth B. Smith. Tel. (312)752-5757. Fax (312)752-5925

Chicago, University of (Divinity School), (Interdenominational), 1025 E. 58th St., Chicago, IL 60637. W. Clark Gilpin. Tel. (312)702-8221. Fax (312)702-6048

Christ the King Seminary, (Catholic), 711 Knox Rd., P.O. Box 607, East Aurora, NY 14052. Frederick D. Leising. Tel. (716)652-8900. Fax (716)652-8903

Christ the Savior Seminary, (Amer. Carpatho-Russ. Orth. Greek Cath.), 225 Chandler Ave., Johnstown, PA 15906. Nicholas Smisko. Tel. (814)539-8086. Fax (814)536-4699

Christian Theological Seminary, (Christian Church, Disciples of Christ), 1000 W. 42nd St., Indianapolis, IN 46208. Richard D. N. Dickinson. Tel. (317)924-1331. Fax (317)923-1961

Church Divinity School of the Pacific, (Episcopalian), 2451 Ridge Rd., Berkeley, CA 94709. Charles A. Perry. Tel. (415)848-3282. Fax (415)644-0712

Cincinnati Bible College and Seminary, (CC/CC), 2700 Glenway Ave., Cincinnati, OH 45204. C. Barry McCarty. Tel. (513)244-8100. Fax (513)244-8140

Circleville Bible College, (Churches of Christ in Christian Union), P.O. Box 458, Circleville, OH 43113. David Van Hoose. Tel. (614)474-8896

Claremont, School of Theology at (United Methodist) 1325 N. College Ave., Claremont, CA 91711. Robert W. Edgar. Tel. (714)626-3521. Fax (714)626-7062

Clear Creek Baptist Bible College, (Southern Baptist), 300 Clear Creek Rd., Pineville, KY 40977. Bill Whittaker. Tel. (606)337-3196

Colegio Biblico Pentecostal de Puerto Rico, (Church of God (Cleveland, TN)), P.O. Box 901, Saint Just, PR 00750. Ernesto L. Rodriguez. Tel. (809)761-0640

Colgate Rochester/Bexley Hall/Crozer, (Multidenominational), 1100 S. Goodman St., Rochester, NY 14620. James H. Evans. Tel. (716)271-1320. Fax (716)271-2166

Colorado Christian University, (Interdenominational), 180 S. Garrison St., Lakewood, CO 80226. L. David Beckman. Tel. (303)238-5386. Fax (303)233-2735

Columbia Bible College and Seminary, (Interdenominational), P.O. Box 3122, Columbia, SC 29230. Johnny Miller. Tel. (803)754-4100. Fax (803)786-4209

Columbia Theological Seminary, (PCUSA), P.O. Box 520, Decatur, GA 30031. Douglas Oldenburg. Tel. (404)378-8821. Fax (404)377-9696

Concordia Seminary, (Lutheran Church - Missouri Synod), 801 DeMun, St. Louis (Clayton), MO 63105. John F. Johnson. Tel. (314)721-5934. Fax (314)721-5902

Concordia Theological Seminary, (Lutheran Church - Missouri Synod), 6600 N. Clinton St., Ft. Wayne, IN 46825. Robert Preus. Tel. (219)481-2100. Fax (219)481-2121

Covenant Theological Seminary, (Presbyterian), 12330 Conway Rd., St. Louis, MO 63141. Paul Kooistra. Tel. (314)434-4044. Fax (314)434-4819

Cranmer Seminary, (Anglican Orthodox Church), P.O. Box 329, 323 Walnut St., Statesville, NC 28677. James P. Dees. Tel. (704)873-8365

Criswell Center for Biblical Studies, (Baptist), 4010 Gaston Ave., Dallas, TX 75246. W. A. Criswell. Tel. (214)821-5433

Criswell College, The, (Baptist), 4010 Gaston Ave., Dallas, TX 75246. Richard Melick. Tel. (214)818-1300. Fax (214)818-1320

Crown College, (Christian and Missionary Alliance), 6425 County Rd., 30, St. Bonifacius, MN 55375. Bill W. Lanpher. Tel. (612)446-4100. Fax (612)446-4149

Dallas Christian College, (Christian Churches), 2700 Christian Pky., Dallas, TX 75234. Gene Shepherd. Tel. (214)241-3371. Fax (214)241-8021

Dallas Theological Seminary, (Interdenominational), 3909 Swiss Ave., Dallas, TX 75204. Donald K. Campbell. Tel. (214)841-3614. Fax (214)841-3625

De Sales School of Theology, (Catholic), 721 Lawrence St. NE, Washington, DC 20017. John W. Crossin. Tel. (202)269-9412

Denver Conservative Baptist Seminary, (Conservative Baptist), Box 10,000, Denver, CO 80210-0100. Tel. (303)761-2482. Fax (303)761-8060

Disciples Divinity House, University of Chicago, (Christian Church, Disciples of Christ), 1156 E. 57th St., Chicago, IL 60637. Kristine A. Culp. Tel. (312)643-4411

Dominican House of Studies (Pontif. Fclty. Immcl Conception), (Roman Catholic), 487 Michigan Ave. NE, Washington, DC 20017-1585. Philip Smith. Tel. (202)529-5300. Fax (202)636-4460

Drew University (Theological School), (United Methodist), 36 Madison Ave., Madison, NJ 07940-4010. Robin Warren Lovin. Tel. (201)408-3258. Fax (201)408-3939

Dubuque, University of (Theological Seminary), (PCUSA), 2000 University Ave., University of Dub, Dubuque, IA 52001. John J. Agria. Tel. (319)589-3222. Fax (319)556-8633

Duke University (Divinity School), (United Methodist), Duke U. Divinity School, Box 90968, Durham, NC 27708. Dennis M. Campbell. Tel. (919)660-3400. Fax (919)660-3473

Earlham School of Religion, (Friends), 228 College Ave., Richmond, IN 47374. Andrew P. Grannell. Tel. (800)432-1377. Fax (317)983-1304

East Coast Bible College, (Church of God), 6900 Wilkinson Blvd., Charlotte, NC 28214. Ronald Martin. Tel. (704)394-2307. Fax (704)394-2308

Eastern Baptist Theological Seminary, (American Baptist), P.O. Box 12438, Philadelphia, PA 19151-0438. Manfred T. Brauch. Tel. (215)896-5000. Fax (215)649-3834

Eastern Mennonite Seminary, (Mennonite Churches), Eastern Mennonite Seminary, Harrisonburg, VA 22801. George R. Brunk. Tel. (703)432-4260. Fax (703)432-4444

Eden Theological Seminary, (United Church of Christ), 475 E. Lockwood Ave., St. Louis, MO 63119. Eugene S. Wehrli. Tel. (314)961-3627. Fax (314)961-5738

Emmanuel College School of Christian Ministries, (Pentecostal Holiness Church), P.O. Box 129, Franklin Springs, GA 30639. David Hopkins. Tel. (404)245-7226. Fax (404)245-4424

Emmanuel School of Religion, (Christian Churches & Churches of Christ), One Walker Dr., Johnson City, TN 37601. Calvin L. Phillips. Tel. (615)926-1186. Fax (615)461-1556

Emmaus Bible College, (Independent), 25720 Asbury Rd., Dubuque, IA 52001. Daniel Smith. Tel. (319)588-8000. Fax (319)588-1216

Emory University (The Candler School of Theology), (United Methodist), Bishops Hall 202, Emory University, Atlanta, GA 30322. R. Kevin LaGree. Tel. (404)727-6324

Episcopal Divinity School, (Episcopalian), 99 Brattle St., Cambridge, MA 02138. Otis Charles. Tel. (617)868-3450. Fax (617)864-5385

Episcopal Theological Seminary of the Southwest, (Episcopalian), P.O. Box 2247, Austin, TX 78768-2247. Durstan R. McDonald. Tel. (512)472-4133. Fax (512)472-3098

Erskine Theological Seminary, (Associate Reformed Presbytarian Church), Drawer 668, Due West, SC 29639. R. T. Ruble. Tel. (803)379-8885. Fax (803)379-8759

Eugene Bible College, (Open Bible Standard Churches), 2155 Bailey Hill Rd., Eugene, OR 97405. Jeffrey E. Farmer. Tel. (503)485-1780. Fax (503)343-5801

Evangelical School of Theology, (Evangelical Congregational Ch.), 121 S. College St., Myerstown, PA 17067. Ray A. Seilhamer. Tel. (717)866-5775. Fax (717)866-4667

Evangelical Theological Seminary, Inc., 2400 E. Ash St., Goldsboro, NC 27534. William Ralph Painter. Tel. (919)735-0831

THE YEAR IN IMAGES

Religious News Service Photo

Ministry building

Habitat for Humanity will become the No. 1 home builder by 1994, according to founder Millard Fuller, seen here working out his theology of the hammer. The organization, based on biblical principles, enlists volunteers to help the poor to build or refurbish homes, then to sell the homes, at cost, to the poor.

Faith Baptist Bible College and Seminary, (Baptist), 1900 NW 4th St., Ankeny, IA 50021. Robert Domokos. Tel. (515)964-0601. Fax (515)964-1638

Florida Bible College, (Ind. Fundamental Churches of America), 1701 N. Poinciana Blvd., Kissimmee, FL 34758. Paul Goodnight. Tel. (407)933-4500. Fax (407)4500

Florida Christian College, (Christian Church), 1011 Bill Beck, Kissimmee, FL 34744. A. Wayne Lowen. Tel. (407)847-8966

Franciscan School of Theology, (Catholic), 1712 Euclid Ave., Berkeley, CA 94709. William M. Cieslak. Tel. (510)848-5232

Free Will Baptist Bible College, (Free Will Baptist), 3606 West End Ave., Nashville, TN 37205. Tom Malone. Tel. (615)383-1340

Fuller Theological Seminary, (Multidenominational), 135 N. Oakland Ave., Pasadena, CA 91182. David A. Hubbard. Tel. (818)584-5200. Fax (818)795-8767

Garrett-Evangelical Theological Seminary, (United Methodist), 2121 Sheridan Rd., Evanston, IL 60201. Neal F. Fisher. Tel. (708)866-3900. Fax (708)866-3957

General Theological Seminary, The (Episcopal), 175 Ninth Ave., New York, NY 10011-4977. Craig B. Anderson. Tel. (212)243-5150. Fax (212)727-3907

George Mercer, Jr. Memorial School of Theology, (Episcopalian), 65 Fourth St., Garden City, NY 11530. Lloyd A. Lewis. Tel. (516)248-4800. Fax (516)248-4883

God's Bible School and College, (Independent), 1810 Young St., Cincinnati, OH 45210. Bence Miller. Tel. (513)721-7944. Fax (513)721-3971

Golden Gate Baptist Theological Seminary, (Southern Baptist), Strawberry Point, Mill Valley, CA 94941. William O. Crews. Tel. (415)388-8080. Fax (415)383-0723

Gordon-Conwell Theological Seminary, (Interdenominational), 130 Essex St., South Hamilton, MA 01982. Robert E. Cooley. Tel. (508)468-7111. Fax (508)468-6691

Grace Bible College, (Grace Gospel Fellowship), P.O. Box 910, Grand Rapids, MI 49509. E. Bruce Kemper. Tel. (616)538-2330

Grace College of the Bible, (Independent), 1515 S. 10th St., Omaha, NE 68108. Warren E. Bathke. Tel. (402)449-2800

Grace Theological Seminary, (Fellowship of Grace Brethren), 200 Seminary Dr., Winona Lake, IN 46590. John J. Davis. Tel. (219)372-5100. Fax (219)372-5265

Graduate Theological Union, (Nondenominational), 2400 Ridge Rd., Berkeley, CA 94709. Glenn R. Bucher. Tel. (510)649-2410. Fax (510)649-1417

Grand Rapids School of the Bible and Music, (Independent), 109 School St. NE, Comstock Park, MI 49321. Ronald Chadwick. Tel. (616)785-8703. Fax (616)785-8708

Great Lakes Christian College, (Church of Christ/Christian Church), 6211 W. Willow Hwy., Lansing, MI 48917. Kenneth E. Henes. Tel. (517)321-0242. Fax (517)321-5902

Greenville College, (Free Methodist Church of North America), 315 E. College Ave., Greenville, IL 62246. W. Richard Stephens. Tel. (800)345-4440. Fax (618)664-1748

Hartford Seminary, (Interdenominational), 77 Sherman St., Hartford, CT 06105. Barbara Brown Zikmund. Tel. (203)232-4451. Fax (203)236-8570

Harvard Divinity School, (Nondenominational), 45 Francis Ave., Cambridge, MA 02138. Ronald F. Thiemann. Tel. (617)495-5761. Fax (617)495-9489

Hebrew Union College—Jewish Inst. of Religion, (Jewish), 1 W. 4th St., New York, NY 10012. Alfred Gottschalk. Tel. (212)674-5300. Fax (212)533-0129

Hebrew Union College—Jewish Inst. of Religion, (Jewish), 3077 University, Los Angeles, CA 90007. Tel. (213)749-3424. Fax (213)747-6128

Hebrew Union College—Jewish Institute of Religion, (Jewish), 3101 Clifton Ave., Cincinnati, OH 45215. Alfred Gottschalk. Tel. (513)221-1875. Fax (513)221-2810

Hobe Sound Bible College, (Independent), P.O. Box 1065, Hobe Sound, FL 33475. Robert E. Whitaker. Tel. (407)546-5534. Fax (407)546-9379

Holy Cross Gk. Orthodox School of Theology(Hellenic College), (Greek Orthodox), 50 Goddard Ave., Brookline, MA 02146. Alkiviadis Calivas. Tel. (617)731-3500. Fax (617)738-9169

Holy Trinity Orthodox Seminary, (Russian Orthodox Ch. Outside of Russia), P.O. Box 36, Jordanville, NY 13361. Archbishop Laurus. Tel. (315)858-0940. Fax (315)858-0505

Hood Theological Seminary, (A.M.E. Zion), 800 W. Thomas St., Salisbury, NC 28144. James R. Samuel. Tel. (704)638-5505

Howard University School of Divinity, (Interdenominational), 1400 Shepherd St. NE, Washington, DC 20017. Clarence G. Newsome. Tel. (202)806-0500. Fax (202)806-0711

Huntington College, Graduate School of Christian Ministries, (United Brethren in Christ), 2303 College Ave., Huntington, IN 46750. Paul R. Fetters. Tel. (800)642-6493. Fax (219)356-9448

Iliff School of Theology, The, (United Methodist), 2201 S. University Blvd., Denver, CO 80210. Donald E. Messer. Tel. (303)744-1287. Fax (303)744-3387

Immaculate Conception Sem. Sch. of Theol. of Seton Hall Univ, (Catholic), 400 S. Orange Ave., South Orange, NJ 07079. Robert E. Harahan. Tel. (201)761-9575. Fax (201)761-9577

Indiana Wesleyan University, (Wesleyan Church), 4201 S. Washington, Marion, IN 46953. Joseph W. Seaborn. Tel. (317)677-2241. Fax (317)677-2499

Interdenominational Theological Center, (Interdenominational), 671 Beckwith St. SW, Atlanta, GA 30314. Clarence L. James. Tel. (404)527-7702. Fax (404)527-0901

Jesuit School of Theology at Berkeley, (Catholic), 1735 LeRoy Ave., Berkeley, CA 94709. Thomas F. Gleeson. Tel. (510)841-8804. Fax (510)841-8536

Jewish Theological Seminary of America, (Jewish), 3080 Broadway, New York, NY 10027. Ismar Schorsch. Tel. (212)678-8000. Fax (212)678-8947

John Wesley College, 2314 N. Centennial St., High Point, NC 27265. Brian C. Donley. Tel. (919)889-2262

Johnson Bible College, (Christian Chs.), 7900 Johnson Dr., Knoxville, TN 37998. David L. Eubanks. Tel. (615)573-4517. Fax (615)579-2336

Kansas City College and Bible School, (Church of God-Holiness), 7401 Metcalf Ave., Overland Park, KS 66204. Noel Scott. Tel. (913)722-0272. Fax (913)722-0351

Kenrick-Glennon Seminary, (Catholic), 5200 Glennon Dr., St. Louis, MO 63119. Ronald W. Ramson. Tel. (314)644-0266. Fax (314)644-3079

Kentucky Christian College, (Christian Chs.), 617 N. Carol Malone Blvd., Grayson, KY 41143-1199. Keith P. Keeran. Tel. (606)474-6613. Fax (606)474-3502

Kentucky Mountain Bible College, (Kentucky Mountain Holiness Assn.), Box 10, Vancleve, KY 41385. Wilfred Fisher. Tel. (606)666-5000. Fax (606)666-7744

L.I.F.E. Bible College, (Intnatl. Church Foursquare Gospel), 1100 Covina Blvd., San Dimas, CA 91773. Ronk Mehl. Tel. (714)599-5433. Fax (714)599-6690

La Sierra University, (Seventh-day Adventist), 4700 Pierce St., Riverside, CA 92515-8247. Fritz Guy. Tel. (714)785-2000. Fax (714)785-2901

Lancaster Bible College, (Nondenominational), 901 Eden Rd., Lancaster, PA 17601. Gilbert A. Peterson. Tel. (717)569-7071. Fax (717)560-8213

Lancaster Theological Seminary of the Unit. Church of Christ, (United Church of Christ), 555 W. James St., Lancaster, PA 17603-2897. Peter M. Schmiechen. Tel. (717)393-0654. Fax (717)393-4254

Lexington Theological Seminary, (Christian Church, Disciples of Christ)), 631 S. Limestone St., Lexington, KY 40508. Herbert Sledd. Tel. (606)252-0361. Fax (606)281-6042

Lincoln Christian College and Seminary, (Church of Christ/Christian Churches), 100 Campus View Dr., Lincoln, IL 62656. Charles A. McNeely. Tel. (217)732-3168. Fax (217)732-5914

Louisville Presbyterian Theological Seminary, (PCUSA), 1044 Alta Vista Rd., Louisville, KY 40205. John M. Mulder. Tel. (502)895-3411. Fax (502)895-1096

Luther Northwestern Theological Seminary, (Evangelical Lutheran Church in America), 2481 Como Ave., St. Paul, MN 55108. David L. Tiede. Tel. (612)641-3456. Fax (612)641-3425

Lutheran Bible Institute in California, (Lutheran), 641 S. Western Ave., Anaheim, CA 92804. Clifton Pederson. Tel. (714)827-1940

Lutheran Bible Institute of Seattle, (Lutheran), 4221 - 228th Ave. SE, Issaquah, WA 98027. Trygve R. Skarsten. Tel. (206)392-0400. Fax (206)392-0404

Lutheran Brethren Seminary, (Church of the Lutheran Brethren), 815 W. Vernon, Fergus Falls, MN 56537. Joel Egge. Tel. (218)739-3375. Fax (218)739-3372

Lutheran School of Theology at Chicago, (Evangelical Lutheran Church in America), 1100 E. 55th St., Chicago, IL 60615-5199. William E. Lesher. Tel. (312)753-0700. Fax (312)753-0782

Lutheran Theological Seminary, (Evangelical Lutheran Church in America), 61 NW Confederate Ave., Gettysburg, PA 17325. Darold H. Beekmann. Tel. (717)334-6286. Fax (717)334-3469

Lutheran Theological Seminary at Philadelphia, (Evangelical Lutheran Church in America), 7301 Germantown Ave., Philadelphia, PA 19119. Robert G. Hughes. Tel. (215)248-4616. Fax (215)248-4577

Lutheran Theological Southern Seminary, (Evangelical Lutheran Church in America), Lutheran Theological Southern Seminary, Columbia, SC 29203. H. Frederick Reisz. Tel. (803)786-5150

Magnolia Bible College, (Churches of Christ), P.O. Box 1109, Kosciusko, MS 39090. Cecil May. Tel. (601)289-2896

Manhattan Christian College, (Christian Churches), 1415 Anderson Ave., Manhattan, KS 66502. Kenneth Cable. Tel. (913)539-3571. Fax (913)539-0832

Manna Bible Institute, (Independent), 700 E. Church La., Philadelphia, PA 19144. Tel. (215)843-3600

Mary Immaculate Seminary, (Catholic), 300 Cherryville Rd., Box 27, Northampton, PA 18067. Richard J. Kehoe. Tel. (215)262-7866

Maryknoll School of Theology, (Cath. Foreign Miss. Soc. of Amer., Inc.), Maryknoll School of Theology, Maryknoll, NY 10545. John K. Halbert. Tel. (914)941-7590. Fax (914)941-5753

McCormick Theological Seminary, (PCUSA), 5555 S. Woodlawn Ave., Chicago, IL 60637. David Ramage. Tel. (312)947-6300. Fax (312)947-6273

Meadville/Lombard Theological School, (Unitarian Universalist Assoc.), 5701 S. Woodlawn Ave., Chicago, IL 60637. Spencer Lavan. Tel. (312)753-3195. Fax (312)753-1323

Memphis Theol. Sem. of the Cumberland Presbyterian Church, (Cumberland Presbyterian), 168 E. Parkway S, Memphis, TN 38104. J. David Hester. Tel. (901)458-8232. Fax (901)452-4051

Mennonite Brethren Biblical Seminary, (Mennonite Brethren Church), 4824 E. Butler Ave. (at Chestnut Ave.), Fresno, CA 93727. John E. Toews. Tel. (209)251-8628

Methodist Theological School in Ohio, (United Methodist), 3081 Columbus Pk., P.O. Box 1204, Delaware, OH 43015-0931. Norman E. Dewire. Tel. (614)363-1146. Fax (614)362-3135

Mid-America Bible College, (Church of God), 3500 SW 119th St., Oklahoma City, OK 73170. Forrest R. Robinson. Tel. (405)691-3800. Fax (405)692-3165

Midwestern Baptist Theological Seminary, (Southern Baptist), 5001 N. Oak St., Kansas City, MO 64118. Milton Ferguson. Tel. (816)453-4600. Fax (816)455-3528

Minnesota Bible College, (Church of Christ), 920 Mayowood Rd. SW, Rochester, MN 55902. Donald Lloyd. Tel. (507)288-4563. Fax (507)288-9046

Moody Bible Institute, (Interdenominational), 820 N. La Salle Blvd., Chicago, IL 60610. Joseph M. Stowell. Tel. (312)329-4000

Moravian Theological Seminary, (Moravian), 1200 Main St., Bethlehem, PA 18018. David A. Schattschneider. Tel. (215)861-1516. Fax (215)861-3919

Moreau Seminary (Holy Cross Fathers), (Roman Catholic), Moreau Seminary, Notre Dame, IN 46556. Thomas K. Zurcher. Tel. (219)239-7735

Morehouse School of Religion, (Amer.Bapt.; Prog. Natl. Bapt; Natl. Bapt. Conv., USA, So.Bapt.Conv.), 645 Beckwith St.SW, Atlanta, GA 30314. Clarence L. James. Tel. (404)527-7777. Fax (404)527-0901

Mount Angel Seminary, (Catholic), Mount Angel Seminary, St. Benedict, OR 97373. Patrick S. Brennan. Tel. (503)845-3951. Fax (503)845-3126

Mt. St. Mary's Seminary, (Catholic), Emmitsburg, MD 21727-7797. Kenneth W. Roeltgen. Tel. (301)447-5295. Fax (301)447-5755

Mt. St. Mary's Seminary of the West, (Catholic), 6616 Beechmont Ave., Cincinnati, OH 45230. Robert J. Mooney. Tel. (513)231-2223. Fax (513)231-3254

Multnomah Graduate School of Ministry, (Interdenominational), 8435 NE Glisan St., Portland, OR 97220. Joseph C. Aldrich. Tel. (503)255-0332. Fax (503)254-1268

Mundelein Seminary of the Univ. of St. Mary-of-the-Lake, (Catholic), Mundelein Seminary, Mundelein, IL 60060. Gerald F. Kicanas. Tel. (708)566-6401. Fax (708)566-7330

Nashotah House (Theological Seminary), (Episcopalian), 2777 Mission Rd., Nashotah, WI 53058-9793. Gary W. Kriss. Tel. (414)646-3371. Fax (414)646-2215

Nazarene Bible College, (Nazarene), 1111 Chapman Dr., Box 15749, Colorado Springs, CO 80916. Jerry Lambert. Tel. (719)596-5110. Fax (719)550-9437

Nazarene Theological Seminary, (Nazarene), 1700 E. Meyer Blvd., Kansas City, MO 64131. A. Gordon Wetmore. Tel. (816)333-6254. Fax (816)822-9025

Nebraska Christian College, (Christian Church), 1800 Syracuse Ave., Norfolk, NE 68701. Ray D. Stites. Tel. (402)371-5960

New Brunswick Theological Seminary, (Reformed Church in America), 17 Seminary Pl., New Brunswick, NJ 08901-1107. Norman J. Kansfield. Tel. (908)247-5241. Fax (908)249-5412

New Orleans Baptist Theological Seminary, (Southern Baptist), 3939 Gentilly Blvd., New Orleans, LA 70126. Landrum P. Leavell. Tel. (504)282-4455. Fax (504)944-4455

New York Theological Seminary, (Interdenominational), Five W. 29th St., 9th Floor, New York, NY 10001. M. William Howard. Tel. (212)532-4012. Fax (212)684-0757

North American Baptist Seminary, (North American Baptist Conference), 1321 W. 22nd St., Sioux Falls, SD 57105. Charles M. Hiatt. Tel. (605)336-6588. Fax (605)355-9090

North Central Bible College, (Assemblies of God), 910 Elliot Ave. S, Minneapolis, MN 55404. Don Argue. Tel. (612)332-3491. Fax (612)343-4778

North Park Theological Seminary, (Evangelical Covenant Church), 3225 W. Foster Ave., Chicago, IL 60625. David G. Horner. Tel. (312)583-2700. Fax (312)583-0858

Northern Baptist Theological Seminary, (American Baptist), 660 E. Butterfield Rd., Lombard, IL 60148. Ian M. Chapman. Tel. (708)620-2100. Fax (708)620-2194

Northwest Col. of the Assemblies of God, (Assemblies of God), 5520 108th Ave. NE, P.O. Box 579, Kirkland, WA 98083-0579. Dennis A. Davis. Tel. (206)822-8266. Fax (206)827-0148

Notre Dame, University of, (Dept. of Theology), (Roman Catholic), University of Notre Dame, Notre Dame, IN 46556. Laurence S. Cunningham. Tel. (219)239-7811

Notre Dame Seminary, (Catholic), 2901 S. Carrollton Ave., New Orleans, LA 70118. Gregory M. Aymond. Tel. (504)866-7426

Oak Hills Bible College, (Independent), 1600 Oak Hills Rd. SW, Bemidji, MN 56601. Mark Hovestol. Tel. (218)751-8670. Fax (218)751-8825

Oblate College, (Catholic), 391 Michigan Ave. NE, Washington, DC 20017. George F. Kirwin. Tel. (202)529-6544

Oblate School of Theology, (Catholic), 285 Oblate Dr., San Antonio, TX 78216-6693. Patrick Guidon. Tel. (512)341-1366. Fax (512)341-4519

Ozark Christian College, (Churches of Christ/Christian Churches), 1111 N. Main St., Joplin, MO 64801. Ken Idleman. Tel. (417)624-2518

Pacific Christian College, (Nondenominational), 2500 E. Nutwood Ave., Fullerton, CA 92631. E. Leroy Lawson. Tel. (714)879-3901. Fax (714)526-0231

Pacific Lutheran Theological Seminary, (Evangelical Lutheran Church in America), 2770 Marin Ave., Berkeley, CA 94708. Jerry L. Schmalenberger. Tel. (415)524-5264. Fax (415)524-2408

Pacific School of Religion, (Interdenominational), 1798 Scenic Ave., Berkeley, CA 94709. Eleanor Scott Meyers. Tel. (510)848-0528. Fax (510)845-8948

Payne Theological Seminary, (A.M.E.), P.O. Box 474, Wilberforce, OH 45384. Louis-Charles Harvey. Tel. (513)376-2946. Fax (513)376-2948

Pepperdine University, (Churches of Christ), Pepperdine University, Religion Division, Malibu, CA 90263. Thomas H. Olbricht. Tel. (213)456-4352. Fax (213)456-4314

Perkins School of Theology (Southern Methodist University), (United Methodist), Perkins School of Theology, Kirby Hall, Dallas, TX 75275-0133. James E. Kirby. Tel. (214)692-2138. Fax (214)692-4295

Philadelphia College of Bible, (Interdenominational), 200 Manor Ave., Langhorne, PA 19047-2990. W. Sherrill Babb. Tel. (215)752-5800. Fax (215)752-5812

Philadelphia Theological Seminary, (Reformed Episcopal Church), 4225 Chestnut St., Philadelphia, PA 19104. Ray R. Sutton. Tel. (215)222-5158. Fax (215)222-2939

Phillips Graduate Seminary, (Christian Church, Disciples of Christ), Box 2335, University Sta., Enid, OK 73702. William Tabbernee. Tel. (405)237-4433. Fax (405)237-1607

Piedmont Bible College, (Baptist), 716 Franklin St., Winston-Salem, NC 27101. Howard L. Wilburn. Tel. (919)725-8344

Pittsburgh Theological Seminary, (PCUSA), 616 N. Highland Ave., Pittsburgh, PA 15206. Carnegie Samuel Calian. Tel. (412)362-5610. Fax (412)363-3260

Point Loma Nazarene College, (Nazarene), 3900 Lomaland Dr., San Diego, CA 92106. Jim Bond. Tel. (619)221-2200. Fax (619)221-2579

Pontifical College Josephinum, (Catholic), 7625 N. High St., Columbus, OH 43235. Blase J. Cupich. Tel. (614)885-5585. Fax (614)885-2307

Pope John XXIII National Seminary, (Catholic), 558 South Ave., Weston, MA 02193. Cornelius M. McRae. Tel. (617)899-5500. Fax (617)899-9057

Practical Bible Training School, (Independent Baptist), Box 601, Bible School Park, NY 13737. Dale E. Linebaugh. Tel. (607)729-1581. Fax (607)729-2962

Presbyterian School of Christian Education, (PCUSA), 1205 Palmyra Ave., Richmond, VA 23227. Wayne G. Boulton. Tel. (804)359-5031. Fax (804)254-8060

Princeton Theological Seminary, (PCUSA), Box 552, Princeton, NJ 08542-0803. Thomas W. Gillespie. Tel. (609)921-8300. Fax (609)924-2973

Protestant Episcopal Theolopgical Seminary in Virginia, (Episcopal), 3737 Seminary Rd., Alexandria, VA 22304. Richard Reid. Tel. (703)370-6600. Fax (703)370-6234

Puget Sound Christian College, (Christian Church), 410 Fourth Ave. N, Edmonds, WA 98020-3171. Glen R. Basey. Tel. (206)775-8686

Rabbi Isaac Elchanan Theol. Sem. (affil. of Yeshiva Univ.), (Orthodox Jewish), 2540 Amsterdam Ave., New York, NY 10033. Zevulun Charlop. Tel. (212)960-5344. Fax (212)960-0061

Reconstructionist Rabbinical College, (Jewish), Church Rd. and Greenwood Ave., Wyncote, PA 19095. Arthur Green. Tel. (215)576-0800. Fax (215)576-6143

Reformed Bible College, (Interdenominational), 3333 East Beltline NE, Grand Rapids, MI 49505. Edwin D. Roels. Tel. (616)363-2050. Fax (616)363-9771

Reformed Presbyterian Theological Seminary, (Reformed Presb. Church of North America), 7418 Penn Ave., Pittsburgh, PA 15208. Bruce C. Stewart. Tel. (412)731-8690

Reformed Theological Seminary, (Independent), 5422 Clinton Blvd., Jackson, MS 39209. Luder G. Whitlock. Tel. (601)922-4988. Fax (601)922-1153

Roanoke Bible College, (Churches of Christ), 714 First St., Elizabeth City, NC 27909. William A. Griffin. Tel. (919)338-5191. Fax (919)338-0801

SS. Cyril and Methodius Seminary, (Catholic), Orchard Lake, MI 48324. Francis B. Koper. Tel. (313)682-1885. Fax (313)683-0402

Saint Bernard's Institute, (Catholic), 1100 S. Goodman St., Rochester, NY 14620. Sebastian A. Falcone. Tel. (716)271-1320. Fax (716)271-2166

Saint Paul School of Theology, (United Methodist), 5123 Truman Rd., Kansas City, MO 64127. Lovett H. Weems. Tel. (816)483-9600. Fax (816)483-9605

Saint Thomas Theological Seminary, (Catholic), 1300 S. Steele St., Denver, CO 80210. John E. Rybolt. Tel. (303)722-4687. Fax (303)722-7422

San Francisco Theological Seminary, (PCUSA), 2 Kensington Rd., San Anselmo, CA 94960. J. Randolph Taylor. Tel. (415)258-6500. Fax (415)454-2493

San Jose Christian College, (Nondenominational), 790 S. 12th St., P.O. Box 1090, San Jose, CA 95108. Bryce L. Jessup. Tel. (408)293-9058. Fax (408)293-7352

Savonarola Theological Seminary, (Polish National Catholic), 115 Lake Scranton, Scranton, PA 18505. John F. Swantek. Tel. (717)343-0100

Seabury-Western Theological Seminary, (Episcopal), 2122 N. Sheridan Rd., Evanston, IL 60201. Mark S. Sisk. Tel. (708)328-9300. Fax (708)328-9624

Seminario Evangelico de Puerto Rico, (Interdemoninational), 776 Ponce de Leon Ave., Hato Rey, PR 00918. Luis Fidel Mercado. Tel. (809)751-6483. Fax (809)751-0847

Seminary of the Immaculate Conception, (Catholic), 440 West Neck Rd., Huntington, NY 11743. John J. Strynkowski. Tel. (516)423-0483. Fax (516)423-2346

Seventh Day Baptist Center on Ministry, (Seventh Day Baptist General Conference), 3120 Kennedy Rd., P.O. Box 1678, Janesville, WI 53547. Rodney Henry. Tel. (608)752-5055. Fax (608)752-7711

Seventh-day Adventist Theological Seminary, Andrews Univ., (Seventh-day Adventist), Berrien Springs, MI 49104. Werner Vyhmeister. Tel. (616)471-3536

Shaw Divinity School, (National Baptist), P.O. Box 2090, Raleigh, NC 27102. Joseph C. Paige. Tel. (919)832-1701

Simpson College, (Christian and Missionary Alliance), 2211 College View Dr., Redding, CA 96003. Leonard Wallmark. Tel. (916)224-5600. Fax (916)224-5608

Southeastern Baptist College, (Baptist Missionary Assn. of Mississippi), Highway 15N, Laurel, MS 39941. Gerald D. Kellar. Tel. (601)426-6346

Southeastern Baptist Theological Seminary, (Southern Baptist Convention), 222 N. Wingate, P.O. Box 1889, Wake Forest, NC 27587. L. Paige Patterson. Tel. (919)556-3101. Fax (919)556-3101

Southeastern Bible College, (Interdenominational), 3001 Highway 280 E, Birmingham, AL 35243. John D. Talley. Tel. (205)969-0880. Fax (205)969-0880

Southeastern College of the Assemblies of God, (Assemblies of God), 1000 Longfellow Blvd., Lakeland, FL 33801. James L. Hennesy. Tel. (813)665-4404. Fax (813)666-8103

Southern Baptist Theological Seminary, (Southern Baptist Convention), 2825 Lexington Rd., Louisville, KY 40280. Roy Lee Honeycutt. Tel. (502)897-4011. Fax (502)897-4202

Southern Christian University, (Churches of Christ), 1200 Taylor Rd., P.O. Box 240240, Montgomery, AL 36124-0240. Rex A. Turner. Tel. (205)277-2277. Fax (205)277-0002

Southwestern Assemblies of God College, (Assemblies of God), 1200 Sycamore St., Waxahachie, TX 75165. Delmer R. Guynes. Tel. (214)937-4010. Fax (214)923-0488

Southwestern Baptist Theological Seminary, (Southern Baptist Convention), P.O. Box 22000, Fort Worth, TX 76122. Russell H. Dilday. Tel. (817)923-1921. Fax (817)923-0610

Southwestern College, (Baptist), 2625 E. Cactus Rd., Phoenix, AZ 85032. Donald R. Engram. Tel. (602)992-6101

St. Charles Borromeo Seminary, (Catholic), 1000 East Wynnewood Rd., Overbrook, PA 19096. Daniel A. Murray. Tel. (215)667-3394

St. Francis Seminary, (Catholic), 3257 S. Lake Dr., St. Francis, WI 53207. David A. Lichter. Tel. (414)747-6400. Fax (414)747-6442

St. John's Seminary, (Catholic), St. John's Seminary, Brighton, MA 02135. Timothy Moran. Tel. (617)254-2610

St. John's Seminary College, (Catholic), 5118 E. Seminary Rd., Camarillo, CA 93012-2599. Rafael Luevano. Tel. (805)482-2755. Fax (805)987-5097

St. John's University, School of Theology, (Catholic), St. John's University, Collegeville, MN 56321. Dale Launderville. Tel. (612)363-2100. Fax (616)363-2115

St. Joseph's Seminary, (Catholic), 201 Seminary Ave., (Dunwoodie) Yonkers, NY 10704. Raymond T. Powers. Tel. (914)968-6200

St. Louis Christian College, (Christian Churches), 1360 Grandview Dr., Florissant, MO 63033. Thomas W. McGee. Tel. (314)837-6777. Fax (314)837-8291

St. Mary Seminary, (Catholic), 28700 Euclid Ave., Wickliffe, OH 44092. Allan R. Laubenthal. Tel. (216)943-7600. Fax (216)585-3528

St. Mary's Seminary, (Catholic), 9845 Memorial Dr., Houston, TX 77024. Chester L. Borski. Tel. (713)686-4345. Fax (713)681-7550

St. Mary's Seminary and University, (Catholic), 5400 Roland Ave., Baltimore, MD 21210. Robert F. Leavitt. Tel. (301)323-3200. Fax (301)323-3554

St. Meinrad School of Theology, (Catholic), St. Meinrad Seminary, St. Meinrad, IN 47577. Eugene Hensell. Tel. (812)357-6611. Fax (812)357-6964

St. Patrick's Seminary, (Catholic), 320 Middlefield Rd., Menlo Park, CA 94025. Gerald D. Coleman. Tel. (415)325-5621. Fax (415)322-0997

St. Paul Seminary School of Divinity, (Catholic), 2260 Summit Ave., St. Paul, MN 55105. Charles Froehle. Tel. (612)647-5715. Fax (612)647-4361

St. Tikhon's Orthodox Theological Seminary, (Orthodox Church in America), P.O. Box 130, South Canaan, PA 18459-0121. Herman. Tel. (717)937-4686. Fax (717)937-4939

St. Vincent Seminary, (Catholic), St. Vincent Seminary, Latrobe, PA 15650. Thomas Acklin. Tel. (412)537-4592

209

St. Vincent de Paul Regional Seminary, (Catholic), 10701 S. Military Trail, Boynton Beach, FL 33436. Arthur Bendixen. Tel. (407)732-4424. Fax (407)737-2205

St. Vladimir's Orthodox Theological Seminary, (Eastern Orthodox), 575 Scarsdale Rd., Crestwood, NY 10707. Thomas Hopko. Tel. (914)961-8313. Fax (914)961-4507

Starr King School for the Ministry, (Unitarian Universalist), Starr King School for the Ministry, Berkeley, CA 94709. Rebecca Parker. Tel. (415)845-6232

Swedenborg Sch. of Religion (formerly New Church Theol. Sch.), (Gen. Conv. of the Swedenborgian Church), 48 Sargent St., Newton, MA 02158. Mary Kay Klein. Tel. (617)244-0504. Fax (617)964-3258

Talbot School of Theology, (Interdenominational), 13800 Biola Ave., La Mirada, CA 90639. Dennis H. Dirks. Tel. (310)903-4816. Fax (310)903-4759

Temple Baptist Seminary, (Baptist), 1815 Union Ave., Chattanooga, TN 37404. Roger Martin. Tel. (615)493-4221. Fax (615)493-4497

Theological School of the Protestant Reformed Churches, (Protestant Reformed Churches in America), 4949 Ivanrest Ave., Grandville, MI 49418. Robert D. Decker. Tel. (616)531-1490. Fax (616)531-3033

Toccoa Falls College, (Christian and Missionary Alliance), Toccoa Falls College, Toccoa Falls, GA 30598. Paul L. Alford. Tel. (706)886-6831. Fax (706)886-0210

Trevecca Nazarene College (Religion Dept.), (Nazarene), 333 Murfreesboro Rd., Nashville, TN 37210. H. Ray Dunning. Tel. (615)248-1200. Fax (615)248-7728

Trinity Bible College, (Assemblies of God), Trinity Bible College, Ellendale, ND 58436. Ray W. Trask. Tel. (800)523-1603. Fax (701)349-5443

Trinity College at Miami, (Interdenominational), 500 NE 1st Ave., P.O. Box 019674, Miami, FL 33101-9674. Kenneth Meyer. Tel. (305)577-4600. Fax (305)577-4612

Trinity College of Florida/Tampa Bay Seminary, (Independent), P.O. Box 9000, Holiday, FL 34690. Richard Williams. Tel. (813)376-6911. Fax (813)376-0781

Trinity Evangelical Divinity School, (Evangelical Free Church of America), 2065 Half Day Rd., Deerfield, IL 60015. Kenneth M. Meyer. Tel. (708)945-8800. Fax (708)317-8090

Trinity Lutheran Seminary, (Evangelical Lutheran Church in America), 2199 E. Main St., Columbus, OH 43209-2334. Dennis A. Anderson. Tel. (614)235-4136. Fax (614)238-0263

Union Theological Seminary, (Interdenominational), 3041 Broadway, New York, NY 10027. Holland L. Hendrix. Tel. (212)662-7100. Fax (212)280-1416

Union Theological Seminary in Virginia, (PCUSA), 3401 Brook Rd., Richmond, VA 23227. T. Hartley Hall. Tel. (804)355-0671. Fax (804)355-3919

United Theological Seminary, (United Methodist Church), 1810 Harvard Blvd., Dayton, OH 45406. Leonard I. Sweet. Tel. (513)278-5817. Fax (513)278-1218

United Theological Seminary of the Twin Cities, (United Church of Christ), 3000 Fifth St. NW, New Brighton, MN 55112. Benjamin Griffin. Tel. (612)633-4311. Fax (612)633-4315

University of the South (School of Theology), (Episcopal), School of Theology, Sewanee, TN 37375-1000. Guy Fitch Lytle. Tel. (615)598-1288. Fax (615)598-1165

Valley Forge Christian College, (Assemblies of God), Charlestown Rd., Phoenixville, PA 19460. Wesley W. Smith. Tel. (215)935-0450

Vanderbilt University (Divinity School), (Interdenominational), Vanderbilt University, Nashville, TN 37240. Joseph C. Hough. Tel. (615)322-2776. Fax (615)343-9957

Vennard College, (Interdenominational), Box 29, University Park, IA 52595. Blake J. Neff. Tel. (515)673-8391

Virginia Union University (School of Theology), (Baptist), 1601 W. Leigh St., Richmond, VA 23220. John W. Kinney. Tel. (804)257-5715

Walla Walla College (School of Theology), (Seventh-day Adventist), Walla Walla College, College Place, WA 99324. Douglas Clark. Tel. (509)527-2194. Fax (509)527-2253

Wartburg Theological Seminary, (Evangelical Lutheran Church in America), 333 Wartburg Pl., Dubuque, IA 52003-7797. Roger Fjeld. Tel. (319)589-0200. Fax (319)589-0333

Wash. Theological Consortium & Washington Inst. of Ecumenics, 487 Michigan Ave. NE, Washington, DC 20017. David Trickett. Tel. (202)832-2675

Washington Theological Union, (Catholic), 9001 New Hampshire Ave., Silver Springs, MD 20903. Vincent D. Cushing. Tel. (301)439-0551. Fax (301)445-4929

Wesley College, (Cong. Methodist), P.O. Box 1070, Florence, MS 39073. Samuel Bruce. Tel. (601)845-2265

Wesley Theological Seminary, (United Methodist), 4500 Massachusetts Ave. NW, Washington, DC 20016. G. Douglass Lewis. Tel. (202)885-8600. Fax (202)885-8605

Western Baptist College, (General Association of Regular Baptist), 5000 Deer Park Dr. SE, Salem, OR 97301. David F. Miller. Tel. (503)581-8600. Fax (503)585-4316

Western Conservative Baptist Seminary, (Conservative Baptist Assoc.), 5511 SE Hawthorne Blvd., Portland, OR 97215. Lawrence W. Ayers. Tel. (503)233-8561. Fax (503)239-4216

Western Evangelical Seminary, (Interdenominational), 4200 SE Jennings Ave., Portland, OR 97267. David LeShana. Tel. (503)654-5466. Fax (503)654-5469

Western Theological Seminary, (Reformed Church in America), 86 E. 12th St., Holland, MI 49423. Marvin D. Hoff. Tel. (616)392-8555. Fax (616)392-7717

Westminster Theological Seminary, (Independent), Chestnut Hill, P.O. Box 27009, Philadelphia, PA 19118. Samuel T. Logan. Tel. (215)887-5511. Fax (215)887-5404

Weston School of Theology, (Catholic), 3 Phillips Pl., Cambridge, MA 02138. Robert Wild. Tel. (617)492-1960. Fax (617)492-5833

William Tyndale College, (Interdenominational), 35700 W. Twelve Mile Rd., Farmington Hills, MI 48331. James C. McHann. Tel. (313)553-7200. Fax (313)553-5963

Winebrenner Theological Seminary, (Churches of God, General Conference), 701 E. Melrose Ave., P.O. Box 478, Findlay, OH 45839. David E. Draper. Tel. (419)422-4824. Fax (419)424-3433

Wisconsin Lutheran Seminary, (Wisconsin Lutheran), 11831 N. Seminary Dr., 65W, Mequon, WI 53092. Armin Panning. Tel. (414)242-7200. Fax (414)242-7255

Yale University (Divinity School), (Nondenominational), 409 Prospect St., New Haven, CT 06511-2167. Thomas Ogletree. Tel. (203)432-5303. Fax (203)432-5756

8. THEOLOGICAL SEMINARIES AND BIBLE SCHOOLS IN CANADA

The following list includes theological seminaries and departments in colleges and universities in which ministerial training is given. Many denominations have additional programs. The lists of Religious Bodies in Canada should be consulted for the address of denominational headquarters.

The list has been developed from direct correspondence with the institutions. Inclusion in or exclusion from this list implies no judgment about the quality or accreditation of any institution.

The listing includes the institution name, denominational sponsor when appropriate, location, the head of the institution, telephone number, and fax number when known.

Acadia Divinity College, (Un. Bapt. Conv. of Atlantic Provinces), Acadia University, Wolfville, NS B0P 1X0. Andrew D. MacRae. Tel. (902)542-2285. Fax (902)542-7527

Alberta Bible College, (CC/CC), 599 Northmount Dr. N.W., Calgary, AB T2K 3J6. Ronald A. Fraser. Tel. (403)282-2994. Fax (403)282-3084

Aldersgate College, (Free Methodist Church in Canada), Box 460, Moose Jaw, SK S6H 4P1. Joseph F. James. Tel. (306)693-7773. Fax (306)692-8821

Arthur Turner Training School, (The Anglican Church of Canada), Pangnirtung, NT X0A 0R0. Rev. Roy Bowkett. Tel. (819)473-8375

Atlantic Baptist College, (Un. Bapt. Conv. of the Atlantic Province), Box 6004, Moncton, NB E1C 9L7. W. Ralph Richardson. Tel. (506)858-8970. Fax (506)858-9694

Atlantic School of Theology, (Ecumenical (Anglican, Catholic, UCC)), 640 Francklyn St., Halifax, NS B3H 3B5. Gordon MacDermid. Tel. (902)423-6801. Fax (902)492-4048

Baptist Leadership Training School, (Bapt. Un. of Western Canada), 4330 16th St. S.W., Calgary, AB T2T 4H9. Kenneth W. Bellous. Tel. (403)243-3770. Fax (403)287-1930

Bethany Bible College—Canada, (Wesleyan Church), 26 Western St., Sussex, NB E0E 1P0. David S. Medders. Tel. (506)432-4400. Fax (506)432-4425

Bethany Bible Institute, (Mennonite Brethren Church, Can. Con. of), Box 160, Hepburn, SK S0K 1Z0. Dr. James Nikkel. Tel. (306)947-2175. Fax (306)947-4229

Briercrest Bible College and Biblical Seminary, (Interdenominational), 510 College Dr., Caronport, SK S0H 0S0. John Barkman. Tel. (306)756-3200. Fax (306)756-3366

Brockville Bible College, (Stand. Ch. of Am.), Box 1900, Brockville, ON K6V 6N4. Tel. (613)345-5001

Canadian Bible College, (Chr. and Miss. All.), 4400-4th Ave., Regina, SK S4T 0H8. Robert A. Rose. Tel. (306)545-1515. Fax (306)545-0210

Canadian Lutheran Bible Institute, (Lutheran), 4837 52A St., Camrose, AB T4V 1W5. Ronald B. Mayan. Tel. (403)672-4454

Canadian Mennonite Bible College, 600 Shaftesbury Blvd., Winnipeg, MB R3P 0M4. John H. Neufeld. Tel. (204)888-6781

Canadian Mennonite Bible College, (Mennonite), 600 Shaftesbury Blvd., Winnipeg, MB R3P 0M4. Tel. (204)888-6781

Canadian Nazarene College, (Church of the Nazarene), 1301 Lee Blvd., Winnipeg, MB R3T 2P7. Riley Coulter. Tel. (204)269-2120. Fax (204)269-7772

Canadian Reformed Churches, Theol. College of the, (Can. Ref. Chs), 110 West 27th St., Hamilton, ON L9C 5A1. L. C. Van Dam. Tel. (416)575-3688. Fax (416)575-0799

Canadian Theological Seminary, (Chr. and Miss. All.), 4400-4th Ave., Regina, SK S4T 0H8. Robert A. Rose. Tel. (306)545-1515. Fax (306)545-0210

Central Baptist Seminary, (Fell. of Evan. Bapt. Chs.in Canada), 6 Gormley Industrial Ave., Box 28, Gormley, ON L0H 1G0. Stan Fowler. Tel. (416)888-9600. Fax (416)888-9603

Central Pentecostal College, University of Saskatchewan, (Pentecostal Assemblies of Canada), 1303 Jackson Ave., Saskatoon, SK S7H 2M9. J. Harry Faught. Tel. (306)374-6655. Fax (306)373-6968

Centre d'Études Théologiques Évangeliques, (Un. d'Églises Bapt. Françaises), 2285, avenue Papineau, Montréal, QC H2K 4J5. Dr. Nelson Thomson. Tel. (514)526-6643

Centre for Christian Studies, (Ang. Ch. of Canada; Un. Ch. of Canada), 77 Charles St. W., Toronto, ON M5S 1K5. Trudy Lebans. Tel. (416)923-1168. Fax (416)923-5496

Christianview Bible College, (Pent. Holiness Chs. of Canada), 164 George St., ON N0M 1A0. Alisa Graig. Tel. (519)293-3506

Church Army College of Evangelism, (Anglican Church of Canada), 397 Brunswick Ave., Toronto, ON M5R 2Z2. Capt. Roy Dickson. Tel. (416)924-9279. Fax (416)924-2931

College Biblique, Québec - Formation Timothie, (Pentecostal Assemblies of Canada), 1320 rue St-Paul Est, ste. 200, Ancienne Lorette, QC G2E 1Z4. Tel. (418)871-5292

College Dominicain de Philosophie et de Théologie, (Catholic), 96 avenue Empress, Ottawa, ON K1R 7G3. Michel Gourgues. Tel. (613)233-5696. Fax (613)233-6064

College of Emmanuel and St. Chad, (Anglican Church of Canada), 1337 College Dr., Saskatoon, SK S7N 0W6. J. Russell Brown. Tel. (306)975-3753

Columbia Bible College, (Menn. Breth.; Gen. Conf. Menn), 2940 Clearbrook Rd., Clearbrook, BC V2T 2Z8. Walter Unger. Tel. (604)853-3358. Fax (604)853-3063

Concord College, (Mennonite Brethren), 1 169 Riverton Ave., Winnipeg, MB R2L 2E5. James N. Pankratz. Tel. (204)669-6583. Fax (204)654-1865

Concordia Lutheran Seminary, (Lutheran Church—Canada), 7040 Ada Blvd., Edmonton, AB T5B 4E3. Dr. Milton L. Rudnick. Tel. (403)474-1468. Fax (403)479-3067

Concordia Lutheran Theological Seminary, (Lutheran Church—Canada), 470 Glenridge Ave., Box 1117, St. Catharines, ON L2R 7A3. Jonathan Grothe. Tel. (416)688-2362. Fax (416)688-9744

Covenant Bible College, (Evangelical Covenant Church of Canada), 245 21st St. E., Prince Albert, SK S6V 1L9. W. B. Anderson. Tel. (306)922-3443. Fax (306)922-5414

Eastern Pentecostal Bible College, (The Pentecostal Assemblies of Canada), 780 Argyle St., Peterborough, ON K9H 5T2. R. W. Taitinger. Tel. (705)748-9111. Fax (705)748-3931

Emmanuel Bible College, (Missionary Church of Canada), 100 Fergus Ave., Kitchener, ON N2A 2H2. Dr. Thomas E. Dow. Tel. (519)894-8900

Emmanuel College, (United Church of Canada), 75 Queen's Park Crescent, Toronto, ON M5S 1K7. John C. Hoffman. Tel. (416)585-4539. Fax (416)585-4584

Faith Alive Bible College, (Charismatic - Word of Faith), 637 University Dr., Saskatoon, SK S7N 0H8. Tel. (306)652-2230

Full Gospel Bible Institute, (Apostolic Ch. of Pentecost), Box 579, Eston, SK S0L 1A0. Alan B. Mortensen. Tel. (306)962-3621. Fax (306)962-3810

Gardner Bible College, (Church of God, Anderson, Ind.), 4704 55th St., Camrose, AB T4V 2B6. Bruce Kelly. Tel. (403)672-0171. Fax (403)672-6888

Great Lakes Bible College, (Churches of Christ), 4875 King St. E., Beamsville, ON L0R 1B0. Dave McMillan. Tel. (416)563-5374. Fax (416)563-0818

Huron College, (Ang. Ch. of Canada, Faculty of Theology), 1349 Western Rd., London, ON N6G 1H3. Dr. Charles J. Jago. Tel. (519)438-7224. Fax (519)438-3938

Institut Biblique Beree, (Pentecostal Assemblies of Canada), 1711 Henri-Bourassa Est, Montréal, QC H2C 1J5. Tel. (514)385-4238. Fax (514)462-1789

Institut Biblique Béthel, (Interdenominational), 1175 Chemin Woodward Hill, RR1, Lennoxville, QC J1M 2A2. Richard Strout. Tel. (819)823-8435. Fax (819)569-7887

Institut Biblique Laval, (Mennonite Brethren), 1775, boul. Édouard-Laurin, Ville Saint-Laurent, QC H4L 2B9. Tel. (514)331-0878. Fax (514)331-0879

Institute for Christian Studies, 229 College St., Toronto, ON M5T 1R4. Tel. (416)979-2331. Fax (416)979-2332

International Bible College, (Church of God, Cleveland, Tenn.), 401 Trinity La., Moose Jaw, SK S6H 0E3. Tel. (306)692-4041

Jubilee Bible College, (Apostolic Church of Pentecost), Box 322, 21746 Lougheed Highway, Maple Ridge, BC V2X 7G2. Tel. (604)467-4728. Fax (604)467-9234

Key-Way-Tin Bible Institute, (Interdenominational), Box 540, Lac La Biche, AB T0A 2C0. Tel. (403)623-4565

Knox College, (Presbyterian Church in Canada), 59 St. George St., Toronto, ON M5S 2E6. Iain G. Nicol. Tel. (416)978-4500. Fax (416)971-2133

Living Faith Bible College, (Fellowship of Christian Assemblies), Box 100, Caroline, AB T0M 0W0. Dr. Virgil Stauffer. Tel. (403)722-2225. Fax (403)722-3400

London Baptist Bible College/Seminary, (Baptist), 30 Grand Ave., London, ON N6C 1K8. Marvin Brubacher. Tel. (519)434-6801

Lutheran Theological Seminary, (Evangelical Lutheran Church in Canada), 114 Seminary Crescent, Saskatoon, SK S7N 0X3. Roger Nostbakken. Tel. (306)975-7004. Fax (306)975-0084

Maritime Christian College, (CC/CC), Box 1145, 223 Kent St., Charlottetown, PE C1A 7M8. Stewart J. Lewis. Tel. (902)894-3828. Fax (902)892-3959

McMaster Divinity College, (Baptist Convention of Ontario and Québec), McMaster Divinity College, Hamilton, ON L8S 4K1. Dr. William H. Brackney. Tel. (416)525-9140. Fax (416)577-4782

Millar College of the Bible, (Interdenominational), Box 25, Pambrun, SK S0N 1W0. Tel. (306)582-2033. Fax (306)582-2027

Montréal Diocesan Theological College, (Anglican Church of Canada), 3473 University St., Montréal, QC H3A 2A8. John Simons. Tel. (514)849-3004

Mount Carmel Bible School, (Christian Brethren), 4725 106 Avenue, Edmonton, AB T6A 1E7. Tel. (403)465-3015. Fax (403)449-1409

National Native Bible College, (Elim Fellowship), Box 478, Deseronto, ON K0K 1X0. Tel. (613)396-2311. Fax (613)396-2555

Newman Theological College, (Catholic), 15611 St. Albert Trail, Edmonton, AB T5L 4H8. D. MacDonald. Tel. (403)447-2993. Fax (403)447-2685

Nipawin Bible Institute, (Interdenominational), Box 1986, Nipawin, SK S0E 1E0. Mark Leppington. Tel. (306)862-5095. Fax (306)862-3651

North American Baptist College/Edmonton Baptist Seminary, (North American Baptist Conference), 11525 - 23rd Ave., Edmonton, AB T6J 4T3. Paul Siewert. Tel. (403)437-1960. Fax (403)436-9416

Northwest Baptist Theological College and Seminary, (Fellowship of Evangelical Baptists), 22606 76A Ave., P.O. Box 790, Langley, BC V3A 8B8. Doug Harris. Tel. (604)888-3310. Fax (604)888-3354

Northwest Bible College, (Pentecostal Assemblies of Canada), 11617-106 Ave., Edmonton, AB T5H 0S1. G. K. Franklin. Tel. (403)452-0808. Fax (403)452-5803

Okanagan Bible College, (Interdenominational), Box 407, Kelowna, BC V1Y 7N8. Dr. Stewart Simpson. Tel. (604)768-4410. Fax (604)768-0631

Ontario Christian Seminary, (CC/CC), P.O. Box 324, Stn. D, 260 High Park Ave., Toronto, ON M6P 3J9. Nelson Deuitch. Tel. (416)769-7115. Fax (416)769-7115

Ontario Theological Seminary, (Multidenominatinal), 25 Ballyconnor Ct., North York, ON M2M 4B3. Dr. Wm. J. McRae, Chancellor. Tel. (416)226-6380. Fax (416)226-6746

Pacific Bible College, (Non-denominational), 15100 66 A Ave., Surrey, BC V3S 2A6. Tel. (604)597-9331. Fax (604)597-9090

Peace River Bible Institute, (Interdenominational), Box 99, Sexsmith, AB T0H 3C0. Reuben Kvill. Tel. (403)568-3962

Prairie Bible Institute, (Interdenominational), Box 4000, Three Hills, AB T0M 2A0. Ted S. Rendall. Tel. (403)443-5511. Fax (403)443-5540

Presbyterian College, (Presbyterian), 3495 University St., Montréal, QC H3A 2A8. W. J. Klempa. Tel. (514)288-5256. Fax (514)398-6665

Providence College and Theological Seminary, (Non-denominational), General Delivery, Otterburne, MB R0A 1G0. William R. Eichhorst. Tel. (204)433-7488. Fax (204)433-7158

Queen's College, (Anglican Church of Canada), Queen's College, St. John's, NF A1B 3R6. Rev. Canon Frank Cluett. Tel. (709)753-0640. Fax (709)753-1214

Queen's Theological College, (United Church of Canada), Queen's Theological College, Kingston, ON K7L 3N6. Hallett Llewellyn. Tel. (613)545-2110. Fax (613)545-6879

Regent College, (Transdenominational), 5800 University Blvd., Vancouver, BC V6T 2E4. Walter C. Wright, Jr.. Tel. (800)663-8664. Fax (604)224-3097

Regis College, (Catholic), 15 St. Mary St., Toronto, ON M4Y 2R5. John E. Costello. Tel. (416)922-5474. Fax (416)922-2898

Rocky Mountain College: Centre for Biblical Studies, (Evangelical Church and Missionary Church), 4039 Brentwood Road NW, Calgary, AB T4L 1L1. Kervin Raugust. Tel. (403)284-5100. Fax (403)220-9567

Salvation Army College for Officer Training, The, (Salvation Army), 2130 Bayview Ave., Toronto, ON M4N 3K6. Lt. Col. John E. Carew. Tel. (416)481-6131. Fax (416)481-6810

St. Andrew's Theological College, (United Church of Canada), 1121 College Dr., Saskatoon, SK S7N 0W3. Tel. (306)966-8970

St. Augustine's Seminary of Toronto, (Catholic), 2661 Kingston Rd., Scarborough, ON M1M 1M3. Rev. James M. Wingle. Tel. (416)261-7207. Fax (416)261-2529

St. John's College, Univ. of Manitoba, Faculty of Theology, (Anglican Church of Canada), St. John's College, Univ. of Manitoba, Winnipeg, MB R3T 2M5. Murdith McLean. Tel. (204)474-6852. Fax (204)275-1498

St. Peter's Seminary, (Catholic), 1040 Waterloo St., London, ON N6A 3Y1. Patrick W. Fuerth. Tel. (519)432-1824. Fax (519)432-0964

St. Stephen's College, Grad. and Continuing Theological Ed., (United Church of Canada), St. Stephen's College, 8810 112th St., Edmonton, AB T6G 2J6. Garth I. Mundle. Tel. (403)439-7311. Fax (403)433-8875

Steinbach Bible College, (Non-denominational), Box 1420, Steinbach, MB R0A 2A0. Gordon Daman. Tel. (204)326-6451. Fax (204)326-6908

Swift Current Bible Institute, (Mennonite), Box 1268, Swift Current, SK S9H 3X4. Ray Friesen. Tel. (306)773-0604. Fax (306)773-9250

Temple Bible School, (Fellowship of Christian Assemblies), 3715-85 Street, Edmonton, AB T6K 3R9. Tel. (403)462-6572

The Salvation Army Catherine Booth Bible College, (Salvation Army), 447 Webb Pl., Winnipeg, MB R3B 2P2. Lt. Col. Earl Robinson. Tel. (204)947-6701. Fax (204)942-3856

Toronto Baptist Seminary and Bible College, (Baptist), 130 Gerrard St., E., Toronto, ON M5A 3T4. Norman Street. Tel. (416)925-3263

Toronto School of Theology, (7 theol colleges , of 4 denominations), 47 Queens Park Crescent E., Toronto, ON M5S 2C3. E. James Reed. Tel. (416)978-4039. Fax (416)978-7821

Trinity College, Faculty of Divinity, (Anglican Church of Canada), 6 Hoskin Ave., Toronto, ON M5S 1H8. R. H. Painter. Tel. (416)978-2370. Fax (416)978-2797

United Theological College/Le Séminaire Uni, (United Church of Canada), 3521 rue Universite, Montréal, QC H3A 2A9. Pierre Goldberger. Tel. (514)849-2042. Fax (514)398-6665

Université Laval, Faculté de théologie, (Catholic), Cité Universitaire Ste-Foy, Ste-Foy, QC G1K 7P4. Rene-Michel Roberse. Tel. (418)656-7823. Fax (418)656-2809

Université Saint-Paul, Faculté de théologie, (Catholic), 223 rue Main, Ottawa, ON K1S 1C4. M. Hubert Doucet. Tel. (613)236-1393. Fax (713)782-3004

Université de Montréal, Faculté de théologie, (Catholic), C. P. 6128, Montréal, QC H3C 3J7. Laval Letourneau, Dean. Tel. (514)343-7160. Fax (514)343-5738

Université de Sherbrooke, Faculté de théologie,, (Catholic), 2500 boul. Université, Sherbrooke, QC J1K 2R1. Lucien Vachon. Tel. (819)821-7600

University of St. Michael's College, Faculty of Theology, (Catholic), 81 St. Mary St., Toronto, ON M5S 1J4. Michael A. Fahey. Tel. (416)926-7140. Fax (416)926-7276

University of Winnipeg, Faculty of Theology, (Interdenominational), 515 Portage Avenue, Winnipeg, MB R3B 2E9. H. J. King. Tel. (204)786-9390. Fax (204)786-1824

Vancouver School of Theology, (Interdenominational), 6000 Iona Dr., Vancouver, BC V6T 1L4. Arthur Van Seters. Tel. (604)228-9031. Fax (604)228-0189

Victory Bible College, (Victory Churches of Canada International), Box 1780, Lethbridge, AB T1J 4K4. Tel. (403)320-1565. Fax (403)327-9013

Waterloo Lutheran Seminary, (Evangelical Lutheran Church in Canada), 75 University Avenue West, Waterloo, ON N2L 3C5. Richard C. Crossman. Tel. (519)884-1970. Fax (519)725-2434

Western Christian College, (Churches of Christ), Box 5000, Dauphin, MB R7N 2V5. V. V. Anderson. Tel. (204)638-8801. Fax (204)634-7054

Western Pentecostal Bible College, (Pentecostal Assemblies of Canada), Box 1700, Abbotsford, BC V2S 7E7. James G. Richards. Tel. (604)853-7491. Fax (604)853-8951

Western Pentecostal Bible College, (Pentecostal Assemblies of Canada), Box 1700, Abbotsford, BC V2S 7E7. Tel. (604)853-7491. Fax (604)853-8951

Winkler Bible Institute, (Mennonite Brethren), 121 7 Street S, Winkler, MB R6W 2N4. Eldon DeFehr. Tel. (204)325-4242. Fax (204)325-9028

Wycliffe College, (Anglican Church of Canada), 5 Hoskin Ave., Toronto, ON M5S 1H7. H. St. C. Hilchey. Tel. (416)979-2870. Fax (416)979-0471

9. RELIGIOUS PERIODICALS IN THE UNITED STATES

This list of religious periodicals contains two types of periodicals. First, there are official national publications of denominations. Regional publications and newsletters are not included. The denominational listings in sections 3 and 4 include the names of periodicals found in this listing.

The second type of periodical listed here is the independent national religious publication.

Probably the most inclusive list of religious periodicals published in the United States can be found in *Gale Directory of Publications and Broadcast Media, 1992*, Gale Research, Inc., P.O. Box 33477, Detroit MI 48232-5477).

Each entry lists the title of the periodical, frequency of publication, religious affiliation, editor's name, address, telephone number and fax number when known.

21st Century Christian, Churches of Christ, M. Norvel Young, Box 40304, Nashville, TN 37204. Tel. 800-331-5991

A.M.E. Review, African Methodist Episcopal, Paulette Coleman, 500 Eighth Ave., S., Nashville, TN 37203. Tel. (615)320-3500. Fax (615)244-7604

ALERT, Metropolitan Community Churches, Stephen Pieters, 5300 Santa Monica Blvd., Los Angeles, CA 90029. Tel. (213)464-5100. Fax (213)464-2123

Action, (10/yr.), Churches of Christ, Tex Williams, Box 9346, Austin, TX 78766. Tel. (512)345-8191. Fax (512)345-6634

Adult Quarterly, The, Associate Reformed Presbyterian(General Synod), W. H. F. Kuykendall, One Cleveland St., Greenville, SC 29601

Advance, Assemblies of God, Harris Jansen, Gospel Publishing House, Springfield, MO 65802. Tel. (417)862-2781. Fax (417)862-8558

Advancer, The, Baptist Missionary Association, Larry Silvey, P.O. Box 7270, Texarkana, TX 75505-7270. Tel. (903)793-6531. Fax (903)792-0619

Advent Christian News, Advent Christian, Robert Mayer, P.O. Box 23152, Charlotte, NC 28212. Tel. (704)545-6161. Fax (704)573-0712

Advent Christian Witness, The, Advent Christian Church, Robert Mayer, P.O. Box 23152, Charlotte, NC 28212. Tel. (704)545-6161. Fax (704)573-0712

Adventist Review, Seventh-day Adventist Church, W. G. Johnsson, 12501 Old Columbia Pike, Silver Spring, MD 20904-6600. Tel. (301)680-6560. Fax (301)680-6638

Advocate, The, Baptist Missionary Association, Ronald J. Beasley, 8101 Joffree Dr., Jacksonville, FL 32210.

Allegheny Wesleyan Methodist, The, Allegheny Wesleyan Methodist Connection, John B. Durfee, 1827 Allen Dr., Salem, OH 44460. Tel. (216)337-9376

Alliance Life, (bi-w), Christian and Missionary Alliance, Maurice Irvin, P.O. Box 35000, Colorado Springs, CO 80935. Tel. (719)599-5999. Fax (719)593-8692

America, Catholic, George W. Hunt, 106 W. 56th St., New York, NY 10019. Tel. (212)581-4640. Fax (212)399-3596

American Baptist Quarterly, American Baptist, William R. Millar, P.O. Box 851, Valley Forge, PA 19482. Tel. (215)7682378

American Baptists in Mission, (12/yr), American Baptist, Martha M. Cruz, P.O. Box 851, Valley Forge, PA 19482. Tel. (215)768-2301. Fax (215)768-2320

American Bible Society Record, (10/yr), Nondenominational, Clifford P. Macdonald, 1865 Broadway, New York, NY 10023. Tel. (212)408-1480. Fax (212)408-1456

American Jewish History, Jewish, Marc Lee Raphael, 2 Thornton Rd., Waltham, MA 02154. Tel. (617)891-8110. Fax (617)899-9208

American Presbyterians: Journal of Presbyterian History, Presbyterian (U.S.A.), James H. Smylie, 425 Lombard St., Philadelphia, PA 19147. Tel. (215)627-1852. Fax (215)627-0509

Anglican & Episcopal History, Episcopal, J. F. Woolverton, Box 2247, Austin, TX 78768.

Anglican Theol. Review, Episcopal, James Griffiss, 600 Haven St., Evanston, IL 60201. Tel. (708)864-6024. Fax (708)328-9624

Anglican and Episcopal History, Episcopal, John F. Woolverton, P. O. Box 261, Center Sandwich, NH 03227

Associate Reformed Presbyterian, The, Associate Reformed Presbyterian, Ben Johnston, One Cleveland St., Greenville, SC 29601. Tel. (803)232-8297

At Ease, (bi-m), Assemblies of God, Lemuel McElyea, Gospel Publishing House, Springfield, MO 65802. Tel. (417)862-2781. Fax (417)862-8558

Awake!, Watchtower Society, 25 Columbia Heights, Brooklyn, NY 11201. Tel. (718)625-3600. Fax (718)624-8030

Banner of Truth, The, Netherlands Reformed Congregations, Joel R. Beeke, 2115 Romence Ave., N.E., Grand Rapids, MI 29503.

Banner, The, Christian Reformed, 2850 Kalamazoo Ave., S.E., Grand Rapids, MI 49560. Tel. (616)246-0732. Fax (616)246-0834

Baptist Bible Tribune, The, Baptist Bible Fellowship, James O. Combs, P.O. Box 309 HSJ, Springfield, MO 65801. Tel. (417)831-3996. Fax (417)865-0794

Baptist Bulletin, General Association of Regular Baptist, Vernon D. Miller, 1300 N. Meacham Rd., Schaumburg, IL 60173-4888. Tel. (708)843-1600. Fax (708)843-3757

Baptist Herald, (10/yr.), North American Baptist, Barbara J. Binder, 1 S. 210 Summit Ave., Oakbrook Terrace, IL 60181. Tel. (708)495-2000. Fax (708)495-3301

Baptist Herald, Baptist Missionary Association, Jerry Derfelt, P.O. Box 218, Galena, KS 66739

Baptist History and Heritage, Southern Baptist, Lynn E. May, 901 Commerce St., Ste. 400, Nashville, TN 37203-3630. Tel. (615)244-0344. Fax (615)242-0344

Baptist Leader, American Baptist Churches, Linda Isham, P.O. Box 851, Valley Forge, PA 19842-0851. Tel. (215)768-2153. Fax (215)768-2056

Baptist Message, Southern Baptist, Lynn Clayton, Box 311, Alexandria, LA 71309. Tel. (318)442-7728

Baptist Program, (11/yr.), Southern Baptist, Ernest E. Mosley, SBC, 901 Commerce St., Nashville, TN 37203. Tel. (615)244-2355. Fax (615)742-8919

Baptist Progress, Baptist Missionary Association, Danny Pope, P.O. Box 2085, Waxahachie, TX 85165. Tel. (214)923-0756. Fax (214)923-2679

Baptist True Union, (b-m), Southern Baptist, Robert Allen, 10255 Old Columbia Rd., Columbia, MD 21046. Tel. (410)290-5290. Fax (410)290-7040

Baptist Trumpet, Baptist Missionary Association, David Tidwell, P.O. Box 192208, Little Rock, AR 72219. Tel. (501)565-4601

Baptist Witness, Primitive Baptists, L. Bradley, Box 17037, Cincinnati, OH 45217. Tel. (513)821-7289

Baptist and Reflector, Southern Baptist, W. Fletcher Allen, P.O. Box 728, Brentwood, TN 37024. Tel. (615)371-2003. Fax (615)371-2014

Being In Touch, Mennonite, General Conference, David Linscheid, Box 347, 722 Main St., Newton, KS 67114. Tel. (316)283-5100. Fax (316)283-0454

Biblical Recorder, R. G. Puckett, P.O. Box 26568, Raleigh, NC 27611. Tel. (919)847-2127. Fax (919)847-6939

Brethren Evangelist, The, Brethren (Ashland, Ohio), Richard C. Winfield, 524 College Ave., Ashland, OH 44805. Tel. (419)289-1708. Fax (419)281-0450

Brethren Journal, Unity of Brethren, Milton Maly, Rte. 3, Box 558N, Brenham, TX 77833

Brethren Missionary Herald, Grace Brethren, Fellowship of, Charles Turner, P.O. Box 544, Winona Lake, IN 46590. Tel. (219)267-7158. Fax (219)267-4745

Bridegroom's Messenger, The, Intnatl. Pent. Ch. of Christ, Janie Boyce, 121 W. Hunters Trail, Elizabeth City, NC 27909. Tel. (919)338-3003

Builder, David R. Hiebert, 616 Walnut Ave., Scottdale, PA 15683. Tel. (412)887-8500. Fax (412)887-3111

Burning Bush, The, (bi-m), Metropolitan Church, E. L. Adams, Metropolitan Church Assoc., Lake Geneva, WI 53147. Tel. (414)248-6786

Calendarul Credinta, Romanian Orthodox Church in America, Vasile Vasilachi, 19959 Riopelle St., Detroit, MI 48203

Calvary Messenger, The, Beachy Amish Mennonite, Ervin N. Hershberger, Rt. 1, Box 176, Meyersdale, PA 15552. Tel. (814)662-2483

Campus Life, (10/yr), Independent, Jim Long, 465 Gunderson Dr., Carol Stream, IL 60188. Tel. (708)260-6200. Fax (708)260-0114

Capital Baptist, Southern Baptist, Victor Tupitza, 1628 16th St. NW, Washington, DC 20009. Tel. (202)265-1526. Fax (202)677-8258

Capsule, General Association of General Baptists, Charles Carr, 100 Stinson Dr., Poplar Bluff, MO 63901. Tel. (314)785-7746. Fax (314)785-0564

Caring, (9/yr.), Assemblies of God, Owen Wilkie, Gospel Publishing House, Springfield, MO 65802. Tel. (417)862-2781. Fax (417)862-8558

Cathedral Age, Episcopal, Kelly Ferguson, Office of Public Affairs, WNC, Washington, DC 20016-5098. Tel. (202)537-6247. Fax (202)364-6600

Catholic Chronicle, (bi-w), Catholic, Richard S. Meek, Jr., P.O. Box 1866, Toledo, OH 43603. Tel. (419)243-4178. Fax (419)243-4235

Catholic Digest, Catholic, Henry Lexau, P.O. Box 64090, St. Paul, MN 55164. Tel. (612)647-5296. Fax (612)647-4346

Catholic Herald, Catholic, Ethel M. Gintoft, 3501 S. Lake Dr., St. Francis, WI 53235-0913. Tel. (414)769-3500. Fax (414)769-3468

Catholic Light, (bi-w), Catholic, James B. Earley, 300 Wyoming Ave., Scranton, PA 18503. Tel. (717)346-8915. Fax (717)346-8917

Catholic Review, The, Catholic, Daniel L. Medinger, P.O. Box 777, Baltimore, MD 21203. Tel. (410)547-5327. Fax (410)385-0113

Catholic Standard and Times, Catholic, Paul S. Quinter, 222 N. 17th St., Philadelphia, PA 19103. Tel. (215)587-3660. Fax (215)587-3979

Catholic Transcript, The, Catholic, David M. Fortier, 785 Asylum Ave., Hartford, CT 06105-2886. Tel. (203)527-1175. Fax (203)541-6110

Catholic Universe Bulletin, (bi-w), Catholic, Patrick Hyland, 1027 Superior Ave., N.E., Cleveland, OH 44114. Tel. (216)696-6525. Fax (216)696-6519

Catholic Worker, (8/yr), Catholic, Jo Roberts, 36 E. First St., New York, NY 10003. Tel. (212)254-1640

Catholic World, The, (bi-m), Catholic, Laurie Felknor, 997 Macarthur Blvd., Mahwah, NJ 07430. Tel. (201)825-7300. Fax (201)825-8345

Cela Biedrs, (10/yr.), Latvian Evangelical Lutheran, Eduards Putnins, 1468 Hemlock St., Napa, CA 94559. Tel. (707)252-1809

Celebration!, Seventh-day Adventist, John R. Calkins, 55 W. Oak Ridge Dr., Hagerstown, MD 21740.

Celebration: An Ecumenical Worship Resource, Catholic, William Freburger, P.O. Box 419493, Kansas City, MO 64141. Tel. (816)531-0538. Fax (816)531-7466

Cerkovnyj Vistnik—Church Messenger, (bi-w), American Carpatho-Russian Orthodox Greek Catholic, James S. Dutko, 280 Clinton St., Binghamton, NY 13905

Charisma Courier, The, Full Gospel Assemblies, C. E. Strauser, P.O. Box 1230, Coatesville, PA 19320. Tel. (215)857-2357

Childlife, Independent, Terry Madison, 919 W. Huntington Dr., Monrovia, CA 91016. Tel. (818)357-7979. Fax (818)357-0915

Christadelphian Advocate, Christadelphians, 1023 Green Hill Rd., South Hill, VA 23970.

Christadelphian Tidings, Christadelphians, Donald H. Styles, 30480 Oakleaf Ln., Franklin, MI 48025. Tel. (317)851-3028. Fax same

Christadelphian Watchman, Christadelphians, George Booker, 2500 Berwyn Cir., Austin, TX 78745.

Christian Baptist, The, Primitive Baptist, S. T. Tolley, P.O. Box 68, Atwood, TN 38220. Tel. (901)662-7417

Christian Bible Teacher, Churches of Christ, J. J. Turner, Box 1060, Abilene, TX 79604.

Christian Century, The, (38/yr), Independent, James M. Wall, 407 S. Dearborn St., Chicago, IL 60605. Tel. (312)427-5380. Fax (312)427-1302

Christian Chronicle, Churches of Christ, Howard W. Norton, Box 11000, Oklahoma City, OK 73136.

Christian Community, The, Community Churches, J. Ralph Shotwell, 7808 College Dr., Suite 2SE, Palos Heights, IL 60463. Tel. (708)361-2600. Fax (708)361-3649

Christian Echo, The, Churches of Christ, R. N. Hogan, Box 37266, Los Angeles, CA 90037.

Christian Endeavor World, The, Independent, David G. Jackson, P.O. Box 1110, Columbus, OH 43216-1110. Tel. (614)258-9545. Fax (614)252-2311

Christian Index, The, (bi-m), Christian Methodist Episcopal, P.O. Box 665, Memphis, TN 38101. Tel. (901)345-1173

Christian Index, The, Southern Baptist, R. Albert Mohler, Jr., 2930 Flowers Rd., S., Atlanta, GA 30341. Tel. (404)936-5312. Fax (404)936-5160

Christian Leader, (bi-w), Mennonite Brethren, U.S. Conf., Don Ratzlaff, Hillsboro, KS 67063. Tel. (316)947-5543. Fax (316)947-3266

Christian Living, (10/yr), Mennonite, David Graybill, 616 Walnut Ave., Scottdale, PA 15683. Tel. (412)887-8500. Fax (412)887-3111

Christian Ministry, The, (6/yr), Independent, James M. Wall, 407 S. Dearborn St., Chicago, IL 60605. Tel. (312)427-5380. Fax (312)427-1302

Christian Monthly, Apostolic Lutheran, Alvar Helmes, Apostolic Lutheran Book Concern, Brush Prairie, WA 98606. Tel. (206)687-7088

Christian Outlook, Pentecostal Assemblies of the World, Jane Sims, 3939 Meadow Dr., Indianapolis, IN 46208.

Christian Pathway, The, Mennonite, Kenneth Mast, Hwy. 172, Crockett, KY 41413.

Christian Reader, The, (bi-m), Independent, Bonne Steffen, 465 Gundersen Dr., Carol Stream, IL 60188. Tel. (708)260-6200. Fax (708)260-0114

Christian Record, Seventh-day Adventist, R. J. Kaiser, P.O. Box 6097, Lincoln, NE 68506.

Christian Recorder, The, (bi-w), African Methodist Episcopal, Robert H. Reid, 500 8th Ave., S., Nashville, TN 37203. Tel. (615)256-8548

Christian Science Journal, The, Church of Christ, Scientist, William E. Moody, One Norway St., Boston, MA 02115. Tel. (617)450-2000

Christian Science Monitor, The, (d & w), Church of Christ, Scientist, Richard Cattani, One Norway St., Boston, MA 02115.

Christian Science Quarterly, Church of Christ, Scientist, William E. Moody, One Norway St., Boston, MA 02115.

Christian Science Sentinel, Church of Christ, Scientist, William E. Moody, One Norway St., Boston, MA 02115. Tel. (617)450-2000

Christian Social Action, United Methodist, Lee Ranck, 100 Maryland Ave. NE, Washington, DC 20002. Tel. (202)488-5621. Fax (202)488-5619

Christian Standard, Christian Churches and Churches of Christ, Sam E. Stone, 8121 Hamilton Ave., Cincinnati, OH 45231. Tel. (513)931-4050. Fax (513)931-0904

Christianity and Crisis, (bi-w), Independent, Leon Howell, 537 W. 121st St., New York, NY 10027. Tel. (212)662-5907. Fax (212)662-6210

Church & Society Magazine, (bi-m), Presbyterian (U.S.A.), Kathy Lancaster, 100 Witherspoon St., Louisville, KY 40202-1396. Tel. (502)569-5810. Fax (502)569-8034

Church Advocate, The, Churches of God, General Conference, Linda Draper, P.O. Box 926, Findlay, OH 45839. Tel. (419)424-1961. Fax (419)424-3433

Church Bytes, Neil B. Houk, 562 Brightleaf Square No. 9, Durham, NC 27701. Tel. (919)479-5242

Church Herald, The, (11/yr), Reformed Church in America, Jeffrey Japinga, 4500 60th St. SE, Grand Rapids, MI 49512. Tel. (616)698-7071

Church History, Independent, Martin E. Marty, and Jerald C. Brauer, The Univ. of Chicago, Chicago, IL 60637. Tel. (312)702-8215. Fax (312)702-6048

Church Management: The Clergy Journal, (10/yr), Independent, Manfred Holck, Jr, P.O. Box 162527, Austin, TX 78716. Tel. (512)327-8501

Church School Herald, African Methodist Episcopal Zion, Mary A. Love, P.O. Box 32305, Charlotte, NC 28232-2305. Tel. (704)332-9873. Fax (704)333-1769

Church of God Missions, Church of God (Anderson, Ind.), Dondeena Caldwell, Box 2337, Anderson, IN 46018. Tel. (317)649-7597

Church of God Progress Journal, (bi-m), Church of God General Conference (Oregon, Ill.), David Krogh, Box 100,000, Morrow, GA 30260. Tel. (404)362-0052. Fax (404)362-9307

Church of God Quarterly; COG Newsletter, The, Church of God, Voy M. Bullen, Box 13036, 1207 Willow Brook, Apt. #2, Huntsville, AL 35802. Tel. (205)881-9629

Church of the Lutheran Confession Directory, (b-a), Church of the Lutheran Confession, Rollin Reim, 994 Emerald Hill Rd., Redwood City, CA 94061. Tel. (415)364-2200

Churchman's Human Quest, The, (bi-m), Edna Ruth Johnson, 1074 23rd Ave. N., St. Petersburg, FL 33704. Tel. (813)894-0097

Churchwoman, (bi-m), Church Women United, Margaret Schiffert, 475 Riverside Dr., New York, NY 10115. Tel. (212)870-2344. Fax (212)870-2338

Clarion Herald, (bi-w), Catholic, Peter P. Finney, P. O. Box 53247, New Orleans, LA 70153. Tel. (504)596-3030. Fax (504)596-3020

Co-Laborer, (bi-m), Free Will Baptist, National Association of, Melissa L. Riddle, Woman's Natl. Auxiliary Convention, Antioch, TN 37011-5002. Tel. (615)731-6812

Columban Mission, (10/yr), Catholic, Richard Steinhilber, St. Columbans, NE 68056. Tel. (402)291-1920. Fax (402)291-8693

Columbia, Catholic, Richard McMunn, One Columbus Plz., New Haven, CT 06510. Tel. (203)772-2130. Fax (203)777-0114

Commission, The, (9/yr), Southern Bapt., Leland F. Webb, Box 6767, Richmond, VA 23230. Tel. (804)353-0151. Fax (804)358-0504

Commonweal, (bi-w), Catholic, Margaret O'Brien Steinfels, 15 Dutch St., New York, NY 10038. Tel. (212)732-0800

Congregational Journal, (2/yr), Congregational Christian, American Congregational Center, Henry David Gray, 298 Fairfax Ave., Ventura, CA 93003. Tel. (805)644-3397

Congregationalist, The, (bi-m), Congregational Christian, Joseph B. Polhemus, 1105 Briarwood Rd., Mansfield, OH 44907. Tel. (419)756-5526. Fax (419)524-2621

Congregationalist, The, Louis B. Gerhardt, P. O. Box 9397, Fresno, CA 93792. Tel. (209)227-6936

Conqueror, United Pentecostal, Darrell Johns, 8855 Dunn Rd., Hazelwood, MO 63042.

Conservative Judaism, Jewish, Rabbi Shamai Kanter, 3080 Broadway, New York, NY 10027. Tel. (212)678-8060. Fax (212)749-9166

Contact, Free Will Baptists, Jack Williams, P.O. Box 5002, Antioch, TN 37011-5002. Tel. (615)731-6812. Fax (615)731-0049

Contempo, Southern Baptist, Cindy Lewis Dake, P.O. Box 830010, Birmingham, AL 35283. Tel. (205)991-8100

Cornerstone Connections, Seventh-day Adventist, Gary B. Swanson, 12501 Old Columbia Pike, Silver Spring, MD 20904. Tel. (301)680-6160. Fax (301)680-6155

Courage in the Struggle for Justic and Peace, (10/yr), Office for Church in Society, Rubin Tendai, 110 Maryland Ave., NE, Washington, DC 20002. Tel. (202)543-1517. Fax (202)543-5994

Covenant Companion, Evangelical Covenant, James R. Hawkinson, 5101 N. Francisco Ave., Chicago, IL 60625. Tel. (312)784-3000. Fax (312)784-4366

Covenant Home Altar, Evangelical Covenant, James R. Hawkinson, 5101 N. Francisco Ave., Chicago, IL 60625.

Covenant Quarterly, Evangelical Covenant, Wayne C. Weld, 5101 N. Francisco Ave., Chicago, IL 60625. Tel. (312)478-2696. Fax (312)583-0858

Covenanter Witness, The, Reformed Presbyterian, James Pennington, 7408 Penn Ave., Pittsburgh, PA 15208. Tel. (412)241-0436

Credinta—The Faith, Romanian Orthodox Church in America, Vasile Vasilachi, 19959 Riopelle St., Detroit, MI 48203. Tel. (313)893-8390

Criterion, The, Catholic, John F. Fink, P. O. Box 1717, Indianapolis, IN 46206. Tel. (317)236-1570

Cumberland Flag, The, Cumberland Presbyterian Church in America, Robert Stanley Wood, 226 Church St., Huntsville, AL 35801. Tel. (205)536-7481. Fax (205)536-7482

Cumberland Presbyterian, The, Cumberland Presbyterian, Mark Brown, 1978 Union Ave., Memphis, TN 38104. Tel. (901)276-4572. Fax (901)276-4578

Currents in Theology and Mission, (6/yr), Lutheran School of Theology, Ralph W. Klein, 1100 E. 55th St., Chicago, IL 60615. Tel. (312)753-0751. Fax (312)753-0782

Decision, (11/yr), Billy Graham Evangelistic Assn., Roger C. Palms, 1300 Harmon Pl., Minneapolis, MN 55403. Tel. (612)338-0500. Fax (612)335-1299

Directory of the Ministry, Christian Churches and Churches of Christ, Zella M. McLean, 1525 Cherry Rd., Springfield, IL 62704. Tel. (217)546-7338

Disciple, The, Christian Church (Disciples of Christ), Robert L. Friedly, Box 1986, Indianapolis, IN 46206. Tel. (317)353-1491. Fax (317)359-7546

Doors and Windows, (5/yr), The Evangelical, Timothy Christman & Dirk Pogue, Dr. W. Joel Copeland, E.C. Church Center, Myerstown, PA 17067. Tel. (717)866-7581

EMC Today, Evangelical Mennonite, Donald W. Roth, 1420 Kerrway Ct., Fort Wayne, IN 46805. Tel. (219)423-3649

Ecumenical Trends, William Carpe, P.O. Box 16136, Ludlow, KY 41016. Tel. (606)581-6216

El Interprete, (6/ySpanish), United Methodist, Edith LaFontaine, P.O. Box 320, Nashville, TN 37202. Tel. (615)742-5115. Fax (615)742-5460

Eleventh Hour Messenger, (bi-m), Wesleyan Holiness, J. Stevan Manley, 108 Carter Ave., Dayton, OH 45405. Tel. (513)278-3770

Elim Herald, L. Dayton Reynolds, 7245 College St., Lima, NY 14485. Tel. (716)582-2790

Emphasis on Faith and Living, (bi-m), Missionary, Robert Ransom, P.O. Box 9127, Ft. Wayne, IN 46899. Tel. (219)747-2027. Fax (219)747-5331

Ensign, The, Jay M. Todd, 50 E. North Temple St., Salt Lake City, UT 84150.

Episcopal Church Annual, The, Episcopal, E. Allen Kelly, Morehouse Publishing, Ridgefield, CT 06877-2801. Tel. (203)431-3927. Fax (203)431-3964

Episcopal Life, Episcopal, Jerrold Hames, 815 Second Ave., New York, NY 10017. Tel. (212)867-8400. Fax (212)949-8059

Episcopal Recorder, Reformed Episcopal, Walter G. Truesdell, 4225 Chestnut St., Philadelphia, PA 19104. Tel. (212)222-5158

Evangel, Homer G. Rhea, P.O. Box 2250, Cleveland, TN 37320.

Evangel, The, Lutheran Churches, American Association of, Christopher Barnekov, 214 South St., Waterloo, IA 50701.

Evangelical Beacon, (8/yr), Evangelical Free Church, Carol Madison, 901 East 78th St., Minneapolis, MN 55420-1300.

Evangelical Friend, (6/yr), Paul Anderson, 600 East Third St., Newberg, OR 97132. Tel. (503)538-7345. Fax (503)538-7033

Evangelical Visitor, Brethren in Christ, Glen A. Pierce, P.O. Box 166, Nappanee, IN 46550. Tel. (219)773-3164

Evangelist, The, Catholic, James Breig, 40 N. Main Ave., Albany, NY 12203. Tel. (518)453-6688. Fax (518)453-6793

Extension, (9/yr), Catholic, Bradley Collins, 35 East Wacker Dr., Rm. 400, Chicago, IL 60601. Tel. (312)236-7240. Fax (312)236-5276

Focus, (2/yr.), Friends General Conference, Meredith Walton, 1216 Arch St., 2B, Philadelphia, PA 19107. Tel. (215)561-1700

Foresee, (bi-m), Conservative Congregational Christian, Wanda Evans, 7582 Currell Blvd., #108, St. Paul, MN 55125. Tel. (612)739-1474

Faith & Fellowship Press, David Rinden, P.O. Box 655, Fergus Falls, MN 56538.

Faith-Life, (bi-m), Protes'tant (Lutheran), Marcus Albrecht, P.O. Box 2141, LaCrosse, WI 54601.

Fellowship Magazine, The, (6/yr), Assemblies of God Intl. Fell. (Independent), T. A. Lanes, 8504 Commerce Ave., San Diego, CA 92121. Tel. (619)530-1727. Fax (619)530-1543

Fellowship Tidings, Full Gospel Fell., Chester P. Jenkins, 4325 W. Ledbetter Dr., Dallas, TX 75233. Tel. (214)337-1865. Fax (214)337-1865

Firm Foundation, Churches of Christ, H. A. Dobbs, P.O. Box 690192, Houston, TX 77269-0192.

First Things: A Monthly Journal of Religion and Public, Independent, Richard J. Neuhaus, 156 Fifth Ave., Ste. 400, New York, NY 10010. Tel. (212)627-2288. Fax (212)627-2184

Flaming Sword, The, Fire Baptized Holiness (Wesleyan), Susan Davolt, 10th St. & College Ave., Independence, KS 67301.

For the Poor, Primitive Baptist, W. H. Cayce, Hwy. 172, Crockett, KY 41413.

Forum Letter, Lutheran, Russell E. Saltzman, P.O. Box 327, Delhi, NY 13753. Tel. (607)746-7511

Forward, United Pentecostal, J. L. Hall, 8855 Dunn Rd., Hazelwood, MO 63042.

Forward Day by Day, Episcopal, Charles H. Long, 412 Sycamore St., Cincinnati, OH 45202. Tel. (513)721-6659. Fax (513)421-0315

Foursquare World Advance, (6/yr.), Foursquare Gospel, Ron Williams, 1910 W. Sunset Blvd., Ste 200, Los Angeles, CA 90026. Tel. (213)484-2400. Fax (213)413-3824

Free Will Baptist Gem, Free Will Baptist, Nathan Ruble, P.O. Box 991, Lebanon, MO 65536.

Free Will Baptist, The, Original Free Will Bapt., Janie Jones Sowers, P.O. Box 159, Ayden, NC 28513. Tel. (919)746-6128. Fax (919)746-9248

Free Will Bible College Bulletin, Free Will Baptist, Bert Tippett, 3606 West End Ave., Nashville, TN 37205. Tel. (615)383-1340. Fax same

Friends Journal, Religious Society of Friends, Vinton Deming, 1501 Cherry St., Philadelphia, PA 19102-1497. Tel. (215)241-7277. Fax (215)568-1377

Front Line, Fricke, Gill, and Ralph Monsen, Dir. of Chaplaincy Ministries, P.O. Box 66, Wheaton, IL 60189

Gem, The, Churches of God, General Conference, Marilyn Rayle Kern, P.O. Box 926, Findlay, OH 45839.

General Baptist Messenger, General Baptists, Wayne Foust, 100 Stinson Dr., Poplar Bluff, MO 63901. Tel. (314)785-7746. Fax (314)686-5198

Gleaner, The, Baptist Missionary Association, F. Donald Collins, 721 Main St., Little Rock, AR 72201

Global Witness, The, United Pentecostal, Mervyn Miller, 8855 Dunn Rd., Hazelwood, MO 63042

God's Field, (bi-w), Polish National Catholic, Anthony M. Rysz, 1002 Pittston Ave., Scranton, PA 18505. Tel. (717)346-9131

Gospel Advocate, Churches of Christ, Furman Kearley, Box 150, Nashville, TN 37202. Tel. (615)254-8781

Gospel Herald, Mennonite, J. Lorne Peachey, 616 Walnut Ave., Scottdale, PA 15683. Tel. (412)887-8500. Fax (412)887-3111

Gospel Herald, The, Church of God, Mountain Assembly, Dennis McClanahan, P.O. Box 157, Jellico, TN 37762.

Gospel Messenger, The, Congregational Holiness, Franklin Creswell, 3888 Fayetteville Hwy., Griffin, GA 30223. Tel. (404)228-4833. Fax (404)228-1177

Gospel News, The, Church of Jesus Christ (Bickertonites), Anthony Scolaro, 20 Byrd Ave., Bloomfield, NJ 07003. Tel. (313)429-5080. Fax (313)429-4714

Gospel Tidings, (bi-m), Fell. of Evangelical Bible Churches, Robert L. Frey, 5800 S. 14th St., Omaha, NE 68107. Tel. (402)731-4780. Fax (402)731-1173

Gospel Tidings, Churches of Christ, Travis Allen, Box 4355, Edgewood, CO 80155. Tel. (303)694-3560

THE YEAR IN IMAGES

Religious News Service Photo

Rating entertainment

The church was at the forefront of a call for the entertainment system to use a new rating system. Cardinal Roger Mahony of Los Angeles addressed a February 1992 news conference calling for a rating system.

Guardian of Truth, (b-w), Churches of Christ, Mike Willis, Box 9670, Bowling Green, KY 42101.

Guide, Seventh-day Adventist, Jeannette R. Johnson, 55 W. Oak Ridge Dr., Hagerstown, MD 21740. Tel. (301)791-7000. Fax (301)791-7012

Heartbeat, (b-m), Free Will Baptist, Don Robirds, Foreign Missions Office, Antioch, TN 37011-5002. Tel. (615)731-6812. Fax (615)731-0049

Helping Hand, (bi-m), Pentecostal Holiness, Doris Moore, P.O. Box 12609, Oklahoma City, OK 73157.

Herald of Christian Science, The, Church of Christ, Scientist, William E. Moody, One Norway St., Boston, MA 02115. Tel. (617)450-2000

Herald of Holiness, Nazarene, Wesley D. Tracy, 6401 The Paseo, Kansas City, MO 64131. Tel. (816)333-7000. Fax (816)333-1748

Heritage, Assemblies of God, Wayne E. Warner, 1445 Boonville Ave., Springfield, MO 65802. Tel. (417)862-1447. Fax (417)862-8558

High Adventure, Assemblies of God, Marshall Bruner, Gospel Publishing House, Springfield, MO 65802-1894. Tel. (417)862-2781. Fax (417)862-8558

Holiness Union, The, United Holy Church, Joseph T. Durham, 13102 Morningside La., Silver Spring, MD 20904.

Homelife, United Pentecostal, Mark Christian, 8855 Dunn Rd., Hazelwood, MO 63042.

Homiletic and Pastoral Review, Catholic, Kenneth Baker, 86 Riverside Dr., New York, NY 10024. Tel. (212)799-2600

Horizons, (bi-m), Presbyterian (U.S.A.), Barbara A. Roche, Presbyterian Women, Louisville, KY 40202. Tel. (502)569-5367. Fax (502)569-8085

Horizons, Christian Churches and Churches of Christ, Norman L. Weaver, Box 2427, Knoxville, TN 37901. Tel. (615)577-9740. Fax (615)577-9743

Insight, Advent Christian, Millie Griswold, P.O. Box 23152, Charlotte, NC 28212.

Insight and Insight/Out, Seventh-day Adventist, J. Christopher Blake, 55 W. Oak Ridge Dr., Hagerstown, MD 21740. Tel. (301)791-7000. Fax (301)791-7012

Interest, Christian Brethren, William W. Conard, P.O. Box 190, Wheaton, IL 60189. Tel. (708)653-6573. Fax (708)653-6595

International Bulletin of Missionary Research, Independent, Gerald H. Anderson, 490 Prospect St., New Haven, CT 06511. Tel. (203)624-6672. Fax (203)865-2857

Interpretation, Interdenominational, Jack D. Kingsbury, 3401 Brook Rd., Richmond, VA 23227. Tel. (804)355-0671. Fax (804)355-3919

Interpreter, (8/yr), United Methodist, Ralph E. Baker, P.O. Box 320, Nashville, TN 37203. Tel. (615)742-5104. Fax (615)742-5469

Jewish Action, Jewish, Charlotte Friedland, 333 Seventh Avenue, New York, NY 10001. Tel. (212)244-2011. Fax (212)564-9058

Jewish Education, Jewish, Alvin I. Schiff, 426 W. 58th St., New York, NY 10019. Tel. (212)713-0290

John Three Sixteen, Fire Baptized Holiness (Wesleyan), Mary Cunningham, 10th St. & College Ave., Independence, KS 67301.

Journal of Adventist Education, (5/yr.), Seventh-day Adventist, Beverly Rumble, 12501 Old Columbia Pike, Silver Spring, MD 20904-6600. Tel. (301)680-5075. Fax (301)680-6090

Journal of Christian Education, African Methodist Episcopal, Kenneth H. Hill, 500 Eighth Ave., S., Nashville, TN 37203. Tel. (615)242-1420. Fax (615)726-1866

Journal of Ecumenical Studies, Independent, Leonard Swidler, Temple Univ. (022-38), Philadelphia, PA 19122. Tel. (215)787-7714. Fax (215)787-4569

Journal of Pastoral Care, The, Independent, Orlo Strunk, 1549 Clairemont Rd., Ste. 103, Decatur, GA 30030-4611.

Journal of Reform Judaism, Jewish, Lawrence Englander, 192 Lexington Ave., New York, NY 10016. Tel. (212)684-4990. Fax (212)689-1649

Journal of Theology, (4/yr.), Church of Lutheran Confession, John Lau, Immanuel Lutheran College, Eau Claire, WI 54701-7199. Tel. (715)836-6621

Journal of the American Academy of Religion, Independent, William Scott Green, Univ. of Rochester, Rochester, Rochester, NY 14627. Tel. (716)275-5415

Judaism, Jewish, Ruth B. Waxman, 15 E. 84th St., New York, NY 10028. Tel. (212)879-4500. Fax (212)249-3672

Keeping in Touch, Metropolitan Community Churches, Kittredge Cherry, 5300 Santa Monica Blvd, #304, Los Angeles, CA 90029. Tel. (213)464-5100. Fax (213)464-2123

Leadership: A Practical Journal for Church Leaders, Independent, Marshall Shelley, 465 Gundersen Dr., Carol Stream, IL 60188. Tel. (708)260-6200. Fax (708)260-0114

Leaves of Healing, Christian Catholic (Evangelical-Protestant), Roger W. Ottersen, 2500 Dowie Memorial Dr., Zion, IL 60099.

Liberty, (bi-m), Seventh-day Adventist, R. R. Hegstad, 12501 Old Columbia Pike, Silver Spring, MD 20904. Tel. (301)680-6691. Fax (301)680-6695

Light of Hope, The, (bi-m), Apostolic Faith Mission of Portland, Oregon, Loyce C. Carver, 6615 S.E. 52nd Ave., Portland, OR 97206. Tel. (503)777-1741

Liguorian, Roman Catholic, Allan J. Weinert, 1 Liguori Dr., Liguori, MO 63057. Tel. (314)464-2500. Fax (314)464-8449

Listen, Seventh-day Adventist, Lincoln E. Steed, P.O. Box 7000, Nampa, ID 83707.

Living Church, The, Episcopal, David A. Kalvelage, 816 E. Juneau Ave., Milwaukee, WI 53202. Tel. (414)276-5420. Fax (414)276-7483

Long Island Catholic, The, (51/yr), Roman Catholic, Francis J. Maniscalco, P.O. Box 700, Hempstead, NY 11551. Tel. (516)538-8800. Fax (516)538-8858

Lookout, The, Christian Churches and Churches of Christ, Simon J. Dahlman, 8121 Hamilton Ave., Cincinnati, OH 45231. Tel. (513)931-4050. Fax (513)931-0904

Lutheran Ambassador, The, (bi-w), Free Lutheran, Robert Lee, 3110 East Medicine Lake Blvd., Minneapolis, MN 55441. Tel. (612)545-5631

Lutheran Educator, The, Wisconsin Evangelical Lutheran, John R. Isch, Dr. Martin Luther College, New Ulmsa, MN 56073. Tel. (507)354-8221. Fax (507)354-8225

Lutheran Forum, Lutheran, Paul R. Hinlicky, P.O. Box 327, Delhi, NY 13753. Tel. (607)746-7511

Lutheran Sentinel, Evangelical Lutheran Synod, P. Madson, 813 S. Willow Ave., Sioux Falls, SD 57104. Tel. (605)334-4225

Lutheran Spokesman, The, Lutheran Confession, Paul Fleischer, 238 Nicollet Ave., North Mankato, MN 56003. Tel. (507)345-4217

Lutheran Synod Quarterly, Evangelical Lutheran Synod, W. W. Peterson, Bethany Lutheran College, Mankato, MN 56001. Tel. (507)625-2977. Fax (507)625-1849

Lutheran Witness, The, Lutheran Church—Missouri Synod, David Mahsman, 1333 S. Kirkwood Road, St. Louis, MO 63122. Tel. (314)965-9917. Fax (314)965-3396

Lutheran, The, Evangelical Lutheran Church in America, Edgar R. Trexler, 8765 W. Higgins Rd., Chicago, IL 60631. Tel. (312)380-2540. Fax (312)380-2751

Lutherans Alert-National, Michael Adams, P.O. Box 7186, Tacoma, WA 98407. Tel. (800)228-4650. Fax (206)759-1790

Magyar Egyhaz, (6/yr.), Hungarian Reformed, Stefan Torok, 331 Kirkland Pl., Perth Amboy, NJ 08861.

Majallat Al-Masjid, Muslims, Dawud Assad, 99 Woodview Dr., Old Bridge, NJ 08857. Tel. (908)679-8617. Fax (908)679-1260

Maranatha, Advent Christian, Robert Mayer, P.O. Box 23152, Charlotte, NC 28212. Tel. (704)545-6161. Fax (704)573-0712

Marriage Partnership, Independent, Ron Lee, 465 Gundersen Dr., Carol Stream, IL 60188. Tel. (708)260-6200. Fax (708)260-0114

Maryknoll, Roman Catholic, Joseph R. Veneroso, Maryknoll Fathers and Brothers, Maryknoll, NY 10545. Tel. (914)941-7590. Fax (914)945-0670

Mature Years, United Methodist, Marvin W. Cropsey, 201 Eighth Ave. S, Nashville, TN 37202. Tel. (615)749-6292. Fax (615)749-6079

Media&Values, Independent, Elizabeth Thoman, Center for Media and Values, Los Angeles, CA 90034. Tel. (310)559-2944. Fax (310)559-9396

Memos: A Magazine for Missionettes Leaders, Assemblies of God, Linda Upton, Gospel Publishing House, Springfield, MO 65802. Tel. (417)862-2781

Mennonite Historical Bulletin, Mennonite, Levi Miller, 1700 S. Main, Goshen, IN 46526. Tel. (219)535-7477. Fax (219)535-7293

Mennonite Quarterly Review, Mennonite, John S. Oyer, 1700 S. Main St., Goshen, IN 46526.

Mennonite Yearbook, Mennonite, James E. Horsch, 616 Walnut Ave., Scottdale, PA 15683. Tel. (412)887-8500. Fax (412)887-3111

Mennonite, The, (semi-m), Mennonite , General Conference, Gordon Houser, Box 347, 722 Main St., Newton, KS 67114. Tel. (316)283-5100. Fax (316)283-0454

Message, (bi-m), Seventh-day Adventist, Stephen P. Ruff, 55 West Oak Ridge Dr., Hagerstown, MD 21740.

Message of the Open Bible, (10/yr), Open Bible Standard , Delores A. Winegar, 2020 Bell Ave., Des Moines, IA 50315-1096. Tel. (515)288-6761. Fax (515)288-2510

Messenger, Church of the Brethren, Kermon Thomasson, 1451 Dundee Ave., Elgin, IL 60120. Tel. (708)742-5100. Fax (708)742-6103

Messenger of Truth, (bi-w), Church of God in Christ (Mennonite), Gladwin Koehn, P.O. Box 230, Moundridge, KS 67107. Fax (316)345-2582

Messenger, The, The (Original) Church of God, Johnny Albertson, 2214 E. 17th St., Chattanooga, TN 37404. Tel. (615)629-4505

Messenger, The, Presbyterian Ch. in America, Robert G. Sweet, 1852 Century Pl., Ste. 101, Atlanta, GA 30345. Tel. (404)320-3388. Fax (404)320-7964

Messenger, The, Swedenborgian, Patte LeVan, 1592 N. 400 W., LaPorte, IN 46350. Tel. (219)325-8209. Fax (219)325-8209

Messenger, The, Pentecostal Free Will Baptist Church, Inc., Donna Hammond, P.O. Box 1568, Dunn, NC 28335. Tel. (919)892-0297

Methodist History, United Methodist, Charles Yrigoyen, P.O. Box 127, Madison, NJ 07940. Tel. (201)822-2787. Fax (201)408-3909

Mid-Stream: An Ecumenical Journal, Christian Church (Disciples of Christ), Paul A. Crow, P.O. Box 1986, Indianapolis, IN 46206. Tel. (317)353-1491. Fax (317)359-7546

Midwest Missionary Baptist, Baptist Missionary Association, Bill Brevette, 202 Romona Ave., Portage, MI 49002.

Ministry, Seventh-day Adventist, J. David Newman, 12501 Old Columbia Pike, Silver Spring, MD 21029-6600. Tel. (301)680-6510. Fax (301)680-6502

Ministry Today, (bi-m), Missionary Church, Robert Ransom, P.O. Box 9127 Ave., Ft. Wayne, IN 46899. Tel. (219)747-2027. Fax (219)747-5331

Mission Grams, (bi-m), Free Will Baptist, National Association, Roy Thomas, Home Missions Office, Antioch, TN 37011-5002. Tel. (615)731-6812. Fax (615)731-0049

Mission Herald, (bi-m), National Baptist, William J. Harvey, 701 S. 19th Street, Philadelphia, PA 19146. Tel. (215)878-2854. Fax (215)735-1721

Mission, Adult and Junior-Teen, Seventh-day Adventist, Janet Kangas, 12501 Old Columbia Pike, Silver Spring, MD 20904. Tel. (301)680-6167. Fax (301)890-3965

Missionary Messenger, The, Christian Methodist Episcopal, P. Ann Pegues, 2309 Bonnie Ave., Bastrop, LA 71220. Tel. (318)281-3044

Missionary Messenger, The, Cumberland Presbyterian, Clay J. Brown, 1978 Union Ave., Memphis, TN 38104. Tel. (901)276-4572. Fax (901)276-4578

Missionary Seer, African Methodist Episcopal Zion, Kermit J. DeGraffenreidt, 475 Riverside Dr., Rm. 1935, New York, NY 10115. Tel. (212)870-2952. Fax (212)870-2055

Missions, USA, William Junker, 1350 Spring St., N.W., Atlanta, GA 30367. Tel. (404)873-4041

MissionsUSA, Southern Baptist, Phyllis Thompson, 1350 Spring St. NW, Atlanta, GA 30367. Tel. (404)898-7000. Fax (404)898-7228

Monday Morning, (bi-m), Presbyterian (U.S.A.), Theodore A. Gill, 100 Witherspoon St., Louisville, KY 40202. Tel. (502)569-5755. Fax (502)569-5018

Moody Magazine, (11/yr), Independent, Bruce Anderson, 820 N. LaSalle Dr., Chicago, IL 60610. Tel. (312)329-2163. Fax (312)329-2144

Moravian, The, (10/yr), Moravian Ch. in America (Unitas Fratrum), Herman I. Weinlick, P.O. Box 1245, Bethlehem, PA 18016. Tel. (215)867-7566. Fax (215)866-9223

Mother Church, The, Armenian Church of NA, Sipan Mekhsian, 1201 N. Vine St., Hollywood, CA 90038. Tel. (213)466-5265. Fax (213)466-7612

Mountain Movers, Assemblies of God, Joyce Wells Booze, Gospel Publishing House, Springfield, MO 65802. Tel. (417)862-2781. Fax (417)862-0085

Muslim World, The, Independent, Ernest Hamilton, 77 Sherman St., Hartford, CT 06105. Tel. (203)232-4451

NBCA Lantern, E. Edward Jones, 1540 Pierre Ave., Shreveport, LA 71113.

National Baptist Voice, (s-m), National Baptist, U.S.A., Inc., Roscoe Cooper, 2800 Third Ave., Richmond, VA 23222. Tel. (804)321-5115

National Catholic Reporter, (44/yr), Roman Catholic Church, Thomas C. Fox, P.O. Box 419281, Kansas City, MO 64141. Tel. (816)531-0538. Fax (816)531-7466

National Christian Reporter, The, Independent, John A. Lovelace, P.O. Box 222198, Dallas, TX 75222. Tel. (214)630-6495. Fax (214)630-0079

National Spiritualist Summit, The, National Spiritualist Association, Sandra Pfortmiller, 2020 W. Turney Ave., Phoenix, AZ 85015. Tel. (602)274-3161

New Church Life, New Jerusalem, Donald L. Rose, Box 277, Bryn Athyn, PA 19009. Tel. (215)947-6225. Fax (215)947-3078

New Horizons in the Orthodox Pres. Ch., (10/yr), Thomas E. Tyson, 303 Horsham Rd., Ste. G, Horsham, PA 19044-2029. Tel. (215)956-0123

New Oxford Review, (10/yr), Roman Catholic, Dale Vree, 1069 Kains Ave., Berkeley, CA 94706. Tel. (510)526-5374

New World Outlook, (bi-m), United Methodist, Alma Graham, 475 Riverside Dr., Rm. 1351, New York, NY 10115. Tel. (212)870-3765. Fax (212)870-3940

New World, The, Roman Catholic, Thomas J. Widner, 1144 W. Jackson Blvd., Chicago, IL 60607. Tel. (312)243-1300. Fax (312)243-1526

News, The, Anglican Orthodox, Margaret D. Lane, Anglican Orthodox Church, Statesville, NC 28677. Tel. (704)873-8365

Newscope, United Methodist, J. Richard Peck, P.O. Box 801, Nashville, TN 37202. Tel. (615)749-6488. Fax (615)749-6079

Newsletter, FWCC of the Americas, (3/yr.), Stephen Serafin, 1506 Race St., Philadelphia, PA 19102. Tel. (215)241-7250

North American Catholic, The, North American Old Roman Catholic, Nan Simpson, 4200 N. Kedvale Ave., Chicago, IL 60641.

Northwest Profile, Baptist Missionary Association, Leo Hornaday, 5575 Barger St., Eugene, OR 97402. Tel. (503)687-6874

Northwestern Lutheran, Wisconsin Evangelical Lutheran, James P. Schaefer, 2929 N. Mayfair Rd., Milwaukee, WI 53222. Tel. (414)771-9357. Fax (414)771-3708

On the Line, Mennonite, Mary C. Meyer, 616 Walnut ave., Scottdale, PA 15683. Tel. (412)887-8500. Fax (412)887-3111

One Church, (bi-m), Russian Orth. Ch. in USA, Patriarchal Parishes, Feodor Kovalchuk, 727 Miller Ave., Youngstown, OH 44502. Tel. (216)788-0151. Fax (216)788-9361

Orthodox Observer, The, Greek Orthodox Archdiocese of North and South America, Jim Golding, 8 E. 79th St., New York, NY 10021. Tel. (212)628-2590

Orthodox Tradition, (4/yr.), True (Old Calendar) Orthodox Church of Greece (Synod of Metropolitan Cyprian), American Exarchate, Auxentios and Fr. James Thornton, St. Gregory Palamas Monastery, Etna, CA 96027.

Our Daily Bread, Swedenborgian, Richard H. Tafel, 8085 Lagoon Rd., Ft. Myers Beach, FL 33931. Tel. (813)463-5030

Our Family, New Apostolic, Friedrich Bischoff, Gutleutstrasse 298, 6000 Frankfurt am Main, Germany. Tel. (069)2696-0. Fax (069)252915

Our Little Friend, Seventh-day Adventist, Aileen Andres Sox, P.O. Box 7000, Nampa, ID 83707.

Our Sunday Visitor, Roman Catholic, Tricia Hempel, 200 Noll Plaza, Huntington, IN 46750. Tel. (219)356-8400. Fax (219)356-8472

Outreach, Armenian Apostolic, Iris Papazian, 138 E. 39th St., New York, NY 10016. Tel. (212)689-7810. Fax (212)689-7168

Outreach Magazine, (2/yr), Open Bible Standard, Paul V. Canfield, 2020 Bell Ave., Des Moines, IA 50315-1096. Tel. (515)288-6761. Fax (515)288-2510

Outreach, The, United Pentecosta/General Home Missions Div., J. L. Fiorino, 8855 Dunn Rd., Hazelwood, MO 63042.

Paraclete, Assemblies of God, David Bundrick, Gospel Publishing House, Springfield, MO 65802. Tel. (417)862-2781. Fax (417)866-1146

Pastor's Journal, The, Community Churches, Robert Puckett, 7808 College Dr., 2 SE, Palos Heights, IL 60463.

Pastoral Life, Roman Catholic, Anthony Chenevey, Rte. 224, Canfield, OH 44406. Tel. (216)533-5503. Fax (216)533-1076

Path of Orthodoxy (Eng.), The, Serbian Orthodox Church, U.S.A. and Canada, Rade Merick and Mirko Dobrijevich, P.O. Box 36, Leetsdale, PA 15056. Tel. (412)741-8660. Fax (412)741-9235

Path of Orthodoxy (Serbian), The, Serbian Orthodox Church, U.S.A. and Canada, Nedeljko Lunich, 300 Striker Ave., Joliet, IL 60436. Tel. (815)741-1023

Paul, (bi-m), Netherlands Reformed, J. R. Beeke, 2115 Romence Ave., N.E., Grand Rapids, MI 29503.

Pentecost Today, Full Gospel Assemblies (Pentecostal), C. E. Strauser, P.O. Box 1230, Coatesville, PA 19320. Tel. (215)857-2357

Pentecostal Evangel, Assemblies of God, Richard G. Champion, Gospel Publishing House, Springfield, MO 65802. Tel. (417)862-2781. Fax (417)862-8558

Pentecostal Herald, The, United Pentecostal, J. L. Hall, 8855 Dunn Rd., Hazelwood, MO 63042. Tel. (314)837-7300. Fax (314)837-4503

Pentecostal Holiness Advocate, The, Pentecostal Holiness, International, Shirley Spencer, P.O. Box 12609, Oklahoma City, OK 73157.

Pentecostal Interpreter, The, The Church of God in Christ, H. Jenkins Bell, P.O. Box 320, Memphis, TN 38101.

Pentecostal Messenger, The, Pentecostal Church of God, Donald K. Allen, P.O. Box 850, Joplin, MO 64802. Tel. (417)624-7050. Fax (417)624-7102

Perspectives on Science & Christian Faith, Independent, J. W. Haas, P.O. Box 668, Ipswich, MA 01938. Tel. (508)356-5656. Fax (508)356-4375

Pillar of Fire, (bi-m), Pillar of Fire, Donald J. Wolfram, Zarephath, NJ 08890.

Pilot, The, Roman Catholic, Peter V. Conley, 49 Franklin St., Boston, MA 02110. Tel. (617)482-4316. Fax (617)482-5647

Pockets, United Methodist, Janet R. McNish, P.O. Box 189, Nashville, TN 37202. Tel. (615)340-7333. Fax (615)340-7006

Polka, Polish National Catholic, Cecelia Lallo, 1002 Pittston Ave., Scranton, PA 18505.

Power for Today, Churches of Christ, Steven S. and Emily Y. Lemley, Box 40526, Nashville, TN 37204.

Praying, (bi-m), Roman Catholic, Art Winter, P.O. Box 419335, Kansas City, MO 64111. Tel. (816)531-0538. Fax (816)931-5082

Preacher's Magazine, Nazarene, Randal Denny, 10814 E. Broadway, Spokane, WA 99206. Tel. (509)926-1545

Preacher, The, (bi-m), Baptist Bible Fellowship, James O. Combs, P.O. Box 309 HSJ, Springfield, MO 65801. Tel. (417)831-3996

Presbyterian Layman, The, (6/yr), Presbyterian (USA), Parker Williamson, 1489 Baltimore Pike, Ste. 301, Springfield, PA 19064-3989. Tel. (215)543-0227. Fax (215)543-2759

Presbyterian Outlook, Independent, Robert H. Bullock, Box 85623, Richmond, VA 23285-5623. Tel. (804)359-8442. Fax (804)353-6369

Presbyterian Survey, Presbyterian, (U.S.A.), Kenneth Little, 100 Witherspoon St., Louisville, KY 40202-1396. Tel. (502)569-5637. Fax (502)569-5018

Presbyterian Survey, Kenneth E. Little, 100 Witherspoon St., Louisville, KY 40202-1396. Tel. (502)569-5637. Fax (502)569-5018

Primary Treasure, Seventh-day Adventist, Aileen Andres Sox, P.O. Box 7000, Nampa, ID 83707.

Primitive Baptist, Primitive Baptist, W. H. Cayce, P.O. Box 38, Thornton, AZ 71766. Tel. (501)352-3694

Priority, Missionary Church, Ken Stucky, P.O. Box 9127, Ft. Wayne, IN 46899. Tel. (219)747-2027. Fax (219)747-5331

Providence Visitor, Roman Catholic, Michael Brown, 184 Broad St., Providence, RI 02903. Tel. (401)272-1010. Fax (401)421-8418

Pulpit Digest, The, Independent, David Albert Farmer, 1160 Battery St., 3rd Fl., San Francisco, CA 94111. Tel. (415)477-4400. Fax (415)477-4444

Purpose, Mennonite, James E. Horsch, 616 Walnut Ave., Scottdale, PA 15683. Tel. (412)887-8500. Fax (412)887-3111

Pursuit, Evangelical Free Church, Carol Madison, 901 East 78th St., Minneapolis, MN 55420-1300. Tel. (612)853-1750

Qala min M'Dinkha (Voice from the East), Apostolic Catholic Assyrian, Akhitiar Moshi, Diocesan Offices, Chicago, IL 60626. Tel. (312)465-4777. Fax (312)465-0776

Quaker Life, (10/yr), Friends United Meeting, James R. Newby, 101 Quaker Hill Dr., Richmond, IN 47374-1980. Tel. (317)962-7573. Fax (317)966-1293

Quarterly Review, United Methodist, Sharon Hels, Box 871, Nashville, TN 37202. Tel. (615)340-7334. Fax (615)340-7048

Quarterly Review, African Methodist Episcopal Zion, James D. Armstrong, P.O. Box 31005, Charlotte, NC 28231.

Reconstructionist, The, (bi-m), Jewish, Joy Levitt, Church Rd. & Greedwood Ave., Wycote, PA 19095. Tel. (215)887-1988

Reflections, (bi-m), United Pentecostal, Melissa Anderson, 8855 Dunn Rd., Hazelwood, MO 63402. Tel. (314)837-7300

Reform Judaism, Jewish, Aron Hirt-Manheimer, 838 5th Ave., New York, NY 10021. Tel. (212)249-0100. Fax (212)734-2857

Reform Judaism, (4/yr), Jewish, Aron Hirt-Manheimer, 838 Fifth Ave., New York, NY 10021. Tel. (212)249-0100. Fax (212)734-2857

Reformation Today, (bi-m), Sovereign Grace Baptist, Erroll Hulse, c/o Tom Lutz, Anderson, IN 46011-3008. Tel. (317)644-0994. Fax (317)644-0994

Reformed Herald, Reformed Church in U. S., P. Grossmann, Box 362, Sutton, NE 68979. Tel. (402)773-4227

Rejoice!, Inter-Mennonite, Katie Funk Wiebe, 836 Amidon, Wichita, KS 67203-3112. Tel. (316)269-9185

Religious Broadcasting, (11/yr), National Religious Broadcasters, Ron J. Kopczick, 7839 Ashton Ave., Manassas, VA 22110. Tel. (703)330-7000. Fax (703)330-7100

Religious Education, Independent, Jack D. Spiro, Virginia Commonwealth Univ., Richmond, VA 23284. Tel. (804)257-1224

Religious Herald, (44/yr), Southern Baptist, Michael Clingenpeel, P.O. Box 8377, Richmond, VA 23226. Tel. (804)672-1973

Reporter, (24/yr), Lutheran Church—Missouri Synod, David Mahsman, 1333 S. Kirkwood Rd., St. Louis, MO 63122. Tel. (314)965-9917. Fax (314)965-3396

Rescue Herald, The, American Rescue Workers, Robert N. Coles, 1209 Hamilton Blvd., Hagerstown, MD 21742. Tel. (301)797-0061. Fax (301)797-1480

Response, United Meth., Dana Jones, 475 Riverside Dr., Room 1363, New York, NY 10115. Tel. (212)870-3755. Fax (212)870-3940

Restitution Herald, The, (bi-m), Church of God Gen. Conf. (Oregon, Ill.), Hollis Partlowe, Box 100, Oregon, IL 61061. Tel. (815)732-7991. Fax (404)362-9307

Restoration Herald, Christian Churches and Churches of Christ, Thomas D. Thurman, 5664 Cheviot Rd., Cincinnati, OH 45247-7071. Tel. (513)385-0461

Restoration Quarterly, Churches of Christ, Everett Ferguson, Box 8227, Abilene, TX 79699. Tel. (915)674-3734

Restoration Witness, (bi-m), Reorganized Church of Jesus Christ, LDS, Barbara Howard, P.O. Box 1059, Independence, MO 64051. Tel. (816)252-5010. Fax (816)252-3976

Review for Religious, (bi-m), Roman Catholic, David L. Fleming, 3601 Lindell Blvd., St. Louis, MO 63108. Tel. (314)535-3048. Fax (314)535-0601

Review of Religious Research, (4/yr), D. Paul Johnson, Texas Tech. U., Lubbock, TX 79409. Tel. (806)742-2400. Fax (806)742-2007

Rocky Mountain Christian, Churches of Christ, Jack W. Carr, 2247 Highway 86 E., Castlerock, CO 80104.

Sabbath Recorder, Seventh Day Baptist, Kevin J. Butler, 3120 Kennedy Rd., Janesville, WI 53547. Tel. (608)752-5055. Fax (608)752-7711

Saint Anthony Messenger, Roman Catholic, Norman Perry, 1615 Republic St., Cincinnati, OH 45210. Tel. (513)241-5616. Fax (513)241-0399

Saints Herald, Reorganized Church of Jesus Christ of Latter Day Saints, Roger Yarrington, P.O. Box 1770, Independence, MO 64055. Tel. (816)252-5010. Fax (816)252-3976

Salt, Catholic, Mark J. Brummel, 205 W. Monroe St., Chicago, IL 60606. Tel. (312)236-7782. Fax (312)236-7230

Schwenkfeldian, The, Schwenkfelder, Brittney Pettis, 1 Seminary Street, Pennsburg, PA 18073.

Secret Chamber, African Methodist Episcopal Church, Yale B. Bruce, 5728 Major Blvd., Orlando, FL 82819. Tel. (305)352-6515

Secret Place, The, American Bapt. Ch., Kathleen Hayes, P.O. Box 851, Valley Forge, PA 19482. Tel. (215)768-2240. Fax (215)768-2056

Shabbat Shalom, Seventh-day Adventist, Clifford Goldstein, 55 W. Oak Ridge Dr., Hagerstown, MD 21740.

Share, (bi-m), James Lanz, Evangelical Church Board of Missions, Minneapolis, MN 55444.

Sharing, Mennonite, Steve Bowers, P.O. Box 438, Goshen, IN 46526. Tel. (219)533-9511. Fax (219)533-5264

Shiloh's Messenger of Wisdom, Israelite House of David, William Robertson, P.O. Box 1067, Benton Harbor, MI 49023.

Signs of the Times, Seventh-day Adventist, Gregory Brothers, P.O. Box 7000, Boise, ID 83707. Tel. (208)465-2577. Fax (208)465-2531

Skopeo, Fellowship of Fundamental Bible Churches, Doughty, Mark Franklin & James Korth, 134 Delsea Dr., Westville, NJ 08093.

Social Questions Bulletin, (bi-m), United Methodist (Independent), George McClain, 76 Clinton Ave., Staten Island, NY 10301. Tel. (718)273-6372. Fax (718)273-6372

Sojourners, (10/yr), Independent, Jim Wallis, Box 29272, Washington, DC 20017. Tel. (202)636-3637. Fax (202)636-3643

Southwestern News, Southern Baptist, Jay Chance, Box 22,00-3E, Fort Worth, TX 76122. Tel. (817)923-1921

225

Spectrum, Walter Fricke, P.O. Box 66, Wheaton, IL 60189

Spectrum, Wendy Gill, P.O. Box 66, Wheaton, IL 60189

Spirituality Today, Richard Woods, 7200 W. Division St., River Forest, IL 60305. Tel. (312)771-4270

St. Willibrord Journal, Christ Catholic, Charles E. Harrison, P.O. Box 271751, Houston, TX 77277-1751. Tel. (417)587-3951

Standard, The, Baptist General Conference, Donald E. Anderson, 2002 S. Arlington Heights Rd., Arlington Heights, IL 60005. Tel. (312)228-0200. Fax (708)228-5376

Star of Zion, African Methodist Episcopal Zion, Morgan W. Tann, P.O. Box 31005, Charlotte, NC 28231. Tel. (704)377-4329

Stewardship USA, Independent, Raymond Barnett Knudsen, P.O. Box 9, Bloomfield Hills, MI 48303-0009. Tel. (313)737-0895. Fax (313)737-0895

Story Friends, Mennonite, Marjorie Waybill, 616 Walnut Ave., Scottdale, PA 15683. Tel. (412)887-8500. Fax (412)887-3111

Sunday, Interdenominational, Jack P. Lowndes, 2930 Flowers Rd., S., #16, Atlanta, GA 30341-5532. Tel. (404)936-5376

Sunday School Counselor, Assemblies of God, Sylvia Lee, Sunday School Promotion and Training, Springfield, MO 65802. Tel. (417)862-2781. Fax (417)862-8558

Sunday School Curriculum & Literature, Assemblies of God, Gary Leggett, Gospel Publishing House, Springfield, MO 65802. Tel. (417)862-2781. Fax (417)862-8558

Sunday School Literature, Pentecostal Holiness, Shirley Spencer, P.O. Box 12609, Oklahoma City, OK 73157

Sunday School Literature, Church of God in Christ, Roy L. H. Winbush, Church of God in Christ, Memphis, TN 38103

Tablet, The, Catholic, Ed Wilkinson, 653 Hicks St., Brooklyn, NY 11231. Tel. (718)858-3838. Fax (718)858-2112

Teens Today, Church of the Nazarene, David W. Caudle, Nazarene Publishing House, Kansas City, MO 64141. Tel. (816)333-7000

The Challenge, John F. Sills, 3000 Market St., NE, Ste. 528, Salem, OR 97301

The Evangelical Advocate, (3/yr), Rob Rice, 1670 60 128th Ave., SE, Renton, WA 98055.

The Orthodox Church, Leonid Kishkovsky, P.O. Box 675, Syosset, NY 11791

The Silver Lining, David Bertsch, Grabill, IN 46741

The Southern Methodist, Thomas Owens, P.O. Drawer A, Orangeburg, SC 29116-0039

The Syrian Antiochian Persepective, Archdiocesan Editorial Board, 49 Kipp Ave., Lodi, NJ 07644

The Wave, General Baptists, Sandra Trivitt, 100 Stinson Dr., Poplar Bluff, MO 63901. Tel. (314)785-7746. Fax (314)785-0564

Theological Education, The, (semi-a), James Waits, 10 Summit Park Dr., Pittsburgh, PA 15275. Tel. (412)788-6505

Theology Digest, Catholic, Bernhard A. Asen & Rosemary Jermann, 3634 Lindell Blvd., St. Louis, MO 63108. Tel. (314)658-2857

Theology Today, Long and Patrick D. Miller, P.O. Box 29, Princeton, NJ 08542. Tel. (609)497-7714. Fax (609)924-2973

These Days, (bi-m), Presbyterian Church (U.S.A.), Arthur M. Field, 100 Witherspoon St., Louisville, KY 40202. Tel. (502)569-5474. Fax (502)569-5018

Thought, Catholic, G. Richard Dimler, Fordham Univ., Bronx, NY 10458. Tel. (718)579-2322. Fax (212)579-2708

Tidings, The, Roman Catholic, Tod M. Tamberg, 1530 W. Ninth St., Los Angeles, CA 90015. Tel. (213)251-3360. Fax (213)386-8667

Today's Christian Woman, (6/yr), Independent, Julie A. Talerico, 465 Gunderson Dr., Carol Stream, IL 60188. Tel. (708)260-6200. Fax (708)260-0114

Tradition: A Journal of Orthodox Jewish Thought, Jewish (Rabbinical Council of America), Rabbi Emanuel Feldman, Rabbinical Council of America, New York, NY 10001. Tel. (212)807-7888. Fax (212)727-8452

Truth, (bi-m), Grace Gospel Fellowship, Roger G. Anderson, 2125 Martindale SW, Grand Rapids, MI 49509

U.S. Catholic, Mark J. Brummel, 205 W. Monroe St., Chicago, IL 60606. Tel. (312)236-7782. Fax (312)236-7230

UB, United Brethren in Christ, Steve Dennie, 302 Lake St., Huntington, IN 46750. Tel. (219)356-2312

Ubique: American Province, Liberal Catholic, Rev. Joseph Tisch, P.O. Box 1117, Melbourne, FL 32902. Tel. (407)254-0499

Ukrainian Orthodox Herald, Ukrainian Orthodox Ch. in America), Anthony Ugolnik, c/o St. Mary's Church, Allentown, PA 18102.

United Church News, (10/yr), W. Evan Golder, 700 Prospect Ave., Cleveland, OH 44115.

United Evangelical Action, (bi-m), Interdenominational, Donald R. Brown, 450 E. Gundersen Drive, Carol Stream, IL 60188. Tel. (708)665-0500. Fax (708)665-8575

United Foursquare Women's Magazine, International Church of the Foursquare Gospel, Beverly Brafford, 1910 W. Sunset Blvd., Los Angeles, CA 90026

United Methodist Reporter, The, (bi-w), United Methodist. Ronald Patterson, P.O. Box 660275, Dallas, TX 75266. Tel. (214)630-6495. Fax (214)630-0079

United Synagogue Review, (bi-a), Jewish, Lois Goldrich, 155 - 5th Ave., New York, NY 10010. Tel. (212)533-7800

Upreach, Churches of Christ, Randy Becton, Box 2001, Abilene, TX 79604. Tel. (915)698-4370

Vanguard, Christian Church (Disciples of Christ), Ann Updegraff Spleth, 222 S. Downey Ave., Box 1986, Indianapolis, IN 46206-1986.

Vibrant Life, (bi-m), Seventh-day Adventist, Barbara L. Jackson-Hall, 55 W. Oak Ridge Dr., Hagerstown, MD 21740. Tel. (301)791-7000. Fax (301)791-7012

Victory Leader (Youth Magazine), William M. Wilson, P.O. Box 2910, Cleveland, TN 37320-2910

Vindicator, The, Old German Baptist, M. Keith Skiles, 1876 Beamsville-Union City Rd., Union City, OH 45390. Tel. (513)968-3877

Vista, Christian Ch. of North A.m, David Perrello, 35 Millbrook Dr., Williamsville, NY 14221

Vital Christianity, (12/yr), Church of God (Anderson, Ind.), Arlo F. Newell, Box 2499, Anderson, IN 46018. Tel. (317)644-7721. Fax (317)649-3664

Voice, General Baptists, Gene Koker, 100 Stinson Dr., Poplar Bluff, MO 63901. Tel. (314)785-7746. Fax (314)785-0564

Voice, (11/yr.), Mennonite, Eve MacMaster, 256 Grove St., Bluffton, OH 45817. Tel. (419)358-8230

Voice of Missions, African Methodist Episcopal, Anne R. Elliott, 475 Riverside Dr., Rm. 1926, New York, NY 10115. Tel. (212)870-2258. Fax (212)870-2242

Voice of Missions, The, Church of God in Christ, Jenifer James, 1932 Dewey Ave., Evanston, IL 60201

Voice, The, Independ. Fundamental, Paul J. Dollaske, P.O. Box 810, Grandville, MI 49418. Tel. (616)531-1840. Fax (616)531-1814

Voice, The, Bible Church of Christ, Montrose Bushrod, 1358 Morris Ave., Bronx, NY 10456. Tel. (212)588-2284

Worldorama, Pentecostal Holiness, Jesse Simmons, P.O. Box 12609, Oklahoma City, OK 73157. Tel. (405)787-7110. Fax (405)787-7729

WSBC Horizons, Southern Baptist, John Thomason, P.O. Box 3074, Casper, WY 82602. Tel. (307)472-4087. Fax (307)235-9945

War Cry, The, (b-w), Salvation Army, Col. Henry Gariepy, 615 Slaters Lane, Alexandria, VA 22313. Tel. (703)684-5500. Fax (703)684-5539

Wesleyan Advocate, The, Wesleyan, Jerry Brecheisen, P.O. Box 50434, Indianapolis, IN 46250-0434. Tel. (317)576-8156. Fax (317)577-4397

Wesleyan Woman, Wesleyan, Karen Disharoon, P.O. Box 50434, Indianapolis, IN 46250. Tel. (317)576-1312. Fax (317)573-0679

Wesleyan World, Wesleyan, Wayne MacBeth, P.O. Box 50434, Indianapolis, IN 46250. Tel. (317)576-8172. Fax (317)841-1125

Western Recorder, Southern Baptist, Marv Knox, Box 43969, Louisville, KY 40253. Tel. (502)244-6470. Fax (502)244-1688

White Wing Messenger, John Pace, P.O. Box 2910, Cleveland, TN 37320-2910

White Wing Messenger, The, (bi-w), Church of God of Prophecy, Billy Murray, P.O. Box 2910, Cleveland, TN 37320-2910. Fax (615)476-6108

Whole Truth, Church of God in Christ, David Hall, P.O. Box 2017, Memphis, TN 38101

Window to Mission, Mennonite, Gen. Conf., Bek Linsenmeyer, Box 347, Newton, KS 67114. Tel. (316)283-5100. Fax (316)283-0454

Wisconsin Lutheran Quarterly, Wisc. Evangelical Lutheran, Wilbert R. Gawrisch, 11831 N. Seminary Dr., 65 W. Mequon, WI 53092. Tel. (414)242-1842. Fax (414)242-7255

With, (8/yr), Mennonite, Eddy Hall &. Carol Duerksen, P.O. Box 347, Newton, KS 67114. Tel. (316)283-5100

Witness, Pentecostal Holiness, Joe Iaquinta, P.O. Box 12609, Oklahoma City, OK 73157. Tel. (405)787-7110. Fax (405)789-3957

Woman's Touch, (bi-m), Assemblies of God, Sandra Clopine, Gospel Publishing House, Springfield, MO 65802. Tel. (417)862-2781. Fax (417)862-8558

Women's Missionary Magazine, African Methodist Episcopal, Bertha O. Fordham, 800 Risley Ave., Pleasantville, NJ 08232.

Word and Way, Southern Baptist, Bob Terry, 400 E. High, Jefferson City, MO 65101. Tel. (314)635-7931. Fax (314)659-7436

Word and Work, Independent, Alex V. Wilson, 2518 Portland Ave., Louisville, KY 40212.

Word, The, (10/yr), Antiochian Orthodox, George S. Corey, 52 78th St., Brooklyn, NY 11209. Tel. (718)748-7940. Fax (718)855-3608

Workman, The, Ch. of God, Gen. Conf., Marilyn Rayle Kern, P.O. Box 926, Findlay, OH 45839

World Mission, Nazarene, Roy Stults, Nazarene Publishing House, Kansas City, MO 64141. Tel. (816)333-7000. Fax (816)363-3100

World Monitor, Church of Christ, Scientist, Earl W. Foell, One Norway St., Boston, MA 02115. Tel. (617)450-2000. Fax (617)450-2654

World Parish, (s-m), United Methodist, Joe Hale, P.O. Box 518, Lake Junaluska, NC 28745. Tel. (704)456-9432. Fax (704)456-9433

World Partners, (bi-m), Missionary Church, Charles Carpenter, P.O. Box 9127, Ft. Wayne, IN 46899-9127. Tel. (219)747-2027. Fax (219)747-5331

World Vision, Open Bible Standard, Paul V. Canfield, 2020 Bell Ave., Des Moines, IA 50315-1096. Tel. (515)288-6761. Fax (515)288-2510

World Vision, (bi-m), Terry Madison, 919 W. Huntington Dr., Monrovia, CA 91016. Tel. (818)357-7979. Fax (818)357-0915

World, The, (6/yr.), Unitarian Universalist, Linda C. Beyer, 25 Beacon St., Boston, MA 02108. Tel. (617)742-2100. Fax (617)367-3637

Worship, (6/yr), Catholic, R. Kevin Seasoltz, St. John's Abbey, Collegeville, MN 56321. Tel. (612)363-2600. Fax (612)363-2504

Y.P.W.W. Topics, Church of God in Christ, James L. Whitehead, 67 Tennyson, Highland Park, MI 48203

Young Educator, The, Juanita Roby-Arrington, AOH Publishing Department, Birmingham, AL 35234.

Youth Ministry Accent, Seventh-day Adventist, Michael H. Stevenson, 12501 Old Columbia Pike, Silver Spring, MD 20904-6600.

Zion's Advocate, Church of Christ, Gary Housknecht, P.O. Box 472, Independence, MO 64051.

Zion's Herald, United Zion, Martha Harting, 75 Hickory Rd., Denver, PA 17517. Tel. (215)267-5849

10. RELIGIOUS PERIODICALS IN CANADA

The religious periodicals below constitute a basic core of important newspapers, journals and periodicals circulated in Canada. Consult the religious bodies in Canada listing (section 4) for the names of periodicals published by each denomination.

Each entry gives the title of the periodical, frequency of publication, religious affiliation, editor's name, address, telephone number and fax number when known.

A.C.O.P. Messenger, Apost. Ch. of Pent. of Canada, Irwin W. Ellis, 105, 807 Manning Rd. NE, Calgary, AB T2E 7M8. Tel. (403)273-5777. Fax (403)273-8102

ARC, (1/yr), Fac. of Rel. Studies/McGill Univ., Faculté of Religious Studies, McGill University, Montréal, QC H3A 2A7. Tel. (514)398-4121. Fax (514)398-6665

Advance, Assoc. Gospel, Wayne Foster, 8 Silver St., Paris, ON N3L 1T6. Tel. (519)442-6220

Alberta Alert, The, Baptist Gen. Conf. of Alberta, Virgil Olson, 10727 - 114 St., Edmonton, AB T5H 3K1. Tel. (403)438-9126

Anglican Journal/Journal Anglican, Anglican, Ian Storey and Elwood Jones, c/o The General Synod Archives, Toronto, ON M4Y 2J6. Tel. (416)924-9192. Fax (416)968-7983

Anglican Montré Anglican, (10/yr), Anglican, Joan Shanks, 1444 Union Ave., Montréal, QC H3A 2B8. Tel. (514)843-6344. Fax (514)843-6344

Anglican, The, (10/yr.), Anglican, Vivian Snead, 135 Adelaide St. E, Toronto, ON M5C 1L8. Tel. (416)363-6021. Fax (416)363-7678

Atlantic Baptist, The, Un. Bapt. Conv. of the Atlantic Provinces, Michael Lipe, Box 756, Kentville, NS B4N 3X9. Tel. (902)681-6868. Fax (902)681-0315

Atlantic Wesleyan, Atlantic Dist. of The Wesleyan Ch., Ray E. Barnwell, P.O. Box 20, Sussex, NB E0E 1P0. Tel. (506)433-1007. Fax (506)432-6668

Aujourd'hui Credo, (French m), Église unie du Canada (United Church of Canada), Gérard Gautier, 132 Victoria, Greenfield Park, QC J4V 1L8. Tel. (514)466-7733

B.C. Conference Call, British Columbia Baptist, Walter W. Wieser, 7600 Glover Rd., Langley, BC V3A 6H4. Tel. (604)888-2246. Fax (604)888-1905

B.C. Fellowship Baptist, Evang. Bapt. in B.C. and Yukon, Gordon Reeve, Box 800, Langley, BC V3A 8C9. Tel. (604)888-3616. Fax (604)888-3601

BGC Canada NEWS, (4/yr), Baptist General, Abe Funk, 4306 97th St., Edmonton, AB T6E 5R9. Tel. (403)438-9127. Fax (403)435-2478

Banner of Truth, Netherlands Reformed, Joel R. Beeke, 2115 Romence NE, Grand Rapids, MI 49503. Tel. (616)459-6565. Fax (616)459-7709

Baptist Herald, (10/yr), North American Bapt., Barbara J. Binder, 1 S. 210 Summit Ave., Oakbrook Terrace, IL 60181

Baptist Horizon, The, Canadian Conv. of Southern Baptists, Nancy McGough, Postal Bag 300, Cochrane, AB T0L 0W0. Tel. (403)932-5688. Fax (403)4937

Bible Tidings, (bi-m), Canadian Lutheran Bible Institute, Felicitas Ackermann, 4837-52A St., Camrose, AB T4V 1W5. Tel. (403)672-4454

Blackboard Bulletin, Old Order Amish, Elizabeth Wengerd, Rt. 4, Aylmer, ON N5H 2R3

Briercrest Echo, The, Interdenominational, Donna Lynne Erickson, Briercrest Schools, Caronport, SK S0H 0S0. Tel. (306)756-3200. Fax (306)756-3359

British Columbia Catholic, The, Cath., Vincent J. Hawkswell, 150 Robson St., Vancouver, BC V6B 2A7. Tel. (604)683-0281. Fax (604)683-8117

Budget, The, Old Order Amish/Mennonite, George R. Smith, P.O. Box 249, Sugarcreek, OH 44681. Tel. (216)852-4634. Fax (216)852-4421

Cahiers de Joséphologie, (2/yr), Catholic, Roland Gauthier, Centre de recherche, Montréal, QC H3V 1H6. Tel. (514)733-8211. Fax (514)733-9735

Canada Lutheran, (11/yr), Evang. Luth., Kenn Ward, 1512 St. James St., Winnipeg, MB R3H 0L2. Tel. (204)786-6707. Fax (204)783-7548

Canadian Adventist Messenger, (12/yr), Seventh-day Adventist, June Polishuk, Maracle Press, Oshawa, ON L1H 7N4. Tel. (416)723-3438. Fax (416)428-6024

Canadian Baptist, The, (10/yr.), Baptist, Larry Matthews, 217 St. George St., Toronto, ON M5R 2M2. Tel. (416)922-5163. Fax (416)922-4369

Canadian Bible Society Quarterly Newsletter, Floyd Babcock, 10 Carnforth, Toronto, ON M4A 2S4. Tel. (416)757-4171. Fax (416)757-3376

Canadian Disciple, (4/yr.), Christian Church (Disciples of Christ), Raymond A. Cuthbert, 240 Home St., Winnipeg, MB R3G 1X3. Tel. (204)783-5881

Canadian Ecumenical News, (5/yr.), Multi-faith, Joan Craker, 2040 W. 12th Ave., Vancouver, BC V6J 2G2. Tel. (604)736-1613. Fax (604)875-1433

Canadian Foursquare Challenge, Foursquare Gospel, Timothy J. Peterson, #200-3965 Kingsway, Burnaby, BC V5H 1Y7. Tel. (604)439-9567. Fax (604)439-1451

Canadian Friend, The, (bi-m), Religious Soc. of Friends, Dorothy Parshall, General Delivery, Highland Grove, ON K0L 2A0

Canadian Jewish Herald, (irreg.), Jewish, Dan Nimrod, 17 Anselme Lavigne Blvd., Dollard des Ormeaux, QC H9A 1N3. Tel. (514)684-7667

Canadian Jewish News, (47/yr), Jewish, Patricia Rucker, 10 Gateway Blvd., Ste. 420, Don Mills, ON M3C 3A1. Tel. (416)422-2331. Fax (416)422-3790

Canadian Jewish Outlook, Jewish, Henry M. Rosenthal, 6184 Ash St., #3, Vancouver, BC V5Z 3G9. Tel. (604)324-5101. Fax (604)325-2470

Canadian Lutheran, (bi-m), Lutheran Church—Canada, Frances A. Wershler, Box 163, Stn. A, Winnipeg, MB R3K 2A1. Tel. (204)832-0123. Fax (204)888-2672

Canadian Trumpeter Canada-West, Church of God of Prophecy, Vernon Van Deventer, 130 Centre Street, Strathmore, AB T1P 1G9. Tel. (403)934-4787. Fax (403)934-4787

Canadian Zionist, (5/yr.), Jewish, Meyer Krentzman, 5250 Decarie Blvd., Ste. 550, Montréal, QC H3X 2H9. Tel. (514)486-9526

Catalyst, The, (10/yr), Citizens for Public Justice, Harry J. Kits, 229 College Street, #311, Toronto, ON M5T 1R4. Tel. (416)979-2443. Fax (416)979-2458

Catholic New Times, (bi-w), Catholic, Anne O'Brien, 80 Sackville St., Toronto, ON M5A 3E5. Tel. (416)361-0761

Catholic Register, The, Catholic, Carl Matthews, 67 Bond St., Ste. 303, Toronto, ON M5B 1X6. Tel. (416)362-6822. Fax (416)362-8652

Catholic Times, The, (10/yr), Cath., Eric Durocher, 2005 St. Marc St., Montréal, QC H3H 2G8. Tel. (514)937-2301. Fax (514)937-5548

Cela Biedrs, (10/yr.), Latvian Evangelical Luth., Edwards Putnins, 1468 Hemlock St., Napa, CA 94559. Tel. (707)252-1809

Central Canada Clarion, Wesleyan Ch., S. A. Summers, 3 Applewood Dr., Ste. 102, Belleville, ON K8P 4E3

Channels, Renewal Fellowship Within Presby. Ch. in Canada, J. H. (Hans) Kouwenberg, 5800 University Blvd., Vancouver, BC V6T 2E4. Tel. (604)224-3245. Fax (604)224-3097

China and Ourselves, Ecum., Canada China Prog., Cynthia K. McLean, 40 St. Clair Ave. E, #201, Toronto, ON M4T 1M9. Tel. (416)921-4152. Fax (416)921-7478

Christian Courier, Nondenominational, Bert Witvoet, 261 Martindale Rd., Unit 4, St. Catharines, ON L2W 1A1. Tel. (416)682-8311. Fax (416)682-8313

Clarion: The Canadian Reformed Magazine, (bi-w), Canadian and American Reformed, J. Geertsema, One Beghin Ave., Winnipeg, MB R2J 3X5. Tel. (204)663-9000. Fax (204)663-9202

Coast to Coast, Presbyterian Ch. in America , J. Cameron Fraser, Box 490, Sechelt, BC V0N 3A0. Tel. (604)885-9707. Fax (604)885-4696

College News & Updates, (6/yr), Gardner Bible College, Bruce Kelly, 4704 - 55 St., Camrose, AB T4V 2B6. Tel. (403)672-0171. Fax (403)672-6888

College Newsletter, Mennonite Brethren, Katherine Urruh, Concord College, Winnipeg, MB R2L 2E5. Tel. (204)669-6583. Fax (204)654-1865

Communauté Chrétienne, (8/yr), Richard Guimoud, Pères Dominicains, 2715 chemin de la Côte, Montréal, QC H3T 1B6. Tel. (514)739-9797. Fax (514)739-1664

Communicator, The, (4/yr), Assoc. of R.C. Communicators of Can., Ron Pickersgill, Box 2400, London, ON N6A 4G3. Tel. (519)439-7514. Fax (519)439-0207

Connexions, (4/yr), Ecumenical, Ulli Diemer, P.O. Box 158, Stn. D, Toronto, ON M6P 3J8. Tel. (416)537-3949

Consensus: A Canadian Lutheran Journal of Theology, (bi-a), Luth., Saskatoon Luth. Theol. Sem. and Waterloo Luth. Sem., Eduard R. Riegert, 75 University Ave. W, Waterloo, ON N2L 3C5. Tel. (519)884-1970. Fax (519)725-2434

Contact, The, Menn. Breth., George Dirks, Bethany Bible Institue, Hepburn, SK S0K 1Z0. Tel. (306)947-2175. Fax (306)947-4229

Covenant Messenger, The, Evangelical Cov., Elizabeth A. Stroman, 245 21st St. E, Prince Albert, SK S6V 1L9. Tel. (306)922-3449

Crusader, The, (2/yr), Anglican Ch. of Canada, W. Marshall, 397 Brunswick Ave., Toronto, ON M5R 2Z2. Tel. (416)924-9279

Crux, Donald Lewis, Regent College, Vancouver, BC V6T 2E4. Tel. (604)224-3245. Fax (604)224-3097

Dimanche et fête, (7/yr), Cath., Revue Vie Liturgique, 1073 boul. St-Cyrille ouest, Sillery, QC G1S 4R5. Tel. (418)688-1211. Fax (418)688-0868

Discover the Bible, Cath., Guy Lajoie, P.O. Box 2400, London, ON N6A 4G3. Tel. (519)439-7211. Fax (519)439-0207

EMMC Recorder, Mennonite, Adina Kehler, Box 126, Winnipeg, MB R3C 2G1. Tel. (204)477-1213. Fax (204)477-1214

Ecumenism/Oecuménisme, Canadian Centre for Ecumenism, Thomas Ryan, 2065 Sherbrooke St. W, Montréal, QC H3H 1G6. Tel. (514)937-9176. Fax (514)935-5497

Edge, The, Salvation Army, Bruce Power, 455 N. Service Rd. E, Oakville, ON L6H 1A5. Tel. (416)845-9235. Fax (416)845-1966

Eglise et Theologie: Review of the Faculty of Theology, (3/yr-bil), Cath., bi-lingual, Leo Laberge, St. Paul University, Ottawa, ON K1S 1C4. Tel. (613)236-1393. Fax (613)782-3005

En Evant!, Salvation Army, David McCann, 455 N. Service Rd. E, Oakville, ON L6H 1A5. Tel. (416)845-9235. Fax (416)845-1966

Enterprise, Canadian Bapt. Federation, Frank M. Byrne, 7185 Millcreek Dr., Mississauga, ON L5N 5R4. Tel. (416)821-3533. Fax (416)826-3441

Entre-nous, Can. Council of Chs., James Hodgson, 40 St. Clair Ave. E, Toronto, ON M4T 1M9. Tel. (416)921-4152. Fax (416)921-7478

Esprit, (bi-m), Evangelical Luth. Church, Melanie Scott, 1512 St. James St., Winnipeg, MB R3H 0L2. Tel. (204)786-6707. Fax (204)783-7548

Evangel: The Good News of Jesus Christ, Canadian and American Ref. Chs., Reformed Evangelical Task Force, Box 3012, Langley, BC V3A 4R3

Evangelical Baptist, Evangelical Bapt. Church in Canada, Roy W. Lawson, 679 Southgate Dr., Guelph, ON N1G 4S2. Tel. (519)821-4830. Fax (519)821-9829

Evangelical Baptist Magazine, Evangelical Baptist Churches in Canada, R. W. Lawson, 679 Southgate Dr., Guelph, ON N1G 4S2. Tel. (519)821-4830. Fax (519)821-9829

Exchange, (3/yr), United Ch. of Canada, Lynda Newmarch, Div. of Mission in Canada, Toronto, ON M4T 1M8. Tel. (416)925-5931. Fax (416)925-3394

Expression, Menn. Breth., Dan Block, 225 Riverton Ave., Winnipeg, MB R2L 0N1. Tel. (204)667-9576. Fax (204)669-6079

Faith Today, (bi-m), Evang. Fell. of Canada, Brian C. Stiller, Box 8800, Sta. B, Willowdale, ON M2K 2R6. Tel. (416)479-5885. Fax (416)479-4742

Faith and Fellowship, (bi-m), Lutheran Breth., David Rinden, 704 Vernon Ave. W, Fergus Falls, MN 56537. Tel. (218)739-3336. Fax (218)739-5514

Family Life, (11/yr), Old Order Amish Ch., Joseph Stoll, Rt. 4, Aylmer, ON N5H 2R3

Fellowship Magazine, (5/yr), Un. Ch. Renewal Fellowship, Edward McCaig, Box 237, Barrie, ON L4M 4T3. Tel. (705)737-0114. Fax (705)726-7160

Free Methodist Herald, The, Free Methodist, Donald G. Bastian, 42 Conalda Cres., Agincourt, ON M1S 1Nf. Tel. (416)848-2600

Free Methodist Herald, The, Free Methodist, Donald G. Bastian, 69 Browning Ave., Toronto, ON M4K 1W1. Tel. (416)463-4536

Glad Tidings, (10/yr), Presbyterian Ch. in Canada, L. June Stevenson, Women's Missionary Society, Don Mills, ON M3C 1J7. Tel. (416)441-1111. Fax (416)441-2825

Global Village Voice, Canadian Cath. Org. for Development and Peace, Jack J. Panozzo, 3028 Danforth Ave., Toronto, ON M4C 1N2. Tel. (416)698-7770. Fax (416)698-8269

Good News West, (bi-m), Chs. of Christ in Canada, Jim Hawkins, 3460 Shelbourne St., Victoria, BC V8P 4G5. Tel. (604)592-4914

Good Tidings, Pent. Assemb. of Newfoundland, Roy D. King, 57 Thorburn Rd., St. John's, NF A1B 3T2. Tel. (709)753-6314. Fax (709)753-4945

Gospel Contact, The, (4/yr), Ch. of God in Western Canada (Anderson, Ind.), Lloyd Moritz, 4717 56th St., Camrose, AB T4V 2C4. Tel. (403)672-0772. Fax (403)672-6888

Gospel Herald, Churches of Christ in Canada, C. Perry and Roy Merritt, 4904 King St., Beamsville, ON L0R 1B6. Tel. (416)563-7503

Gospel Standard, The, (bi-m), Free Will Bapts., Fred D. Hanson, Box 355, Hartland, NB E0J 1N0. Tel. (506)375-6735. Fax (506)375-4199

Gospel Standard, The, Fund., Perry F. Rockwood, Box 1660, Halifax, NS B3J 3A1. Tel. (902)423-5540

Gospel Witness, The, (18/yr.), Regular Baptist., W. P. Bauman, Toronto, ON M5A 3T4. Tel. (416)925-3261. Fax (416)925-8305

Grail, Ecum., Michael W. Higgins, Univ. of St. Jerome's College, Waterloo, ON N2L 3G3. Tel. (519)884-8110. Fax (519)884-5759

Hallelujah, (bi-m), Bible Holiness Movement, Wesley H. Wakefield, Box 223, Postal Stn. A, Vancouver, BC V6C 2M3. Tel. (604)498-3895

Herold der Wahrheit, Old Order Amish, Cephas Kauffman, 1829 110th St., Kalona, IA 52247

Horizons, (bi-m), Salvation Army, Dudley Coles, 455 N. Service Rd. E., Oakville, ON L6H 1A5. Tel. (416)845-9235. Fax (416)845-1966

Huron Church News, (10/yr), Anglican, Roger McCombe, 220 Dundas St., 4th Fl., London, ON N6A 1H3. Tel. (519)434-6893. Fax (519)673-4151

IdeaBank, Menn. Breth., David Wiebe, Christian Ed. Office, Winnipeg, MB R2L 2E5. Tel. (204)669-6575. Fax (204)654-1865

In Holy Array, Canadian and American Reformed, E. Kampen, Canadian Ref. Young Peoples' Societies, Edmonton, AB T5P 4B7

Insight Into, (bi-m), Netherlands Reformed, H. Hofman, 46660 Ramona Dr., Chilliwack, BC V2P 7W6. Tel. (604)792-3755

Intercom, Evang. Bapt. Chs. in Canada, R. W. Lawson, 679 Southgate Dr., Guelph, ON N1G 4S2. Tel. (519)821-4830. Fax (519)821-9829

Iskra, (bi-w), Un. of Spiritual Communities of Christ (Orth. Doukhobors in Canada), D. E. Popoff, Box 760, Grand Forks, BC V0H 1H0. Tel. (604)442-8252. Fax (604)442-3433

Islamic Horizons, The, Muslims, Kamran Memon, P.O. Box 38, Plainfield, IN 46168. Tel. (317)839-8157. Fax (317)839-1840

Jewish Post and News, Jewish, Matt Bellan, 117 Hutchings St., Winnipeg, MB R2X 2V4. Tel. (204)694-3332

Jewish Standard, (semi-m), Jewish, Julius Hayman, 77 Mowat Ave., Ste. 016, Toronto, ON M6K 3E3. Tel. (416)537-2696

Jewish Western Bulletin, Jewish, Samuel Kaplan, 3268 Heather St., Vancouver, BC V5Z 3K5. Tel. (604)879-6575. Fax (604)879-6573

Journal of Psychology and Judaism, Jewish, Reuven P. Bulka, 1747 Featherston Dr., Ottawa, ON K1H 6P4. Tel. (613)731-9119. Fax (613)521-0067

Kerygma, (2/yr), Cath. (bilingual), Martin Roberge, St. Paul Univ., Inst. of Mission Studies, Ottawa, ON K1S 1C4. Tel. (613)236-1393. Fax (613)782-3005

L'Église Canadienne, (15/y), Cath., Rolande Parrot, 1073 boul. St-Cyrille ouest, Québec, QC G1S 4R5. Tel. (418)688-1211. Fax (418)681-0304

Laval Théologique et Philosophique, (3/yr), Cath., René Michael Roberge, Pavillon Félix-Antoine Savard, Québec, QC G1K 7P4. Tel. (418)656-4115. Fax (418)656-7267

Lien, Le, (11/yr), Menn. Breth., Annie Brosseau, 1775 Édouard-Laurin, St. Laurent, QC H4L 2B9. Tel. (514)331-0878. Fax (514)331-0879

MCC Contact, Mennonite, John Longhurst, 134 Plaza Dr., Winnipeg, MB R3T 5K9. Tel. (204)261-6381. Fax (204)269-9875

Majallat Al-Masjid, (4/yr), Muslims, Dawud Assad, 99 Woodview Dr., Old Bridge, NJ 08857. Tel. (908)679-8617. Fax (908)679-1260

Mandate, (6/yr), United Ch. of Canada, Rebekah Chevalier, Div. of Communication, Toronto, ON M4T 1M8. Tel. (416)925-5931. Fax (416)925-9692

Mantle, The, Ind. Assemblies of God—Canada, A. W. Rassmussen, 24411 Ridge Route Dr., Laguna Hills, CA 92653.

Marketplace, The: A Magazine for Christians in Business, Menn., Wally Kroeker, 402-280 Smith St., Winnipeg, MB R3C 1K2. Tel. (204)944-1995. Fax (204)942-4001

Mennonite Brethren Herald, (bi-w), Menn. Breth., Ron Geddert, 3-169 Riverton Ave., Winnipeg, MB R2L 2E5. Tel. (204)669-6575. Fax (204)654-1865

Mennonite Historian, Menn. Breth., Abe Dueck and Peter Rempel, Ctr. for Menn. Brethren Studies, Winnipeg, MB R2L 2E5.

Mennonite Mirror, (10/yr), Inter-Menn., Ruth Vogt, 207-1317A Portage Ave., Winnipeg, MB R3G 0V3. Tel. (204)786-2289

Mennonite Reporter, (bi-w), Inter-Mennonite; independent, Ron Rempel, 3-312 Marsland Dr., Waterloo, ON N2J 3Z1. Tel. (519)884-3810. Fax (519)884-3331

Mennonite, The, (semi-m), General Conference Mennonite Church, Gordon Houser, Box 347, 722 Main, Newton, KS 67114. Tel. (316)283-5100. Fax (316)283-0454

Mennonitische Post, Die, (bi-m), Inter-Menn., Isbrand Hiebert, Box 1120, Steinbach, MB R0A 2A0. Tel. (204)326-6790. Fax (204)326-4860

Mennonitische Rundschau, (bi-w), Menn. Breth., Lorina Marsch, 3-169 Riverton Ave., Winnipeg, MB R2L 2E5. Tel. (204)669-6575. Fax (204)654-1865

Messenger (of the Sacred Heart), Cath, F. J. Power, Apostleship of Prayer, Toronto, ON M4J 4B3. Tel. (416)466-1195

Messenger, The, (bi-w), Evangelical Menn. Conf., Menno Hamm, Bd. of Church Ministries, Steinbach, MB R0A 2A0. Tel. (204)326-6401. Fax (204)326-1613

Ministry to Women Sketch, The, Salvation Army, David Hammond, 455 N. Service Rd. E, Oakville, ON L6H 1A5. Tel. (416)845-9235. Fax (416)845-1966

Mission News, (bi-m), Canadian and American Reformed, Clarence Stam, 4th & Gerald Crescent, Stoney Creek, ON L8S 2G8. Tel. (416)578-5758. Fax (416)578-5758

Monitor, The, Cath., Patrick J. Kennedy, P.O. Box 986, St. John's, NF A1C 5M8. Tel. (709)739-6553. Fax (709)739-6458

National Bulletin on Liturgy, (4/yr), Cath., J. Frank Henderson, Novalis, Outremont, QC H2V 4S7. Tel. (514)948-1222

New Church Canadian, New Jerusalem, Glenn Alden, 40 Chapel Hill Dr., Kitchener, ON N2G 3W5. Tel. (519)748-5302

New Church Life, New Jerusalem, Donald L. Rose, Box 277, Bryn Athyn, PA 19009. Tel. (215)947-6225. Fax (215)947-3078

New Freeman, The, Cath., Theresa M. Nowlan, One Bayard Dr., Saint John, NB E2L 3L5. Tel. (506)632-9226. Fax (506)632-9272

Newfoundland Churchmen, William Abraham, 28 Woodwynd, St. John's, NF A1C 3E6. Tel. (709)754-7627

News & Views, (3/yr), Foursquare Gospel, Timothy J. Peterson, #200-3965 Kingsway, Burnaby, BC V5H 1Y7. Tel. (604)439-9567. Fax (604)439-1451

News of Québec, Christian Breth. (aka Plymouth Breth.), Richard E. Strout, 222 Alexander St., Sherbrooke, QC J1H 5L3. Tel. (819)820-1693. Fax (819)821-9287

Newsletter, (3/yr), Faith at Work, E. Milliken, 29 Albion St., Belleville, ON K8N 3R7. Tel. (613)968-7409

Newsletter of the Diocese of London, (5/yr), Cath., Ron Pickersgill, P.O. Box 2400, London, ON N6A 4G3. Tel. (519)439-7514. Fax (519)439-0207

Nor Serount, Armenian Ch. of North America, Antranik Tchilingirian, 20 Progress Ct., Scarborough, ON M1G 3T5. Tel. (416)431-3001. Fax (416)431-0269

Northwest Canada Echoes, Evangelical Church, A. W. Riegel, c/o 2805-13th Ave. SE, Medicine Hat, AB T1A 3R1.

Ottawa Jewish Bulletin & Review, (bi-w), Jewish, Cynthia Engel, 151 Chapel St., Ottawa, ON K1N 7Y2. Tel. (613)232-7306

PMC: The Practice of Ministry in Canada, (5/yr.), PMC Board (Ecumenical), Jim Taylor, 60 St. Clair Ave. E, Ste. 302, Toronto, ON M4T 1N5. Tel. (416)928-3223. Fax (416)928-3223

Paul, (bi-m), Netherlands Reformed, Joel R. Beeke, 50420 Castleman Rd., Chilliwack, BC V2P 6H4. Tel. (604)794-7114. Fax (604)794-3502

Pentecostal Herald, The, United Pentecostal, J. L. Hall, 8855 Dunn Rd., Hazelwood, MO 63042. Tel. (314)837-7300. Fax (314)837-4503

Pentecostal Testimony, Pent. Assemblies, R. J. Skinner, 6745 Century Ave., Mississauga, ON L5N 6P7. Tel. (416)542-7400. Fax (416)542-7313

Peoples Magazine, The, Peoples Church, The, Paul B. Smith, 374 Sheppard Ave. E, Toronto, ON M2N 3B6. Tel. (416)222-3341. Fax (416)222-3344

Pourastan, Église Armenienne, Dioc. de Canada, V. Ketli, 615 Stuart Ave., Montréal, QC H2V 3H2. Tel. (514)279-3066. Fax (514)276-9960

Prairie Messenger, Cath., Andrew M. Britzh, Box 190, Muenster, SK S0K 2Y0. Tel. (306)682-5215. Fax (306)682-5285

Presbyterian Message, The, (10/yr), Presbyterian, Janice Carter, Kouchibouguac, NB E0A 2A0. Tel. (506)876-4379

Presbyterian Record, Presbyterian, John Congram, 50 Wynford Drive, Don Mills, ON M3C 1J7. Tel. (416)441-1111. Fax (416)441-2825

Reformed Perspective: A Magazine for the Christian Fam., Canadian and American Reformed, C. L. Stam, Box 12, Transcona Postal Sta., Winnipeg, MB R2C 2Z5. Tel. (204)663-9000. Fax (204)663-9200

Regent College World, Dan Schindell, Regent College, Vancouver, BC V6T 2E4. Tel. (604)224-3245. Fax (604)224-3097

Relations, Cath., Compagnie de Jésus, Giselle Turcot, 25 ouest, Jarry, Montréal, QC H2P 1S6. Tel. (514)387-2541. Fax (514)387-0206

Religious Studies and Theology, (5/yr), P. Joseph Cahill, Religious Studies, Edmonton, AB T6G 2E5. Tel. (403)492-2174. Fax (403)492-2174

Revival Fellowship, Interdenom., Dan Erickson, Canadian Revival Fellowship, Regina, SK S4P 3A3. Tel. (306)522-3685. Fax (306)522-3686

Rivers of Living Water, Interdenom., Mark Leppington, Box 1986, Nipawin, SK S0E 1E0. Tel. (306)862-5095. Fax (306)862-3651

Rupert's Land News, (10/yr), Anglican, J. D. Caird, 935 Nesbitt Bay, Winnipeg, MB R3T 1W6. Tel. (214)453-6130

SR: Studies in Religion: Sciences religieuses, Peter Richardson, c/o Wilfrid Laurier University Press, Waterloo, ON N2L 3C5. Tel. (416)978-7149. Fax (416)978-8854

Sally Ann, Salvation Army, Margaret Hammond, 455 N. Service Rd. E, Oakville, ON L6H 1A5. Tel. (416)845-9235. Fax (416)845-1966

Saskatchewan Anglican, (10/yr), Anglican, W. Patrick Tomalin, 1501 College Ave., Regina, SK S4P 1B8. Tel. (306)522-1608. Fax (306)352-6808

Scarboro Missions, (9/yr), Scarboro For. Miss. Soc., G. Curry, 2685 Kingston Rd., Scarborough, ON M1M 1M4. Tel. (416)261-7135. Fax (416)261-0820

Science et Esprit, (3/yr), Cath., Gilles Langevin, Science et Esprit, Montréal, QC H3T 1W4. Tel. (514)737-1465. Fax (514)387-5637

Servant Magazine, (bi-m), Interdenom., Phil Callaway, Prairie Bible Institute, Three Hills, AB T0M 2A0. Tel. (403)443-5511. Fax (403)443-5540

Servant, The, Inter-Menn., Jake Ginter, Steinbach Bible College, Steinbach, MB R0A 2A0. Tel. (204)326-6451. Fax (204)326-6908

Shantyman, The, (bi-m), Non-denom., Arthur C. Dixon, 6981 Millcreek Dr., Unit 17, Mississauga, ON L5N 6B8. Tel. (416)821-1175. Fax (416)821-8400

Social Questions Bulletin, (bi-m), United Methodist (Independent), George McClain, Shalom House, Staten Island, NY 10301. Tel. (718)273-6372. Fax (718)273-6372

Solia/The Herald, Romanian Orth., David Oancea, P.O. Box 185, Grass Lake, MI 49240-0185. Tel. (517)522-3656. Fax (517)522-5907

Studia Canonica, (2/yr), Cath., Francis G. Morrisey, Faculté de Droit Canonique, Ottawa, ON K1S 1C4. Tel. (613)236-1393. Fax (613)782-3005

Trait D'Union, Le, (4-5/yr), Union d'Églises Baptistes Françaises au Canada, Amar Djaballah, 2285 Ave. Papineau, Montréal, QC H2K 4J5. Tel. (514)526-6643

Tidings, (10/yr), Can.Bapt. Fed., Atl.Prov., Bapt. Women's Missionary Un., H. May Bartlett, 225 Massey St., Fredericton, NB E3B 2Z5. Tel. (506)455-9674

Topic, Anglican, Lorie Chortyk, #302-814 Richards St., Vancouver, BC V6B 3A7. Tel. (604)684-6306

Touchstone, (3/yr), United Ch. of Canada, A. M. Watts, Faculty of Theology, Winnipeg, MB R3B 2E9. Tel. (204)786-9390. Fax (204)786-1824

Undzer Veg, (irreg.), (Yiddish, English) Jewish, Joseph Kage, 272 Codsell Ave., Downsview, ON M3H 3X2. Tel. (416)636-4024

United Church Observer, United Ch. of Canada, Muriel Duncan, 84 Pleasant Blvd., Toronto, ON M4T 2Z8. Tel. (416)960-8500. Fax (416)960-8477

Update, Multidenom., William J. McRae, Ontario Bible College and Theological S., North York, ON M2M 4B3. Tel. (416)226-6380. Fax (416)226-6746

Update, (bi-m), Lutheran Church, Frances A. Wershler, Box 163, Sta. A, Winnipeg, MB R3K 2A1. Tel. (204)832-0123. Fax (204)888-2672

Vie Chrétienne, La, (French, m), Presbyterian, Jean Porret, 2302 Goyer, Montréal, QC H3S 1G9. Tel. (514)737-4168

Vie des Communautés religieuses, La, (5/yr), Cath., Laurent Boisvert, 5750 boul. Rosemont, Montréal, QC H1T 2H2. Tel. (514)259-6911. Fax (514)259-7407

Visnyk: The Herald, Ukrainian Orthodox, Stephan Jarmus, 9 St. John's Ave., Winnipeg, MB R2W 1G8. Tel. (204)582-0996. Fax (204)582-5241

Voce Evangelica/Evangel Voice, Italian Pent., Joseph Manafo, Daniel Ippolito, 6724 Fabre St., Montréal, QC H2G 2Z6. Tel. (514)766-8014. Fax (514)593-1835

War Cry, The, Salv. Army, David E. Hammond, 455 N. Service Rd. E, Oakville, ON L6H 1A5. Tel. (416)845-9235. Fax (416)845-1966

Western Catholic Reporter, (47/yr), Cath., Glen Argan, Great Western Press, Edmonton, AB T6A 0L1. Tel. (403)465-8030. Fax (403)465-8031

Windsor Jewish Federation Bulletin, (3/yr), Jewish, Allen Juris, 1641 Ouellette Ave., Windsor, ON N8X 1K9. Tel. (519)973-1772. Fax (519)973-1774

Word Alive, (5/yr), Interdenom., Dwayne Janke, Wycliffe Bible Translators of Canada, Calgary, AB T2M 4L6. Tel. (403)250-5411. Fax (403)250-2623

Word, The, (10/yr), Antiochian Ortho. Christian, George S. Corey, 52 78th St., Brooklyn, NY 11209. Tel. (718)748-7940. Fax (201)871-7954

Worldwind/Worldview, United Ch. of Can., Rebekah Chevalier, 85 St. Clair Ave. E, Toronto, ON M4T 1M8. Tel. (416)925-5931. Fax (416)925-9692

Yearbook - Canadian and American Reformed Churches, Canadian and American Reformed, W. W. J. Vanoene, One Beghin Ave., Winnipeg, MB R2J 3X5. Fax (204)663-9202

Young Companion, (11/yr), Old Order Amish, Joseph and Christian Stoll, Rt. 4, Aylmer, ON N5H 2R3.

Young Soldier, The, Salvation Army, Judy Power, 455 N. Service Rd. E, Oakville, ON L6H 1A5. Tel. (416)845-9235. Fax (416)845-1966

11. INTERNATIONAL CONGREGATIONS

This directory lists International Congregations seeking to serve an international and ecumenical constituency using the English Language.

The churches are listed within global regions, and then alphabetically by country.

This list was provided by INTERNATIONAL CONGREGATIONS/Christians Abroad, 475 Riverside Dr., 6th Floor, New York, NY 10115-0050. Tel. (212)870-2463. Fax (212)870-3112.

EUROPE

Austria
Vienna Community Church, Schelleingasse #2/6, A-1040 Vienna. Tel. (0222)50 55 233
United Methodist Church, Sechshauser Strasse 56, A-1150 Vienna. Tel. (01)83 62 67

Belgium
American Protestant Church, Kapelsesteenweg 637 B-2180 Ekeren, Antwerp. Tel. (03)665 37 05
International Protestant Church, Kattenberg, 19 (campus of Int'l School), B-1170 Brussels. Tel. (02)673 05 81 or 660 27 10

Czechoslovakia
International Church of Prague, Dusikova 2/1869 16200 Praha 6. Tel. (02) 35-38-096

Denmark
International Church, Gjorlingsvej 10 DK-2900 Hellerup. Tel. (031) 62 47 85

England
American Church in London, Whitefield Memorial Church, Tottenham Court Road, 79 London WIP 9HB. Tel. (071) 580 2791 or 722 58 46 Fax (071)580 5013
St. Anne & St. Agnes Church, 8 Collingham Gardens, London SW5 OHW. Tel. (071) 373 5566 or (081) 769 2677
International Community Church, Vine House, 41 Portsmouth Road, Cobham, Surrey. Tel. (0932) 868 283 or 222 781

Estonia
International Christian Fellowship, Meeting at Puhavaium Church, Tallinn. Tel. (358) (090) 446 776

Finland
International Evangelical Church, Runeberginkatu 39 A 56 SF-00100 Helsinki. Tel. (0) 0-406 091 or 684 8051

France
Holy Trinity Episcopal Church, 11 rue de la Buffa, F-06000 Nice. Tel. (093) 87 19 83
American Cathedral of the Holy Trinity, 23 Avenue George V, F-75008 Paris. Tel. (01) 47 20 17 92
American Church in Paris, 65 Quai d'Orsay, F-75007 Paris. Tel. (01) 47 05 07 99 or 45 55 98 48

Germany
American Church in Berlin, Onkel Tom Strasse 93 D-1000 Berlin 37. Tel. (030) 813 2021

American Protestant Church of Bonn, c/o American Embassy, Box 270, APO AE 09080. Tel. (0228) 374 193 or 373 393
Church of Christ the King, Sebastian Rinzstrasse 22, D-6000 Frankfurt am Main 1. Tel. (069) 550 184
Trinity Lutheran Church, Am Schwalbenschwanz 37, D-6000 Frankfurt am Main 50. Tel. (069) 599 478, 512 552 or 598 602. Fax (069) 599 845
United Methodist Church, Ministries with Laity Abroad, Kirchenkanzlei, Wilhelm-Leuschner 8, D-6000 Frankfurt (M) 1. Tel. (069) 239 373 or (06192) 41554. Fax (069) 239 375
Kaiserslautern Lutheran Church, Bruchstrasse 10, D-6750 Kaiserslautern. Tel. (0631) 92 210
Church of the Ascension, Seyboth Strasse 4, D-8000 Munich 90. Tel. (089) 648 185
Peace United Methodist Church, Frauenlobstrasse 5, D-8000 Munich 2. Tel. (089) 265 091 or 300 6100

Greece
St. Andrew's Protestant Church, Xenopoulou 5, GR-15451 New Psychiko, Athens. Tel. (01) 647 9585 or 652 1401. Fax (01) 652 8191

Hungary
International Church, Box 44, Budapest 1525. Tel./Fax (01) 176 4518

Italy
St. James Episcopal Church, Via Bernardo Rucellai 13, Florence, I-50123. Tel. (055) 294 417
All Saints Anglican Church, Via del Babuino 153B 00187, Rome. Tel. (06) 679 4357
St. Andrew's Church, Via XX Settembre 7, I-00187, Rome. Tel. (06) 482 7627
Ponte Sant'Angelo Methodist Church, Via del Banco di Santo Spirito, 3 I-00186, Rome. Tel. (06) 475 1627
Rome Baptist Church, Piazza San Lorenzo in Lucina, 35 I-00186, Rome. Tel. (06) 892 6487 or 687 6652
St. Paul's Within the Walls, Via Napoli 58, Rome I-00184. Tel. (06) 474 3569 or 463 339
Protestant English Church, Chiesa Evanglica Valdese, Via S. Pio V 15, 17 Turin I-10125. Tel (011) 669 28 38 or 65 26 01 Fax (011) 650 75 42

The Netherlands
Trinity Church Eindhoven, Pensionaat Eikenburg Chapel, c/o Prof. van der Grintenlann, 18 NL-5652 Eindhoven. Tel. (040) 512 580
American Protestant Church, Esther de Boer Van Rijklaan, 20, NL-2597 TJ The Hague. Tel. (070) 324 44 90 or 324 44 91

Norway

American Lutheran Congregation, Postboks 3012, Elisenberg N-0207 Oslo 2. Tel. (02) 44 35 84 or 53 26 17

Stavanger International Church, Vaisenhusgt 41, 4012 Stavanger. Tel. (0474) 56 48 43 or 52 21 21

Poland

Warsaw International Church, ul. Obserwatorow 13, 02-714 Warszawa. Tel. 43 29 70

Russia

Moscow Protestant Chaplaincy, c/o AmEmbassy, Moscow APO AE 09721. Tel. (095) 143 3562

Spain

Community Church of Madrid, Los Alamos, Portal 9, 2-A E-28270 Colmenarejo (Madrid). Tel. (01) 302 0176

Sweden

Immanuel International Church, Kungstensgatan 17, S-113 57 Stockholm. Tel. (08) 15 12 25 or 673 68 03 Fax (08) 31 53 25

United Christian Congregation Stockholm, Box 2122, S-103 13 Stockholm. Tel. (08) 723 3029 Fax (08) 21 31 09

Switzerland

Emmanuel Episcopal/American Church, 3 rue de Monthoux, CH-1201 Geneva. Tel. (022) 732 8078

Evangelical Lutheran Church, 20 rue Verdaine, CH- 1204 Geneva. Tel. (022) 310 50 89 or 348 75 95 Fax (022) 798 86 16

International Church, Swiss Methodist Ch., Hirtenhofstr. 52, CH-6005 Luzern Tel. (041) 44 39 16

International Protestant Church/Zurich, French Reformed Church, Haringstrasse 20, CH-8001 Zurich. Tel. (01) 262 5525 or (01) 825 6483

MIDDLE EAST

Bahrain

National Evangelical Church, P.O. Box 1, Manama. Tel. 254 508

Egypt

Alexandria Community Church, P.O. Box 258, Saraya, Alexandria E-21411. Tel. (03) 857 525

Heliopolis Community Church, 25 Ramses Street, E-11341 Heliopolis, Cairo. Tel. (02) 290 9885

St. Andrew's United Church, Box 367, Dokki, Cairo. Tel. (02) 759 451 or 360 3527

Maadi Community Church, Box 218 Maadi, Cairo. Tel. (02) 351 2755 or 353 2118

Jerusalem

Church of the Redeemer, P.O. Box 14076, Old City, Jerusalem. Tel. (02) 89 47 50 or 82 84 01 Fax (02) 89 46 10

Kuwait

National Evangelical Church, P.O. Box 80 Safat, 13001 Kuwait. Tel. 243 1087

Libya

Union Church of Tripoli, Box 6397, Tripoli. Tel. (021) 70531

Oman

Protestant Church in Muscat, P.O. Box 4982 Ruwi. Tel. 70 23 72

Salalah English-Speaking Congregation, Salalah Christian Centre, P.O. Box 19742, Salalah. Tel. 23 56 77

Tunisia

Community Church in Tunis, 5 rue des Protestants, 1006 Tunis, Bab Souika. Tel. (01) 24 36 48

Turkey

Union Church of Istanbul, Istiklal Caddesi 485 TR-80050 Beyoglu, Istanbul. Tel. (01) 144 5212 or 144 5763

United Arab Emirates

United Christian Church of Dubai, P.O. Box 8684, Dubai, U.A.E. Tel (04) 697 629

AFRICA

Kenya

Uhuru Hiway Lutheran Church, P.O. Box 44685, Nairobi

Methodist Community Church, P.O. Box 25030, Nairobi

South Africa

St. Peter's by the Lake, P.O. Box 72023 - Parkview 2122, Johannesburg. Tel. (011) 646 5740

Tanzania

International English Congregation, Azania Front Lutheran Church, P.O. Box 1594, Dar es Salaam. Tel. (051) 25127

NORTH AMERICA

Canada

Chalmers-Wesley United Church, 36 rue des Jardins, Quebec City, Quebec, Canada G1R 4L5. Tel. (418) 692-2640 or 692-0431 Fax (418) 692-3876

Illinois

O'Hare Airport Interdenominational Chapel, Mezzanine level/Terminal 2, P.O. Box 66353, Chicago, IL 60666. Tel. (708) 596-3050 or 333-0020

CENTRAL AMERICA/CARIBBEAN

Costa Rica

Escazu Christian Fellowship, Country Day School, Apartado 1462-1250, Escazu. Tel. (506) 32-14-07 or 34-32-92

Union Church of San Jose, Apartado 4456, San Jose

Dominican Republic
Union Church of Santo Domingo with Epiphany Episcopal Church, Apartado 935, Santo Domingo. Tel. (809) 689-2070 or 687-3707 Fax (809) 685-1635 or 541-6550

El Salvador
Union Church of San Salvador, VIPSAL No. 238, P. O. Box 52-5364, Miami, FL 33152-5364. Tel. (503) 23 5505

Guatemala
Church Union of Guatemala, Apartado Postal 6-A, Guatemala City. Tel. (502) 2-316904

Honduras
Union Christian Church, Apartado 1869, Tegucigalpa. Tel. (504) 32 3386 or 32-4454

Mexico
Union Evangelical Church, Reforma 1870-Lomas Chapultepec, Mexico City 11000 D.F. Tel. (05)520-0436 or 520-9931

Union Church of Monterrey, Apartado 1317, 64000 Monterrey, N.L. Tel. (083) 46-05-41 or 47-17-27

Panama
Balboa Union Church, Box 3664, Balboa. Tel. (507) 52-2295

Margarita Union Church, Apartado 2401, Cristobel. Tel. (507) 89 39 54 or 46 44 98

Gamboa Union Church, Apartado 44, Gamboa. Tel. (507) 56 64 70 or 56 68 30

Puerto Rico
Wesleyan Community Church, P.O. Box 2906, Guaynabo. Tel.(809) 720-2595 or 790-4818

Second Union Church of San Juan, Apolo Avenue & Mileto Street, Guaynabo 00969. Tel. (809) 720-4423 or 789-7178 Fax (809) 789-1380

Grace Lutheran Church, Calle del Parque 150, Santurce 00911. Tel. (809) 722-5372 or 722-1137

St. John's Episcopal Cathedral, P.O. Box 9262, 1401 Ave. Ponce de Leon, Santurce. Tel. (809)722-3254 or 784 7883

Union Church of San Juan, 2310 Lauel Street, Punta Las Marias, Santurce 00913. Tel. (809) 726-0280

SOUTH AMERICA

Argentina
United Community Church, Avenida Santa Fe 839, Acassuso (1640), Buenos Aires. Tel. (01) 792 1375

Bolivia
Community Church, Castilla 4718, La Paz. Tel. (02) 78-6515 or 78-6525

Brazil
Campinas Community Church, Caixa Piostal 1114, 13.100 Campinas, Sao Paolo.

Union Church of Rio, Caixa Postal 37154 2600, Rio de Janeiro. Tel. (021) 325-8601

Fellowship Community Church, Rua Carlos Sampaio, 107, 01333 Bela Vista, Sao Paulo S.P. Tel. (011) 287-2294 or 844-1153

Chile
Santiago Community Church, Avenida Holanda 151, Santiago, 9

Colombia
Union Church of Bogota, Apartado Aereo 52615, Bogota. Tel. (01) 248-5115

Ecuador
Advent-St. Nicholas Lutheran/Episcopal Church, Casilla 17.03-415, Quito. Tel. (02) 23 43 91

English Christian Fellowship, Casilla 691, Quito

Peru
Union Church of Lima, Casilla 18-0298, Miraflores, Lima. Tel. (14) 41-1472 or 41-4882

Uruguay
Christ Church, Arocena 1907, Montevideo. Tel. (02) 61 03 00 or 60 27 11

Venezuela
United Christian Church, Apartado 60320, Caracas. Tel. (02) 71 39 01, 71 39 02 or 751-6438

Christ Church, Apartado 10160, Maracaibo. Tel. (061) 77 548

Protestant Church of Puerto Ordaz, Apartado 229, Estado Bolivar, Puerto Ordaz, 8015A. Tel. (086) 22 89 48

ASIA

Bangladesh
Dhaka International Christian Church, American International School, P.O. Box 6010 Gulsha, Dhaka 12

China
Beijing International Christian Fellowship at the International Club, Jianguomenwai Dajie, Beijing

English-Language Christian Fellowship, St. Paul's Church, c/o Amity Foundation, 17 Da Jian Tin Xiang, Nanjing 210029

Hong Kong
Church of All Nations (Lutheran), 8 Repulse Bay, Hong Kong. Tel. 812-0375 Fax 812-9508

Hong Kong Union Church, 22A Kennedy Road, Victoria. Tel. 522-1515 or 523-7247

Kowloon Union Church, 4 Jordan Road, Kowloon. Tel. 367-2585

India
St. Andrew's Church, 15 B.B.D. Bag, Calcutta 700 001. Tel. (033) 20-1994

St. Paul's Cathedral, Cathedral Road, Calcutta 700 001. Tel.(033) 28-2801 or 28-5127

Church of the Redemption, Church Road (North Avenue), New Delhi 110 001. Tel. (011) 301-4458

Centenary Methodist Church, 25, Lodi Road at Flyover, New Delhi 110 003. Tel. (011) 36-5396

Free Church, 10, Sansad Marg, New Delhi 110 001. Tel. (011) 31-1331

Free Church Green Park, A24 Green Park, New Delhi 110 016. Tel. (011) 66-4574

Indonesia

Jakarta Community Church, Jalan Iskandarsyah II/176, Jakarta 12160. Tel. (021) 7723325

Japan

Kobe Union Church, 2-4 Nagamindai, Nada-ku, Kobe 657. Tel. (078) 871-6844

All Soul's Episcopal Church, 935 Makiminato, Urasoe City, Okinawa 901-21

Nagoya Union Church, Kinjo Church UCC, Tatedaikan-cho 17, Higashi-ku, Nagoya 461. Tel.(052) 932-1066 or 772-3043 Fax (052) 931-6421

St. Alban's Anglican/Episcopal Church, 6-25 Shiba-koen 3-chome, Minato-ku, Tokyo 105. Tel.(03) 431-8534 or 432-6040 Fax (03) 5472-4766

Tokyo Union Church, 7-7, Jingumae 5-chome, Shibuya-ku, Tokyo 150. Tel.(03) 3400-0047 or 3461-4537 Fax (03) 3400-1942

West Tokyo Union Church, 6-10-27 Osawa, Mitaka-shi, Tokyo 181. Tel. (0422) 33-0993 Fax (0422) 32-8140

St. Paul International Lutheran Church, 1-2-32. Fujimi, 1-chome, Chiyoda-ku, Tokyo 102. Tel.(03) 261-3740 or 262-8623

Yokohama Union Church, 66 Yamate-cho, Naka-ku, Yokohama 231. Tel.(045) 651-5177 Fax (045) 625-4656

Korea

Seoul Union Church, Memorial Chapel at Foreigners' Cemetery Park, 144 Hapchung-Dong, Mapo-ku, Seoul. Tel. (02) 333-7393 or 333-0838 Fax (02) 333-7493

International Lutheran Church, 726-39 Hannam-2 Dong, Yongsan-ku, Seoul 140-212. Tel.(02) 794-6274

Onnuri Presbyterian Church, CPO Box 1125, Seoul 100-611. Tel. 793-9686 or 336-9690 Fax 796-0747

Malaysia

St. Andrew's International Church, 31 Jalan Raja Chulan. 50200 Kuala Lumpur. Tel. (03) 232-5687

Nepal

International Protestant Congregation, Lincoln School, Raki Bahwan, Box 654, Kathmandu. Tel.(01) 270 966

Pakistan

Protestant International Congregation, No. 21A, St 55, F-7/4, Isalamabad. Tel(051) 818 397

International Church of Karachi, P.O. Box 12251, Karachi 75500. Tel. (021) 57 07 76

International Christian Fellowship, 11 Forman Christian College, Lahore. Tel. (042) 879955 or 305867

Philippines

Union Church of Manila, MCCPO Box 184, Makati, Metro Manila. Tel. (02) 818-1634 or 817-4474 Fax (01) 818-2888

Singapore

Lutheran Church of Our Redeemer, 28-30 Dukes Road, Singapore 1026. Tel. (65)466-45590 or 467-5093

Orchard Road Presbyterian Church, 3 Orchard Road, Singapore 0923. Tel. (65)337-6681

St. George's Church (Anglican), Minden Road, Tanglin, Singapore 1024. Tel. (65)473-2783

Sri Lanka

St. Andrew's Church, 73 Galle Road, Colombo 3. Tel. (01) 23765

Taiwan

Kaohsiung Community Church, 151 Ren Yi Street, Kasohsiung 80208. Tel. (07) 331-8131

Church of the Good Shepherd, 509, Chung Cheng Road, Shihiin 111. Tel. (02) 883-3490

Taipei International Church, Taipei American School, 800 Chung Shan North Road, Sec. 6, Tienmou, Taipei. Tel. (02) 872-4073

Thailand

International Church of Bangkok, 61/2 Soi Saen Sabai, Sukhumvit 36 (Rama IV Road), Bangkok 10110. Tel. (02) 258-5821 Fax (02) 253-7291

Chiang Mai Community Church, Cort Hall, Chiang Mai. Tel. (053) 242661

OCEANIA

American Samoa

Community Christian Church, P.O. Box 1016, Pago Pago. Tel. (684) 699-1544 or 699-9184

Guam

Guam United Methodist Church, P.O. Box 20279 GMF, Barrigada 96291. Tel. (761) 734-3251 or 477-8357

Hong Kong

Trinity Union Church, Casilla 5941, Santa Cruz. Tel. (03) 32-3091

12. DEPOSITORIES OF CHURCH HISTORY MATERIAL

Kenneth E. Rowe
Drew University

Most American denominations have established central archival-manuscript depositories. In addition, many large communions have formed regional (conference, diocesan, synodical, or provincial) depositories. Denominations with headquarters in the United States may also have churches in Canada. Historical material on Canadian sections of these denominations will occasionally be found at the various locations cited below. The reader is also referred to the section "In Canada," which follows.

The section for the United States was compiled by Kenneth E. Rowe. Neil Semple and Jean Dryden contributed to the Canadian section.

IN THE UNITED STATES

The most important general guide is *Directory of Archives and Manuscript Repositories* in the United States, 2d edition, compiled by the National Historical Publications and Records Commission. New York : Oryx Press, 1988.

Major Ecumenical Collections:

American Antiquarian Society, 185 Salisbury St., Worcester, MA 01609 Tel (617)755-5221

American Bible Society Library, 1865 Broadway, New York, NY 10023-9980. Tel (212)408-1495 FAX (212)408-1512. Peter Wosh

Amistad Research Center, Old U.S.Mint Building, 400 Esplanade Ave., New Orleans, LA 70116. Tel (504)522-0432

Billy Graham Center Archives, Wheaton College, 510 College Ave., Wheaton, IL 60187-5593. Tel (708)752-5910. Robert Schuster

Boston Public Library, Copley Square, Boston, MA 02117-0286. Tel (617)536-5400 FAX (617)236-4306

Graduate Theological Union Library, 2400 Ridge Road, Berkeley, CA 94709 Tel (415)649-2540 FAX (415)649-1417. Oscar Burdick

Harvard University (Houghton Library) Cambridge, MA 02138 Tel (617)495-2440

Howard University, Moorland-Springarn Research Center, 500 Howard Place, N.W., Washington, DC 20059 Tel (202)636-7480

Huntingdon Library, 1151 Oxford Road, San Marino, CA 91108 Tel (213)792-6141.

National Council of Churches Archives, in Presbyterian Church USA Office of History Library, 425 Lombard St., Philadelphia, Pa 19147. Tel (215)627-0509. FAX (215)627-0509. Gerald W. Gillette

Newberry Library, 60 W. Walton St., Chicago, IL 60610-3394. Tel (312)943-9090.

New York Public Library, Fifth Ave. & 42nd St. New York, NY 10018. Tel (212)930-0800 FAX (212)921-2546.

Schomburg Center for Research in Black Culture, 515 Malcolm X Blvd., New York, NY 10037. Tel (212)862-4000. Howard Dodson

Union Theological Seminary (Burke Library) 3041 Broadway, New York, NY 10027. Tel (212)280-1505 FAX (212)280-1416. Richard D. Spoor. Includes Missionary Research Library

University of Chicago (Regenstein Library) 1100 E.57th St. Chicago, IL 60637-1502. Tel (312)702-8740 Curtis Bochanyin

University of Texas Libraries, P.O. Box P, Austin, TX 78713-7330. Tel (512)471-3811 FAX (512)471-8901.

Yale Divinity School Library, 409 Prospect St. New Haven, CT 06510 Tel (203)432-5291. Includes Day Missions Library

Yale University (Sterling Memorial Library) 120 High St., P.O. Box 1603A Yale Station, New Haven, CT 06520. Tel (203)432-1775. FAX (203)432-7231 Katharine D. Morton

Adventist:

Andrews University (James White Library), Berrien Springs, MI 49104 Tel (616) 471-3264. Mr. Warren Johns.

Auroro University (Charles B. Phillips Library) 347 S. Gladstone, Aurora, IL 60506 Tel (708) 844-5437. Ken VanAndel. Advent Christian Church archives

Berkshire Christian College (Linden J. Carter Library) Lenox, MA 01240

Seventh Day Adventists General Conference Archives, 6840

Eastern Ave. NW, Washington, DC 20012 Tel (212)722-6000

Baptist:

American Baptist Archives Center, P.O. Box 851, Valley Forge, PA 19482-0851. Tel (215)768-2000. Beverly Carlson, administrator.

American Baptist-Samuel Colgate Historical Library, 1106 S. Goodman St., Rochester, NY 14620-2532. Tel (716)473-1740. James R. Lynch.

Andover Newton Theological School, (Franklin Trask Library) 169 Herrick Road, Newton Centre, MA 02159 Tel (617) 964-1100. Ms. Sharon A. Taylor. Includes Backus Historical Library.

Bethel Theological Seminary Library, 3949 Bethel Dr., St. Paul, MN 55112 Tel (612)638-6184. Dr. Norris Magnuson. Swedish Baptist collection.

Elon College (Iris Holt McEwen Library) P.O. Box 187, Elon, NC 27244-2010 Tel (919)584-2479. Diane Gill, archivist. Primitive Baptist Archives.

Seventh Day Baptist Historical Society Library, 3120 Kennedy Rd., P.O. Box 1678, Janesville, WI 53547 Tel (608)752-5055. Janet Thorngate.

Southern Baptist Historical Library & Archives, 901 Commerce St., Suite 400, Nashville TN 37203-3620. Tel (615)244-0344. FAX 615-242-2153. Bill Sumner, director of library and archives.

Brethren in Christ:

Messiah College (Murray Learning Resources Center) Grantham, PA 17027-9990 Tel (717)691-6042. E. Morris Sider.

Church of the Brethren:

Bethany Theological Seminary Library, Butterfield and Meyers Roads, Oak Brook, IL 60521. Tel (708) 620-2214. Dr. Helen K. Mainelli.

Brethren Historical Library and Archives, 1451 Dundee Ave., Elgin, IL 60120 Tel (708)742-5100. Kenneth M. Shaffer Jr.

Juniata College (L. A. Beeghly Library) 18th & Moore, Huntingdon, PA 16652. Tel (814)314-6286. Peter Kupersmith.

Churches of Christ:

Abilene Christian University (Brown Library) 1700 Judge Ely Blvd., ACU Station, P.O. Box 8177, Abilene, TX 79699-8177. Tel (915)674-2344. Marsha Harper

Harding Graduate School of Religion (L.M.Graves Memorial Library) 1000 Cherry Rd., Memphis, TN 38117. (901)761-1354. Don Meredith.

Pepperdine University (Payson Library) Malibu, CA 90263. Tel (213)456-4243. Harrold Holland

Churches of God, General Conference:

University of Findlay (Shafer Library) 1000 N. Main St., Findlay, OH 45840-3695. Tel (419)424-4612. FAX (419)424-4757. Robert W. Shirmer. Archives/Museum of the Churches of God in North America.

Congregational: (See United Church of Christ)

Disciples of Christ:

Brite Divinity School Library, Texas Christian University, P.O. Box 32904, Fort Worth, TX 76219. Tel (817)921-7106. FAX (817) 921-7110. Robert Olsen, Jr.

Christian Theological Seminary Library, P.O. Box 88267, 1000 W. 42nd St., Indianapolis, IN 46208. Tel (317)924-1331. David Bundy.

Culver-Stockton College (Johnson Memorial Library) College Hill, Canton, MO 63435. Tel (314)288-5221. FAX (314)288-3984. John Sperry, Jr.

Disciples Divinity House, University of Chicago,1156 E. 57th St., Chicago, IL 60637 Tel (312)643-4411

Disciples of Christ Historical Society Library, 1101 Nineteenth Ave., S., Nashville, TN 37212-2196. Tel (615)327-1444. Dr. James Seale.

Lexington Theological Seminary (Bosworth Memorial Linbrary) 631 South Limestone St., Lexington, KY 40508 Tel (606)252-0361 FAX (606)281-6042. Philip N. Dare

Episcopal:

Archives of the Episcopal Church, P.O. Box 2247 606 Rathervue Pl., Austin, TX 78768 Tel (512)472-6816. V. Nelle Bellamy.

Episcopal Divinity School Library, 99 Brattle St. Cambridge, MA 02138 Tel (617)868-3450. James Dunkly

General Theological Seminary (Saint Mark's Library) 175 Ninth Ave., New York, NY 10011. Tel (212)243-5150. David Green.

Nashotah House Library, 2777 Mission Road, Nashotah, WI 53058-9793. Tel (414)646-3371 FAX (414)646-2215 Mike Tolan.

National Council, The Episcopal Church, 815 2nd Ave., New York, NY 10017. Tel (212)867-8400.

Yale Divinity School Library, 409 Prospect Street, New Haven, CT 06510 Tel (203)432-5291. Berkeley Divinity School Collection.

Evangelical United Brethren:

(see United Methodist Church)

Evangelical Congregational Church:

Evangelical School of Theology (Rostad Library), 121 S. College St., Myerstown, PA 17067. Tel (717)866-5775. FAX (717) 866-4667. Terry Heisey. Historical Society Library of the Evangelical Congregational Church

Friends:

Friends' Historical Library, Swarthmore College, 500 College Ave., Swarthmore, PA 19081. Tel (215)328-8557. FAX (215)328-8673. Mary Ellen Chijioke, curator.

Haverford College (Magill Library) Haverford, PA 19041-1392. Tel (215)-896-1175. FAX (215)896-1224. Edwin Bronner

Jewish:

American Jewish Archives, 3101 Clifton Ave., Cincinnati, OH 45220 Tel (513)221-1875. Kevin Proffit.

Friedman Memorial Library, American Jewish Historical Society, 2 Thornton Rd., Waltham, MA 02154 Tel (617)891-8110. FAX (617)899-9208. Bernard Wax, director of special projects.

YIVO Institute for Jewish Research, Library & Archives, 1048 Fifth Ave., New York, NY 10028. Tel (212)535-6700. Zachary Baker, librarian; Marek Weber, archivist.

Latter-Day Saints:

Church of Jesus Christ of the Latter-Day Saints Library-Archives, Historical Department, 50 E. North Temple St., Salt Lake City, UT 84150. Tel (801)240-2745. Steven Sorenson

Family History Library, 35 North West Temple St., Salt Lake City, UT 84150. Tel (801) 240-2331 FAX (801)240-5551 David M. Mayfield.

Lutheran:

Augustana College (Swenson Swedish Immigration History Center) Box 175, Rock Island, IL 61201. Tel (309)794-7221. Kermit Westerberg.

Evangelical Lutheran Church in American Archives, 8765 West Higgins Road, Chicago, IL 60631-4198. Tel 1-800-NET-ELCA or (312)380-2818. Elisabeth Wittman

Region 1 (Alaska, Idaho, Montana, Oregon and Washington) Pacific Lutheran University (Mortvedt Library) Tacoma, WA 98447 Tel (206)535-7587 Kerstin Ringdahl

Region 2 (Arizona, California, Colorado, Hawaii, New Mexico, Nevada, Utah, Wyoming) Pacific Lutheran Theological Seminary, 2770 Marin Ave., Berkeley, CA, 94708; contact Ray Kibler III, 4249 N. LaJunta Drive, Claremont, CA 91711-3199.

Region 3 (Minnesota, North Dakota, South Dakota) Paul Daniels, Region 3 Archives, ELCA, 2481 Como Avenue West, Saint Paul, MN 55108-1445. Tel (612)641-3205

Region 4 (Arkansas, Kansas, Louisiana, Missouri, Nebraksa, Oklahoma, Texas) No archives esablished by 1992.

Region 5 (Illinois, Iowa, Wisconsin, Upper Michigan) Robert C. Wiederaenders, Region 5 Archives, ELCA, 333 Wartburg Place, Dubuque, IA 52001

Region 6 (Indiana, Kentucky, Michigan, Ohio) No archives established by 1992

Region 7 (New York, New Jersey, Eastern Pennsylvania, New England and the non-geographic Slovak-Zion Synod) John E. Peterson, Region 7 Archives, ELCA, 7301 Germantown Ave., Philadelphioa, PA 19119 Tel (215)248-4616. For Metropolitan New York Synod : David Gaise, 32 Neptune Road, Toms River, NJ 08753

Region 8 (Delaware, Maryland, Central and Western Pennsylvania, West Virginia, Washington, DC) Paul A. Mueller, Thiel College, Greenville, PA 16125 Tel (412)588-7000; (Central Pennsylvania, Delaware, Eastern Maryland, and Washington, DC) Lutheran Theological Seminary (Wentz Library) 66 Confederate Ave., Gettysburg, PA 17325 Tel (717)334-6286. Donald Matthews

Region 9 (Alabama, North and South Carolina, Florida, Georgia, Mississippi, Tennessee, Virginia, and the Caribbean Synod) Lutheran Theological Southern Seminary, 4201 N. Main St., Columbia, SC 29203-5898. Tel (803)786-5150. Lynn A. Feider

Concordia Historical Institute (Dept. of Archives and History, Lutheran Church-Missouri Synod) 801 De Mun Ave., St. Louis, MO 63105-3199. Tel (314)721-5934, Ext 320,321. August R. Suelflow

Concordia Seminary (Fuerbringer Hall library) 801 DeMun Avenue, St. Louis, MO 63105. Tel (314) 721-5934. David O. Berger.

Finnish-American Historical Archives, Suomi College, Hancock, MI 49930. Tel (906)482-5300, ext 273.

Luther College (Preus Library) Decorah, IA 52101. Tel (319)387-1191. FAX (319)382-3717. Ted Stark.

Lutheran School of Theology at Chicago (Jesuit/Kraus/ McCormick Library) 1100 East 55th St., Chicago, IL 60615 Tel (312)753-0739. Mary R. Bischoff

Saint Olaf College (Rolvaag Memorial Library) 1510 St. Olaf Ave., Northfield, MN 55057-1097. Tel (507)663-3225 Joan Olson. Norwegian Lutheran collection.

Wisconsin Lutheran Seminary Archives, 11831 N. Seminary Drive, 65W, Mequon, WI 53092. Tel (414)272-7200. Martin Westerhaus

Mennonite:

Archives of the Mennonite Church, 1700 South Main, Goshen, IN 46526. Tel (219)533-3161, Ext 477

Associated Mennonite Biblical Seminaries, Library, 1445 Boonveille Ave, Northwest Dock, Springfield, MO 65802. Tel (417)862-3344. Joseph F Marics, Jr.

Bethel College, Historical Library, P.O. Dramer A, North Newton, KS 67117-9998. Tel (316)283-2500, Ext 366. FAX (316)284-5286. Dale R. Schrag.

Bluffton College (Mennonite Historical Library) Bluffton, OH 45817 Tel (419)358-8015, ext 271.

Center for Mennonite-Brethren Studies, 4824 E. Butler, Fresno, CA 93727 Tel (209)251-7194, Ext 1055.

Eastern Mennonite College (Menno Simons Historical Library and Archives) Eastern Mennonite College, Harrisonburg, VA 22801 Tel (703)433-2771, ext 177

Goshen College (Mennonite Historical Library) Goshen, IN 46526 Tel (219)535-7418

Mennonite Historians of Eastern Pennsylvania Library and Archives, P.O. Box 82, 656 Yoder Road, Harleysville, PA 19438. Tel (215)256-3020. Joel D. Alderfer

Methodist:

Asbury Theological Seminary (B.L.Fisher Library) Wilmore, KY 40390-1199. Tel (606)858-3581. David W. Faupel

Boston University School of Theology (New England Methodist Historical Society Library) 745 Commonwealth Ave., Boston, MA 02215. Tel (617)353-3034. Stephen Pentek.

Cincinnati Historical Society (Nippert German Methodist Collection) The Museum Center, Cincinnati Union Terminal, 1301 Western Ave., Cincinnati, OH 45403. Tel (513)287-7068. Jonathan Dembo

Drew University Library, Madison, NJ 07940. Tel (201) 408-3590. Kenneth E. Rowe, Methodist Librarian.

Duke Divinity School Library, Duke University, Durham, NC 27706. Tel (919)684-3234. Roger Loyd

Emory University, Candler School of Theology (Pitts Theology Library) Atlanta, GA 30322. Tel (404)727-4166. Channing Jeschke

Free Methodist World Headquarters (Marston Memorial Historical Center) Winona Lake, IN 46590. Tel (219)267-7656. Frances Haslam

Garrett-Evangelical Theological Seminary (United Library) 2121 Sheridan Rd, Evanston, IL 60201. Tel (708)866-3900. David Himrod

General Commission on Archives and History, The United Methodist Church, PO Box 127, Madison, NJ 07940. Tel (201) 822-2787 FAX (201)408-3909 Susan M. Eltscher, Asst. Gen. Sec.

Indiana United Methodist Archives, DePauw University (Roy O. West Library) Greencastle, IN 46135. Tel (317)658-4434. FAX (317)658-4789. Wesley Wilson.

Interdenominational Theological Center (Woodruff Library) 6111 James P. Brawley Drive, S.W., Atlanta, GA 30314. Tel (404)522-8980. Joseph E. Troutman. African American Methodist collection

Livingstone College and Hood Theological Seminary (William J. Walls Heritage Center) 701 W. Monroe St., Salisbury, NC 28144 Tel (704)638-5500 A.M.E.Zion archives

Miles College (W.A.Bell Library) 5500 Avenue G., Birmingham, AL 35208 Tel (205)923-2771. C.M.E. collection

Mother Bethel African Methodist Episcopal Church, 419 South 6th St., Philadelphia, PA 19147 Tel (215)925-0616

Office of the Historiographer, African Methodist Episcopal Church, P.O. Box 301, Williamstown, MA 01267. Tel (413)597-2484 (413)458-4994. Dennis C. Dickerson, historiographer.

Paine College (Candler Library) Augusta, GA 30910 Tel (404)722-4471 C.M.E. collection

Perkins School of Theology (Bridwell Library Center for Methodist Studies) Southern Methodist University, Dallas, TX 75275-0476. Tel (214)692-3483. Dr. Richard P. Heitzenrater

United Methodist Historical Library, Beeghley Library, Ohio Wesleyan University, 43 University Ave., Delaware, OH 43015. Tel (614)369-4431, Ext 3245 FAX (614)363-0079.

United Methodist Publishing House Library, Room 122, 201 Eighth Ave., South, Nashville, TN 37202. Tel (615)749-6437. Rosalyn Lewis

United Theological Seminary (Center for Evangelical United Brethren Studies) 1810 Harvard Blvd., Dayton, OH 45406. Tel (513)278-5817. Elmer J. O'Brien

Upper Room Library, 1908 Grand Avenue, P.O. Box 189, Nashville, TN 37202-0189. Tel (615)340-7204. FAX (615)340-7006. Sarah Schaller-Linn.

Vanderbilt University, Divinity Library, 419 21st Avenue, South, Nashville, TN 37240-0007 Tel (615)322-2865. William J. Hook

Wesley Theological Seminary Library, 4500 Massachusetts Ave., NW, Washington, DC 20016 Tel (202)885-8691 Allen Mueller. Methodist Protestant Church collection

Wesleyan Church Archives & Historical Library, International Center Wesleyan Church, P.O. Box 50434, Indianapolis, IN 46250-0434 Tel (317)842-0444. Daniel L. Burnett

Wilberforce University and Payne Theological Seminary (Rembert E. Stokes Learning Resources Center) Wilberforce, OH 45384-1003 Tel (513)376-2911 ext 628 A.M.E. Archives

World Methodist Council Library, P.O. Box 518, Lake Junaluska, NC 28745 Tel (704)456-9432. Evelyn Sutton

For United Methodist annual conference depositories, see *United Methodist Church Archives and History Directory 1989-1992*. Madison, NJ : General Commission on Archives and History, UMC, 1989.

Moravian:

The Archives of the Moravian Church, 41 W. Locust St., Bethlehem, PA 18018 Tel (215)866-3255 Vernon H. Nelson

Moravian Archives, Southern Province of the Moravian Church, 4 East Bank St., Winston-Salem, NC 27101 Tel (919) 722-1742

Nazarene:

Nazarene Archives, International Headquarters, Church of the Nazarene, 6401 The Paseo, Kansas City, MO 64131. Tel (816) 333-7000, Ext 437 Stan Ingersoll

Nazarene Theological Seminary (Broadhurst Library) 1700 East Meyer Blvd., Kansas City, MO 64131. Tel (816)333-6254 William C. Miller

Pentecostal:

Assemblies of God Archives, 1445 Boonville Ave., Springfield, MO 65802.Tel (417)862-2781. Wayne Warner

Oral Roberts University Library, P.O. Box 2187,777 S. Lewis, Tulsa, OK 74171 Tel (918)495-6894. Oon-Chor Khoo

Pentecostal Research Center, Church of God (Cleveland, Tenn.), P. O. Box 3448, Cleveland, TN 37320. Tel (615)472-3361 FAX (615)478-7052. Joseph Byrd

Polish National Catholic:

Commission on History and Archives, Polish National Catholic Church, 1031 Cedar Ave., Scranton, PA 18505. Chmn., Joseph Wielczerzak

Presbyterian:

Department of History, Presbyterian Church (USA) Library, 425 Lombard St., Philadelphia, PA 19147 Tel (215)627-1852 FAX (215)627-0509. Gerald W. Gillette.

Department of History, Presbyterian Church (USA), Historical Foundation Library, P.O. Box 847, Montreat, NC 28757. Tel (704)669-7061 FAX (704)669-5369. Robert Benedetto

McCormick Theological Seminary (Jesuit/Kraus/McCormick Library) 1100 East 55th St., Chicago, IL 60615 (312)753-0739 Mary R.Bischoff

Princeton Theological Seminary (Speer Library) Library Place and Mercer St., P.O. Box 111, Princeton, NJ 08540 Tel (609)497-7940. James S. Irvine

Presbyterian Church in America, Historical Center,12330 Conway Rd., St. Louis, MO 63141

Reformed:

Calvin College and Seminary Library, 3207 Burton St, S.E., Grand Rapids, MI 49546 Tel (616)949-4000. Harry Boonstra (Christian Reformed)

Commission on History, Reformed Church in America, Gardner A. Sage Library, New Brunswick Theological Seminary, 21 Seminary Place, New Brunswick, NJ 08901-1159. Tel (908)247-5243 FAX (908)249-5412 Russell Gassaro

Lancaster Theological Seminary, Evangelical and Reformed Historical Society (Philip Schaff Library) 555 West James St., Lancaster, PA 17603. Tel (717)393-0654. Richard R. Berg. Reformed in the U.S., Evangelical and Reformed)

Roman Catholic:

Archives of the American Catholic Historical Society of Philadelphia, Ryan Memorial Library, St. Charles Boromeo Seminary, 1000 E. Wynnewood Rd., Overbrook, Philadelphia, PA 19096-3012. Tel (215)667-3394. FAX (215)664-7913. Joseph S. Casino

Catholic University of America (Mullen Library) 620 Michigan Ave., NE Washington, DC 20064 Tel (202)319-5055. Carolyn T. Lee.

Georgetown University (Lauinger Library) P.O.Box 37445, Washington, DC 20013-7445. Tel (202)687-7425 Eugene Rooney

St. Louis University (Pius XII Memorial Library) 3650 Lindell Blvd., St. Louis, MO 63108 Tel (314)658-3100 Thomas Tolles

St. Mary's Seminary & University (Knott Library) 5400 Roland Ave, Baltimore, MD 21210-1994. Tel (301)323-3200, Ext 64. David P. Siemsen

University of Notre Dame Archives (Hesburg Library) Box 513, Notre Dame, IN 46556 Tel (219)239-5252. Sophia K. Jordan.

Salvation Army:

The Salvation Army Archives and Research Center, 615 Slaters Lane, Alexandria, VA 22313. Tel (703)684-5500, Ext 669. Connie Nelson

Schwenkfelder:
Schwenkfelder Library, 1 Seminary Ave., Pennsburg, PA 18073. Tel (215)679-3103. Dennis Moyer

Shaker:
Ohio Historical Society, Archives Library, 1982 Velma Ave., Columbus, OH 43211-2497. Tel (614)297-2510. Wendy Greenwood

Western Reserve Historical Society,10825 E. Blvd. Cleveland, OH 44106-1788. Tel (216)721-5722 FAX (216)721-0645. Kermit J. Pike

Swedenborgian:
Academy of the New Church Library, 2815 Huntingdon Pike, P.O. Box 278-68, Bryn Athyn, PA 19009. Tel (215)938-2547. Carroll C. Odhner

Unitarian and Universalist:
Harvard Divinity School (Andover-Harvard Theological Library) 45 Francis Ave., Cambridge, MA 02138 Tel (617)495-5770. Alan Seaburg

Meadville/Lombard Theological School Library, 5701 S. Woodlawn Ave., Chicago, IL 60637. Tel (312)753-3196 Neil W. Gerdes

Rhode Island Historical Society Library, 121 Hope St., Providence, RI 02906. Tel (401)331-8575. FAX (401)751-7930. Madeleine Telfeyan

Unitarian-Universalist Association Archives Library, 25 Beacon St., Boston, MA 02108 Tel (617)742-2100. Deborah Weiner

The United Church of Christ:
Chicago Theological Seminary (Hammond Library) 5757 University Ave., Chicago, IL 60637 Tel (312)752-5757. Neil W. Gerdes

Congregational Library, 14 Beacon St., Boston, MA 02108 Tel (617)523-0470. Harold Worthley

Eden Archives, 475 E. Lockwood Ave., Webster Groves, MO 63119-3192. Tel (314)961-3627. Lowell H. Zuck.

Evangelical and Reformed
Hartford Seminary (Educational Resources Center) 77 Sherman St., Hartford, CT 06105 Tel (203)232-4451. William Peters

Harvard Divinity Schol (Andover Harvard Theological Library) 45 Francis Ave., Cambridge, MA 02138. Tel (617)495-5770. Russell O. Pollard.

Lancaster Theological Seminary, Archives of the United Church of Christ (Philip Schaff Library) Lancaster Theological Seminary, 555 W. James St., Lancaster, PA 17603 Tel (717)393-0654. Richard R. Berg

Yale Divinity School Library, 409 Prospect Street, New Haven, CT 06510. Tel (203)432-5291

Yale University (Sterling Memorial Library) Yale University, 120 high St., Box 1603A Yale Station, New Haven, CT 06520 Tel (203)436-0907

Wesleyan, see Methodist

STANDARD GUIDES TO CHURCH ARCHIVES
William Henry Allison, Inventory of Unpublished Material for American Religious History in Protestant Church Archives and other Depositories (Washington, D. C., Carnegie Institution of Washington, 1910, 254 pp.).

John Graves Barrow, A Bibliography of Bibliographies in Religion (Ann Arbor, Mich., 1955), pp. 185-198.

Edmund L. Binsfield, "Church Archives in the United States and Canada: a Bibliography," in American Archivist, V. 21, No. 3 (July 1958) pp. 311-332, 219 entries.

Nelson R. Burr, "Sources for the Study of American Church History in the Library of Congress," 1953. 13 pp. Reprinted from Church History, Vol. XXII, No. 3 (Sept. 1953).

Homer L. Calkin, Catalog of Methodist Archival and Manuscript Collections. Mont Alto, PA: World Methodist Historical Society, 1982—(4 vols. to date)

Church Records Symposium, American Archivist, Vol. 24, October 1961, pp. 387-456.

Mable Deutrich, "Supplement to Church Archives in the United States and Canada, a Bibliography," Washington, DC: 1964.

Andrea Hinding, ed. Women's History Sources: A Guide to Archives and Manuscript Collections in the U.S. New York: Bowker, 1979. 2 vols.

E. Kay Kirkham, A Survey of American Church Records, for the Period Before The Civil War, East of the Mississippi River (Salt Lake City, 1959-60, 2 vols.). Includes the depositories and bibliographies.

Peter G. Mode, Source Book and Bibliographical Guide for American Church History (Menasha, Wisc., George Banta Publishing Co., 1921, 735 pp.).

Society of American Archivists. American Archivist, 1936/37 (continuing). Has articles on church records and depositories.

Aug. R. Suelflow, A Preliminary Guide to Church Records Repositories, Society of American Archivists, Church Archives Committee, 1969. Lists more than 500 historical-archival depositories with denominational and religious history in America.

U. S. National Historical Publications and Records Commission, Directory of Archives and Manuscript Repositories in the United States. 2d edition. New York : Oryx Press, 1988.

United States, Library of Congress, Division of Manuscripts, Manuscripts in Public and Private Collections in the United States (Washington, D.C., 1924).

U. S. Library of Congress, Washington, D. C.: The National Union Catalog of Manuscript Collections, A59—22 vols., 1959-1986. Based on reports from American repositories of manuscripts. Contains many entries for collections of church archives. This series is continuing. Extremely valuable collection. Researchers must consult the cumulative indexes.

IN CANADA
A few small Canadian religious bodies have headquarters in the United States, and therefore the reader is advised to consult "Main Depositories of Church History Material and Sources in the United States," which immediately precedes this section for possible sources of information on Canadian religious groups. Another source: Directory of Canadian Archives, edited by Marcel Caya.

The use of the term "main" depositories in this section implies that there are some smaller communions with archival collections not listed below and also that practically every judicatory of large religious bodies (e.g., diocese, presbytery, conference) has archives excluded from this listing. For information on these collections, write directly to the denominational headquarters or to the judicatory involved.

The major libraries in the United States listed above "Major Ecumenical Collections" contain material relating to Canadian church history.

Most American Protestant denominational archives have important primary and secondary source material relating to missionary work in Canada during the pioneer era.

Ecumenical:

Canadian Council of Churches Archives, on deposit in National Archives of Canada, 395 Wellington, Ottawa, Ontario K1A 0N3. Some records remain at the Canadian Council of Churches office located at 40 St. Clair Ave. E., Toronto, ON M4T 1M9. The National Archives of Canada also contains a large number of records and personal papers related to the various churches.

Anglican:

General Synod Archives, 600 Jarvis St., Toronto, ON M4Y 2J6. Archivist: Mrs. Terry Thompson (416)924-9192

Baptist:

Canadian Baptist Archives, McMaster Divinity College, Hamilton, ON L8S 4K1. Librarian: Judith Colwell (416)525-9140, ext. 3511
Evangelical Baptist Historical Library, 679 Southgate Dr., Guelph, ON N1G 4S2 (519)821-4830
Baptist Historical Collection, Vaughan Memorial Library, Acadia University, Wolfville, NS B0P 1X0. Archivist: Mrs. Pat Thompson (912) 542-2205

Disciples of Christ:

Canadian Disciples Archives, 39 Arkell Rd., R.R. 2, Guelph, ON N1H 6H8. Archivist: Gordon Reid (519)824-5190
Reuben Butchart Collection, E.J. Pratt Library, Victoria University, Toronto, ON M5S 1K7, (416) 585-4470

Jewish:

Jewish Historical Society of Western Canada, 404-365 Hargrave St., Winnipeg, MB R3B 2K3. Archivist: Bonnie Tregobov (204) 942-4822
Canadian Jewish Congress (Central Region) Archives, 4600 Bathurst St., Toronto, ON M3T 1Y6. Archivist: Stephen A. Speisman (416)635-2883

Lutheran:

Evangelical Lutheran Church in Canada, 1512 St. James St., Winnipeg, MB R3H 0L2. Archivist: Rev. Leon C. Gilbertson (incorporating archives of the Evangelical Lutheran Church of Canada, the Lutheran Church in America—Canada Section's Central Synod Archives and those of the Western Canada Synod) (204)786-6707. The Eastern Synod Archives are housed at Wilfrid Laurier University, Waterloo, ON N2L 3C5. Archivist: Rev. Erich R.W. Schultz (519)745-3505

Lutheran Church in Canada, Eastern Synod, 50 Queen St. N., ON N2H 6P4. Archivist: Rev. Roy Gross (519)743-1461 @ADDRESS PARA = Concordia College, Edmonton, AB T5B 4E4. Archivist: Mrs. Hilda Robinson (405)479-8481

Mennonite:

Conrad Grebel College, Archives Centre, Waterloo, Ontario N2L 3G6. Archivist: Sam Steiner (519)885-0220

Mennonite Brethren Bible College, Centre for Mennonite Brethren Studies in Canada, 1-169 Riverton Ave., Winnipeg, MB R2L 2E5. Archivist: Kenneth Reddig (204)669-6575

Mennonite Heritage Centre. Archives of the General Conference of Mennonites in Canada, 600 Shaftesbury Blvd., Winnipeg, MB R3P 0M4. Tel (204)888-6781. Historian-archivist: LPeter H. Rempel (204)888-6781

Free Methodist:

4315 Village Centre Ct., Mississauga, ON L4Z 1S2 (416)848-2600

Pentecostal:

The Pentecostal Assemblies of Canada, 6745 Century Ave., Streetsville, ON L5N 6P7. Archivist Douglas Rudd (416) 595-1277

Presbyterian:

Presbyterian Archives, 59 St. George St., Toronto, ON M5S 2E6. Archivist: Miss Kim Arnold (416)595-1277

Roman Catholic:

For guides to many Canadian Catholic diocesan religious community, and institutional archives, write: Rev. Pierre Hurtubise, O.M.I., Dir. of the Research Center in Religious History in Canada, St. Paul University, 223 Main St., Ottawa, ON K1S 1C4 (613) 236-1393

Salvation Army:

The George Scott Railton Heritage Centre (Salvation Army), 2130 Bayview Ave., Toronto, ON M4N 3K6. Contact: Elayne Dobel (416)481-4441

The United Church of Canada:

Central Archives, Victoria University, Toronto, ON M5S 1K7. (Methodist, Presbyterian, Congregational, Evangelical United Brethren.) Also Regional Conference Archives. Chief Archivist Jean Dryden (416)585-4563

III

STATISTICAL SECTION

GUIDE TO STATISTICAL TABLES

Earl Brewer
World Network of Religious Futurists

Since there are no religious questions in the U.S. census, the *Yearbook of American and Canadian Churches* becomes as near an "official" record of denominational statistics as is available. It is often supplemented by several sample studies, such as Gallup, National Opinion Research Center, and others.

Students, denominational, ecumenical, or congregational policy-makers may use these statistics to gain insights for program planning. Trends in religious adherents and the population of the countries may be related to these statistics.

In spite of these and other values, there are limitations of these statistics which need to be kept in mind by users:

1. The data are not for a single year. Each year the *Yearbook* staff sends questionnaires to appropriate officers of religious bodies in Canada and the United States. The responses are shown in Tables 1-4.

Denominations have different report schedules and some do not report on a regular basis. Only data that has been reported within the last 10 years is included. Denominations that are not listed have not provided data for at least 10 years.

2. The statistics are not comparable in all cases. Definitions of membership and other important characteristics differ from denomination to denomination. In Tables 1-4 of this section, full or confirmed membership refers to those with full, communicant, or confirmed status. Inclusive membership refers to those who are full communicants or confirmed members plus other members baptized, non-confirmed or non-communicant.

3. The data are incomplete. Different methods and times are used in collecting them. Some denominations don't keep or report statistics in some of the categories listed in the tables.

4. This statistical information is based on reports made by denominational leaders rather than "head counts" of the population. In many cases denominations keep careful records. Other denominations only make estimates.

The *Yearbook* staff wants to make every effort to improve the quality and the quantity of the statistics of the vast number of religious bodies. It is hoped that continued cooperation of religious bodies and ecumenical groups will enhance and make more useful this part of the *Yearbook*.

Statistics collected from other sources than the questionnaire are often included in the *Yearbook*.

Tables 1-4 are based largely on the responses to the questionnaires mailed to appropriate officials in all known religious bodies in Canada and the United States. However, in several cases it was impossible to obtain information directly from a denominational official. Wardell Payne from Howard University School of Divinity kindly provided additional information.

The religious bodies are listed alphabetically. The financial data are based on the currency of the country.

TABLE 1: CANADIAN CURRENT STATISTICS

Religious Body	Year Reported	No. of Churches	Full, Communicant or Conf- firmed Members	Inclusive Membership	Pastors Serving Parishes	Total No. of Clergy	No. of Sunday or Sabbath Schools	Total Enrollment
The Anglican Church of Canada	1990	1,767	529,943	848,256	1,907	3,463	1,623	82,022
The Antiochian Orthodox Christian Archdiocese of North America	1989	12		20,000	25	25		
Apostolic Christian Church (Nazarene)	1985	14		830	49	49		
The Apostolic Church in Canada	1989	14		1,600	14	19		
Apostolic Church of Pentecost of Canada Inc.	1991	132	10,629	13,842	180	287	97	6,200
Associated Gospel Churches	1992	126	9,284		118	239		
Bahá'í Faith		398	27,000	27,000				
Baptist Convention of Ontario and Quebec	1991	372	33,144	44,713	315	564		
Baptist General Conference of Canada	1987	70		6,066	80	84		
Baptist Union of Western Canada	1991	172	15,528	20,719	263	336	154	
The Bible Holiness Movement	1991	14	358	904	6	11		
Brethren in Christ Church, Canadian Conference	1992	36	3,069	3,069	51	100	32	2,293
Canadian and American Reformed Churches	1992	44	6,729	13,182	30	51		
Canadian Baptist Federation	1992	1,165	129,720	129,720	1,124	1,292T		
Canadian Convention of Southern Baptists	1990	104	6,001	6,001	51	104	104	6,482
Canadian Yearly Meeting of the Religious Society of Friends	1991	52	1,112	1,556	30	26	26	
The Central Canada Baptist Conference	1992	37						
Christian and Missionary Alliance in Canada	1991	336	27,923	76,119	544	680	336	35,837
Christian Brethren (Also known as Plymouth Brethren)	1985	600		52,000		250	60	
Christian Church (Disciples of Christ) in Canada	1990	36	2,496	4,251	25	48	36	1,006
Christian Churches and Churches of Christ in Canada	1989	140		7,500	95	100		
Christian Reformed Church in North America	1992	240	50,075	86,281	193	262	44	2,639
Church of God (Anderson, Ind.)	1990	50	3,151	3,151	39	57		
Church of God (Cleveland, Tenn.)	1991	98	5,958	5,958			49	2,644
The Church of God of Prophecy in Canada	1991	50	2,915	2,915	114	114		

TABLE 1: CANADIAN CURRENT STATISTICS—Continued

Religious Body	Year Reported	No. of Churches	Full, Communicant or Confirmed Members	Inclusive Membership	Pastors Serving Parishes	Total No. of Clergy	No. of Sunday or Sabbath Schools	Total Enrollment
The Church of Jesus Christ of Latter-day Saints in Canada	1990	380	126,000	126,000	380	380	380	
Church of the Lutheran Brethren	1992	7	318	918	8	8	7	532
Church of the Nazarene	1991	161	10,915	10,915	117	243	159	15,957
Churches of Christ in Canada	1991	147	7,181	7,181	133		108	
Conference of Mennonites in Canada	1991	150	28,648	28,648	310	440		
Congregational Christian Churches in Canada	1991	6	762	762	5	14	4	247
The Coptic Church in Canada	1992	12			20		17	
The Estonian Evangelical Lutheran Church	1990	13	6,268	6,478	13	15		
Evangelical Baptist Churches in Canada, The Fellowship of	1989	484		57,780				
The Evangelical Church in Canada	1990	46	3,688	3,688	46	79	39	3,431
The Evangelical Covenant Church of Canada	1991	23	1,278	1,278	16	31	18	1,753
Evangelical Free Church of Canada	1991	124	6,358	13,299	51	126	124	
Evangelical Lutheran Church in Canada	1991	656	148,630	206,187	486	859	475	25,715
The Evangelical Mennonite Conference	1990	50	6,000	6,000	175	200	50	3,092
Evangelical Mennonite Mission Conference	1990	28	3,528	3,559	25	51	25	1,375
Foursquare Gospel Church of Canada	1990	46	2,019	2,019	78	94		
Free Methodist Church in Canada	1989	147		7,479	132	235		
Free Will Baptists	1992	17	450	1,125	5	7	15	1,340
General Church of the New Jerusalem	1992	3	275	825	4	6	3	185
Greek Orthodox Diocese of Toronto (Canada)	1984	58		230,000	45	49		
Independent Holiness Church	1987	13		600	13	21		
The Italian Pentecostal Church of Canada	1990	21	3,300	3,300	20	24		
Jehovah's Witnesses	1992	1,312	106,052	106,052	0		0	0
The Latvian Evangelical Lutheran Church in America	1990	8	2,200	2,380	6	8	5	
Lutheran Church—Canada	1991	321	58,792	78,566	251	353	293	18,034
Mennonite Brethren Churches, Canadian Conference of	1991	193	27,597	27,597			193	24,119

TABLE 1: CANADIAN CURRENT STATISTICS—Continued

Religious Body	Year Reported	No. of Churches	Full, Communicant or Conf-firmed Members	Inclusive Membership	Pastors Serving Parishes	Total No. of Clergy	No. of Sunday or Sabbath Schools	Total Enrollment
Metropolitan Community Churches, Universal Fellowship	1992	12	500	1,500	8	9	1	36
The Missionary Church of Canada	1984	92		6,431	73	129		
Moravian Church in America, Northern Province, Canadian District of	1991	9	1,498	2,126	11	14	9	499
Netherlands Reformed Congregations of North America	1991	9	2,148	4,660	2	3		
North American Baptist Conference	1992	120	18,125	18,125	83	173	120	9,421
Old Order Amish Church	1992	17			61	61		
The Open Bible Standard Churches of Canada	1987	4		1,000	5	6		
Orthodox Church in America (Canada Section)	1991	59			37	41	13	
The Pentecostal Assemblies of Canada	1990	976	192,706	194,972	1,372	1,593	159	14,200
Pentecostal Assemblies of Newfoundland	1991	160	16,000	33,700	254	376		
Presbyterian Church in America (Canadian Section)	1990	16	538	886	17	23		392
The Presbyterian Church in Canada	1990	1,023	156,513	245,883	1,218	1,218	637	35,321
Reformed Church in Canada	1991	40	4,082	6,779	47	73	40	2,160
Reformed Doukhobors, Christian Community and Brotherhood of	1986	1		2,108				
The Reformed Episcopal Church	1991	4	330	780	8	9	1	22
Reinland Mennonite Church	1987	7		800	10	10		
Reorganized Church of Jesus Christ of Latter Day Saints	1990	83	12,258	12,258	1,088	1,088		
The Roman Catholic Church in Canada	1990	11,286		11,852,350		44,669		
The Romanian Orthodox Episcopate of America (Jackson, MI)	1990	13	8,600	8,600	11	12	10	663
Russian Orthodox Church in Canada, Patriarchal Parishes	1991	24	6,000	7,000	4	5	3	46
The Salvation Army in Canada	1992	402	24,597	99,658	793	2,098	420	16,873
Serbian Orthodox Church in the U.S.A. and Canada, Diocese of Canada	1983	17		18,494	11	13		

TABLE 1: CANADIAN CURRENT STATISTICS—Continued

Religious Body	Year Reported	No. of Churches	Full, Communicant or Conf-firmed Members	Inclusive Membership	Pastors Serving Parishes	Total No. of Clergy	No. of Sunday or Sabbath Schools	Total Enrollment
Seventh-day Adventist Church in Canada	1991	320	41,085	41,085	173	308	357	26,525
Ukrainian Orthodox Church of Canada	1988	258		120,000	75	91		
Union D'Églises Baptistes Francaises Au Canada	1991	23	1,169	1,969	15	21	18	763
Unitarian Universalist Association	1990	40	6,003	6,003	20	20	34	1,303
United Baptist Convention of the Atlantic Provinces	1991	558	45,897	64,093		518		
United Brethren Church in Canada	1991	10	818	857	5	13	9	410
The United Church of Canada	1991	4,044	785,726	2,018,808	2,090	3,939	3,384	192,385
United Pentecostal Church in Canada	1992	213			327			
The Wesleyan Church of Canada	1992	72	4,945	5,232	98	141	72	

247

TABLE 2: UNITED STATES CURRENT STATISTICS

Religious Body	Year Reported	No. of Churches	Full, Communicant or Conf-firmed Members	Inclusive Membership	Pastors Serving Parishes	Total No. of Clergy	No. of Sunday or Sabbath Schools	Total Enrollment
Advent Christian Church............	1992	335	28,000	28,000	267	498	330	15,000
African Methodist Episcopal Church #..........	1991			3,500,000				
African Methodist Episcopal Zion Church........	1991	3,000	1,000,000	1,200,000	2,500	2,686	1,556	50,046
Albanian Orthodox Diocese of America........	1992	2	1,873	1,873	1	3	2	128
Allegheny Wesleyan Methodist Connection (Original Allegheny Conference)	1991	117	2,007	2,130	90	191	117	5,908
Amana Church Society.............	1990	1	400	450			1	44
The American Baptist Association.............	1986	1,705		250,000	1,740	1,760		
American Baptist Churches in the U.S.A........	1991	5,862	1,527,840	1,527,840	5,346	8,421		323,371
The American Carpatho-Russian Orthodox Greek Catholic Church.............	1991	72	17,981	17,981	73	84	73	
American Evangelical Christian Churches	1992				75	160		
American Rescue Workers	1984	20		2,700	35	53		
The Anglican Orthodox Church	1983	40		6,000	8	8		
The Antiochian Orthodox Christian Archdiocese of North America.............	1992	170	350,000	350,000	225	275	170	5,850
Apostolic Catholic Assyrian Church of the East, North American Dioceses.............	1989	22		120,000	92	109		
Apostolic Christian Church (Nazarene)	1985	48		2,799	178	178		
Apostolic Christian Churches of America	1989	80		11,450	300	340		
Apostolic Faith Mission Church of God	1989	18		6,200	27	32		
Apostolic Faith Mission of Portland, Oregon	1990	50	4,100	4,100	76	86	50	6,600
Apostolic Lutheran Church of America..........	1989	53		7,583	29	34		
Apostolic Overcoming Holy Church of God, Inc........	1988	177		12,479	127	130		
Armenian Apostolic Church of America........	1992	30	25,000	150,000	22	28	17	963
Armenian Church of America, Diocese of the	1991	72	14,000	150,000	49	70	38	2,370

TABLE 2: UNITED STATES CURRENT STATISTICS—Continued

Religious Body	Year Reported	No. of Churches	Full, Communicant or Confirmed Members	Inclusive Membership	Pastors Serving Parishes	Total No. of Clergy	No. of Sunday or Sabbath Schools	Total Enrollment
Assemblies of God	1991	11,536	1,324,800	2,234,708	17,047	30,746	11,123	1,414,922
Associate Reformed Prebyterian Church (General Synod)	1991	189	33,494	38,552	158	247	168	17,011
Bahá'íFaith	1992	1,700	110,000	110,000			355	
Baptist Bible Fellowship International	1992	3,500						
Baptist General Conference	1992	821	134,658	134,658	1,200	1,700	821	81,896
Baptist Missionary Association of America	1991	1,312	230,127	230,127	1,200	2,400	1,310	93,025
Beachy Amish Mennonite Churches	1989	99		6,872	376	376		
Berean Fundamental Church	1991	51	2,768	2,768	60	60	51	4,063
The Bible Church of Christ, Inc.	1992	6	4,200	6,700	8	54	6	725
Brethren Church (Ashland, Ohio)	1991	124	13,322	13,322	93	178	119	6,847
Brethren in Christ Church	1992	194	17,454	17,454	252	388	165	12,818
Buddhist Churches of America	1989	67		19,441	65	107		
Bulgarian Eastern Orthodox Church	1991	9	10,000	10,000	15	20	6	230
Christ Catholic Church	1991	10	1,190	1,435	9	26	1	9
The Christian and Missionary Alliance	1991	1,900	141,077	267,853	1,639	2,475	1,683	143,540
Christian Brethren (also known as Plymouth Brethren)	1984	1,150		98,000		500	1,000	
Christian Catholic Church (Evangelical-Protestant)	1990	6	2,500	2,500	10	19T6		
Christian Church (Disciples of Christ)	1991	4,031	663,336	1,022,926	3,729	6,912	4,031	303,823
Christian Church of North America, General Council	1985	104		13,500	107	169		
Christian Churches and Churches of Christ	1988	5,579		1,070,616	5,525	6,596		
The Christian Congregation, Inc.	1991	1,447	110,716	110,716	1,447	1,450	1,302	47,219
Christian Methodist Episcopal Church	1983	2,340		718,922	2,340	2,650		
Christian Nation Church U.S.A.	1989	5		200	4	23		
Christian Reformed Church in North America	1992	739	146,582	224,921	671	1,180		
Christian Union	1984	114		6,000	80	114		
Church of God (Anderson, Ind.)	1992	2,330	214,743	214,743	3,000	4,743	2,320	164,752

249

TABLE 2: UNITED STATES CURRENT STATISTICS—Continued

Religious Body	Year Reported	No. of Churches	Full, Communicant or Conf-firmed Members	Inclusive Membership	Pastors Serving Parishes	Total No. of Clergy	No. of Sunday or Sabbath Schools	Total Enrollment
Church of God by Faith, Inc.	1991	145	6,819	8,235	155	170		
Church of God (Cleveland, Tenn.)	1990	5,841	620,393	620,393	4,665	6,585	5,514	389,093
Church of God General Conference (Oregon, IL and Morrow, GA)	1992	89	4,251	5,526	62	78	87	3,252
The Church of God In Christ	1991	15,300	5,499,875	5,499,875	28,988	33,593		
Church of God in Christ, International	1982	300		200,000	700	1,600		
Church of God in Christ (Mennonite)	1991	78	9,999	9,999	344	344	78	6,600
Church of God, Mountain Assembly, Inc.	1992	111	5,052	5,052	112	116	111	6,600
Church of God of Prophecy	1992	2,072	72,465	72,465	12,211	12,307	1,592	67,421
The Church of God (Seventh Day), Denver, Colo.	1990	153		5,749	127			
Church of God (Which He Purchased with His Own Blood)	1991	7	800	800		16	7	22
The Church of Illumination	1992	8			18	27		
The Church of Jesus Christ (Bickertonites)	1989	63		2,707	183	262		
The Church of Jesus Christ of Latter-day Saints	1991	9,468	3,814,000	4,336,000	28,404	31,890	9,860	3,485,511
Church of the Brethren	1990	1,095	148,253	148,253	1,084	1,541		
Church of the Living God (Motto: Christian Workers for Fellowship)	1985	170		42,000		170		
Church of Lutheran Brethren of America	1992	111	8,224	22,478	133	235	111	10,868
Church of the Lutheran Confession	1991	70	6,363	8,722	57	82	67	1,429
Church of the Nazarene	1991	5,172	572,152	573,834	4,416	9,363	4,945	860,099
Churches of Christ	1992	13,200	1,290,000	1,690,000			12,000	
Churches of Christ in Christian Union	1991	240	10,349	10,349	255	479	240	14,210
Churches of God, General Conference	1991	354	33,584	33,584	258	437	354	27,000
Community Churches, International Council of	1991	398	250,000		600			
Congregational Christian Churches, National Association of	1992	405	90,000	90,000	600	600	370	7,150
Congregational Holiness Church	1991	176	7,116	7,116	312	349	176	7,150

TABLE 2: UNITED STATES CURRENT STATISTICS—Continued

Religious Body	Year Reported	No. of Churches	Full, Communicant or Conf-firmed Members	Inclusive Membership	Pastors Serving Parishes	Total No. of Clergy	No. of Sunday or Sabbath Schools	Total Enrollment
Conservative Baptist Association of America	1989	1,126		210,000	1,126	1,324		
Conservative Congregational Christian Conference	1991	176	28,035	28,035	294	505	162	12,035
Conservative Lutheran Association	1987	12		1,530	18	27		
Coptic Orthodox Church	1992	55		260,000	60			
Cumberland Presbyterian Church	1991	784	260,000	92,433		783		44,974
Elim Fellowship	1990	177		20,000	151	272		
Episcopal Church	1991	7,367	1,615,505	2,471,880	8,040	14,878		531,813
The Estonian Evangelical Lutheran Church	1989	24		7,298	17	19		
Ethical Culture Movement	1988	21		3,212	19	43		
The Evangelical Church	1990	185	16,398	16,398	240	349	185	17,428
The Evangelical Congregational Church	1990	155	24,437	32,700	141	222	153	17,100
The Evangelical Covenant Church	1991	596	89,648	89,648	542	1,028	514	77,903
The Evangelical Free Church of America	1992	1,113	110,456	187,775	1,631	1,858	T	
Evangelical Friends International—North America Region	1991	246		26,322		455	246	14,881
Evangelical Lutheran Church in America	1991	11,074	3,890,947	5,245,177	9,929	17,426	9,639	1,113,033
Evangelical Lutheran Synod	1991	126	16,004	21,347	97	151	116	3,845
Evangelical Mennonite Church	1992	27	4,059	4,059	28	55	27	3,671
Evangelical Methodist Church	1990	126	8,514	8,514	133	269	126	8,930
Evangelical Presbyterian Church	1992	180		56,000		375		
Fellowship of Evangelical Bible Churches	1988	14		1,925	18	47		
Fellowship of Fundamental Bible Churches	1992	26	1,461	2,087	35	52	26	1,362
The Fire Baptized Holiness Church (Wesleyan)	1991	49	695	695	49	64		
Free Lutheran Congregations, The Association of	1991	210	21,150	27,650	114	170	182	8,705
Free Methodist Church of North America	1991	1,063	57,794	73,572	956	1,862		93,629
Free Will Baptists, National Association of	1991	2,495	209,223	209,223	2,800	2,900	2,495	45,870
Friends General Conference	1991	520	30,902	30,902				

TABLE 2: UNITED STATES CURRENT STATISTICS—Continued

Religious Body	Year Reported	No. of Churches	Full, Communicant or Confirmed Members	Inclusive Membership	Pastors Serving Parishes	Total No. of Clergy	No. of Sunday or Sabbath Schools	Total Enrollment
Friends United Meeting	1991		50,803	50,803	341	637	354	17,566
Full Gospel Assemblies International	1984	150		3,800	122	399		
Full Gospel Fellowship of Churches and Ministers International	1985	450		65,000	850	850		
Fundamental Methodist Church, Inc.	1990	12	675	1,075	14	25	12	431
General Association of Regular Baptist Churches	1992	1,532		160,123		1,384		
General Baptists (General Association of)	1990	876	74,156	74,156	1,384			
General Conference of the Church of God (Seventh Day)	1990	153		5,700		130		
General Baptists (General Association of)	1990	876						
Grace Brethren Churches, Fellowship of	1991	322	39,237	39,237		600	300	
Grace Gospel Fellowship	1990	50	2,500	4,500	68	120	50	
Hungarian Reformed Church in America	1989	27		9,780	29	32		
The Hutterian Brethren	1992	95		6,700		195	95	2,455
Independent Fundamental Churches of America	1991	700	78,174	78,174	745	1,510	700	74,566
International Church of the Foursquare Gospel	1991	1,516	203,218	208,150		2,516	1,043	37,595
The International Pentecostal Church of Christ	1992	77	2,532	3,840	77	177	77	3,535
International Pentecostal Holiness Church	1990			131,674				
Jehovah's Witnesses	1992	9,890	914,079	914,079				
Jewish Organizations	1990	3,416	3,750,000	5,981,000		6,500		
Korean Presbyterian Church in America, General Assembly of the	1992	203	21,788	26,988	326	381		
The Latvian Evangelical Lutheran Church in America	1990	56	11,432	12,553	34	48	19	
The Liberal Catholic Church—Province of the United States of America	1987	34		2,800	64	127		
Liberty Baptist Fellowship	1992	100			100	110		
The Lutheran Church—Missouri Synod	1991	5,364	1,952,845	2,607,309	5,417	8,389	5,783	668,298

TABLE 2: UNITED STATES CURRENT STATISTICS—Continued

Religious Body	Year Reported	No. of Churches	Full, Communicant or Confirmed Members	Inclusive Membership	Pastors Serving Parishes	Total No. of Clergy	No. of Sunday or Sabbath Schools	Total Enrollment
Lutheran Churches, The American Association of	1988	78		15,150	63	80		
Mennonite Brethren Churches, The United States Conference of	1991	144	16,843	16,843	196	470		11,299
Mennonite Church	1992	1,053	99,431	99,431	1,631	2,754		
Mennonite Church, The General Conference	1991	229	33,937	33,937	212	394	229	16,250
Metropolitan Community Churches, Universal Fellowship of	1990	195	12,576	25,076	276	304		
The Missionary Church	1991	303	27,320	27,320	437	714	286	26,940
Moravian Church in America, Alaskan Province	1987	23		5,159	11	15		
Moravian Church in America, Northern Province	1991	98	22,887	29,805	89	175	97	7,053
Moravian Church in America, Southern Province	1991	56	17,300	21,513	63	95	56	8,691
National Baptist Convention, U.S.A., Inc.	1992	36,000		8,000,000	30,000		30,000	
National Baptist Convention of America (DAARB)	1987	2,500		3,500,000		8000		
National Missionary Baptist Convention of America	1992			2,500,000				
National Organization of the New Apostolic Church of North America	1991	523	39,816	39,816	793	884	523	2,540
National Spiritualist Association of Churches	1992	137	2,883	3,883	83	95	48	508
Netherlands Reformed Congregations	1991	15	2,770	5,250	5	7		
North American Baptist Conference	1992	265	43,087	43,087	243	451	265	23,082
North American Old Roman Catholic Church (Archdiocese of New York)	1992	5	400	400	9	10	3	37
Old German Baptist Brethren	1991	55	5,475	5,475	242	242		
Old Order Amish Church	1992	876	78,840	78,840		3,504	65	
Open Bible Standard Churches	1992	368	33,000	40,000	535	1,004	350	
Orthodox Church In America	1992	1,000	1,000,000	1,030,000	750	1,150	600	
The Orthodox Presbyterian Church	1991	170	12,265	18,137		315		
Pentecostal Assemblies of the World #	1989	1,005		500,000				

TABLE 2: UNITED STATES CURRENT STATISTICS—Continued

Religious Body	Year Reported	No. of Churches	Full, Communicant or Confirmed Members	Inclusive Membership	Pastors Serving Parishes	Total No. of Clergy	No. of Sunday or Sabbath Schools	Total Enrollment
Pentecostal Church of God	1991	1,160	40,750	92,060		1,679		
The Pentecostal Free Will Baptist Church, Inc.	1992	148	11,757		163	228	148	11,734
Presbyterian Church in America	1991			233,770				
Presbyterian Church (U.S.A.)	1991	11,468	2,805,548	3,778,358	10,042	20,357	9,943	1,140,999
Primitive Advent Christian Church	1992	10	343	343	11	11	8	310
Primitive Methodist Church in the U.S.A.	1989	85		8,244	54	84		
Progressive National Baptist Convention, Inc.	1991	1,400	2,500,000	2,500,000	1,400	1,400	1,400	
The Protes'tant Conference (Lutheran), Inc.	1992	7	850	1,150	9	9	6	160
Reformed Church in America	1991	967	197,688	340,991	926	1,617	967	110,213
Reformed Church in the United States	1985	34		3,778	28	34		
Reformed Episcopal Church	1990	83	5,882	6,565	88	147	72	2,938
Reformed Methodist Union Episcopal Church	1983	18		3,800	24	33		
Reformed Presbyterian Church of North America	1988	68		5,174	59	127		
Religious Society of Friends (Conservative)	1984	28		1,744		17		
Reorganized Church of Jesus Christ of Latter Day Saints	1992	1,001	150,143	150,143	16,742	16,742		
The Roman Catholic Church	1991	19,971		58,267,424		52,277		
The Romanian Orthodox Episcopate of America	1990	37	65,000	65,000	37	81	30	1,800
Russian Orthodox Church in the U.S.A., Patriarchal Parishes of the	1985	38		9,780	37	45		
The Salvation Army	1991	1,151	133,214	446,403	2,710	5,241	1,181	107,833
The Schwenkfelder Church	1991	5	2,489	2,489	9	10	5	798
Separate Baptists in Christ	1988	101		10,000	101	165		
Serbian Orthodox Church in the U.S.A. and Canada	1986	68		67,000	60	82		
Seventh-day Adventist Church	1991	4,229	733,026	733,026	2,312	4,485	4,409	394,598
Seventh Day Baptist General Conference, USA and Canada	1992	90	5,250	5,250	48	81	90	
Southern Baptist Convention	1991	36,168	15,232,347	15,232,347	38,700	65,450	36,615	8,178,345

TABLE 2: UNITED STATES CURRENT STATISTICS—Continued

Religious Body	Year Reported	No. of Churches	Full, Communicant or Confirmed Members	Inclusive Membership	Pastors Serving Parishes	Total No. of Clergy	No. of Sunday or Sabbath Schools	Total Enrollment
Southern Methodist Church	1992	133	7,745	7,745	100	139		
Sovereign Grace Baptists	1992	300	3,000	3,000	400	500	300	7,000
The Swedenborgian Church	1988	50		2,423	45	54		
Syrian Orthodox Church of Antioch (Archdiocese of the United States and Canada)	1988	28		30,000	20	25		
True (Old Calendar) Orthodox Church of Greece (Synod of Metropolitan Cyprian)	1992	8	900	900	8	17		
Ukrainian Orthodox Church of America (Ecumenical Patriarchate)	1986	27		5,000	36	37		
Unitarian Universalist Association	1991	1,020	141,315	141,315	650	1,210		48,888
United Brethren in Christ	1990	260	25,775	25,775	320	382	260	14,748
United Christian Church	1987	12		420	8	11		
United Church of Christ	1991	6,301	1,583,830	1,583,830	4,581	10,171		413,255
The United Methodist Church	1991	37,100	8,785,135	8,785,135	20,607	38,502		3,851,864
United Pentecostal Church International	1992	3,500	550,000	550,000	7,474			
United Zion Church	1987	13		850	19	20		
Unity of the Brethren	1991	26	2,615	3,615	22	28	21	1,444
Vedanta Societies	1988	13		2,500	14	14		
The Wesleyan Church (USA)	1992	1,612	106,397	114,174	1,755	2,539	1,592	49,395
Wisconsin Evangelical Lutheran Synod	1990	1,211	316,813	420,039	1,167	1,607	1,173	

Figures obtained from the *Directory of African American Religious Bodies, 1991*

Table 3: SOME STATISTICS OF CHURCH

Communion	Year	Full or Confirmed Members	Inclusive members	Total Contributions	Per Capita Full or Confirmed Members	Per Capita Inclusive Members
Associated Gospel Churches	1992	9,284	9,284	12,353,009	1,330.57	1,330.57
Baptist Union of Western Canada	1991	15,528	20,719	21,896,817	1,410.15	1,056.85
Brethren in Christ Church, Canadian Conference	1992	3,069	3,069	4,778,774	1,557.11	1,557.11
Christian and Missionary Alliance in Canada	1991	27,923	76,119	62,842,447	2,250.56	825.58
Conference of Mennonites in Canada	1991	28,648	28,648	23,825,000	831.65	831.65
Congregational Christian Churches in Canada	1991	762	762	1,095,306	1,437.41	1,437.41
The Evangelical Covenant Church of Canada	1991	1,278	1,278	1,754,167	1,372.59	1,372.59
Evangelical Lutheran Church in Canada	1991	148,630	206,187	53,709,785	361.37	260.49
Lutheran Church—Canada	1991	58,792	78,566	26,106,560	444.05	332.29
Moravian Church in America, Northern Province, Canadian	1991	1,498	2,126	1,585,068	1,058.12	745.56
North American Baptist Conference	1992	18,125	18,125	19,564,622	1,079.43	1,079.43
Reformed Church in Canada	1991	4,082	6,779	4,282,776	1,049.19	631.77
The Reformed Episcopal Church	1991	330	780	161,680	489.94	207.28
Seventh-day Adventist Church in Canada	1991	41,085	41,085	43,022,443	1,047.16	1,047.16
Union D'Eglises Baptistes Francaises Au Canada	1991	1,169	1,969	822,335	703.45	417.64
United Brethren Church in Canada	1991	818	857	970,601	1,186.55	1,132.56
The United Church of Canada	1991	785,726	2,018,808	290,431,072	369.63	143.86
The Wesleyan Church of Canada	1992	4,945	5,232	9,215,129	1,863.52	1,761.30

Table 4: SOME STATISTICS OF CHURCH

Communion	Year	Full or Confirmed Members	Inclusive members	Total Contributions	Per Capita Full or Confirmed Members	Per Capita Inclusive Members
Albanian Orthodox Diocese of America	1992	1,873	1,873	188,100	100.43	100.43
Allegheny Wesleyan Methodist Connection (Original Allegheny Conference)	1991	2,007	2,130	3,933,987	1,960.13	1,846.94
American Baptist Churches USA	1991	1,527,840	1,527,840	368,107,929	240.93	240.93
Baptist General Conference	1992	134,658	134,658	123,112,848	914.26	914.26
Baptist Missionary Association of America	1991	230,127	230,127	59,003,603	256.40	256.40
Brethren in Christ Church	1992	17,454	17,454	16,663,994	954.74	954.74
Christian Church (Disciples of Christ)	1991	663,336	1,022,926	374,968,316	565.28	366.56
Church of God (Anderson, Ind.)	1992	214,743	214,743	168,051,017	782.57	782.57
Church of God General Conference	1992	4,251	5,526	3,611,297	849.52	653.51
Church of the Lutheran Confession	1991	6,363	8,722	3,288,167	516.76	377.00
Churches of God, General Conference	1991	33,584	33,584	19,359,884	576.46	576.46
Conservative Congregational Christian Conference	1991	28,035	28,035	22,064,342	787.03	787.03
The Episcopal Church	1991	1,615,505	2,471,880	1,433,467,803	887.32	579.91
Evangelical Covenant Church	1991	89,648	89,648	90,753,171	1,012.33	1,012.33

FINANCES—CANADIAN CHURCHES

	CONGREGATIONAL FINANCES			BENEVOLENCES		
Total Congregational Contributions	Per Capita Full or Confirmed Members	Per Capita Inclusive Members	Total Benevolences	Per Capita Full or Confirmed Members	PerCapita Inclusive Members	Benevolences As a Percentage of Total Contributions
9,542,661	1027.86	1027.86	2,810,348	302.71	302.71	22.75
17,997,310	1159.02	868.64	3,899,507	251.13	188.21	17.81
3,965,699	1292.18	1292.18	813,075	264.93	264.93	17.01
51,175,818	1832.75	672.31	11,667,629	417.85	153.28	18.57
12,000,000	418.88	418.88	11,825,000	412.77	412.77	49.63
983,215	1290.31	1290.31	112,091	147.1	147.1	10.23
1,363,635	1067.01	1067.01	390,532	305.58	305.58	22.26
47,950,593	322.62	232.56	5,759,192	38.75	27.93	10.72
21,359,985	363.31	271.87	4,746,575	80.74	60.42	18.18
1,415,127	944.68	665.63	169,941	113.45	79.93	10.72
14,740,178	813.25	813.25	4,824,444	266.18	266.18	24.66
3,518,893	862.05	519.09	763,883	187.13	112.68	17.84
148,000	448.48	189.74	13,680	41.45	17.54	8.46
11,656,327	283.71	283.71	31,366,116	763.44	763.44	72.91
769,209	658.01	390.66	53,126	45.45	26.98	6.46
653,323	798.68	762.34	317,278	387.87	370.22	32.69
250,588,097	318.93	124.13	39,842,975	50.71	19.74	13.72
7,147,494	1445.4	1366.11	1,769,000	357.74	338.11	19.20

FINANCES—UNITED STATES CHURCHES

	CONGREGATIONAL FINANCES			BENEVOLENCES		
Total Congregational Contributions	Per Capita Full or Confirmed Members	Per Capita Inclusive Members	Total Benevolences	Per Capita Full or Confirmed Members	PerCapita Inclusive Members	Benevolences As a Percentage of Total Contributions
170,000	90.76	90.76	18,100	9.66	9.66	9.62
3,062,677	1,526.00	1,437.88	871,310	434.14	409.07	22.15
315,777,005	206.68	206.68	52,330,924	34.25	34.25	14.22
99,753,153	740.79	740.79	23,359,695	173.47	173.47	18.97
48,900,045	212.49	212.49	10,103,558	43.90	43.90	17.12
13,327,414	763.57	763.57	3,336,580	191.16	191.16	20.02
331,629,009	499.94	324.20	43,339,307	65.32	42.34	11.56
146,249,447	681.04	681.04	21,801,570	101.52	101.52	12.97
3,077,291	723.90	556.87	534,006	125.62	96.64	14.79
2,764,278	434.43	316.93	523,889	82.33	60.07	15.93
16,141,658	480.64	480.64	3,218,226	95.83	95.83	16.62
17,760,290	633.50	633.50	4,304,052	153.52	153.52	19.51
1,187,757,178	735.22	480.51	245,710,625	152.10	99.40	17.14
74,154,515	827.17	827.17	16,598,656	185.15	185.15	18.29

Table 4: SOME STATISTICS OF CHURCH

Communion	Year	Full or Confirmed Members	Inclusive Members	TOTAL CONTRIBUTIONS		
				Total Contributions	Per Capita Full or Confirmed Members	Per Capita Inclusive Members
Evangelical Lutheran Church in America	1991	3,890,947	5,245,177	1,561,455,955	401.30	297.69
Evangelical Lutheran Synod	1991	16,004	21,347	7,687,783	480.37	360.13
Evangelical Mennonite Church	1992	4,059	4,059	6,133,865	1,511.18	1,511.18
Free Methodist Church of North America	1991	57,794	73,572	67,757,203	1,172.39	920.96
International Pentecostal Church of Christ	1992	2,532	3,840	2,276,361	899.04	592.80
The Lutheran Church-Missouri Synod	1991	1,952,845	2,607,309	866,755,839	443.84	332.43
Mennonite Church	1991	99,431	99,431	97,390,523	979.48	979.48
Missionary Church, Inc.	1991	27,320	27,320	35,288,286	1,291.66	1,291.66
Moravian Church in America, Northern Province	1991	22,887	29,805	11,300,672	493.76	379.15
National Association of Free Will Baptists, Inc.	1991	209,223	209,223	60,300,000	288.21	288.21
North American Baptist Conference	1992	43,087	43,087	35,128,115	815.28	815.28
The Orthodox Prebyterian Church	1991	12,265	18,137	14,400,000	1,174.07	793.96
Presbyterian Church (U.S.A.)	1991	2,805,548	3,778,358	2,061,418,737	734.77	545.59
Reformed Church in America	1991	197,688	340,991	151,871,896	768.24	445.38
The Schwenkfelder Church	1991	2,489	2,489	954,894	383.65	383.65
Seventh-Day Adventist Church	1991	733,026	733,026	657,654,178	897.18	897.18
Southern Baptist Convention	1991	15,232,347	15,232,347	5,015,095,825	329.24	329.24
Sovreign Grace Baptists	1992	3,000	3,000	195,000	65.00	65.00
True (Old Calendar) Orthodox Church of Greece (Synod of Metropolitan Cyprian),	1992	900	900	32,000	35.56	35.56
United Church of Christ	1991	1,583,830	1,583,830	616,953,639	389.53	389.53
United Methodist Church	1991	8,785,135	8,785,135	3,099,522,282	352.81	352.81

SUMMARY STATISTICS

Communion	Number Reporting	Full or Confirmed Members	Inclusive members	TOTAL CONTRIBUTIONS		
				Total Contributions	Per Capita Full or Confirmed Members	Per Capita Inclusive Members
Canadian Communions	17	1,151,692	2,520,393	578,417,591	502.23	229.50
United States Communions	36	40,358,175	44,745,703	17,183,751,078	425.78	384.03

	CONGREGATIONAL FINANCES			BENEVOLENCES			
	Total Congregational Contributions	Per Capita Full or Confirmed Members	Per Capita Inclusive Members	Total Benevolences	Per Capita Full or Confirmed Members	PerCapita Inclusive Members	Benevolences As a Percentage of Total Contributions
1,375,439,787	353.50	262.23	186,016,168	47.81	35.46	11.91
6,657,338	415.98	311.86	1,030,445	64.39	48.27	13.40
3,834,001	944.57	944.57	2,299,864	566.61	566.61	37.49
57,880,464	1,001.50	786.72	9,876,739	170.90	134.25	14.58
1,779,315	702.73	463.36	497,046	196.31	129.44	21.84
741,823,412	379.87	284.52	124,932,427	63.97	47.92	14.41
68,926,324	693.21	693.21	28,464,199	286.27	286.27	29.23
29,372,723	1,075.14	1,075.14	5,915,563	216.53	216.53	16.76
10,095,337	441.09	338.71	1,205,335	52.66	40.44	10.67
48,000,000	229.42	229.42	12,300,000	58.79	58.79	20.40
27,335,239	634.42	634.42	7,792,876	180.86	180.86	22.18
11,700,000	953.93	645.09	2,700,000	220.14	148.87	18.75
1,636,407,042	583.28	433.10	425,011,695	151.49	112.49	20.62
121,350,787	613.85	355.88	30,521,109	154.39	89.51	20.10
747,238	300.22	300.22	207,656	83.43	83.43	21.75
201,411,183	274.77	274.77	456,242,995	622.41	622.41	69.37
4,283,283,059	281.20	281.20	731,812,766	48.04	48.04	14.59
35,000	11.67	11.67	160,000	53.33	53.33	82.05
25,000	27.78	27.78	7,000	7.78	7.78	
543,803,752	343.35	343.35	73,149,887	46.19	46.19	11.86
2,421,078,608	275.59	275.59	678,443,674	77.23	77.23	21.89

	CONGREGATIONAL FINANCES			BENEVOLENCES			
	Total Congregational Contributions	Per Capita Full or Confirmed Members	Per Capita Inclusive Members	Total Benevolences	Per Capita Full or Confirmed Members	PerCapita Inclusive Members	Benevolences As a Percentage of Total Contributions
456,975,564	396.78	181.35	121,144,392	105.19	48.08	20.94
13,960,997,845	345.93	312.01	3,222,753,233	79.85	72.02	18.75

TABLE 5: CONSTITUENCY OF THE NATIONAL COUNCIL OF THE CHURCHES IN THE U.S.A.

A separate tablulation has been made of the constituent bodies of the National Council of Churches of Christ in the U.S.A.

Religious Body	Year	Number of Churches	Inclusive Membership	Pastors Serving Parishes
African Methodist Episcopal Church.	1991	8,000	3,500,000	8,000
African Methodist Episcopal Zion Church.	1991	3,000	1,200,000	2,500
American Baptist Churches in the U.S.A.	1991	5,862	1,527,840	5,346
The Antiochian Orthodox Christian Archdiocese of North America.	1992	170	350,000	225
Armenian Church of America, Diocese of the.	1991	72	414,000	49
Christian Church (Disciples of Christ).	1991	4,031	1,022,926	3,729
Christian Methodist Episcopal Church.	1983	2,340	718,922	2,340
Church of the Brethren.	1990	1,095	148,253	1,084
Community Churches, International Council of.	1991	398	250,000	400
Coptic Orthodox Church.	1992	55	260,000	60
Episcopal Church.	1991	7,367	2,471,880	8,040
Evangelical Lutheran Church in America.	1991	11,074	5,245,177	9,929
Friends United Meeting.	1991		50,803	341
Greek Orthodox Archdiocese of North and South America.	1977	535	1950000	610
Hungarian Reformed Church in America.	1989	27	9,780	29
Korean Presbyterian Church in America, General Assembly of the.	1992	203	26,988	326
Moravian Church in America, Northern Province.	1991	98	29,805	89
Moravian Church in America, Southern Province.	1991	56	21,513	63
National Baptist Convention, U.S.A., Inc.	1991	30,000	7,800,000	30,000
National Baptist Convention of America.	1990	5,600	3,500,000	5,600
Orthodox Church in America.	1992	1,000	1,030,000	750
Philadelphia Yearly Meeting, Society of Friends.	1991	105	12,627	141
Polish National Catholic Church of North America.	1960	162	282,411	
Presbyterian Church (U.S.A.).	1991	11,468	3,778,358	10,042
Progressive National Baptist Convention, Inc.	1991	1,400	2,500,000	1,400
Reformed Church in America.	1991	967	340,991	926
Russian Orthodox Church in the U.S.A., Patriarchal Parishes of the.	1985	38	9,780	37
Serbian Orthodox Church in the U.S.A. and Canada.	1986	68	67,000	60
The Swedenborgian Church.	1988	50	2,423	45
Syrian Orthodox Church of Antioch (Archdiocese of the United States and Canada).	1992	28	30,000	20
Ukrainian Orthodox Church of America (Ecumenical Patriarchate).	1986	27	5,000	36
United Church of Christ.	1991	6,301	1,583,830	4,581
The United Methodist Church.	1991	37,100	8,785,135	20,607
Totals.		138,697	48,925,442	117,405

TRENDS IN SEMINARY EDUCATION
1987-1992

Gail Buchwalter King, Ph.D.
Associate Director, The Association of Theological Schools

More students enrolled in seminaries in 1992 than in 1991.

The following tables offer an update for fall 1992 enrollment in ATS member schools. In 1992, nine schools were admitted to membership at the June 1992 Biennial Meeting. Enrollment at the nine new schools was 1,148 (760 full time equivalent, FTE). Two of the schools were Canadian with 228 students (206 FTE).

Opening fall 1992 enrollment in ATS schools was 63,171. This represents an increase of 5.1% over the previous year (1991). If, however, we exclude the nine new member schools we find only a 3.2% increase. The 1992 figure of 63,171 includes the increase in schools applying for membership.

TABLE 1 Enrollments in ATS Member Schools

	1987	1988	1989	1990	1991	1992
Number of schools	201	202	202	208	208	215
Total enrollment	53,766	55,745	56,171	59,190	60,086	63,171
By Nation						
Canada	3,572	4,024	4,113	4,053	4,648	4,831
United States	52,194	51,721	52,058	55,137	55,438	58,430
By Membership						
Accredited	52,464	52,129	52,913	54,235	55,217	55,727
Not Accredited	3,302	3,616	3,258	4,955	4,869	5,444

Comparisons of Total Enrollment to Full-time Equivalents

Table 2 reflects for the fall of 1992 an increase in the full-time equivalent (FTE) enrollment of 13.4%. With the removal of the new schools the FTE percentage of total person enrollment is even slightly higher, 13.6%. Although this looks like a major turnaround, it in part reflects different reporting in the FTE categories for the Professional Doctoral and Unclassified programs from 1991 to 1992. Even if you remove these two programs, there is still an increase in FTE of 9.8%, the highest increase recorded by ATS. Schools have made major efforts to increase endowments for student aid and this may reflect some of this shift.

TABLE 2 Total Enrollments and Full-time Equivalents

Year	Total Persons (HC)	Percent Change	FTE Enrollment	Percent Change	Percent of Total Enrollment
1978	46,460		36,219		78.0
1979	48,433	+ 4.2	36,795	+ 1.6	76.0
1980	49,611	+ 2.4	37,245	+ 1.2	75.1
1981	50,559	+ 1.9	37,254	0.0	73.7
1982	52,620	+ 4.1	37,705	+ 1.2	71.7
1983	55,112	+ 4.7	38,923	+ 3.3	70.6
1984	56,466	+ 2.5	39,414	+ 1.3	69.8
1985	56,377	- 0.2	38,841	- 1.5	68.9
1986	56,328	- 0.1	38,286	- 1.4	68.0
1987	55,766	- 1.0	38,329	+ 0.1	68.7
1988	55,745	0.0	36,802	- 4.0	66.0
1989	56,171	+ 0.8	38,178	+ 3.7	68.0
1990	59,190	+ 5.4	40,847	+ 7.0	69.0
1991	60,086	+ 1.5	40,922	+ 0.2	68.1
1992	63,171	+ 5.1	46,404	+13.4	73.5

STATISTICAL SECTION

Table 3 represents enrollment by degree so that the reader can actually see where the growth points are. As mentioned above, the Professional Doctoral and the Special/Unclassified programs were counted differently for the FTE, so comparisons are not appropriate. There are however, significant increases in the Head Count of those two programs as well as in the Certificate programs. When you take into account the addition of nine new member schools the increase in the M.Div. program is not substantial.

TABLE 3 Total Enrollment by Degree Types

Degree Types	1991	1992	Percent of 1992 total HC	Percent of 1992 total FTE
Professional/Academic 1 or 2 years post-baccalaureate				
Head Count	11,910	12,514	19.81%	
Full-time Equivalent	7,760	8,400		8.10%
Professional 3 & 4 year post-baccalaureate				
M.Div. (excluding intern year)				
Head Count	25,511	26,234	41.53%	
Full-time Equivalent	20,840	21,389		46.09%
Professional post-baccalaureate doctoral programs				
Head Count	7,598	7,960	12.60%	
Full-time Equivalent	5,665	7,038		15.17%
Certificate and diploma programs (non-preordination only)				
Head Count	3,348	4,349	6.88%	
Full-time Equivalent	1,924	2,743		5.91%
Special/Unclassified				
Head Count	5,646	6,075	9.2%	
Full-time Equivalent	577	2,004		4.32%
Interns				
Head Count	809	813	1.29%	
Full-time Equivalent	758	758		1.63%
Academic post-M.A./M.Div. programs				
Head Count	5,264	5,226	8.27%	
Full-time Equivalent	3,398	4,072		8,78%
Total				
Head Count	60,086	63,171	100%	
Full-time Equivalent	40,922	46,404		100%

Women in Seminaries

Table 4 reports the ratio of women seminary students for each year since 1972, when collection of data was begun. Twenty years ago women constituted only 10.2% of the total student group. This year they constituted 31.1% of the student body. Growth during the past year was 6.9%. This number continues the trend of increased enrollment of women with some of the Protestant schools showing even higher percentages of women students. When one looks at administrative positions across the board in theological education there is a similar increase in women personnel. When one looks at the two top administrative positions, that of the CEO and Academic Dean, there is not a similar increase. Representation on the faculty is improving but does not match the student ratio because change and turnover of full-time faculty members is slower.

TABLE 4 Women Enrollment

Year	Number of Women	Percentage Annual Change	Percentage of Total Enrollment
1972	3,358		10.2
1973	4,021	+ 19.7	11.8
1974	5,255	+ 30.7	14.3
1975	6,505	+ 23.8	15.9
1976	7,349	+ 13.0	17.1
1977	8,371	+ 13.9	18.5
1978	8,972	+ 7.2	19.3
1979	10,204	+ 13.7	21.1
1980	10,830	+ 6.1	21.8
1981	11,683	+ 7.9	23.1
1982	12,473	+ 6.8	23.7
1983	13,451	+ 7.8	24.4
1984	14,142	+ 5.1	25.0
1985	14,572	+ 3.0	25.8
1986	14,864	+ 2.0	26.4
1987	15,310	+ 3.0	27.0
1988	16,344	+ 6.8	29.3
1989	16,461	+ 0.7	29.3
1990	17,571	+ 6.7	29.7
1991	18,384	+ 4.6	30.6
1992	19,653	+ 6.9	31.1

African American Student Enrollment

African American enrollment continued its steady growth, which has averaged 5.6 percent per year for the past five years. In order to meet the shortage of African American faculty, more of these students need to be encouraged to seek a Ph.D. degree.

TABLE 4 African American Enrollment

Year	Number of African American Students	Percentage Annual Change	Percentage of Total Enrollment
1970	808		2.6
1971	908	+ 12.4	2.8
1972	1,061	+ 16.9	3.2
1973	1,210	+ 14.0	3.6
1974	1,246	+ 3.0	3.4
1975	1,365	+ 9.6	3.3
1976	1,524	+ 11.6	3.5
1977	1,759	+ 15.4	3.9
1978	1,919	+ 9.1	4.1
1979	2,043	+ 6.5	4.2
1980	2,205	+ 7.9	4.4
1981	2,371	+ 7.5	4.7
1982	2,576	+ 8.6	4.9
1983	2,881	+ 11.8	5.2
1984	2,917	+ 1.2	5.2
1985	3,046	+ 4.4	5.4
1986	3,277	+ 7.6	5.8
1987	3,379	+ 3.1	6.0
1988	3,662	+ 8.4	6.6
1989	3,961	+ 8.2	7.1
1990	4,303	+ 8.6	7.3
1991	4,671	+ 8.6	7.8
1992	5,554	+ 18.9	8.8

Hispanic Enrollment

After a huge increase in 1990, Hispanic enrollment declined in 1991. Enrollment remains at its second-highest level ever, however. Given the shifting population and demographics in the United States and Canada, efforts of denominations to reach out to this group will continue to be important to the existing program of theological schools.

TABLE 5 Hispanic Enrollment

Year	Number of Hispanic Students	Percentage Annual Change	Percentage of Total Enrollment
1972	264		0.8
1973	387	+ 46.8	1.1
1974	448	+ 15.8	1.2
1975	524	+ 17.0	1.3
1976	541	+ 3.2	1.3
1977	601	+ 11.1	1.3
1978	681	+ 13.3	1.5
1979	822	+ 20.7	1.7
1980	894	+ 8.8	1.8
1981	955	+ 6.8	1.9
1982	1,180	+ 23.6	2.2
1983	1,381	+ 17.0	2.5
1984	1,314	- 4.9	2.3
1985	1,454	+ 10.6	2.6
1986	1,297	- 10.8	2.3
1987	1,385	+ 6.8	2.5
1988	1,415	+ 2.2	2.5
1989	1,490	+ 5.3	2.7
1990	1,904	+ 27.8	3.2
1991	1,625	- 14.7	2.7
1992	1,670	+ 2.8	2.6

Pacific/Asian Students

The numbers of Pacific/Asian American students have risen faster than those of any other ethnic constituency, during the past 14 years. Last year's increase was smaller than the average during that span, but was still the greatest increase of any ethnic constituency. The determination to provide an educated ministry is obvious in these statistics.

Table 6 Pacific/Asian Enrollment

Year	Number of Pacific/Asian American Students	Percentage Annual Change	Percentage of Total Enrollment
1977	494		1.1
1978	499	+ 1.0	1.1
1979	577	+ 15.6	1.2
1980	602	+ 4.3	1.2
1981	716	+ 18.9	1.4
1982	707	- 1.3	1.3
1983	779	+ 10.2	1.4
1984	1,130	+ 45.1	2.0
1985	1,195	+ 5.8	2.1
1986	1,393	+ 16.6	2.5
1987	1,645	+ 18.0	2.9
1988	1,963	+ 19.3	3.5
1989	2,065	+ 5.2	3.7
1990	2,439	+ 18.1	4.1
1991	2,653	+ 8.8	4.4
1992	3,072	+ 15.8	4.9

IV
A CALENDAR FOR CHURCH USE
1993-1996

This Calendar presents for a four-year period the major days of religious observance for Christians, Jews, and Muslims; and, within the Christian community, major dates observed by Roman Catholic, Orthodox, Episcopal, and Lutheran churches. Within each of these communions many other days of observance, such as saints' days, exist, but only those regarded major are listed. Thus, for example, for the Roman Catholic Church, mainly the "solemnities" are listed. Dates of interest to many Protestant communions are also included.

Many days of observance, such as Christmas and Easter, do not carry the list of communions observing them, since it is assumed that practically all Christian bodies do. In certain cases, a religious observance will be named differently by various communions, and this is noted.

In the Orthodox dates, immovable observances are listed in accordance with the Gregorian calendar. Movable dates (those depending on the date of Easter) often will differ from Western dates, since Pascha (Easter) in the Orthodox communions does not always fall on the same day as in the Western churches. For Orthodox churches that use the old Julian calendar, observances are held thirteen days later than listed here. Ecumenical dates, such as Week of Prayer for Christian Unity and World Communion Sunday, also are included. For Jews and Muslims, who follow differing lunar calendars, the dates of major observances are translated into Gregorian dates. For Muslim observances, the festivals are dated according to astronomical calculations that have been published in Paris, not in the United States, and this could lead to slight variations. Since the actual beginning of a new month in the Islamic calendar is determined by the appearance of the new moon, the corresponding dates given here on the Gregorian calendar may vary slightly. It is also possible for a festival to occur twice in the same Gregorian year. Only 'Id al-Fitr and the 'Id al-Adha are religious holidays prescribed by the texts of Islam. Other Islamic dates are nevertheless key moments in the lives of Muslim believers. Jewish observances begin at sundown of the day previous to those listed below and end at sundown of the last day.

(Note: In the Calendar, "RC" stands for Roman Catholic, "O" for Orthodox, "E" for Episcopal, "L" for Lutheran, "ECU" for Ecumenical.)

Event	1993	1994	1995	1996
New Year's Day (RC-Solemnity of Mary;O-Circumcision of Jesus Christ; E-Feast of the Holy Name; L-Name of Jesus	Jan 01	Jan 01	Jan 01	Jan 01
Epiphany (Armenian Christmas)	Jan 06	Jan 06	Jan 06	Jan 06
Feast Day of St. John the Baptist (O)	Jan 07	Jan 07	Jan 07	Jan 07
First Sunday After Epiphany (Feast of the Baptism of Our Lord)	Jan 10	Jan 09	Jan 08	Jan 07
Week of Prayer for Christian Unity (ECU)	Jan 18 to Jan 25	Jan 18 to Jan 25	Jan 18 to Jan 25	Jan 18 to Jan 25
Week of Prayer for Christian Unity, Canada (ECU)	Jan 24 to Jan 31	Jan 23 to Jan 30	Jan 22 Jan 29	Jan 21 to Jan 28
Ecumenical Sunday (ECU)	Jan 24	Jan 23	Jan 22	Jan 21
Presentation of Jesus in the Temple (O-The Meeting of Our Lord and Savior Jesus Christ)	Feb 02	Feb 02	Feb 02	Feb 02
Brotherhood Week (Interfaith)	Feb 21 to Feb 27	Feb 20 to Feb 26	Feb 19 to Feb 25	Feb 18 to Feb 24
Last Sunday After Epiphany (L-Transfiguration)	Feb 21	Feb 13	Feb 26	Feb 18
Ash Wednesday (Western churches)	Feb 24	Feb 16	Mar 01	Feb 21
Easter Lent Begins (Eastern Orthodox)	Mar 01	Mar 14	Mar 06	Feb 25
World Day of Prayer (ECU)	Mar 05	Mar 04	Mar 06	Mar 01
Purim (Jewish)	Mar 07	Feb 25	Mar 16	Mar 05
Joseph, Husband of Mary (RC,E,L)	Mar 19	Mar 19	Mar 19	Mar 19
The Annunciation (O) (Apr 01 for L; Apr 08 for RC and E)	Mar 25	Mar 25	Mar 25	Mar 25
First Day of the Month of Ramadan (M)	Feb 23	Feb 12	Feb 02	Jan 21
Id al-Fitr (Festival of the End of Ramadan, celebrated on the first day of the month of Shawwal)	Mar 25	Mar 14	Mar 03	Feb 19
Holy Week (Western Churches)	Apr 04 to Apr 10	Mar 27 to Apr 2	Apr 09 to Apr 15	Mar 31 to Apr 07
Holy Week (Eastern Orthodox)	Apr 12 to Apr 16	Apr 25 to Apr 29	Apr 17 to Apr 21	Apr 08 to Apr 12
Sunday of the Passion (Palm Sunday) (Western Churches)	Apr 04	Mar 27	Apr 09	Mar 31
Palm Sunday (Eastern Orthodox)	Apr 11	Apr 24	Apr 16	Apr 07

Event	1993	1994	1995	1996
Holy Thursday (Western Churches)	Apr 08	Mar 31	Apr 13	Apr 04
Holy Thursday (Eastern Orthodox)	Apr 15	Apr 28	Apr 20	Apr 11
Good Friday (Friday of the Passion of Our Lord) (Western Churches)	Apr 09	Apr 01	Apr 14	Apr 05
Holy (Good) Friday, Burial of Jesus Christ (Eastern Orthodox)	Apr 16	Apr 29	Apr 21	Apr 12
Easter (Western Churches)	Apr 11	Apr 03	Apr 16	Apr 07
First Day of Passover (Jewish, 8 days)	Apr 06	Mar 27	Apr 15	Apr 04
Pascha (Eastern Orthodox Easter)	Apr 18	May 01	Apr 23	Apr 14
National Day of Prayer	May 06	May 05	May 04	May 02
May Fellowship Day (ECU)	May 07	May 06	May 05	May 03
Rural Life Sunday (ECU)	May 09	May 08	May 14	May 12
Ascension Day (Western Churches)	May 20	May 13	May 25	May 16
Ascension Day (Eastern Orthodox)	May 27	Jun 09	Jun 01	May 23
First Day of Shavuot (Jewish, 2 days)	May 26	May 16	Jun 04	May 24
Pentecost (Whitsunday) (Western Churches)	May 30	May 22	Jun 04	May 26
Pentecost (Eastern Orthodox)	Jun 06	Jun 19	Jun 11	Jun 02
Visitation of the Blessed Virgin Mary (RC,E,L)	May 31	May 31	May 31	May 31
Holy Trinity (RC,E,L)	Jun 06	Jun 29	Jun 04	Jun 02
Corpus Christi (RC)	Jun 13	Jun 05	Jun 11	Jun 09
Nativity of St. John the Baptist (RC,E,L)	Jun 24	Jun 24	Jun 24	Jun 24
Sacred Heart of Jesus (RC)	Jun 20	Jun 10	Jun 16	Jun 14
Saint Peter and Saint Paul, Apostles (RC,E,L)	Jun 29	Jun 29	Jun 29	Jun 24
Feast Day of the Twelve Apostles of Christ (O)	Jun 30	Jun 30	Jun 30	Jun 30
Id al-Adha (Festival of Sacrifice at time of annual pilgrimage to Mecca)	Jun 01	May 21	May 10	Apr 28
First Day of the Month of Muharram (Beginning of Muslim Liturgical Year)	Jun 21	Jun 10	May 31	May 19
Transfiguration of the Lord (RC,O,E)	Aug 06	Aug 06	Aug 06	Aug 06
Feast of the Blessed Virgin Mary (E; RC-Assumption of Blessed Mary the Virgin; O-Falling Asleep (Dormition) of the Blessed Virgin Mary; L-Mary, Mother of Our Lord)	Aug 15	Aug 15	Aug 15	Aug 15
The Birth of the Blessed Virgin (RC, O)	Sep 08	Sep 08	Sep 08	Sep 08
First Day of Rosh Hashanah (Jewish, 2 days)	Sep 16	Sep 06	Sep 25	Sep 14
Holy Cross Day (O-The Adoration of the Holy Cross; RC-Triumph of the Cross)	Sep 14	Sep 14	Sep 14	Sep 14
Yom Kippur (Jewish)	Sep 25	Sep 15	Oct 04	Sep 23
First Day of Sukkot (Jewish, 7 days)	Sep 30	Sep 20	Oct 09	Sep 28
World Communion Sunday (ECU)	Oct 03	Oct 02	Oct 01	Oct 06
Mawlid al-Nabi (Anniversary of Prophet Muhammad's birthday)	Aug 31	Aug 20	Aug 09	Jul 28
Laity Sunday (ECU)	Oct 10	Oct 09	Oct 08	Oct 13
Shemini Atzeret (Jewish)	Oct 07	Sep 27	Oct 16	Oct 05
Simhat Torah (Jewish)	Oct 08	Sep 28	Oct 17	Oct 06
Thanksgiving Day (Canada)	Oct 11	Oct 10	Oct 09	Oct 14
Reformation Sunday (L)	Oct 31	Oct 30	Oct 29	Oct 27
Reformation Day (L)	Oct 31	Oct 31	Oct 31	Oct 31
All Saints (RC,E,L)	Nov 01	Nov 01	Nov 01	Nov 01
World Community Day (ECU)	Nov 05	Nov 04	Nov 03	Nov 01
Stewardship Day (ECU)	Nov 14	Nov 13	Nov 12	Nov 10
Bible Sunday (ECU)	Nov 21	Nov 20	Nov 19	Nov 17
Last Sunday After Pentecost (RC, L-Feast of Christ the King)	Nov 21	Nov 20	Nov 26	Nov 24
Presentation of the Blessed Virgin Mary in the Temple (also Presentation of the Theotokos) (O)	Nov 21	Nov 21	Nov 21	Nov 21
Thanksgiving Sunday (U.S.)	Nov 21	Nov 20	Nov 19	Nov 24
Thanksgiving Day (U.S.)	Nov 25	Nov 24	Nov 23	Nov 28
First Sunday of Advent	Nov 28	Nov 27	Dec 03	Dec 01
Feast Day of St. Andrew the Apostle (RC,O,E,L)	Nov 30	Nov 30	Nov 30	Nov 30
Immaculate Conception of the Blessed Virgin Mary (RC)	Dec 08	Dec 08	Dec 08	Dec 08
First Day of Hanukkah (Jewish, 8 days)	Dec 09	Nov 28	Dec 18	Dec 06
Fourth Sunday of Advent (Sunday before Christmas)	Dec 19	Dec 18	Dec 24	Dec 22
Christmas (Except Armenian)	Dec 25	Dec 25	Dec 25	Dec 25

IV
INDEXES

ORGANIZATIONS

INDEXES

271

INDIVIDUALS

This list contains the names of people included in the listings of Cooperative Organizations, Religious Bodies, Regional Ecumenical Agencies, Seminaries and Bible Schools, and Publications.

279

282

INDEXES

300